1969

may be k

Germany:
The Symbol and The Deed

and Germany:
The Symbol and The Deed

Jonas Lesser

New York

Germany:
The Symbol
and The Deed

Jonas Lesser

New York · Thomas Yoseloff · London

To the memory of the six million
Jews and six million Slavs
murdered by the Germans.

Thomas Yoseloff, *Publisher*
South Brunswick, N.J.

Thomas Yoseloff, Ltd
18 Charing Cross Road
London W.C.2, England

6246
Printed in the United States of America

Contents

Germany:
The Symbol and The Deed

"You will not persuade Europe that a nation of sixty-five millions could have been barbarised against its will."

Karl von Tschuppik

"Nobody goes to the Devil against his own free will. Neither did Germany."

Franz Werfel

Introduction

"WAS THE NAZI STATE AND ITS ATTENDANT HORRORS A PECULIARLY German phenomenon?" Mr. James Joll (Oxford) asked when reviewing Dr. Gerald Reitlinger's book about the SS.[1] The historian A. J. P. Taylor asked: "How on earth did it happen? It remains incomprehensible that this highly civilised nation should have plunged into a nightmare of barbarism. We understand the Bolshevik revolution . . . but Hitler's Germany? The concentration camps, the barefaced illegality, the gas-chambers, a whole nation run mad—these are beyond us . . . How on earth did it happen?"[2]

If one gets an opportunity to put these questions to a German, he invariably suspects that they have been prompted by resentment or hatred. "Resentment" is indeed the favorite word of all Germans of today to ward off any criticism of their past and present. They prefer to talk of "the unsolved riddle of the Third Reich" or of the "blind" fate which brought National Socialism about. "Fate," they say, "let the political power slip into the hands of Hitler." They also say: "No nation is safe from abysses."[3] Utterances like these have been published in innumerable variations in post-war Germany. But Germans speak about the numerous German precursors of Hitler. Everything on earth has its roots and causes; can National Socialism have sprung from nothing?

Professor Gerhard Ritter, too, tells the Germans that Hitler came from nowhere. When he asserted that it was doubtful whether other nations would have less easily succumbed to the seductive glory of Hitler's political and military triumphs, Dr. F. L. Carston of London University retorted that a less emotional, less obedient, a politically more mature nation than the Germans, would never have allowed a Hitler to assume power.[4] Professor Ritter tells his compatriots that National Socialism is part and parcel of our "age of general cultural decline, irreligion and nihilism."[5] Germans are apt eagerly to believe such a fallacy, but we ask why only Germany deteriorated into the worst tyranny in all history. Ritter represents something of a split personality, for various of his statements cancel each other out. On the one hand he says that National Socialism only became possible by "the separation of German political thought from Western European thought, a separation which led from Fichte and Hegel through Ranke and his disciples to Treitschke," and that "the general decline of the cultural tradition of the West is no excuse for the millions of Germans who followed Hitler before 1933 without being scandalized by the intellectual and moral inferiority of his associates and the wild hatred expressed in all pronouncements of the agitator and his party."[6] On the other hand, however, Ritter emphatically asserts: "National Socialism was something fundamentally new in German history and came as unexpectedly as Fascism in Italy or Bolshevism in Russia."[7] He goes even further and makes the West responsible for it. The modern "totalitarian state" derives from Rousseau's *Contrat Social*. The French Revolution coined new ideas and slogans with the help of which "the modern Führer state" was established. Does Professor Ritter not remember that Goebbels repeatedly declared that the liberal epoch of the French revolution had been replaced by the authoritarian state of Hitler? Does he not know that the Führer compelled the French to change their world-famous slogan *"Liberté, Egalité, Fraternité"* ("France's greatest words," as President Eisenhower has called them) into *Travail, Famille, Patrie* on their coins? He does not, for he speaks of the "democratic-totalitarian state" as if the two adjectives did not exclude each other. The state, he continues, is sovereign, it acknowledges no judge, it is responsible to no one. "The liberty of the sovereign nation can at any moment change into totalitarian tyranny," if a gifted demagogue succeeds in winning the confidence of the masses and "credibly personifying the mythical will of the nation."[8] No explanation is given why that change only happened in Germany. Professor Johannes Albrecht von Rantzau called Ritter a disappointed nationalist who does not really believe in democratic freedom. Rantzau condemns the typically German concept that every state is an *individuum per se,* and turns against those unteachable German historians of the old and of a new school who called Professor Friedrich Meinecke unpatriotic because of his uncompromising assertion that the Third Reich and the German catastrophe were the inevitable result of Germany's alienation from the main lines of European development towards political liberty.[9] Professor Ludwig Dehio, another of the honest but small group of German post-war historians, deplored the reappearance of *Epochs of German History* by Johannes Haller, a nationalistic standard work in which Hitler was praised in 1939 as the fulfiller of German history. "It is as if you met a ghost," he said.[10]

Winfried Martini popularized Ritter's ideas in a separate book. While blaming the Germans for following a half-educated

Führer who preached hatred of the Jew and promised the conquest of Europe, he asserts, like Ritter, that National Socialism
derives from Rousseau's concept of the sovereign people. "For
decades democracy was on the way towards the Third Reich.
The sovereign people was resolved to abolish the legal state,"
and Hitler was "the outcome of democracy." Again no explanation is given why only in Germany a Hitler arose. We are only
given the advice not to adhere to the superstitious belief "that
today only democracy can safeguard freedom and the rights of
the individual."[11]

Sane and responsible German students of history try to tell
the Germans what consequences of their behavior they have to
accept today, but their voices have been completely drowned.
Professor Hans Herzfeld, remembering the Austrian ultimatum
in 1914 and the "blank check" the Germans gave them, and
President Wilson's words in 1918 that the Germans knew no
pity against the Russians, says that the First World War destroyed "the hegemony of Europe," and that the Second World
War resulted "in the establishment of two giants as world powers," the United States and Soviet Russia.[12] Professor Golo
Mann, Thomas Mann's son, says: "A new epoch in the history
of mankind began in the spring, in the summer of 1945."[13]
Professor K. D. Bracher calls militarism and racial mania the
two main tenets of National Socialism and traces them back to
Nietzscke's "superman" and "blond beast" and to Spengler's
visions of a barbaric Caesarism. Hitler's "anti-Communism"
was "in reality" Hitler's aim "to conquer new living space for
his racially superior Germans" and "to germanize it recklessly."
In 1938 he said: "It would be utterly irresponsible not to make
use of an instrument as the German *Wehrmacht.*" His pact with
Stalin "opened the door to the Second World War but at the same
time, the road to the West to the Soviet Union." Bracher quotes
the Professor Hofer who called Hitler "the greatest pace-maker
of Bolshevism in Europe," and adds: "His terror regime

brought that revenge upon Germany which fell on the heads of guilty and innocent alike. More than six million dead Germans, twice as many German refugees, the mutilation and division of our country, the end of our existence: this was the sum total of the Third Reich."[14]

These things are stated in Volume IX of the *Propyläen World History*, which is illustrated with many terrible photographs and charts. One of them shows 500 slave worker camps and 20 concentration camps whose names have become world-famous. Another photograph shows the Italian, German and Japanese flags hanging from an official building in Tokyo. These were the three aggressor states which President Roosevelt suggested be put in "quarantine" on October 5, 1937. Professor P. F. Langer describes Japan in words which equally apply to Mussolini's Italy and Hitler's Germany. "The creators of modern Japan," he says, "were the product of a feudal and authoritarian society. They were men of the sword educated in the Samurai spirit. Their main impulse was an immense national arrogance." That nationalism "destroyed the last remnants of the parliamentary system. They created a totalitarian state which started on the declivitous road to aggression and led the Japanese nation into a suicidal war against the United States."[15]

Count Coudenhove-Kalergi, descendant of one of the most ancient noble families going back to the Byzantine emperors, said, in a memorandum which he sent to the West German Government and politicians in February 1959, that the Germans had learned nothing from their history, that they repeated the mistakes of earlier times and hindered a peaceful development of world politics. The existence of two independent German states was a basic fact of world politics, reunification in freedom mere wishful thinking. But a policy nurtured by illusions could only lead to a catastrophe.[16]

Klaus Mehnert, a German expert on Russian affairs and an irredentist like most Germans, says all the same: "The Russians remember their recent past more vividly than does the forgetful West, especially the 'a-historical' Germans. . . . The older generation (of Russians) have twice witnessed how German armies penetrated deep into Russia, the second time up to the doors of their capital and the banks of Mother Volga. . . . Just as our grandfathers had on the walls of their flats reproductions of the famous picture showing the foundation of the German Reich on January 18, 1871 in the Hall of Mirrors at Versailles, so one can find in Russian flats reproductions of a picture by P. A. Kriwonogow showing the capture of the Berlin Reichstag by the Red Army."[17]

The German historian Eduard Meyer said in 1914 (but this was meant as a retort to the Western allies, not as applying to the Kaiser's Germany): "Every nation is responsible for the kind of government which it has chosen for itself and under which it lives. It is a vain undertaking to shift the responsibility to the government of the ruling party."[18]

But the voices of sanity have never reached the German masses, who, as a judicious German said ironically, "call everybody a fellow-traveller of the Russians who does not bow to the official opinion, just as in the old days everybody was called a hireling of the Jews and a criminal who did not shout: Heil Hitler."[19]

Day in, day out, the Germans of today are told things like this: "Our territorial claims go far beyond the Oder-Neisse line. We want our old German frontiers back." Or: "We must not forget that Germany needs more living space again. We have no such space, but can find it with our neighbors who do not need it. Empty regions beyond our frontiers, in the East, are waiting for us."[20] Or: "We shall and can never resign if we want to remain a nation of vitality which can do justice to its European task."[21] Hitler's slogans again in many variations. Professor Eugen Rosenstock-Huessy, however, who now lives in the United States, said: "All those who still dream of the *Reich* of the Germans do not see that it went off in the smoke of the great World War."[22]

Such people hold, of course, no brief for Communism. These people, liberals or conservatives, clearly see the consequences of Hitler's war and try to convince the Germans that the present situation cannot be changed without a war which would destroy all of us. They are joined by Englishmen who are as little sympathetic to Communism as they are.

Professor Geoffrey Barraclough, former director of the Royal Institute of International Affairs, says that after twelve years of illusions the West Germans must now realize that they entertained fictitious hopes which have been intentionally encouraged. It would be a wholesome process if West Germany, which up to now was living in a cloudland, realized the political realities of the 1960's. The division of Germany into two sovereign states is a fact. Nobody regards the German frontiers of 1938 as being sacrosanct. Just as Bismarck excluded Austria in 1871, although it was a German country, in the same sense there is no reason in 1961 not to recognize the existence of the other German state—not because we like that state, but because its recognition is unavoidable. The division of Germany as a result of the war is part of a historical process which has gone on for centuries and led to the loss of Holland, the German part of Switzerland, Alsace and Lorraine, and Austria. These facts cannot be ignored nor altered, least of all in the fallacious name of self-determination which Hitler misused to destroy Austria, Czechoslovakia, and Poland.[23]

Lord Boothby, who visited the East in the summer of 1961, reported: "The Poles, the Czechs, and the Hungarians fear and hate the Germans to an extent which we cannot even begin to comprehend. . . . The Germans killed and killed and killed for five interminable years. The killing was not confined to the Jews; and it is not forgotten. In defence of the Oder-Neisse line the Poles are ready to fight at any moment. Every time Herr

Willy Brandt talks about a rectification of the Oder-Neisse line, or says that it is simply not possible for the German people to recognise a dictated division of their country, every Polish peasant reaches for his harness and his gun. . . . Only twenty years ago the satellite countries were under the Nazi jackboot, and the Russians had the Germans at their throats. For sixteen years the policy of the West has been based on the fiction that somehow or other Germany can be reunited. For the last ten years no one has seriously believed it, and the bluff has now been called." Lord Boothby concludes that "the *Drang nach Osten* was not an invention of Hitler's," and the nations of the East "fear an all-out attack on the part of a rearmed Germany, with the full support from a United Western Europe and the United States to recover the 'lost provinces.'" He quotes the words of the German minister Dr. Hans Seebohn who once said: "We are the vanguard in the fight to shake off the yoke of Bolshevik colonialism from Eastern Europe."[24] An Israeli journalist, Uri Dan, who made a special study of the spirit of the new German army in 1961, asked himself "whether Germany, with her military power, could not endanger world peace. There are in the new army a number of officers of the old (Hitlerian) *Wehrmacht*. Most officers do not show their real opinion because they are clever enough to know that you must play 'democracy' today, but they are waiting eagerly for the day when the military power of Germany can, with the help of her Western allies, defeat Communism in Europe and enforce German reunification."[25]

Field Marshal Montgomery, however, said on January 29, 1961: "It is an illusion indeed illogical to expect Russia to agree that a reunited Germany armed with nuclear weapons should be integrated into the Western Alliance—with nuclear launching sites on the Polish frontier. Further illusions could be quoted—that the East German Government doesn't exist . . ."[26] On September 2, 1961, he repeated: "To describe Germany as one Germany is just a pious fraud. You cannot have one Germany."[27] In 1959, he had tried to remind the world of the German record since 1864. "Europe has never known durable peace since Bismarck created the German Empire." In the Kaiser's war "some 20 million men perished or shed their blood. After it, Winston Churchill wrote in *The World Crisis.* 'Surely, Germans, for history it is enough.' But it wasn't. In 1939 we had Hitler's war in which it is estimated that some 40 millon men, women and children perished in battle, in concentration camps, in gas chambers or by starvation. Hitler's war left Germany divided. Can we wonder why some nations are frightened about any reunification of the two Germanys?"[28] On another occasion he said that we all know what a nation of seventy million could do when united under a Führer. Englishmen who have not forgotten the German past agree with Montgomery.

G. M. Trevelyan says that National Socialism was "immeasurably worse than anything in the experience of modern Europe," as the "Nazi form of Government" was "based on wholesale torture and massacre."[29] Elizabeth Wiskemann wrote that the Third Reich "surpasses the horror of all other recorded tyranny."[30]

Professor Hugh Trevor-Roper says: "The Russian people at least resisted Communism. It was only during a disastrous foreign war that the Bolsheviks seized power, only after a long and bitter civil war that they established it. But Hitler was voted into power by the Germans in time of peace . . . and he was able to proceed to mass-murder at once with the co-operation, or at least permission, of the existing non-Nazi establishment. . . . This massive acquiescence in the most monstrous tyranny in Western history is a phenomenon which it would be foolish, perhaps dangerous, to forget. . . . The German apologists, of course, have their answer. According to them, other countries should have stopped it. Such an answer is absurd. Sovereign

States must make and unmake their own Governments. Hitler called his Russian war 'the be-all and end-all of Nazism.' Russia, to him, was simply land to be occupied when the natives (conveniently dismissed as 'submen') had been cleared off. 'In so far as we don't need them, they may die.' . . . Hitler's aggression against Russia was of a murderous brutality unexampled in history: a deliberate, calculated brutality which finally deprives the Germans of any moral claims in Eastern Europe."[31] Colin Welch says: "Why on earth did such a richly gifted people as the Germans prostitute themselves to become the tools of a maniac? The imaginative insight of a Dostoevsky is required to show how Hitler dulled in them their sense of right and wrong; how he drew them on into great unimaginable atrocities . . . Did he feel any sympathy for any human being? Not clearly for any Jew or Slav. They were subhuman. . . . The Nazi party was his brush; the German nation his palette, Europe—the world—his canvas."[32] Brigadier Sir Otto Prior-Palmer said in Parliament on November 1, 1960: "I am getting extremely worried about the irredentist movement in West Germany . . . The gist of what they were saying was that if Germany stood fast with the West, one day the West would see that East Prussia was freed. That sends a cold shiver down my spine. Are they not just the sort of noises we heard in 1936, 1937 and 1938? It is said there that the present situation is impossible. Impossible for whom? Certainly not for the Poles. They regard the Oder-Neisse line as their one security. The situation is certainly not impossible for the Czechs. . . . I hope that one day I may not regret having voted for German rearmament."[33] The historian A. J. P. Taylor said a few years ago that a divided Germany was a Godsend after all that a unified Germany had done to Europe. When a reference to his utterance was made in the German Bundestag, a shout came from the Christian Democratic ranks: "A Jew of course."[34] Hitlerism is still in the back of the mind of many a German. But this did not prevent Mr. Taylor from saying in 1961: "East Germany exists as a separate state, and has done for many years. Recognition does not mean approval. If it did, there are few states in the world we should recognise." He also said: "Berlin is certainly a great problem, and Germany a greater. But the Russians did not create it all alone. The Germans created this problem by supporting Hitler in aggressive war."[35] Walter Lippmann, most judicious of all American columnists, said in 1958: "The defenders of the existing European policy of the Western Powers consider themselves great realists. On what calculation in the power relationships of great states do they base their expectation that Russia will withdraw from Europe while the United States and Great Britain remain and are allowed to advance their military frontiers at least to the borders of Poland? In Bonn, in London, in Paris and in Washington there have long been leading persons who, when they are speaking privately, say quite frankly that they prefer a divided and occupied Germany to a reunited and unoccupied Germany. They are afraid that a united and unoccupied Germany will dominate Europe."[36]

We must, therefore, tell the Germans that they should listen to what the few sensible of their fellow citizens say about the consequences of the Hitler madness. We must also tell them that we can do no more for them than protect West Germany from any Russian attack, but cannot go to war for the restoration of what they have destroyed themselves. To tell them this does not mean to hate them or to ostracize them.

Hitler once said to Dr. Ranschning: "If, however, we should not be victorious and go down, we shall take half of the universe with us into our ruin."[37] His Foreign Secretary Ribbentrop said in the end: "If we National Socialists should be defeated and disappear, we shall close the door behind us with a bang that the whole earth will tremble."[38]

On the reunification of the two German republics almost all

Western politicians seem agreed on the fact that a divided Germany is a danger to the peace of Europe. Nobody stops to consider that a reunited and remilitarized Germany which, apart from the Ruhr coal, would also own the Silesian coal mines, is bound, within fifteen or twenty years, to become a great danger to all other European nations. Germany had been united for only seven decades and proved a nuisance, a thorn in the flesh of Europe as Thomas Mann said. In spite of the pious words of present-day German politicians, a reunited Germany will soon clamor for the lost Eastern provinces, and being militarized, it might involve Europe in another, a third, world war. A notable Austrian publicist, Dr. Ernst Winter, spoke in 1956 of Germany's *Drang* toward the southeast of Europe, from Frederick II to Hitler, and said that the existence of two separate Germanies would have a paralyzing effect on those German tendencies to expansion while a reunited Germany between Rhine and Vistula would "of necessity constitute the greatest possible danger for Austria's independence, and, indeed, for all nations of the Danube basin. The division of Germany is infinitely preferable to a new German unification, as far as Central Europe is concerned."[39] The French writer François Mauriac, Nobel Prize winner, agreed fully with him when he said: "Even at the risk of people gnashing their teeth, I ask myself whether all the evil that came and comes from Russia is not abundantly outweighed by the invaluable benefit which we owe her: a divided Germany." When two German writers of the younger generation deplored his attitude he answered a few months later that in spite of what these two young Germans said he had not changed his opinion—not out of hatred, as he explained, but out of fear, "out of admiration for the dangerous virtues of your nation."[40] When various Germans showed "surprise" and "indignation," one (only one) German again had the courage to say that Mauriac was, of course, unable and unwilling to forget. "He still sees the red flags" of the Nazis "floating in the streets of Paris, their swastikas looking to him like spiders sucked full with blood. When, thinking of Germany today, he still sees death in the depth of our souls, this should compel us to search our conscience." For one must not forget that the Germans have fought France three times within the last seventy years, the motto being: "God with us." That sober German reminded his fellow countrymen that Mauriac's skepticism against Germany is shared by more people in Great Britain and Italy than the Germans think.[41] Among the resistance fighters against the Hitler regime from 22 European countries who, in the autumn of 1959, attended the unveiling of a memorial for the 92,000 women and children who died at Ravensbruck concentration camp, were many French delegates who wore their former concentration camp clothes: the men, grey and white cotton jackets and the women, shapeless dresses of the same design.

General Sir Lewis Halliday, V.C., wrote in 1955 when the Geneva Conference was about to start: "Is it pertinent to remember that Germany was not 'united' until within 90 years ago, when Prussia forced war on Austria in 1866? The object was, in the words of Bismarck, 'to unite Germany' (including Austria) 'by force against France.' There was then little in common between Prussia and the various German states, such as Bavaria and Baden. In 1868 von Moltke began his 'Projects for war with France.' In 1870, 'united' Germany attacked and crushed the French armies. In 1914, united Germany again attacked France and menaced the world. In 1938 united Germany attempted world domination. Germany should never again be united."[42] In 1959, General Halliday reminded us of this letter and said: "It is no use blinding ourselves to the fact that East Germany now is, and so far as is humanly foreseeable will be, a satellite of Russia. That being so, West Berlin is not only a stumbling block and menace to world peace, but has become an absurd anomaly. Consequently, West Berlin should now, of course, with due compensation from East Germany, be evacuated and a new Berlin be established in West Germany."[43] The Marqess of Bristol said two years later: "In the not too distant future Berlin may be a dead city anyhow. The people are getting out. . . . It would be much better if the West Germans agreed to cede West Berlin to the East, and then compensate appropriately those who wished to leave and did not already possess a stake elsewhere."[44]

As to Communism in general, we can only hope that it will gradually become less rigid, less dogmatic, less totalitarian. It is bound to change as time goes on, but it may take generations, as it took Western Europe many centuries to free itself from totalitarian dogmatism in 1789. Cardinal Spellman said in the summer of 1960 that the day would come when the Communist rulers of today would be swept away, and that we must not relax in our efforts to hasten this. With all due respect, such a policy can only lead to a third war which will destroy the world. Communism would never have arisen if the European states had worked out satisfactory social conditions everywhere before the *Communist Manifesto* was published in the middle of the 19th century. Communism won the masses only in backward countries, like Russia, China, Germany, and the Balkan states. It never appealed to many people in the democratic states of Western Europe and the United States. Now we have about 1,000 million Communists who cannot just be swept away. We must try to come with them to a *modus vivendi,* a sort of peaceful co-existence. If we treat them as enemies, we shall certainly make enemies of them. In the meantime, we must go on hoping that they will become more liberal in their practical philosophy, although still retaining nationalization of the soil and state ownership of industry. Of Poland, Professor Carlo Schmid said that it is "no longer a totalitarian police state"; even Roman Catholics told him so in Warsaw. Professors can openly say that they had never mentioned, and never would, the names of Marx and Lenin in their lectures and books. Science is free in Poland; only a very few professors are Communists. Roman Catholic professors base their juridical lectures on Catholic natural law. The Churches are often overfull with worshippers, young and old.[45]

We can only hope that things will slowly become better also in Czechoslovakia and even in the Eastern Zone of Germany if we leave these states alone. Constant propaganda against them can only harden their minds. This is also the opinion of Professor J. P. Corbett, Sussex University, who said that the policy of the West during the last twelve years "rested on the vague assumption" that Russia could be "rolled back." The Russians who "withstood the Nazi onslaught" will not collapse, nor will the West go to war for the reunification of Germany. It has always been an illusion that if West Germany was integrated into the NATO system and powerfully rearmed, "the East German regime would disintegrate, Germany would be reunited, and all would be well." But this policy brought about "precisely the opposite result." Professor Corbett reminds us that the Germans, "by supporting or condoning the activities of the Nazis," brought the Russians into Europe, and this resulted in the establishment of a German Communist state. As a liberal Englishman he does, of course, not agree with the Communist creed but he stresses the fact that we must try to live with it. "We should go out to meet them intellectually without fear or carping or calculation but patiently and calmly, neither to praise nor to blame, as Spinoza put it, but to understand. In this way an intellectual and moral atmosphere can be created in which practical negotiations might emerge from endless misunderstanding and recrimination, and turn unsettled into settled peace; while if we continue to meet the Communist intellectual challenge with flat hostility we shall only help to confirm it precisely in those dogmatic and unprincipled habits of thought which is our highest interest to dispel."[46]

This is the language of sensible men, Germans and Englishmen alike, but the Germans do not want to listen to reason. They try to shift German responsibility onto the shoulders of the Western nations. They have always possessed a congenital gift for putting the blame on other people. An enlightened German, however, Christian Lichtenberg, who had visited England several times, said already two hundred years ago: "Nowhere is man as esteemed as in England. Everything is being enjoyed here in a way of which others under the government of soldiers can only dream." The British constitution, combining as it did, republican liberty with the idea of monarchy, "prevented any change from a democracy into a plain monarchy or despotism."[47]

The present book intends to answer in detail Mr. Joll's, and Mr. Taylor's questions, to explain the German present (the Third Reich and the post-war period) by the German past, and to put things into their proper perspective. Innumerable German books have appeared since 1945, books by reasonable and books by unteachable Germans, and it is now possible—and indeed very necessary—to draw the balance, all the more so as Mr. Taylor felt compelled to state: "We are all rather ashamed of having told the truth about the German behaviour. We like to pretend that it did not happen, and we try to treat the German past as much like the past of any other country."[48] This forgetful attitude has far-reaching political consequences. Very few people in this country seem to know anything of the German past of the last ten or fifteen decades, not only the political but also, and even more so, the intellectual history, and hardly anyone knows what a decent German minority has always said about and against German developments since the days of Goethe or even Luther. Nobody seems to know anything of what the decent German minority of today has to say about the consequences of Hitlerism and the German post-war behavior. Their voices are constantly drowned in the noise which German politicians and newspapers make day in, day out about the "wrongs" which have been, and are still being, done to Germany.

Things have gone from bad to worse in Germany since Sir Lewis Namier pointed to the first post-war falsifications of German history by German writers, since Professor H. R. Trevor-Roper stated that the Germans prefer to forget the National Socialist period rather than understand it, and since Professor Barraclough complained that German historians who try to convey an unvarnished picture of the German past are in a hard-pressed minority.[49] Also in Germany, so decent a writer as Stefan Andres has complained bitterly that only the petty thieves have been hanged but that the big are at large and back again in their old, or even in new, positions. "They get their pensions and write their memoirs without a word of shame and self-accusation, and are only occupied with the restoration of their honor and the dishonesty of the others."[50] A number of Hitler's generals, admirals, and other "experts" of the Third Reich have combined and written a *Balance of the Second World War*. All aspects of this war are reviewed in detail from a purely German point of view and much is told in some 500 pages about what the Germans did to help Hitler win the war. The German soldiers, airmen, and parachutists are highly praised, the partisans of the enemies of the Third Reich condemned. Hitler, says one of Hitler's generals, made a peace offer after the defeat of Poland but the West unfortunately declined. General Guderian is grieved that Hitler did not knock out Great Britain after the defeat of France. Others blame the West for not allowing the Germans to defeat Russia and quote Dönitz's words of May 1, 1945: "The Anglo-Americans continue the war not for the sake of their own safety but for the spreading of Bolshevism in Europe."[51] This is the new stab-in-the-back legend of which we shall hear more on later pages. Hardly a word is uttered in this history about the unspeakable crimes perpetrated by innumerable Germans. The deportation to Germany of millions of foreigners as slave workers is glossed over with a few mitigating words. Schwerin von Krosigk, Hitler's Finance Minister, gives details of how the war was financed without remembering his Führer's words that 18 million slave workers would pay for the war. The extermination of the Jewish race is hardly mentioned.

The writer of the present book aims at restoring the *full* truth about the German past, and in doing this he bases his arguments entirely on German documents, political and literary. Extensive quotations will be unavoidable, and the author would like to apologize for this here. Only in this manner can he hope that his book will be really persuasive. If he himself were to say all the things that a decent German minority has been saying since the days of Bismarck, he might be accused, even by benevolent readers, of bias, distortion, and exaggeration. Truly, this is not a book of hatred nor does it intend to arouse or renew hatred. It is a dispassionate appraisal of German history and mentality during the last two centuries. I follow the advice of the German historian Walter Goetz who said to the Germans in 1924, in vain: "It is not the historian's task to treat a misunderstood past with reverence, but to explore it mercilessly."[52] But to really understand what established itself in Germany in 1933 we must go far back in history—indeed, two thousand years back.

Notes

1. *The National and English Review,* London, January, 1957.
2. *New Statesman,* London, March 7, 1959.
3. *Sueddeutsche Zeitung,* Muenchen, January 5, 1957; *Club Republikanischer Journalisten,* Koeln, June, 1957; Picht, et al. *Bilanz des Zweiten Weltkrieges.* Oldenburg, 1953, p. 21.
4. *The Listener,* London, March 10, 1955.
5. Gerhard Ritter. *Europa und die deutsche Frage.* Muenchen, 1948, pp. 199-200.
6. Professor Hans Kohn (ed.). *German History: Some New German Views,* London, 1954, pp. 27, 200.

7. Ritter, *op. cit.*, p. 194.
8. *Ibid.*, pp. 45, 47, 51, 52, 199; Kohn, *op. cit.*, pp. 164ff.
9. *Die Sammlung*, Goettingen, May, 1950; *Deutsche Rundschau*, Stuttgart, January, 1956.
10. *Historische Zeitschrift*, Muenchen, Vol. CLXXII/2, October, 1951.
11. Winfried Martini. *Das Ende Aller Sicherheit*. Stuttgart, 1954, pp. 113, 312.
12. *Propyläen-Weltgeschichte*, Berlin, 1960, Vol. IX, p. 77.
13. *Ibid.*, p. 13.
14. *Ibid.*, pp. 394, 389, 400, 403, 429, 456, 457.
15. *Ibid.*, pp. 257, 264.
16. *Nuernberger Nachrichten*, February 18, 1959.
17. Klaus Mehnert. *Der Sowjetmensch*. Stuttgart, 1959, p. 329.
18. *Kriegsschriften des Kaiser-Wilhelm Dank*. Berlin, 1914, Pamphlet No. 3.
19. *Nuernberger Nachrichten*, March 18, 1958.
20. *Deutsche Woche*, Muenchen, September 6, 1961.
21. *Nuernberger Nachrichten*, September 8, 1959.
22. H. J. Schultz (ed.). *Deutsche, Juden, Christen*. Stuttgart, 1961, p. 202.
23. *Blaetter fuer deutsche und internationale Politik*, Koeln, September, 1961.
24. *Sunday Times*, London, July 16, July 30, 1961.
25. *Blaetter*, Koeln, January, 1962.
26. *Daily Telegraph*, London, September 2, 1961.
27. *Ibid.*
28. *Sunday Times*, London, July 12, 1959.
29. *Bulletin of the Wiener Library*, London, 1960, III.
30. *The Listener*, London, November 10, 1960.
31. *Sunday Times*, London, November 6, March 13, 1960.
32. *Daily Telegraph*, London, November 7, 1960.
33. *Parliamentary Debates*. Hansard, London, November 1, 1960.
34. *Observer*, London, March 23, 1958.
35. *Sunday Express*, London, November 19, 1961.
36. *Sunday Times*, London, March 30, 1958.
37. H. Rauschning. *Gespraeche mit Hitler*. New York, 1940, p. 11.
38. Lali Horstmann. *Unendlich viel ist uns geblieben*. Muenchen, 1954, p. 83.
39. *Die oesterreichische Nation*, Wien, April, 1956.
40. *Blaetter*, Koeln, March, 1959.
41. *Nuernberger Nachrichten*, May 3, 1958; *Dokumente*, Koeln, February, 1959.
42. *Die Kultur*, Muenchen, June 15, 1958.
43. *Daily Telegraph*, London, July 16, 1955, September 11, 1959.
44. *Ibid.*, December 12, 1961.
45. *Die Zeit*, Hamburg, March 20, 1958.
46. *The Listener*, London, November 2, 1961.
47. Carl Brinitzer. *Lichtenberg*. Tuebingen, 1956, pp. 60, 70.
48. *New Statesman*, London, October 6, 1956.

49. Sir Lewis Namier. *In the Nazi Era.* London, 1952, p. 5; H. R. Trevor-Roper, *Foreign Affairs,* New York, January, 1953, p. 225; Barraclough, *The Listener,* London, May 27, 1954.

50. *Sueddeutsche Zeitung,* Muenchen, June 18, 1955.

51. *Bilanz des zweiten Weltkrieges,* p. 433.

52. G. A. Mueller. *Regierte der Kaiser?* Goettingen, 1959, p. 27.

1
Jesus as a Jewish Prophet

EVER SINCE THE FOUR GOSPELS WERE WRITTEN DOWN SOME nineteen hundred years ago, innumerable books and essays have been written by theologians and historians to explain their meaning, to praise them uncritically or to criticize—more or less severely—their meaning. Some scholars even went as far as to regard them as mere myths comparable to the myths of the ancient Greeks. But most scholars of our day are of the opinion that the reports according to St. Mark, St. Matthew, St. Luke, and St. John contain a core of historical truth, although it seems impossible to them to differentiate between what really happened and what was only based on unverifiable rumors. "Of Jesus of Nazareth," said Paul Goodman, a famous Jewish scholar, "as he was in reality, we know no more than we choose to fancy according to the descriptions left of him in his biographies in the New Testament."[1] Julius Wellhausen, the most famous of all Protestant biblical scholars of the 19th century, said long ago: "Mark left but a few really historic facts to his successors, and what they assert beyond those facts, is of doubtful value."[2] Rupert Furneaux said more recently: "An historical Jesus, a real man, does not exist in the pages of the New Testament. The idealized picture was the creation of the later Church. . . . The Jesus of the Gospels remains an enigma, unexplained and unexplainable. He is the creation of a later period which conceived him in its own image."[3]

We must not forget that the Gospels were written 40 to 80 years after the events which they narrate. The gospel writers collected—more or less uncritically—different (and often contradictory) tales, and put words into the mouth of Jesus and the other characters which may never have been spoken or may have been altered and distorted many times through oral tradition, as is usual even today. They describe the same events in different ways and in different orders, one adding new things, another leaving out certain episodes. Take, for instance, the last words of Jesus on the cross. Mark makes him say in Aramaic: "My God, my God, why hast thou forsaken me?" Matthew repeats these words, a quotation from the 22nd Psalm, which appears to mean that Jesus had realized that his mission had ended in failure. Luke gives as Jesus' last words: "Father, into they hands I commend my spirit," while John makes him say: "It is finished."

So what Jesus really said on this or that occasion will forever remain an unanswerable riddle. But it is clear to a minority of unprejudiced scholars that, to quote Wellhausen again, "Jesus was not a Christian; he was a Jew."[4] And so was John the Baptist, whose Jewish name was Jochanan. When he preached to his fellow Jews, "Repent ye, for the kingdom of heaven is at hand," he repeated the preachings of the Jewish prophets from Amos to Jeremiah. According to the evangelists, Jesus refers again and again to the Old Testament. He says, for instance, "The first of all commandments is, Hear O Israel, The Lord our God is one Lord. . . . And the second is like, namely this, Thou shalt love thy neighbor as thyself" (Mark 12:29-31). We must remember these commandments when we deal with the history of Christian and German anti-Semitism. Luke (18:20) makes Jesus say: "Do not commit adultery, Do not kill, Do not steal, Do not bear false witness, Honour thy father and thy mother." John (15:10) puts these words into his mouth: "If ye keep my commandments, ye shall abide in my love; even as I kept my Father's commandments, and abide in his love." Jesus also warns his followers (Matt. 7:15). "Beware of false prophets which come to you in sheep's clothing, but inwardly they are ravening wolves." His first followers are Jews, too, who quote the Old Testament: "Blessed is he that cometh in the name of the Lord."

What is known to all Christians as the Lord's Prayer—"Our Father which art in heaven"—is called by Professor F. C. Grant "one of the most beautiful, most searching, most comprehensive of all Jewish prayers."[5] The Jewish scholar, Gerald Friedlander, agrees with this when calling the Lord's Prayer "quite Jewish in structure, a type of the seven-fold Jewish prayer that was in vogue before the destruction of the temple."[6] When Jesus blesses the poor in spirit, the pure in heart, the merciful, the peacemakers and those who hunger and thirst after righteousness (Matt. 5) he is referring to similar utterances by Jewish prophets, the Psalmists, and to other passages in the Old Testament. Also his habit of speaking in parables is Jewish. One need only compare his words, "For the kingdom of heaven is like unto a man that is an householder which went out early in the morning to hire labourers into his vineyard" (Matt. 20), with Isaiah's parable (5:1-7), "For the vineyard of the Lord is the house of Israel," to realize that Jesus was a Jew also in his manner of speaking. "With what measure ye mete, it shall be measured to you again" (Matt. 7:2), can also be found in the Talmud. Jesus stressed his Jewishness by asserting: "Think not that I am come to destroy the law or the prophets. I am not

come to destroy, but to fulfill" (Matt. 5:17). Luke (16:16-17)
seems to quote another tradition when he makes Jesus say:
"The law and the prophets were until John: since that time the
Kingdom of God is preached." But in the very next sentence
he retreats from this position and makes Jesus say: "It is easier
for heaven and earth to pass, then one tittle of the law to
fall."

Matthew (5:43-44) makes Jesus say: "Ye have heard that it
was said, Thou shalt love thy neighbour, and hate thine enemy:
but I say unto you, Love your enemies, and pray for them that
persecute you." Christian commentators tell us that these words
refer to Deuteronomy (23:1-6): "Thou shalt not seek their
peace nor their prosperity all thy days for ever." These words
refer to the special case of the Ammonites and Moabites who
"met you not with bread and with water in the way when ye
came forth out of Egypt; and because they hired against thee
Balaam the son of Baor to curse thee. . . . but the Lord turned
the curse into a blessing unto thee." Why, one may ask, should
Matthew make Jesus refer to that ancient episode? Jesus could
have referred to many another command in the Old Testament
which allows for no "but I say unto you." In Exodus (23:4-5,
9) we read: "If thou meet thine enemy's ox or his ass going
astray, thou shalt surely bring it back to him again. If thou see
the ass of him that hateth thee lying under his burden, and
wouldst forbear to help him, thou shalt surely help with him.
. . . Also thou shalt not oppress a stranger: for ye know the heart
of a stranger, seeing ye were strangers in the land of Egypt." In
Leviticus (19:17-18, 34) we read: "Thou shalt not hate thy
brother in thine heart. . . . Thou shalt not take vengeance but
thou shalt love thy neighbor as thyself. . . . The stranger that
sojourneth with you shall be unto you as the homeborn among
you, and thou shalt love him as thyself." In Proverbs (24:17
and 25:21) we read: "Rejoice not when thine enemy falleth,
and let not thine heart be glad when he stumbleth. . . . If thine

enemy be hungry, give him bread to eat; and if he is thirsty, give him water to drink." That all these commandments were obeyed by the Jews we can see from what some rabbis living at the age of Jesus said. Rabbi Nachman said: "He is strong who turns an enemy into a friend." Another rabbi: "If a friend wants thy help in loading up, first help thy enemy, so that the evil impulse may be conquered." In the Talmud we read: "A pagan who does the good from all his heart is as highranking as the High Priest of Israel."[7]

It is therefore that Furneaux says: "Nothing in his [Jesus'] teaching was new; it can all be found in Jewish tradition. . . . It has frequently been observed that Jesus taught nothing more than was already well known in Jewish thought."[8] Goodman denies that Jesus "gave a unique significance to the Fatherhood of God."[9] Friedlander, too, denies "that the Fatherhood of God is expounded by Jesus with more depth and intensity than by the great prophets and teachers of Israel."[10] Shalom ben Chorin says Jesus "did not teach anything that was new. We find to nearly everyone of his teachings and parables parellels in the Old Testament and in Rabbinic literature." The Gospels tell the Jews "no new wisdom, no new law."[11]

The greatest German writer, Goethe, who called the history of the Church a mixture of error and terror, once said:

> Jesus fühlte rein und dachte
> Nur den einen Gott im stillen.
> Wer ihn selbst zum Gotte machte,
> Kränkte seinen heiligen Willen.[12]

Who was it who first made a God of Jesus? We shall never know. The idea of dying and reborn savior-gods was common heritage of the pre-monotheistic religions of the Middle East, and that belief was still alive among various sects of Graeco-Roman Palestine. Did Jesus regard himself as the Son of God, or was it only after his death that some of his first followers conceived the idea that he had been a God who had come down to earth to deliver humanity from original sin? Again, we shall never know. In the Gospels, at any rate, we read questions like: "Art thou the Christ, the Son of the blessed?" (Mark 14:61 and Matt. 26:63) and hear the answer: "I am" or "Thou hast said." Luke (9:20) makes Jesus ask: "But who say ye that I am?" and Peter answer: "The Christ of God." According to Mark, the centurion, when seeing that Jesus gave up his ghost, says: "Truly this man was the son of God." But Luke (23:47) makes the centurion only say: "This was a righteous man." John, the latest of the Gospel writers, calls Jesus (3:18) "the only begotten Son of God."

Once the idea of Jesus being the Son of God was conceived, people (and, consequently, the Gospel writers) furnished his life with motifs from the Old Testament. Matthew traces his origin back to King David because, as we can see from the Psalms of Solomon, written two or three generations before the Gospels, the Messianic expectations of the Jews were expressed in these words: "Behold, O Lord, and raise unto them their King, the Son of David . . . that he may purge Jerusalem from nations that trample her down to destruction." In Isaiah (7:14) we read: "Behold, a virgin"—Jews say the Hebrew word means a young woman—"shall conceive and bear a son, and shall call his name Immanuel." Matthew (1:22) refers these words to the birth of Jesus saying "that it might be fulfilled which was spoken of the Lord by the prophet." Matthew (2:13-15) also makes Jesus and his mother flee to Egypt and return to Palestine after the death of Herod "that it might be fulfilled which was spoken by the Lord through the prophet, saying: Out of Egypt did I call my son"—an allusion to Hosea (11:1): "When Israel was a child, then I loved him, and called my son out of Egypt,"—a perfectly arbitrary method of taking words out of their context and using them for an entirely different purpose.

And so it went on through the whole story of Jesus' "life." The story of his birth and the wise men from the East being guided by a star to the child and presenting him with gold, frankincense and myrrh is taken from Isaiah 9: "The people that walked in darkness have seen a great light. . . . For unto us a child is born, unto us a son is given . . . and his name shall be called the everlasting Father, The Prince of Peace"; from Isaiah 60: "The Gentiles shall come to thy light. . . . all they gather themselves together, they come to thee, they shall bring gold and incense," and from Psalm 81: "The Kings of Tarshish and of the isles bring presents: the Kings of Sheba and Seba shall offer gifts." The scene of Jesus' coming up out of the water after being baptized and hearing a voice from heaven saying, "Thou art my beloved Son, in whom I am well pleased," has its origin in Isaiah 42: "Behold my servant whom I uphold; mine elect in whom my sense delighteth. I have put my spirit upon him," and in Psalm 2: "The Lord hath said unto me, Thou art my Son; this day have I begotten thee." Jesus as a good shepherd—this idea is taken from Isaiah 40: "He shall feed his flock like a shepherd: he shall gather the lambs with his arm, and carry them in his bosom." Jesus entering Jerusalem on an ass—see Zechariah IX: "Rejoice greatly, O daughter of Zion . . . behold, thy King cometh unto thee . . . riding upon an ass."

The famous German scholar, Rudolf Bultmann, says about the predictions of the passion which are to be found in the gospels: "Can there by any doubt that all are *vaticinia ex eventu?*"[13] Professor Grant says Jesus knew that he was facing death, and went forward unhesitatingly. "Why? I believe we can understand Jesus better by contemplating the fearless, unhesitating courage of those young men who gave their lives in battle, not long ago, to save our world from tyranny and servitude."[14]

We now come to the last supper of Jesus and his disciples. Jesus, we read (Mark 14), "took bread, and blessed, and broke it, and gave to them, and said, Take, eat: this is my body. And he took the cup, and when he had given thanks, he gave it to them, and they all drank of it. And he said unto them, This is my blood of the new testament." In the Old Testament (Ex. 24) we read of Moses telling the people all the words of the Lord and building an altar, "and twelve pillars, according to the twelve tribes of Israel." The people make peace offerings of oxen. "And Moses took the blood, and sprinkled it on the people, and said, Behold the blood of the covenant, which the Lord hath made with you concerning all these words." Thomas Mann says about "Take, eat: this is my body" and "This is my blood": "Is there anybody who does not realise that Christianity, by gruesomely renewing ancient religious and psychological conceptions of blood and sacrificial meals of the flesh of a god, must have appeared to civilised Greeks and Romans as a true horror of regression and atavism by which the nethermost in the world was turned up literally and in every sense of the word?"[15]

When Jesus is brought before Pilate (Mark 15) and the chief priests accuse him "of many things," he "answered nothing," and "Pilate marvelled." This strange behavior goes back to what Isaiah (53) says: "He was oppressed, and he was afflicted, yet he opened not his mouth: he is brought as a lamb to the slaughter, and as a sheep before her shearers is dumb, so he opened not his mouth." After the crucifixion the Roman soldiers, according to all four Gospel writers—I am quoting John 19—"took his garments and made four parts, to every soldier a part; and also the coat: They said, Let us not rend it, but cast lots for it whose it shall be." This is taken from Psalm 22: "They pierced my hands and my feet . . . They part my garments among them, and cast lots upon my vesture." John says: "That the scripture might be fulfilled which saith" and quotes Psalm 22.

Professor Grant says: "Certainly Jesus was a complete and thorough Jew. The 'Nordic' nonsense popular in Germany in the 1930's, with its purely 'Aryan' Christ, was utterly impossible."[16] That nonsense was popularized in Germany by many forerunners of Hitler. Many a Jew has claimed Jesus back: Professor Klausner, Rabbi Leo Baeck, Claude Montefiore, Shalom Asch in three novels, Max Brod, a German-Jewish writer now living in Israel, in his novel, *The Master,* and the Israeli writer Abraham Kabak in his novel, *The Narrow Path.* Martin Buber said: "From my early youth on I regarded Jesus as my elder brother."[17] Constantin Brunner, a German-Jewish thinker who left Germany in 1933 and died in Holland of a broken heart while his books were being burned by the Gestapo, said long ago that the words of Jesus "show not the slightest connection with 'religious philosophy,' let alone with philosophy. . . ." John does not dare to put "the Word"—"In the beginning was the Word"—"into the mouth of Christ." None of the words of Jesus have anything to do with Greek wisdom, "everything sounds like the wisdom of Israel." But "to this very day, 'Christians' refuse to agree that Christ was a thorough Jew." Brunner reminds us of those German racialists who used to say: "Christ possessed also Aryan blood, Christ possessed only Aryan blood. It is a Jewish lie that Christ was a Jew. He was an Aryan. Only Aryans, only Germans, only anti-Semites can produce a genius. Christ is a German, a Westphalian, a Saxon anti-Semite."[18] Shalom ben Chorin says that Jesus brought "no peace and no redemption. 'Thy Kingdom come': the faith of Jesus unites us, but the faith in Jesus divides us. Jesus of Nazareth was not the saviour and redeemer promised by the prophets of the Old Testament, because he did not redeem the world. I cannot see the cross of Golgatha as an isolated fact. It stands amidst the terrible smoke which went up to heaven from the crematoria of Auschwitz and Maidanek where innocent Jewish children were gassed and burned, all of them suffering servants of God who had to suffer for the others. And I see the stakes of the *auto-da-fés* of the Spanish Inquisition which burned Jews for the higher honor of God. And I see the German Rhine reddened by the blood of murdered Jews

during the crusades. . . . Since I have moved from Christian
Europe into Jewish Israel, Jesus is much nearer to me. When I
lift my chalice at the passover meal and break the unleavened
bread, I am doing what he did, and I know I am nearer to him
than many a Christian. Jesus, the Jew, the image of a Jew, is
near to us as he can never be to Christians, because he was
ours."[19]

Notes

1. Thomas Walker. *Jewish Views of Jesus*. London, 1931, p. 27.
2. A. Drews. *Das Markusevangelium als Zeugnis gegen die Geschicht-
lichkeit Jesu*. Jena, 1921, p. 2.
3. R. Furneaux. *The Other Side of the Story*. London, 1953, pp. 1, 6.
4. *Ibid.*, p. 7.
5. F. C. Grant. *Ancient Judaism and the New Testament*. Edinburgh,
1960, p. 187.
6. Walker, *op. cit.*, p. 43.
7. F. W. Foerster. *Die juedische Frage*. Freiburg, 1959, p. 123.
8. Furneaux, *op. cit.*, pp. 8, 52.
9. Walker, *op. cit.*, p. 43.
10. *Ibid.*, pp. 32-33.
11. *Juden und Christen: Unterwegs* No. 12, Berlin, 1960, pp. 29, 35.
12. "Jesus in his pure heart only thought of one God. Those who made
a God of him offended his holy will." *Westoestlicher Divan*. Grosse Weimarer oder Sophien-ausgabe. Weimar—1887-1919. Part I, Vol. VI, p. 288.
13. Oscar Cullmann. *The Christology of the New Testament*. London,
1959, pp. 60, 61.
14. Grant, *op. cit.*, p. 144.
15. *Die Forderung des Tages*. Berlin, 1930, p. 200.
16. Grant, *op. cit.*, p. 117.
17. *Juden und Christen*, p. 14.
18. Constantin Brunner. *Unser Christus*. Re issued Koeln, 1958, pp. 193,
212, 545.
19. *Deutsche, Juden, Christen*, pp. 140-150.

2
Early Christianity
and Anti-Semitism

THOSE WHO ARE FAMILIAR WITH THE HISTORY OF EUROPEAN
Christianity tell us that Nazism has its roots in Christian anti-
Semitism. Rev. Dr. James Parkes said: "In our own day more
than six million deliberate murders are the consequence of the
teachings about the Jews for which the Christian Church is
ultimately responsible, and of an attitude to Judaism which is
not only maintained by all the Christian Churches, but has its
ultimate resting place in the teaching of the New Testament
itself."[1] Professor Helmut Gollwitzer, a German Protestant, said:
"We still find in many Christian communities an aversion
against penance for what has happened, because racial anti-
Semitism was preceded by Christian anti-Semitism and paved,
and is still paving, the way for it."[2] Professor Jules Isaac, a
French Jew, and Shalom ben Chorin said the same. Dr. Ernst
Ludwig Ehrlich, a Swiss Jew, says that what the National So-

cialists did to the Jews was nothing new for it had been "done, not by pagan barbarians, but by Christians for 2,000 years." The Church has for too long a time been telling the world that the Jews were guilty and had to suffer, and this conception led to "all devilish deeds" against them being justified. He reminds us of a picture by the Jewish painter Chagall showing a burning village and fleeing Jews, and Christ on the Cross who wears Jewish phylacteries and looks at his Jewish brethren knowing that he himself is being persecuted in every persecuted Jew. "It is the tragedy of all Christian-Jewish relationships that only the most wicked of all criminals"—Adolf Hitler—"opened the eyes of the Christians so that they realise now what fatal companionship they have kept for 2,000 years."[3] Sir Lewis Namier says that the other nations built "on the rock of our existence, the Book," but "the Jews have suffered the most incredible persecutions and tortures in the two thousand years of Dispersion."[4]

As to the New Testament, quite a number of biblical scholars —Jews, Germans, Englishmen, Dutchmen, Frenchmen, Swedes, Norwegians, and Americans—have been pointing out for more than two centuries that the story told in the four Gospels is at variance with the historical facts as far as they are known to us from other sources. They have shown that the tradition that reached the evangelists was already an interpreted tradition, a Christological interpretation of the things that had happened one, two, or three generations earlier. The stories told in the Gospels are not historical facts but a conglomeration of facts and fiction, that is, an interpretation of these facts in the light of opinions held by the early adherents of Jesus. The text of the Gospels only preserves fragments of his many discurses with them, intermingled with interpretations of his messages in the light of ideas that had sprung up after his death.

Various German and other biblical scholars have stressed that the record of the trial of Jesus cannot have been based on facts because nobody had witnessed it to tell what had actually happened. "The events," says Dr. Parkes (and various German scholars, for instance Walter Bauer, Martin Dibelius, Wilhelm Brandt, Wilhelm Heitmueller, Paul Wernle agree with him), "which succeeded each other between the time when Jesus disappeared with his guard within the doors of the high-priestly palace and when he appeared again from the palace of the Roman governor, could only be pieced together by hearsay, none of his followers were present."[5] He rebukes Christian scholars, who have been unwilling to listen to the objections of Jewish scholars to these narratives for a long time past. Shalom ben Chorin calls the Gospels "biased missionary texts, but no history books."[6]

Pontius Pilate as pictured in the Gospels is entirely different from the haughty governor whom we know from other sources. The famous German classical scholar, Eduard Norden, said several decades ago that Pontius Pilate was "an irascible, rough and offhandish boss without the slightest understanding for the peculiar character of his subjects" but the Gospels surrounded him with "a tendentious legend."[7] Dr. Parkes speaks of "the unconvincing details of Pilate's pusillanimous pity which we have in the Gospel narratives." The procedures adopted for the trial "are incomprehensible from our knowledge of both Jewish and Roman law."[8]

What the Gospels put into the mouth of Jesus, Julius Wellhausen, the most famous German biblical scholar of the nineteenth century, argued a long time ago, nowhere amounted to a blasphemy from the Jewish point of view. Matthew makes Jesus say: "Hereafter shall ye see the Son of man sitting on the right hand of power, and coming in the clouds of heaven." Hans Lietzmann said about these words in 1931: "This could have been abhorred as a mad fantasy, fought as a corrupting superstition but it was no blasphemy."[9] Jack Finegan, in 1934, thought the examination before the High Priest (Mark 55-65) fictitious.

"If the Synedrion had found Jesus guilty of blasphemy, it would have had him stoned without delay."[10]

T. A. Burkill says: "It is part of St. Mark's doctrinal purpose to make it plain to his readers that the ill-will [of the Jews] was the determining factor behind the crucifixion."[11] The same can be said (and was said) of St. John's narrative, (19:7): "We have a law, and by our law he ought to die because he made himself the Son of God." Orazio Marucchi, a Roman Catholic scholar, said in 1908: "Jesus Christ was condemned for the crime of sedition and tumult."[12] Professor F. X. Arnold, a German Roman Catholic, said in 1960: "The myth of the Jewish guilt for the crucifixion of Jesus has been tenaciously preserved in the catechisms of all Christian denominations. It is an historical fact that the Roman Pilate pronounced the death sentence against Jesus, and that the crucifixion was a Roman, not a Jewish, way of execution. And did the crucified Jesus not say from the cross: 'Father, forgive them for they know not what they are doing'?"[13] Maurice Goguel, a French Protestant, said: "Jesus was arrested as an agitator, or as a person who might become the occasion of a political agitation."[14] Heinz Lietzmann said: Crucifixion was "a typical Roman punishment. So it is pretty clear that Pilate condemned him, not the Synedrion. He condemned him as 'King of the Jews' and had him crucified. This was the usual punishment for rebels."[15] Another German scholar, Gustav Hoelscher, said: "The religious movements caused by St. John the Baptist and Jesus belonged, from a political point of view, to the series of many disturbances of which Josephus tells us between 6 and 66 B.C. The political authorities intervened in both cases."[16] The same was said by Oscar Cullmann and William Reuben Farmer. Dr. Parkes is of exactly the same opinion: "Nobody knew what had passed behind the closed doors of the palace of Jerusalem; but Christians must often have reproached Jews with 'having killed the Messiah'. . . . The Romans would not care what he taught, but would merely see a man who was capable of attracting an immense following among a turbulent subject people. From their point of view a man who cleansed the temple might suddenly try to 'cleanse' Jerusalem of the Roman eagles."[17]

While Christians have been asserting for two thousand years that Jesus brought something entirely new into the world, Herbert J. Muller Professor of Indiana University, says: "Nothing seems more certain that neither he nor his first followers had any intention of founding a new religion. . . . He died, as he had lived, a devout Jew." The "famous Rabbi Hillel also taught that true religion was summed up in the two commandments, to love God and love thy neighbour." Jesus' teaching was "essentially that of the great prophets of Israel"; he never boasted of the Davidic ancestry attributed to him by Luke and Mark. "The New Testament was the product of the early Churches, not their basis." He can neither be made responsible for the success or the failure of Christianity. His followers "transfigured" him. "He became the Christ, a Greek word he was unaquainted with. He was identified with the Logos that he never heard of."[18] Rev. James Parkes asks: "Did Jesus teach that he was replacing Sinai, and that the old Israel was thereby rejected to be replaced by a new Israel? . . . The general assumption has led to extravagant interpretations by both Roman Catholic and Protestant theologians."[19] When Matthew, however, (10:34-35) makes Jesus say: "Think not that I am come to send peace on earth: I came not to send peace, but a sword. For I am come to set a man at variance against his father, and the daughter against her mother"—Ben Chorin answers that these words, as the history of Jews and Christians prove, "have come true to a most terrible extent."[20]

In Acts (3:18) we read: "God had shewed by the mouth of all his prophets that Christ should suffer." Dr. Parkes says: "Jesus was not the Messiah as envisioned by the prophets. No prophet envisaged a Messiah who would be rejected by his own people." A Messiah who would be regarded as an outcast and, by his death, would atone for the sins of humankind "was foreign to such messianic expectation as is found in the prophets." Jesus, as impartial scholars agree, never claimed such a messianic role, but the evangelists sought "to fit him into the pattern of the Messiah foretold by the prophets."[21] The most famous passage used for this purpose was Isaiah 53: "He is despised and rejected of men . . . surely he hath borne our griefs, and carried our sorrows: yet we did esteem him stricken, smitten of God, and afflicted. But he was wounded for our transgressions, he was bruised for our iniquities: the chastisement of our peace was upon him; and with his stripes we are healed."

Jewish rabbis and scholars have, from the very beginning, denied that these ancient and mysterious words had anything to do with the life and death of Jesus, but, as the Jews have been a persecuted minority for two thousand years, their protesting voices have been drowned by the others. We cannot quote all these Jewish protestants, but a few may serve our purpose. Saadia, the Gaon of Sura, who lived in the 10th century, identified the "righteous servant" with the prophet Jeremiah.[22] Rabbi Abraham Ibn Ezra applied the words of Isaiah to the suffering of the Jews by the other nations. Rabbi Shlomo ben Yizhak of Troyes, Rabbi Yizhak Lopez of Aleppo, and Rabbi David Kimchi (13th century) agreed with him. Rabbi Moses ben Nachman, a Spanish Jew of the 13th century, looking around at the ways of the world, denied that the Messiah of the Jews had already come by quoting Isaiah 2:4 and Micah 4:3: "And they shall beat their swords to plowshares, and their spears into pruning-hooks: nation shall not lift up sword against nation, neither shall they learn war any more."[23] He probably did not know that Origen had said centuries before him: "We have come, listening to the teachings of Jesus, to destroy the swords with which we fought for our opinions and attacked our adversaries. For we do not lift up the sword against a nation nor do we learn war any more after we have become children of peace by Jesus."[24] Who has ever listened to these words?

Rabbi Shem Tow ben Shaprut of Toledo (14th century) referred Isaiah 53 "to the depression of Israel among the Gentiles". Don Abarbanel (16th century) called the Christian opinions "perverted interpretations."[25] Solomon Levi of Salonica (16th century) and Rabbi Abraham of Cordoba (16th century) agreed with what many of their predecessors had said, and so did Isaac Orobio de Castro, a Jewish doctor who fled from Spain to Amsterdam in the 17th century: "With his stripes we are healed—the prophet says that from the troubles of Israel health resulted to the nations. We know that from these troubles and sufferings good will result not only for Israel, but also for many nations. The nations will be cured of their envy, their hatred. This health the nations will enjoy at the redemption of Israel. And this the nations will confess, saying: The chastisment of our peace was upon him, and with his stripes we are healed."[26]

By and by, from the 18th century onward, Christian biblical scholars also, especially German Lutherans, began to agree with the Jewish point of view that the righteous servant was the nation Israel. The famous Professor Alfred Jeremias said in 1906 that the righteous servant of Isaiah was "a prophetic-Israelite Tammuz-figure who offers himself willingly. It is possible that the prophet had in mind a definite royal martyr-figure of his own time."[27] Rabbi Epstein says today: "The Suffering Servant is the symbol of suffering mankind. The suffering of the Jewish people down all ages is no mark of their guilt, but symptomatic of the world. Their miseries throw a grave reproach on other peoples."[28]

But we must return to the times of Jesus. Rev. Robert Travers Herford complained long ago that the Gospels picture the Pharisees as the opponents of Jesus, while, in reality, Jesus and the Pharisees "shared in common a Judaism in the terms of a spiritual Theism." But for two thousand years innumerable

Christian scholars regarded the Pharisees as hair-splitting hypocrites. All these scholars—Herford especially mentions the Germans Bousset, Ewald, Hilgenfeld, Schuerer, Weber, and Wellhausen—only showed that they had "not the slightest comprehension of the real nature and intention of Pharisaism . . . Pharisaism is usually judged from the outside, as seen by not friendly eyes." The only real contributions to the knowledge of Pharisaism have been made by Jewish scholars who, rightly, stress the similarity between the teachings of Jesus and the teachings of the rabbis of his time. "Psalm CXIX," Herford says, "is one long joyous hymn of praise, in glorification of Torah and of God who gave it. And, if anyone desires to know what a Pharisee meant by Torah, and even more, what Torah meant to a Pharisee, let him study this Psalm." When Judaism and Christianity parted, "it was the dividing, not of the living from the dead, but of the living from the living." The high conception of Torah enabled the Jews "to endure through the centuries of persecution and the world's ill-will down to the present day." Non-Jews who speak of "the mechanical formalism of Jewish prayers" have little knowledge of Jewish liturgy.[29]

Rev. James Parkes endorsed Rev. Herford's view in our time. Jesus and the Pharisees were agreed on the fundamentals of Judaism and only quarrelled about minor things. He quotes with approval a Jewish scholar, Louis Finkelstein, as saying: "The Pharisees constituted a religious Order of singular influence in the history of civilisation; Judaism, Christianty, and Mohammedanism all derive from this ancient Palestinian Society." Rev. Parkes adds that Christian readers will be astonished or even shocked by these words of a Jew because their "knowledge of the Pharisees rests on the New Testament." But have not already Jean Bodin in the 16th century and the great Cambridge Hebraist, John Selden, and the still greater Dutchman, William Surenhuis, Travers Herford, George Foot Moore challenged the traditional Christian picture of the Pharisees? Rev. Parkes rebukes German-Lutheran scholars for regarding Jewish history between the return of the Jews from their Babylonian exile and the destruction of Jerusalem as "a period of decline," while that period had been very rich in spiritual development. A period that inaugurated popular worship based on prayer and praise, created the vision of man "as fully personal," and deepened the understanding "of the nature of sin and the holiness of God"—such a period could not be called "a period of decay," as was done by many Christian scholars. The Pharisees were "the sole authentic heirs of the line of development which opens with the Babylonian exile . . . and which is still giving the world the worship of synagogue, church and mosque." The sanctity of the Sabbath, a Jewish idea, "played a large part in preserving the Jewish spirit through the centuries of dispersion." Dr. Parkes rebukes W. J. Pythian-Adams, who appreciates the history of the Jews only "from Moses to David," and later on finds nothing but "apostasy, schism and corruption." What, asks Dr. Parkes, about "the great prophets, the many psalmists, the courage of the return, the up-building of synagogue worship, and the steady progress of teaching the people the meaning of loyalty to the will of God?"[30]

Professor Muller speaks of the typical "Christian bias" that calls the Pharisees "legalists" and identifies the word "Pharisaic" with "self-righteous and hypocritical." In reality, the Pharisees were liberals who tried "to adapt the traditional faith to the new conditions" and tolerated "wide differences in opinion." Formalism is common to all religions; Christianty, too, stressed the importance of forms and ceremonies.[31] "A Roman Catholic priest," as Rev. Parkes reminds us, "in celebrating the mass uses a great number of very precise gestures which express spiritual truth and which the congregation accepts as such."[32] Travers Herford says: "The dogmatic theology of the Christian Church has been worked out to a degree of detail and subtle refinement fully equal to anything which the Rabbinical literature can show."[33]

Much anti-Semitism is to be found in the first three Gospels. St. John makes Jesus say: "Ye are of your father the devil and the lusts of your father ye will do. He was a murderer from the beginning." Rev. Herford and Rev. Parkes call the fourth Gospel a stage in the development of anti-Jewish feeling. The charge of the collective guilt of the Jews was repeated a thousand times during the whole Christian era. To mention but a few accusers, Tertullian said: "The whole synagogue of the sons of Israel killed him."[34] Origen said: "One of the proofs for the godly and holy character of Jesus lies in the fact that the Jews have been visited by terrible sufferings up to now. They will never find peace because they have committed the most terrible crime. It was therefore that the city in which Jesus suffered was utterly destroyed and the Jewish race exterminated."[35] Athanasius said: "The Jews are no longer the people of God, but the masters of Sodom and Gomorrah."[36] Jerome said: "That curse is on the Jews up to this day, the blood of our Lord will never be taken from them.[37] John Chrysostom called the Synagogue "a brothel, a place of vice, the Devil's abode."[38] Thomas Aquinas said in immaculate Latin: *"Iudaei peccaverunt non solum tamquam hominis Christi sed etiam tamquam Dei crucfiores."*[39] Until, in our days, Hitler took up this charge in *Mein Kampf* and Streicher, as was said at Nuremberg, recommended "the extermination of that people whose father is the Devil." But even after the last war, a French Roman Catholic writer, R. Rochefort, renewed that charge in a book on the Jewish novelist Kafka. Kafka, he says, who was filled with "an infinite feeling of guilt tried to find in the certainty of negation a reassurance of his conscience. . . . The history of Israel is the story of man in his relation to God, of man, who, having been created for paradise, lost it by his fall and by his guilt moved further and further away from Heaven and still denies the redemption by Christ." The Jews are "the chosen people but, at the same time, the faithless, apostate people on which the curse of God lies."[40] But an open-minded Austrian Roman Catholic, Friedrich Heer, calls Kafka's writings "one of the greatest religious works of our time. It centres in the idea of the Father and is a pilgrimage of the son erring through the labyrinth of the olden times and the olden space . . . to his face which remains hidden, as it remained hidden to Moses. German Jews like Scheler, Husserl, Rosenzweig, Buber, Edith Stein, Landsberg, and French Jews, like Bergson, Simone Weil, Raissa Maritain, also John Newman and many others, whether convertites or Jews, have always considered that hidden face."[41]

A British Jew, Richard Yaffe, who visited Germany in 1961, made the acquaintance of a German who was twenty in 1945, had been in the Hitler Youth and a fighter pilot during the last two years of the war. He was "a devout Catholic who dipped a finger into the holy water and crossed himself as he took me from one lovely Munich church to another. He was an anti-Nazi, of course; I found no pro-Nazis in Germany. I found no one who had ever met a pro-Nazi in Germany. The Hitler hordes which overran Europe must have been composed not of men but of spirits." Mr. Yaffe reports a very interesting conversation which he had with that Roman Catholic, who told him: "Nothing happens in life without plan. God not only knows everything but plans everything."

" 'Even the murder of the six million Jews?'

" 'Yes.'

" 'But why?'

" 'Perhaps for some mortal sin.'

" 'But what sin?'

" 'Perhaps as the final atonement.'

" 'For what sin?'

"He did not reply. He could not get himself to say, in front of a Jew, that which he had learned in his Catechism: the perfidious Jews had killed his Lord.

" 'And God chose the Nazis as the vessel for His terrible wrath against the Jews?'

" 'Yes.'

" 'And, therefore, the Nazis were the chosen of God?'

" 'Yes.' "[42]

We now come to the role played by St. John in the history of Jewish-Christian relations. "Paul's presentation of Judaism," says Rev. Travers Herford, "is at its best a distortion and at its worst a fiction." He "inflicted upon the Jews an injury without excuse," because what he said about them does not correspond with the facts. He told people who were willing to listen to him (and we know that the Jews were not willing to do so) that the "Torah" was a sort of curse. He simply translated it by the Greek word "nomos" (law) and by doing so conjured up a misshapen phantom" which still figures in many books written by Christian theologians of the traditional school. The Law, according to Paul, only plunged the Jews into deeper and deeper despair, increasing, as it allegedly did, the occasions of sin and burdening the sinner with a guilt before God whose many commands he had failed to obey. "No Jew before Paul ever thought of the Torah in a way or ever felt the despair which, according to this theory, he should have felt." On the contrary, the Jew was "full of joy that God had given him something that he could do for His sake." Every command—the Hebrew word for it is *mitzvah*—which a Jew fulfilled, and fulfills, assures him that he fulfills "some part of the divine will" and that God gave him these opportunities because he loved Israel. But Christians still speak of the "burden of the Law," the "bondage" under which the Jews live, because Paul has taught them to do so, and they are convinced of the "superiority of the Gospel over the Law," "the freedom under the Gospel."[43] Charles Guignebert says: "Delight in the Law is the keynote of the lives of the Rabbis."[44]

Rev. Parkes fully agrees with what these scholars say. "Jesus made no wholesale onslaught on the Law. Paul condemns Torah itself in a number of passages. It is one of the mysteries of history that it is Paul and not Jesus who has been the determinant in the Christian attitude to Judaism." He quotes "one of the greatest Christian scholars of rabbinic Judaism," George Foot Moore, who said about "Torah": "It is a source of manifold misconceptions that the word is customarily translated 'Law'. . . . 'Law' must, however, not be understood in the restricted sense of legislation, but must be taken to include the whole of revelation. The prophets call their own utterances Torah." Dr. Parkes finds "repulsive" Paul's words to the Thessalonians (2:1, 7-10) about Jesus coming down from heaven one day and pouring out "vengeance" with fire falling upon those who refuse obedience to the Gospel of Christ, because they stand "in total dissonance from the actual life of Jesus." What Matthew says (25:31-46) about Jesus coming "in his glory" and cursing those who never gave him food or drink and throwing them into the eternal fire which had been prepared for the devil, Dr. Parkes calls "an odd idea of glory," and what Luke makes Jesus say (13:28) of weeping and gnashing of teeth, he calls a "horrifying picture," an "appalling misunderstanding of the life of Jesus of Nazareth."[45]

Professor Muller, another impartial scholar, says that Jesus "preached a simple ethical and apocalyptic gospel in the prophetic tradition." He never said anything of the Davidic ancestry that Luke and Matthew bestowed on him. "The Messiah of tradition was not the Son of God." Jesus taught that man could earn the kingdom of heaven "by his own efforts," by repentance and righteousness. He might have been regarded as one of the Jewish prophets if Paul had not "taken liberties with the Law. . . . He was largely responsible for the violent break with Judaism." When Jews and Christians parted, the Christians took the Old Testament with them and proclaimed "that no virtue was left in Judaism. They were now the chosen people;

the Jews were something worse than pagans, because they had rejected Christ." As time went on, the Church made Jesus "the equal of God" and taught "that salvation was possible only through Christ." For all this Paul is responsible. "He sacrificed the historic Jesus," whom he only knew by hearsay. By his new doctrine of Christ as "the Redeemer who atones the sins of all men since the Fall of Adam," he laid the foundations of orthodox Christianity. "Paul transformed the gospel of Jesus," as, in our time, "Lenin transformed the gospel of Marx."[46]

While neither the Jewish prophets nor Jesus had made anything of the ancient myth of the Garden of Eden, Paul "introduced the idea of Original Sin." He was "the first of a long line of Christian saints whose spirituality involved a morbid fear or hatred of sex"; he taught "a radical dualism of flesh and spirit, unwarranted by the teachings of Jesus."[47] Rabbi Epstein is of the same opinion—"Christian doctrine of the irreconcilable antagonism between the flesh and the spirit." Paul also "relentlessly disparaged the Law as worthless and obsolete, contrasting the slavery of those who live under the Law with the freedom of those who believe in Jesus." Paul's belief was that Christ, by his death on the cross, had atoned for the sins of mankind. "This was in opposition to the teachings of Judaism that atonement and consequent salvation are procured through observance of the Law." Paul "is guilty of deliberate perversion of the significance of the Law."[48]

Professor Muller blames Paul for yet another doctrine which had catastrophic consequences throughout European history. "He provided the text that became perhaps the most influential argument for bondage to absolute monarchs: 'The powers that be are ordained of God. Whosoever therefore resisteth the power, resisteth the ordinance of God; and they that resist shall receive to themselves damnation.'"[49] One has only to look at the history of Europe in order to see the consequences of this doctrine.

As Rev. Parkes reminds us, the Church, from the very beginning, "emphasized every passage in the prophets denouncing the rebelliousness of the children of Israel, and quoted with relish every passage in which their destruction is foretold."[50] The Jewish scholar Cecil Roth says that the Jews revolted against the barbaric rule of the Romans, and their leaders "either perished sword in hand, or were subjected to the ruthless judgment of the Roman conqueror." But very soon after the destruction of Jerusalem, Christian theologians eagerly began "to emphasize the lesson. The Jews, so recently responsible for the most grievous of crimes, were now to receive their punishment."[51] Professor F. W. Foerster, the most decent of all Germans today, says: "Vespasian ordered his son Titus finally to destroy the whole city since it was the only power which still offered resistance to the world-empire of Rome." The triumphal arch erected in Rome to Titus "in gratitude for having subjected the Jewish people and destroyed the city of Jerusalem" is a towering monument to the heroism of Israel."[52] Professor Muller quotes Rabbi Johanan ben Zakkai, who lived to see the destruction of Jerusalem, as saying that now "the Jews would have only the Almighty and his Law, but this would suffice." Professor Muller adds: "That it did indeed suffice, and through far worse trials than he could have foreseen, is the unique glory of Judaism."[53] Rev. Parkes says that Rabbi Johanan ben Zakkai "made of the teaching of Torah the basis of survival," and adds: "There is no sadder or more touching verdict on the destruction of the Temple than the words of a third century rabbi that, since the destruction of the Temple, the gates of prayer are locked but the gates of tears are always open."[54]

Notes

1. Malcolm Hay. *The Foot of Pride*. Boston, 1950, p. 11.
2. *Rundbrief XII*, Freiburg, 1959.

3. *Ibid.*
4. *Conflicts.* London, 1942, pp. 126-127.
5. J. Parkes. *The Foundations of Judaism and Christianity.* London, 1960, p. 160.
6. *Juden und Christen,* pp. 33-34.
7. Paul Winter. *On the Trial of Jesus.* Berlin, 1961, p. 176.
8. Parkes *op. cit.,* pp. 160, 164.
9. *Der Prozess Jesu. Sitzungsberichte der Preussischen Akademie der Wissenschaften.* Berlin, Jahrgang, 1931. Philosophisch-historische Klasse.
10. Winter, *op. cit.,* p. 163.
11. *Ibid.,* p. 207.
12. *Ibid.,* p. 173.
13. *Deutsche, Juden, Christen,* Stuttgart, 1961, pp. 317-322.
14. Winter, *op. cit.,* p. 173.
15. *Der Prozess Jesu.*
16. Winter, *op. cit.,* p. 175.
17. Parkes, *op. cit.,* pp. 162, 164.
18. H. J. Muller. *The Uses of the Past.* Galaxy Books, Oxford University Press, London, 1957. pp. 72, 73, 148-150, 155.
19. Parkes, *op. cit.,* p. 181.
20. *Juden und Christen,* pp. 27-28.
21. Parkes, *op. cit.,* pp. 145, 149.
22. Sheldon H. Blanck. *Prophetic Faith in Isaiah.* Cincinnati, 1958, p. 100.
23. H. J. Schoeps. *Juedisch-christliches Religionsgespraech.* Berlin, 1937, p. 64.
24. Blaetter, Koeln, September, 1960.
25. Adolf Neubauer and S.R. Driver. *The Fifty-Third Chapter of Isaiah.* Oxford, 1877, Vol. II, pp. 92-98, 153-197.
26. *Ibid.,* Vol. II, pp. 450-531.
27. C. R. North. *The Suffering Servant.* London, 1956, p. 70.
28. Dr. Isidore Epstein. *The Faith of Judaism.* London, 1954, pp. 301-303.
29. *Pharisaism.* London, 1912, pp. 2, 3, 126; *The Pharisees.* London, 1924, pp. 13, 65, 68.
30. Parkes, *op. cit.,* pp. 126-140, 167.
31. Muller, *op. cit.,* p. 73.
32. Parkes, *op. cit.,* p. 354.
33. *The Pharisees,* pp. 106-107.
34. Winter, *op. cit.,* p. 58.
35. *Deutsche, Juden, Christen,* p. 119.
36. Malcolm Hay. *The Foot of Pride,* p. 25.
37. *Deutsche, Juden, Christen,* p. 119.
38. *Ibid.,* p. 109.
39. "The sin of the Jews is not only that they crucified the man but also the God." Winter, *op. cit.,* p. 1.
40. Robert Rochefort. *Kafka.* Wien, 1955, pp. 22-24.
41. *Europaeische Geistesgeschichte.* Stuttgart, 1953, p. 633.
42. *The Jewish Chronicle,* London, February 17, 1961.
43. *Pharisaism,* pp. 193, 196, 197, 198; *The Pharisees,* pp. 75, 78, 161, 220.

44. Parkes, *op. cit.*, p. 135.
45. *Ibid.*, pp. 41, 149-150, 202.
46. Muller, *op. cit.*, pp. 72, 150, 157, 300.
47. *Ibid.*, pp. 160-161.
48. Epstein, *op. cit.*, pp. 287, 291.
49. Muller, *op. cit.*, p. 159.
50. Parkes, *op. cit.*, p. xii.
51. *The Listener,* London, September 22, 1960.
52. Foerster. *Die juedische Frage,* pp. 49-50.
53. Muller, *op. cit.*, p. 94.
54. Parkes, *op. cit.*, pp. 243, 247.

3
Later Christian
Anti-Semitism

REV. PARKES, WHO WAS BEATEN UP BY HOOLIGANS OF THE SWISS
Fascist organization, The Iron Front, in 1935, and who has
devoted his life to clearing up the religious origins of anti-
Semitism culminating, in our time, in the slaughter of six million Jews by the Germans, says: "The Fathers made me
sick."[1] When Christianity was made legal by the Edict of Milan
in 313, it did not "take long for the persecuted Church to turn
persecutor." A law, promulgated in 315, threatened converts to
Judaism with the penalty of burning—in unbelievably vulgar
language calling Judaism "a *feralis* or a *nefaria* sect" and the
synagogue a *conciliabulum,* a brothel. "It is difficult for the
modern Christian to understand how it came to be acceptable to
his Christian ancestors to speak with such vulgar and unbridled
abuse of Judaism and the Jewish people." This vulgar abuse can
be found in the works of Eusebius of Caesarea and John

Chrysostom,[2] who wrote about "the wretched and uncanny Jews who resist the truth in a shameless manner": "The Jews collect choruses of debauchees, the rabble of lascivious women and bring the actors of the theatre into their synagogue, for there is no difference between theatre and synagogue. The synagogue is not just a theatre, it is a brothel, a den of thieves, a refuge of unclean beasts, a house of the devil. The souls of Jews are houses of devils." The Roman Catholic Professor Josef-Maria Nielen (Cologne) who quotes these words, says that John Chrysostom would be "brought to trial today for such a sermon."[3] Rev. Travers Herford says Christians soon forgot the persecution they had suffered under barbaric Roman Emperors and began to persecute the Jews. What they themselves had had to suffer was "but a trifle in comparison with what they have inflicted on Jews."[4] Bertrand Russell is of the same opinion.[5] Professor Muller compared the fanaticism of the Christians with the mild philosophy of the pagan Themistius who said: "God likes the variety of human thought, and is pleased to see his subjects struggle in rivalry to honour his majesty or confess by their differences their difficulty in comprehending it."[6] Not so the Fathers of the Church, who preached the collective guilt of the Jews in the most barbaric manner. St. Justin called the Jews idolators, morbid, cunning, unjust, fornicators, and capable of every evil under the sun. Their sinfulness, he said, was so immense that even the waters of all the seas would not suffice to cleanse them.[7] Gregor of Nyssa repeated this in similar words. St. Ambrose approved of the burning of the synagogue of Rome. Pope Leo the Great, as Professor Muller reminds us, "endorsed the death for erroneous belief. The Church adopted his doctrine."[8] Up to about 800, Christians used to kneel down when, in the Good Friday liturgy, praying *"pro perfidis Judaeis,"* but later they were told not to kneel down any longer because the Jews had derided Christ by mockingly kneeling down before him.[9] Pope Stephan, in the 10th century, called the Jews "dogs," and Pope Innocent III said the Jews, by crucifying Christ, had been condemned to eternal slavery.[10]

Speaking of slavery, we must add that the Christian peasants were no better than slaves in the Middles Ages. "The masses of men," Professor Muller says, "were taught to seek their well-being in the life to come, and to endure without complaint the hard lot that enabled the ruling classes to enjoy well-being in this life." The Church did nothing to better the lot of the peasants because it regarded "serfdom as the natural social order of man." St. Ambrose argued "that slaves had an unusual advantage for the exercise of the Christian virtues of humility, patience, and forgiveness of enemies, and that men cursed with original sin were not fit to govern themselves anyway."[11]

Professor Muller sees in the social conditions of the Middle Ages a repetition of the conditions prevailing in pagan Rome. The conquest of the Roman imperialists "enriched the patricians and the rising business class," but "left the plebeians worse off." Tiberius Gracchus complained: "The wild animals that range over Italy have a hole, and each of them has its lair and nest, but the men who fight and die for Italy have no part in anything but the air and the sunlight. They are called the lords of the World, and they have not a clod of earth to call their own." Professor Muller compares these words with what Jesus said: "Foxes have holes, and birds of the air have nests; but the son of man hath no where to lay his head." Augustus, in his turn, "merely encouraged the city bourgeoisie" but did nothing for the proletarian masses, which, too apathetic to make revolution, invested "their faith and hope in dying gods, instead of living emperors or revolutionists."[12]

These conditions remained unchanged in Europe until the French Revolution in 1789, which was "the inspiration of popular causes all over the Western world."[13] Liberty, equality, and fraternity were true ideals which were, however, falsified by the rising bourgeoisie. Professor Muller rightly blames Protestant ethics for this deplorable development. Calvin "made the pursuit of wealth and preservation of property a Christian duty." Capitalism came to be regarded as God's plan for society. . . . Money-making was the only worldly activity blessed by their gospel." Bitter words by a non-Marxist! People confuse democratic idealism by identifying Freedom with economic freedom; their curious theory remains that uncontrolled economic strife will automatically promote the good of all." Looking at the present state of American affairs, Muller complains of "the depreciation of all values that do not 'pay,'" of "the routine hypocrisy in politics, advertising, publicity, commercialized sport, commercialized art, commercialized piety."[14]

The next terrible chapter in the history of the Jews was the age of the crusades. The crusaders started their belligerent pilgrimage to the Holy Land by murdering thousands of Jews at Cologne, Mayence, Treves, Worms, Speyer, and other places along the Rhine. When the Jews of Treves asked Bishop Egilbert for protection, he told them: "Now your sins are falling upon your heads."[15] Many Jews were given the choice to become Christians or die. Most of them preferred to die and drowned themselves and their families in the Rhine. This, according to Michael Müller-Claudius, a German Roman Catholic who fought German anti-Semitism in the years of Hitler's rise, was "the super-human courage of the followers of a creed who did not fear death but regarded it as a gateway to God. Remembering this, all frivolous talk of the inborn cowardice of the Jews becomes miserable libel."[16] By sacrificing their lives rather then betraying God, those Jews of the Middle Ages followed the legacy of their earliest ancestors, the Maccabeans. In the words of Rabbi Dr. S. Rappaport, whose parents and brother were murdered by the Germans: "The victorious struggle of Matthatias, a village priest from Modin near Jerusalem, his five stalwart sons and a band of loyal Jews, for the integrity of their religion and the preservation of their liberty, constitutes a wonderful chapter in the history of Israel and humanity. . . . It set a glorious example to subsequent generations who believed that rebellion against tyrants is obedience to God." But for the resistance and martyrdom of the Maccabeans, "not only would Judaism have lost its unique spiritual quality, but neither Christianity nor Mohammedanism would ever have arisen and the values of ethical monotheism might have disappeared from the consciousness of men." Rabbi Rappaport reminds us that Sir (then Mr.) Winston Churchill, after the retreat from Dunkirk, roused his country and the freedom-loving world with words spoken by Judas Maccabeus in 165 B.C.: "Arm yourselves and be men of valour, and be in readiness for the conflict, for it is better for us to perish in battle than to look upon the outrage of our nation and our altars."[17]

When the crusaders conquered Jerusalem on July 15, 1099, under their leader Godfrey of Bouillon, they massacred the Moslem population and burned the Jews in their synagogue. Professor Muller reminds us of what an ecstatic crusader, Raimundus de Agiles, wrote at the time: "In the temple and porch of Solomon one rode in blood up to the knees and even the horses' bridles, by the just and marvellous Judgment of God."[18] Lessing, in his *Nathan the Wise,* makes the wise Jewish hero tell the fate of the Jews after the fall of Jerusalem. Rabbi Meir, who lived in France, probably in the 11th century, said: "They murder us, and the murderers deride their victims. They call us a pest of swindlers, damned and cursed. Oh, Lord, can you bear it? Why did you deliver the good into the hands of the tyrants? Can you bear this, Oh Lord?"[19]

Bernard of Clairvaux wrote to the Emperor Lothar that he found it difficult to put up with the fact that a descendant from Jews had been made Pope Anaclet II "to shame Christ"—Professor Foerster retorts today that Petrus was also a Jew by Birth.[20] Bernard of Clairvaux exhorted the soldiers of the second crusade with these words: "Fight courageously and with bold hearts the enemies of Christ so that neither life or death can sever you from the love of God. The soldiers of Christ should wage the wars of their Lord cheerfully and not fear the sin of exterminating the enemy."[21] We know that this and all the following crusades came to nothing.

But the same Bernard of Clairvaux said ten years later, when the Jews, excluded from agriculture, commerce, and trade and allowed only to become money-lenders, were accused of being money-lenders: "Where there are no Jews Christians are much worse money-lenders."[22] A Jewish rabbi of the time, Jacob Tam, wrote: "We have been left no other way of earning our living and paying the high taxes which kings and princes burden us with." Three centuries later Rabbi Isserles complained: "It is true we are mostly earning our living by usury, but this is what the mighty force us to do."[23] In the 13th century many German Jews were accused of the desecration of hosts, and, during the plague (1340-1350), of having poisoned wells and rivers. Duke Amadeus of Savoy had one of the most famous Jewish doctors tortured until he admitted that he had poisoned the water. King Ludwig of Bavaria said in 1343: "All Jews belong to me with their lives and their property, and I can do with them what I like." Margrave Albrecht of Brandenburg said: "When a Roman King or Emperor is being crowned, he can rob the Jews of all their property and even kill them."[24] To give out one example of how this was put into practice in medieval Germany, on September 13, 1377, all Jews of Deggendorf in Bavaria were murdered on the pretext that they had mutilated the sacred Host. In one of the churches of Deggendorf twelve plates are being shown to this very day outlining that untrue accusation. One of the tables glorifies an earlier massacre of Jews in 624. The caption of this table reads: "The Jews were murdered and exterminated by the Christians for rightful and God-pleasing reasons. May God grant our fatherland remaining free for ever from these hellish rabble." In 1879, Father Braunmueller of the Order of Benedict composed a *Gnadenbuechlein* which was reissued recently by Father Fink. There we read of "the herd of scabby Jewish dogs," "a pack of monsters," "Jewish tramps," "the Devil's hordes," "poison-mixers," and an old rhyme: "Oh, let me say it in frank German: It would have been better if your Moses had been drowned in the morass of the Nile, and Abraham, Isaac and Jacob as well. The world would have had peace from you dirty Jews."[25] Pope Paul IV decreed that the Jews of Rome must live in a ghetto, own no houses or land, and wear yellow hats. They were not allowed to employ Christian servants nor could Jewish doctors treat Christians or Jews be addressed as 'Masters' by poor Christians.[26]

The European Jews of the Middle Ages had only peace in the Mohammedan parts of Spain, ruled by caliphs more civilized and tolerant than the "Christian" kings who reconquered southern Spain. Mohammedans, Jews, and Christians lived peacefully together. Arabian philosophers translated Aristotle; Jewish poets and philosophers like Yehuda Halevy and Maimonides, physician to the Caliph of Cordoba, published their books in peace. A famous work by the Jewish philosopher Salomon ibn Gabirol, *The Font of Life,* won the admiration of the Christian philosophers Duns Scotus, St. Thomas Aquinas, and Albertus Magnus who, it is true, did not know that Ibn Gabirol was a Jew. The famous library at Cordoba was the center of the highest culture in Europe at the time. All this came to an abrupt end after two illustrious centuries, "a truly enlightened age of political and spiritual liberty," as the German professor F. W. Foerster calls it,[27] when fanatical Christian rulers succeeded in defeating a pacifist caliph and expelling the educated Mohammedans while ensalving the rest as they enslaved and humiliated the Jews. Archbishop Ferrabd Martinex of Sevilla ordered that the Jewish synagogue be destroyed, and he himself led the Christian thugs when they pulled the synagogue down. "Jews," the Archbishop said, "who refuse baptism are to be killed."[28] So 30,000 Jews were murdered and 4,000 sold into slavery.

Many Jews, to save their lives, accepted baptism *pro forma* while remaining Jews in their hearts. When they were found out, they were burned alive in their thousands. The most infamous fanatic of the time was the Grand Inquisitor Torquemada. What would have happened to Jesus himself, if he had returned to Seville at the time of Torquemada, was described by Dostoevsky in *The Brothers Karamazov*. Christ appears when fires were lighted every day to the glory of God and wicked heretics burnt by the cardinal, the Grand Inquisitor, in the presence of the King, the court, the knights, the Cardinals, the most charming ladies of the court, and the whole population of Seville. The old Inquisitor bids the guards to arrest him, and when he visits him later in a prison cell of the Holy Inquistion, asks him: "Why art thou come to hinder us?" and tells him that he will have him burnt at the stake to-morrow. Christ does not open his mouth to utter a word. He only softly kisses the bloodless lips of the old Inquisitor who opens the door and says to him: "Go and come no more."[29] The Jewish playwright Richard Beer-Hofmann described in our time how the Jews were burned at the stake in totalitarian Spain. In one of his plays, he makes a Jew describe how his father was burned. The Christian orders, the whole clergy, and the court witnessed the *auto-da-fé*. "What an honour that was for a Jew!" The King himself lighted the fire whereupon the choir "began to sing *our* psalms and praised *our* God."[30] Rev. Parkes says: "There were many harsh practices in the legal procedures of Christendom which owed nothing to the authority of the Old Testament. Jewish law knew nothing of physical torture as practiced even by the Church in the courts of the Inquisition."[31]

In 1492 all Jews were expelled from Spain under circumstances which remind us of what happened to the Jews of Europe under Hitler. Many Jews found refuge in Byzantium, which had been conquered by the Moslems a few decades before. Professor Muller, who describes the barbaric history of the Byzantine empire in vivid words—Justinian "surpassed all his predecessors in the persecution of heretics"—quotes what the historian Ducas said when Byzantium fell: "O city, city, head of all cities! O city, city, centre of the four quarters of the world! O city, city, pride of the Christians and ruin of the barbarians! Where is thy beauty, O paradise!"[32] But Rabbi Salomon Rappaport reminds us that the Jewish historian Joseph Ha-Cohen (1496-1577) who described in detail the siege and fall of Byzantium, declared that with the wicked city the Lord had fulfilled the prophecy of Jeremiah: "The cup of punishment shall also pass unto thee, thou shalt be drunken and make thyself naked." Rabbi Rappaport adds: "The Jewish people have every reason to remember the conquest of Byzantium with feeling of gratitude to the Turkish Empire, which in one of the darkest hours of their history offered generous asylum to hunted Jewish fugitives."[33]

I cannot retell here the whole history of the Church's behavior towards the Jews, and not only towards them. John Milton, in a celebrated sonnet, wrote about the massacre of the Waldenses of Piedmont:

> Avenge, O Lord, the slaughtered saints whose bones
> Lie scattered on the Alpine mountains cold.[34]

About the Jews, in about the same days, Pascal wrote: "It is an astonishing thing, and worth particular notice, to see this Jewish people lasting for so many years, and to see them always unfortunate. This is necessary for the proof of Jesus Christ, which requires that they should survive in order to prove Him, and that they should be unfortunate because they crucified Him; and though to be unfortunate and to continue in existence are contradictory, the Jews nevertheless endure, despite their misfortunes."[35] Pierre Bayle, however, whose *Dictionaire Historique et Critique* was "the bible of the Age of Reason," criticized Christian fanaticism in the person of the Jesuit Father Maimbourg and said that there was more Christianity in Seneca than in the Father's history of the Calvinists. When the Edict of

Nantes was revoked in 1685, Bayle wrote: "You have made our Christianity stink and its name has become justly odious to infidels."[36] Voltaire called the crusades an "epidemic fury" which had proved "that the human race was to be spared no curse."[37] When, only a few decades later, the great Napoleon gave the Jews of France full rights of citizenship, the Greek Orthodox Synod, the main pillar of Tsarist absolutism, protested in these words: "Napoleon assembled the Judaean Synagogues in France and established a great Sanhedrin of the Jews, the same ungodly assembly which had once dared to pass the sentence of crucifixion on our Lord Jesus and now plans to unite the Jews whom the wrath of the Almighty has scattered over the face of the whole earth."[38] In Rome, even as late as 1895, an enthusiastic prelate wrote a hymn in prose to the Inquisition: "Oh, you blessed flames of the stakes! By exterminating the few wholly corrupt men, you saved thousands and thousands of souls from the abyss of error and damnation. . . . Oh, glorious and venerable memory of Thomas Torquemada!"[39]

It is, therefore, not surprising that an honest Englishman summed up the two thousand years of Jewish-Christian relations in these words: "Unconsciously all Gentiles are anti-Semites."[40] And another Englishman, Sidney R. Campion, recalls his elementary school days, "when it was constantly impressed upon me that the Jews crucified Jesus Christ and that Shylock demanded a pound of Christian flesh. My sense of justice was outraged, and I found myself hating the Jews. When I passed the synagogue I threw stones at the windows by way of revenge, and this daily act gave me intense satisfaction."[41]

Jews and God-fearing Christians had something more to say about these things.

The late British Chief-Rabbi Dr. H. Hertz calls the Jews "the classical people of martyrdom," and quotes the lines of a modern Jewish poet, J. L. Gordon:

We have sacrificed all. We have given our wealth,
Our homes, our honours, our land and our health,
Our lives—like Hannah her children seven—,
For the sake of the Torah that came from Heaven.[42]

Rabbi Epstein said: "No people has suffered more cruelly from 'man's inhumanity to man' than have the Jews. They endured such trials as no other people have been called upon to bear," and quotes the words of G. K. Chesterton: "Christianity has not failed, it has never been tried." Rabbi Epstein asks: "How is it that 2,000 years of Christian teaching have not been able to eradicate from Christian peoples those bestial instincts of murder and hate that have laid waste the world twice within a generation?"[43] The French-Jewish scholar, Jules Isaac, asks: "How could Christianity, born Jewish, of a Jewish belief, of the preaching of a Jew, Jesus-Joshua, and of his disciples and apostles, all Jews—how could this Christianity succumb to anti-Semitism?" He has no answer but he quotes the answer of Christian theology, "a very simple explanation: the fault lies entirely with Israel; the Jewish people condemned itself in rejecting Jesus and refusing to recognise him as Messiah and Son of God." And theologians too often add: "Thereby the Jews completely identified themselves with the murderers of Christ." In reality, the number of Jews accepting the belief in Jesus as Messiah first increased with extraordinary speed, but when Christianity, turning to Gentiles, "totally rejected obedience to the Torah," the gulf between Judaism and Christianity inevitably widened. Christian anti-Semitism became much worse than its pagan predecessor. Judaism was regarded as degenerate, the Jews were regarded as reproved by God, and they became a convenient scapegoat for every evil that befell the European nations. Jews cannot forget "that Hitlerian racialism appeared on ground which previous centuries had prepared for it. Did the Nazis spring from nothing or from the bosom of a Christian people? . . . I well understand how hurtful and wounding such a statement may appear to a Christian. But is this a reason for not facing it?"[44]

Rabbi Georg Salzberger (of German origin but now living in Great Britain) said in 1962 in a conversation with a Roman Catholic and a Lutheran theologian that 19 centuries of Christian hatred were responsible for the massacre of the Jews by the Germans. "The Jews never suffered under the Moslems as much as under the Christians." The Gospel writers made the Jews the sole culprits. Paul called them "stubborn and blinded," and Luther called them *stocksteineisenteufelhart.* Origen asserted that "the blood of Jesus has come not only upon those at the time but upon all generations of Jews." The church never adhered to the commandment of Jesus to "Love thy enemy" as far as the Jews were concerned. The yellow patch the Jews had on their clothes in the Third Reich was no invention of Hitler nor were the Hitlerites the first to burn Jewish books. Pope Gregor IX had 24 wagon loads of copies of the Talmud burned in 1242. "A devout Jew cannot believe that God can become man, die, rise from the dead and fly to heaven. Jews cannot believe that Jesus was the Messiah whom the Jewish prophets had prophesied." They see in him "one of the most noble and pious of their race." While the church asserts that *nulla salus extra ecclesiam,* Jews are of the belief "that the pious of all nations will have part of the other world."[45]

Professor Hugo Bergmann of Jerusalem University wrote to a German Roman Catholic lady, who was a victim of Nazi persecution herself: "Unfortunately, a grave historical memory lies between your Church and my Synagogue, which cannot be eradicated within a few years. We Jews have all in our blood the inquisition and the memory of your fanatical chaplains."[46] Ben Chorin says that Christians betrayed the teachings of Jesus by the crimes of the crusaders, the stakes of the inquisition, by Luther's anti-Semitism. "Things being what they are, and bitterly undeceived as we are by the bloody period which we ourselves have experienced and suffered, we can no longer believe in the fairy-tale of moral progress." The disciples of Jesus, he says, "have persecuted the Jews, the brothers of Jesus, through the centuries and perverted the gospel of love. The degeneration of Christianity stands as a terrible shadow between us and our eternal brother from Nazareth. The Church must apologize before the world, just as the world must apologize before the Bible. We have never been waiting for a Son of God but we know that we are all children of the living God. A Son of God, born by a virgin, this is more like a hellenistic and oriental belief than a biblical fulfillment." People misinterpreted Isaiah VII, 14, who speaks of an *almo,* i.e., a young woman not of a virgin. The Jews only believe in one God and cannot believe in a trinity. As to the question of the suffering servant, all Jews martyred because of their belief in one God have been suffering servants, and not only Jews but also "the martyrs of humanism and justice, the inflexible Servet and Giordano Bruno and the nameless martyrs of all nations and ages." In a poem which Ben Chorin, born in Munich and once called Fritz Rosenthal, wrote in 1945, he said: "If we have gone back to our fatherland, it would not have looked at us out of shame, because all stones confess what they have done to us."[47]

Dr. Paul Winter, a biblical scholar now living in London after having fled from Czechoslovakia, says: "The accusers of old are dead. The trial of Jesus goes on. His is a trial in which the rôles of judge and accused are strangely reversed. . . . Many have come in his name and have joined the accusers. . . . Never spoken when Jesus was tired, the words 'His blood upon us and upon our children, (Matt. 27:25), have come true—a thousand times."[48] An Israeli writer of German origin, M. Y. Ben-Gavriel, said: "I think anti-Semitism goes back to the theology of the Fathers of the Church who taught that 'the sons of the murderers of Christ, are in close touch with the Devil. Modern German anti-Semitism is the secularised form of this belief."[49]

Various Christian writers and theologians are in full agreement with these Jewish statements. Professor Muller said that Christianity has "a record of religious atrocity unmatched by any other high religion." It persecuted the Jews for two thousand years, segregated them in ghettos, forced them to wear "a yellow badge of infamy," spoke of "an international conspiracy of Jewry," accused them of avarice, burned them on the stake—one enthusiastic contemporary spoke of "a holocaust very great and pleasing to God." Christendom made the history of the Jews as much "heroic" as "appalling." The martyrdom that Christians suffered in their early history "was negligible compared with the martyrdom they later inflicted on the Jews. In the Roman Empire, they could fight and die heroically, in Christendom they were simply massacred."[50]

Professor F. C. Grant says that Jesus "was put to death by the Roman procurator of Judea for fear that he might start a revolution," and crucified "as a claimant to the vacant throne of David"; but Matthew (27:25) makes the Jews blame themselves for his death: "His blood be on us and our children," and John (8:44) makes Jesus say to the Jews: "Ye are of your father the devil." Later Paul came along, "a convert who exaggerates the faults of the creed he has abandoned," and later still the most eminent of the Church Fathers held "the Jews responsible for the death of Christ" and explained the fall of Jerusalem and the scattering of the Jews "as a divine punishment for this awful deed." Fanatical hatred of the Jews was as characteristic of the early church as it was of the medieval and post-Reformation churches. The religion of the Jews was defamed as being moribund, formalistic, insincere, purely formal and hypocritical." Professor Grant, bewildered by so much bigotry, retorts: "A religion in decline does not produce saints and martyrs" from the time of the Maccabees to the death of Akiba. "Judaism is still alive in spite of the repeated efforts of its enemies to exterminate it, chiefly in our times." He complains that even today one reads "the most grotesque descriptions of ancient Judaism." He feels the warmth of Judaism in "the oldest parts of the Jewish liturgy, the *Shema* with its three great prayers, or the *Shemoneh Esreh,* the *Kaddish,* the Psalms," and praises Judaism because it has never been overwhelmed by any system of dogmatic theology. As Judaism has demonstrated, it is perfectly possible for a religion to live without dogmas, without attempting to define the indefinite."[51]

The Anglican Rev. W. W. Simpson said in a B.B.C. television program early in January, 1961 that the social and political anti-Semitism of modern times developed from the anti-Semitism of the Middle Ages. Anti-Semitic prejudice had its roots in the conflict between Church and Synagogue. Pope Innocent III was the first to decree that Jews should wear a distinctive badge. On the south porch of Strasbourg Cathedral there were two figures representing the Church and the Synagogue. The figure of the Synagogue is blindfolded, the tables of the Law slipping from her hand, and her spear broken.[52] That Pope said in a bull of 1208: God made Cain an errant and fugitive but made a sign on his forehead that he should not be killed. In the same manner, the Jews must remain errants until their faces are covered with shame and they search for the name of Jesus. For his blood cries out against them."[53] Pope Innocent III also was the inaugurator of the Inquisition, set up for the persecution of Jews and "heretics." One shudders to remember the innumerable innocent victims of this institution. On Easter Sunday, 1962, Rev. Simpson wrote: "Many Jews find this a disturbing time of the year . . . partly because they find the constant reiteration of phrases in music, drama, and sermons which seem to involve 'the Jews' of all time with responsibility for the crucifixion of Jesus very distressing, and partly because they do not find it easy to forget the suffering inflicted on generations of their forebears on this very charge. Pilate, known to his contemporaries as a man of inflexible disposition, hard and obdurate, has been cast in the traditional Christian presentation of the Passion Story for the vacillating role of a weak provincial governor." Of the words in the first Gospel, "All the people answered and said: His blood be on us and on our children," Claude Montefiore, founder of the Liberal Jewish Synagogue of Great Britain, said: "A horrible invention, one of the phrases which have been responsible for oceans of human blood, and a ceaseless stream of misery and desolation." Rev. Simpson reminds us of Dr. Paul Winter's book, *The Trial of Jesus* (1961), which destroys the legends told by the Gospel writers, and is dedicated "To the dead in Auschwitz, Izbica, Maidanek, Theblinka, among whom are those who were dearest to me." Rev. Simpson adds: "I cannot help wondering whether, in this generation of ours, the Jew on the Cross is not to be found more closely identified with the Jew in the gas chamber than with those who still present the historic events which led to the crucifixion, so as to fasten upon the Jewish people of today responsibilities which belong to our corporate humanity and not to one race or community."[54]

A German Jesuit, Karl Rahner, in 1952 warned the Catholic Church to avoid giving the impression of a totalitarian system.[55] Another German Jesuit, Gustav A. Wetter, spoke of the parallelism of Roman Catholicism and Communism and said "that the analogies between Bolshevism and Christianity, especially in its Roman Catholic persuasion, revealed something deeper than mere superficial similarities."[56] A Swiss Jesuit, Richard Gutzweiler, said after the last war: "The aiming at a totalitarian church is a great danger. Under no circumstances should the church try to extend her influence and her power as much as possible and submit to it all spheres of life."[57] Thomas Mann says of the Third Reich: "Freedom was given to thought to justify terror, just as, seven centuries earlier, reason had been free to analyse faith, to prove dogma.[58] In 1925 he quoted the words of Pope Gregor the Great: "Cursed be the man who keeps his sword back from blood."[59] A German Lutheran, Gerd Theunissen, said in a lecture, *Between Golgotha and Auschwitz:* "Who of us Christians dares to assert that the face of the Lord has not darkened in his eyes? Are the Christians exempt from the ungodly darkness reigning today? By no means. For if this were not the case, how could there have been a place like Auschwitz? Christians must realise that they have not taken the Old Testament seriously enough, that they must be reborn in the spirit of the Jews on whom, since the days of Golgotha, they have seen fit to take revenge for Him who, on the Cross, had cried out in the words of the 22nd Psalm of the Old Testament: 'My God, my God, why hast thou forsaken me?' On the road from Golgotha to Auschwitz throughout the history of Christianity, Christians have cursed the Jews again and again until the worst of them exterminated the Jews."[61] Professor Helmut Gollwitzer, a Lutheran theologian, said after Hitler's war: "The Christian contempt of the Jews through the centuries was the breeding-ground from which those exterminations stemmed. If anybody, Christians should have known from the Sermon of the Mount that he who despises his brother sows the seed of murder which will grow up one day."[62] Professor Karl Jaspers said: "European Christianity is burdened with anti-Semitism."[63] Professor Hans Joachim Kraus of Hamburg University reminds us in Hegel's words of Luther's outburst against the Jews returning: "The Infinite Spirit finds no room in the prison of a Jewish soul," and traces all this back to the Gospels and the early Christian theologians who said that the Jews were punished and scattered all over the earth for their crime against Jesus, that Judaism was done with "wholly and entirely" and the Jews "cursed for all time." He warns Christians that they should not try to evade their responsibility by saying that the persecution of the Jews had nothing to do with the true Church. "It would be better for us to put the hands on our mouths and keep silent."[64] Yet another Lutheran Professor, Hans Walter

Wolff, said: "Whenever Christians sever the ties with the Old Testament, the Gospels have been falsified; it was so with Marcion, with Adolf Harnack, and with Hitler."[65] A Roman Catholic writer, the Austrian Friedrich Heer, says: "We stand terrified before the ruins of a perennial misunderstanding of the Jewish faith by European Christianity. Auschwitz, Maidanek, and the burning of millions of Jewish children, women and men had not been possible if Christians had not burned Jews in the fire of their hatred for a thousand years[66]. . . . The Church has gone to bed with all dictators."[67] The Swiss novelist Ruth Schaumann who, already in 1942, had written a novel, *The Outlawed,* in honor of a murdered Jewess, said that the thought of the persecution of the Jews would torment her unto her last day. With her new novel, *I.H.S.,* she wrote, as she said, "a flaming confession of guilt on all the walls of Christian hearts, if these should not already be artificial hearts without any love and remorse."[68] Another German writer, Karlheinz Deschner, agrees with her: "Before the Nazis persecuted the Jews, Church and Christianity have bred and nursed anti-Semitism for 2,000 years. I make bold to assert that without that example of the Christian pogromists the bestialities of the Nazis would never have become possible."[69]

The most outspoken critic of Roman Catholic crimes against the Jews is German Professor F. W. Foerster of whom his Roman Catholic publisher says that he has "scourged, during his long life, the false development of his nation, ardently warning and pitilessly fighting it. . . . The wrong way which the Germans have taken in modern times and which has led them into the catastrophe of the Second World War, was not wrong because of a false policy. This false and fateful policy only became possible because the nation had taken a wrong turn spiritually and morally." Professor Foerster says in his latest book, to which he also gave the Hebrew title *Haschaala Haivrith,* that as soon as the Christian Church had established itself, it began to persecute the Jews "with an unbelievable hatred and persecution mania. Who could enumerate all the cruelties to which the Jews fell victims in their thousands in Christian Europe?" He quotes the Jewish historian Josef Kastein as saying: "No age, no nation, no church has ever committed such bloody deeds of torture, unless we think of the extermination of the Inkas by their Spanish conquerers." The Jews, Professor Foerster continues, have shown in their history more "uplifting courage and greatness of character" than any other nation. "Great heroic deeds have often been performed for temporal fatherlands," but the Jews have "sacrificed themselves, their youth and their fatherland to keep faith to the invisible God. . . . A Jewish king wrote psalms which have not only brought the Jews nearer to the understanding of godly truth, but also permeated the Christian church like a heavenly music for many centuries. . . . Where is the thanks of the Christians for these mighty fundaments of their own faith?" Christian theologians assert to this very day in sermons and books that the fate of the Jews and their "wanderings among the nations who despise them" is the appropriate punishment for the crucifixion of Christ. Professor Foerster also quotes a German Protestant writer, M. J. Schleiden, who said recently: "Christians have such a splendidly bad memory of their own sins that they hardly ever mention the terrible fate of the Jews in the Middle Ages in their history books." It is therefore that Professor Foerster bids Christians to beat their hearts and confess: *"Mea culpa, mea maxima culpa."*[70]

Professor Muller complains that "to this day orthodox churchmen have ignored its (Israel's) independent claims to truth, treating it as a poor, wayward relation rather than an elder brother."[71] What is meant by this complaint can best be illustrated by various German statements which the author of this book came across in the course of his studies; for instance:

"The religion of the Old Testament comes to maturity in the religion of Jesus Christ."[72]

"It is strange that the chosen people which should have accepted the Messiah and proclaimed him to the world, has followed their leaders and rejected and condemned Him."[73]

Ernst Ludwig, a Swiss Jew, complained: "Catholic children are confirmed, or at least left, in their belief that the Jews of today are the descendants of the murderers of Christ."[74] Jules Isaac quotes examples from Roman Catholic catechisms which French children study: "The religious life of the Jews was reduced in the time of Jesus to pure exterior formalism." "The Jews had neither the fear nor the love of God." "For more than 19 centuries, the Jewish people have been dispersed throughout the world, and have kept the stain of their deicide." "Until the end of time, children of Israel in dispersion will carry the curses which their father have called down upon them."[75]

Martin Buber said in 1933, when innumerable Germans shouted "Germany awake—perish Judah": "We feel that the world is still unredeemed. We do not see a caesura in history. We know of no centre, we only know an aim, the aim of God who does not stop on his way."[76] Ben Chorin says today: "The world is unredeemed in the sense of the prophets as long as war and robbery defame the world, anxiety and death are ruling and Israel is exposed to the bloody hatred to their enemies."[77] Rabbi Epstein takes Professor Emil Brunner, a Lutheran theologian, to task for saying: "Pious Jews (having rejected Jesus as the Messiah) are still waiting for the Christ who is to come; this means that they are still waiting for the revelation which we Christians believe and confess to be one that has already come." Rabbi Epstein answers: "Jews are not waiting, nor have they ever waited, for any Messiah in the Christian sense. All the work of fulfilment which the Christians claim for Jesus, is left by the Jews entirely to God, who alone, without the need of a Christ or mediator, can do what He thinks best for His children, and enfold them in His eternal and gracious love."[78] Professor Helmut Gollwitzer, whom we have already quoted several times, saw in Jerusalem a book describing 2,000 years of pressure on the Jews, and said therefore: "The word of our missionary task among the Jews sticks chokingly in our throats."[79] Ben chorin tells of a German-Lutheran pastor who had come to Israel to do missionary work there but left it again out of deep love for the Jews. Remembering the terrible guilt of the Germans, he found it impossible for the Church to behave as an *ecclesia triumphans* towards a Synagogue with a broken sceptre.[80]

Rev. Parkes says: "It is the rarest thing to find a Christian who would accept the statement that 'Judaism still carries as much the divine imperative as Christianity'. . . . It is surely unnecessary to seek to substitute one conception for the other or to deny the validity, in the present world, of both. Christianity is not a substitute for Israel. . . . Judaism is not a substitute for Christianity."[81] The same spirit of conciliation was shown by Pope John XXIII when he received a delegation of American Jews who had come to thank him for what many dignitaries of the Church had done for the Jews during the Nazi terror, rescuing many of them at the risk of their own lives. He said: "When I see you all here in front of me I am reminded of Joseph who, for a long time, withheld from his brethren the fact that he was their brother. But eventually he could not restrain himself. I feel today and I say to you 'I am your brother.' "[82] The French sculptor, Jacques Lipschitz, a Jew of Lithuanian descent, presented a Holy Virgin to a Catholic church, writing on the back of it: "Jacob Lipschitz, Jew, loyal to the faith of his ancestors, has made this Virgin for the sake of understanding between men on earth, so that the spirit may prevail."[83]

Notes

1. *Observer*, London, September 18, 1960.
2. Parkes, *op. cit.*, pp. 226, 319, 323.
3. *Christlicher Antisemitismus*. Koeln, pp. 17-18.
4. Herford. *The Pharisees*, p. 225.

5. *Wisdom of the West.* London, 1959, p. 130.
6. Muller, *op. cit.,* p. 164.
7. *Die Kultur,* February, 1960.
8. Muller, *op. cit.,* p. 186.
9. *Rundbrief* XII, 1959.
10. Foerster. *Die juedische Frage,* p. 75.
11. Muller, *op. cit.,* pp. 13, 188.
12. *Ibid.,* pp. 216ff.
13. *Ibid.,* p. 286.
14. *Ibid.,* pp. 272-275, 316.
15. Foerster. *Die juedische Frage,* p. 81.
16. Michael Müller-Claudius. *Deutsche und jüdische Tragik.* Frankfurt, 1955, pp. 36-37.
17. *Jewish Horizons.* Johannesburg, 1959, pp. 3-4.
18. Muller, *op. cit.,* p. 244.
19. Kurt Fassmann (ed.). *Gedichte gegen den Krieg.* Muenchen, 1961, pp. 40-41.
20. F. W. Foerster. *The Jews.* London, 1961, pp. 97-98.
21. *Blaetter,* Koeln, September, 1960.
22. Foerster. *Die juedische Frage,* p. 60.
23. *Ibid.,* p. 63.
24. *Ibid.,* p. 97.
25. *Deutsche Rundschau,* Stuttgart, October, 1961, pp. 900-901.
26. Ludwig von Pastor. *Geshichte der Paepste.* Freiburg, Vol. VI, 1913, pp. 515-516.
27. Foerster. *Die juedische Frage,* pp. 85-86.
28. *Ibid.,* p. 87.
29. Fyodor Dostoevsky. *The Brothers Karamazov.* London, 1912, impression 1915, pp. 263, 277.
30. *Der Graf von Charolais.* Berlin, 1905, pp. 64-65.
31. Parkes, *op. cit.,* p. 81.
32. Muller, *op. cit.,* pp. 7, 10.
33. *Jewish Horizons,* p. 155.
34. *The Poetical Works of John Milton.* London, 1961, p. 550.
35. *Pensées.* Everyman's Library No. 874, ed. 1960, p. 169.
36. G. P. Gooch. *French Profiles.* London, 1961, pp. 6, 7.
37. *Ibid.,* pp. 107, 108.
38. *Jewish Horizons,* pp. 157-160.
39. J. S. Whale. *The Protestant Tradition.* Cambridge University Press, 1955, p. 242.
40. *New Statesman,* London, September, 1960.
41. *Observer,* London, April 29, 1962.
42. *The Pentateuch and Haphtoras.* London, 1937, p. 201.
43. Epstein, *op. cit.,* pp. 58, 73.
44. *World Jewry,* London, November, 1960.
45. *Christlicher Antisemitismus,* pp. 7, 10, 11, 13, 35.
46. *Rundbrief,* Freiburg, February, 1954.
47. *Juden und Christen,* pp. 48-49, 61. *An den Wind geschrieben.* Collected by Manfred Schloesser. Koeln, 1960, p. 227.

48. *On the Trial of Jesus*, p. 149.
49. *Die Kultur*, August, 1961.
50. Muller, *op. cit.*, pp. 76, 94-96, 160, 246.
51. Grant. *Ancient Judaism and the New Testament*. Sec. Edition, 1960, pp. 3, 5, 15, 16, 19, 23, 51, 143, 144, 149, 168.
52. *The Jewish Chronicle*, London, January 13, 1961.
53. *Deutsche, Juden, Christen*, p. 120.
54. *Observer*, London, April 22, 1962.
55. Friedrich Heer. *Europäische Geistesgeschichte*, p. 657.
56. *Ibid.*, p. 657.
57. Friedrich Heer. *Die dritte Kraft*. Frankfurt, 1959, p. 632.
58. *Doktor Faustus*. Stockholm, 1947, p. 632.
59. *Der Zauberberg*. Berlin, 1924, Vol. II, p. 103.
60. *Zwischen Golgatha und Auschwitz*. Koeln, 1959, pp. 14-15.
61. *Israel und wir*. Berlin, 1958, p. 16.
62. *Philosophie und Welt*. Muenchen, 1958, p. 161.
63. *Deutsche, Juden, Christen*, pp. 112-113.
64. *Ibid.*, p. 289.
65. *Ibid.*, p. 189.
66. *Blaetter*, Koeln, June, 1959.
67. *Die Kultur*, February, 1960.
68. *Ibid.*
69. *Die juedische Frage*, pp. 7, 29, 35, 74, 78, 79, 89, 114.
70. Muller, *op. cit.*, p. 72.
71. F. König. *Christus und die Religionen der Erde*. Freidburg, 1956, Vol. III, p. 521.
72. *Ibid.*, p. 527.
73. *Rundbrief* XII, Freidburg, 1959.
74. *World Jewry*. London, November 1960.
75. A. J. Schoeps. *Jüdisch-Christliches Gespräch*. Berlin, 1937, p. 138.
76. *Juden und Christen*, pp. 47-48.
77. Epstein, *op. cit.*, p. 322.
78. *Rundbrief* XII.
79. *Juden und Christen*, pp. 3-4, 7.
80. Parkes, *op. cit.*, p. 330.
81. *The Jewish Chronicle*, London, October 21, 1960.
82. *Observer*, London, November 22, 1959.

4
German Anti-Semitism

THOMAS MANN MAKES A COSMOPOLITAN JEW SAY IN *Doctor Faustus:* "We Jews have everything to fear from the German character *qui est essentiellement anti-semitique.*"[1] Let us have a closer look at this side of the German problem.

The Jews, who had come to Western Germany in the wake of the Romans, generally speaking aroused no hatred in the early Middle Ages and lived side by side with the Christians as peasants and wine-growers. Medieval German emperors sometimes took them under their protection. This state of affairs changed terribly in the age of the crusades when so-called "Knights of Christ" on their way to the East began to murder Jews because they were made responsible for the crucifixion of Christ. After those terrible days, the German Jews never enjoyed peace and freedom in Germany. Many books tell of their plight in the following centuries. Since the middle of the 14th century, when the German Jews were made responsible for the Black Death and many were murdered by the German mob, the Jews began to flee in great numbers. It was Poland which received them, and there they lived for nearly six centuries, until the catastrophe of Auschwitz and the other German death camps. Jose Orabuena, a Spanish-Jewish writer, describes the life of the Eastern Jews in a moving novel of some 600 pages. "Free?" one of them asks. "A terribly exciting word for the ear of a Jew." And another says: "Is Wilna a home or a place of suffering? Does the Bible, does the Talmud speak of Wilna? But they speak of Jerushalayim, of Palestine." Ben Orabuena who lives in Great Britain says: "I live there because I love the country very much. I esteem the English because I found only among them that important and orderly freedom which I like."[2]

In the year 1700, the German Professor Johann Andreas Eisenmenger published two huge volumes under the title, *Entdecktes Judenthum*. The subtitle ran like this: "A thorough and true record of how the stubborn Jews slander and defame the holy trinity, God Father, Son and the Holy Spirit in a terrible manner, and of many other things which are either wholly or partly unknown among Christians." Rev. Travers Herford speaks of "the scurrilous rancour of Eisenmenger" censuring him and another German scholar, Wagenseil, because they "explored the Rabbinical literature well-nigh from end to end" mainly "for the purpose of reviling what they found."[3]

Things in Germany changed very little in those centuries as far as the Jews were concerned, although the American and French Revolutions in the 18th century spoke of unalienable human rights, of freedom, equality, and pursuit of happiness. When Germany reached its pinnacle of culture in the 18th century, Professor Christian Lichtenberg said: "It is we Christians who must be the first to be ashamed of even the real defects of the Jews."[4] Herder called the Jews "the most excellent nation on earth . . . All laws which treat the Jews as inferior to cattle, mistrust them and call them lousy bear witness to the continuing barbarism of the state which tolerates such laws derived from barbaric times.[5] Johann Georg Haman, another East Prussian philosopher, said: "Every Jew is to me the miracle of all miracles of God's providence and government." He called the Jew "the real and original nobleman of the whole human race."[6] The great poet Klopstock said in a wonderful verse: "Who is not filled with awe and pity when he sees our mob dehumanize the nation of Israel! And does the mob not do so because our princes put them into iron chains?"[7] In the same 18th century Lessing wrote his *Nathan the Wise* in praise of true humanism and tolerance, and said: "I do not, as yet, know of any place where this play could be performed at present. I wish health and happiness to the place where it is first performed."[8] In the wise humanist Nathan he portrayed his friend Moses Mendelssohn whom Kant, too, praised for combining religion with freedom of conscience in a way as to give an example to Christianity. Three times in Lessing's play we hear the voice of fanaticism: "Never mind, the Jew shall burn!" This reminded the Germans, as it reminds us today, of the intolerance of the Christian Church against Jews and other "heretics" as long as it had the political power to persecute them in the name of the love of Christ.

Lessing's Nathan tells the story of how Christians at Gath murdered all Jews together with their wives and children, among them his own wife and seven sons. When *Nathan* was rehearsed on the Weimar stage Goethe wrote to Schiller: "May the divine sentiments of patience and tolerance expressed there ever remain precious and sacred in our nation's view."[9] As the totalitarian Church had also persecuted Christian 'heretics' through the centuries, Goethe says:

> The few who aught thereof have known or learned,
> Who their hearts' fulness foolishly unsealed,
> And to the vulgar herd their thoughts and dreams revealed,
> Men in all times have crucified and burned.[10]

A few years after Lessing's death, the philosopher Fichte was the first German in modern times to preach the collective guilt of the Jews by saying in 1793 that everywhere in Europe they represented a powerful and inimical state within the state which was based "on the hatred of the whole of mankind. But you are speaking sweet words of tolerance and human rights. Do you not foresee that the Jews, if you grant them civil rights, will tread the other citizens under their feet?"[11] Hitler said exactly the same in *Mein Kampf,* and between Hitler and Fichte many Germans said the same, as we shall presently show.

In the days before the advent of Napoleon the German Jews still lived in ghettoes and when they went from one town to another they had to pass the customs-house of the new place in a manner described by the 19th century liberal novelist Wilhelm Raabe: "Today, . . . January, 178-, Duties Paid at the Cross Gate for 1) three cows; 2) fourteen pigs; 3) three calves; 4) one Jew, calling himself Moses Mendelssohn from Berlin." Raabe adds: "The battle of Jena, which put an end to many infamies and much nonsense, ended also this scandal."[12] Napoleon did not only do much for the unification of Germany, but also freed the Jews, opening the gates of their ghettoes, in the name of *liberté, egalité, fraternité.* One of the many liberated Jews was young Heinrich Heine, who remained grateful to Napoleon for this all his life and mourned the fall of the French emperor in his famous ballad of the two grenadiers. Bismarck referred to this a few decades later, saying that, like Heine, he would have hated, had he been born a Jew, to see the gates of the ghettoes being closed at eight o'clock in the evening and the Jews restricted by very severe special laws. "Naturally, Heine praised the man who brought French laws into the Rhineland and abolished all exceptional laws, as a liberator from excruciating pressure."[13]

After Napoleon's downfall, however, as Raabe tells us, "Anno 1815 many a loving father of the fatherland would have liked to reintroduce the good, old custom."[14] They really did so all over Germany by and by. At the Congress of Vienna Napoleon's new laws regarding the Jews were approved by the German princes on the advice of two humane Germans, Humboldt and Hardenberg. But very soon after this many a prince evaded the approved regulations by various legal niceties. Jews could neither become officers nor civil servants and they remained excluded from society which was mainly Christian and reactionary. They were even excluded from the commercial guilds, forbidden to buy houses, and had not even a right of domicile. Very soon people began to complain of Jewish supremacy, although the Jews represented a tiny minority and most of them were very poor. As they were not allowed to open shops, many wandered up and down the country as hawkers. Nobody cared to look at the real facts. More and more spoke of Jewish usury, Jewish materialism, although the worst of the early German capitalists were Christians.

After Fichte, by the end of the 18th century, had established the fashion, a certain Carl Grattenauer in 1802 published his pamphlet, *Against the Jews,* which influenced many German intellectuals. In 1816 the philosopher J. F. Fries published a book about the danger to the German character which the Jews represented and advised the Germans "to put an end to this scandal by an outrageous act" like Spain had done, "where the whole nation enjoyed seeing thousands of Jews at the stake. It is very important that these chaps should be exterminated root and branch."[15] Another professor, Friedrich Rühs, wrote in the same year that a nation which wanted to preserve its character and dignity must remove "those aliens which it cannot digest, namely the Jews."[16] He suggested new exceptional laws to render the Jews less dangerous. It was of no avail that two distinguished Jews in 1817 tried to refute these hateful allegations and to remind the public that the Jews had again been excluded from all professions and offices and could only earn a miserable living in a miserable way.[17] *Turnvater* Jahn spoke contemptuously of the Jews and praised the Germans as "the

saviours of the world." He was therefore praised by the racialist
Ludwig Schemann in 1931 because his "teachings about the
purity of race and against mixing of races are by far the best
and healthiest things that can be said about these problems."[18]
In 1831, however, a solitary German voice cried in the wilderness of growing German anti-Semitism: "Hatred of the Jews
begins where common sense ends."[19] Four years later, Professor Anton Theodor Hartmann of Rostock published his diatribe
against the Jews, *Fundaments of Orthodox Jewry,* which is full
of libellous allegations and extracts from the Bible, taken from
their context, their meaning distorted. When a Jewish scholar
quietly replied by drawing attention to the true fundamentals of
Jewish religion as expressed in the commandments: "Love thy
neighbor as thyself" and: "Do not withdraw thy help even from
thine enemy," the professor exclaimed in a truly Streicherian
manner: "Rejoice, ye lucky sons of Abraham, at the new and
decisive victory which our celebrated hero Salomon (blessed be
his memory!) has gained over the bitter enemy of our nation
who liveth at Rostock (cursed be his name!) reducing him to
nought."[20]

All these anti-Semites were Protestants, and this is not a mere
chance. In 1841 the Roman Catholic poetess, Annette Droste,
published her famous short story, *The Jew's Beech,* telling the
story of the murder of a Jew in the 18th century. Fellow-Jews
carved into the bark of the beech under which he had been
murdered these words in Hebrew: "If thou shouldst ever come
near this place, the same shall happen to thee as thou hast done
to me."[21] And so it happened. In 1840 the great German
dramatist, Friedrich Hebbel, published his tragedy, *Judith,* in
which we cannot fail to recognize today the situation which
prevailed in the Third Reich. While the Jews revere their "invisible God," the captains of the Moabites and Ammonites say:
"This nation is contemptible." Judith decides to murder Holofernes, the enemy of her people, by sacrificing her honor, pre-

tending to love him, and killing him when he is drowsy with
lust. Before she goes to the camp of Holofernes she prays to
God: "If thou putest sin between me and my deed, before thee
the unclean becometh clean. Thou hast made me beautiful. Now
I know why." Her aim achieved, she kills herself. When Holofernes calls himself "a lightning which threatens to burn the
world," when he says: "The world looks miserable to me, I
think I was born to destroy it,"[22] we are reminded of what
Hitler said to Dr. Rauschning in 1932. In about 1848 Heine
wrote: "I once saw with amazement in a beer cellar at Goettingen with what thoroughness my old-German friends drew up
their proscription-lists for the day when they would gain political power. Whoever was descended, in the seventh degree, from
a Frenchman, a Jew, a Slav would die by the axe. Whoever had
written anything against Jahn or against the old-German nonsense in general, could expect to be murdered."[23] In 1855 he
wrote: "Those remnants or descendants of the Teutomaniacs of
1815 who have but little modernised their old clothes of ultra-
German fools,—oh, I detested and fought them all my life. . . .
These nationalists and the whole wicked rearguard of 1815 are
ruling Germany once again. The day will come when the inevitable kick will crush you all. I leave the world with this
hopeful conviction."[24]

By and by, various German historians, psychologists, scientists, and diplomats began to differentiate between the "German" and the "Semitic" races, and to call the latter inferior.
Even two liberal writers wrote novels which could not have but
a devastating influence on the minds of German intellectuals. In
1854, Gustav Freytag published a novel, *Debit and Credit,*
depicting the "good" hard-working Germans and the "bad"
Jews, who are swindlers and receivers. Anton Wohlfahrt, the
son of a decent German, never strays from the path of virtue,
but his former schoolmate, the Jew Veitel Itzig, is out from the
beginning to make his way in life by foul means. He despises

"the Gentiles," gets rich in time but flees when the police find
him out and ends by suicide. Two other antagonistic characters
are Baron Rothsattel, descendant of an old noble family, and
the Jew Hirsch Ehrenthal who left his father's house as a poor
barefooted boy and has become a rich old usurer who goes mad
in the end. Of the virtuous Anton the author says: "The poetic
dreams which the boy Anton once dreamt in his father's house,
under the blessings of his good parents, were honest dreams.
They came true."[25] Ten years later, in 1864, Wilhelm Raabe
published a similar novel, *The Hungerpastor,* in which we meet
again good Germans and bad Jews—absolute opposites. Hans
Unwirrsch, the son of a German shoemaker who reads Jacob
Boehme, is filled with hunger for the ideal. Moses Freudenstein,
the son of a Jewish secondhand dealer, is filled with "terrible
hunger" for material things. Hans ends as a pastor to poor
fishermen somewhere on the northern coast of Germany.
Moses becomes a careerist and seducer of women, a "world
citizen," who says to Hans: "We are much better off than all of
you, whatever your names, you Aryans." He ends as a very high
official but "civilly dead in the most terrible sense of the word."
Of the virtuous Hans the author says in the last sentence of his
novel: "Hand *your* weapons over to another, Hans Unwirrsch!"[26]

In the 1870s the Court Chaplain Adolf Stöcker began to
preach a mixture of Christianity and anti-Semitism and found
many followers. The Emperor Frederick III said with regard
to his activities: "The anti-Semitic agitation is a disgrace for
Germany. I cannot understand how men who are, or should be,
in accordance with their vocation, on a spiritual level, can get
mixed up with an agitation equally objectionable in its presuppositions and aims."[27] He was not listened to but when Stöcker
came to London on a lecture tour in 1883 people staged demonstrations against him.

In 1879 another anti-Semite, W. Marr, complained in a book

that Lessing had got on a "wrong philosophical track" by writing *Nathan the Wise*. He spoke of the "world supremacy" held by the Jews and exclaimed in Hitlerian despair: "Future and life belong to the Jews, and only the past and death to Germandom."[28] In the same year a German nobleman, Gustav von Linden, published a strong refutation of Marr's allegations and reminded the public that the Christian nations of Europe had treated the Jews "in a most cruel and vulgar manner," that "our great Lessing" had rightly advocated the emancipation of the Jews, and that "every enlightened man" must do likewise. In angry words he attacked Marr's "abracadabra" and asked his readers to use their commonsense to refute him.[29] The German intellectuals, however, did not listen to this nobleman, they preferred to listen to the anti-Semitic Rector Ahlwardt and to another nobleman and wild nationalist, Heinrich von Treitschke.

The Jews, Treitschke wrote, are a nomadic nation, and even in Berlin there were "many Jews who have remained, in spite of their using the German language, unadulterated orientals in their hearts." The main characteristics of the Jewish nature were "their wild and passionate commercial instinct, their monstrous racial pride and their deadly hatred of Christians." They had no fatherland and no political instinct. "The Jews are our misfortune."[30] Rev. Professor Paulus Cassel in 1880 turned against Treitschke, who, he said, "has not inaugurated the attack against the Jews but does not disdain to bring his own wood to the burning stake." He asserted: "There has been a gulf between the European and the Semitic spirit since the days of Tacitus who had spoken of the *odium generis humani.*" This "infamous phrase of the haughty Roman," retorted Cassel, was hurled against the Christians. While Jesus had said that salvation comes from the Jew, Treitschke keeps on saying: "The Jews are our misfortune." Such an un-Christian and cowardly teaching, Cassel retorted again, is the misfortune of our nation. When a Jewish critic reviews the books of a German unfavorably Germans cry out about the insolence of the Jews. When Wagner sees that some Jews pay more homage to Mendelssohn than to him he writes about the Jews in music. Now Treitschke cries out against "the vigorous young Jews who immigrate to Germany from the East, selling trousers today, while their children and grandchildren will rule our exchange and Press one day." These Jews, Cassel reminded the raving historian, fled from Germany during the cruel persecutions by the crusaders and "thousands of them have become excellent men in all walks of life in Germany and in Europe."[31] Instead of deriding these Jews as sellers of trousers Treitschke had better help them to become useful men.

A Jewish rabbi, too, a Dr. J. Glueck, turned against Treitschke in 1880. The Jews, he wrote, are no "alien elements" in Germany. "Our and our forefather's cradles stood on German soil, German is our mother tongue, German are our customs, and we give our blood when our fatherland calls on us to defend it in war." He reminded the "biased" professor of history that many a rapacious bishop, prince, count, and baron had found in the "unfortunate Jews" of bygone centuries "a convenient object of plunder."[32] A Jewish journalist, Dr. S. Meyer, refuted Treitschke's charges by saying that there were more Jews living in France than in Germany, but in France there was no Treitschke, no Stoecker, no Marr. He quoted what the Catholic *Koelnische Zeitung* had written about German anti-Semitism: "Some of our modern Jew-baiters probably regret that the fine days are gone when one could get rid of 'the Semitic intruders' simply by killing them." That newspaper also censured those Lutheran "servants of our Lord who unscrupulously fill the mostly unthinking masses with a fanatical hatred against a part of their fellow men instead of preaching to them the love of their neighbor."[33]

A year later Rev. Cassel published another pamphlet in which he enumerated Treitschke's precursors. In 1798 and in

1804 two anonymous broadsheets were published in Germany, full of accusations against the Jews. In later years new Jew-baiters appeared on the German stage: Dühring, "Father of the Church of modern anti-Semites," who called Lessing a Jew; Bernhard Foerster (who later married Nietzsche's infamous sister); Wilhelm Marr, "one of the *triarii* of the anti-Semites"; and Adolf Stöcker, a Lutheran pastor, who tells large audiences that "the Jews are responsible for all our misfortunes," instead of telling them: "You yourselves are guilty. You do worse things than those with which you reproach the Jews." Stöcker, continues Cassel, "increases the arrogance of his listeners who pharisaically beat their breasts and shout: Away with the Jews. Afterwards we shall have a paradise like that—in Spain."[34] Stoecker, court preacher to Wilhelm I, called the Jews "a great danger to the national life of the Germans." It was true that the Jews had "carried the belief in a personal and only God through ancient times like a holy flame," but they had fallen back "into the worst idolatry" again and again. "It was only German Christianity which has cured these abuses." The Jews of modern times were "an irreligious power bitterly fighting against Christianity and uprooting the Christian belief as well as the national feelings" of the Germans. In flaming words swallowed by the population he spoke of the danger of Germany being dominated by the Jews and proposed laws against them to "combat Jewry's overrunning of German life." If these special laws were not promulgated, "our future is endangered, the German spirit will be judaised, the economic life of Germany impoverished."[35] Thus spoke the leading Lutheran pastor of his time. Pastor Cassel called him "a fatal personality"[36] and revealed that a coin had been minted and distributed among pupils of high-schools, showing on one side the names of the anti-Semites, Stöcker, Forster, and Henrici, and on the other the war-cry against the Jews, "Hepp, Hepp." Cassel quoted the anxious words of a Christian German lady that that "fanatical anti-Semitism must of necessity lead to murderous deeds by the uncivilised masses. Are not the intellectuals doubly guilty?"[37] This lady foresaw already then what Germans were doing sixty years later. Cassel was also very angry with the philosopher Eduard von Hartmann's anti-Semitic book, *The Jews in Present and Future,* and called him "a philosophical opportunist and industrious journalist," and advised him to study the Jewish problem "a little more closely" before attempting to pass judgment on the Jews; he would then have something to tell not only of "Jews at the stock-exchange" but also of their terrible sufferings through twenty centuries and of their "rich religious and poetic literature."[38] He had not much hope that the Germans would ever become sensible. The greatest German-Jewish scholar, Leopold Zunz, said at about the same time: "If a literature is called rich only because it possesses a few classical tragedies, which place does a tragedy merit which has been lasting for fifteen hundred years, written and produced by its own heroes?"[39] It was of no avail. In 1881 Eugen Duehrung published his pernicious book, *The Jewish Problem as a Problem of Race, Morals and Culture.* In 1940 the National Socialist Dr. Josef Müller said of him: "His warning: 'It is flesh and blood rather than iron and blood by which the fate of nations and individuals is decided' is very characteristic of the foresight of this man at a time when others spoke of humanity and equality."[40]

In the same year Berthold Auerbach, a writer of Jewish origin, famous all over Germany for his stories of Black Forest peasants, expressed the hope that the centenary of Lessing's death, which was about to be celebrated in Germany, might help "to push into the background the crude agitation against the Jews." The German Empress attended the Lessing festival at Berlin and wrote to Auerbach, whom she revered, that she was continuing the celebrations by reading his *Genesis of Nathan.* A month later Auerbach saw the Grand-Duke of Baden who was also one of his admirers, and they spoke about the assassination of Czar Alexander II. Auerbach told the Grand-Duke that the German agitation against the Jews was no less dangerous "than throwing bombs." The Grand-Duke agreed with him in that the minds of the Germans were poisoned by anti-Semitism, and he only hoped that it would cease soon. When Auerbach saw the Empress and the Grand-Duchess of Baden together he complained that it was very painful for him to be told that he was not a German and had no fatherland after having "done all that was in his power for the German nation for forty-six years"; the Grand-Duchess said: "Believe me, this ugly thing is prevalent only in Berlin." The Empress: "And even there it is only transitory."[41] They were mistaken.

Pope Leo XIII, in his encyclical of February 15, 1882, admonished all Catholic priests and the Catholics in general to avoid sinful generalizations about the Jews and repudiate anti-Semitism as contrary to the spirit of Christianity.[42] But the great German-Jewish novelist of the 1920s, Jakob Wassermann, shows in his novel, *The Goose-Herd* (1915), what difficulties a Jewish scholar had to overcome in 1882 when he tried to get a university chair. He did not even look like a Jew! "This," an anti-Semite retorts, "is the new Jewish trick. In olden times they wore the yellow badge and had noses like vultures and hair like bushmen."[43]

Yet another anti-Semite was Professor Paul de Lagarde who called the Jews foreigners who "ruined the fulfilment of the peculiar (*arteigen*) mission" of the German nation. He made the Jews responsible for capitalism and for plundering the other nations. One day, he asserted they would gain world supremacy. "It wants a heart as hard as a crocodile's skin not to feel pity with the poor fleeced Germans, not to hate the Jews and all those who talk of 'humanity' to please the Jews and are too cowardly to crush these vermins. You do not argue with trichinas and bacilli. You cannot 'educate' them, they must be exterminated as quickly and thoroughly as possible."[44] The noble professor also taught the Germans a foggy mysticism which made him say things like these: "The nation does not speak at all when the single individuals speak of which the nation is composed. The nation speaks only when nationhood (*Volkheit*) finds its expression in the words of the individuals. The nation remains completely mute with regard to single laws, even if you ask man by man for their opinion and man by man answers. Where general suffrage is the height of wisdom voices are not weighed but counted. My pupils should know that this is an immoral way of achieving an aim."[45] Are we not hearing the voice of Hitler? Lagarde's *German Writings* were republished in the Third Reich. Their editor said "Lagarde goes down in our history as the most powerful instigator of the ideas on which the Third Reich was built. It took fifty years until what he said about the Jews asserted itself successfully against the most unprecedented odds." The publisher sent a copy of the new edition to Hitler with these words: "The work of the old prophet of the German nation, dedicated to his successor by J. F. Lehmann."[46] Alfred Rosenberg learned his "philosophy" from Lagarde and H. S. Chamberlain.[47] He could have studied it also from Theodor Fritsch's *Catechism for Anti-Semites,* published in 1891. Hitler certainly studied it. It contains all the ideas which Hitler repeated in *Mein Kampf.* Fritsch spoke of the catastrophic role of the German Jews in the political, economic, and cultural life of Germany. They have, he alleged, ruined the peasants, the merchants, the officers, and suppress large parts of the population in a degree that revolts seem to be imminent. They try to shift their guilt to the Junkers, and they are the most daring seducers of German womanhood. Through their international connections they influence all governments in Europe so that no state dares to do anything against a Jew.[48] In 1892 Rector Hermann Ahlwardt was much acclaimed because he had said: "A dense cloud of Jews surrounds all the thrones so that the princes do not see the misery of the people nor hear their cries. I wish a man may arise and fight his way through the cloud of Jews to the monarch to bring before him, with a voice of love and faithfulness, the call for help of his people enslaved by the Jews, and to tell him that the claws of the Jewish dragon enclosed a diamond which is more precious than all treasures of the world, the bleeding heart of his people; and to ask him whether he would like, as a new Siegfried, to kill that dragon with the glorious sword of his ancestors and win the diamond. Millions and more millions would greet him enthusiastically. Oh God, let arise that man! This should be our prayer every Sunday in every church."[49]

Early in the 20th century *Rembrandt as an Educator* by Julius Langbehn was one of the most read books in Germany. What did the Germans find in that book? That they had been ruined by democracy and that the Jews were responsible for it, because they worked for disintegration in accordance with their racial essence. The modern Jew has no religion, no character, no home, no children. He is a part of the human race that has gone sour, just as hell is a part of heaven that has gone sour. The youthful Aryan spirit revolts against both. The youth against the Jews! We must remember that the first German students' corporations excluded Jews and that the German officers' corps and the order of the Jesuits did and still do the same. The youth, the church, the army follow ideals and are therefore anti-Jewish."[50]

The poet Richard Dehmel protested early in the 20th century against the German intrigues connected with the erection of a monument to Heine in his poem, *Ein Heine-Denkmal*. In it a German prince invites a sculptor and asks him to make a statue of "the ailing Jew and great artist who spoke our mother-tongue more forcefully than all the German Mullers or Schulzes." He gives the artist a few hints as to how he would like him to execute the job. In the eyes of the poet he must show the

Greeks' "free power," the ancient Indians' "free fervour," the Germans' "free passion," and the Jews' "sick longing, sick with the long servitude of Israel." The prince thanks the artist for his willingness to give preference to this task rather than to the other work he is planning, "The German Michel Awakening from his Sleep." Dehmel did not foresee what sort of "Germany awake" would take place three decades later.[51]

In 1901, Count Heinrich Coudenhove, the father of the founder of the Pan-European movement, a much-travelled scholar and devout Roman Catholic, refuted the allegations of German anti-Semites in a lengthy book, *The Essence of Anti-Semitism*. As he knew the ways of the anti-Semites, he said they would not succeed in making a Jew or a Freemason of him, there was not a drop of Jewish blood in his forefathers, and he was a pious son of the Roman Catholic Church. He called the "alleged difference of the races" a hateful heresy and said that the word "Aryan" was a linguistic, a philological term, and that it was madness to derive from it anatomic and moral differences. Friedrich Schlegel, who invented the word "Indo-German," would turn in his grave if he could see "the devastations" it had caused in German minds. "There are no Semitic peculiarities of character." He showed that the "Aryan" Parsees had developed very much like the Semitic Jews in Europe because they had had to endure similar hardship from their Mohammedan overlords. As they had been excluded from agriculture and military service like the Jews, they had got a good deal of Indian commerce into their hands, like the Jews. And like these, they remained faithful to their religion in spite of all persecution. "Racial hatred," said Count Coudenhove, "is the expression of backward men who have remained on a lower level of moral education." He reminded the backward Germans of what Herder had once said about the Jews, quoted on an earlier page.[52]

Count Coudenhove was not heeded. In 1911 Professor

Werner Sombart published a lengthy book about the role of the Jews in the economic history of Europe. He quoted with "scientific" satisfaction everything that had been said against the Jews in earlier barbaric centuries. In the Germany of the 18th century somebody had written that "the mean nature of the Jews, as is well known, is obnoxious and ruinous to everybody." The learned professor added it was true that Christians also sometimes acted against law and custom, but with Jews it was an entirely different matter. "When a Jew acts against law and custom it is by no means a question of the isolated immorality of a single sinner. . . . Their offences are the result of the general business morality characteristic of the Jews." Sombart found "in the religion of the Jews the same leading ideas which characterise capitalism." Jewish religion had rationalized the life of the Jews and had thus made them more susceptible to capitalism than others.[53] The Pan-Germans of the 20th century developed a program which advocated a German religion, the creed of a Nordic master race, and, naturally, also violent anti-Semitism.

When the First World War broke out it was a high official of Jewish origin, Councillor Riezler, who drafted the Kaiser's proclamation "To My People." When the German armies crossed the Russian frontier ("victoriously, by the help of God," as they boasted) the German High Command addressed a proclamation of the Jews of Poland: "We come as your friends and liberators. Our colours bring you justice and freedom, full and equal civil rights, a genuine freedom of worship and equality in all cultural and economic matters. Every one of you must help us with all his strength."[54] These were, as usual in Germany, empty promises. The shops and factories of the Jews were closed, and all raw material they had was confiscated.

Many thousands of German Jews fought as valiantly as the other Germans, just as German Jews had fought Napoleon a hundred years earlier. Twelve thousand Jews fell in the Kaiser's war, fifteen hundred were awarded the Iron Cross (First Class), one Jew received the *Pour le Mérite,* the highest German order, only to find himself in Dachau on November 10, 1935. Two Jews saved Germany from early disaster, Walther Rathenau, by organizing all German raw materials, and Professor Fritz Hager, by his invention of a method of gaining nitrogen from the air without which, Professor Max Planck said, "the First World War would have been lost at the very beginning."[55] A few years after the war, as Müller-Claudius reports, a Nazi headmaster remarked in a discussion: "If it was a Jew who worked out that method, he did not do it for the benefit of Germany but for his own profit." Asked how he got his information he replied: "From the unalterable racial character of the Jew."[56]

Towards the end of the war the Austrian playwright, Richard Beer-Hofmann, author of the haunting *Cradle-Song for Miriam* published his play in blank verse, *Jacob's Dream,* in which Jacob, fleeing from the wrath of Laban, is tempted by the Devil to forsake God. The Devil foretells him that he would have to wander among the nations of the world and never find a home, that the earth would be like iron under his feet, the heavens like iron above his head, that everybody would wrong and persecute him, that even the scabby beggars would ridicule him and praise themselves that they were not his like. To all these prophecies Jacob answers: "I love Him just as He is. Cruel and full of grace, sheer light and dark abyss. I know I belong to Him! I am not lured by promises nor terrified by horrors. Look, Devil: deep in my soul, where your word cannot penetrate, rests that in me from which you have been alienated: Blissful confidence." And turning to God: "Oh Lord! Whatever your will may put on my shoulders I shall bear it like a crown, not like a yoke!"[57] (Twenty years later, when Hitler invaded Vienna, the aged poet had to flee for his life and died in exile.)

While the war was still on, the Jewish philosopher Constantin

Brunner said that the belief in racialism was synonymous with haughtiness and hate. He implored Germany, which he called his "holy fatherland," to change her mind and realize "that hate is not only and not always catastrophic for the hated but also and always for the hater. The patriotic behavior of the German Jews during the war did not prevent the German anti-Semites from continuing their wild agitation against them. Dr. Brunner wrote another book in defence of the Jews in 1918. Why, he asked, do you call us swindlers without a fatherland, seducers, enemies of mankind, out to conquer the whole world? He recalled the German anti-Semites of an earlier generation, Stöcker, Ahlwardt, Foerster, Henrici, Chamberlain, and quoted a word of one of them: "The God of Moses is a personality just as the Jews needed to do business with." But he also quoted two decent Germans who had said very different things. Varnhagen von Ense, a century earlier, said a Jew-baiter must have "a dark spot in his heart on in his reason or in his life." Gottlieb August Schueler said in 1880 that the Germans treated the Jews "in a most characterless, most ignoble and most unworthy manner," and "ill-used the poor Jews for centuries by stupid arrogance, never-heard-of contempt, bitter mockery, the greatest possible cruelty, and cold hatred."[58]

The answer to this desperate appeal was given, in March 1919, when the name of Hitler was still unknown in Germany, by a Pan-German who hid behind the Goethean pen-name of Wilhelm Meister. In *The Account of Guilty Jewry* he accused the Jews of being responsible for Germany's defeat, which spelled victory for them. He called them a "pest for the human soul" and alleged that by their money they exercised a world supremacy and were out to arrange a "world revolution, the Jews' last and terrible method to achieve their highest aim, the Jewish World Republic." But he would not despair. "The Jews will die through the national German idea, as miasmata die when they get into the light of the sun. Up now and take up this task so that our hope be fulfilled! Judas Ischariot will then go the way which he has already gone once, and the German hope will become a certainty: the world will be saved by Germandom. Let nobody believe that the Jews are invincible!"[59] Two years later the Pan-German Otto Bonhard published his book, *From the Ghetto to Power,* under the pen-name Otto Kernholt. He quoted his anti-Semitic forerunners, Luther, Duehring, Lagarde, Wagner, Stoecker, and Treitschke, who had always spoken of "the alien drop" which has found its way "into our blood" and must be secreted again if it is not to poison us, and whose words "The Jews are our misfortune" had had "the effect of a bombshell" in 1879. He denounced as friends of the Jews the brothers Humboldt, Hardenberg, and Lessing who, with his *Nathan,* has wiped out again everything that he may have done for the Germans, Bonhard said: "Only whole measures can help. Away with all half-hearted measures, away with our fear of unavoidable cruelty!"[60] Adolf Bartels wrote in his *Our Right to Antisemitism:* "Cast off those who stultify our nation, and get out of the way those who disgrace our culture!"[61] In Switzerland, however, Leonhard Ragaz, a devout Christian, said at about the same time: "Jews were always the first to fight nationalism, militarism, imperialism, the whole domination of the world powers, and to replace it by the law of justice. They have thus been following their old vocation to be the nation of all nations and to keep the nations together by the Kingdom of God.[62]

In the same period two noble Germans tried to stem the new tide of anti-Semitism. One was Professor F. W. Foerster, who for many years had also been fighting Germany's false ideologies under Bismarck and the Kaiser. He called it a lie that the Semitic race "represented a dangerous and paralysing element," and told the Germans if they met a disagreeable Jew, to think of "all the malicious wrongs which the Christian nations had done to the Jews and were still doing "by words and books. The

Germans bear a heavy guilt because of their generalising anti-Semitism in the last decades." Being a devout Christian, not just calling himself one, he said that "the world-historical cooperation of the Aryan genius and the Semitic genius has been the will of God," that "the perfectly human can only be realized by the union of Semitism and Aryanism in Christianity. The fundamental idea of the Kingdom of God is the great gift of the Hebrews. The Jews have a stronger feeling of the spiritual fundamentals of life and society than any other nation." The Germans did not listen to him nor did they take note of the books which Martin Buber wrote about the Jewish spirit, and of his translations of the legends of great Jewish rabbis and saints who had lived in Russia and Poland in the 18th century and had inaugurated the mystical movement of Chassidism, based on a concept of life in the face of God, the joy in God in everyday doings, very much like that of St. Francis. It was only F. W. Foerster again who said about it: That old and devout Judaism still thrives today unadulterated in the closed Jewish communities among the Eastern Slavs. Many German anti-Semites have not the slightest inkling of how much nearer such a highly disciplined Judaism is to the spirit of Christ than their crude and uncharitable racial arrogance."[63] In the years between 1924 and 1932, Otto Hauser published seven books about *Racial Discipline, Racial Pictures, Race and Health, Racial Thinking, The Jews and Half-Jews in German Literature, Race and Philosophy*. Johannes von Leers, who after 1945 fled to Egypt, published these books during the same period: *Jews Look at You, History on a Racial Basis, Odal: The Life-Law of Eternal Germany, Fourteen Years of a Jewish Republic, Blood and Race in Law, The Criminality of Jewry, How Did the Jews Win Their Money, Jews Behind Stalin, The Criminal Nature of the Jews, Away with the Jews*. All these books were devoured by many Germans. The brave Professor E. R. Curtius, however, in his book, *German Spirit Endangered,* turned against the hateful allegation that the Jewish spirit was "essentially national and abstract. It is only necessary to remember the Jewish prophets and the mysticism of the Chassidic movement in order to refute such generalising assertions."[64] It was of no avail.

Arrogance and hatred went on and became more and more violent. So much so that the only decent general among the many reactionaries under the leadership of Ludendorff, Count von Schönaich, called German anti-Semitism the "infamy of the ages in which potentates tried to avert the attention from their own sins."[65] He turned against the military, political, and economic leaders of defeated Germany, naming especially the wildly reactionary Baron von Freytag-Loringhoven, "who, in their innermost hearts, feel responsible for the downfall but do not want to confess their guilt and look for a whipping-boy." He derided the balderdash of a "Nordic master race of which the racialists are drivelling," but which has never existed.[66] "For centuries," he told them, "we have excluded the Jews from the honourable careers of officer and civil servant, and forced them into the trades. Jews at the war front have done their duty throughout but our Hakenkreuz youth see in Walther Rathenau only the Jew, not the man of genius, the noble spirit, the ardent patriot."[67] In 1958, a German poet addressed a moving poem to the son of an unknown Jewish soldier who had fought for Germany in the First World War. Your father, he said, was a good patriot, spent four years in the trenches, received a shot in his lungs and the Iron Cross—"therefore he was gassed by the canaille of the Third Reich. Of the corpse they made useful things for our countrymen, artificial fertilizers or soap—miracles of chemistry . . ."[68]

In 1925 the famous novelist Jacob Wassermann tried to draw the German's attention to the history of suppression and persecution of the Jews and said: "An absurd idea of race today triumphs in Germany, which furthers all sorts of demagogical madness. No reason, no humanism, no historic and philosophic truth can assert itself against that lapidary and narrowminded cry: 'The Jew shall burn!'" In 1925 he also spoke of German "mass-psychosis."[69] But the Lutheran *General-superintendent* of the Prussian province, Otto Dibelius, on April 3, 1928, addressed a confidential letter to the pastors of his province in which he said: "We all must have not only understanding but also full sympathy for the deepest reasons of the racialism movement. I have always been an anti-Semite in spite of the bad ring of this word. We cannot fail to see that the Jews played a leading part in all the negative sides of modern civilization. May God bless our Easter festival and the Easter gospel!"[70]

Joseph Roth, a German novelist of Jewish origin who came from the Austrian province of Galicia, said in 1927 that for the Eastern Jews Germany was still "the country of Goethe and Schiller whom every studious young Jew knows better than our schoolboys with their Hakenkreuz."[71] His novel, *Hiob* (1930), depicted the life of those Eastern Jews. In 1933 he had to emigrate, and died in despair the death of a drunkard in Paris. Today he is praised in Germany as one of the best prose writers of his age.

Therefore the Roman Catholic writer Müller-Claudius said after the war that the racial anti-Semitism of the Germans after the First World War had been developed to "a singular degree until it went down in a series of innumerable crimes." Unlike the democratic nations of the West the Germans have never freed themselves from "the idea of an autocratic state" which they regarded as "an unalterable heritage of their racial substance." Democracy seemed to them to be the result of treachery by "seducers of alien race, the instrument," as Hitler put it, "of that race which, because of its aims, must fear the light of the sun. Only the Jew can praise an institution which is as dirty and untrue as he is himself."[72] Rabbi Salomon Rappaport, who was once beaten up by Nazi thugs in Vienna, says that the

Kingdom of God and the brotherhood of all men are the fundament of the Jewish religion. It was, he adds, the tragedy of the German Jews that Germany has never reached mature democracy; only in Great Britain and the United States Jews have been able to amalgate their own culture with those of the two ancient democracies of the world.[73] Professor Foerster, when reading of the unspeakable crimes committed by Hitler's "Aryan" thugs against the Jews, was reminded of the prophecy of a medieval German abbot of the monastery of Lehnin "that such a great crime would one day be committed in Germany that it could only be expiated by death. *Infandum nefas—morte piandum.*"[74] This was the death of Germany in 1945.

And today? The Germans say today they did not know anything. Hjalmar Schacht alluded to "Jewish" scandals in the years between the two wars.[75] There were many more "Aryan" scandals in the same period of German history. Heinrich Mann in 1925 drew attention to the fact that the authors and beneficiaries of the inflation had "acquired all Germany for nothing," but that Germany found consolation in the fact: "Thank God, we have Stinnes."[76] General von Schönaich said in 1923 that Stinnes had immensely enriched himself as the main purchaser of British coal, and that the German nation had been brought into "the repute of a foul bankrupt" by his and his friends' policy. Why, he asked Stinnes, do you not sacrifice half of your mines, blast-furnaces, wood and cement works, and newspapers in order to help our economy "to break through the shameless and usurious prices which force the nation to suffer cold and hunger?" Stinnes, like all the other unteachable Germans, preferred to ascribe their misery to the Versailles reparations. In 1925 Schönaich said that "the honest and silly Germans" only knew of the Stinnes concern as much as it suited the purposes of Stinnes because nine-tenths of all German newspapers and news agencies were in the hands of Stinnes and his like, the big industrialists and agrarians, whose protégés were Ludendorff and Hitler.[77] "Or were perhaps those Teutonic heroes with their long beards and Jaeger shirts and the myth of the blond master race not a perpetual challenge?" asked the writer Rudolf Pechel after the German collapse. "The shortcomings of a few Jews mean nothing compared to the fact that 60 millions attacked a defenceless minority of 600,000 Jews."[78]

When one Jewish captain, Alfred Dreyfus, was wrongly persecuted by French reactionaries, half of the French nation rose in disgust. George Clémenceau and Anatole France took up the case, Émile Zola published his world-famous *J'Accuse* in which he accused the French Government of corruption. In the years of Hitler's ascendancy a Dreyfus film ran in Germany for many months, but nobody connected the story of the unlucky French captain with what was going on in Germany. Millions of Germans hailed Hitler fanatically because of his anti-Semitism. When after the war some Germans behaved badly abroad, in Florence or Denmark, and foreign newspapers criticized "the" Germans for their bad behavior, innumerable German journalists protested that it was wrong to generalize. I searched in vain in German newspapers of the pre-Hitler years for similar protests by German journalists and writers against the preaching of the general guilt of the Jews. Post-war Germany is full of scandals of bribery and corruption among high officials. If, after each scandal had become known, we had started to exterminate five or six million Germans, how many would be alive today? There are some Jewish M.P.s in the British Labor Party and there are some others in the Conservative Party, but who has ever ventured to call a Conservative or a Labor government of Great Britain Jewish? Who in Great Britain or in the United States speaks of Marxism as a Jewish movement? Marxism is always analyzed and judged on its merits, praised by some and criticized by others, but never called Jewish as in Germany. Why? Because anti-Semitism is negligible in these countries. The Jewish writer Robert Henriques said in 1957 that the

Anglo-Jewish pattern of life and the British traditions of fairness and decency would never connive at anti-Semitism. The Jewish writer David Daiches, who grew up in Edinburgh, said that anti-Semitism was unknown in Scotland. The English writer T.L. Jarman said that the Englishman acts empirically, learns by trial and error and knows how to make compromises; the German, however, finds all this very difficult. If he considers the Nordic race the best, he must suppress all other races, and if he dislikes the Jews, he must exterminate them.

Why? Goethe, as usual, knew the answer: "General ideas" (his term for ideologies) "and great conceit are always apt to bring about terrible misfortune."[79] Thomas Mann agrees with him and says that the Germans are "too docile" and live "too willingly on theory."[80] He has something more to say about his nation. In 1930, when trying to warn the Germans against National Socialism, he asked them whether their behavior was German. "Is there any deep stratum of the German soul where all that fanaticism, that bacchantic frenzy, that orgiastic denial of reason and human dignity is really at home?"[81] After the collapse of Germany he said that the German soul was full of "the poison of isolation, provincial boorishness, neurosis, implicit Satanism. . . . This state of their mind had always had something scurrilously spooky, something hiddenly uncanny about it, a quality of secret daemonism."[82] The Germans, he holds, only seemed to be men of the 20th century; in reality they still moved in the Gothic Middle Ages. In the German atmosphere "something had clung of the state of mind of the final decades of the fifteenth century, the hysteria of the dying Middle Ages, something of a latent spiritual epidemic . . . a secret union of the Germans with the daemonic."[83] This appears in many variations in *Doctor Faustus,* which deals with Germany's pact with the devil in the years 1933 to 1945. "The Satanic covenant to win all treasures and power on earth for a time at the cost of the soul's salvation, strikes me as something exceedingly typical of German nature."[84] When Hitler said that the war could only end with the complete annihilation of either Germany or Great Britain and that he was sure that it would end with the destruction of Great Britain, while Sir Winston Churchill thought that it would end with the destruction of Germany, he asked Sir Winston to believe him this time, only this time, because he was speaking "as a prophet." How could an emissary from hell ever be a true prophet?

Notes

1. *Doktor Faustus,* p. 620.
2. José Orabuena. *Gross ist deine Treue.* Paderborn, 1959, pp. 277, 310, 413.
3. *Pharisaism,* p. 332.
4. Müller-Claudius. *Deutsche und juedische Tragik,* p. 66.
5. *Deutsche Blaetter,* Santiago de Chile, 1944/II.
6. *Rundbrief* XII.
7. J. Wolf and G. Salomon. *Der Charakter des Judentums.* Leipzig, 1817, p. 135.
8. G. E. Lessing. *Nathan der Weise.* London, re-ed. 1962, p. xvii.
9. G. E. Lessing. *Werke.* Edited by F. Bornmueller. Leipzig. Vol. II, p. xxxii.
10. *Faust.* Part I, first conversation with Wagner.
11. *Saemtliche Werke.* Vol. VI, 1845, pp. 149-150.
12. *Der Hungerpastor.* Berlin, no year of publication given, p. 47.
13. *Telegraf.* Berlin, February 18, 1956.
14. *Der Hungerpastor,* p. 4.
15. Erich Kahler. *Die Verantwortung des Geistes.* Frankfurt, 1952, p. 83.
16. *Ueber die Ansprueche der Juden an das deutsche Buergerrecht.* Berlin, 1816, p. 32.
17. Wolf Salomon, *op. cit.,* p. 153.
18. *Die Rassenfragen im Schrifttum der Neuzeit.* Muenchen, 1931, p. 369.
19. *Deutscher Horizont* (a periodical of the time).
20. *Grundsaetze des orthodoxen Judentums.* Rostock, 1835, p. 1.
21. Annette von Droste. *Die Judenbuche. Saemtliche Werke.* Muenchen, 1952, p. 936.
22. *Saemtliche Werke.* Berlin, 1911. *Erste Abteilung: Dramen,* Vol. I, pp. 12, 26, 63.
23. *Bulletin of the Leo Baeck Institute.* Tel Aviv, 1958/II-III, p. 76.
24. Hans Mayer. *Von Lessing bis Thomas Mann.* Pfullingen, 1959, pp. 281-282.
25. G. Freytag. *Soll und Haben.* Leipzig, 1886, Vol. II, p. 410.

26. *Der Hungerpastor,* pp. 135-136, 497, 499.

27. Gabriele Tergit. *Effingers.* Hamburg, 1951, p. 161.

28. *Der Sieg des Judentums über das Germanentum.* Bern, 1879, pp. 18, 39.

29. *Der Sieg des Judentums über das Germanentum, Eine Widerlegung der W. Marrischen Polemik.* Leipzig, 1879, pp. 26, 33, 39, 48.

30. *Politik.* Leipzig, 1897, Vol. I, pp. 276, 294-295.

31. *Wider Heinrich von Treitschke.* Berlin, 1880, pp. 3, 6, 9-10, 15-17, 24.

32. *Ein Wort an den Herrn Professor Heinrich von Treitschke.* Oldenburg, 1880, pp. 2, 3ff.

33. *Ein Wort an Herrn von Treitschke.* Berlin, 1880, pp. 18-19.

34. *Die Antisemiten und die evangelische Kirche.* Berlin, 1881, pp. 6, 7, 25-26, 30.

35. *Das moderne Judentum in Deutschland.* Berlin, 1880.

36. *Ahasverus: Die Sage vom ewigen Juden.* Berlin, 1885, p. 5.

37. *Ibid.,* pp. 5, 68.

38. *Ibid.,* pp. 11-12.

39. Foerster. *Die juedische Frage,* p. 78.

40. *Die Entwicklung des Rassenantisemitismus in den letzten Jahrzehnten des 19. Jahrhunderts.* Berlin, 1940, p. 31. The author of this book asserted in its first sentence: "The German nation has now entered the last phase of its fight against world Jewry."

41. *Briefe an Jakob Auerbach.* Frankfurt, 1884, Vol. II, pp. 448ff.

42. Foerster. *Die juedische Frage,* p. 77.

43. *Das Gänsemännchen.* Berlin, 1915, edition 1917, pp. 71-72.

44. *Deutsche Woche,* December 20, 1961.

45. Thomas Mann. *Betrachtungen eines Unpolitischen.* Berlin, 1919, p. 261.

46. *Deutsche Schriften,* Muenchen, 1940; *Deutsche Rundschau,* September, 1954.

47. International Military Tribunal (IMT), July 10, 1946.

48. *Deutsche Woche,* October, 1961.

49. H. Pross. *Die Zerstoerung der deutschen Politik.* Frankfurt, 1959, pp. 250-251.

50. *Deutsche Woche,* December 20, 1961.

51. Richard Dehmel. *Saemtliche Werke.* Berlin, 1913, Vol. I, pp. 171-176.

52. *Das Wesen des Antisemitismus.* Berlin, 1901, pp. 21, 96, 109, 110, 198, 257, 475.

53. *Die Juden und das Wirtschaftsleben.* Leipzig, 1911, pp. 138, 153, 242, 281, 328.

54. S. Adler-Rudel. *Ostjuden in Deutschland.* Tuebingen, 1959, p .156.

55. H. Hartmann. *Max Planck.* Basel, 1953, p. 69.

56. Müller-Claudius. *Deutsche und juedische Tragik,* p. 114.

57. *Jaakobs Traum.* Berlin, 1918. Reissued 1956, pp. 75-81.

58. *Deutschenhass, Judenhass und der Judenhass der Deutschen.* Berlin, 1919, pp. 14-15; *Der Judenhass und die Deutschen.* Berlin, 1918, pp. 1, 3, 8, 11-13, 182, 381.

59. *Judas Schuldbuch.* Muenchen, 1919, pp. 21, 159, 169, 171.

60. Otto Kernholt. *Vom Ghetto zur Macht.* Leipzig, 1921, pp. v, 193, 259, 296.

61. Franz Schonauer. *Deutsche Literatur im Dritten Reich*. Olten, 1961, pp. 31-33.

62. *Juden und Christentum*. A London Library Pamphlet of 1922, p. 39.

63. *Politische Ethik und Politische Paedagogik*. Muenchen, 1918, pp. 353-354, 376, 378, 385.

64. *Deutscher Geist in Gefahr*. Stuttgart, 1932, pp. 19-20, 24, 84.

65. *Mein Damaskus*. Berlin, 1926, p. 14.

66. *Zehn Jahre Kampf fuer Frieden*. Hamburg, 1929. Entry for July 4, 1926.

67. *Mein Damaskus*, p. 216.

68. *Deutsche Rundschau*, January, 1958.

69. *Lebensdienst*. Leipzig, 1928, pp. 150-173.

70. I found this letter in Germany and wrote to Bishop Dibelius. He did not deny having written it, but pleaded that it had been long ago, as if this were an excuse.

71. *Juden auf Wanderschaft* (1927). *Werke*. Koeln, 1956, Vol. III, p. 629.

72. Müller-Claudius. *Deutsche und juedische Tragik*. Frankfurt, 1955, pp. 96, 98-105, 108.

73. *Jewish Horizons*, p. 42.

74. *Rundbrief*, September, 1954.

75. *Merkur* (a periodical), May, 1954.

76. *Sieben Jahre*. Wien, 1929, p. 216.

77. *Zehn Jahre Kampf fuer Frieden*. October 18, November 1, 1923.

78. Rudolf Pechel. *Deutsche Gegenwart*. Darmstadt, 1953, pp. 166-168.

79. *Grosse Weimarer oder Sophien-Ausgabe*. Part I, Vol. 42/II, p. 169.

80. *Doktor Faustus*, p. 731.

81. *Achtung, Europa!* Stockholm, 1938, p. 55.

82. *Doktor Faustus*, p. 475.

83. *Ibid.*, p. 57.

84. *Aufbau*, New York, September 28, 1945.

85. Walther Hofer. *Der Nationalsozialismus*. Frankfurt, 1957. p. 241.

5
Luther

GERMANY'S POLITICAL DISASTER BEGAN WITH LUTHER. BY SAYING
this we do not intend to enter into the age-old and still
unsettled controversy between Catholics and Protestants as to
the rights and wrongs of Luther's deed. Only it must be said in
passing that German Catholics are convinced that German history would have been very different and much happier without
Luther.

Erasmus wrote to Luther on May 30, 1519 that more can be
achieved by politeness than by violence and hatred. But Luther
would not listen. Ten years later Erasmus said: "When you see
terrible cataclysms arise in the world, remember that Erasmus
predicted them."[1] Two hundred and fifty years later, Goethe
stated with regard to the French Revolution: "What Luther
once did, France does now in our troublesome days. It represses
quiet culture." These words, Thomas Mann says, show that in
the 16th century Goethe would have been on the side of
Erasmus. Thomas Mann agrees with both of them.[2] After Hit-

ler's war he stated twice with a sorrow which comes near despair that Germany would have been spared the Thirty Years' War, the religious schism, her depopulation and cultural as well as political disaster, "if Luther had not restored the Church."[3] Many decades before these words were written, the novelist Wilhelm Raabe had stated in a short story depicting life in the Germany of the 16th century: "The division of the German nation had become a fact for the benefit of the world, for the misery of the fatherland!"[4]

Luther, one can read in many books, was disgusted with the abuses of the Church. But as early as 1522, Pope Adrian VI, the devout successor of three rather un-Christian Popes, promised publicly through the mouth of his nuncio at the Nuremberg Diet to reform the Church and free it from all unworthy things which he did not deny. Early in 1523 the nuncio read to the Diet letters which he had received from Pope Adrian. The Pope blamed Luther for thinking himself the only wise man in Europe and creating a religious confusion, and he repeated his willingness to re-arrange everything in a quiet manner. God, he said, had punished the Church because of the sins of many prelates and priests, and detestable things had occurred even in the Vatican itself. He would do everything in his power to rid it and the Church from all abuses, but he asked for patience; age-old grievances could not be abolished in a day or two.[5]

If Luther had really wanted to restore the Church, he could have come around now. Instead he called that pious Pope an Antichrist. Satan, he said, spoke out of him.[6] This boorish way of talking was inherent in Luther's language. Thomas Mann quotes also Luther's word "the Divil's sow, the Pope" and reminds us that Luther called Canon Crotus Rubeanus, a peace-loving scholar who was inclined to reasonable compromise, "Dr. Kröte, lickspittle of the Mainz Cardinal."[7] When in 1538 Pope Paul III published a memorandum about the planned Church reform, Luther called the authors liars and "desperate rascals" and cursed the Pope "with his God, the Devil."[8] In his pamphlet *Against the Papacy in Rome* he delighted in even more obscene words, like His Hellishness, the Ass Pope with long asses' ears, Roman Hermaphrodite, Pope of Sodomites, the cursed dregs of the Devil at Rome.[9] We cannot fail to recognize Hitler's wild language against the Jews in these Lutheran apostrophes. Thomas Mann speaks of the "specifically Lutheran, the choleric coarseness, the invective, the fuming and raging, the extra-ordinary rudeness," and calls Luther not only anti-Roman but also anti-European and wildly nationalistic and anti-Semitic to boot. This Germanism in its unalloyed state, he confesses, is frightening and shocking. "I do not love him, I should not have liked to be Luther's dinner guest. I should probably have felt as comfortable as in the cosy home of an ogre."[10] Luther, he says, was "a mighty hater, willing from the depth of his heart to shed blood." A revolutionary and a reactionary at the same time, as a man of the Middle Ages he constantly "wrestled with the Devil and dogmatically believed in demons." His Devil, like Faust's Devil, is "a typically German figure." Thomas Mann declines to recognize the antithesis of popular robustness and civilization, "the antithesis of Luther and Erasmus," as inevitable. Goethe overcame it.[11] When Thomas Mann said this publicly, the German Lutheran bishops, who had never uttered a public protest against Hitler's persecution of the Jews, protested vehemently; up to this very day no German permits anybody to say anything against German heroes such as Luther, Bismarck, Wagner, Nietzsche and Hindenburg.

Now, Thomas Mann is a Lutheran himself, and when he wrote his essay on the Lutheran Lessing he was very conscious of being his spiritual descendant. He is not blind to the important fact that Luther is the creator of the modern German language which is as unthinkable without the Lutheran Bible as the English language would be without the Authorized Version; he therefore calls Luther "a gigantic incarnation of the German spirit."[12] He praises him for breaking the scholastic fetters and thus inaugurating, much against his own will, the age of reasoning and free philosophic speculation. Yet another Lutheran writer, Ricarda Huch, praised the immense importance of Luther's German Bible, adding that without it neither Lessing nor Goethe, Schiller, or any of the great German writers would have been what they were.[13] Of Luther's pamphlet, *Of the Jews and Their Lies,* however, she said during the barbaric reign of Hitler that Luther had once called the Jews the noblest of nations because God became flesh among them, but later changed his mind in a terrible manner.[14] This is what Luther said in that pamphlet and in another, *Shem Hamphoras:* "Burn down their synagogues, take away their books including their Bible. They should be condemned to forced labour. If they dare to pronounce the name of God, denounce them to the authorities or pelt them with cow dung. Moses already said, 'Don't suffer an idolator'; were he alive he would be the first to burn their temples down. May they follow him and return to Canaan. I would rather be a pig than a Jewish Messiah." And again, "What shall we do with this depraved and infamous people? I offer this for your good counsel: that their synagogues or schools should be burned by fire, that their houses and dwelling places, too, be broken up and destroyed, that we take away their prayer-books and their Talmud which teaches them all their idolatry, their lies, sacrilegious wickednesses and blasphemy, that their rabbis are forbidden on pain of death, to teach forthwith, that Jews be forbidden the right of way and the use of our streets."[15] Ricarda Huch asked whether Luther had forgotten that he had once been a Reuchlinist? With these words she alluded to the attack launched by the Cologne Dominicans and the baptized Jew Pfefferkorn against the Talmud and other Jewish books. The Emperor Maximillian then asked several experts, among them the famous biblical scholar Johannes Reuchlin, to investigate the accusations of the Dominicans. Reuchlin defended the Jews and said there was nothing wrong with their literature and they had a right to follow their religion without being molested. Luther was then on the side of Reuchlin. Later, however, he wrote his anti-Semitic pamphlets—did he not know, asked the famous and courageous Ricarda Huch, that the governments in those days "only needed to open a sluice in order to unleash a pogrom?"[16] A contemporary of Luther, the Swiss reformer Heinrich Bullinger, was shocked by Luther's coarse language, which he called the language of "a shepherd of pigs, not a famous shepherd of souls."[17] Professor Ritter, however, defends Luther by pointing out that he did not act from "racial" but "religious and moral" motives."[18] A Jew, when murdered by an incited mob, would probably not consider the subtle ideological differences which led to his being murdered. Julius Streicher at Nuremberg wondered on April 29, 1946 whether Luther, if still alive, would have sat in his stead in the prisoner's dock, for he had urged the burning of synagogues, and he, Streicher, had only followed his command. The Austrian historian Friedrich Heer says that Luther suffered from an anxiety complex which made him speak of his "confident despair." When he wrote to Erasmus: "You are not pious," this meant: "You do not share my anxiety." His anxiety complex made him say: "Wherever you are, sleep, talk, go and stand, whatever you do, the Devils are always around you like bumblebees." It is therefore not surprising, argues Heer, "that he regarded all his adversaries as Devils who must be exterminated. The papists, the enthusiasts, the baptists, the Romans, the Slavs, the Jews, the non-Germans were monsters. Succumbing to the old hatred of the mob and whipping it up even more violently, he told them to burn the synagogues and murder the Jews. In 1534, he composed a detailed program for the liquidation of the Jews." Many historians, says Heer, have spoken of "the catastrophic consequences of Luther. He opened a gulf between Germany and Western Europe by unclogging German irrationalism."[19] Quite a number of non-Catholic theologians, socialists, and politicians called Luther one of the main inaugurators of National Socialism, among them Karl Barth, Reinhold Niebuhr and Dean Inge.[20] Heer also wrote this: "He who wants to understand the lack of all tolerance, humanism, religious, spiritual, and political freedom in the Protestant parts of Germany and Europe must consider Luther's too great opinion of the *Father*."[21]

Various Lutheran writers in Germany are today accusing Luther of still other things. Ricarda Huch says that Luther called the rulers of earthly states the lieutenants of God, and that "the German princes eagerly and gladly lapped up these new teachings."[22] Professor Wilhelm Roepke says that Luther's teachings "no doubt had influenced the political, spiritual, and social history of Germany in a manner which can only be called catastrophic. Luther's Reformation bears the main responsibility for the separation of political and private life in Germany, and his teachings about the evil world resulted in the German non-resistance against the power of the state, their uninterestedness in politics and their resigned submissiveness to their rulers."[23] This we see recurring in Goethe's *Faust* where somebody starts a song:

The good old Holy Roman Realm,
How hangs it still together?

and his fellow-drunkard will have nothing of it:

A scurvy song! Faugh! A political song!
A filthy song! Thank God, with day's return,
The Holy Roman Empire's none of your concern.[24]

These words were the life motto of the philosopher Schopenhauer, who reacted furiously against the revolution of 1848, and in later years Richard Wagner, who had been a revolutionary for a short while, declared that democracy was something un-German; later still Hitler declared democracy to be something which the dirty Jews had invented. The romantic writer ETA. Hoffmann said that an artist could not be bothered by political events of his day. Nietzsche proudly called himself the last unpolitical German. He was not the last unpolitical man among German writers. This was Thomas Mann and he defended his position with vigour and much pessimistic wit during the First World War. But it is his glory that he changed his mind in time to warn his fellow countrymen against the danger of political uninterestedness. He made one of his characters in *The Magic Mountain,* the democrat Settembrini, say that everything is political—but the Germans between the two German wars did not listen to him. Therefore he censured them some twenty years later and stated: "The German cultural idea lacking in political will, in democracy was revenged on us in a terrible way."[25]

The philosopher Leopold Ziegler spoke in 1925 of "this nation of inborn Protestantism" which "is beaten up like a dog and submissive like a beggar."[26] Fritz Fischer wrote after Germany's second downfall about German Protestantism and Germany's politics in the 19th century, summarizing the consequences of Luther's doctrine: because of his strong belief in original sin Luther was "deeply pessimistic about man and world, excluding all optimistic progress. While people in the West saw in the misuse of power a sin, German Lutherans regarded revolution against power as a sin." Fischer finds this attitude in many German thinkers between Luther and Ranke.[27]

Even Professor Ritter recognizes this. In Luther's pessimism with regard to the world, he says, "lies the danger of remaining passive against the evil powers of this world. Luther's unpolitical piety revealed its catastrophic consequences in the 19th century—in a far too close relationship between *Thron* and *Altar,"* that is, the Prussian Kings and the Lutheran church which showed too little understanding for the drive of the nation towards political responsibility and too much servility to the Hohenzollern monarchy. "The Lutheran church of the 19th Century has given some nauseating proofs of the naïve collaboration of catechism, monarchism and Prussian militarism."[28] It gave still more disconcerting proofs of this naïvety in the 20th Century. The famous poet and novelist Hermann Hesse, Nobel Prize Winner, said that "the German pastors and their God went over to Hitler *en masse*."[29] The most nauseating proofs of their servility to the state were given by many leaders of the Protestant Church in the Third Reich. While the devout Lutheran writer Jochen Klepper entered in his diary on March 8, 1933: "Anti-Semitism is terrible now", and on March 11, 1933: "What has this much-advertised national revolution brought about? An atmosphere of pogrom"; and on March 30, 1933: "I believe in the mystery of God revealing itself in the Jews, and can therefore only see with sorrow that the Church puts up with the present happenings"[30]—the "Leaders of all German-Lutheran Churches" published the following on January 27, 1934: "Under the impression of the great hour when the leaders of the Lutheran Church met the Chancellor, they reaffirm unanimously their unconditional devotion to the Third Reich and its Führer. They condemn most vigorously all intrigues and criticisms of State, Nation and the (National Socialist) Movement which are apt to endanger the Third Reich."[31] In Klepper's diary we also find the following statements: "The Church recedes point by point. Truly, Judgment of the House of God had begun. The Church is afraid of the State, not of God." And: "We found deep comfort in what Pastor Wiese said of the Church's terrible failing with regard to the treatment of the Jews by the Third Reich."[32] Therefore, Pastor Martin Niemoeller said in 1945: "Our Church knew that the road taken would lead to a catastrophe. But we did not warn the nation, we did not uncover the wrongs done. We, the Church, must beat our

breasts and confess: *Mea culpa, mea culpa, mea maxima culpa!*
It is not for us now to accuse the Nazis, we have to accuse
only ourselves."[33] The resistance fighter Ernst Niekisch says
that many Lutheran pastors had supported the National Socialist movement, approved of the so-called "German Christians"
and prayed for Hitler in their sermons; they even hoisted the
National Socialist swastika on their churches during festivals of
the Nazis. When imprisoned for his activities against the Third
Reich, the Lutheran prison pastor, adorned with a swastika,
reproached him for his unrepentant behavior because "high
treason is a grave crime." When the pastor asked him why he
had left the Lutheran church, he received the answer: "Because
I saw already in 1919 that the Protestant Church was on a
declivitous road."[34] Of the consequences of Lutherism in Germany (by their fruits ye shall know them) we shall hear more
when we deal with Hitler's professors.

To return to Thomas Mann, he says that Luther applied
Paul's words "Let every soul be subject unto the higher powers"
to the petty princes of the small German states, while Paul had
in mind the authority of the Roman empire which was to become the political realm for the Christian religion. In this way
Luther's servility became German servility down the ages to the
time of Hitler. Specifically German also—this was the fault of
Luther, who was unpolitical and anti-political—was the dualism
of bold philosophical speculation and political infantilism.
Thirdly, Luther is to be blamed for the typically German separation of nationalism from the ideal of political liberty. The
Reformation was a nationalistic movement in contrast to the
international order of medieval Europe. Luther is responsible
for the fatal development which caused the German idea of
liberty to become "racial" (*voelkisch*) and anti-European and,
consequently, barbaric. Certain rude elements in Germany's war
of liberation against Napoleon proved this again and alienated
Goethe from his nation; he remained very cold amidst the gen-

eral enthusiasm. Hitler's barbarians also called what they inaugurated "a German liberation movement," as if a nation
which was internally as little free and self-responsible as the
politically immature Germans could dare to speak of freedom
and deserved external freedom. Freedom means primarily internal political freedom. The Germans, however, had never
learned to combine the national idea with the idea of political
liberty and humanism. Their idea of liberty had always been
narrow and self-centered; it only meant the right to be nothing
but German, and from this limitless egotism sprang the Hitlerian idea of enslaving the whole of Europe.[35]

Thomas Mann goes on to blame Luther for his catastrophic
attitude in the war of the German peasants. When these most
unfortunate people, inspired by the idea of evangelical freedom,
tried to better their social status, their serfdom, and revolted
against their inhuman masters, Luther condemned them in a
pamphlet, *Against the Rapacious and Murderous Peasant
Rabble,* fuming with anger, and told the princes to kill the
peasants like mad dogs and so gain the Kingdom of Heaven.[36]
He used the berserk language which is still in our ears from
Hitler's speeches. Ricarda Huch says that Luther, instead of
mediating between the princes and the peasants, took sides with
the princes against the peasants. His friends, says that famous
poet, novelist, and historian of the Reformation, looked with
terror at "that demon whose imperiousness and obstinancy
came near to satanism."[37] Golo Mann, when speaking of
Ricarda Huch in 1938, said: "Never have Luther's nature, his
satanical imperiousness and obstinancy, his barbaric attitude
towards the revolt of the peasants, and the catastrophic consequences of his activity for science and humanism, for the political servitude of religion, been as terribly indicted as in the book
of this Protestant writer."[38] Even Professor Ritter exclaims:
"What language is this? Is this still the voice of the liberator of
the Germans, or is it the hard and angry tone of the anathemas

of a new spiritual tyrant?"[39] When it was too late, Luther
recognized his catastrophic errors and accused himself: "I,
Martin Luther, have murdered all those peasants, for I bade
them murder. Their blood is on my head."[40] Thomas Mann
says that the revolt of the peasants, if successful, could have
given German history a turn to the better, a turn toward political freedom. He contrasts Luther's attitude with that of Tilman
Riemenschneider, a fine sculptor and wood-carver "to whom all
my sympathy goes out."[41] His compassionate heart compelled
him to side with the peasants against their tyrannic masters, but
the revolt was suppressed, and he was imprisoned and tortured.
Luther's example is the cause why "all German revolutions
have failed, that of 1525, of 1813, of 1848 and of 1918."[42]
Even Friedrich Ebert, the first President of the German Republic, a Social Democrat, once said: "I hate revolution like sin."
This, Thomas Mann continues," was genuinely Lutheran, genuinely German."[43] He also says that German revolutions are
"the puppet-shows of world history."[44] While Protestantism
paved the way towards political freedom in other countries, in
Germany it had a contrary effect.

Thomas Mann compared Luther and Goethe. In the latter
too, he finds much demonic power apt to frighten the mere
humanitarian. But Goethe, who was as different from Luther
as from Bismarck, knew how to unite mystery and clarity,
genius and reason. Him, not the other two, Thomas Mann calls
"a German miracle"[45] among mere Germans. Hermann Hesse,
the other great German writer of our time, who speaks in his
novels and in many of his poems, by way of various images, of
his own way from demonism to clarity and humanism, praises
Goethe for his perfectly unique attempt at a synthesis "of
German genius with rationality, of irresponsible musical diony-
sian ecstasy with belief in responsibility and moral obligation."[46] In Goethe, Thomas Mann underlines, Germany made
"a tremendous stride in human culture—or should have made
it, for in reality she kept always closer to Luther than to

Goethe."[47] Goethe once called himself a "liberator" of the Germans, but this remained wishful thinking. There is a straight line from the petty princes of Luther's time to the Hohenzollerns and from Kaiser Wilhelm to Hitler, whom they called their liberator.

As the Germans kept closer to Luther than to Goethe, Thomas Mann in 1947 settled his accounts with them in a novel of distinctly Lutheran flavor. We mean, of course, *Doctor Faustus,* in which we meet the theologian Ehrenfried Kumpf, "a nationalist of the Lutheran brand,"[48] who mixes his modern German with phrases of the German of Luther's time, if not of Luther himself. The modern Luther, too, sees the Devil in a corner of his room and throws his ink-pot (or rather a roll) after him. The Devil with whom Nazi Germany has made a pact, plays a major, a decisive, part in this novel, in which everything that has to do with him is described in Luther's German and which is full of quotations both from the old Faust story of the 16th century and from Goethe's *Faust.* This language, the Devil once remarks, "happens to be just precisely my favoured language."[49] The hero and his biographer come from Kaisersaschern, which lies "in the midst of the native home of the Reformation, in the heart of Lutherland" and is "rich with meaning for the inner life of the Lutheran Leverkühn."[50]

The air of Kaiseraschern is "good old German air, from anno MD or thereabouts, shortly before Dr. Martinus came ... long before the thirty years' frolic."[51] And when the Devil adds, "Bethink thee what lively movement was with you in Germany's midst," his words allude both to the Reformation and National Socialism. The words "in Germany's midst"—*"in Deutschland's Mitten"*—also allude to Nuremberg where Hitler held his pompous Party meetings, and, as they are taken from Wagner's *The Mastersingers of Nuremberg,* they remind us of one of the most important teachers, in racial and anti-Semitic matters, of the Führer.[52]

The hero of this novel, like his parents, has features which seem to have been molded in an earlier age, in the time "before the Thirty Years' War."[53] When the Devil visits him somewhere in Italy and Adrian Leverkühn finds this visit not in style, for the Devil should have called on him in Germany, in Wittenberg, on the Wartburg or in Leipsic, the Devil quietly retorts: "If you only had the courage to say unto yourself: 'Where I am there is Kaiseraschern.' "[54]

We make also the acquaintance of several of Adrian's university friends and hear from them that the idea of youth is the special prerogative of the Germans. German youth, they assert, embodies the German spirit which is young and full of future, "immature if you like—but what does ripe mean? German deeds were always done out of a certain mighty immaturity, and not for nothing are we the people of the Reformation. That too was a work of immaturity . . . where would the world be if maturity were the last word? We shall in our immaturity inflict on her many a renewal, many a revolution."[55] They did, and the world will never forget it; only they have forgotten it.

These hopeful young men—the elite of both German wars, who declared themselves under Kaiser Wilhelm and under Hitler, like the Italians under Mussolini, to be *the* young nation of Europe—also speak of the German Becoming, of the German Wandering, of the endless migrations of the German soul: "If you like, the German is the eternal student."[56] In 1925 the German philosopher Leopold Ziegler stated that the Germans were a nation of seekers and wanderers, something "unfinished, raw, half-grown among so many finished, disciplined, grown-up peoples. . . . We have always remained half-finished barbarians; we appear to the other nations driven about and about by the demonism of Becoming and never of Being."[57] According to the National Socialist writer Guido Kolbenheyer, that nation was young which still had much plasma to use in its battles for life, and that nation old which had already used up its biological resources. The nations of the West, he said, had spent all their biological heritage. In the words of the Führer, in 1932, "We are barbarians, we want to be barbarians."[58]

Thomas Mann, his most famous enemy, makes those hopeful young Germans say: "To be young means to be able to stand up and shake off the fetters of an outlived civilisation, to dare— where others lack the courage—to plunge again into the elemental."[59] This daring plunge cost the innocent lives of twelve million people murdered by youthful Nordic heroes. Following this plunge the whole of Europe was twice devastated. Hermann Hesse, although a Lutheran himself, the son and grandson of Lutheran missionaries, said in 1948: "The minimizing of 'good deeds,' the idea of salvation by faith (Luther's *fide sola*), was already with Luther a terrible and even impudent foolhardiness which helped unspeakably bad things into being. The Germans, especially the Germans of today, are by no means a nation which could be told that 'deeds' do not matter, that they can be dispensed with if only the will be good. The 'will,' with most of them, will only be a genuine or alleged patriotism, and in the name of the fatherland they would be capable of committing the same crimes tomorrow the consequences of which threaten to destroy the nation today."[60]

The political consequences of the Reformation were catastrophic for all future German history. The Germans have never recovered from it. Goethe once said to Eckermann that German history cannot be compared with English history, and a few decades later the great dramatist Friedrich Hebbel sadly stated: "It is perfectly true: we Germans are not connected with the history of our nation. Why? Because this history has been without any result, because we cannot regard ourselves as products of an organic development, as, for instance, the English and the French. What we cannot help calling our German history, is not the history of our lives but of our illness."[61] It was their "archenemy" Napoleon who contributed most to their unification by abolishing the innumerable petty German states.

Notes

1. *Die Neue Rundschau,* Stockholm, October, 1945.
2. *Bemuehungen.* Berlin, 1925, p. 96.
3. *Doktor Faustus,* p. 140.
4. Wilhelm Raabe. *Der heilige Born. Complete Works,* Berlin, 1913, First Series, Vol. 3, p. 24.
5. Ludwig Pastor. *Geschichte der Päpste.* Vol. IV/II, 1907, pp. 88-96.
6. *Ibid.,* p. 98.
7. *Doktor Faustus,* p. 139.
8. Pastor, *op. cit.,* Vol. V, 1909, p. 127.
9. *Ibid.,* p. 516.
10. Thomas Mann. "Deutschland und die Deutschen." In *Die Neue Rundschau,* Stockholm, October, 1945.
11. Thomas Mann. "Goethe, das deutsche Wunder." In *Der Monat,* Berlin, August, 1949; "Deutschland und die Deutschen."
12. "Deutschland und die Deutschen."
13. *Luther.* Wiesbaden, 1951. Inselausgabe, p. 6.
14. *Das Zeitalter der Glaubensspaltung.* Zürich, 1937, pp. 288 ff.
15. *The Jewish Quarterly,* London, Summer, 1961.
16. *Das Zeitalter der Glaubenssapaltung,* p. 378.
17. Foerster. *Die juedische Frage,* p. 96.
18. Gerhard Ritter. *Luther.* Muenchen, 1950, p. 226.
19. *Die dritte Kraft,* pp. 195, 208, 698.
20. *Ibid.,* p. 698.
21. *Ibid.,* pp. 232-233.
22. *Das Zeitalter der Glaubensspaltung,* p. 178.
23. Wilhelm Roepke. *Die deutsche Frage.* Zürich, 1945, pp. 136-137, 163-164.
24. *Faust.* Part I. Auerbach's Cellar.
25. *Altes und Neues.* Frankfurt, 1953, p. 651.
26. *Das heilige Reich der Deutschen.* Darmstadt, 1925, Vol. I, p. 22.
27. *Historische Zeitschrift,* 1951, pp. 474-476.
28. *Aussenpolitik,* Stuttgart, December, 1954, pp. 773ff.
29. *Briefe.* Frankfurt, 1954, p. 241.
30. *Unter dem Schatten deiner Fluegel.* Stuttgart, 1956, pp. 40, 41, 47.
31. Kurt Pritzkoleit. *Die neuen Herren.* Muenchen, 1955, p. 99.
32. *Unter dem Schatten deiner Fluegel.* April 11, 1939, January 14, 1940.
33. Martin Niemoeller. *Reden 1945-1954.* Darmstadt, 1958, p. 12.
34. *Gewagtes Leben.* Koeln, 1958, p. 342.
35. "Deutschland und die Deutschen."
36. *Ibid.*
37. *Das Zeitalter der Glaubensspaltung,* pp. 178, 211-213, 378.
38. *Geschichte und Geschichten.* Frankfurt, 1960, p. 48.
39. Ritter. *Luther,* p. 187.
40. Heyck (ed.). *Luther.* Bielefeld, 1933, p. 78.
41. "Deutschland und die Deutschen."
42. *Ibid.*

43. *Ibid.*
44. *Doktor Faustus*, p. 185.
45. "Goethe, das deutsche Wunder."
46. *Gesammelte Schriften*. Frankfurt, 1957, Vol. VII, p. 376.
47. "Deutschland und die Deutschen."
48. *Doktor Faustus*, p. 96.
49. *Ibid.*, p. 346.
50. *Ibid.*, p. 16.
51. *Ibid.*, p. 358.
52. *Ibid.*, p. 358.
53. *Ibid.*, p. 12.
54. *Ibid.*, p. 226.
55. *Ibid.*, p. 184.
56. *Ibid.*, p. 185.
57. *Das heilige Reich der Deutschen*. Vol. I, pp. 13-15, 31.
58. *Gespraeche mit Hitler*, p. 78.
59. *Doktor Faustus*, p. 185.
60. *Briefe*, p. 272.
61. W. Muschg. *Tragische Literaturgeschichte*. Bern, 1948, p. 229.

6

Goethe, the Exception

THE GERMANS PRIDED THEMSELVES ON BEING A NATION OF poets and thinkers. Even in the Third Reich a Hitler poet said: "Also as a nation of doers we have no less remained a nation of poets."[1] He proved this by quoting a number of poems in praise of Hitler and his totalitarian Reich, his own poem for instance, *To the Führer,* in which he addressed him as the incarnation of the old-German custom of choosing "a Führer out of their midst." Or a poem of Baldur von Schirach's in which this criminal said that the Germans should not behave like praying ascetics but "like soldiers who say their prayers by deeds!" Gerhard Schumann, who had become a high SA officer, prayed to God to guard the Führer and the country; "we shall do everything else ourselves." What they all have done the world knows by now. Or has it already forgotten it?

A nation of poets and thinkers! What have their great poets said and what did they make of them during Hitler's "millennium"? What have their great poets and writers said of them?

Let us start with Lessing. In *Emilia Galotti* he condemned
absolutism, in *Nathan the Wise* he condemned fanaticism and
the hatred of the Jews.

> For is not Christianity all built
> Upon the Jewish creed? Oh oft, too oft,
> It vexes me and cost me bitter tears,
> To think that Christians will so constantly
> Forget that Christ our Saviour was a Jew.[2]

In the days of growing National Socialism Thomas Mann said
in a lecture that Lessing never wanted to be praised as a patriot
because he considered himself a citizen of the world, and longed
for men in all countries who knew when patriotism was no
longer a virtue. Thomas Mann stressed this point because the
nationalists called him unpatriotic after he had denounced nationalism and National Socialism. A writer to their liking, he
retorted, must not see anything of what was going on in Germany. As they despised Lessing for being rationalist, Thomas
Mann answered: "We are far gone in the irrational—to the joy
of all the baser enemies of light, all priests of the dynamic
orgasm . . ."[3]

Now to Goethe. He called his work the triumph of the purely
humane and found in the Gospels "the reflection of a greatness
which emanated from the person of Jesus and which was of as
divine a nature as was ever seen on earth. . . . I bow before Him
as the divine manifestation of the highest principle of morality."[4] He said that genuine tolerance is best attained by leaving
the peculiar characteristics of individuals and nations where
they are, and sticking to "the conviction that the truly great
belongs to all mankind."[5] National hatred, however, was
"strongest and most violent in the lowest civilisations."[6]
Twenty years earlier he had said that "our life did not lead us to
separation from other nations but to the greatest intercourse."[7]
On a later occasion he said: "We Germans are of yesterday.
True, we have civilised ourselves for a hundred years, but several centuries will be needed before our compatriots generally

acquire so much spirit and higher culture to admire beauty as the Greeks did, and people will be able to say of us that it had been long ago that we were barbarians."[8] On yet another occasion he said of the Germans: "Oh, that wretched people, they will find a bad end, because they do not want to understand themselves, and every misunderstanding of oneself arouses, not only the laughter, but also the hatred of the world. Fate will smash them because they betrayed themselves and did not want to be what they are."[9] Goethe also thought that patriotism ruined history, and that despotism encouraged the autocracy of all and sundry.[10] He did not think much of the enthusiasm of the romantics for German antiquities and asked what we could find in "those gloomy old-German times."[11] He ridiculed "the patriotic German who arrogated to himself all the virtues of other nations and stressed that the other nations had originated from the Germans."[12] While forgetting "everything which he has been owing to other nations for the last fifty years and still owed it to them."[13]

What did Goethe think of the Germans and English? The individual German, he said, is often respectable, but the nation as a whole is miserable;[14] that, like the Jews, they should be scattered all over the earth in order to develop "fully and for the benefit of the nations" the good that lies in them.[15] But after what they had done to the peoples of Europe between 1938 and 1945, Thomas Mann said that the Germans would have to live shut in like the Jews of the ghettoes because the frightful hatred they have aroused against themselves will not allow them to emerge from behind their frontiers. Goethe once confessed to a feeling of terror when comparing his Germans with other nations. He escaped from it into science and literature, which are not limited by national frontiers.[16] He was very impatient with patriotic Germans who asserted that they could exist with themselves, that the other nations stemmed from them, and who had the effrontery to arrogate to themselves the merits of all other nations. "We Germans fall too easily into pedantic conceit when we do not look beyond the walls of our surroundings." He called national literature a senseless term and coined the new term 'world-literature.' Everybody, he said, must strive to bring about the period of world literature.[17] Did the Germans listen to him? He complained that they had always pushed away what he had done and performed. In verse he asserted that he was a burden on all of them and that they hated him mortally.

Unlike Kleist, Goethe revered Napoleon. After the battle of Jena, in which Napoleon had defeated the old-fashioned Prussian armies, the historian Luden asked Goethe how he felt in these days of shame and misfortune, and received, to his consternation, the answer that the poet felt all right and had no reason to complain. He compared himself to a man who was looking down from a secure cliff into the raging sea whose breakers could not reach him. As early as 1792, witnessing the first onslaught of the French army of revolution at Valmy which routed the Prussian army with a vigor never before experienced, Goethe had said to his entourage that they were witnessing a new epoch of world history and would be able to boast that they had been there. The old-fashioned Frederican army was not reformed after that defeat, and in 1806 Napoleon routed it again at Jena.

In 1813 Goethe said to Luden that he was by no means indifferent to great ideas like freedom and fatherland, but that he could not agree with the historian's enthusiasm about the German rising. "Has the nation really been awakened? Did it know what it wanted?" He no longer saw Frenchmen and Italians in Weimar, but instead he saw Cossacks, Bashkirs, Croats, Magyars, Cassubs, brown and other hussars—was that better? he asked.[18] For it did not matter to him that these were "friends" and the French "enemies." He could not, he said, hate the French because he owed so much to their culture. He was over eighty years when he confessed to being "a moderate liberal, as every sensible man is."[19] He considered himself lucky as having been born at a time "when the greatest world events were happening and are still happening." He mentioned the Seven Years' War, America's separation from England, the French Revolution and the Age of Napoleon. "So I arrived at opinions and results very different from those who have been born only now."[20]

One day the old man said to his secretary Riemer that the antipathy which the nation felt against the Jews, and in which there was mingled respect with aversion, could only be compared to the antipathy felt against the Germans, whose role and position among the nations had the strangest kinship with that of the Jews. He confessed he "felt at times a choking anxiety that the accumulated world-hatred might one day turn against the Germans."[21] A century later, in 1914, Count Hermann Keyserling said that the Germans had embodied an evil principle with German thoroughness and self-intoxicating success at a time when the other nations were already longing for a new level of international life—"Germany has therefore accumulated the hatred of all the world on her own head."[22] After the First World War the novelist Hermann Hesse said to the Germans: "Have you ever asked yourselves why you are so little loved, so much, so deeply hated, so much feared and so passionately shunned?" He gave them the explanation: "You are always talking of 'German virtues,' faithfulness and other virtues you thought had been invented by the Kaiser and your nation. But you have not been faithful, you have betrayed yourselves, and it is exactly this which has caused the world to hate you. You played a role which was not yours. With the help of your Kaiser and of Richard Wagner you made an opera of the 'German' virtues which nobody in the world took seriously except you yourselves. Behind the pretty humbug of that operatic power you allowed all your dark, slavish and megalomaniac instincts to grow and blossom. You Germans are more accus-

tomed to obedience than any other nation, you have obeyed so
easily, so enthusiastically, you did not like to make even one
step without feeling the satisfaction that you were fulfilling a
command. Your country has been covered as with a forest with
boards promulgating laws and more especially decreeing:
'Verboten.' "[23]

To return to Goethe, he knew how much he owed to English
literature. "I owe," he said, "very, very much to Shakespeare,
Sterne and Goldsmith."[24] German novels derived, as he knew,
from Fielding and Goldsmith.[25] He thought Fielding's *Tom
Jones* one of the most famous novels, "and rightly so," he
thought Goldsmith's *Vicar of Wakefield* "one of the best novels
ever written," and his *Deserted Village* was for a long time "one
of my most decisive passions."[26] He also had much praise for
Byron and Scott's novels, and admired Sterne's deep humor
which had inaugurated "the great epoch of a purer knowledge
of man, of noble toleration and tender love."[27] He called him
"the most beautiful spirit who had ever been active," and said
he had first freed us "from pedantism and philistinism."[28] Of
himself he said in a poem that he had freed the Germans from
"the nets of philistinism," that is to say, he had tried to free
them but had succeeded only with a tiny minority.

The most expressive homage, however, he paid to Shakespeare through all his long life. He called himself a man who
had been born blind but whose eyes had been opened in one
second by a miraculous hand. Shakespeare's tragedies, he said,
are "not mere poems. You see the huge books of Fate
opened."[29] Shakespeare and "Ossian" helped to free him from
coquettish rococo and reach the deeper layers of the human
heart. At the age of seventy-five he confessed that he had never
dared to compare himself with Shakespeare. "He is a being of a
higher race to whom I look up and whom I must revere."[30]

He admired the English and the French for their clear way of
writing and condemned the German philosophers for the ob-

scurity and pomposity which not even the Germans could understand, let alone foreigners. He ridiculed Fichte's metaphysical fancies and called him "the absolute Ego" and was unhappy
about Hegel's unfortunate influence on the German language.
Once he received a book by a "Super-Hegel" and tried to de-
cipher it but gave it up as "an experience with a rattle-snake."
He read a passage of that "damned stuff" aloud to Eckermann
and said that these philosophers were ruining the language.[31]
To Wilhelm Humboldt he once wrote that the Germans had
been condemned "to live in the chimerical night of speculation."[32] They did not listen to him and went on enjoying those
chimerical regions up to this very day. One metaphysical school
followed the other during the 19th and 20th centuries, and not
even the terrible catastrophe of 1945 changed anything in that
respect. There was Fichte and Hegel, there were the New-
Kantians and New-Hegelians, there were many other schools,
and today there is an existentialist abracadabra in Germany
with the philosopher Martin Heidegger, who once praised the
Third Reich, in the lead. He is back again although he said this
in 1933: "We want our nation to fulfil its historical mission.
The young and youngest power of the nation has already decided this question. But we shall only understand the glory and
greatness of this *Aufbruch* if we carry in us that deep circum-
spection from which the ancient wisdom of the Greeks sprang:
Everything great stands in a storm." As he spoke to students he
added: "No dogmas and ideas should be the rules of your existence. The *Führer* alone represents the German reality of
today and tomorrow, he is the law."[33]

Many young Englishmen came to Weimar and Jena and
Goethe often invited them to his home. One day, nearly eighty,
he spoke about them to Eckermann. "There is," he said, "nothing vitiated or spoilt about them, nothing half-way or crooked,"
and he pondered why this was so; was it their race, their free
political institutions or their healthy education? "They have a

much freer development than is the case with us Germans."
And in vivid words he described to his listeners a scene which
he had recently observed fom his window. It had snowed, and
the children of his neighbors had taken their little sledges out
into the street. But immediately a policeman had come around,
"I saw the poor little things fly as quickly as they could."[34]
What a symbolic little scene! What far-reaching consequences it
conjures up before our eyes today! Goethe did not know that
Frederick William III, the King of Prussia, had only eighteen
months earlier warned the editor of the *Vossische Zeitung* to
restrict announcements about birthdays of "private individuals"
to a minimum. That newspaper had published a lengthy article
about a celebration, held by a private club, of Goethe's and
Hegel's birthdays on August 27 and 28 respectively. Articles of
such length, the Prussian King wrote, were only suitable for
descriptions of "a monarch's accession to the throne."[35] A few
decades later, a German racialist, Hans Hermann, said of
Goethe: "If you look at him (more closely), these dark eyes
with their slight melancholy, this curved nose, this long body on
short legs—you recognise the prototype of a descendant of
Abraham. But not only these physical traits but also his spiritual attitude reveal Goethe as a descendant of the Old Testament
heroes. His glowing sensuality, and eternal infatuation, his immorality, his servility, his perfect lack of patriotism, his cowardly behaviour towards the war events of his time, and many
another trait, speak too clearly not to reveal to an unbiased man
that Goethe had much more of a Semite than of a German."[36]
Another mad anti-Semite, Eugen Duehring, said the same of
Lessing in days when nobody knew anything of Hitler: "From
early on I realised that Lessing must have had Jewish blood in
his veins. This explains all sorts of things in his behaviour."[37]
   In the hundred years between Goethe and Hitler, the Germans gradually began to think differently of Great Britain.
Early in the First World War Professor Werner Sombart, also

famous for his anti-Semitism, published a book, *Händler und Helden,* the heroes being the Germans, the shop-keepers, the British. One could also speak of "soldiers" and "retailers," he said. The present war, he explained, was a war for "predominance between the heroic and the tradesmen-like *Weltanschauung.*" He ridiculed Herbert Spencer's "rights of men" as "a merchant's shallow idea of a state" and exclaimed: "What does the Englishman know of liberty!"[38] Professor Sombart's forerunner, Treitschke, had found everywhere in the world, except in Germany, "an economic idea of the state, the longing for much money and little authority, while the Germans alone knew how to reconcile the ancient antithesis of "state power and liberty of the nation." He added: "The foreigners know this in their hearts and hate us therefore."[39] In the Second World War this megalomania took the form of "Why do they do all this to us? Because they envy us, because they envy us our Führer, because they envy us our achievements. Out of envy, out of envy!"[40] An SS criminal rounding up Jews in Denmark in 1941 said to the wife of a Dane who was in the meantime rescuing Jews and bringing them secretly to Sweden: "We Germans are a nation of heroes."[41]

In the Second World War the Hitler professor Friedrich Schoenemann said the English would never understand anything of "a living community formed by the principle of blood and soil," because they knew only "a state based on a strictly lawful constitution"; they were representatives "of a liberal *Weltanschauung,* as Sombart had already recognised." He saw "an elective affinity between the Anglo-Saxons and the Jews," and asked scornfully: "Who, apart from the Jews, has ever been interested in cosmopolitism? Who has ever intellectually puzzled out pacifism, an abstract peace without regard to a true, life-warm peace? The Anglo-Saxons have taken over this and other things with the utmost readiness and conviction from the Jews because and insofar as they were in agreement with their plans for world domination."[42] This professor was not the only madman who propagated such falsehoods.

Nietzsche once said that Goethe had been "an event without consequence in German history,"[43] and that he "cavilled as if from abroad, with impatient vigour, at everything of which the Germans were proud."[44] He apparently alluded to an entry in Goethe's diaries: "Question whether great men have left any impression in their respective countries. No trace of them in Germany."[45] Goethe once said: "Germany? But where is it? I cannot find this country. You Germans are striving in vain to become a nation. Try to become free men, and you will succeed."[46] Of Weimar he said in a poem: "Oh, Weimar, yours was a peculiar lot! Like Bethlehem in Judah you are small and great at the same time." A headline in a British newspaper of 1962, *Weimar and Buchenwald,* shows Germany's downfall from Goethe to Hitler. We read in that article: "Goethe's Weimar and Hitler's Buchenwald in the space of a single morning formed a contrast that made it hard to believe that both had originated in human thought and endeavour. Yet there they were in the countryside only a couple of miles or so apart with the turrets of the one plainly visible from the torture chambers of the other. . . . The guide who showed us the cells, the whipping blocks, the execution chambers where gramophone records had drowned the screams of the dying, the ovens where their corpses were burnt and the tiled sinks in which Ilse Koch had tanned human skin into lampshade parchment, had himself spent eleven years as a prisoner there."[47]

While H. S. Chamberlain, a savage German nationalist, hailed Hitler as the Saviour of Germany, celebrated Goethe as the model of an "Aryan man" and impudently denied his deep esteem for the "Jew" Spinoza, the great German poet Stefan George early in the 20th century ridiculed the hypocritical lip-service the Germans paid to Goethe and said that if he came back suddenly, they would not recognize him, "a king who passed you by."[48] He derided their animosity against Goethe's cosmopolitism which made them grudgingly say that the lotus of Hellas had killed his love for his own country, that he had been an enemy of the fatherland and had sacrificed on the altars of false gods.[49] In 1939 the exiled Thomas Mann, in *Lotte in Weimar,* put into Goethe's mouth highly scornful words against the Germans of the Third Reich who had gambled away all honesty and thought they were great, and looked "with jaundiced eyes on those whom foreigners love and respect, seeing in them the true Germany. . . . They do not like me—so be it, I do not like them either, we are quits. They think they are Germany —but I am Germany. Let the rest perish, root and branch, it will survive in me."[50] Ten years later, after Germany's downfall, Thomas Mann said on the occasion of Goethe's 200th birthday that the whole civilized world "celebrated the solemn return of his Epiphany."[51] But the commentators of the racial laws of Nuremberg, State Secretary Dr. Wilhelm Stuckart and Dr. Hans Globke, one dead by now and in Wotan's Walhall, the other State-Secretary in Adenuaer's *Bundeskansleramt,* founded those infamous laws not only on the saying of Hitler and race "experts" but also on these lines of Goethe:

> After laws mighty,
> Brazen, eternal,
> Must all we mortals
> Finish the circles
> Of our existence.

It did not concern them in the least that this poem begins with the words:

> Noble be man,
> Helpful and good.[52]

Goethe once said: "What does it mean to love one's fatherland and to work as a patriot? When a poet has endeavoured all his life to fight harmful prejudices, to eliminate narrow opinions, to

enlighten the soul of his people, to purify its taste, and to en-
noble its ideas what could he do better? How could he work
more patriotically?"[53]

Notes

1. Will Vesper. *Die Ernte der Gegenwart*. Muenchen, 1941, p. 386.
2. *The Dramatic Works*. London, 1878, p. 346.
3. *Die Forderung des Tages*, p. 91.
4. J. P. Eckermann. *Gespraeche mit Goethe*. Leipzig, 1837, Part III, p. 371.
5. In a letter to Carlyle, July 20, 1827. *Grosse Weimarer oder Sophien-ausgabe*. Weimar 1887-1919. Part IV, Vol. 42, p. 278.
6. Eckermann. *Gespraeche mit Goethe*. Part III, p. 316.
7. Riemer. *Gespraeche mit Goethe*, November 18, 1806.
8. Eckermann. *Gespraeche mit Goethe*. Part III, p. 166.
9. Wilhelm Roepke. *Die deutsche Frage*, p. 260.
10. Riemer. *Gespraeche mit Goethe*, March 23, 1810.
11. Eckermann. *Gespraeche mit Goethe*. Part II, p. 13, October 3, 1828.
12. Letter to J. H. Meyer, April 24, 1817. *Grosse Weimarer Ausgabe*. Part IV, Vol. 28, p. 68.
13. "Deutsche Sprache." *Kunst und Altertum* (a periodical), 1818.
14. To the historian Luden on December 13, 1813. *Goethe's Gespraeche ohne die Gespraeche mit Eckermann*. Leipzig, no year given, p. 304.
15. F. W. Foerster. *Deutsche Geschichte und politische Ethik*. Nuremberg, 1961, p. 7.
16. To Luden on December 13, 1813. *Ibid.*, p. 304.
17. Eckermann. *Gespraeche mit Eckermann*. Part I, p. 325.
18. *Goethe's Gespraeche ohne die Gespraeche mit Eckermann*, pp. 305-306.
19. Eckermann. *Gespraeche mit Goethe*. Part III, p. 289, February 3, 1830.
20. *Ibid.*, Part I, p. 118.
21. Wilhelm Roepke. *Die deutsche Frage*. Zürich, 1945, p. 11.
22. F. W. Foerster. *Weltpolitik und Weltgewisson*. Muenchen, 1919, p. 12.
23. *Gesammelte Schriften*. Frankfurt, 1957, Vol. VII, pp. 224-226.
24. Eckermann. *Gespraeche mit Goethe*, Part II, p. 43.
25. *Ibid.*, Part I, p. 173.
26. *Versuch ueber Dichtungen. Grosse Weimarer-oder Sophienausgabe*. Part I, Vol. 40, p. 234; *Dichtung und Wahrheit. Buch 10. Ibid.*, Vol. 27, p. 343 and Vol. 28, pp. 156-157.
27. *Ibid.*, Part I, Vol. 41/II, p. 252.
28 *Maximen und Reflexionon. Ibid.*, Part I, Vol. 42/II, p. 197; *Tage-buch, Ibid.*, Part III, Vol. 12, p. 311.
29. *Zum Shaekspears Tag. Ibid.*, Part I, Vol. 37, p. 130; *Wilhelm Meisters Lehrjahre. Ibid.*, Part 3, Vol. 21, pp. 309ff.

30. Eckermann. *Gespraeche mit Goethe*. Part I, pp. 143-144.

31. *Ibid.*, Part III, pp. 123-124.

32. In a letter to W. Humboldt, September 16, 1799. *Grosse Weimarer Ausgabe*. Part IV, Vol. 14, p. 180.

33. H. Pross. *Die Zerstoerung der deutschen Politik*, pp. 97-98; *Geist und Zeit*, Darmstadt, 1959, III.

34. Eckermann. *Gespraeche mit Goethe*. Part III, pp. 250-251.

35. Wolfgang Leppmann. *The German Image of Goethe*. Clarendon Press, Oxford, 1961, p. 54.

36. Constantin Brunner. *Der Judenhass und die Juden*. Berlin, 1918, pp. 88-89.

37. *Die Ueberschaetzung Lessings*. Karlsruhe, 1881, p. 25.

38. Werner Sombart. *Händler und Helden*. Leipzig, 1915, pp. 6, 24, 84.

39. W. Bussmann. *Treitschke*. Goettingen, 1952, p. 352.

40. *Die Zeit*, Hamburg, August 19, 1954.

41. Aage Bertelsen. *October 43*. London, 1955, p. 139.

42. *Weltkampf* (a periodical), January-March, 1942.

43. Nietzsche. *Menschlich-Allzumenschliches*. Vol. II, aphorism 125.

44. Nietzsche. *Jenseits von Gut und Boese*. Aphorism 244.

45. *Nuernberger Nachrichten*, June 28, 1958.

46. Pross. *Die Zerstoerung der deutschen Politik*, p. 15.

47. *Daily Telegraph*, London, March 15, 1962.

48. *Der siebente Ring*. Berlin, edition 1920, p. 11.

49. *Das neue Reich*. Berlin, p. 11.

50. *Lotte in Weimar*. Stockholm, 1939, p. 330.

51. *Der Sonntag*, Berlin, August 7, 1949.

52. *Das Goettliche. Saemtliche Werke. Insel-Ausgabe* Leipzig, Vol. XIV; *Lyrische und epische Dichtungen*, Vol. I, p. 250.

53. *Deutsche Rundschau*, November, 1961.

7
Romanticism

GOETHE ALSO SAID: "THE CLASSICAL IS THE HEALTHY, THE ROMANTIC the morbid."[1] How right he was! The novelist Heinrich Mann quoted these words in 1946 and said: "This great lover of life disliked the whole lot of them. . . . The sense of life of the German romantics was the lowest that literature can have. . . . Fairy-tales, old-German masquerades, artificial ecstasies, bottomless depths of thought—who could continue that way? Those poets wrote as if they were the last men." As for the thinkers of the period "politics was out of the question. History served as a substitute. As consolation they developed a fateful fanaticism of national pride."[2]

Of Goethe, however, a judicious observer once said that he was a sedate poet. Goethe explained: "He meant to convey that for all my poetical activity I continued to be a sensible man according to bourgeois standards."[3] German romantic poets, however, craved for the infinite, the unutterable, night and death. The romantic poet August Platen begins one of his most famous and enchanting poems with these words:

> He whose eyes have once encountered death
> Cannot live: he is to death surrendered.[4]

What strange logic! He called his poem *Tristan*. This glorification of death returns in Wagner's *Tristan* which also contains allusions to Novalis's hymns to the night. Death is also the inspiring genius of the post-Wagnerian romantic opera *Palestrina* by Hans Pfitzner.

Novalis, one of the earliest German romantics, has written most enchanting poems, full of seraphic vision and extravagances, but none of them is bolder or more sublime than Goethe's best poems. Novalis, however, said of him ironically: "Goethe is a thoroughly practical poet. He is in his writings what the Englishman is in his wares: thoroughly simple, tasteful, well-adapted and durable." Goethe's *Wilhelm Meister* he called "a Candide directed against poetry." He himself, a hectic mystic, wrote fantastically romantic novels full of bewitching prose-poetry but leading nowhere. Goethe's novel seemed to him to ruin poetry and the miraculous, and he complained that it only dealt "with ordinary human things, nature and mysticism being completely forgotten." He was disgusted with the "bourgeois and domestic" affairs which he found in it.[5]

Goethe never liked the romantics, not even their greatest representative, Heinrich von Kleist, that demonic, ecstatically glowing, but problematic and unredeemed genius. This poet, he said, was out to "disarrange our feelings."[6] Thomas Mann, who tries to defend Kleist against Goethe's accusations, cannot help finding in his *Hermannsschlacht* the tragedy of ancient Germany's fight against Rome, a reminder of Luther's raging language: "Berserk nationalism raging against Rome," that is against France and Napoleon. The "blue-eyed hero" of his drama, he says, is "a warning against the German character."[7] The breath-taking story of *Michael Kohlhaas,* too, contains much of that berserk spirit which ruined Europe in the years 1939 to 1945.

Thomas Mann, who considered Germany's romanticism in the light of what happened in Germany during the last three decades, speaks of the iridescent ambiguity of this romanticism. It gave the world, he stated, much fascinating poetry and music, but at the same time was full of "a certain dark richness and piousness, an antiquarianism of the soul which feels very close to the chthonian, irrational and daemonic forces of life."[8] In the years of growing National Socialism he quoted the romantic poet Wackenroder as speaking of the "wicked guilelessness, the terrible, oracular, equivocal darkness of music," and confessed that everybody (that is to say he himself and the other great German writer, his beloved friend Hermann Hesse) who regarded it of importance "to give the German soul clarity and shape in order to make it possible and esteemed in the world, was forced to fight the equivocal mysticism of music in Germany, though he might thus most painfully cut his own flesh."[9] He dealt with the problem of romantic music and romantic love of death in *The Magic Mountain,* which was much hailed when it appeared in 1925 but had no influence whatever on the German mind already intoxicated with Hitler's ideas. A rationalist and democrat in that book calls music a half articulate, equivocal, and irresponsible art, "politically suspect."[10] The same man corrects the hero's romantic ideas about life and death and advises him to think of death "as part and parcel of life," and never to sever it from life.[11] The hero, Thomas Mann's alter ego, is more teachable than the other Germans and learns in the end that life and death must never be regarded as opposites, that man is the lord of all opposites, and that the sympathy with death in his heart must become one with the freedom of his living mind. "I will keep faith with death in my heart, yet will well remember that sympathy with death is evil, is hostile to humankind, as soon as we give it power over thought and action."[12]

As to music, romantic music, Wagnerian music, the young

hero and Thomas Mann find that Death was the inspiring genius of even so enchanting a song as Schubert's *The Linden Tree;* it is "a fruit of life, conceived of death." Wagner, Mann continues, without mentioning his name, possessed not more genius, only more talent than Schubert, but he enchanted the German soul ("we were all his sons") and subjugated the world. The most faithful son of that soul-enchanting romanticism, however, would be "he who consumed his life in self-conquest. . . ."[13] Who was this man? Not Nietzsche, as Mann mistakenly thought at the time (he changed his views of Nietzsche radically in later years); it was Thomas Mann, it was Hermann Hesse, and it was Stefan George, who never liked romantic music.

Thomas Mann returned to the problem of music after the Second World War, to the role which music played in Germany, the influence it had on the German mind. The Germans, he says, have given to a grateful world "the most beautiful, certainly its deepest music." But such musicality of soul, he continues, is "paid for dearly in another sphere," namely in politics. This musicality is the reason for the estrangement of all speculative German thinking from all socio-political philosophy, the contempt felt for all this as being of second importance or of no importance whatever. The relation of the German intellectual to the world around him, and especially to that beyond the German borders, always remained "abstract and mystical, that is musical"; it was "the relation of a professor with a touch of daemonism, filled with the arrogant knowledge that he surpassed the world in 'depth.'" The Germans are "the people of the romantic counter-revolution against the philosophical intellectualism and rationalism of the Enlightenment—a revolt of music against literature"; they have glorified the vital in contrast to the purely moral. In their pride they have always repudiated European humanism and democracy. At the beginning of the 19th century, when German poets, philosophers, and historians

revolted against the intellectualism of the 18th century, these
ideas seemed new, revolutionary, grand. But in the course of a
century they more and more deteriorated until, under Hitler,
"German romanticism broke out into hysterical barbarism, into
a drunkenness and a paroxysm of arrogance and crime which
now finds its horrible end in a regional catastrophe, a physical
and psychical collapse without parallel." National Socialism has
deep roots in German intellectual and political life; it is the
result of what a hundred years earlier was proudly called
"Romanticism."[14] Professor Wilhelm Roepke says there was
lurking in German romanticism "an immoderate extravagance,
an unbridled lawlessness and wildness which had broken
through four times in the last two centuries: in the Storm and
Stress of the 18th century, in the romanticism of the early 19th
century, in the Young German movement and, in the highest
excess, in National Socialism, which is not only Prussianism but
also the last degeneration of the inborn romanticism and mysticism of the German."[15] Professor Werner Kohlschmidt attested
that Thomas Mann had more deeply than anybody else seen
that the German romantic movement was "in a large degree
responsible for the German catastrophe which also became a
European catastrophe."[16]

What Thomas Mann said after the war was not wisdom after
the event. He had foreseen all this very clearly and said so to
the Germans, trying to warn them against what was inevitably
to come. Professor Ernst Troeltsch had shown him the way in a
lecture which he gave in 1922 on *Natural Law and Humanism
in World Politics*. He told the Germans that their political and
ethical philosophy wanted a revision. It derived from Germany's romantic counter-revolution, which had alienated Germany from Western Europe. The West was dominated by the
belief in an eternal and godly natural law, the equality of men,
the uniform destiny of all mankind. In Germany, however,
reigned the belief in a multiplicity of historical individuals who

again and again founded new structures out of a new law. The Germans saw in the Western schools of thought only shallow and sterile rationalism while the West saw in the German teachings about the state a strange mixture of mysticism and brutality. Troeltsch, a Lutheran, stressed that only Protestant Germany had severed itself by its state theory from the rest of Europe, while Catholic Germany had always remained in its way of thinking within the Catholic European tradition. The result had been, he said, that the German state theory, while showing certain traits of sublime romanticism, had become cynical and perfectly indifferent to all spirit, all morality. Turning to the German philosophers of the day he admonished them to come nearer to Western thought and to make up for what they had missed. No self-denial was needed, he said. You have only to turn to a lost heritage where what now seems specifically Western had once been commonly European.[17]

Most German professors remained perfectly deaf to what Troeltsch said and became more and more impressed by Hitler's sermons. Only Thomas Mann confessed publicly that Troeltsch's lecture had opened his eyes.

Mann went on to utter his warnings against the "revolutionary obscurantism" which wanted the Germans to believe that they had once again come to some crossroads, that Goethe's "classicism" had been overtaken by a new romantic revolution preached by the philosopher Ludwig Klages. Klages had rediscovered the romantic archaeologist J. J. Bachofen and Alfred Baeumler re-edited his works, with a lengthy introduction in which he celebrated the holy past, night and death, the chthonic, the demonic, the romantic, the national—ideas which Goethe had abhorred in his day. These irresponsible thinkers, Mann said, stressed the powerlessness of reason and hallowed the irrational depths of the soul, the dynamism of the unconscious. If the mind, reason, and intellect are really as feeble as they pretend, why not protect them? Why defame them "as though there was a danger that they might ever become too strong?" Why call them "grave-diggers of life?"[18]

Freud's psychoanalysis, Thomas Mann asserted, was the only form of modern irrationalism which did not lend itself to reactionary misuse. Freud, he said, was interested in the night-side of the soul, but he never glorified the power of the unconscious. He tried to unravel it in order to cure the disturbed soul and let reason triumph. Freud was no obscurantist, but, worse, he was a Jew and psychoanalysis was a Jewish invention;[19] even C. G. Jung called it that in the early days of the Third Reich.

The influence of these pernicious ideas of Klages, Baeumler, and Bachofen on the German mind was catastrophic. Thomas Mann noticed a thousand lectures of the irrational, which had "mushroomed out of the ground all over Germany" and made the highly obscure and intricate new philosophies popular among the intellectuals and even the German masses. They preached a confused anti-intellectualism and anti-idealism and were resolved to break the predominance of reason, which they defamed as the most sterile of all the illusions. They themselves, Thomas Mann retorted, were the most dangerous illusion, inclining as they did to orgiastic excess and poisoning all politics, making of the nationalism of the 19th century, with its trend of cosmopolitanism and humanism, an entirely new barbarism, National Socialism, which, while being "the foulest racial reaction," pretended to be, and was hailed as, "a wonderfully attractive new way of life."[20]

Since nobody listened to him, he used the occasion of the Pan-Europe Congress in 1930 to deliver another warning lecture which he entitled *The Trees in the Garden, i.e.,* of Eden. (He was then working at the first of his novels about *Joseph and His Brethren,* into which he inserted many of his ideas on irrationalism, romanticism and National Socialism.) He contrasted the two opposite worlds of rationalism and irrationalism, using as symbols the olive tree and the fig tree, or, in other terms, the words *day* and *night*. The day-world, he said, is the world of manly spirit, of reason, consciousness, freedom, and the love of the future. The other, the night-world, is the world of the soul, the unconscious, bondage, the love of the night and the past. The nations of the West are fond of the first while the Germans resist all one-sided (as they think) belief in reason and argue that they have a more intimate relationship with the world of the soul and of creative unconsciousness than the other nations. They love bondage more than freedom, formless becoming more than form and being, the past more than the will towards the future. This German attitude, while containing a grain of truth, Mann continued, has caused the other nations again and again to resist Germany as the enemy of reason and liberty, the enemy of mankind, all the more so as the Germans, with a doctrinaire and fanatical passion, had torn open a gulf between spirit and life, intellect and soul. What are you doing? he asked his countrymen. Are you not mad in calling "the intellect the henchman of life" and tearing asunder soul and spirit with a religious passion at a time when it has become absolutely necessary to unite them, to fill reason with soul and soul with reason?[21]

It was of no avail. If you think that your teachings are true, he asked the philosophers of the new irrationalism on yet another occasion, would it not have been wiser to keep them, during those dangerous days, within a small circle of experts, instead of offering them to a wider and incompetent public? The result was catastrophic. The masses had heard with astonishment and delight of "the dethronement of reason and intellect," they had heard that reason was something Jewish, they had "learnt to pronounce the tongue-twisting but heart-warming word *irrationalism*," and had coined the word "intellectual beast." What a pitiful spectacle! The air, Mann said warningly, is full of the foul vapors of this new irrationalism, this "mystagogic balderdash," of "blood and soil," and the end of it all, he told them despairingly, will be "war, all-embracing catastrophe, the collapse of civilization."[22]

He proved right in terrible literalness. After the German collapse he reminded them (but they do not listen to him even now) that he had fought the catastrophic movement because he had foreseen all its brutal consequences: "I foresaw the hideous danger of National Socialism to Germany and Europe very early, at a time when that menace could have been killed very easily, and warned against it when it called itself a conservative revolution. They were no 'simple fools,' those chthonic betrayers of the spirit. They knew what they were doing. They were politicians."[23] In his *Doctor Faustus* he puts these words into the mouth of a decent German: "We Germans perennially yearn for intoxication. Under its spell we committed, through years of deluded high living, an excess of shameful deeds which must now be paid for."[24] But they do not want to pay. They behave as if nothing had happened. They left it to him to feel responsible for it all. He confessed that he had once loved romanticism "down to its sins and vices," and that he had been "through it all. . . . Everyone who was born a German *does* have something in common with German destiny and German guilt."[25]

Of the synthesis of intellect and soul which he had advocated to them in his warning lectures, he spoke twice during and after the last war. In *Joseph and His Brethren* he speaks again of the soul "which clings to the past and the graves and the solemn 'it was.' But may the spirit too be with thee, and enter into thee genuinely, may the two principles permeate and hallow one another and create a humanity which would be blest from heaven above and from the depths beneath."[26] It is Jacob's blessing for humanity, it is the blessing which Thomas Mann sees fulfilled in the personality of the greatest German, Goethe. After the war he expressed the same idea in *Doctor Faustus,* both at the beginning and at the end of this novel, now in Bachofenian terms. Even the most benevolent and dignified sphere of human activities, he says, is not "inaccessible to the influence of the powers of the depth beneath, nay, it wants a fruitful contact with them." True culture aims at "including, in a pious, orderly and propitiatory manner, the dark and uncanny into the cult of the gods of light." He returns to this synthesis on one of the last pages of the novel, stressing the need for a cultural idea "in which the reverence for the deities of the depths and the moral cult of Olympic reason and clarity become *one* piety."[27]

Notes

1. Eckermann. *Gespraeche mit Goethe*. Part II, p. 92.
2. *Ein Zeitalter wird Besichtigt*. Berlin, 1946, p. 23.
3. Thomas Mann. *Adel des Geistes*. Stockholm, 1945, p. 110.
4. *Collected Works*. Leipzig, 1910, Vol. II, p. 94.
5. *Ibid.*, pp. 119-120.
6. Goethe. *Grosse Weimarer Ausgabe*. Part III, Vol. 3, p. 239.
7. Thomas Mann. *Nachlese*. Frankfurt, 1956, p. 16.
8. "Deutschland und die Deutschen." *Die Neue Rundschau*, Stockholm, October 1945, p. 17.
9. Thomas Mann. *Bemuehungen*, p. 254.
10. *Der Zauberberg*. Vol. I, p. 191.
11. *Ibid.*, p. 337.
12. *Ibid.*, Vol. II, p. 260.
13. *Ibid.*, pp. 524-525.
14. "Deutschland und die Deutschen" and "Deutsche Hoerer!" Stockholm, 1945, p. 41.
15. Roepke, *op. cit.*, pp. 158-159.
16. *Form und Innerlichkeit*. Muenchen, 1955, p. 158.
17. *Deutscher Geist und Westeuropa*. Tuebingen, 1925, pp. 6, 7, 12, 18, 23, 25.
18. *Achtung, Europa!*, pp. 84-92.
19. *Die Forderung des Tages*, pp. 220-224.
20. *Achtung, Europa!*, pp. 84-92.
21. *Altes und Neues*. Frankfurt, 1953, pp. 360-363.
22. *Achtung, Europa!*, pp. 84-92.
23. *Altes und Neues*, p. 13.
24. *Doktor Faustus*, p. 271.
25. "Deutschland und die Deutschen."
26. *Joseph und seine Brueder*. Berlin, 1933, Vol. I. p. lvii.
27. *Doktor Faustus*, pp. 18-19, 765.

8
From Napoleon
to Bismarck

THE DECADES BETWEEN THE DOWNFALL OF NAPOLEON AND THE RISE
of Bismarck are best characterized by the name of Metternich,
who suppressed every vestige of political liberty in Germany
and Austria. Georg Büchner, the only revolutionary writer
of high rank in that time, died young and was soon forgotten.
In 1834 he had said: "Because the German Reich had been
rotten and putrid, God let the Reich fall to pieces."[1] In
1956 these words were used as a caption beneath a photograph
showing the damaged *Garnisonskirche* at Potsdam amidst the
ruined houses of the town.

The revolutionary poet Heinrich Heine realized early that the
outdated regime of the Prussian kings was doomed. He ridiculed the writers who sang of the good days of the Holy Roman
Empire, and wrote biting verse against Frederick William IV,
who flirted with the Middle Ages, and against the reactionary
politics of his contemporaries. "Since I have known the German

philistine, he has been a lazy-bones. In March"—the abortive revolution—"I thought he had taken courage and become more sensible" because he spoke of "princely traitors. But when the black, red, and golden flag was unfurled, that old-German rubbish, I soon got disillusioned. I already saw Arndt and Jahn, the heroes of other times, come out of their graves and fight for the *Kaiser,* and I saw the students from the days of my youth, full of enthusiasm for the *Kaiser* [of the Middle Ages] because they were drunk."[2] And, "we Germans know how to hate. This German hatred springs from the depths of our souls and poisons them."[3] When the poet Georg Herwegh waxed enthusiastic about the German "spring," Heine asked: "Do you really see the flowers of spring? This spring is only in your poems."[4] Shortly before 1848 Heine had written his famous poem, *The Weavers,* in which the poor Silesian weavers say:

> The shuttle flies in the creaking loom
> And night and day we weave your doom.
>
> Old Germany, listen ere we disperse,
> We weave your shroud with a triple curse.[5]

He foresaw the social revolution which would put an end to Prussian feudalism, and made another even more astonishing prophecy about the coming of Hitlerism: "Christianity has in some way subdued that brutal Germanic lust for war, but it could not root it out, and when once the Cross breaks down then the barbaric rage of the old fighters, that mad berserk frenzy of which the Nordic bards have sung and said so much, will storm forth again. The day will come when it will break out. Do not smile at my counsel, the counsel of a dreamer, who warns you against Kantians, Fichtians and philosophers of nature. . . . When you hear the cracking, such cracking as has never been heard before in the history of the world, then know that the German thunder has struck. Then a drama will be performed on the German stage compared to which the French Revolution will appear as a harmless idyll. That day will come and the other nations will group themselves around Germany as on the steps of an amphitheatre to watch the great games of the gladiators."[6] Young Karl Marx couched his prophecy in different words: "Germany will find herself one morning on the level of European decadence before ever having reached the level of European emancipation."[7]

The revolution of 1848 was unsuccessful both in Austria and Germany. In Austria they sang that the Devil was black, and envy yellow, wherefore only the Devil could stick to the black and yellow colors of the Hapsburgs. The Czech and Hungarian struggles for freedom were crushed. The Austrian reactionaries even called in Tsarist troops to fight the brave Hungarians. Kossuth fled to the United States. The German revolutionaries were few and unrealistic. "Even the Pan-German discussions of the St. Paul's Parliament," says Thomas Mann, "had a tinge of medieval imperialism, reminiscent of the Holy Roman Empire."[8] Robert Blum, a fighter for the rights of the Poles, fell into the hands of the Austrian army and was shot. F. T. Vischer, a staunch liberal, was deeply disappointed and left Germany to become a professor at Zurich University. Carl Schurz was forced to flee in 1848, but returned secretly in 1850, rescued Professor Gottfried Kinkel from Spandau prison, and helped him to escape to Scotland. Schurz himself went to the United States where he became famous under Lincoln, fought as a general in the Civil War, and became a Senator.

Richard Wagner, a revolutionary in his young days, fled to Switzerland, Ferdinand Freiligrath, who had written passionate poems about freedom and revolution, came to England. The best Germans, Thomas Mann once bitterly remarked, are always living in exile. The German dream of liberty and equality Heine sang, was just "bubbles of the best foam,"[9] and the Spanish diplomat Donoso Cortes said in 1850 that the Germans had hailed the Frankfort Parliament like a goddess of freedom but had let her perish a year later "like a street woman in the gutter."[10] Ludwig Uhland, the famous Swabian poet, who, as a liberal member of the Württemberg Parliament, courageously fought his reactionary king, once said: "No crowned head will ever again shine upon Germany which was not annointed with a drop of democratic oil."[11] These words died away unheard till all the German dynasties were driven out in 1918. The Germans submitted to their autocratic rulers and took refuge in the romanticism and the idylls and dreams which their writers and artists offered them. Nothing could be more characteristic of this period than Eichendorff's *Life of a Good-for-Nothing* and Mörike's dream of "Orplid, my land, which shines from afaɪ" and his prayer "Leave, oh world, leave me alone!"[12] The German nation as a whole remained good-hearted and amiable—till Bismarck appeared on the political horizon.

Not all Germans were happy with his successes. As usual, a tiny minority of Germans saw immediately the danger which was threatening the nation. Baron Ludwig von Gerlach, a man of genuine religiosity, was early disheartened by Bismarck's war against the Danes, the "sinful war among brothers" against Austria, and the annexation of Hanover made him an irreconcilable adversary of the Iron Chancellor. Prussia, he said publicly, had "shamelessly violated the Ten Commandments, harmed her soul by the vice of pseudo-patriotism and stained her conscience." Bismarck's war policy seemed to him a renewal of Frederick's aggressive policy in the 18th century, and he changed the king's motto *"Suum cuique"* to read: *"Suum cuique rapere."*[13] The poet and short story writer Theodor Storm who, in 1862, called the "reactionary" Prussian government "abominable" said two years later: "The nobility (and the Church) are the poison in the blood of the nation," spoke in 1864 of "the robber's policy of Bismarck" and was furious when the Prussians annexed "his" Schleswig-Holstein. "Although," he wrote, "the Prussians have every reason to behave modestly in Schleswig-Holstein because they have annexed our

country, every Prussian official puts on the air of a little personal conqueror, as if he had brought us a higher wisdom. The
naïve rudeness of these chaps is incredible and deepens the
wrinkles of hatred which their behavior has engraved in
the forehead of every upright man here."[14]

Bishop von Ketteler as famous in his day as Bishop Count
von Galen in the days of Hitler, said in 1866: "Borussianism is
a fixed idea of Prussia's vocation, the foggy conception of Prussia's world-mission. The friends of this Borrussianism regard
this Prussian calling as the highest thing in the world, higher
than all rights."[15] Constantin Frantz, another righteous man,
said that Prussianism did not possess the spiritual stamina to
create a new Germany and that a German Reich under Prussia's
leadership was an absurdity. Could Goethe have written his
Faust if he had been a Prussian?[16] Did not Humboldt feel better
in Paris than in Berlin? Nietzsche, when still young, sane, and
near to Goethe and Schopenhauer, said that in 1870 Germany
had exchanged the German spirit for a German Reich. He
called the era of Bismarck an "era of German stupidity," solely
interested as it was in problems of power.[17] How can you call a
statesman great, he asked the Germans, who compels his people
"to practice high politics for which they are by nature
badly endowed and prepared and stimulates the slumber-
ing passions and avidities of his people, subverts their conscience, makes their minds narrow and their taste 'national'?"
He foretold that they would have to do penance for all this
throughout their whole future.[18] The historian Onno Klopp and
the politician Franz von Roggenbach, whom Bismarck regarded
as his possible successor under the emperor Frederick III, asserted early that Bismarck's Reich would have no future. The
historian Hermann Baumgarten wrote to the historian Sybel in
1881 that Bismarck would leave behind a terrible chaos and
that Germany would have to pay dearly for her blindness.[19]
Theodor Mommsen, too, regarded the failures of the Bis-

marckian era as infinitely greater than its successes. The enslavement of the German personality, of the German spirit, he
regarded as a fatal illness from which Germany would never
recover. "Bismarck," he said, "broke the backbone of our
nation."[20] Professor Wilhelm Uhde said in 1899 that Prussian
discipline and absolute obedience could only delay the day of
Germany's downfall.[21] When Thomas Mann wrote his first
novel, *Buddenbrooks,* early in the 20th century, he compared
the high school in his native Lübeck in the days before and after
1870. The old school had been governed by "a sense of joyous
idealism," which completely disappeared with the arrival of
Bismarck in Germany and the Prussian professor Dr. Wulicke
as headmaster of Lübeck high school. He brought new ideas to
Lübeck: "Authority, duty, power, service, career. The school
became a state within a state, in which not only the masters but
also the pupils regarded themselves as officials."[22] When, early
in the 20th century, the poet Stefan George wrote his famous
Time-Poems, he celebrated, among others, Goethe and Pope
Leo XIII, and also sketched, but never finished, a poem about
Bismarck. The famous (or infamous) words "We Germans fear
God but nothing else on earth," which Bismarck once spoke in
the German Parliament, were called by George a "blasphemy"
and he said of the Iron Chancellor: "You never moved us or
did what makes our blood get hotter."[23] After Germany's first
downfall, Heinrich Mann said that Germany had hardly been
united when it began "to deny the idea of liberty and self-
determination of other nations. The German *Drang* towards
unity fell into the hands of violent men who trampled down the
slow ripening of a peaceful democracy."[24]

The amiable writer Bogumil Goltz thanked God in the years
before 1870 that the German genius had developed in a cosmopolitan way and warned the Germans not to exchange this
happy state of affairs for a national phantom and become
blockheaded and arrogant. But this was exactly what was done

in 1871. It was not enough for Bismarck to found the German
Reich, it had to be done in the Hall of Mirrors at Versailles,
defeated France had to feel the Prussian boot on her neck. (The
hubris of this arrogance, never forgotten by Clemenceau, led to
the retribution of 1918, when defeated Germany had to sign the
Peace Treaty in the same hall at Versailles.) Furthermore, Bismarck was not satisfied with incorporating German Alsace in
the newly founded Reich; France was also robbed of the wholly
French province of Lorraine. The Alsatian and Lorrainese
members of the First German Parliament claimed their right
to remain with France but were laughed at. Arthur Rimbaud,
hardly seventeen at the time, prophesied Germany's ruin, stating
that a nation was the nearer to its decline the more self-assertive
it was; history has proved it. "As soon as a nation is out to
conquer and dominate others it commits suicide."[25] After
Germany's downfall in 1918, Heinrich Mann said: "Between
then and now lies the history of a German sin."[26] The liberal
writer Gustav Freytag had already said in 1870: "Our princes
move now, like actors on the stage, between flowers and loud
applause of enthusiasts, while the destructing demons lurk in
the depth."[27] The old diplomatist Alexander von Villers whom
Thomas Mann calls "a noble man and European," said in
1870: "I am so fed up with this singing nation of empty phrases
that I tore up in disgust all the thousand threads which connected my soul with Germany."[28] And Nietzsche, still young,
still sane, wrote in 1873: "A great victory is a great danger.
Of all bad consequences of our last war against France the
worst is the common error that also German culture was victorious in that war. This madness is very catastrophic because it
might turn our victory into a complete defeat, the extirpation of
the German spirit for the benefit of the German *Reich*."[29]

The Reich which Bismarck created represented only the interests of the Hohenzollern dynasty and the Prussian Junkers.
When Bismarck once said "It is now a question of Prussian

interests, and when they are at stake I know of no justice,"[30] it shows him as a precursor of Hitler, although he was more moderate than the Führer. Sated after three wars, he tried to secure his spoils by concluding the cynical Reinsurance Treaty with Russia against Austria, after having made a pact with Austria against Russa. But he remained a dictator in questions of politics; his infamous Three Class franchise remained in force up to the First World War. The German Reichstag was a mere façade. Parliamentarians and journalists, he was fond of saying, should "not meddle in high politics, because only the initiated could really understand it."[31] The first Kaiser, Wilhelm I, who had once helped to crush the revolution of 1848 and who, in 1862, as King of Prussia, resisted any change in the constitution which would as he put it, make him "a slave of Parliament," was an autocrat like his predecessors and complained when the President of Parliament once spoke of "the nation beside the throne." Beside? Surely that would mean "that there should no longer be any subjects who were mentioned in the church prayers."[32] Luther again!

Bismarck hated the wife of the Crown Prince Frederick, the Englishwoman, as he called her, and all the official biographers of Bismarck agreed with him in this respect, as in many others. She was a liberal and influenced her husband in the direction of a liberalization of her new fatherland. Patriotism meant to her freedom for the individual and it grieved her when everything dear to her liberal heart was ridiculed as impracticable, untimely, romantic. Blood and Iron had made Germany great. The Germans learned to cherish autocracy more and more and as late as 1917 General Ludendorff saw "no reason why Germany should become democratised and parliamentarised"; in his opinion every concession could only lead to a "downfall."[33] H. S. Chamberlain, born as a free Englishman, became, in Bismarck's and the Kaiser's Germany, a raving Pan-German who found it "incomprehensible that our German democrats regard Great

Britain as the birthplace of political liberty. Parliamentarism is the main vice of our age." Just like Hitler, whom ten years later he hailed as Germany's savior, he translated "Parliament" by "talking-shop."[34] In the Third Reich, the Hitler Professor, Fritz Hartung, in 1941 praised Bismarck for "having resisted the intrusion of West European Parliamentarism" into Germany. "In this spirit, which does not leave government to parliamentary majorities, I recognise the very essence of the German State which has again and again asserted itself successfully against alien influences."[35] The famous historian Max Weber, however, said in 1918: "Bismarck's political heritage? He left behind him a nation without any political education, a nation without any political will, accustomed to the idea that the great statesman at the helm will settle all political questions for them, a nation which accepted fatalistically what has been decided above their heads."[36]

Since 1945 a number of German historians have again begun to whitewash Bismarck, calling him a Chancellor of Peace, an honest dealer, and what-not. Not so those Germans who love the truth—a tiny minority of Germans, as usual.

Professor Friedrich Meinecke said: "The tragic history of the First and even more of the Second World War compels us to ask ourselves whether the seeds of the later catastrophes are not to be found in Bismarck's nature. . . . A whole generation allowed itself to be hypnotised by Bismarck and did not realize the catastrophic consequences of his politics. . . . Whatever we may say about the differences of his unsocial autocracy and Hitler's National Socialism, Bismarck must still be regarded as his predecessor."[37] Professor Gerhard Ritter, too, sees a big difference between Bismarck and Hitler, but he is forced to admit that Bismarck's war against Austria in 1866 was "a long prepared war of aggression," that the foundation of the German Reich by "monarchistic authorities, not by a liberal movement of the nation, was detrimental to the development of German liberalism. . . . By his autocratic attitude, Bismarck strangled all political independence and will to responsibility."[38] Professor Eduard Hemmerle said: "Bismarck's old-Prussian ideas of faithfulness to the throne and to Prussianism prevented him from building into the constitution of the Reich those precautions which could have made a modern state of the German Reich. The Prussian Kaisers were not annointed with the democratic drop of oil of which the poet Uhland had once spoken."[39] Professor Karl Barth, the famous theologian, said that the Germans of today see in National Socialism a deplorable incident and taboo their past. They refuse to see in Hitlerism "the last consequence of Bismarck's policy which united Germany by violent means, with blood and iron, creating a nationalistic, capitalistic and imperialistic Reich and becomig the grave-digger of the living freedom of 1848."[40] Professor Joachim Schoeps says that Bismarck paved the way to a Prussian hegemony over Europe by incorporating all Germany into Prussia instead of doing it the other way round, as Gerlach would have done. "Not many Germans have realised that in 1866 the great decision had fallen when Bismarck opened a road which ended in the two world wars of 1914 and 1939."[41] Professor Wilhelm Roepke, too, speaks of Germany's fateful policy since 1866 and adds that "Bismarck imitated a way of thinking which ruined Germany inwardly and outwardly. His violent solution urged Germany towards a road which inevitably led her through 1914, 1933, and 1939 to the present catastrophe, the catastrophe both of Germany and Europe." He quotes Schiller's words: "There is no salvation for despotic states except in their downfall."[42]

Professor Friedrich Wilhelm Foerster says that Bismarck had "inaugurated the moral dissolution of Europe, and that Germany had gone on militarising until the threatened world organized itself so effectively that a German attack led inevitably to a German defeat."[43] Professor Levin L. Schuecking says that

Bismarck "hated democracy from the bottom of his heart." The Iron Chancellor erred when he said that Germany, once seated in the saddle, would be able to ride by herself. "When Germany threw off the leading-strings of authoritarian government" in 1918 and could have enjoyed the democracy of the Weimar republic, it became clear "that the German nation was unable to shape its own history." They hailed "a mad criminal" and gave him all the power. "Already Bismarck was uncritically deified, and this deification, which disgusted men like Mommsen, ruined Germany's democratic development in an irreparable manner and deteriorated into the hero-worship of the Third Reich."[44] Professor Ludwig Dehio says that Germany always lacked a universal and normative idea such as was produced by other European nations; Great Britain was the champion of freedom, France in 1789 appealed to the whole of mankind, and even Russia in 1917 seemed to inaugurate a new era for the down-trodden masses. Germany, however, never had an equally per-suasive mission. "We prided ourselves on our steel-like Prussian objectivity. But this objectivity gained no human warmth and attraction when it tried to ally itself to socialism. The alliance of socialism and Prussianism was only the forerunner of the ten-dencies of the Third Reich."[45] Dehio sums his verdict up in these words: "Behind the coffin of Germany's power there was only a small mourning-retinue in 1918—to say nothing of 1945."[46] Karl Buchheim said "that Bismarck's system was a reversion to autocracy which, after his death, developed into the 'personal rule' of Wilhelm II, the dictatorial High Command under Ludendorff, the authoritarian power of Hindenburg down to the 'Führer' Adolf Hitler who had only to give orders which all followed in blind obedience or weakness—into a catastrophe without a parallel."[47]

Now for the two greatest German writers of our time. Her-mann Hesse, a Swabian, pondering "the German tragedy," thinks of "what would have happened and matured if a very different Germany had been created around the nucleus of old democratic Swabia, not a Roman or a Bismarckian-Prussian but just a Swabian Germany."[48] Thomas Mann draws an unflattering portrait of Bismarck, "a hysterical colossus, brutal and sentimental, a giant with unfathomable cunning and cynical frankness." His appetite was gargantuan, and in his capacity and passion for hatred he resembled Luther; he, too, was "Germanic-anti-European." A thorough Machiavellian, he deeply disconcerted liberal Europe by his triumphal successes; "in Germany he intensified a servile worship of power quite as much as he weakened the belief in more tender, more noble ideas and values." Thomas Mann compares Bismarck with Goethe, as he compared him with Luther, and says that Goethe was "a genuine and real brother both of Luther and Bismarck, an expression of German powerfulness," but, he adds, "the most sublime, most humanised, most disciplined variation of it."[49] Personalities like Bismarck, Luther, Wagner, Nietzche compel Mann to confess that "great Germans embody as much of goodness as greatness can embody it at all, the 'bad' Germany is always embodied in it, too."[50] Of Bismarck's achievement he says that the German Reich did not represent a "nation" in the democratic sense. "It was a pure power structure and aimed at getting the hegemony over Europe." It seemed a modern state but it "clung to memories of medieval glory." Just this made the Bismarckian Reich so dangerous, "the mixture of robust timeliness, efficient modernity, and dreams of the past—in a word, a highly technological romanticism." Born of wars, the Unholy German Empire of the Prussian nation could never be anything but a war empire. "As such it lived, a thorn in the flesh of Europe, and as such it perished."[51]

Notes

1. *Denk ich an Deutschland.* Muenchen, 1956, p. 68.
2. *Collected Works.* Leipzig, no year given, Vol. II, pp. 187-188.
3. *Ibid.,* pp. 77-78.

4. *Ibid.*, p. 169.
5. *Ibid.*, pp. 177-178.
6. W. Stigand. *Life of Heine.* London, 1875, Vol. I, pp. 442-443.
7. Georg Lukacs. *Die Zerstoerung der Vernunft.* Berlin, 1955, p. 32.
8. "Deutschland und die Deutschen."
9. *Collected Works.* Vol. II, p. 221.
10. Veit Valentin. *1848. Chapters of German History.* London, 1940, p. 263.
11. *Nuernberger Nachrichten,* July 3, 1954.
12. *Collected Works.* Stuttgart, 1961, Vol. I, pp. 82 and 101.
13. H. J. Schoeps. *Das andere Preussen.* Stuttgart, 1952, pp. 44-45, 50.
14. Fritz Boettger. *Theodor Storm in seiner Zeit.* Berlin, 1959, pp. 199, 207, 227, 264.
15. Schoeps. *Das andere Preussen,* pp. 257-258.
16. *Deutschland und der Foederalismus.* Re-issued Stuttgart, 1921, p. 83.
17. Thomas Mann. *Betrachtungen eines Unpolitischen,* p. 220.
18. *Jenseits von Gut und Boese.* Aphorism 241.
19. *Deutsche Rundschau,* November, 1957.
20. *Ibid.,* November, December, 1957.
21. *Ibid.,* November, 1957.
22. *Buddenbrooks.* Berlin. Edition 1920, Vol. II, p. 430.
23. R. Boehringer. *Mein Bild von Stefan George.* Muenchen, 1951, p. 90.
24. *Deutsche Rundschau,* October, 1957.
25. *Die Zeit,* Hamburg, October 21, 1954.
26. *Macht und Mensch.* Muenchen, 1919, p. 205.
27. *Denk ich an Deutschland.* Muenchen, 1959, p. 6.
28. Thomas Mann. *Briefe.* Vol. I. Frankfurt, 1961, p. 374.
29. Schonauer, *op. cit.,* p. 21.
30. F. W. Foerster. *Mein Kampf gegen das militaristische und nationalistische Deutschland.* Stuttgart, 1920, p. 49.
31. W. Bussmann. *Treitschke.* Goettingen, 1952, p. 55.
32. In a letter to Von der Heydt, January 26, 1862.
33. *Blaetter,* Koeln, March 1960.
34. *Demokratie und Freiheit.* Muenchen ,1917, pp. 6, 74.
35. *Das Reich und Europa.* Leipzig, 1941, p. 90.
36. *Gesammelte politische Schriften.* Muenchen, 1921, pp. 138-139.
37. *Deutsche Rundschau,* January, 1952, January, 1956; F. Meinecke. *Die deutsche Katastrophe.* Wiesbaden, 1947, p. 39.
38. *Europa und die deutsche Frage.* Muenchen, 1948, pp. 80-81, 85-86, 106.
39. Eduard Hemmerle. *Der Weg in die Katastrophe.* Muenchen, 1948, p. 18.
40. *Ibid.,* p. 17.
41. Schoeps. *Das andere Preussen,* p. 49.
42. Roepke, *op. cit.,* pp. 13, 15, 100, 179.
43. F. W. Foerster. *Erlebte Weltgeschichte,* p. 172.
44. *Blaetter,* Koeln, December, 1959.
45. L. Dehio. *Deutschland und die Weltpolitik.* Muenchen, 1955, p. 95.
46. *Ibid.,* p. 105.

47. Karl Buchheim. *Leidensgeschichte des zivilen Geistes*. Muenchen, 1951, pp. 21-22.

48. *Neue Zuercher Zeitung*, August 18, 1954.

49. *Der Monat*, Berlin, August, 1949.

50. "Deutschland und die Deutschen."

51. *Ibid.*

9
Wagner, Nietzsche, H. S. Chamberlain

RICHARD WAGNER'S MUSIC IS THE LATE RESULT OF THE DEVELopment of European music. After writing a few operas of the more conventional type, he got involved in the revolution of 1848 and was forced to flee. In his exile he developed his revolutionary musical style which was much attacked before it conquered Europe. One of his earliest admirers was Nietzsche who was introduced to him in Switzerland. Nietzsche immediately succumbed to his spell, wrote an enthusiastic essay on Wagner's mission and, in *The Birth of Tragedy,* distorted the historical facts about the origin of Greek tragedy in order to prove that Wagner's music was the acme of a development of more than two thousand years. With the help of the enthusiastic king of Bavaria, Wagner at last succeeded in laying the foundation stone of his own theater at Bayreuth and Nietzsche was invited to attend the happy event. He was terribly disappointed.

Wagner had changed in a way that smashed all Nietzsche's romantic illusions. Wagner had become a German master, although Nietzsche knew too well that his music spoke to sophisticated artists of cosmopolitan taste. Wagner had even become an anti-Semite. Nietzsche fled and never saw Wagner again. Wagner had always been an anti-Semite. He had already in 1852 spoken of the reign of Jewish money and ridiculed Mendelssohn. He had advised the Jews: "Remember that one thing only can deliver you from the curse which weighs upon you: the deliverance of the wandering Jew—extinction."[1] He wrote an essay which, in the Third Reich, was used as an introduction to a selection from Gobineau's racial writings, *Aryan Man,* and rightly so, for Wagner says in it that Gobineau had tested the blood of modern mankind and found it "corrupted past recovery." Very true, Wagner added. In his view Gobineau had rightly asserted that humanity consisted "of unequal races which cannot be equalised. The noblest race can rule the inferior ones but it cannot make them equal to itself, by mixing with them, it can only become less noble itself."[2] Again, if this is not National Socialism, what is? Alexis de Tocqueville, however, foresaw the dangers inherent in Gobineau's false teachings and wrote to him that they would lead to a complete annihilation of human freedom, to "arrogance, violence, contempt of other nations, tyranny, and baseness in every respect"; in a word, to Hitler's Third Reich.[3]

A Lutheran theologian, Professor Paulus Cassel, turned against Wagner and his anti-Semitic circle in 1880, because Wagner had blasphemed "the Jewish Creator God" and said it was "doubtful whether Jesus had come from Jewish stock," whereupon one of his circle, Ernst von Wolzogen, made of Jesus "a Celto-German." As Wagner, in *The Jews in Music,* had said that the Jews had never been creative in art, Rev. Cassel quoted St. Jerome who had said that the Psalms were our Simonides, Pindar, Alcaeus, Horace, and Catullus. "Which musical and poetical effect in the history of the world can be compared to that of the Psalms? They have become the hymnbook of the world and have stilled many tears and placated many hearts." He quoted Psalm XXVII: "Deliver me not over unto the will of mine enemies: for false witnesses are risen up against me, and such as breathe out cruelty." For weeks on end Niblungs and Valkyries were moving on Wagner's stage. What had their effect been, what would it be? What can we learn from Sigurd, the dragon killer, who is worse than the dragon which he kills treacherously? Wotan is deceitful, the woman are demonic, the dwarfs insidious. "Passion burns hotter than the flames encircling Brunhilde. What can the nation learn from it than to feel its own passions set ablaze! If we become furious at Wagner's blasphemous article, 'Know Thyself,' should we listen to his *Ring of the Niblung* in order to become calm again? For it teaches nothing but revenge and lust for revenge." He suggested a little more Christian humility to the composer of *Tristan* and the *Ring* who, with his "Religion and Art," had "erected a Babylonian battering-ram against the truth of the eternal God and will suffer the fate of Babel. He will experience what is said in Psalm II."[4]

In 1899, Professor Arthur Drews wrote a book on the meaning of Wagner's musical dramas in which he reminded the Germans especially of the composer's article, "Know Thyself," in which Wagner had reproached the Germans with acknowledging the German Jews as Germans. He himself called them "the plastic demon of mankind's degeneration." Drews stressed Wagner's originality, for he had written that article without knowing anything of Gobineau's "gigantic work on human races." He read it only later and was so impressed by it that he wrote an essay on it—the essay which was reprinted in Nazi Germany as an introduction to Gobineau's ideas. Gobineau later visited Wagner in Bayreuth and they became intimate friends, as one "in their belief in Germanism, in their love of

Nordic mythology."[5] Professor Drews shared their belief so enthusiastically that, in 1935, he published a book, *German Religion*, in which he preached a religion "independent of the alleged revelation of a God alien to our race."[6]

Wagner had conceived his *Ring of the Niblung* as an optimistic drama of human progress, of the rejuvenation of the world by a revolutionary hero. But later, under the influence of Schopenhauer's philosophy, he completely changed its meaning, turning it into a tragedy about the downfall of gods and men. When Bernard Shaw, in a brilliant essay, analyzed the *Ring* he showed that, in spite of Wagner's intention, it had remained what it had originally been, a drama of today, "a frightfully real" and modern story of capitalism and the lust for money. Shaw drew attention to the fact that Wagner in 1848 had been a revolutionary who managed to flee from Germany while his fellow revolutionary, Bakunin, was caught and imprisoned. Shaw identified Wagner's hero, who breaks Wotan's power, with the Russian revolutionary who was out to overthrow capitalism. "The political philosophy of Siegfried is exactly contrary to the political philosophy of Schopenhauer." But Wagner preferred to persuade himself that he had always been a pessimist and denounced optimism "as rank Judaism, the Jew having at that time become for him the whipping boy for all modern humanity."[7]

A Swedish critic, Wilhelm Petersen, once remarked that Wagner's music had an unmistakably cosmopolitan cachet. Nietzsche saw the kinship of Wagner's music with French romantic music. Thomas Mann compared the *Ring* with Zola's cycle of the Rougon-Macquarts and found in them striking similarities of spirit, aims and methods, of the love of the grandiose and massive. He came early under Wagner's spell and loved his music immensely but not without a deep Nietzschean distrust as to the healthiness of its fascinating artistry. He compares Wagner to a very cunning magician who has at his command all sorts of allurements both simple and diabolic. His music, he says, is not music in any Mozartian or Beethovenian sense, but literature, psychology, and symbolism. It does not spring, as the Germans would have it, from mythical sources. Certain things in it undoubtedly bear the mark of blissful inspiration but for the most part the music is very intelligent, shrewdly thought out and calculated, showing the diligence of a dwarf. Wagner, he stresses, is not German in a simple and conservative way; he is analytical, intellectual, well versed in European art and artistry; he does not personify Germanness as such but rather represents the most sensational self-portraiture and self-critique of the German character. His Siegfried is not only the hero of a northern sun-myth but also a most modern 19th century man and social-revolutionary, whom Shaw was right in comparing with Bakunin. Thomas Mann ironically reminds us that Wagner, who was very fond of bourgeois elegance and luxury, of silk and satin, of gorgeous dressing gowns lined with eiderdowns, and of voluptuous bed-covers, was inspired by this bourgeois extravagance to compose music containing more than a suggestion of satin dressing gowns, a music for his Nordic hero Seigfried which, he adds, swelled "the breast of German youth with lofty feelings of manly glory." They sacrificed their lives by the hundreds of thousands for the false glory of the Kaiser's war. They followed the tune of Pied Piper Hitler with unparalleled enthusiasm. Wagner's music, described by Thomas Mann as "blissfully sensuous, searing, sensually consuming, deeply intoxicating, hypnotically caressing, heavily and voluptuously upholstered," poisoned a whole nation.[8]

The Viennese professor Leopold von Schröder, however, a good friend of H. S. Chamberlain, celebrated the *Ring* as "the completion of the Aryan mystery at Bayreuth."[9] In reality the *Ring,* as Wagner found it in Nordic sagas, is a myth of "Nordic" frauds, breaches of contract, incest, treacherous murder, and the going up of the world and the gods in flames—in a word, the myth of the Third Reich as it was shattered to pieces by Allied bombing. Hitler saw in the *Ring* a myth of the fight of Aryan heroes against inferior World Jewry which he almost succeeded in exterminating. The *Heil Siegfried* of the *Ring* became the *Heil Hitler* of millions in Nazi Germany. In his testament Hitler again spoke of World Jewry which had stabbed him in the back—the fate of Siegfried! Was it for this reason that he told his SS thugs to burn him on a pyre when Germany was going up in flames in 1945? Thomas Mann speaks of Hitler in Wagnerian terms. Germany was "the Sleeping Beauty surrounded by a hedge of roses instead of Brunhilde's circling flames, and smiling as her Siegfried hero awakens her with a kiss. 'Germany awake!' "[10] In Shaw's description of Alberich we again recognize Hitler. He describes how the dwarf longs for the gold "with a brutish narrowness of intelligence and selfishness of imagination . . . incapable of seeing anything from anyone else's point of view." After he has got the gold (power) "hordes of his fellow-creatures are henceforth condemned to slave miserably, overground and underground, lashed to their work by the invisible whip of starvation."[11]

In Wagner, Thomas Mann said after the war, there was "too much of Hitler, really too much latent and very soon manifest Nazism."[12] He also resembled Hitler very much in that he was always full of himself, incredibly immodest, always monologuising, always rodomontading, always lecturing everybody. The words of his Hans Sachs to his admirers,

> Your hearts you ease—mine you oppress;
> I feel my own unworthiness,

could in no way be applied to himself because he could never get too much honor.[13] Thomas Mann, however, confessed that he himself always applied to himself the words "You come in such a questionable shape."[14]

Not Wagner alone, but also his wife, Cosima, was an anti-Semite. Her daughter Daniela in 1923 sent Hitler her husband's book, *Luther and German Culture,* with the dedicatory words, *"Beatus qui venit."*[15] Hitler entered Villa Wahnfried for the first time shortly before his abortive revolt and was enthusiastically received by Winifred Wagner. She later sent him all sorts of things when he was imprisoned in Landsberg, including, among other things, the paper on which he wrote *Mein Kampf.* She regarded him, as her daughter Friedelind told us, as "the saviour of Germany." She tried "to indoctrinate us with Nazism and appreciation of Hitler's supreme personality."[16] When Friedelind fled to Switzerland in disgust, her mother tried to induce her to return to Germany because her flight had annoyed Hitler. But Friedelind refused and spent the war years in Great Britain and the United States.

Thomas Mann's brother Heinrich dealt with Wagner in 1919. He depicted him as a typical son of his age, the imperialistic epoch of united Germany, "lusty of success, possessed by materialism, on the best of terms with lies—and he made music in order to throw a smoke-screen over everything questionable." This music was "full of the noise of victory, of the bombast of Germanism, iridescent with anti-Semitism in order to brighten the colours and effects." He venerated power, which was holy to him. He symbolized power "by magical men with swan helmets," and the German nation by "a chorus drawn up in line, blinded by the resplendance of their masters and always surprised by the course of events." The Germans recognized themselves in "the amoral simpleton Siegfried. Without the Wagnerian heroes they would never have become so utterly evil." In Heinrich Mann's opinion, two different Germanys are to be found in, on the one side, the cosmopolitan and harmonious Mozart, Goethe, and Schiller, and, on the other, in Wagner and Treitschke, who taught the Germans "to found their tortuous Germanism on the hatred of the world."[17] Hermann Hesse characterized Wagner—"the Pied Piper and favourite musician of the Second and even more the Third Reich,"—with a quotation from the ancient Chinese book, *Lü Bü We:* "The more thundering the music the more melancholy the nation, the more dangerous the country, the deeper sinks the ruler."[18]

While Hitler persecuted and exterminated the Jews, Thomas Mann, in *Joseph and His Brethren,* wrote an epic in praise of the Jews and their religion. This epic structurally resembles Wagner's *Ring of the Niblung,* but spiritually it is the very opposite of Wagner's voluptuous music-drama. Wagner tells the story of a Nordic myth which fascinated Hitler. Thomas Mann retells the myth of monotheism, the property of Jews and Christians. We read of how the three principles, soul, spirit, and matter, were "laid down from the beginning" and constituted the universe created by God. It is the role of the spirit, on the Father's command, to show to the soul that this world is not her place, to make it clear to her that her worldly enterprise is a mistake, and make her "strive to regain once more that lofty sphere of peace and happiness" in God's bosom.[19] What could be more opposed to the end of *The Ring of the Niblung* than this end which is a beginning, the human soul gaining salvation?

The story of the salvation of mankind is told by Thomas Mann, in accordance with the Jewish-Christian religion, as the story of Jacob and his children. The light and the dark are not, as in the Third Reich, the "Aryans" and the Jews but the monotheists and the idolators. The light are Abraham, Jacob, Joseph; the dark, Cain, the first murderer, Laban, Jacob's pagan uncle, and Esau, Jacob's pagan brother. Thomas Mann also contrasts the God of Abraham, Isaac, and Jacob with the false and "dead" gods of the Egyptians of which the children of Israel think nothing. When, in very telling words, he describes the arrogance of the Egyptians we realize that he is thinking of the arrogance of Nazi Germany. Every Egyptian, we read, is "too expressly aware of his status as 'man' to have much esteem left over for non-Egyptians, such as Negroes . . . and Asiatic louse-beards," i.e., Jews.[20] The arrogance of the Nazi-Egyptians is contrasted with the pride of Abraham, his veneration of, and search for, God, "the highest of all, whom alone to serve he was resolved in pride and love."[21]

A representative of Egyptian anti-Semitism is the arrogant dwarf Dudu, who speaks, as did the Nazis, of "scabbed Asiatics," and declines to eat at the same table as Joseph.[22] He and Potiphar's wife, Mut-em-enet, another anti-Semite, repeat the slogans of the fanatical high-priest Beknechons whose looks betray "a total rejection of the modern world," who hates "the laxity of foreign ways and the disregard of pious old customs because these enervate the country," and who wishes the Egyptians to "walk in the path of patriotic tradition."[23] Potiphar hates all this Nordic and Aryan balderdash when it emanates from the lips of his wife. "The marrow of the land, and the good old ways, and the laxity of foreign ways—all this is Beknechons, these are his disagreeable and crafty words,"[24] retorts Potiphar because he hates all this as much as Thomas Mann hated the words *"rassisch, völkisch, bündisch, heldisch"* when he tried in vain to warn the Germans against the barbarism of Hitler in 1930.[25]

Nietzsche's case is more complicated. His mental development is full of contradictions. There actually was more than one Nietzsche. He was a great poet, a great psychologist, a great master of the German language. He analyzed the spiritual shortcomings of European civilization with great intuition and insight, and set out to conquer its nihilism. But he furthered it and stimulated totalitarianism by many of his teachings.

In his younger years he declared a man backward if he could not understand that different opinions could co-exist among men. He would not mix with men who had a share in the mendacious lies about race and said that the German nation was made up of the most extraordinary mixture of races. In

1870 he said that the German Reich had extirpated the German spirit, and that united Germany had adopted *Deutschland, Deutschland über alles* as its state principle. He reproached Bismarck for having made the taste of the Germans "national" so that they were suffering from a "national nervous fever," now an anti-French, now an anti-Jewish, now an anti-Polish fever of Wagnerian Teutonic, and Prussian "stupidity."[26] He, on the other hand, was priding himself on being a good European and said he accused the Germans with loving clouds and everything foggy, dim, damp, and overcast, of being more intangible, more contradictory, more incalculable, and even more terrifying than other nations. They are, he said, "well acquainted with the by-paths to chaos."[27]

So far, so good. On the other hand, however, he detested "the ascendancy of parliamentarian nonsense, the democratic man and the stultification of Europe and the diminution of European man."[28] He ridiculed the ideas of "freedom" and "equal rights" and spoke contemptuously of shopkeepers, Christian cows, women, Englishmen, and other democrats.[29] To arrest this European deterioration, as he saw it, he developed the heroic philosophy of the "superman" in his panegyric *Thus Spake Zarathustra,* in which Thomas Mann finds the first signs of his growing megalomania. He himself, however, was of the opinion that a new epoch in the history of mankind was inaugurated by the teachings of this gospel with which he began to transvaluate all values. The greatest danger, we hear, comes from "the good and the just," wherefore the new prophet exclaims: "Break, break the good and the just!" and: "Oh my brethren, become ye hard!"[30] Good is what increases your feeling of power, bad is everything which springs from weakness. The new prophet who brings this strange message does not want to be mixed up "with the preachers of equality" who tell you "all men are equal." He knows better: "All gods are dead: we want that the superman should live!"[31]

He ridiculed as absurd the idea that "all men are equal before God." He knew better. People, he said, have forbidden deeds and opinions which had been "the prerogatives of strong men, as if they were something unworthy of man. They defamed the passions of strong men."[32] Nietzsche set out to undo this crime against the strong men by differentiating anew between the morality of masters" and "the morality of slaves."[33] For the former he put up the equation: "Good=noble=powerful= beautiful=happy=loved by God," and the motto: "Evil is what is evil for me." As to the latter, the morality of the slaves, "the revolt of the slaves in the field of morality," was an invention of the Jews and the Christians. Of Jesus he said: "Did not the Jews exactly by the round-about way of this 'saviour' achieve the last aim of their sublime lust for revenge?"[34] On another occasion he said: "When Socrates and Plato started talking about truth and justice, they were not Greeks any longer, but Jews."[35] If all this is not National Socialism, what is? "Evil is what is evil for me"—in the Third Reich they said: "Good is what is useful for the Germans," and acted accordingly. The nations of Europe will remember this for many generations to come.

Nietzsche wrote a book which he entitled *The Antichrist,* calling Christianity "the one immoral blemish of mankind."[36] Himself, however, he called an "evangelist" of a new creed which was to bring about the millennium. In 1921, Karl Kraus cursed his memory in a poem, *The Antichrist,* in which he said that Nietzsche had not, as he thought, been "a wise and knowledgeable healer of his age but the deepest expression of its illness from which it had not yet recovered." Did he not ridicule God and his Saints and all that they had suffered and taught? Did he not teach the worthless to transvaluate all values? The Christian God was good enough for the rest of us and He would redeem us from evil.[37]

In the same year Hitler appeared on the German horizon.

Fifteen years later one of his paladins, Baldur von Schirach, published a photograph of him looking at a Nietzsche bust in the Nietzsche archives at Weimar, and said that this "German philosopher's ideas fertilised two great national movements: National Socialism and Fascism."[38] As early as 1915 Professor Sombart had called Nietzsche "the last poet and seer who had come down from high heaven and announced unto us the tidings that the son of God will be born out of us; in his language he called him the Superman."[39] A National Socialist said that the Third Reich was "the true fulfilment of the prophetic philosophy of the great seer," Nietzsche,[40] and Professor Alfred Baeumler wrote a treatise to the same effect. He praised Nietzsche's "Nordic" character and his "Germanic" philosophy in which he had gone back to "the Germanic undercurrents in the German character." He was a "Siegfried" who fought Christianity because he knew that "life had no judge above itself." It was Nietzsche's greatest achievement that "he visualised the ancient mission of our race: to be the leader of Europe. The creator of a Europe which would be more than a Roman colony can only be Nordic Germany."[41]

After Nordic Germany had perished, leaving behind a devastated Europe, Thomas Mann called Nietzsche the pacemaker and prompter of European Fascism. His word of the "dangerous life" was part of the Fascist creed in Mussolini's Italy, and his superman was an ideal of Hitler's.[42] As Nietzsche had blasphemously called himself a new evangelist, Thomas Mann turns this blasphemy against him and says with allusion to Isaiah 53: "Of your madness they will feed in health, and in them you will become healthy."[43] The barbarism that Nietzsche had made possible was all the more barbaric because it came a century *after* the German humanism of Goethe and Schiller. Nietzsche, an ultra-romantic philosopher, glorified instinct, power, dynamism, and never cared for the political consequences of his ideas. Typically German. In the countries of his exile, Thomas

Mann learned that a lofty pragmatism reigned there in spiritual matters "which put spirit and thought in a position of responsibility for the consequences of thinking upon life and reality."[44] This had always been alien to Germany, where philosophy and politics had always been widely separated. Thomas Mann quotes an Englishman who confessed that he had felt a deep and genuine sympathy for German culture which, however, had "always been accompanied by a feeling of despair. It is as though every road taken by German poets and philosophers led to the edge of an abyss from which they could not withdraw but must fall into headlong."[45] This, Thomas Mann says, was exactly Nietzsche's case, a clear case "of the fatality hanging over Germany and her ways of thought." With his drive "into the uncharted wastes of thought," his "romantic passion," his urge "to unfold the ego into the limitless without a definite object," he "once more exemplarily demonstrated to the Germans everything by which they have become a terror and a scourge for the world and have ruined themselves."[46]

The third example of the German inclination towards the intellectual abyss which bears the name of National Socialism was H. S. Chamberlain, Wagner's son-in-law, whom the composer Hans Pfitzner called "one of the best Europeans."[47] In 1876, about to become a rabid Wagnerian and a German nationalist, he had impatiently addressed Germany as a country the ways of which "must not be like those of other nations" because "the whole future of Europe" depended on the Germans.[48] Under the influence of Wagner's and Gobineau's writings he conceived and wrote his *Foundations of the Nineteenth Century*. It was a great success in Germany. The Kaiser, a lifelong friend of Chamberlain's, wrote to him that the "Aryo-Germanic which slept in the deep layers of my soul had often rebelled against tradition, but in a bizarre manner. . . . Now you have come, and like a magician you have brought order into the tangled yard, light into the darkness. You have shown aims we must pursue for the benefit of the Germans and, indeed, the whole world."[49] Thus Wilhelm II. But the most dangerous reader of Chamberlain's book was Adolf Hitler.

A fanatical hater of the Jews, Chamberlain tried to make Christ an "Aryan" with the help of "seems," "perhaps," "very likely," "anyway," "so to say," "must." He celebrated the superiority of the Aryan and Nordic race and described world history as a fight between Germanism and Judaism. His dilettante heresies were very soon disproved by the historian Friedrich Hertz, who in 1933 had to leave Germany and died in England. The German intellectuals preferred to listen to Chamberlain, and one edition after another of his pernicious book was published in anti-Semitic and megalomaniacal Germany between 1900 and the ascendancy of Hitler. In 1921, Fritz Kahn published his book, *The Jews as a Race and a Cultural Nation,* in which the Chamberlain-intoxicated Germans could have read, if they had cared to read this book, the words of Professor Max Muller, the famous ethnologist who lived at Oxford. Muller said this with regard to Chamberlain's infamous book: "I have declared again and again that, when I speak of Aryans, I mean neither blood nor bones nor hairs nor skulls; I only speak of those who speak an Aryan language. An ethnologist who speaks of Aryan language, Aryan blood, Aryan eyes and Aryan hair is in my opinion, the same sort of sinner as a linguist who speaks of a long-headed dictionary or a short-headed grammar. This is worse than the Babylonian confusion and a downright swindle."[50] Or they could have read what a famous German professor, Konrad Burdach, said shortly before the First World War and repeated in 1925, in the days of growing National Socialism: He called the pan-German racial mythology a "fantastic dogma" which "even traces the achievement of the Jew Jesus back to heaven knows what addition of blond-haired, master-headed Germanism! One could dismiss these dreams with a laugh if they did not present a world danger. One cannot foresee how much damage they will do to German honour, how much understandable and justified ridicule and hatred they will arouse against us among the nations of the world."[51]

During the First World War Chamberlain was one of the most rabid Pan-Germans and asserted that Germany had been "the true home of liberty ever since," and that the political liberty of Great Britain was a lie, a "democratic tyranny."[52] He exchanged many letters with the Kaiser, and hailed Hitler in 1923 with these words: "That Germany has given birth to a Hitler in the hour of her greatest distress proves that the nation is alive."[53] When Hitler visited his revered teacher in Bayreuth, Friedelind Wagner, the only member of the family who preferred to leave Germany rather than serve the Führer, would very much have liked to be present, as she tells us in *The Royal Family of Bayreuth*, in order to hear whether Chamberlain realised what his teachings had inaugurated in Germany.[54]

Professor F. W. Foerster speaks of "the incomparable spiritual greatness of the Jews" who "only worshipped the *one* and *only* God" and prayed to God to establish His temple on earth, to create it soon, in our time. "No doubt, Jewry was the highest center of monotheism in the whole world." All other nations separated God from the world, only the Jews experienced Him in the reality of life. German nationalism "betrayed all great German traditions", which betrayal became no less "the misfortune of the Jews than of the Germans themselves." H. S. Chamberlain exalted the Aryan race without seeing the one-sidedness of the Aryans who "separated the metaphysical, supernatural from the physical, and this was the tragedy of the Aryans ... In Germany, unworldly idealism led to a wholly godless deification of power." National Socialist racialism had been prepared by Austrian Anti-Semitism. But the Hebrew spirit always saw God not only beyond all things, but also in the fate of the Jews themselves, "in the secret connection between the guilt and the misfortune of the nation."[55]

In spite of the truth of what Theodor Haecker had secretly—he was not allowed to publish a word in the Third Reich—entered in his diary in 1941: "Nietzsche, Wagner, and Chamberlain are the main instigators of the present German mentality. They are the movers of the deeds and misdeeds", after 1945 many Germans tried to whitewash them.[56]

Notes

1. T. Adorno. *Versuch ueber Wagner*. Frankfurt, 1952, p. 28.
2. Gobineau. *Der arische Mensch*. Kampen auf Sylt, 1940, pp. iv-viii.
3. *Deutsche Rundschau*, August, 1955.
4. *Der Juden Gott und Richard Wagner. Eine Antwort an die Bayreuther Blaetter*. Berlin, 1881, pp. 4, 5, 11, 12, 26-29.
5. *Der Ideengehalt von Richard Wagners dramatischen Dichtungen.* 1899, re-issued Leipzig, 1931, pp. 329-330.
6. *Deutsche Religion*. Muenchen, 1935, p. 223.
7. *The Perfect Wagnerite*. London, 1898, pp. 10, 29, 101-103.
8. "Leiden und Groesse Richard Wagners." *Adel des Geistes*. Stockholm, 1945, pp. 398-472; Richard Wagner und der Ring des Nibelungen. *Ibid.*, pp. 472-502.
9. *Die Vollendung des arischen Mysteriums in Bayreuth*. Muenchen, 1911.
10. "Bruder Hitler" (1938). *Altes und Neues*. Frankfurt, 1953, pp. 622-630.
11. *The Perfect Wagnerite*, pp. 8-10.
12. *Altes und Neues*, p. 581.
13. *Die Forderung des Tages*, p. 10.
14. *Ibid.*, p. 11.
15. *Deutsche Rundschau*, September, 1954.
16. *The Royal Family of Bayreuth*. London, 1948, pp. 9, 17, 29.
17. *Macht und Mensch*, pp. 226-27.
18. *Briefe*, pp. 137-38.
19. *Joseph und seine Brueder*. Vol. I, pp. xlvii-lii.
20. *Ibid.*, Vol. III, p. 214.
21. *Ibid.*, Vol. I, p. xiv.
22. *Ibid.*, Vol. III, p. 344.
23. *Ibid.*, Vol. III, pp. 348, 464.
24. *Ibid.*, Vol. III, p. 465.
25. *Achtung, Europa!*, p. 53.
26. *Jenseits von Gut und Boese*. Aphorisms 241, 251.
27. *Ibid.*, aphorism 244.
28. Thomas Mann. *Betrachtungen eines Unpolitischen*, p. 223.
29. Thomas Mann. *Neue Studien*. Stockholm, 1948, p. 137.
30. *Also Sprach Zarathustra*. Leipzig, 1927, pp. 236-237.

31. *Ibid.*, pp. 84, 108.
32. *Der Wille zur Macht.* Leipzig, 1928, aphorism 871.
33. *Jenseits von Gut und Boese.* Aphorism 260.
34. *Zur Genealogie der Moral.* First Essay No. 7.
35. Thomas Mann. *Neue Studien*, p. 137.
36. *Ibid.*, p. 118.
37. *Die Fackel* (a periodical), Wien, November, 1921.
38. Heinrich Hoffmann. *Hitler—wie ihn Keiner Kennt.* With a Foreword by Baldur von Schirach. Berlin, no year of publication given, p. 92.
39. Werner Sombart. *Händler und Helden*, p. 53.
40. F. Griese. *Nietzsche, die Erfuellung.* Tuebingen, 1934, p. 2.
41. *Nietzsche, der Philosoph und Politiker.* Leipzig, 1931, pp. 49, 57, 66, 103, 110, 181-183.
42. *Neue Studien*, pp. 144-146.
43. *Doktor Faustus*, p. 376.
44. *Altes und Neues*, pp. 215-216.
45. *Ibid.*, p. 218.
46. *Neue Studien*, p. 156.
47. Hans Grimm. *Warum, Woher—aber wohin?* Lippoldsberg, 1954, p. 495.
48. *Lebenswege meines Denkens.* Muenchen, 1919, pp. 59-60.
49. Schonauer, *op. cit.*, pp. 33-34.
50. *Deutsche Woche*, December 20, 1961.
51. Jonas Fraenkel. *Dichtung und Wissenschaft.* Heidelberg, 1954, pp. 254-255.
52. *Ideal und Macht.* Muenchen, 1916, p. 29.
53. Schonauer, *op. cit.*, p. 33.
54. *The Royal Family of Bayreuth*, pp. 39-40.
55. Foerster. *Die juedische Frage*, pp. 24, 25, 30, 52, 69, 70, 108.
56. *Tag-und Nachtbuecher*, Muenchen, 1947, p. 30.

10
Megalomania and Subservience: The Deification of the State

WE HAVE ALREADY SEEN HOW LUTHER INAUGURATED GERMAN obedience and subservience, and how these German characteristics became strong under Bismarck. Many educated Germans who knew "their" Schiller did not like to quote the many revolutionary lines in his *Wilhelm Tell,* but rather two lines of his unfinished *Demetrius:* "Majority, what is it? Majority is madness. Reason has always been only with the few." In Schiller's play, this is the creed of a feudal prince of the sixteenth century. In 1901 the liberal historian Theodor Mommsen wrote: "Our nation is about finally to establish the fateful government of the Junkers. The guilt for this rests not only with the governing class but above all with the governed nation."[1] The infamous pan-German general Bernhardi, however, told the Germans in

1912: "No nation is as little fit to take its fate into its own hands, for instance by a parliamentarian or republican constitution, as the Germans." The Germans, he said, wanted "powerful personalities capable of arousing the enthusiasm of the masses, the profundity of German feelings. We must see to it that the opportunity remains open for such men to act freely in accordance with their power and thus achieve great things by and for our nation."[2] One can read many sentences like these in *Mein Kampf*. An open-minded conservative like Count Zedlitz-Trützschler stated early in his diary that it was Germany's misfortune that they had not had a Charles I and a Cromwell. "Only the experience of epoch like this, entirely contradictory to the traditions of Prussian history, could have saved us. Something of a slavish submissiveness is inborn in us, therefore fate has imposed on us the lot of slaves."[3] When, after Germany's downfall, his book was published he was ostracized by his fellow noblemen. The playwright Gerhart Hauptmann said in his epic, *Till Eulenspiegel,* in 1918: "Only the British have style and the will to greatness. We have been lacking both at all times, to say nothing of today."[4]

We have already quoted what Goethe thought of the Germans and the British respectively. The philosopher Fichte, his contemporary, did not agree with him. German megalomania begins with Fichte. He told the Germans that they were an *Urvolk* ("A primordial nation" conveys nothing of the mystical sound of that *Ur*), "a paradigm of a nation" in which "the germ of human perfection is most decisively present. . . . If you perish, the whole of mankind will perish." Only the Germans spoke a really "living language" which, therefore, could not be compared with the languages of other nations. The spiritual education of the Germans was manifest in their daily life. With the other nations spirit and life were separated from each other.[5] Goethe said exactly the opposite: "The German nation is ruled by a spirit of sensuous exultation which is alien to me.

Their art and philosophy are of an abstract character, separated from life and from the natural sources which should feed them."[6] The Austrian Hugo von Hofmannsthal said the same thing a hundred years later when comparing the Germans with the French. French literature, he said, is characterized by "clarity, pleasing soberness, disciplined thoughtfulness." French though was always related to reality; "nothing is to be found in the reality of the political life of the nation which is not expressed in their literature." Nothing of all this could be said of Germany. A German spiritual tradition was lacking; what has "once been achieved" in literature did not continue to operate; one could find "no trace" of Goethe in Germany's public life. German literature was made only by titanic, unwordly outsiders whose dramas were "stuffed-up myths of their own egos," whose novels "opened up cosmic mysteries" and were trying to be "fairy-tales, histories, theogonies and confessions in one." German science was full of *hubris,* "severed from life. It does not serve man, man serves it." In the eyes of the Latin nations the Germans were "an impenetrable thicket."[7] Hofmannsthal was hoping for a change to take place so that the spirit could become life and life, spirit. But when he said so in Munich University in 1927, millions of Germans were already hailing Hitler. Fichte told the Germans that only they knew what "real seriousness" meant in things spiritual while the others were fond of "a genial game which was not aiming at anything."[8] One of the many followers of Fichte, Fritz Bley, wrote in 1897: "No doubt we are the best warriors on earth, we saved European culture. We are the most efficient nation in all fields of science and the arts! We are the best seamen and even the best merchants. We have done with our *Voelkische* self-humiliation, the defamation of the German spirit by France, Rome, England, the Slavs and the Huns. Do you not see at last that all he misfortune of our history was the result of our fatal love of cosmopolitan chimeras, ultra-montanism, international socialism, cosmopolitanism?"[9] Thomas Mann refutes this megalomania in his *Doctor Faustus,* the novel of the German pride followed by the German downfall: "It is a German superstition that there is only *valse brillante* outside Germany, and only seriousness inside it."[10] Hans Grimm, post-war Germany's madman Number 1, certified that Hitler's ideas of the "master-race, Nordic blood, re-nordification" meant the same as the ideas which Fichte had uttered in his addresses to the German nation.[11] He is certainly right in that. In the Third Reich Fichte was praised for having called the Germans an *Urvolk,* having judged "history from a racial standpoint" and having invented the word *völkisch.* His *Closed Economic State* appealed to the followers of Hitler because Fichte had called the autarkic state the ideal state, which alone could secure "the true order." People who found that order "tiresome, oppressive, pedantic," should emigrate, the state would lose nothing by it, said the philosopher. This closed economic state would preserve "the particular way of life, the institutions and the morals" of the nation and very soon achieve "a high degree of national honour. The nation would become different, a completely new nation." A National Socialist who analysed Fichte's book said: "As soon as the nation has realized this, German history can begin. This is the teaching of Fichte's economic philosophy. German history has begun."[12]

Another forerunner of Hitlerism was, in various respects, the writer E. M. Arndt. Take, for instance, the sentence in which he expresses his hope for "another great tyrant and inspired general who, conquering and annihilating, would mould the Germans into one mass."[13] He was praised as "a racial prophet who was the first German to depict the history of the European nations above all as a history of blood."[14] Quite. In 1848 Arndt spoke of "the poisonous Jewish humanism that has always been an abomination to me; for behind it all the feebleness and wretchedness of broken souls is hiding." A decent German of today compares these words with certain similar words in

Hitler's *Mein Kampf* about the fight of "stronger nations against the weaker ones because the force of life will, in the last resort, always break the ridiculous fetters of so-called humanism and replace it by the humanism of nature which destroys the weak and gives their place to the strong. But the genuine Jewish insolence retorts with a silly modern pacifism: 'Man conquers nature.' Millions repeat this Jewish nonsense."[15] Arndt also said this: "A good and just dynasty fears the alien and degenerate which can poison and ruin the pure and wonderful seed of his noble nation. The Jews do not fit into our world and our state, and it is therefore that I do not wish them to multiply too much in Germany. For they are a thoroughly alien nation, and I wish to keep the Germans as free as possible from them."[16]

German megalomania began to assert itself more and more in the middle of the 19th century. The great Austrian dramatist, Franz Grillparzer, said of the Germans that he had been fond of praising them as long as they had been modest, now that they had begun praising themselves it was no longer necessary for him to do so. They were, however, less than they thought they were, while the Austrians were more than they seemed to be. Everywhere in the world only the stupid were stupid, in Germany the clever also were stupid.[17] Characteristic of their arrogance was the slogan *Deutschland, Deutschland über alles* which originally was only meant as an expression of the natural and innocent love of one's country but soon acquired another, an insidious, meaning. The Germans began to speak of themselves as a nation of poets and thinkers; their poetry was the greatest in the world, their music was the profoundest on earth; Great Britain, however, was *The Country without Music*.[18] Karl Hillebrand, a very humane writer of the Goethe tradition, spoke disparagingly of "the devilish arrogance of German scientists," and censured his nation which spoke of German faithfulness, German honesty, German frankness, German conscientiousness, German profundity, German depth of feeling, "as if all this were a monopoly of the Germans."[19] Fichte said: "To have character and to be German is, no doubt, one and the same thing."[20] Even Richard Wagner was horrified by the silly speeches and insipid songs in which the Germans persuaded themselves "that they were something very special."[21] And Julius Froebel, a liberal man, wrote in 1858: "Which other nation speaks constantly, as the Germans do, of German power, German faithfulness, German love, German seriousness, German song, German wine, German depth, German thoroughness, German industriousness, German *Frauen*, German *Jungfrauen*, German men?"[22]

When Austen Chamberlain studied in Germany he heard the historian Treitschke say that the Germans stood on a higher level of the created world than other nations, and he wrote home on October 31, 1887 that a professor who spoke like that would naturally become popular and would attract large audiences. Young Austen thought this very dangerous.[23] At about the same time the Austrian Hermann Bahr, who later became a leading figure in modern German literature, studied at Berlin with Professor Eduard Zeller and Professor Heinrich Treitschke. He says in his autobiography: "When I came from the quiet of Zeller's lecture room into the boiling lecture room of Treitschke, which was overflowing with his pupils, the vapour of a different Germany hit my face."[24] Treitschke's teachings are echoed in General Bernhardi's words, who said in 1912 that he could find with no other nation "an equal capability of general thought and depth as has fallen to the share of the Germans. It is this capacity which destines us to become the leading nation in spiritual matters."[25] When the son of the Belgian historian Pironneau studied at Berlin University in the years between the two German wars he wrote home: "Germany has become a danger to civilisation by its power cult, its self-adulation and its contempt for other nations."[26]At about the same time Hugo von Hofmannsthal called the Germans self-conceited, arrogant, schoolmasterly; everyone of them, he said, is the bearer of a part of their authority but is only seemingly manly; he acts according to commands; they are presumptuous and incapable of entering into another nation's thoughts, they lack historic sense.[27] Helmut von Moltke, a representative of the Christian minority of Prussians and consequently one of Hitler's victims, said when about to be hanged that he had always fought "aganst the narrow-mindedness, arrogance and intolerance which was the heritage of the Germans and found its expression in the National Socialist State."[28]

After Germany's downfall, the writer Ricarda Huch said that the Germans had always found it difficult "to combine sure self-confidence with the sincere esteem of other nations. We alternated between self-contempt and self-exaltation. The National Socialist efforts to strengthen the national confidence were poisoned by the denigration of other nations."[29] The writer Friedrich Sieburg said: "We are certainly the loudest and most irritable nàtion, and stagger to and fro. At one time we are the most radical nation on earth, leaving behind all forms and traditions, at another we suffer bitterly, childishly, from our social shortcomings and our want of moderation. If again and again we are a riddle to other nations, if our nation disturbs the sleep of the world, the main cause of this is our passion to look into every abyss. The world fears us, looks down on us, mistrusts us still, fears us again, not only because of what we have done since 1933 but because of what we are and perhaps will always remain."[30] Helmut Hammerschmidt put it even more bitingly: "We all know this, of course: the Germans are more efficient than the French, more civilised than the Russians and the nations of the East, bolder than the Swiss, the Dutch, the Danes and all the other small nations. We are harder than the rest, the only thing we are not is more humane; but this does not matter, we leave humanitarian sentimentality to the others."[31]

We come now to the German deification of the state, which started with Hegel. Wilhelm von Humboldt, a friend and disciple of Goethe's, wrote a treatise on the limits which had to be drawn to the authority of the state in order to prevent its becoming dangerous to the individual. Schopenhauer, another disciple of Goethe's, ridiculed Hegel's "apotheosis" of the state as the height of "philistinism." For Hegel called the state "the incarnation of moral reason," "God's will becoming present, spirit unfolding itself as the real form and organisation of the World."[32] Hegel also said this about great men "whose particular interests conform with the will of the world-spirit": "The others follow these spiritual leaders because they feel the irresistible power of their own inner self embodied in them." These great men are "the *Geschäftsführer* of the world-spirit" and cannot show "much consideration" for others but strive toward "the One goal. . . . They must trample down many on their way. World-history moves on a higher level than where morality resides."[33] From Hegel's statement, "What is reasonable is real, and what is real is reasonable,"[34] stemmed the deification of the Prussian state culminating in the Third Reich. From his statement, "It is of the greatest importance to really understand dialectics which is the principle of all movement, all life and all activity in the world,"[35] and from his ideas of thesis, antithesis, and synthesis, stemmed Marxism. A certain passage in Thomas Mann's *Doctor Faustus* shows this:

Adrian: Freedom always inclines to a dialectical reversal. She recognises herself very soon in constraint, she realises herself in submission to law, rule, coercion, system—she realises herself in all that, that is to say: she does not cease to be freedom.

Zeitblom: In her opinion. But in reality she is no longer freedom, as little as dictatorship born out of revolution is still freedom.[36]

Bertolt Brecht, mistakenly regarded as an orthodox Marxist, makes a German refugee, a physicist Ziffel, ridicule Hegel's abracadabra in these words: "If one talks of humour, I always think of Hegel who was one of the greatest humourists among philosophers. Unfortunately he was born in Prussia and sold himself to the state. His humour was of a kind that he could not think of order without disorder—even: at the same place. . . . This he wittily called dialectics. The greatest revolutionaries call themselves pupils of the greatest champion of the state. The best school of dialectics is emigration. The most acute dialecticians are the refugees. They exist because of changes and study nothing but changes."[37] But inside the frontiers of the Third Reich, one Dr. Alfred Klemmt called Hegel the patron of "the comprehensive new creation which will one day stretch its wide and mightly dome over the Third Reich."[38] Another hireling of Hitler's, Dr. Werner Schmid, praised the Third Reich as the fulfillment of Hegel's dialectics and ridiculed democracy and liberalism. "What Hegel was striving at since his early days has now been realized by the total unity of our nation."[39]

Hegel's successor as official Prussian philosopher of the state was Friedrich August Stahl, a baptized Jew, who taught the Germans things like these: "Authority does not stem from the will of man but from God." This seems all right but he applied it to the Prussian state. And so he said: "Authority, not majority."[40] This soon became a slogan in Prussia and Germany. Paul de Lagarde adopted it, saying that Hegel's philosophy "is being put into praxis in our days."[41] Long before him, the historian J. G. Droysen paid much homage to the state, the highest good, calling it "the royal liberty of moral man." The individual "feels lifted above his little ego and ennobled by a higher right when he acts with all his vigour and devotion in the service of a higher and general interest," i.e., the authoritarian Prussian state.[42] The glorification of Prussia culminates in Heinrich von Treitschke, who won the large majority of German intellectuals over to his narrow-minded nationalism. German liberalism had never been strong and at no time had it meant the same as Western liberalism, which created more and more guarantees of the liberty of the individual against the power of the state. Treitschke was one of the most outspoken betrayers of the liberal spirit in the 19th century. He defined the state as "firstly power, secondly power, and thirdly power." In his young days he had admired Great Britain because of her principle of "immediate succour against all wrongs from above," and called this principle "not only the pillar of British liberty and the pride of every Briton but the necessary result of all higher education of the nation." But Bismarck warped his mind and he changed completely. Now he said: "The individual must be a member of his state and, consequently, have the courage to take also the mistakes of the state upon his shoulders. There can be no question of the right of the subject to resist an authority which he considers to be immoral."[43] Was this not also the Führer's opinion? "It is indeed," Treitschke said, "a deadly sin to play up sentimentally to another state, as we Germans have done so often to the English. . . . Might will remain right to the end of history; just in this lies the holiness of war."[44] A selection from his notorious *German History in the 19th Century* was re-issued in 1941 under the title *England, the Incendiary of Europe,* a phrase coined by Treitschke himself.[45] One of the few democratic German generals, Baron von Schoenaich, author of *My Way to Damascus,* called Treitschke in 1926 "a national misfortune, the main corrupter of the German spirit," because through his teachings the Germans had been persuaded to believe in the dogma that "might went before right."[46] Ten years later a National Socialist said of Treitschke: "His belief in the German nation and his love of the state have become strong in us again, and when we look back to the men who have guarded our best national values and prepared the new way, one man must not be forgotten: Heinrich von Treitschke."[47] Twelve years later, after Germany's second downfall, Eduard Hemmerle, an extremely decent Roman Catholic, said that the cause of the German misfortune lay "in an intellectual attitude which did not start with Hitlerism but in the remote past. A Hitler would never have been possible if he had not found the soil of Germany prepared for his seed. It had been prepared by all those political powers which had deified the state and prevented the Germans from maturing and thinking independently. The new German Reich had inherited an idea of the state characteristic of the Prussian Kings and the East-Elbian nobility. As a symbol we can regard the helmet of the Prussian policeman. For two hundred years an ideology of militarism was developed in Prussia consisting of German feudalism, faithfulness to the *obersten Kriegsherrn,* iron discipline and an extraordinay esteem for the 'King's uniform.' Nowhere in the world have militarism and heroism in war been as glorified as in Germany." This explains why large parts of the German nation succumbed to Hitler and his regime.[48]

Hegel's idolization of the state found many followers in Germany where even Carlyle's *On Heroes, Hero-Worship and the Heroic in History* was much acclaimed—as much as his hero-worshipping *Life of Frederick II of Prussia.* In Hitler's Reich Carlyle was praised as a Nordic seer, while in Great Britain the novelist E. M. Forster found in his contempt of democracy an affinity with the Nazi teachings.[49] In the years of the rising of National Socialism, the German professor Friedrich Gundolf (of Jewish origin) praised Hegel for having "shielded" great men "against the claims of moralists and humanistic enthusiasts."[50] Gundolf did the same with Alexander, Caesar, and Napoleon. "The great man," he held, "is the highest form in which we can experience the divine." These three men, "cosmic" heroes, "a trinity, one in three," always appeared "when a world was ripe for destruction." Do we not in this visualize Hitler? While the old world, continues Gundolf, sees "destroyers" in them, the new world hails them as "fulfillers. What now becomes holy was once a crime."[51] Professor Michael Grant, however, said a few years ago that while admiring the many talents of Caesar, we should not hold him up as a model to our children. Had not some of the German generals who were condemned at Nuremberg been gifted generals, politicians, and writers? He reminded us that Caesar once invited Gallic chieftains to a friendly conversation and in the meantime had the women and children of their tribes murdered by his cavalry. Cato, when hearing of this outrage, suggested to the Senate to hand Caesar over to those tribes as a war criminal.[52] Count Leo Dietrich Geyr von Schweppenburg, who was German Military Attaché in London a few years before the last war, was once told by an English friend: "My dear Geyr, we English have a fundamental antipathy against geniuses. In the last resort, they lead you to disaster."[53]

Militarism was another fateful German heritage. Down to the days of Hitler, most Germans glorified Frederick II, encouraged by Carlyle's romantic biography of the Prussian king which had been a best-seller in Germany during the First World War. But Lessing once remarked bitterly that in Frederick's Berlin freedom was only granted in one respect: people could hurl "as many foolish attacks on religion as one might want to."[54] Harold Nicolson who holds no brief for Germany, says that Frederick, in spite of solemn promises given to the Emperor Charles VI, attacked and robbed Austrian Silesia in 1740 soon after the death of the Emperor. "The question of right," Frederick wrote to his Foreign Secretary, "is for you to elaborate." Macaulay wrote a hundred years later that "the selfish rapacity of the King of Prussia" had set the whole of Europe on fire. Carlyle, Nicolson adds, that worshipper of the superman and of *Realpolitik,* tried to defend Frederick's war of aggression, but Nicolson is of the opinion that Frederick's seizure of Silesia "started a chain reaction which continued until 1763. . . . This flagrant violation of the Law of Nations shocked the conscience of Europe." Frederick's success "did permanent damage to the

Law of Nations and to the political thinking of his own countrymen."[55]

During the 1920's Frederick's reputation was enhanced by the wave of new nationalism, in spite of Werner Hegemann's devastating *Fridericus* (1924) which had as a motto the words of E. M. Arndt in 1805: "We Germans have experienced little pleasure from this King. Nobody has done us more harm." Hegemann had to flee into exile in 1933. Another exile, Heinrich Mann, said that Frederick had represented "the Prussian Germany which was to come . . . the challenging antagonism of one country against the European order."[56]

In 1788 Mirabeau stated: *"La Prusse n'est pas un pays qui a une armée, c'est une armée qui a un pays."* Count von Stein, a conservative nobleman of the Napoleonic age, once said: "It is vain to expect the communal spirit of the English and French to awaken with us if we do not keep the army within bounds which it is not allowed to overstep in countries where a communal spirit reigns."[57] When he suggested constitutional reforms after the English model Friedrich Wilhelm III called him "an obstinate, defiant, stubborn and disobedient civil servant."[58] Scharnhorst, who reformed the Prussian army after its defeat by Napoleon at Jena and regarded the German war against Napoleon not so much as a war of liberation from an enemy but rather as an opportunity for creating a constitutional Prussia freed from feudal shackles, died early without having really democratized the Prussian army. The historian Friedrich Meinecke said 150 years later that a Prussian lieutenant "went through the world like a young god, and a reserve-lieutenant like a demi-god."[59] The German army remained a feudal private army of the Prussian kings down to the days of Wilhelm the Last, obedient solely to him, not to the constitution. Only in Germany was it possible for Ludendorff and Hindenburg to usurp dictatorial power and force Reichs-Chancellor Bethmann to resign; in the same manner Count Waldersee, Chief of the

General Staff of the time, had a hand in the downfall of Bismarck.

Kurt von Schuschnigg, the last Austrian Chancellor before the Second World War, whom Hitler kept seven years in concentration camps, sees a direct line going from the famous Prussian lieutenant of Saverne (Alsace) over the more famous Captain of Köpenick to the most famous "unknown corporal of the First World War," who destroyed Germany for ever.[60] When a Prussian lieutenant in 1913 forced the French inhabitants of Saverne to step off the pavement to make room for him, Count von Galen, still very young at the time, wrote to his brother: "It does not matter if the Reichs-Chancellor and the War Minister expose themselves to ridicule. But if the representatives of authority do not defend right against violence they encourage those who see in power the only source of right. This is the fundamental evil of our policy about which father has always complained when speaking of 'the idolised state.' "[61]

Professor Ritter has on several occasions tried to deny that there had ever existed such a thing as German militarism; for instance: "The army must always remain an unpolitical instrument, otherwise it becomes a deadly danger to every government. This is not at all a militaristic peculiarity of the Prusso-German state, it must, of necessity, remain a fundamental law in all Western democracies."[62] The Germans fall for such nonsense with eagerness. They do not listen to Professor Ludwig Dehio who speaks of Ritter's "narrow conception of militarism and his way of regarding the notion of *raison d'état* as a moral one. This makes it difficult for him to get to the centre of real militarism. . . . The ascending and descending parts of a trajectory must be considered together."[63] German militarism was especially responsible for the ruin of Germany and Europe in the Second World War. The opposite of this militarism was observed by the German poet Hans Carossa when he had an opportunity to observe the behavior of American soldiers in

Bavaria. "Their way of saluting their officers was very different from our German way. It was confined to a cursory indication of standing to attention, with the friendly proviso: Do not forget that I am as free an American citizen as you yourself."[64]

Professor Ritter denies the existence of German militarism but he admits it, without realizing, when he says that "the one-sided overestimation of military virtue (in Germany) led to a confusion of moral and political ideas. To aim at eternal peace was declared utterly immoral, long-lasting peace was called a moral danger."[65] The quick victories of 1870 added much to the glory of the German army. The memory of the victory of Sédan was celebrated every year with much noise and in innumerable speeches. Even Professor Lagarde once called it "a cannibal brutality to tell our neighbouring nation again and again that we have defeated it,"[66] and Mommsen was all for abolishing the *Sédan Day*. In more and more books and speeches war as such was celebrated in immoderate words. When Professor J. K. Bluntschli sent a copy of his textbook on International Law to the Chief of the General Staff, Moltke, he received the following answer: "Eternal peace is but a dream, and not a beautiful one for that matter; war, however, is part of God's cosmic order. The most noble virtues of man blossom in wars, courage and resignation, a sense of duty and the willingness to sacrifice. The world would sink into materialism without wars."[67] Nietzsche had said the same before him: "It is a mere dream of beautiful souls to expect much of mankind when it has unlearnt the waging of war."[68] General Bernhardi took these words as a motto for his book, *Germany and the Next War*. He could also have chosen the following words from Nietzsche's *Thus Spake Zarathustra*: "You say it is the good cause which hallows even a war? I say unto you it is the good war which hallows every cause."[69] The ghost of Hitler seems to rise from his grave when one hears these words. Bernhardi regretted that some Germans regarded war as "a downright danger. The Germans were once the most bellicose and war-loving nation in Europe," but unfortunately they have got accustomed "to regarding war as a misfortune and do no longer see in it the greatest factor of civilisation and power." Study Claus Wagner's book, *War as the Creative Principle of the World,* he told his compatriots, and added that the idea of abolishing war was not only stupid, "but immoral and inhumane."[70] He succeeded in poisoning the German soul. In 1912 one could read in a German newspaper: "Which men are famous in German history, which ones are loved most passionately? Goethe, perhaps, or Schiller or Wagner or Marx? Not at all. They are Barbarossa, Frederick the Great, Bluecher, Moltke, Bismarck—hard men of blood. They have sacrificed thousands of human lives but the soul of the nation is full of adoring gratitude towards them. They have done what we should do now. Salvation lies only in attack."[71] German youth repeated this message in 1913 and called war "the most lofty and holy of all human activities. We, too, shall experience the great and gay hour of war."[72] In the Hitler Youth they said: "We know that we belong to a warlike race. Our lives are empty without war, and our honour cannot thrive."[73]

When the First World War, for which Bernhardi and his like had longed so enthusiastically, had at last started, Professor Sombart ridiculed Thomas More's *Utopia* because in it war was depicted "as something downright bestial," which was very characteristic of the unheroic British. He liked Treitschke much better because this forerunner of Hitler had said that nations became effeminate and egoistic in continuous peace. "Shallow intellects," Treitschke had said, "share the crazy idea that war is the greatest evil. It is salutary for such a generation to be blessed with a great and just war." Professor Sombart was proud to be able to fill many pages, if he so desired, with similar quotations from Fichte, Schopenhauer, Hegel, Hartmann,

Nietzsche. These philosophers differed in their philosophical out-look, but "they were all agreed as to the purifying and elevating effect of war."[74] Militarism, he explained, "is the spirit of heroism enhanced by the spirit of war. It is Potsdam and Weimar in most intimate union. It is *Faust, Zarathustra,* a Beethoven score in the trenches. We are a nation of warriors, and to them go the greatest honours. Militarism awakens the heroic feelings of the last day-labourer in a village. As we are full of this militarism, we regard war as something holy, as the holiest thing on earth."[75] The pan-German H. S. Chamberlain, Hitler's teacher, agreed with him: "The Germans are most gifted for war."[76] And Ludendorff said in 1935: "War is the highest manifestation of the racial will to life."[77]

Professor Arnold Toynbee, in *A Study of History,* spoke of "the emergence, first in Prussia and latterly in Germany at large, of a militarism that had been deadly in the histories of other civilizations." While comparing German militarism with the militarism of Sparta, Professor Toynbee points out that the militarism of the Bismarck era was "still kept within the bounds by a surviving respect for at least some of a civilization's tradi-tional conventions." Less so the militarism of the post-Bis-marckian period. "As to the mad-dog militarism of a National Socialist Germany, this could only be compared with the last phase of the *furor Assyriacus.*"[78] Decent Germans agree with Professor Toynbee. Karl Buchheim, a Roman Catholic writer, reminds us of what Mirabeau said in the 18th century, and continues: "The fusion of the feudalism of the Junkers with the autocracy of military circles resulted in what must be called militarism. It was the Prussian principle to militarise society. The really governing class was the militaristic aristocracy . . . and the great industrialists allied themselves to the Junkers."[79] The Protestant Friedrich Meinecke said that Prussian militarism "hastened the rise of the Third Reich in a decisive manner."[80] A victim of the Reich, Ernst Niekisch, said: "The Germans are born soldiers by nature and by history. They react with their fists rather than with their thoughts. The stupid Siegfried who never discusses but takes his sword and splits heads is the German idol. This heroism, poor in spirit, is the 'Nordic blood heritage' of the Germans. He wants an order to exterminate with voluptuousness. He calls it obedience when he behaves like a berserk. It was therefore that the *Reichswehr* made Hitler their *Führer*."[81] Another German complained in November, 1959 that Hitler's "unsuccessful conquest of Europe has left us some 4,000 possessors of his Order of the Cross. Three hundred and fifty of them met recently at Regensburg, among them the active generals of the new German army, Pensel, Uebelhack und Reichelt. Also army chaplains of both Christian denominations were present (there are no Jewish possessors of the Order of the Cross). Much blood sticks on these Crosses, blood of Germans and blood of our former enemies."[82]

Notes

1. *Deutsche Rundschau,* November, 1957.
2. *Deutschland und der Naechste Krieg.* Stuttgart, 1912, p. 123.
3. Graf Robert Zedlitz-Truetzschler. *Zwoelf Jahre am deutschen Kaiserhof.* Stuttgart, 1924, p. 10.
4. *Till Eulenspiegel.* Berlin, 1918, canto IV.
5. *Reden an die deutsche Nation,* 4th, 7th, 13th addresses.
6. *Goethes Gespraeche ohne die Gespraeche mit Eckermann.* Abridged edition, Leipzig, p. 655, no year of publication given.
7. *Das Schrifttum als geistiger Raum der Nation. Collected Prose Works.* Frankfurt, 1955, Vol. IV, pp. 394-396, 402-404.
8. *Reden die deutsche Nation,* 4th address.
9. Pross. *Die Zerstoerung der deutschen Politik,* pp. 274-275.
10. *Doktor Faustus,* p. 619.
11. *Warum, Woher—oder Wohin?,* p. 138.
12. H. Brunner. *Die Wirtschaftsphilosophie Fichtes.* Nurenberg, 1935, pp. vi, 76-77.
13. *Germanien und Europa.* Altona, 1803, p. 421.
14. L. Schemann. *Die Rassenfragen im Schrifttum der Neuzeit.* Muenchen, 1931, pp. 366ff.
15. *Geist und Zeit,* Darmstadt, August, 1960.
16. *Christlicher Antisemitismus,* p. 30.
17. *Spectrum Austriae.* Wien, 1937, pp. 621ff.

18. O. A. H. Schmitz. *Das Land ohne Musik*. Muenchen, 1914.
19. H. Srbik. *Geist und Geschichte des deutschen Humanismus bis zur Gegenwart*. Muenchen, 1951, Vol. II, p. 361.
20. *Reden an die deutsche Nation*, 12th address.
21. P. A. Loos. *Wagner*. Muenchen, 1952, p. 36.
22. Pross. *Die Zerstoerung der deutschen Politik*, pp. 11-12.
23. *Englische Politik*. Essen, 1938, p. 94.
24. *Selbstbildnis*. Berlin, 1923, p. 180.
25. *Deutschland und der Naechste Krieg*, p. 76.
26. F. W. Foerster. *Erlebte Weltgeschichte*, p. 315.
27. *Spectrum Austriae*, pp. 630-631.
28. A. Leber. *Das Gewissen steht auf*. Berlin, 1954, p. 202.
29. E. Hoppe. *Ricarda Huch*. Stuttgart, 1951, p. 911.
30. *Die Lust am Untergang*. Hamburg, 1955, pp. 27, 30, 32, 35.
31. *Bayrischer Rundfunk*, Muenchen, February 7, 1956.
32. G. Ritter. *Staatsmacht und Utopie*. Muenchen, 1941, p. 129.
33. *Volk, Staat, Geschichte*. Stuttgart, 1942, pp. 38-60, 83.
34. A. Huebscher. *Von Hegel zu Heidegger*. Stuttgart, 1961, p. 21.
35. *Ibid.*, p. 9.
36. *Doktor Faustus*, p. 295.
37. *Fluechtlingsgespraeche*. Frankfurt, 1961, pp. 108-112.
38. *Wissenschaft und Philosophie im Dritten Reich*. Berlin, 1938, p. 14.
39. *Hegel und die Idee der Volksordnung*. Leipzig, 1944, p. 148.
40. J. Loewenstein, *Hegels Staatsidee*. Berlin, 1927, p. 95.
41. *Ibid.*, p. 109.
42. *Deutsche Rundschau*, December, 1957.
43. Bussmann. *Treitschke*, pp. 33ff.
44. *Politik*. Vol. I, pp. 34, 39.
45. Edited by Prof. W. Schneider. Nurenberg, 1941.
46. *Mein Damaskus*. Berlin, 1926, p. 58.
47. E. Leipprand. *Heinrich von Treitschke im deutschen Geistesleben des 19. Jahrhunderts*. Stuttgart, 1935, p. 286.
48. *Der Weg in die Katastrophe*. Muenchen, 1948, pp. 8, 9, 16, 19, 363.
49. *Nordic Twilight*. London, 1940, p. 29.
50. *Caesar im 19. Jahrhundert*. Berlin, 1929, p. 41.
51. *Dichter und Helden*. Heidelberg, 1921, pp. 25, 51, 53.
52. *The Listener*, London, October 9, 1952.
53. *Erinnerungen eines Militaerattachés*. Stuttgart, 1949, p. 22.
54. W. Leppmann. *The German Image of Goethe*, p. 4.
55. *The Age of Reason*. London, 1960, pp. 102-103.
56. A. Kantorowicz. *Thomas und Heinrich Mann*. Berlin, 1956, p. 50.
57. W. Hegemann. *Entlarvte Geschichte*. Leipzig, 1933, p. 210.
58. G. H. Pertz. *Das Leben des Freiherrn vom Stein*. Berlin, 1849, Vol. I, pp. 393-394.
59. F. Meinecke. *Die deutsche Katastrophe*. Wiesbaden, 1946, p. 25.
60. *Ein Requiem in Rot-Weiss-Rot*. Zuerich, 1946, p. 468.
61. M. Bierbaum. *Leben des Kardinals von Galen*. Muenster, 1956, p. 105.
62. *Merkur*, Stuttgart, August, 1954.

63. *Historische Zeitschrift*, Muenchen, August, 1955, p. 64.
64. *Ungleiche Welten*. Wiesbaden, 1951, p. 227.
65. *Europa und die deutsche Frage*, pp. 102-104.
66. Foerster. *Erlebte Weltgeschichte*, p. 51.
67. Pross. *Die Zerstoerung der deutschen Politik*, pp. 29-30.
68. *Menschliches-Allzumenschliches*. Vol. I, aphorism 477.
69. *Also sprach Zarathustra*, p. 49.
70. *Deutschland und der naechste Krieg*, pp. 1, 4, 13, 21, 30.
71. Foerster. *Erlebte Weltgeschichte*, p. 315.
72. Foerster. *Mein Kampf gegen das militaristische und nationalistische Deutschland*, p. 42.
73. Müller-Claudius. *Deutsche und juedische Tragik*, p. 139.
74. *Händler und Helden*, pp. 31, 82.
75. Pross. *Die Zerstoerung der deutschen Politik*, pp. 194-196.
76. *Rasse und Persoenlichkeit*. Muenchen, 1925, p. 21.
77. *Der totale Krieg*. Muenchen, 1935, p. 10.
78. *A Study of History*. London, Vol. IX, 1954, pp. 445-446.
79. Karl Buchheim. *Leidensgeschichte des zivilen Geistes*. Muenchen, 1951, pp. 5-6, 14, 113.
80. *Deutsche Rundschau*, January, 1956.
81. *Das Reich der niederen Daemonen*. Hamburg, 1953, pp. 20-21.
82. *Club republikanischer Journalisten*. Koeln, November, 1959.

11
Germany's First Downfall

THE SELF-ASSERTIVE WILHELM SUDDENLY DROPPED BISMARCK, AL-
though only a short while before, on the Chancellor's birthday, he had loudly proclaimed: "Let him lead us, and we shall
follow him!"[1] Ominous words, which were to be repeated (unconsciously probably) fifty years later by Göring who said after
Hitler had started the war which was to ruin Germany for ever:
"Leader, command and we shall follow you."[2] National Socialists furnished German history after 1945 with yet another variation; "Führer, give your command and we shall bear the consequences."[3]

The "pilot" dropped, the Kaiser was not slow in defaming his
Chancellor by informing the Austrian Emperor of Bismarck's
"secret arrangement à double fonds with Russia which he had
immediately "annulled."[4] Wilhelm was no Hitler, of course, but
in some ways he was his precursor all the same, as when he
boastfully announced: "I shall lead you towards glorious
days."[5] In Hitlerian terms this ran: "After a crisis of 300 or

perhaps 400 years, the rejuvenation of our people has begun. I know for certain that we are at the beginning of a German life and a German future."[6] The Kaiser entered into the guest book of Munich town hall these words: *"Sic volo, sic iubeo."*[7] The medieval phrase "By the grace of God" had a ring of humility; in his mouth it became an arrogant slogan. In 1895 he wrote to Nicholas II of Russia: "Heaven has imposed on us Christian Kaisers and Kings a holy duty: to preserve the principle of God's Grace."[8] In 1901 he said at the consecration of the Kaiser Alexander *Grenadier* Barracks: "If Berlin should again, as they did in 1848, rebel against her King with insolence, you, my *Grenadiers,* will have the duty to repel the insolent and unruly with your bayonets."[9] Ten years earlier he said to new recruits: "Unfaithfulness and displeasure raise their heads more and more in our fatherland, and it can happen that you will have to shoot down your own relatives, brothers or even your parents."[10] In 1910, at a speech at Koenigsberg, referring to the coronation of his grandfather Wilhelm I: "It was here that my gradfather, again in his own right, put the crown of Prussia on his head and stressed that God in his grace had it given to him, neither parliament nor the people, and that he regarded himself as the elect instrument of heaven. I, too, go my way regarding myself as God's instrument without any consideration of the opinions of the day."[11] His great-grandfather, Friedrick Wilhelm IV, was of the same opinion when he wrote in 1841: "I am fully convinced of the Grace of God. No prince, no peasant, no Diet and no Jewish school will acquire any of the rights of the Crown if I do not give it to them. Paternal government is the German way, and as government is my heritage I want to lead children under age, punish the degenerate, but allow the well-bred to take part in the administration of my estate."[12]

To return to the Kaiser, he called the Social Democrats, as later Hitler did, " a rabble without a fatherland," not worthy of

bearing the name of Germans."[13] "National Socialism," Niekisch says, "was a political cancer growing on the body of the
bourgeoise Reich. Its seed is already recognisable in what the
Kaiser wrote to Chancellor Buelow on December 31, 1905:
'First we must kill the Socialists—by a massacre, if necessary—
and then we must go to war.' "[14] When Professor F. W. Foerster said in an article that such insulting words from the throne
could only widen the cleavage between the dynasty and the
workers, and that only an imitation of the English example
could avert the worst, the Kaiser took offense and Professor
Foerster was condemned to three months imprisonment.[15]
Thomas Mann tells us that when his fellow pupils at Lubeck
High School once damaged their classroom benches the headmaster said to them: "You have behaved like the Social Democrats."[16] On June 27, 1900, the Kaiser said to the German
naval troops which he sent to China that they "must give no
pardon to anybody and take no prisoners"; as the Huns were
still, after a thousand years, remembered in stories and fairy-
tales for what they had done, so the name of the Germans
should be remembered in China.[17] His pan-Germans had already said in 1890: "If our Kaiser calls us, we are willing to
stand to attention and allow ourselves, mutely and obediently,
to be led against our enemies. But we can ask for a price to be
paid to us worthy of our sacrifice. This price is: to become a
master race which arrogates to itself a part of the world without
waiting for the grace and the benevolence of other nations.
Germany, awake!"[18]

When the Kaiser went to Turkey as a self-styled patron of the
Muslims and visited Jerusalem, part of the wall had to be demolished so that he could enter the city on a white horse. The
playwright Frank Wedekind wrote a ballad—and recited it on
the stage—in which he made King David rise from his grave
and welcome the visitor which all his "lackeys and excellences
and innumerable policemen." "How proud," King David

sang and plucked his harp, "will Golgatha now be which once heard the last word of Christ and now hears the first word of you. Welcome then, whether you come in tropical uniform or as a sailor, in your purple robes or in a rococo costume of stiff silk."[19] Wedekind got a year's imprisonment for his ballad.

Like Hitler, the Kaiser used to speak of "miserable parliamentarism,"[20] and when he did not get his way in the Reichstag he thundered: "I shall send the half-crazy chaps to the devil!"[21] His Lord Chamberlain, Count Robert Zedlitz-Truetzschler, in 1904 entered in his diary that it became more and more difficult to tell Wilhelm the truth because he only wanted to be admired. He was convinced of his intellectual superiority and called every advice tiresome arrogance.[22] When Bismarck's successor, General Caprivi, said in Parliament that he was there at the command of his sovereign and would continue to manage politics as the Kaiser wanted and as long as he had his confidence, Count Zedlitz remarked that only a sergeant-major, not a Reichs-Chancellor, could speak like that.[23] The famous publicist Maximilian Harden, who had twice been imprisoned for his criticisms of saber-rattling Germany, wrote in his periodical, *Die Zukunft,* on November 21, 1908. "Wilhelm II has never done anything useful for his nation, and only asked subordinance to his will. Now he sees the results. If he still thinks it possible to stick to the throne—all right. But he should never again identify his will with the fate of the German Reich. We have enough of a Zeus who thunders from high above. He has proved utterly incompetent in political matters."[24] A few years after 1918, Harden was terribly beaten up by the first hooligans of Hitler. He died in Switzerland in 1927.

The Kaiser relied only on the Junkers in all questions of domestic and foreign policy. Writers who try to whitewash the reactionary Junkers today can mention only very few Prussian noblemen who opposed the Kaiser and, later, Hitler. They often refer to the poet and novelist Theodore Fontane as being a fine specimen of Prussianism and forget what this writer thought of Prussian policy. About Frederick II he said that great as he may have been he did not outweigh the whole glorious history of a nation of men. He called Prussianism "one of the lowest forms of civilization."[25] He utterly disliked the men around the Kaiser, "that narrow-minded, egoistic and mad nobility, that hypocritical or stupid Christianity, that dreadful Byzantinism."[26] The demands of the Junkers, he complained, became all the more intolerable the more they realized that the world belonged to other powers; their patriotism was "disgraceful claptrap. The sooner we got rid of them the better."[27] In 1896 he wrote to his friend James Morris that what the workers thought had far outstripped the thinking and writing of the ruling classes; "everything was more genuine and true."[28] To a German friend he wrote that the German colossus had "feet of clay. The whole building is shaking."[29] To this Prussian minority of very decent Germans belonged also those Prussian noblemen who were involved in the plot against Hitler and were hanged after July 20, 1944.

Bismarck very early called the Kaiser "the certain destroyer of Germany,"[30] and Crown Prince Rudolph of Austria said of him: "This arch-reactionary, who combines pig-headed obstinacy with the arrogance of a Junker, will bring Germany to ruin!"[31] He opposed his father's alliance with the Kaiser. Vice-Admiral Kurt Assmann, who spent many years in England as a military attaché, said after the Second World War that he "envied" Great Britain nothing more than her "dynasty and the love and veneration it enjoyed among its people."[32] He did not say why, but he assured the Germans that the world would think differently of Hitler a century hence, just as it happened with Napoleon. Goethe, who admired Napoleon but would hardly have admired Hitler, knew well why monarchs were "brushed away as with a broom"[33] and said that revolutions would not happen as long as governments were wise enough to forestall them by timely reforms.[34]

While judicious Germans foresaw Germany's downfall long
before it occurred, the vast majority believed the shameful
legend that Germany was being encircled by her enemies. This
legend is being repeated today again by various unteachable
Germans. What were the facts? The Kaiser did not renew the
Reinsurance Pact with Russia, thus making her suspicious of
Germany's further intentions, and he aroused Great Britain's
suspicions, too. Russia felt isolated and concluded a military
convention with France, which felt isolated, too, as her relations
with Great Britain were not too friendly at the time. It was
Bismarck himself who made the men of the "new course" in
Germany responsible for Russia's pact with France, and he
deeply resented the Kaiser's impudent telegram to President
Krueger. In the difficult days of the Boer War Great Britain
tried to arrange things with Germany, in 1897 through Salisbury, in 1898 through Balfour; and in 1899 Joe Chamberlin
said to the Kaiser that German and British interests were identical. The Kaiser, Chancellor Bulow, and the Grey Emi-
nence, Baron Holstein, refused to commit Germany, relying
on the old enmity between Russia and Great Britain and on the
differences between Great Britain and the French Republic. So
the instigators of the "new course" were also responsible for the
rapprochement between France and Great Britain. Dr. G. P.
Gooch says today that the so-called "encirclement" of the Germans had been of their own doing.

One of the most irresponsible men was Admiral Tirpitz. In
1897 he submitted his ideas about the necessity of a big German navy to Bismarck, who brushed them aside. Tirpitz then
turned to the Kaiser and, as Kuehlmann says in his autobiography, aroused Wilhelm's "ambition to go down in history as the
creator of a powerful German navy."[35] This idea sprang from
Wilhelm's inferiority complex and he treated it as a question of
Germany's prestige. The historian Max Weber wrote in 1908:
"The Hohenzollerns only know the sergeant-major type of
power: commands, submissiveness, boastfulness."[36] The poet

Stefan George said in 1905 that a genuine friend of the Germans must wish them a thorough defeat at sea so that they could learn again that modesty "which would enable them once more to produce spiritual values.[37] When Count Eulenburg asked the English ambassador Lascelles in the same year why England had given up her former good will towards Germany he got the answer: "If I had reported home every word of what your sovereign said to me, we might already have been at war on twenty occasions."[38] The Austrian admiral Spaun said at about the same time that the Kaiser's utterances would "only arouse England's distrust and drive her into the arms of France and Russia."[39]

Eyre Crowe, Permanent Under-Secretary in the Foreign Office at the time, acted as a very responsible man when he submitted his famous memorandum in which he very clearly and convincingly summed up the situation. Unlimited sea power, he pointed out, was a vital matter to England because of her geographical situation. Luckily it coincided with the interests of the other states whose independence could only be threatened by Germany, never by Great Britain; therefore they did not mind the British supremacy of the seas. When this memorandum was published after the First World War various German historians told the Germans that it was full of hatred against Germany. One of the craziest Germans of today, Hans Grimm, repeated this legend after the Second World War, saying that Crowe hated Germany. Why did he not hate France or Italy or Austria? No answer was given but that Great Britain was envious of Germany.

In 1907 Vice-Admiral K. Galster published his book, *What Sort of Sea War Does Germany Want?* He agreed with Tirpitz' policy but argued that to wage war against Great Britain no big ships were necessary, only small cruisers and torpedo boats. British politicians began to ask themselves more and more seriously what Germany was aiming at. Count Hatzfeld and Count

Wolff-Metternich, the two German ambassadors at the time, warned their government more and more poignantly against this mad policy, because they saw in it the main cause of the British estrangement from Germany. Count Wolff-Metternich wrote that Tirpitz and his like seemed to think that once the German naval policy had gone far enough Great Britain would acquiesce to the new situation and would become Germany's best friend. This, the Count said, is a fatal error. Tirpitz, instead of listening to the warnings of a sensible man, had him removed. He hoped, as Küehlmann tells us, that he would one day outgrow the British navy; he told this to a small circle of German parliamentarians. "Great Britain felt threatened by Tirpitz' activities."[40] The Austrian poet and satirist Karl Kraus wrote in 1908: "An apocalyptic horseman moves about in Germany who equals four. He is a jack-of-all-trades, his moustache reaches from East to West and from South to North. And power was given to the horseman to rob the earth of peace so that they should strangle each other. And people adored the beast and spoke: Who is like the beast? Who can fight it? It has got a mouth to utter great things."[41] The Kaiser said on March 18, 1909 that Great Britain's suggestion to limit the armament race was an insult, and Great Britain "can have war immediately if she wanted it."[42] Sir Edward Grey was alarmed by the dreadnoughts which Germany started building; you do not want dreadnoughts to protect your trade, he said in Parliament; Great Britain must have supremacy on the high seas, and a big navy is as vital to her as a big army is to Germany. He said to the German ambassador Marschall that if Germany were as satisfied with a small navy as Great Britain was with her small army, the two countries could never become a meance to each other. But what would Germany's reactions be if Great Britain suddenly tried to build up a huge army? Would she not feel threatened? The German historian, Ludwig Dehio, says today: "We, and we alone, were a meance to the central nerves of Great Britain's world power." He reminded the Germans of what the German historian Plehn had said in 1913: "It is the opinion of almost the whole nation that we can only achieve freedom for our world-political activity by a great European war." He also quoted what the historian Hans Delbrueck had said in 1912, namely that it was not the task of the German navy to protect the German trade but to secure the role which Germany had to play in "world-domination." Germany, Delbrueck had said in 1906, was only out to demolish Great Britain's sea-supremacy, and would not go any further. "Could such a naïve, if candid, assertion reassure an Englishman?" asks Dehio. "If Great Britain lost her supremacy, she would be at the mercy of her continental rival!"[43]

Bismarck had remarked very clearly that after his removal German policy had taken a dangerous course which Germany would not be able to change. R. E. May, a thoughtful Hamburg merchant, in 1897 said in a book of warning: "How can you present yourself to the other nations as such a beast? Will they not combine to kill that beast?"[44] But the Germans never listened to any warning out of their midst. They arranged the affair of the "Panther" in 1905 after telling their German firms at Agadir "to send them cries for help," as was revealed by an Under-Secretary in their Foreign Office.[45] In 1912, General Bernhardi published his notorious book, *Germany and the Next War,* in which he asserted that without a war "inferior or demoralised races could only too easily overrun the healthy ones," and proclaimed the right, and indeed the duty, of the Germans "to acquire the necessary territories by war. Our instinct of self-preservation compels us to wage war and conquer new territories. The right is not on the side of him who possesses but of him who remains victor in a war. Power is the best right." Hitler said exactly the same in *Mein Kampf.* Benhardi recommended the Hitlerian tactics of always speaking of peace while preparing for war. "Our nation," he proclaimed, "must realise that the preservation of peace can and must never be the aim of our policy . . . a peaceful settlement with Great Britain is only a Fata Morgana, and no responsible German statesman should ever aim at it."[46] Sir Winston Churchill said in 1912 that Great Britain had no aggressive intentions against Germany but that a big fleet was a necessity for her and only a luxury for Germany. The German admiral Breusing, however, said a year later: "We have not yet got so far as to conquer the British colonies."[47]

The big noise made by the pan-Germans could not fail to strengthen the distrust of Great Britain. As early as 1890 their first champions proclaimed the Germans as "a master race" and shouted: "Germany, awake!" The Big Chief of the pan-Germans, Heinrich Class, asserted in 1933: "I always advocated a war, a big war, as the best means of rescuing Germany from the fatal situation of today, and the number of those who agreed with me has rapidly grown during the last years."[48] In 1912 he published, under the pen name of Daniel Fryman, his sensational book, *If I Were the Kaiser,* which Hitler read and of which he gained the impression "that it contained everything that was important and necessary for Germany."[49] The book contained indeed everything that Hitler proclaimed ten years later. "A powerful leader is necessary," Class had said, a man "who will enforce the steps necessary to our recovery." Universal franchise, he asserted, was an idea of "the criminal Rousseau who propagated that all men are equal," an idea "undoubtedly ruinous to every state." All enemies of the German state must be banished. "One must not be sentimental." "The saviour of the Reich" will be a man "who uncompromisingly resists the democratisation of the state." Great Britain with her democracy was no model for Germany, rather "a warning example. Quite possibly we may become the teachers of Great Britain one day."

Turning to foreign policy, Class deplored that German

diplomats only thought "of preserving the peace." But Germany wanted an enlargement of her sphere of influence, "she had become hungry again, hungry after territory." Small states like Holland and Belgium had no right to exist, and Germany should not leave the mouth of the Rhine to Franco-British domination. New territories could, of course, only be won by a victorious war because "neither France nor Russia will be philanthropic enough to cede to us parts of their territories." After a victorious war Germany will have to ask for "deserted territories in the East or West," or to evacuate them. The other nations have been warned, he proclaimed, and should in time decide "whether they prefer to give us by good means or bad what we need: territory. Everybody who loves his own nation will long for a war because it awakens all our good, healthy and powerful energies."

Class also dealt with anti-Semitism which, as he said, put the finger on the wounds "which the Jews have inflicted, and are still inflicting, daily on our nation." They should be put under special laws "without pity," and no German should "raise his hands above his head because of such cold cruelty." Study Gobineau, he told them, and you will see "in the history of other nations what you experience in your own. Race is the root of all dangers." Class's motto for his nation was the old megalomaniac couplet:

> *Und es wird am deutschen Wesen*
> *Einmal noch die Welt genesen.*
> (One day the world will be saved by Germandom.)

Looking into the future, he said it would not matter if the Germans were defeated in the war which he envisaged. For then chaos would reign "which could only be conquered by the mighty will of a dictator."[50] Hitler, no doubt, applied this prophecy to himself. The great Austrian poet, satirist, and actor, Karl Kraus, once wrote a "Song of the pan-German" which he sang to a barbarian tune and in which he made the

wildly nationalistic representative of the Kaiser's age say that
Germany was more cultured than anybody else and that the new
Germans were heroes fighting "with God and Krupp for the
fatherland," and going into the trenches to capture for Germany
a place in the sun. "I have been a slave in peace-time, and I am
so even more in times of war. Even if the world were full of
devils, the more enemies we have the more honour we win."[51]

A year after Class had published his ominous book the war
came for which he and many pan-Germans had been longing.
As many Germans of today are still proclaiming Germany's
innocence, we must recall some of the more important events of
the days between the assassination of the Austrian crown prince
and the outbreak of the First World War. When the German
ambassador in Vienna reported to Berlin that he was seriously
warning the Austrian authorities against any rash steps, the
Kaiser scribbled on the margin of this letter: "Who has empow-
ered him to do so? This is very silly. It is no concern of his at all.
. . . A clean sweep must be made of the Serbs, and *soon*."[52]
Count Tisza, the Hungarian Prime Minister, however, warned
Count Berchtold on July 1, 1914 against the "fateful mistake"
of a war against the Serbs. "We shall be regarded as war-
mongers by the whole world," he said, "and shall have to fight a
great war under the worst possible conditions."[53] Berchtold did
not take this advice but induced the Austrian Emperor to write
a letter to the Kaiser in which he stated that it would probably
be impossible to prove the complicity of the Serbian government
in the assassination of Archduke Franz Ferdinand, but that we
"must aim at the isolation and reduction of Serbia" and eliminate her "as a political factor in the Balkans."[54]

Germany allowed Austria to do what she liked although
Reichs-Chancellor Bethmann-Hollweg had already written to
Count Berchtold on February 10, 1913 that if one considered
the situation in the Balkans objectively, one must come to the
conclusion that it was almost impossible for Russia, with her

traditional relations to the Balkan states, not to interfere in an Austrian war against Serbia without a terrible loss of prestige. If Russia interfered, he added, a European war would become inevitable.[55] The Austrian politicians were very pleased with Germany's passivity; the Austrian Chief of Staff, Conrad von Hoetzendorf, had already in 1909 pleaded for a war against Serbia in order to incorporate it into the Austrian monarchy. Serbia accepted the Austrian ultimatum almost in all points and was willing to accept the verdict of the Hague Court or the Great Powers with regard to points which she did not accept. Austria refused to accept Serbia's answer without consulting her German ally. If Germany, Prince Lichnowsky said after the war, had interfered at this moment and told Austria to content herself with her diplomatic success and the Serbian answer, the war could have been avoided. But Germany did nothing of the sort, and this is her war guilt. Why did Bethmann not point to his letter of the previous year? Why did he not remember, and remind the Kaiser, of what Bismarck had said in 1887 when negotiating with Russia about the Reinsurance Pact: "Germany recognised Russia's historical rights in the Balkans"?[56]

Prince Lichnowsky was not wise after the event. He had warned Bethmann on July 25, 1914 that everything would be lost if Austria invaded Serbia, that Germany should beware of a war in which she could win nothing but might lose everything. Sir Edward Grey warned Berlin through his ambassador Goschen that Great Britain could not remain neutral, and offered his good services as mediator so that Germany would not have to be afraid of an aggressive policy against herself. Austria had in the meantime declared war on Serbia and Russia had started mobilizing her forces. Grey went further and promised Berlin that, if Austria were satisfied with the occupation of Belgrade and willing to submit to international settlement the problems in question, he would advise Russia not to push on with her military preparations. The Kaiser's mild advice to Vienna to accept the British suggestion was not heeded. At this moment something more was certainly needed, a threat that Germany would not unconditionally follow Austria's policy if Austria did not heed the German advice. Only when Bethmann realised that neither Russia nor Great Britain would remain neutral in the prospective war did he tell the Austrian war-mongers that Germany would not allow herself to be drawn into a general war if her advice was not followed. But it was already too late. The German historian Erich Brandenburg, although praising Adolf Hitler's leadership, wrote in 1933: "How often has Bismarck warned us not to go to war for the expansion of Austria's influence in the Balkans; but this was just what we did."[57] The German politicians lost their heads, told Russia to cancel her mobilization, and challenged France to declare her neutrality and surrender the fortified places of Toulon and Verdun. All these mad requests were not complied with quickly enough; Germany declared war on Russia on August 1.

The next important event was Germany's violation of Belgian neutrality, which Germany had guaranteed just as solemnly as Great Britain, but which she never meant to respect. The German Chief of Staff, Count Schlieffen, had said as early as 1897: "An offensive which wants to turn Verdun must not be shy about violating the neutrality both of Luxembourg and Belgium."[58] In 1900 he said to Count Hutten-Czapski, private secretary to Reichs-Chancellor Hohenlohe, that a German victory might depend on not allowing Germany to be "hemmed in" by international pacts.[59] Another Hitler long before the actual one! Lichnowsky warned Berlin on August 2 that a violation of Belgian neutrality might cause Great Britain to enter the war; on the other hand she might remain neutral if Germany showed moderation towards France. Germany did not heed Lichnowsky's warning and overran Belgium, whereupon Great Britain declared war on Germany, thus sealing her fate. Great Britain could afford to let Germany become the master of Europe in 1914 as little as in 1939.

There can be no doubt that Germany was responsible for the

First World War, although she has always denied it. Or, to be more specific, the main responsibility rests on the shoulders of the Austrian policy. Professor Friedrich Wilhelm Foerster, who had always warned against the German policy, sums his verdict up in these words: "The real German war guilt does not lie in the decisions of the German politicians and soldiers in the summer of 1914 but in the evil passion, slowly growing through decades, of the great majority of Germans mad with lust for power, especially the pan-German school-masters and pastors, the organisations of soldiers and sailors and the big industrialists intoxicated by success."[60]

When Kaiser Wilhelm, in the first days of the war said that that nation would win it which had the better nerves, the novelist Hermann Hesse considered these words "as the gloomy omen of an earthquake." The Kaiser was fond of "the insipid fairy-tale of the vicious French and of the virtuous Germans with their many children," but for "those in the know that utterance was terrible. They all knew that Germany had not better but, on the contrary, worse nerves than her Western enemies. The words of the leader of the nation therefore gave the impression of awful and fateful *hubris* running blindly into disaster."[61] The poet Stefan George declined to be enthusiastic about "German virtue and Italian malice," and confessed that he had sweated "blood of anguish" for a long time when the Germans "played with fire." He foretold that the war in which he refused to take part would not end "in triumph but only in many downfalls without dignity."[62] Barbara W. Tuchman who describes the first weeks of the First World War, says when dealing with the massacre of the hostages of Dinant and the burning of the library at Louvain: "The gesture intended by the Germans to frighten the world—to induce submission—instead convinced large numbers of people that here was an enemy with whom there could be no settlement and no compromise."[63]

Heinrich Mann, who had always been very critical of the

Wilhelminian age, in 1910 contrasted Germany with France in a masterly essay. France, he said, can be proud of a glorious series of writers who, from Rousseau to Zola, had opposed the powerful of their time and had taught their nation "to doubt the power of the state." There, spirit was not "the pale ghost it was with us. Nobody has ever seen that the power of the German nation has ever been used to turn knowledge into political deeds. We think further than anybody, we think as far as the end of pure reason, as far as nothingness, and the country is ruled by Divine Grace and the fist. Why change anything? Ours is no great nation, there are only single great men."[64] After the outbreak of the First World War he adopted an ingenious new method to criticize his war-mad country and foretell its downfall. Early in the war he published a highly artistic essay on Zola, the political implications of which eluded the strict but illiterate German censorship. He spoke of France and Napoleon III; in reality he meant the Kaiser's Germany. The many admirers of his satirical pre-war novels and essays understood him only too well. This is the picture he drew of Bismarck in retirement: "A man of power, the master *par excellence,* and wholly useless if he cannot be the master. Useless the weight of the massive shoulders of a fallen potentate waiting for his return, only waiting, without any spiritual interests." He called the Kaiser's Germany "the most shameless and immoderate of all countries," her industrialists and bankers "pillars of the dynasty as long as it furthered business," while her officers "went to war for little more than their privileges." He prophesied: "A country which is built only on power, and not on freedom, justice and truth, a country which only knows of order and obedience cannot be victorious, even if it has gone to war with superhuman power. . . . The most evil of all governments is driving the nation into a catastrophe. Democracy will be the gift of defeat."[65]

In those noisy years before the First World War Heinrich

Mann also wrote a bitterly sarcastic novel, *Der Untertan,* which could not be published until 1919. Military life in Germany, he said, was mainly aiming at "crushing all personal dignity. Suddenly and unalterably you became a louse, raw material moulded by an infinite will." The nationalistic young men speak, like the Kaiser, of "subversive tendencies," "the inner enemy," and say that "the grumblers should go elsewhere." They are agreed "that Jewish liberalism is the forerunner of socialism, and that the German Christians must flock to the (anti-Semitic) Court preacher Stöcker." Herr von Barnim, a Prussian Junker, is of the opinion that Germany must become a corporate state, and excludes "the Jewish citizens from his order of things because they represent the principle of disorder and chaos, of disrespect, of evil itself." The hero of the novel, the *Untertan* Diederich Hessling, is already at the elementary school having his fun with the only Jewish boy and "crucifies" him. "Christianity acted through him"—not very much later Hitler said the same in *Mein Kampf,* as we shall see.

The German nation is compared by Heinrich Mann with the chorus in Wagner's *Lohengrin,* which is always surprised by events. Of old Buck, a revolutionary of 1848 who had once been sentenced to death, somebody says that he should be more honored than "certain people who always want to cure everything by blood and iron." He himself says: "We have been defeated because we were foolish enough to believe in our nation." He lives to see that this nation is held down again "by the boots of cuirassiers"; it is "the power which passes over our heads and we kiss its hoofs. We can do nothing against it because we all love it, we have it in our blood because we have submissiveness in it." Diederich Hessling is not only His Majesty's most faithful servant, he is also his master's voice. He defends "our holiest values," he "deals with the Social Democrats himself," he "crushes everybody who opposes him," and he "leads you towards glorious days." He speaks of "German decency and morality," of "German faithfulness," of "the selfless idealism which is a privilege of the Germans." He says that "Germanism is culture," that "to be German means to be objective," that "all the world envies us our Kaiser," and that "it is our sword alone which secures us our position in the world." He agrees with the Kaiser's word that he "hates England as only Frederick the Great had hated it, that nation of thieves and merchants."

The story ends with a nationalistic feast, the unveiling of an equestrian statue of Wilhelm I, whom they call the Great. In a remarkable speech Hessling says: "We are the elite of the nations. . . . The morass of democracy flows nearer and nearer from the country of our hereditary enemy. Only German manliness and German idealism can stem the tide."[66]

In the sequel to this novel, *The Poor,* written during the war, we again meet Diedrich Hessling, now a powerful industrialist like those who ten years later gave Hitler millions.

By contrast we shall now show how the Kaiser's pastors and professors behaved during the First World War. Only a handful of them can be quoted here as specimens of the intellectual depravity already prevailing then in Germany's governing circles. Court preacher Goens assured the Kaiser that Germany was fighting for Protestantism and that the Germans were the chosen people. One pastor said: "It is not our guilt if we must also become henchmen in this bloody war. It is a holy service if a soldier rams his bayonet into the ribs of the enemy." Another said: "Hey! How the sword rushes out of the scabbard, how it glitters in the sunshine, the good German sword! God has put you in our hands. You are transfiguring our character like the word and the spirit. Your words are fireworks which testify for life and light. Come, sword, you are the revelation of the Spirit."[67]

Professor Friedrich Meinecke asserted that the war had been forced on innocent Germany "by the guilt of others. Western envy and hatred have only been waiting for the hour to attack us." Great Britain envied Germany "the fruits of our laborious efforts, and to cover this up they spoke of our aggressiveness. If we conquer, we do not only conquer for ourselves, we do so also for humanity."[68] Professor Adolf Hofmeister said that Germany was fighting "for freedom and justice against all those innumerable millions which mercantile envy, lust for revenge and imperial power have gathered against us."[69] The university professors of the Kaiser's Germany published this manifesto: "We are full of disgust with the attempt of the enemies of Germany to differentiate between the spirit of German science and what they call Prussian militarism. The spirit of the German army is the same as the spirit of the German nation. Both are one, and we are part of it. It is our belief that the salvation of European culture depends on the victory of German militarism."[70]

Professor Dietrich Schäfer reminded the Germans that their ancestors had once fixed "the European boundaries of the Roman Empire" and had ultimately destroyed it. While Germany looked back with pride at her "achievements during the last forty years," the foreigners looked at them "with envy and jealousy." Why? Because Germany had become a great power and had asserted herself in the world, "especially on the high seas." Her "cousin" across the channel remembered "his old maxim of knocking out everybody who makes bold to excel the others on the continent, to navigate the high seas and to do business wherever he likes."[71] Professor Eduard Meyer blamed Edward VII as the man above all responsible for the war. Great Britain and France "hated the German name and were envious of Germany's growing prosperity," and furious because "they could no longer behave in the world as in the olden days." And like Hitler twenty years later, he shouted: "If Germany and Austria should be defeated, Russia will become the master of Europe." Germany was fighting "for the salvation of civilisation from Slav hordes."[72]

Professor Hermann Oncken, too, spoke of "the secret of British policy to defeat an economic competitor in time and plunder him. They regard this war as good business." Edward VII is "the father and spiritual author of the policy of encirclement and the father and spiritual author of this war." Like Hitler and like Bismarck he called the English "hypocrites" and anticipated the Führer when he asserted that the European balance of power "had at all times only been the formula for Great Britain's supremacy at sea and in the world. It is Germany's world-historic mission to unmask her and show her true face to the world."[73] Professor Julius Kaftan, a theologian, denounced Edward VII's policy of encirclement, spoke of Great Britain's envy and jealousy and of the false slogan of German militarism, and called Treitschke "one of the best men Germany had produced in the second half of the nineteenth century, one of the prophets of the new Germany under Prussian guidance."[74] Professor Otto Hintze, too, spoke of Great Britain's hatred; the German navy was intolerable to her; she was fighting for the preservation of her world hegemony; Germany, however, fought for her independence, for a place in the sun, and for the freedom of the nations "which was threatened by the British despotism at sea."[75] Professor Kohler said that the other nations lacked the faculty of systematic thinking, and was of the opinion that an international law based on pacts between nations was outdated because "our enemies are liars and swindlers."[76] Professor Gustav Röthe said: "The long peace had opened all doors to effeminacy."[77]

Professor W. Franz called Russia and Great Britain "aggressors." Russia, he said, had always been "fond of adventures and rapacious," and Great Britain allied herself with Russia to destroy Germany's industries and foreign trade. Why? Because she "hated bitterly the German competitor. . . . Looking down from the height of German culture, this alliance between Great Britain, Russia, and France seems to us unnatural, even unworthy and humiliating." And he spoke contemptuously of British cant, self-righteousness, and national pride, of her cycnical and shameless lies. "We make the whole British nation fully responsible for the crime of this aggressive war," he exclaimed, and added: "The present war has proved that German culture is far superior to the British culture of today."[78]

Professor Johannes Haller said that Russia, France, and Great Britain had forced the war on innocent Germany. Great Britain especially, because it wants "to preserve its supremacy in the world trade without a serious competitor. We call this mean, we call it vile." He compared Great Britain to "a merchant who attacks a competitor who is likely to surpass him, and murders him, or rather, has him murdered by assassins." This policy began on January 22, 1901, when Edward VII ascended to the throne. The aim of Germany must therefore be to break "the British supremacy at sea" and to make an end to "this regime of violence, lie and hypocrisy for ever." The 19th century had been the age of British supremacy; in the 20th "the German nation will march at the top of the European nations." Very fittingly, because the Germans were "the greatest, the strongest, the best ordered of Western civilisations." Germany would establish a *Pax Germanica* so that the word of a German poet would come true:

> *Und es soll am deutschen Wesen*
> *Einmal noch die Welt genesen.*[79]

Professor F. W. Foerster speaks therefore of "the Prussification of German historiography."[80]

"Poets" wrote poems full of the same spirit: *"Gott strafe England!"* They confessed that they were proud to be barbarians, hailed the holy war, and condemned peace as beggarly. The poet Rilke praised himself happy because of the enthusiasm he saw around him, the playwright Gerhart Hauptmann spoke

of three robbers—the English, the French, the Russians—who
had attacked innocent Germany. Karl Kraus quoted all these
poems in his periodical, *Die Fackel,* and so saved them for
posterity: pillories of shame. When yet another of these war
poets defiled one of the most famous poems by Goethe by using
its rhymes and rhythm for a poem in praise of the German U-
boats, Karl Kraus, one of the greatest masters of German
prose, said: "Where in the wide world could the last and deepest breath of the greatest poet be degraded with so little awe to
such horrible clatter?"[81] When a German philosopher, who
called himself a Kantian, professed his enthusiasm for the
Kaiser's war, Kraus confronted him with Kant in a poem called
A Kantian and Kant, and in his poem *On Eternal Peace* he paid
homage to Kant's philosophy as expressed in his famous treatise
on the same theme. "Woe," he said in wonderful couplets, "if
the world amidst the German madness overslept the last German miracle which has called for it!"[82] But the Austrian novelist Hermann Bahr, who as a student had once been very critical
of Germany, wrote: "We all bless, bless, bless this war! We are
now nothing but Germans. Praised be this war which has freed
us from all ancient German evils! What else is German music
from Bach and Beethoven to Wagner if not enthusiasm coupled
with discipline? Our mobilisation was German music—it was
exactly like the score of a Wagnerian drama. . . . The miracle of
the German mobilization—was no miracle at all, it was the sum
total of the whole German history. What a Gothic dome made
us feel in our finest hours, what Beethoven announced, what
Faust sketched, finds now its fulfillment."[83] H. S. Chamberlain
in 1917 called the Germans "the nation of thinkers and poets"
and was sure that history would call them "the nation of heroes
and inventors." The English, he asserted, were wrongly called
a free nation, the Germans were "a nation of free, truthful and
decent men. . . . The different groups of the Aryan race were
fundamentally idealists."[84]

When the German offensive in the autumn of 1914 got stuck on the Marne, old Field-Marshal Haeseler said that the war was already lost, and General Moltke said the same to the Kaiser. But have Germans listened to any warning? They fought on, and early in 1917 they started their unrestrained U-boat warfare. Judicious men had warned them against it. Count Bernstorff, the German ambassador in Washington, implored his government to desist from this step because it would draw the United States into the war. Professor Max Weber sent a warning memorandum to the Foreign Office and the party leaders—nobody listened to him. Ludendorff and the Pan-Germans enforced the new policy.

Early in the war German politicians and generals had begun to dream of huge annexations and became enthusiastic about a "strong peace," a "Hindenburg peace"; this went on at a time when, as Kuehlmann says, "our military situation left no room at all for the hope that we could dictate peace to the sea powers of Great Britain and the United States."[85] The Pan-Germans, under their chief Heinrich Class, in 1914 drew up their list of annexations. The nationalistic industrialist Hugenberg told the Kaiser in 1915 that Belgium should on no account be exchanged for further colonies because Belgium and the northern part of France were "absolutely essential" for Germany's industry. As to the East, Germany wanted there a new area necessary for her agrarian policy, for growing more grain on her own soil and feeding a growing industrialized population.[86] Krupp, Stinnes, Thyssen, Kirdorf, Stresemann, Ludendorff, Tirpitz, and many generals were of the same opinion. General Hans von Seeckt suggested a peace treaty with the West based on a *status quo* and the conquest of ten thousand square miles of Russia. This would "probably cost us a million men, among them the best. Against this what does it mean to expel a lot of riff-raff of Jews, Poles, Masurians, Lithuanians, Latvians, Esthonians, etc? Let us behave according to the customs of the age of migration."[87]

Pan-German professors furthered these lunatic aspirations and spoke of a *Pax Germanica: Oderint dum metuant.* In the East, they needed Poland, Lithuania, and Courland, and, as Professor Brandenburg expressed it, a number of "safety regions" where "a powerful policy of German settlements"[88] would be inaugurated. Others wanted areas up to the mouth of the Dnieper. There were many Hitlers about in Germany at the time when the real one was still "an unknown soldier," as he later was to call himself. In the West they asked for Belgium, Luxembourg, Holland, Flanders ("absolutely necessary to our sea power,"[89] said Professor Brandenburg who also asked for "French Briey and Longwy"[90]), the French coast down to the mouth of the Somme, Verdun, Belfort, and Toulon. When Bethmann-Hollweg tried to resist this madness Hindenburg and Ludendorff forced his dismissal. Even as late as January, 1918 a nationalistic parliamentarian said in the Reichstag that a statesman who would not bring home from the war Belgium, Longwy, Briey, and the coast of Flanders would go down in history as the grave-digger of German honor in the world. It never occurred to him and his like that they themselves were the grave-diggers of Germany, not even after 1918, when they preferred to blame others for Germany's ruin, just as they are still doing today after Germany's second and decisive defeat.

Bethmann-Hollweg had said as early as 1915 that the soul of the Germans had been "so deeply poisoned in the last twenty-five years that they would probably become disheartened if somebody forbade them to be boastful."[91] General Groener was already in 1916 of the opinion that the war could at best end in a draw. Professor Friedrich Meinecke, who had become sober again, said in 1917: "The policy of conquest and violence pursued by the conservatives, the Pan-Germans and the chaps of the Fatherland Party must end in a suppression of the nation's wish for political freedom and in the erection of a despotic militarism. This is a very serious danger which we must guard against. Violent foreign policy is followed by violent policy within our borders."[92] As always, the warnings of reasonable Germans were not heeded. It is true that the Kaiser at the end of 1916 put out tentative peace feelers, but, as he made no concrete proposals at all, they came to nothing. When Matthias Erzberger on July 5, 1917 advocated a reasonable arrangement with Germany's enemies, the many annexationists cried out that this would amount to "a peace of renunciation." On July 19, the Reichstag passed with a small majority a resolution for a peace of reconciliation without any annexations, but Reichs-Chancellor Michaelis destroyed all belief in the seriousness of that vote by the words "As I understand it"—an intentional ambiguity, as we can see from his letter to the Crown Prince of July 26. In it he spoke of the "notorious resolution" which, by his interpretation, he had "robbed of its great dangerousness."[93] One hundred and ten professors protested against the resolution. When Professor F. W. Foerster, because of his criticism of Germany's unreasonable war policy, came into conflict with the professors of Munich University and published a report of it in the *Berliner Tageblatt,* Reichs-Chancellor Michaelis, his uncle, reproached him for it: "How can you, a Christian, publish your defence in a Jewish newspaper!" Foerster answered: "Because this Jewish newspaper is more Christian in its policy than your so-called Christian newspapers."[94] The peace feelers of Pope Benedict XV on August 1, 1917 met with no success; Germany's response was evasive and equivocal. The Pope had stressed the necessity of restoring the independence of Belgium, but on just this point Ludendorff and the annexionists remained adamant.[95]

When, in the autumn of 1917, Russia collapsed, the German annexationists saw their dreams of expansion in the East come true. The Russians proposed a peace without annexations and reparations, and the parties of the Roman Catholics and the Socialists were in agreement with them. Not so the right wing

paries and even less Ludendorff. They were determined to get
a big slice of Russia, almost as much as Hitler conquered
25 years later, and claimed it under the pretext of the self-
determination of nations. The negotiations were protracted,
to the despair of Count Czernin, the Austrian Foreign
Secretary. Hunger reigned in Vienna, and an early peace
treaty securing Ukrainian grain for the Austrian population might have averted the threatening revolution. An early
peace treaty might also have enabled Ludendorff to move all his
Eastern armies to the West and secure a better military position
in the difficult months that lay ahead. But Ludendorff remained
inexorable and in the end asked for unconditional surrender.
(We must remember this when we come to 1945.) When
Kuehlmann asked Hindenburg why he pressed for such huge
conquests the Field-Marshall answered: "I want to secure
enough space for the movement of the left German wing in our
next war against Russia."[96] (We must remember this when we
come to 1941.) The Russians were compelled to accept the
very hard, and indeed unique, conditions of March 3, 1918.
Very hard also was the Treaty of Bucharest of May 7, 1918.
The German nationalists, however, according to Kuehlmann's
report, "attacked the treaty with vehemence, saying that it had
secured them nothing."[97]

Kuehlmann is not as innocent as he wants us to believe. On
December 3, 1917 he had told the Kaiser that it was important
to sever Russia from her Western allies. He had therefore inaugurated subversive activities behind the Russian front with a
view to supporting the Bolsheviks, and had sent them money
through various channels. Once the Russians had been left in
the lurch by their allies, they would turn to Germany for help,
he told the Kaiser. The Kaiser agreed with his clever Foreign
Secretary, and Ludendorff, as is well known, allowed Lenin to
leave Switzerland and travel in a sealed carriage through Germany to Russia. Professor Foerster, then already living in

Switzerland as an exile, told the German ambassador at Berne that that mad step of Ludendorff's would one day be bitterly revenged on the Germans, "But for them," Mr. Edward Crankshaw says today, "there would have been no Bolshevism in Russia, no Lenin, no Stalin—no Ulbricht in Germany."[98]

Now we come to President Wilson's famous Fourteen Points, around which the Germans have spun many a misleading legend. Germany and Austria published their answers to Wilson at the end of January, 1918. Austria accepted his suggestions; Germany, faithful to her war policy up to the bitter end, rejected all Western "interference" in her Eastern plans and evaded an unequivocal answer about Belgium. She was still sure of a victory in the West once she had settled her affairs with Russia. On February 11, Wilson drew the attention of the Germans to their peace resolution of July 19, 1917, by which they had solemnly pledged themselves to a peace of reconciliation, excluding all annexations and reparations. When the Reichstag approved of the dictates of Brest-Litovsk and Bucharest, Wilson, in April, 1918, said that he accepted the challenge. The German generals had given him an answer which he could not fail to understand. Might was again to prevail over right. On September 27, 1918, he told the Germans again that after their peace treaties of Brest-Litovsk and Bucharest they would get no negotiated peace. He knew now, he told them, that they had no honor and knew no justice. These things must be stressed and stressed again because the Germans have spread the lie that Wilson had betrayed them, and this lie sticks in their minds up to this very day. Mr. George F. Kennan has reminded us (and his words were translated into German a few years ago) that the Treaty of Versailles was the consequence of the German behavior in Brest.[99] However, in the minds of the Germans of the period between 1918 and 1933 German history began with the Treaty of Versailles, with nothing behind it, as in the minds of the Germans of today German history begins with 1945.

They always arrogate to themselves the privilege to do what they like and never to feel responsible for what they have done.

The Kaiser complained in August, 1914 that the war was Great Britain's thanks for Waterloo. Admiral Tirpitz assured the Kaiser that the war had its origin in the city of London and was waged to bring down Great Britain's strongest competitor on the European continent. The Kaiser, acclaimed by Admirals Tirpitz and Hoetzendorff, declared unrestricted U-boat warfare in spite of the warnings of his American ambassador, Count Bernstorff. "I could not care less," he said. On the instigation of Hindenburg and Ludendorff he dismissed Bethmann-Hollweg who was hated by many nationalist politicians and professors as a misfortune and a friend of Great Britain. But he said that the Kaiser had thoroughly ruined the Germans for twenty years and had turned them into conceited chauvinists. Even in 1918 the Kaiser spoke of the irreconcilable enmity of the anglo-saxon and the Germanic *Weltanschauung,* and said that if a British officer appeared one day asking for a truce, he would first have to kneel down before the Imperial standard because that would signify the victory of monarchy over democracy. When, in 1917 some German circles began to favor a democratization of Prussia, Colonel General von Plessen said: *"Gegen Demokraten helfen nur Soldaten."* Admiral G. A. von Mueller, a sober conservative, who tells us all this in his autobiography, mentions also that Count Czernin warned on April 3, 1917: "If the war does not come to an end within three months, the nations will end it without their governments." Mueller said on April 23, 1917, that the Germans showed "want of moderation both in the West and East."[100]

It was those same nationalist politicians and generals who, if Germany in 1918 had won the war, would have imposed as hard a peace treaty on the Western Allies as those of Brest and Bucharest, who cried out most about the "injustice" of the

Treaty of Versailles. Worst of all was Ludendorff's behavior.
On April 16, 1917, the famous historian Max Weber complained about the dictatorial behavior of Hindenburg and
Ludendorff who had threatened to resign if Bethmann-Hollweg
were not dismissed without delay. Weber wrote: "They interfere
in politics of which they understand *absolutely nothing*."[101]
Ludendorff also forced the dismissal of Kuehlmann when the
latter cautiously intimated to the Reichstag on June 24, 1918
that the war could not be won by military means. Only a few
weeks later, however, Ludendorff nervously insisted on an
armistice offer being made immediately to the Allies to avoid a
complete breakdown of the German armies. General Ludwig
Beck knew in 1916 that only a compromise could save Germany, "but nobody could prevail against the dictator Ludendorff. He could only be defeated by himself."[102] On Hindenburg's suggestion Erzberger signed the armistice agreement, but
the nationalists very soon began to blame him, not the commanding generals, for it. When a commission of inquiry into the
causes of the defeat was set up later, Hindenburg and Ludendorff testified that they had only been soldiers and had never
bothered about politics, and that the home front had been
weakened by defeatist political parties. This was the origin of
the stab-in-the-back legend with its catastrophic consequences
for the policy of the newly founded republic. Ludendorff conveniently forgot that he had said on October 28, 1918, two days
after his dismissal: "I can only hope that we shall succeed in
bringing home an undefeated army," and that Major von Harben
had immediately said to Captain Breucker: "No doubt we have
been defeated on all fronts."[103] This was an opinion shared by
everybody at headquarters. A few years, later, however, Ludendorff said the Freemasons, Jews, and Jesuits had been responsible for Germany's defeat, and a few more years after that
Hitler asserted that only the bottomless mendacity of the Jews
and Marxists could blame for the German breakdown "the man

who had tried with superhuman willpower to avert the catastrophe which he had foreseen."[104] Millions believed him and shouted "Heil Hitler!" Nobody listened to what the historian Hans Delbrueck had written in 1919: "We perished because we had no aim which could be carried through." Millions began to speak of the "November criminals," whom they blamed for the German revolution.

Karl Kraus, who, as he once said, fought a Thirty Years' War against the Austrian and German mentalities, did not cease to fight them during the First World War. While the misguided Austrians and Germans were jubilant and sure of a decisive victory over perfidious Albion ("May God punish England!"), he said that "from August 1, 1914" he had believed only in "the transformation of the earth into a heap of dirt." The war of the Central Powers was "the greatest crime in all history," a war of "murderers and thieves, outrageous cretins. . . . The only true word" of the war was that uttered by "a Russian Minister at the beginning of the fighting: 'This war is an impudence' "; another true word was uttered towards the end of the war by a leader of the Czechs who said that his compatriots "did not shed even one drop of blood voluntarily" for Habsburg's war. As for Karl Kraus he never had any other wish than "that the sober democratic civilisation of the world should arm itself with all those weapons which are necessary for the extermination of this unchastity, the shortening of this incest." Early in October, 1918 he wrote: "The belief, upheld to the last breath of men and horses, that the world—which heaven forbid—would be saved by Germandom is now buried. The hope revives now that the world will be freed from Germandom."[105]

After the downfall of the Central Powers he published an *Obituary* of 120 pages with a frontispiece showing Count Berchtold in the smart uniform of an Austrian Uhlan captain, decorated with the highest Austrian order, the Golden Fleece. It starts with these words: "Through the night of nights in which we, hungry and freezing, bowed down by the curse to be Viennese, must grope our way towards peace, one consoling and hope-giving star is shining: no longer to be Austrians. We cannot become so miserable by our defeat as not to be richly compensated by our defeat!"[106]

The Austrians of today claim again to be the country of Haydn, Mozart, and Schubert, as if Mozart and Schubert had not died in utter misery, and as if the authoritarian Austria of the Habsburgs had had anything in common with the music of the great composers of the time. Sentimentalists all over the world are also often apt to identify the political reality of Austria between the defeat of Napoleon and the rise of Hitler with Austrian music and Austrian literature. There could be no greater mistake. Post-war Austrians tell us today that many nations had found shelter and a fatherland, the like of which they will never find again, behind the black and yellow boundary-posts of the Dual Monarchy. The victors of 1918, they forgetfully assert, had decided upon the radical dismemberment of a state which for centuries had been a bulwark of European culture, a source of peace, and a defender of justice. Forgetful people sometimes agree with this. The Czech historian František Palacky, however, warned the Austrian government in 1848 that Austria could only survive as a bulwark against Russia if it gave freedom to its many nations and transformed itself into a federal state. Nobody took any notice of this stern warning.[107] It was only in 1916 that the last Austrian emperor, Karl I, asked Professor F. W. Foerster for his advice with regard to transforming Austria into such a state; but by then it was too late.

Of the Kaiser's Germany Karl Kraus said in 1918: "Our enemies ask for the surrender of the German artillery. This is madness. It would only be logical to ask for the surrender of the German *Weltanschauung*."[108] Of himself he said: "If one does not want to pay a more positive tribute to the 2,000 pages of the war issues of my periodical *Die Fackel,* one will at least have to say that I rejected day by day and easily the most filthy demands of Power, to see truth in lies, right in injustice, reason in madness." And he quoted Horatio's words in *Hamlet:*

> And let me speak to the yet unknowing world
> How these things came about: so shall you hear
> Of carnal, bloody, and unnatural acts,
> Of accidental judgments, casual slaughters,
> Of deaths put on by cunning and forced cause,
> And in this upshot, purposes mistook,
> Fall'n on the inventors' heads. . . .[109]

The German *Weltanschauung* of which Kraus spoke in 1918 came to full blossom between 1918 and 1933. Kraus lived to see it and wrote his unique essay of 300 pages, *The Third Walpurgisnight.*[110] He died in 1936. When, in 1938, Hitler entered Vienna his thugs demolished his house and destroyed all the manuscripts they found. The Austrian poet Berthold Viertel, during his American exile, in 1941 addressed a poem to Kraus in one quatrain of which he says: "You foresaw early the horror that materialized [in 1933]. You saw it coming at a time when nobody saw it because your dread was deeper than anybody else's."[111]

After the downfall of the Habsburgs and the Hohenzollerns Karl Kraus also published his unique tragedy, *The Last Days of Mankind,* on which he had worked during the war and scenes from which he had recited before Viennese audiences. All the slogans of the lost war crop up again: a holy war of defense, the lies of our enemies, the uplifting of our hearts, may God punish England, Germany's pride on being the first war nation on earth. We meet the generals who hammer out the fate of the world "in these glorious days," we meet the Kaiser's industrialists, the Lutheran pastors who glorify the war, the poets who are enraptured with "the immense bliss of this moment." Professor Sombart's megalomaniacal book about the British and the Germans is summed up in a little, precious dialogue: "They are shopkeepers."—"We are heroes." Nationalists hope for a victory "which will widen our frontiers in East and West. The world has, up to now, shown too little understanding for our national peculiarity and we shall have to knock it thoroughly into them." Pan-German pastors ask for Belgium, Longwy, Briey, the Flemish coast, Gibraltar, Malta, Cyprus, Egypt to be incorporated into a German Empire. Karl Kraus, who had already in 1908 changed the megalomaniacal German phrase *Ein Volk der Denker und Dichter* (we are a nation of thinkers and poets) into *Ein Volk der Henker und Richter* (a nation of hangmen and judges), makes his mouthpiece say: "No nation lives further away from its language, that is the fountain of its life, than the Germans. Which Neapolitan beggar is not nearer to his language than a German professor to his!" The tragedy ends in a pandemonium, a horrible dance of death.[112] Captain Malcolm Hay, a Roman Catholic writer who was a prisoner of war in the Kaiser's Germany, said afterwards: "We lived in the very midst of an organisation which moved as one for one purpose—the destruction of European civilisation and the substitution of Teutonic conceptions."[113] The Bishop of Muenster, Count von Galen, wrote in 1919: "Prussian Germany did not know how to win the love of its subjects. The eternal authoritarianism of the state alienated its citizens. The state was everything, the individual nothing. He has no other freedom, right and self-determination than that given to him by the state: for the state is the sole source of national guilt, this was the illness of which our German Reich, in spite of its splendour, pined away and died—the idea of the deified state, all powerful and responsible to nobody."[114] Paul Claudel, beyond the Rhine, said this to the Germans in 1919: "Oh Nation, full of blind will and physical gluttony! Badly baptised nation, have you now enough of your gross appetite to be God himself? ... It was the enthusiasm for death which took hold of you, as hope took hold of others. You don't know really what you want. You do not want to conquer, you want to die. It is death alone which you bring with you. It is death alone which can satisfy your desire."[115]

Today, however, after Germany's downfall, a sensible German, the liberal General von Senger und Etterlein, says that Germany has not had a revolution since the 16th century. While Great Britain had developed very differently, Germany had always remained a country which had patiently accepted the authority of its many monarchs and of governments which were only responsible to the rulers, not to the nation. The principle of leadership had always been all-powerful in Germany.[116]

Notes

1. Buchheim, *op. cit.*, p. 85.
2. *Der voelkische Beobachter,* December 31, 1939.
3. E. Salomon. *Der Fragebogen.* Hamburg, 1951, p. 698.
4. *Oesterreichische Rundschau.* Wien, LVIII, p. 109.
5. *Denk ich an Deutschland,* 1959, p. 8.
6. *Ibid.*
7. Zedlitz-Truetzschler, *op. cit.*, p. 215.
8. E. Ludwig. *Wilhelm II.* Berlin 1926, pp. 175-176.
9. *Geist und Zeit,* 1961/III.
10. J. Braunthal. *Geschichte der Internationale.* Hannover, 1961, p. 282.
11. *Ibid.*, p. 275.
12. H. Treitschke. *Deutsche Geschichte im 19.Jahrhundert.* Leipzig, 1875-1894, Vol. IV, p. 57.
13. Foerster. *Erlebte Weltgeschichte,* p. 45.
14. *Gewagtes Leben.* Koeln, 1958, p. 382.
15. Foerster. *Erlebte Weltgeschichte,* p. 115.
16. *Meine Zeit.* Amsterdam, 1950, p. 15.
17. Eduard Hemmerle. *Der Weg in die Katastrophe.* Muenchen, 1948, p. 23.
18. Pross. *Die Zerstoerung der deutschen Politik,* pp. 122-123.
19. F. Wedekind. *Chansons.* Re-issued, Muenchen, after the war, pp. 28-31.
20. Zedlitz-Truetzschler, *op. cit.*, p. 90.
21. Hemmerle, *op. cit.*, p. 29.
22. Zedlitz-Truetzschler, *op. cit.*, p. 81.
23. *Ibid.*, p. 11.
24. *Nuernberger Nachrichten,* October 20, 1961.
25. F. Meinecke. *Die deutsche Katastrophe.* Wiesbaden, 1946, p. 26.
26. Thomas Mann. *Nachlese.* Frankfurt, 1956, p. 179.

27. Theodor Fontane. *Briefe an Friedlaender.* Heidelberg, 1954, p. 256.
28. Thomas Mann. *Der Alte Fontane, Rede und Antwort.* Berlin, 1922, p. 91.
29. Fontane. *Briefe an Friedlaender*, p. 310.
30. *Sueddeutsche Monatschefte*, Muenchen, December, 1921.
31. *Contemporary Review*, London, December, 1950.
32. K. Assmann. *Deutsche Schicksalsjahre.* Wiesbaden, 1950, p. 29.
33. *Grosse Weimarer Ausgabe.* Part I, Vol. V/I, p. 153.
34. *Conversations with Eckermann*, January 4, 1824.
35. Richard von Kuehlmann. *Erinnerungen.* Heidelberg, 1948, p. 291.
36. *Gesammelte Schriften.* Muenchen, 1921, p. 457.
37. Theodor Adorno. *Prismen.* Frankfurt, 1955, p. 269.
38. Zedlitz-Truetzschler, *op. cit.*, p. 132.
39. Foerster. *Mein Kampf gegen das militaristische und nationalistische Deutschland*, p. 90.
40. Kuehlmann. *Erinnerungen*, p. 291.
41. Karl Kraus. *Apokalypse* (1908). *Untergang der Welt durch schwarze Magie.* Re-issued Muenchen, 1960, p. 14.
42. Zedlitz-Truetzschler, *op. cit.*, p. 225.
43. Dehio. *Deutschland und die Weltpolitik*, p. 15.
44. F. W. Foerster. *Weltpolitik und Weltgewissen.* Muenchen, 1919, p. 125.
45. Heinrich Class. *Wider den Strom.* Leipzig, 1932, p. 203.
46. *Deutschland und der naechste Krieg*, pp. 10, 14, 34, 54, 86, 106.
47. Alfred Kruck. *Geschichte des alldeutschen Verbandes, 1890-1939.* Wiesbaden, 1954, p. 7.
48. *Grosse Gegenwart—groessere Zukunft.* 1913, p. 441.
49. Kruck, *op. cit.*, p. 192.
50. Daniel Fryman (one of Class's pen names). *Wenn ich der Kaiser wär.* Leipzig, 1913, 4th edition, pp. viii, 5, 6, 9, 30, 32, 34, 35, 37, 38, 40, 53, 54, 66, 67, 74-77, 136, 140, 142, 146, 153, 155, 187, 209, 214, 229.
51. *Worte in Versen.* Re-issued Muenchen, 1959, pp. 203-207.
52. Max Montgelas and Professor Walter Schuecking. *Die deutschen Dokumente zum Kriegsausbruch.* Berlin, 1919, Vol. I, p. 11.
53. Ludwig Bittner, Alfred F. Pribram, Heinrich Srbik, and Hans Uebersberger. *Oesterreich-Ungarns Aussenpolitik von der Bosnischen Krise 1908 bis zum Ausbruch des Krieges 1914.* Wien, 1930, Vol. VIII, p. 248.
54. Montgelas, *op. cit.*, pp. 19-21.
55. *Die grosse Politik der europaeischen Kabinette 1871-1914.* Berlin, Vol. 34/I, Document No. 12818.
56. Fuerst Lichnowsky. *Meine Londoner Mission, 1912-1914.* Berlin, 1919, p. 33; Foerster. *Mein Kampf*, p. 114, and *Erlebte Weltgeschichte*, p. 327.
57. *Von Bismarck zum Weltkrieg.* Leipzig, 1933, 2nd edition, 1939, p. 594.
58. *Sueddeutsche Zeitung*, Muenchen, October 13, 1956.
59. *Die Welt*, Hamburg, October 6, 1956.
60. *Erlebte Weltgeschichte*, p. 319.
61. *Gesammelte Schriften*, Vol. VII, p. 167.
62. *Das Neue Reich*, pp. 29-30.

63. *Daily Telegraph,* London, June 1, 1962.
64. *Macht und Mensch,* pp. 3-4, 6-7.
65. "Zola." *Macht und Mensch,* pp. 82, 84, 87, 93-94, 98.
66. *Der Untertan.* Leipzig, 1918, 83rd edition, pp. 50, 57, 65, 67, 124, 476, 504.
67. David Luschnat. *Inflation der Worte.* Berlin, 1957, p. 6. (A private printing sent to the author of this book).
68. *Kriegsschriften des Kaiser Wilhelm-Dank.* Berlin, 1914, Pamphlet 3.
69. *Ibid.,* Pamphlets 38-39.
70. Luschnat, *op. cit.,* p. 5.
71. *Kriegsschriften des Kaiser Wilhelm-Dank,* Pamphlet 1.
72. *Ibid.,* Pamphlet 3.
73. *Ibid.,* Pamphlet 8.
74. *Ibid.,* Pamphlet 21.
75. *Ibid.,* Pamphlet 15.
76. Foerster. *Weltpolitik und Weltgewissen,* p. 90.
77. *Kriegsschriften des Kaiser Wilhelm-Dank,* Pamphlet 11.
78. *Durch Kampf zum Frieden, Tuebinger Kriegsschriften.* Tuebingen, 1914, Pamphlets 12-13.
79. *Ibid.,* Pamphlet 1.
80. *Weltpolitik und Weltgewissen,* p. 87.
81. Karl Kraus. *Weltgericht.* Leipzig, 1919, Vol. I, pp. 183-184.
82. Karl Kraus. *Worte in Versen,* pp. 234-235.
83. Karl Kraus. *Unsterblicher Witz.* Muenchen, 1961, pp. 318-322.
84. *Rasse und Persoenlichkeit.* Muenchen, 1925, pp. 7, 13.
85. *Erinnerungen,* p. 573-575.
86. *Krupp und die Hohenzollern. Aus der Korrespondenz der Familie Krupp 1850-1916.* Berlin, 1956, pp. 143.
87. G. Hilger and A. G. Meyer. *Incompatible Allies.* New York, 1953, pp. 191-192.
88-90. *Deutschlands Kriegsziele.* Leipzig, 1917, pp. 41, 42, 50, 53, 72, 75.
91. E. Eyck. *Geschichte der Weimarer Republik.* Zuerich, 1954, p. 226.
92. *Die Hilfe* (a periodical), autumn, 1917.
93. Philipp Scheidemann. *Memoiren eines Sozialdemokraten.* Dresden, 1930, Vol. II, pp. 49-50.
94. *Erlebte Weltgeschichte,* pp. 85, 275-276.
95. F. Meinecke. *Kuehlmann und die paepstliche Friedensaktion von 1917.* Preussische Akademie der Wissenschaften, 1928, XVII.
96. *Erinnerungen,* p. 517.
97. *Ibid.,* p. 562.
98. *Observer,* London, May 11, 1958.
99. George Kennan. *Das amerikanisch-russische Verhaeltnis.* Stuttgart, 1954, p. 37.
100. G. A. von Mueller. *Regierte der Kaiser?,* pp. 45, 84, 251, 273, 278, 302, 366.
101. Letter to Professor Hans Ehrenburg, April 16, 1917. *Gesammelte politische Schriften.* Muenchen, 1921, p. 469.
102. Wolfgang Foerster. *Ein General Kaempft gegen den Krieg.* Muenchen, 1949, p. 13.
103. *Deutsche Rundschau,* January, 1957.

104. *Mein Kampf*, p. 252.
105. *Weltgericht*. Leipzig, 1919, Vol. II, pp. 179, 188, 189.
106. *Die Fackel*, January, 1919.
107. *Nuernberger Nachrichten*, January 24, 1959.
108. Karl Kraus. *Beim Wort genommen*. Muenchen, 1955, p. 441.
109. *Weltgericht*, Vol. II, pp. 179, 182.
110. *Die dritte Walpurgisnacht*. Muenchen, 1952.
111. Berthold Viertel. *Dichtungen und Dokumente*. Muenchen, 1956, p. 46.
112. *Die letzten Tage der Menschheit*. Wien, 1922, re-issued Zuerich, 1945.
113. Malcolm Hay. *The Foot of Pride*, p. xiii.
114. M. Bierbaum. *Das Leben des Kardinals von Galen*. Muenster, 1956, pp. 125-126.
115. H. E. Holthusen. *Kritisches Verstehen*. Muenchen, 1961, pp. 290-291.
116. *The Listener*, London, June 17, 1954.

12
Republic to Reich

BEFORE THE FIRST WORLD WAR, THE GERMANS COMPLAINED
that the wicked world was encircling them, innocent lambs
that they were, and after their defeat they invented the stab-in-
the-back legend. Now they have invented the legend that the
Treaty of Versailles was responsible for the rise of Hitler. Many
said so before 1933, although Hermann Hesse had told them:
"By falsely disclaiming all war-guilt, shifting all responsibility
for the German conditions on to the shoulders of our 'enemies'
and Versailles, you create, I think, an atmosphere of political
stupidity, mendacity and immaturity in Germany which will
contribute very much to the outbreak of a future war."[1] But
now they are renewing this legend again. Admiral F. Ruge, who
served Hitler, said in a nationalistic soldiers' periodical: "The
Second World War has its roots in Versailles."[2] Promptly he
was made chief of the new German navy and after a year or two
decorated with a high order.

What were the facts?

The Germans had hardly recovered from the shock of November 9, 1918, when they began to spread the lie that they had remained "undefeated at the front." It was President Ebert himself who greeted the returning Berlin regiments with this formula when they marched through the Brandenburg gate with their flags and music bands. "The home front has failed"—this was the other formula which spread rapidly. The historian Hans Delbrueck had in 1917 condemned the irresponsible behavior of the Pan-Germans, and in 1919 he wrote: "We have been defeated because we had no aims which could have been achieved, because our policy lacked all reasonable consideration." But the Pan-Germans clamored: "The nation of Luther and Frederick II will not allow Erzberger and Scheidemann to ruin them!" They announced their program in their Bamberg pronunciamento of 1919: "A planned racial superiority of the German nation by selection of, and help for, all those persons who are gifted in the good old German manner; fight against all those powers which hamper and harm the racial development of our nation, especially the predominance of the Jews in all economic and cultural fields. . . . Our League can feel no confidence in the present government nor does it consider the present state as adequate for the German nation."[3] General Ludendorff said to Heinrich Class, leader of the Pan-Germans: "I am persuaded that the guilt of all our misfortune lies in the fact that the leaders of the army and the Pan-German League did not see eye to eye. Therefore, we must now collaborate all the more!" General Fritsch, who became Göring's and Himmler's victim in later years, soon after 1918 came to the conclusion that Germany would have to win three battles if she was to get a great power again: 1) the battle against the workers, 2) the battle against the Roman Catholic Church, 3) the battle against the Jews. In 1938 he wrote to a friend that Hitler had already won the battle against the working class, and that he was about to win the battle against the Church. "The battle against the Jews is the most difficult now. I hope everybody is clear about the difficulties of this undertaking."[4] For Ludendorff it became daily "clearer" after 1918 that the Jews and Rome had ruined Germany.[5] He had fled the country in the beginning of the revolution because he was afraid of the revenge of the revolutionaries, but he returned very soon and said to his wife: "The revolutionaries were very stupid when they spared our lives. If I should regain power I will not pardon them. I would with a quiet conscience hang Ebert, Scheidemann and their comrades and see them dangle from the gallows."[6] The Kaiser called him the "Siegfried of our age," while calling Hindenburg "our Wotan." Wotan and Siegfried invented the stab-in-the-back legend. Wotan Hindenburg said in 1919: "We are at the end! Like Siegfried who was felled by the spear of Hagen, our harrassed front broke down."[7] As a matter of fact, the German dream of a "German" victory had already come to an end in March, 1918. August 8 was *the* black day and on September 29 Ludendorff insisted on an immediate armistice offer being made to the West, while he and Hindenburg kept wisely in the background. Some people advised Prince Max of Baden to let the generals go themselves with white flags in their hands to beg for an armistice, otherwise they would afterwards make the politicians responsible for it—which they did only a year later. General Groener, one of the leading figures of the time, said: "I was only too pleased that the army and Headquarters remained as free as possible from all responsibility for the unfortunate negotiations from which we could expect nothing beneficial."[8] Quite. The infamous stab-in-the-back legend poisoned the political atmosphere more and more because the nationalists and the Nazis recklessly exploited it. When Erzberger was murdered in 1921, a nationalistc and anti-Semitic newspaper wrote that he deserved "to be dragged to the gallows on a cow-hide, to be branded with red-hot irons and to be hanged."[9] The University of Koeningsberg, however, in 1921 awarded an honorary degree to "the leader whose strong arm carried the immaculate glory of our arms and the splendour of German culture from the shores of the Atlantic to the desert of Arabia."[10] One hundred and fifty years earlier the most famous professor of Koenigsberg University, Immanuel Kant, had published his treatise, *On Eternal Peace,* and formulated his categorical imperative: "Act in a manner that your actions could become universal law." The stab-in-the-back legend was incorporated into *Mein Kampf.* Ludwig von Rudolph, who had been awarded the highest Bavarian order for a deed of bravery in the First World War and who in 1924 had publicly testified that the stab-in-the-back legend was a lie, says today that the French of the Dreyfus period had succeeded in "penetrating the hiding places of their generals," while the Germans of the 1920's felt no need for a regeneration, hailed Hitler, and "greeted him with the subservience of slaves."[11]

Under the influence of his second wife, Mathilde, Ludendorff turned into a really pagan Siegfried. They travelled the country up and down and lectured on Aryan religion. Mathilde Ludendorff wrote books like *Deliverance from Jesus Christ* and *Christmas in the Light of Racial Knowledge,* books about the Elders of Zion, the Freemasons, the murder of Schiller by Goethe. Ludendorff left the Church. In 1935, when he had already for tactical reasons parted with Hitler, he published a short book full of Hitlerian ideas, *Total War,* from which Hitler learned a lot. Ludendorff asserted that all misfortunes of the world derived from "the power of the Jews and the Roman Catholic Church." Christianity, he said, is "an alien religion wholly contradictory to our race"; the Germans needed some "German knowledge of God as outlined in the books of my wife." Further, he said that the total war of the future would be waged not against the armies at the front alone but "against the nations," and the motto would be: "as you do to me, we will do to you."[12] His wife survived him and is still with us, working as the leader of a "Community for the knowledge of God (Ludendorff)," and teaching a religion which agrees "with our racial ideas of God." What this means becomes clear from her assertions that Christianity, with its teaching of "humility before God," has broken the ancient Germanic "pride before God." Christianity is "alien to the German soul because it denies the differences between the races and nations by postulating that all men are equal before God."[13]

At first, Ludendorff and Hitler were intimate friends, and like the grumbling general, Hitler spoke publicly of the "November criminals" who were responsible for Germany's misfortune. Secretly, however, he said that the Social Democrats were to be praised for two important reasons: they had abolished the Hohenzollern dynasty and had preserved and consolidated the unity of the Reich.[14] Had they really done this? The annexationist parties of the right which had gone into hiding after November 9, 1918—their leader, Count Westarp, had even fled abroad—began very soon to regain their wits and start their fight against the new republic. Franz Seldte, who was later to become one of Hitler's most eager supporters, founded the Stahlhelm organization as early as December 25, 1918 in order to counteract the dirty revolution with the spirit of the soldiers from the front, to fight, as the nationalistic writer Werner Beumelburg said in 1939, "the ignominy within and in foreign affairs amidst the general upheaval."[15] The Pan-Germans, back again, said in a proclamation: "We can neither have confidence in the present government nor recognise the republic as befitting the German nation. The present government is responsible for our breakdown. As we knew that our main enemies wanted to destroy the German *Reich,* even the Germans themselves, we ask for a war and the use of every weapon to break the malicious will of our enemies."[16] The industrialists, the rich financiers, and various deposed princes and noblemen financed nationalists of all shades—the very same people who, a few years

later, financed Hitler. Count Westarp and his friend, Count
Freytag-Loringhoven, spoke of "the damned republic,"[17] and
the worst of the Pan-Germans, like Alfred Hugenberg, founded
very early a "German-Racial offensive and defensive organization" with the aim of "informing the public about the character
and extent of the Jewish danger, and fighting it with all political
means."[18] Another extreme nationalist was Karl Helfferich,
whom the reactionary Count Westarp praised warmly for having "opposed the march of parliamentary democracy to conquer
Germany," while calling the true democrats "democratic level-
lers who out of envious mediocrity are against the superiority of
a true leader."[19]

In 1919, the leader of the Pan-Germans, Heinrich Class,
published the eighth edition of his *German History* under the
pen name Einhart. It is known that Hitler read this book "with
deep excitement."[20] What did he read in it? "Nation and Reich
have broken down because they had no leadership." A states-
manlike leader and savior was lacking but a nation could
achieve anything "if it followed a leader with a strong will."
Bethmann-Hollweg had been a narrow-minded and dangerous
man; November 9, 1918 was an ignominious downfall caused
by the November criminals, degenerated madmen. "Parliamentary democracy" was fateful for Germany, as fateful as "the
turning away from the idea of power and of a Führer."[21] Hitler
read all this and decided to become a politician.

Other heroes of the day were the many generals who had
become pensioners of a state which they fanatically hated. One
of them, Colonel-General von Einem, in 1933 confessed that he
had always hated the Social Democrats and had always fought
them with a good conscience because their ideas had been
obnoxious to the Reich. The writer Theodor Plievier wrote a
book about and against them, *The Kaiser Went But His Generals Remained*. A few years later he had to flee his fatherland
because Hitler would have murdered him, and after Hitler's

downfall he described Germany's downfall in three novels, *Stalingrad, Moscow, Berlin*. Some of the Kaiser's generals took part in the Kapp revolt; another, the Austrian general Alfred von Krauss, in 1921 published a much-read book, *The Identity of Politics and War as Starting-Point for a German Strategy*, in which he advised the aggressor to lull the adversary into "the belief that peace was the aim while preparing for war in an un-ostentatious and unprovocative manner."[22] One can be pretty sure that Hitler read this book, too.

There was only one general who behaved differently, Count Paul von Schoenaich, whom we mentioned earlier. After a conventional career in a Prussian Guard regiment he in time recognized "the shortsighted egoism of our right-wing parties." He asked himself why Great Britain had been spared serious upheavals during the last centuries and found the answer: "Because English aristocrats have always recognised the changed times at the right moment and have, in wise forethought though centainly not always with a gay heart, voluntarily sacrificed some of their privileges." He contrasted this behavior of the British ruling class with the "pandemonium and agitation" of the German aristocracy and the extremists on the right who were unable to understand that the time of "the Prussian police state" was over, and blamed the German "schools and universities" for never allowing "any other thought" to be instilled into the heads of the young people "than those which were agreeable to the Establishment." He singled out for rebuke General Bernhardi, "the evil spirit of the Pan-German movement" who, by his books, had "much contributed to the unification of the world against us." Bernhardi understood as little as the other generals that "the old powers and forms of government must entirely disappear" because the supremacy of the army over the civil government had resulted in "slavish obedience on the one hand and arrogant leadership on the other." These arrogant leaders have now invented the stab-in-the-back legend, to put "the blame on others." They incessantly defy and defame the democratic government and say: "In former times everything was monarchical and good, now everything is republican and bad." These diehards shout: "He who is not a conservative is not a decent man"; they hate democracy because democracy "asks for an understanding of another man's point of view. But they do not want reasonable men, they want silly subjects." During the war, "the German nation has been deceived by the government and the generals"—and now the diehards favor "a mad policy"; in their eyes "the apostle Paul would be 'nationally pernicious.'" Their ideal is Frederick II. Thus they have "terribly poisoned" the political atmosphere. General Schonaich warned in vain: "The world will not be saved by Germandom."[23] Needless to say, this brave general was as much hated by all reactionaries as were Count von Zedlitz-Truetzschler because of his book about the Kaiser's Court and Professor F. W. Foerster because of his post-war books. But General Schoenaich was not to be deterred. In 1925 he published, in collaboration with Otto Lehmann-Russbüldt, a leader of the German League for Human Rights, and some other courageous Germans, a *White-Book About the Black Reichswehr*. Lehmann-Russbüldt published another book about the *Reichswehr* in 1930. General Schonaich was arrested when Hitler came to power but released after a few months. Lehmann-Russbüldt, who in 1918 had published a paperback about the real causes of Germany's defeat in the West, in 1933 fled to Great Britain where he spent the twelve years of Hitler's millennium. After the war he wrote *Deutsche Generalfeldmarschälle und ihr Generalgeldmarschall,* the latter being Hjalmar Schacht, "more efficient than all the alchemists of the Middle Ages," who succeeded in "giving the lie to the old truth that you can fool some men all the time, everybody for some time, but not everybody all the time." Field-Marshal Hindenberg, however, says Lehmann-Russbüldt, was "the rope on which the Weimar Republic struggled to its death to make room for the military autocracy of an unmilitary paranoic."[24]

Professor Foerster, in his post-war books, told the Germans that it was true that the German nation as a whole had not wanted the war of 1914-1918, but that many industrialists had wanted it. Most fateful had been the fact that Germany, by her silly and challenging behavior during the previous twenty years, had aroused the suspicion that she was aiming at war, and she must blame herself for the consequences of this behavior. It was only a legend that she had been "encircled"; Germany had isolated herself by various false steps and forced the others to face the possibility of a German aggressive war. Germany, the courageous professor said, began this isolation at the Hague when a new peace covenant was negotiated there by many nations. Germany was also to be blamed for giving Austria a free hand against Serbia in July, 1914, and for aiming at a "Hindenburg peace" in 1916 and 1917 when a compromise peace appeared to be possible. Professor Foerster had tried to warn his compatriots at the time through an article "A German Peace or a Christian Peace." Lastly, Germany lost all "trust of the Allies in the seriousness of her will to compromise" by forcing on Russia the atrocious peace treaty of Brest-Litovsk.

Like General Schoenaich, Professor Foerster condemned the German way of "subordinating politics to militaristic interests," while France had already, at the time of the Dreyfus affair, "repelled the last onslaught of a militaristic cast." Now that the war was lost, he suggested to the Germans "to sever post-war Germany completely from its militaristic and autocratic past," to give up the Bismarck tradition and to return to the Humboldt tradition.[25]

But most Germans refused to listen to what these judicious men said. Many preferred to listen to what General Bernhardi told them in his post-war book, namely that he would never have thought possible "the depth of depravity to which the

German nation had sunk in 1918." The Germans listened to this unteachable general who had remained after the Kaiser had gone; it took them only ten years to sink into an abyss of depravity never before heard of in the history of nations. "I most decidedly hope," Bernhardi said, "that the Germans who now seem to have fallen into egoism and materialism will summon up their courage, and that the future will find a regenerated nation, which will prove worthy of its great forefathers and visualise the war dictated by reality."[26] They did. Hitler, one can be sure, had also read Bernhardi's postwar pronunciamento.

The remnants of the German army were commanded by General von Seeckt, a strict monarchist who turned the army of 100,000 men allowed by the Treaty of Versailles into a cadre capable of rapid expansion when the suitable occasion arrived, as it did in 1935. Only reliable officers of the Imperial army and sons of peasants were recruited, but no townspeople with "left-ist" affiliations, that is genuine republicans. Seeckt said in 1931: "The Prussian idea of state is as different from the liberal British idea of state, which regards the state as an insurance agent for business, as from the Marxist idea of state, the automatised bee-state. Prussian spirit is the result of Prussian history, it is a militarist spirit, as represented by the greatest piece of art, the Prussian army."[27] The funds allocated to Seeckt's army often found their way into the coffers of illegal organizations which, a little later, formed the nucleus of the SS and SA.

Germany's unstable democracy was surrounded by enemies. In March, 1920, Kapp and General von Luettwitz started their *coup d'etat,* which broke down only because of the general strike of the workers' unions. After this the enemies of the young German democracy resorted to Vehme murders. They were organized by members of the many secret organizations which sprang up everywhere in Germany, para-militaristic nationalists, at first commanded by Count von der Goltz, and later by other released officers. They, too, spoke of the November criminals and the Jewish republic, and promised revenge for November 9, 1918. The most notorious of those organizations were Consul, Ehrhardt, Oberland, Rossbach, Fridericus Rex, and the Black Reichswehr. When the last mentioned was founded, a "traitor" was shot, and over his corpse ("It was a lofty hour") the members swore an oath of allegiance to their leader. Curt Martens spoke in 1925 of the terrible caricature of the secret organizations and added: "The same powers shovel a grave for the German nation."[28] In 1921 a book was published, *Two Years of Murders,* to be followed by another, *Four Years of Political Murders* in 1924, and by three others in the following years, *Nationalist Conspirators, Traitors Will Be Murdered, Let Heads Roll.* One of the first victims was the former naval captain, Hans Paasche, who, horrified by the abyss torn up by the war between Germany and the rest of the world, had confessed his "war guilt," because he had "recognised the madness already before the war, but had placated his conscience and remained silent. Our guilt consists in the fact that under the pressure of our education and the prejudices of our past we have done nothing for freedom." He had condemned all the Pan-German "agitators" and the German professors who had "served militarism." He had told the Germans to give up their prejudices" and to realize that they had "been educated to be slaves."[29] For this he was murdered in 1920. Mathias Erzberger, member of the Reichstag, was murdered by members of Consul because in 1918 he had signed the armistice. It was he who was responsible, they said, not Ludendorff. Karl von Helfferich, an extremist politician of the right, said on June 29, 1919, at the University of Berlin, that the German politicians had betrayed the nation in the hour of decision, and in the unparalleled confusion that reigned at Weimar "the Reich-destroyer Erzberger who had been Germany's most fateful man during the war, had got to the helm and had brought the ship into the harbour of ignominy." The result of these words were the shots which a year later killed Erzberger. More than 400 honest Germans were murdered in this manner. The murderers, when caught, received only light sentences which encouraged new murders. These murderers later became leaders in Hitler's SS and SA.

The next victim was Foreign Secretary Walter Rathenau. In 1914 he had said that history would prove to be senseless if it permitted the Kaiser to ride as a victor through Brandenburg Gate. But while disliking the Kaiser, he served his fatherland and organized Germany's raw materials. The playwright Gerhart Hauptmann said of him in 1917 that he combined in his personality qualities that cancel each other out in other men. The merchants regarded him as a merchant, the statesmen as a statesman, the philosophers as a philosopher, the sociologists as a sociologist, the technicians as a technician, the artists as an artist.[30]

After Germany's defeat he followed the only policy which could lead Germany out of the cul-de-sac into which the Kaiser had brought her. By fulfilling the terms of the Treaty of Versailles he tried to win the confidence of former enemies in the hope of slowly making them realize that a new friendship with a genuinely democratic Germany would be worthwhile. Mr. Terrence Prittie said of him a few years ago that very likely he would have led Germany onto a path of collaboration with the West. But the nationalistic Finance Minister, Karl von Helfferich, was one of the most fanatical adversaries of Rathenau, and in the streets they sang: "Kill Walther Rathenau, the damned Jewish sow." After a hysterical speech by Helfferich in the Reichstag, Rathenau was murdered on June 24, 1922. Erich von Salomon took part in the murder and got five years' imprisonment. (Today he is earning a lot of money with his cynical autobiography.) By what a pernicious spirit the murderers were filled with can best be gathered from this short dialogue:

" 'No nation which in its vigour is out to become perfect, will give up the claim to rule.'

" 'In what dream is the fulfillment of this vigour revealed,'
" 'In the victory of Germandom over the world.' "[31]

After the murder of Rathenau, German currency began
rapidly to fall. The Germans, as usual, put the blame on the
Western Powers. They could have stemmed inflation if they had
really wanted to do so, but they preferred to use it as a political
weapon for defying the West. Professor M. J. Bonn, who died
in London, had always held that in order to prove Germany's good will stabilization must precede any negotiations
about reparations. The big industrialists and the right wing
parties collaborated in sabotaging the Treaty of Versailles and
went on blaming it for conditions in Germany instead of stabil-
izing the mark. At the time of Rathenau's murder the Reichs-
bank would have had enough money to do this, but there were
too many industrialists prospering on the ruin of German currency. One of them was Hugo Stinnes; another was Hugenberg.
Professor Bonn urgently advised Reichs-Chancellor Wirth to
arrest Stinnes because of his "high treason,"[32] and the publicist Felix Pinner denounced him as one of the main representatives of the hypertrophic materialism which was so very
characteristic of a Germany that had failed really to regenerate
herself after her defeat in 1918. He called him "a superman of
unhealthy blood, drawing strength from the destructive powers
of his age." Germany, by regarding him not as her destroyer but
her leader, had only proved that she was continuing to worship
the god of success.[33] Hugenberg, one of the managing directors
of the Krupp concern, shortly after 1918 bought up two-thirds
of all German newspapers and poisoned large parts of the
German public with a wild nationalism and anti-Semitism.
Many small industrialists and large parts of the middle class
were ruined by the inflation and became more and more susceptible to the fanaticism of a new prophet, Adolf Hitler.

Where did he come from? He was, as Professor Foerster
points out, the product of Austrian anti-Semitism, the product
of the Austrian mentality which, as Karl Kraus tells, made

inhuman judges of the First World War force old Serbian and Ukrainian peasants, condemned to death for alleged spying, to dig their own graves before being shot, and the product of a country where anti-Semitism had been flourishing since the 1870's or earlier. When, around 1850, *The Maccabeans* by Otto Ludwig was performed in Vienna, the public laughed at "the synagogue in the Burgtheater."[34] The worst anti-Semites were among the university students, who refused to duel with Jewish students after they had offended them.

The Viennese Lord Mayor, Karl Lueger, founder of the so-called Christian-Social Party, which was neither Christian nor social but simply anti-Semitic, was one of the main teachers of Hitler. (On February 12, 1913, the brother of the new leader of this party, Paul Kunschak, murdered the Social-Democratic leader Schuhmeier.) Hitler's other Austrian educator was the politician Baron Schönerer, who had written in 1882: "We Pan-Germans regard anti-Semitism as the key point of our national ideology, the strongest expression of a genuine national persuasion. It is the greatest idea of our century."[35] He won young Hitler's full sympathy because of his rhymed slogan: "Without Habsburg, Judah, Rome, we shall build the German dome."[36] During the years when Hitler tramped up and down the streets of Vienna, Dr. Arthur Schnitzler, a famous Jewish playwright, wrote his *Professor Bernhardi,* which was published in 1912 but could only be shown on the stage after the downfall of the Austrian monarchy. Professor Bernhardi is surrounded by representatives of the "united clerical and anti-Semitic parties." Professor Filitz speaks of the "idée fixé" of the Jews and finds their spying of anti-Semitism "ridiculous." Professor Ebenwald calls himself "a leader of the German nationalists of the most extreme kind—Watch on the Rhine, Bismarck Oak, Waidhofen Resolution not to give satisfaction to Jews." We hear of "the Judaisation of the University," we hear "Down with the Jews!" and "Down with the Freemasons!" Professor Bernhardi says:

"May God forgive them—they know damn well what they are doing."[37]

Hitler's third Austrian educator was Georg Lanz, a defrocked monk who had turned into a pagan racialist. In 1900 he founded a secret order, *Novi Templi,* to whom many Austrians and Germans flocked. These new Knight Templars had to be of pure Aryan race, with blonde hair and blue eyes. God's command: "Thou shalt love thy neighbor as thyself," was changed by Lanz into: "Thou shalt love people of thy race." In 1905 he began to publish a periodical, *Ostara,* adopting, without any legitimate right, the noble name of Lanz von Liebenfels. That Aryan periodical soon had 100,000 subscribers. In 1907 he hoisted on the tower of his *Ordensburg* Werfenstein a flag showing the swastika in the middle. Hitler, when living in Vienna in 1908 and 1909, devoured Lanz's periodical and once visited him to ask for some issues which he had not read. Other readers of this pernicious periodical were Ludendorff and his second wife Mathilde, the racialist Hans Gunther, and Hitler's bard, Dietrich Eckart.

What did Hitler read in the issues of *Ostara?* "Are you blonde? Are you fed up with the reign of the rabble? Are you blonde? Then you are the creator and savior of civilisation!" He read an "Easter Sermon for the European Master Race," he read that "the racial idea is the aristrocratic principle of our age," and that "the superior race is the source of justice." He read that Jesus had been a blonde and blue-eyed Aryan who had taught that one should keep one's own race unadulterated, that he was "the prototype of the Aryo-heroic man." He read: "The blonde man is always a Siegfried and Knight who performs heroic deeds for his beloved, kills dragons, passes through flickering flames, defeats giants and frees his princess." Hitler also read a prayer which showed him his role: "Lead us to the last and decisive battle against East and West, so that the earth steams of the blood of the mixed races, a worthy sacrifice

to the Aryan god to thank him for delivery from great distress."
Lanz von Liebenfels boasted in 1928: "It was we who hoisted
the swastika for the first time more than fifty years ago—it is
today the symbol of an important and hopeful movement which
originated from us."[38]

In 1913 Lanz praised Karl Kraus as "the savior of Aryan
Germanism" because of his fight against his corrupt age. When
he learned that that savior was of Jewish origin, he corrected
himself by asserting that the Jews were a Mediterranean and
Mongoloid mixture of races, and that their higher and nobler
types always showed "heroic traits. Among that blond type of
Jews were many men of genius superior partly by intellect,
partly by character. Spinoza and Karl Kraus, dedidedly the
greatest writer of German prose today, belong to this type
which combines great intellect and a noble heart."[39]

At about the same time, the Viennese playwright Arthur
Schnitzler, in *Professor Bernhardi,* made a Jewish doctor say it
was no use turning the left cheek to an anti-Semite who has hit
you on the right cheek, for he would not hesitate to hit the
other, too. Nora, Countess of Wydenbruck, tells that her uncle,
on seeing her play with Jewish children, warned her not to do
this because the Jews had crucified Christ. Martin Freud, the
son of Sigmund Freud, tells the story of an Austrian colonel
who was furious when a Jew entered his office: "He wanted to
see *me.* Well, I expect you can guess what happened. I threw
him out."[40]

It was this kind of Austrian air which Hitler inhaled, not
the air of Mozart and Beethoven, Schubert, Grillparzer, Stifter,
Hofmannsthal. No wonder that he found so many enthusiastic
followers in Austria. In 1925 the Austrian National Scoialists
published a pamphlet, *Depravation of Our Race by the Jews;*
when a Zionist Congress was held in Vienna in the same year,
the leading anti-Semitic newspaper said: "Men, guard your
womenfolk against those dreadful sons of the desert."[41] Sig-

mund Freud wrote to Romain Rolland in 1923: "I belong to a race which in the Middle Ages was held responsible for all epidemics and which today is blamed for the disintegration of the Austrian Empire and the German defeat." In 1933 he said: "My judgment of human nature, above all the Christian-Aryan variety, has little reason to change." A few days after the civil war in Austria, he wrote to his son Ernst: "The future is uncertain; either Austrian fascism or the swastika. Our attitude to the two political possibilities for Austria's future can only be summed up in Mercutio's line in *Romeo and Juliet:* 'A plague on both your houses.'" When he reached the British shores he said: "This England is . . . a blessed, a happy country inhabited by well-meaning, hospitable people."[42] Friedrich Heer, an Austrian Roman Catholic, says today: "No history of Austrian anti-Semitism has yet been written. National-Socialist anti-Semitism is but a late chapter of a centuries-old development." Austrians pretend to be proud of such famous Jewish countrymen as Werfel, Hofmannsthal, Kafka, Roth, Broch, Freud, Lise Meitner, but in reality "they do not want to know anything of these great Austrian Jews."[43]

One of Hitler's first public utterances in post-war Germany was words of praise for the murderers of Rathenau, one of whom was an ardent adherent of his. He praised them warmly as "martyrs" for a better German future. A year later, together with Ludendorff, he attempted his *coup d'etat* which brought him into the dock and into prison. German law said: "Any person trying to change the constitution of the German Reich by force, is liable to imprisonment for life."[44] But Hitler got away with a ridiculously short sentence. Therefore, Hermann Hesse said in 1946: "Hitler could perfectly well be seen through since 1923, and when he was not shot, but spoiled in his prison everybody who cared to know knew what would become of Germany."[45]

Landsberg was a jolly prison for Hitler. He was permitted to write *Mein Kampf,* which was published when he came out and hailed by millions.

What did he tell the Germans in it? The main points must be quoted here because the Germans of today disclaim any responsibility for the man whom they chose to be their leader.

It was a dirty lie of the Jews and the Marxists, he said, that Ludendorff had been responsible for the German disaster of 1918, the man who with super-human will power had actually tried to stem the catastrophe which he had foreseen.[46]

Then he spoke of "the original sin"[47] of mankind, the sin against blood and race. The question of race was the key to any understanding of history and culture. A state which, in an age of the poisoning of the races, devoted its energies to the cultivation of its best racial elements is bound to become the master of the earth one day. "A stronger race will drive out the weaker races as the life force will, in the last resort, break the ridiculous shackles of so-called humanity again and again in order to replace it by the humanity of nature which destroys the weak to make room for the strong."[48] In great contrast to the Aryans, however, were the Jews, those eternal fission-fungi of mankind, those parasites under whom the whole of decent humanity was suffering, particularly in Hitler's day, the Jews, whose lives are "based on a single big lie."[49] They were the masters of Great Britain, while France became daily more and more Negroid. They aim at "the complete destruction of Germany." In short, "while fighting the Jews, I am doing the work of God."[50]

These were the most obscene lies ever uttered by a German anti-Semite. The Jewish community in Germany had contributed more to the German nation that any other Jewish community to the nation in which it lived. It had produced many famous poets, writers, painters, composers, philosophers, professors, doctors, and actors. But, as Mr. A. J. P. Taylor said, "people talk nonsense in every country, but only the Germans take it seriously. . . . Hitler's so-called ideas are merely the disjointed ramblings of talk in a public-house, but Hitler put them in print, took them seriously and counted on the Germans doing the same."[51] The judges in Nuremberg said that from these words of Hitler a direct road led to the gas chambers, that *Mein Kampf* had not been written in a secret language. Dr. Max Domarus, a decent German, says in his introduction to Hitler's speeches: "Antisemitism, hidden or outspoken, prevailed in Germany for centuries. This irrational German antipathy against the Jews was furthered by the state separation of the Jews in ghettos, by restricting them to certain trades and other extraordinary laws. They were socially discriminated against till the First World War and could become neither civil servants nor officers. Both Christian denominations branded the Jews as the crucifiers of Jesus, and if the Devil was depicted in the arts, he was given Jewish features. Jews were blamed for all German political misfortunes from the early Middle Ages till the 19th and 20th centuries."[52]

Hitler called democracy a ridiculous extract from dirt and fire, and a precursor of Marxism; it was "the instrument of that race which, because of its hidden aims, has to fear the lights of the sun," namely the "dirty and lying" Jews. "Genuine, German democracy" was something entirely different, for it allowed for "the free election of a Führer. The Pantheon of history is not for sneaks but for heroes."[53]

In by no means secret words he then spoke of his plans, of the eternal privileges of might and power, of the struggle of the mightier races against the inferior ones and of the annihilation of the latter by the former. Peace, he pronounced, can never be achieved "by the palm branches of weeping, pacific old women but by the victorious sword of a master race enlisting the world into the service of a higher culture."[54] The will to life of the German nation will have to be gathered "for a definite fight against France" before acquiring new living space for this nation "in another direction." He was very precise about it. It was nonsense, it was a crime, he said, only to aim at restoring the pre-war frontiers of 1914. He ridiculed those scribes who said that a war of this sort meant "a violation of holy human rights."[55]

New living space, he said, could only be won "at the cost of Russia." Therefore Germany would have "to set off again on the road of the former Order of Knights to secure, by the German sword, the soil for the German plough and the daily bread for the German nation. Our right to this is not smaller than the right of our forefathers."[56] If the National Socialist movement wants to gain "the pathos of a great mission for our nation" in world history, it must give up all the aimlessness in foreign affairs so characteristic of Germany up to now, and collect all the vigour of the nation for the march on that road which will lead out of the present narrowness of our living space "towards new soil."[57] He decided to put an end to the German foreign policy of pre-war times, and "to start again where things were interrupted . . . six centuries ago. We stop the eternal German march to the South and West and turn our eyes eastwards. If we think of new land and soil in the Europe of today, we can in the first instance only think of Russia and its subjected border states."[58] He and his fellow Germans, he proclaimed, were "chosen by fate to become witnesses to a catastrophe which would be the most gigantic proof of the *voelkische* racial theory."[59] What became of this mad "prophet" twenty years later was described in detail by Professor H. R. Trevor-Roper in *The Last Days of Hitler*.

At the main trial at Nuremberg, on July 30, 1946, we heard these words from *Mein Kampf:* "By clever and constant propaganda you can persuade a nation that heaven is like hell and, vice versa, the most wretched life is like paradise." This persuasion lasted through all the twelve years of Hitler's millennium. The German writer Ernst Niekisch, of whom we shall hear more later on, reminded us after the war of Hitler's opinion, as expressed in *Mein Kampf*, "that a certain factor of 'truth' lies in the magnitude of a lie," that masses "fall easily victims of big lies" as their "minds" are "primitively simple."[60]

The German-Jewish writer Hermann Kesten says today that Hitler, "won the votes of the Germans by preaching hatred. He said heads would be chopped off, and his nation hailed him. He promised to exterminate the minorities in Germany, they hailed him for that, and he exterminated the minorities in Germany." Or another occasion, under the heading *Quo Vadis Germania?*, he said that he had witnessed four different German systems, three of which "went down in blood and fire, like Babylon, like Ninive, like Sodom and Gomorrha." Hitler became "the Führer of the Germans, their demi-god to whom they sacrificed everything, religion and morality, reason and liberty, their brothers, sons, and fathers, their neighbours in Europe, the Jews, their conscience. They murdered to please him, they died to please him."

And today? "Just as under the Kaiser, in the Weimar republic and in the Third Reich, so in the Bundesrepublik political and social morality, reason, art and literature, and a great part of the intellectuals are in opposition again, a minority without any influence."[61] Ludwig von Rudolph says today: "Then [1925] no historian warned against the effusions of a monomaniac. If they had read his book and drawn the right conclusions—who knows what we would have been spared?"[62] Even today, von Rudolph said on another occasion, the German historians adhere to "the methods of the men around Treitschke. They evade the issue by calling the events from 1933 to 1945 a 'tragic fate.' In an earlier period, the seeds of the irresponsible historians of the Kaiser came to full blossom. In the 1920s they blossomed again, and after 1933 they filled the whole earth with their hideous crimes." He reminds us of a spiteful word of Kiderlen's: "A press campaign of four months, and you can persuade the German nation of every stupidity," and adds that even today, after catastrophes, the Germans can still be talked into everything.[63]

Hitler was by no means the first German with a *Drang nach Osten*. Many a German before him conceived the mad idea of "a nation without living space," as Hans Grimm called the Germans. Julius Froebel foresaw the coming of Hitler in 1859 when he said: "What the German nation longs for is power—power—power! The man who gives them power will receive more honour than he can think of."[64] Paul de Lagarde, rightly regarded in the Third Reich as a forerunner of Hitler, told the Russians in 1886 that they should show their good will by "voluntarily" retreating to the Black Sea and leaving the whole interjacent territory to the Germans. "We need land before our door-step. If Russia refuses, we shall be compelled [!] to expropriate her, to go to war against her. The Germans are of the opinion that they have a mission for all nations on earth."

Further he asked for Metz, Luxembourg, and Belfort ("absolutely indispensable") in the West, for Trieste, the mouth of the Danube, and Austria, which had no right to exist and the nations of which were "only material for new Germanic structures."[65] In the 1890's the Pan-Germans took over from there and asked that the German *Drang nach Osten* should be awakened again even if "such inferior little nations like Czechs, Slovenes and Slovaks should forfeit their existence, which is no use to civilization anyway."[66] The Kaiser wrote on July 25, 1895: "I am devoted with all my heart and brain to the aim of forging the German tribes all over the world, especially in Europe, into a unity in order to protect us against a Slav and Czech invasion which is threatening us."[67] In 1896 another forerunner of Hitler said that "if the welfare of our fatherland should make necessary the conquest, subjugation, expulsion, extermination of other nations, we must not allow ourselves to be deterred from it by Christian or humanitarian scruples."[68]

In 1903, the anthropologist Ludwig Woltmann wrote: "It is the mission of the German race to rule the earth, exploit the treasures of nature and human labour, and shape the passive races to be servants of their culture."[69] In 1905 the leader of the Pan-Germans, Ernst Hasse, spoke of the "German master race" and the need "to condemn the Europeans of other tribes which live among us or immigrate to us, namely Poles, Czechs, Jews, Italians, etc., to a position of helots. One has to be consequent and not give these aliens the same political and economic rights as the Germans."[70] In 1904 the anti-Semite Friedrich Lange wrote with a view to the Eastern Europe: "Every manly German deed by which the barriers in these regions are pushed forward, should gain us Germans new territory and make it rapidly German. This is the only lesson we can learn from the history of our wars against the Slavs—no other."[71] In 1907 Erich Dombrowski, editor of an influential German newspaper today, wrote in the influential *Die Neue Rundschau* that the immense regions of sleepy Russia were positively clamoring for cultivation. "Here we have a colonizing task before us which could not be imagined more magnificent and lucrative. Our slogan should be: To the East! Today it is still possible to subjugate Russia economically and make it dependent on us."[72] In 1912 General Bernhardi drew attention to the strange fact that the Dutch, racial kinsmen of the Germans, and their territory, were "outside the German sphere of power," and so were the Baltic provinces of Russia, which had once been flourishing regions of German culture. "It is our duty to recover our losses."[73] In 1922, German Foreign Minister Wirth said to Count Brockdorff Rantzau: "The only chance I see for us to rise as a great power is for the German and Russian peoples to work together as neighbors . . . and there is one thing necessary, that Poland must be destroyed. My policy is directed at this goal."[74] Professor Gerhard Ritter said about the Pan-Germans after Germany's second collapse: "It was they who propagated, in a terrifying manner, all those ideas which we have got accustomed to regard as the poisonous flowers of National-Socialist propaganda. They earned us the enmity of the whole world. The parallelism is so astonishing that it is well worth considering whether Adolf Hitler had been poisoned by the Pan-German literature in his early days."[75]

It was Hitler who promised to the Germans those old German dreams. "Germany is not a world power today. . . . Germany will either be a world power or it will not be at all."[76]

When Hitler after eighteen months left Landsberg he could have been expelled from Germany as an undesirable foreigner; this is what any decent government would have done in a case like this. Count Lerchenfeld, the Bavarian Prime Minister, a liberal and honest man, said to Herr von Kahr when he had to yield his office to him: "Stamp this out, for it will become frightful and set the world on fire!"[77] But Hitler was allowed to take up where he had left off after his abortive revolt. He practiced what he had taught in *Mein Kampf,* namely that revolutions come about by the magic of words. So he spoke and spoke, rambled and cursed and lied, and more and more Germans shouted: "Heil Hitler!," "We thank our Führer!," "All power to the Führer!," "Germany awake, perish Judah!," "When the blood of the Jews will splutter from our knives, we shall feel all the better for it!," "Tremble, ye nation of mazzoth swallowers, the night of the long knives draws nearer!," "We shall march on when everything falls to pieces. For today Germany is ours, and tomorrow the whole world!" The Polish writer Czeslaw Milosz said after the war: "'And tomorrow the whole world,' sang the SS men, while black clouds of smoke were ascending from the crematoria of Auschwitz."[78] Millions of Germans hailed the man who in *Mein Kampf* had spoken of the stupidity of the masses who believe lies all the more eagerly the bigger they are. He knew that people can be made to see heaven in hell, and hell in heaven, by continuous propaganda.

The wild agitation of Count Westarp, Baron Freytag-Loringhoven, Ludendorff, and Hitler went on; Frederick II of Prussia was glorified in films such as *Fridericus Rex, The Choral of Leuthen, The Flute Concert of Sanssouci, The Mill of Sanssouci, The Dancer of Sanssouci, The Old Fritz,* in spite of what E. M. Arndt had said of him more than a hundred years earlier: "His greatness was Germany's ruin, and his memory is Germany's curse. He has never thought of, nor worked for, human freedom, or the honor and the life of the nation."[79] At the same time, Chancellor Stresemann followed the only possible policy, inaugurated by Rathenau. Undeterred by the barbarous right wing slogans of "High Treason" and "Jewish Republic," he took up the much maligned "policy of fulfillment" of the Versailles Treaty in order to win again the confidence of the Western Powers.

After Ebert's sudden death on February 28, 1925, the right wing parties would very much have liked to put up a Hohenzollern prince as their candidate for the presidency, but in the end they chose as their candidate 79-year-old Hindenburg, the man who had once said that he had only read two books in his life, the Bible and the drill-book, and who, in a talk before school children, had told them that it would be they "who would one day enter Paris again as victors, as their forefathers had done."[80] Hermann Hesse said in 1954 that the Germans, by choosing Hindenburg, had "opened the door to the terrible things which were to come. Even my nearest relatives in Germany, even my sisters had voted for the senile soldier."[81] The genuine republicans, who had put up the democrat Marx as their candidate, shouted: "Who chooses Hindenburg, chooses Hitler!" The Germans listened to that warning as little as, a few years later, they listened to the warning: "Who chooses Hitler, chooses war!" But General Konstantin Hierl, who later became one of Hitler's ministers, wrote in 1928: "We Germans were a nation without living space already before the World

War, and it is of vital interest to us whether we shall remain a nation without living space. We demand the space which belongs to us upon this earth. We know that we shall not be presented with land, and that we are as yet not in a position to break our prison by forceful means. But all our thinking must be directed towards this aim."[82]

During Hitler's war against Russia, General Hierl boasted that he had said as early as 1926: "The present German state is the worst hindrance to a recovery of the German nation, it is only the continuation of the obsolete liberal state of pre-war times, a continuation of deterioration and decay . . . of Jewish money supremacy. The road to German freedom leads over the corpse of this dragon alone." In 1931 he said: "We refute the idea that all men are alike, it has been disproved by science long ago." In 1940 he wrote: "The genius of the Führer will give the Germans immense social and cultural tasks after the war."[83] Nine years after the death of his master, Hierl spoke of his "service for Germany from 1918 to 1945" and said people abroad had formed a "caricature of National Socialism dictated by hatred."[84]

Carl von Ossietzky, however, whose mother had been an ardent Jew-hater but whose political horizon had been widened by travels in Great Britain, and who had been imprisoned under the Kaiser for his attack against General von Deimling and the disclosures about the scandalous affair of Saverne, fought, from 1918 on, against the growing German nationalism and militarism, against the "Black Reichswehr" and the Vehme murders. For this he was imprisoned again. Undeterred, he revealed in 1929 the existence of a secret German Air Force Department within the framework of the Ministry of Transport. He was accused of treason and sentenced to eighteen months' imprisonment. When he came out, he began his fight against Hitler and the "fifteen million voters" who hailed him. "The Nazi brutality, boastfulness and lack of brains are not a deterrent, but an attraction," he wrote in 1932. "The evil and ugly instinct that the great Aryan Führer, who looks like a gypsy baron, has aroused will infect the whole public life in Germany for many years."[85]

Stresemann recognised Alsace-Lorrain as French and received from the French the promise that they would leave the Rhineland sooner than had been agreed in Versailles. He and Briand received the Nobel Price for Peace for the Locarno Pact. But Stresemann's health was being constantly undermined by the wild agitation against his reasonable policy. His death in 1929 proved as much a catastrophe for Germany as that of Rathenau. When posters announcing his death were stuck up in Munich, Thomas Mann overheard the following conversation between two nationalists: "He was lucky," said the one, "for sooner or later a bullet would have found its way into his body." The other: "Main thing he is dead."[86] Thomas Mann quotes Lord d'Abernon, the British Ambassador in Berlin, as saying that it had been Stresemann's merit to have won for defeated and demilitarized Germany the status of equality among her former enemies. In 1928, the writer Bruno Frank drew an ideal picture of Stresemann and Briand in his *Political Short Story*. While the two statesmen, we read, are striving for peace and cooperation, Germany is like "a cauldron full of darkly foaming evil," and the Germans are "so childish as to fall for every squint-eyed flatterer. They allow themselves to be persuaded that they are the nation of all nations, and their passion for romantic self-intoxication is so great that they welcome everybody who recommends himself with a flood of vaporous words as their savior and as a symbol of all the national virtues."[87] Bruno Frank had to leave Germany in 1933 and died in exile. Bernhard Letterhaus, a Roman Catholic politician who did not leave Germany in time, was hanged by Hitler in 1944 because he had said in 1928: "If that demagogue should one day succeed in getting to the top, the beginning of our ruin will start, and we shall have war."[88]

Hitler's thugs and private armies were terrorizing Germany

more and more. A few days before the election of September
14, 1930, Professor Wilhelm Roepke wrote: "There are many
who think things cannot get worse. Why not try out the National Socialist experiment? They are mistaken. Things can get
much worse, if our economic crisis is followed by a crisis of the
state. Nobody who votes for Hitler on September 14 should be
allowed to say later that he had not known what the outcome
would be. He should know that he chooses chaos instead of
order. He should know that he votes for civil war and for senseless destruction."[89] He, too, was not listened to. The election
brought more than a hundred National Socialists into the
Reichstag, and their followers celebrated the victory by beating
up Jews in the streets and smashing the windows of Jewish
shops. The Führer said: "We are aiming at creating a new
master class which will know no mercy, a class which will know
that it has a right to rule because of its better race."[90] Shortly
after that catastrophic election three army officers were accused
in court of smuggling National Socialist literature into the army.
One of the accused was Lieutenant Ludin, later sentenced to
death as a war criminal by the Czechs. Hitler appeared as a
witness and, when asked about his ideas, he told the Court that
after his coming into power heads would roll in revenge for
November 9, 1918.

Brüning, who had become Chancellor on March 28, 1930,
had no easy task when trying to bring order into the German
chaos, and his difficulties were increased by the stubbornness of
narrow-minded Hindenburg, who refused to suppress the National Socialists, if necessary by force, which would have been
an easy matter at the time. In September, 1931, Hindenburg
suffered a mental breakdown lasting for more than a week, and
after that the political enemies of Brüning found it very easy to
undermine his position with the President. On May 30, 1932,
Hindenburg urged Brüning to form a cabinet of the right which
the honest Roman-Catholic Chancellor "of course" refused to
do. Then Hindenburg declared that he would not put his signa-

ture under any law which had not passed through all three
stages in the Reichstag—this at a time when Hitler's wild men
purposely made every parliamentary debate impossible. This
was the result of choosing for the presidency an old man of
nearly eighty without any political experience. When Hindenburg had been elected president for a second time, Carl von
Ossietzky wrote on February 2, 1932: "They stake everything
on a single man of patriarchal age. What an abdication of a
democracy which has long ceased to defend its position and
shelters behind a man of eighty-three. This is no longer politics
but Byzantinism and turns one's stomach." Ossietzky also
wrote: "Small murderers are beheaded, but the big murderer
goes a crown of laurels."[91] Fritz von Unruh, descendant of an
old noble family, son of a Prussian general, the revolutionary
friend of Einstein and Thomas Mann, who shared with the
latter the bitter years of exile, had exclaimed after the foul
murder of Rathenau in 1922: "You are not mighty when
armed! Woe to the nation without a spiritual flame! Such a
nation is doomed."[92] He fled in 1933 and his books were
burned. Ossietzky, who refused to flee, was tortured to death in
a concentration camp. Göring did not allow him to accept the
Nobel Prize which he had been awarded.

Hindenburg refused his signature to Brüning's great plan to
liquidate those estates in the East which could not fruitfully be
managed even with the help of public funds. The East Prussian
Junkers, who more and more influenced Hindenburg, hated Brü-
ining because of his plan. The notorious Junker Oldenburg-
Januschau, who had collected money among the industrialists in
order to buy the estate Neudeck and present it to Hindenburg,
became one of the most intimate friends of his "neighbor," the
president, and persuaded him that the parties, which had ruined
the monarchy, were responsible for everything. Hindenburg also
refused to sign a decree providing for the division of Prussia
into various provinces and the handing over of the adminstra-
tion of the police and the law courts of North Germany to the

Reich, as planned by a conference of the German *Länder* in 1930. This would have made impossible the scandalous Nazi behavior in the Prussian Landtag.[93]

On January 27, 1932, Hitler, introduced by Fritz Thyssen, spoke before an audience of industrialists and quoted the words of General Clausewitz: "War is the continuation of politics by different means." He told them that the existence of Germany was at stake. His racial theories, he asserted, were "the great springs of all hope of a regeneration of the people." Internationalism, democracy, "the madness of parliamentarism," pacifism were dangerous; what was necessary was "the authority of a personality." The guess was theirs whom he meant. "Our nation and our state have once been founded by the absolute right of the *Herrensinn* of Nordic man." The parties of the Weimar Republic had ruined the state—he spoke of 50% Communists when the Communists only represented 17%—and he who had once found only a handful of followers now had millions of them. To save Germany "our nation must be taken into a school of iron discipline." The National Socialist Party which he had founded thirteen years ago, would regenerate Germany but it must be "intolerant against everybody who sins against the nation, intolerant and inexorable against everybody who aims at the destruction of the nation."[94] His audience understood him perfectly well. Millions of his followers said: "Hitler is our last hope. Hitler is the redeeming word for millions. He will conquer because his nation wants him to conquer."[95]

The intrigues of General Schleicher, Papen, Hugenberg, Oldenburg-Januschau, General Blomberg, Colonel Reichenau, and others against Brüning will probably never be satisfactorily disentangled. Brüning's fall, on May 30, 1932, sealed Germany's downfall. The historian Meinecke knew then what, after the collapse of Germany, he said, that "the German nation, under Brüning's leadership, would surely have been capable of conquering the difficult economic and intellectual crisis and escaping the fatal experiment of the Third Reich. Soldiers, industrialists, and agrarians combined to bring about Brüning's fall."[96]

The chief of the Pan-Germans, Heinrich Class, an enthusiastic pupil of Treitschke, wrote in 1932 in his book, *Against the Current:* "I see with satisfaction and hope that many a fruitful idea which I and my friends have first expressed and advocated, has found its way into the souls of millions and more millions of our nation. They seem to prepare a better future."[97] What sort of fruitful ideas had found their way into the souls of many million Germans was revealed in 1932 by a decent German university professor who, however, did not dare to reveal his name. The Pan-German League, he said, is "something specifically German." He denounced as its leaders Ernst Hasse, Carl Peters, Heinrich Class, Managing Director Hugenberg, Count Arnim-Muskau, Count Mirbach, Count Pfeil, Count Reventlow, General Manager Kirdorf, General Superintendant Klingermann, many university professors, the Generals Bernhardi, Gebsattel, Keim, Krauss, and Liebert. The slogan "Germany, awake!" he said, had been coined in 1890. In a Pan-German tract, *Germania Triumphans* (1895), it was asserted "that the preservation of the national and economic strength of the Germans can only be safeguarded by an extension of their political domination, and that German economy could never find an equilibrium without the war which we have long dreaded and long prepared." It would be the task of the Germans to conquer Latvia, Estonia, Lithuania, Poland, Wolhynia, Podolia, South Russia including the Crimea, and to establish eight new German states under German princes. The subjugated provinces would be germanized and their inhabitants driven out. Great Britain would have to be "slowly starved" and conquered. Then the time would come to turn to North and South America.

In 1903 Hasse said: "We should not fall into the sin of

praising peace." In 1905 another of the Pan-German madmen, Joseph Ludwig Reimer, wrote: "Everything depends on our achieving absolute hegemony in Central and Western Europe by crushing France and, at the same time, or immediately afterwards, occupying the German provinces of Austria. . . . You should not say every nation has a right to its existence and its language, nor should you despair and think yourselves inhuman. We must aim at a German Reich, a world Reich of Germanic tribes under German hegemony." In 1911 and 1912 Class and Bernhardi wrote the books which I have analyzed in detail earlier.

During the First World War Class confessed that he and his like had long been waiting for the hour when war would break out; it was the loftiest hour of their lives. General Gebsattel said: "We have been longing for this war because we thought it necessary in view of the wrong road our nation was about to take." Peters wrote in 1915: "It is foolish to talk of the rights of others. Foolish is a justice which is to prevent us from doing to others what we do not like to suffer ourselves."

The anonymous professor mentioned earlier also denounced the para-military *Stahlhelm,* the leaders of which had said soon after the First World War: "It is true that war kills and mutilates, that it destroys industries and paralyses trade. But eternal peace, do not doubt it, would kill something in us which is more valuable than all this. It would slowly kill our heroism. All this chatter of peace goes against our soldierly honour." So they promulgated to their young followers a new Ten Commandments. "Thou shalt be proud of arms. Thou shalt study the lessons of war history. Thou shalt honour the soldierly traditions. Thou shalt make propaganda for the idea of rearmament."

As a contrast to all this barbarism the mournful professor quoted these words of Czechoslavakian President Masaryk in 1922: "If I am to say which civilisation I think to be the highest, my answer is: the Anglo-American. During my stay in Great Britain during the war, I observed the British way of life with very critical eyes and am convinced that the English have, on the whole, come nearest to the ideals of reason."[98]

When Papen formed his cabinet, the aim of the Pan-Germans, who had said the year before that their main point was to ruin Brüning as an enemy of nationalism and "to bring about a government of the national opposition," was achieved.[99] On June 16 Papen restored the freedom of the SA and SS and on July 20, contrary to all law, he removed the constitutional government of Prussia. Jochen Klepper, a devout Lutheran writer, entered in his diary the words of the 19th century liberal writer Gustav Freytag: "Aristocracy and mob are bad enough if they act singly in politics. But whenever they combine forces they are sure to destroy the house in which they convene."[100]

In December, 1932, the National Socialists were bankrupt; the election of November 2, 1932 had cost them much and lost them two million votes. But on January 4, 1933 Papen met Hitler in the house of the banker Schröder in Cologne and a few days later a number of industrialists, including Krupp, Thyssen, Siemens, Bosch, Schröder, Schnitzler, Kirdorf, Vögler, gave Hitler many millions of marks for financing a new election campaign. In 1927 he had promised Kirdorf, an enthusiastic adherent of his ideas, to abolish "the Marxist laws."[101] Thyssen in 1932 presented Hitler with a book, *Leadership: 25 Biographies of Generals of All Ages,* and on April 20 of the same year he sent "the Führer of awakening Germany his most heartfelt wishes on his birthday."[102] (Prince August Wilhelm, too, signed the telegram.) Krupp boasted in 1944 of what he and the other industrialists had done in the years before 1933 which had to be kept secret. "I may say that the German industrialists had, in a noble contest and with conscious gratefulness, made the intentions of the Führer their own and had become his faithful followers."[103] He, like many others, even built fac-

tories near the eastern concentration camps where millions had
to slave before being shot or gassed. Even in Nuremburg prison
Krupp said that he was no idealist, that life was a fight for bread
and power. "In our hard fight we needed hard and powerful
leadership. Hitler gave us both."[104] The American prosecutor
at Nuremberg called the name of Krupp a symbol of those
sinister powers which have been threatening the peace of Europe for decades; during Hitler's war the Krupps employed
people of all occupied countries as forced labor and treated
them in a most inhuman manner. Their profits, which amounted
to 57 million marks in 1935, rose to 97 million marks in 1938
and to 111 million marks in 1941.[105] Monsigniore Borgia of
the Vatican Secretariat told the German resistance fighter Ernst
Niekisch that behind Hitler's anti-Russian policy stood the
German industrialists, avid for Russian oil and manganese.[106]
And Hitler said: "The Hitler youth must be as hard as Krupp
steel."[107]

On August 10, 1932, a number of SA and SS men murdered
the Polish miner Konrad Pietrzuch in Potempa, near Gleiwitz.
They pulled him out of bed and in the most bestial manner
trampled him to death before the eyes of his terrified mother.
They were arrested and condemned to death or hard labor.
Hitler addressed to them a telegram on August 23, 1932, in
which he said: "My comrades! I remain connected with you in
immeasurable faithfulness in view of this horrible judgment.
From now on your freedom is a question of our honour."[108]
And a little later he said: "I am not objective, but subjective.
Those who live and fight and die for Germany have every right,
but those who turn against Germany have no right at all."[109]
And millions continued to shout: "Heil, Hitler!" and "Germany, awake!" The high priest of the movement, Rosenberg,
said: "One Polish Communist, according to this sentence,
equals five Germans, soldiers who had fought in the war. For
National Socialists one soul is not like another, one man not

like another. They know no right as such, their aim is the strong Germanic man!"[110] Hitler said: "We want to select a new master type who knows no pity: a type who knows that, being of a better race, he has the right to reign."[111]

A few months later, Hitler was nominated Chancellor by Hindenburg. Only a short while before Hindenburg had still refused to nominate the "Bohemian Corporal." (Bohemian, because the aged General confused Braunau in Bohemia, which he remembered from Prussia's war against Austria, with Braunau in Upper Austria.)

In 1932 the writer Ernst Niekisch published a pamphlet, *Hitler—a German Disaster* in which he called Hitler "the greatest demagogue who Germany had ever produced." National Socialism, he said, was "not a beginning but an end" of a long development. Hitler had renewed the ancient German dream of the medieval German Reich and preached a "national redemption," and those Germans who did not believe in him would "be damned in the Third Reich" which was "not an earthly state but a sort of God's Kingdom on earth." Hitler's success was due to "the German readiness to believe in false prophets." The end of all the frantic noise would be "a catastrophe." The cover of Niekisch's pamphlet showed Death in the uniform of an SA officer raising his skeleton right arm to greet the German masses and their swastika banners. Even more prophetic were the etchings inside. One depicts Death playing a huge double bass to the Nazi armies standing to attention; another shows an open coffin with a swastika, and a never-ending stream of Germans falling headlong into it. A third etching shows a big vulture hovering over a battlefield covered with Germans and their *Hakenkreuz* banners.[112]

From the very first day of the Third Reich, Niekisch knew that it was "the death struggle of Germany as a Great Power."[113] In January, 1933 he published a cartoon in his periodical, *Resistance,* showing a morass out of which stuck innumerable stretched-out arms, SA flags, and swastika banners. The swamp had already closed over the heads. The caption ran: "The End—the Morass."[114] After the war he said: "Hitler was a symbol of everything awful and terrible that is hidden in the Germans, he let loose all that is subhuman and abysmal in the German soul." He did not leave it at that; he looked into the German past and found that the Germans, unlike the French, proved "incapable of creating a national state by revolution"; war was the mid-wife of the new German Reich of 1871—no tribunes of the people "but victorious generals stood at its cradle"; the Germans always put their hopes in generals and emperors, and this "could only end in a great historical catastrophe." In 1914 they wrote on the trains which carried them to the front: "Still more declarations of war are being accepted here." When they violated the neutrality of Belgium, they said: "Necessity knows no commandment." *Mein Kampf* showed beyond any doubt "what would become of the Germans if that adventurer came to power. . . . The day was full of false prophets, and the most mad and irresponsible of those saviours was Adolf Hitler." The result? "The German nation became the enemy of mankind and humanity."[115]

Niekisch, an upright man, kept in touch with members of the resistance from the extreme right to the extreme left. In 1937 he was arrested and tried for high treason. The President of the Court read to him, from a manuscript which he had written and which had been found, passages stating that the nation had converted itself into submissive cannon fodder for a Führer, and asked him: "What do you say now?" He answered that he could prove the truth of everything he had written and wanted to know who was punishable: the man who was committing unspeakable crimes or the man who simply stated them?[116] The Prosecutor asked for twelve years hard labor, but Niekisch was given a life sentence. The Russians opened his prison after eight years. "I should never," he says now, "have witnessed the day of liberation if I had had to wait for the Germans to liberate me. The German nation did not even on the day of the downfall of the Third Reich prove capable of a revolution against the criminal Hitler regime. . . . World history has become world judgment for Germany. She had been weighed and found wanting and been rejected."[117]

He settled his account with the destroyers of Germany in a detailed book which was published after the war. Article 17 of the 25 articles of Hitler's program, published on February 24, 1920, says: "All soil will be expropriated without payment for the common good." But as the years went on and because Hitler wanted to win the favor of the bourgeois he declard on April 13, 1928 that his adversaries had defamed him, and that his party favored "private property." The industrialists and the militaristic Junkers began helping him to prepare the Third Reich. The inflation and the depression made the industrialists richer and richer and the nation poorer and poorer. But the public was told that the victorious Western powers and the Weimar republic were responsible for their misfortune. "The militaristic leaders, with shameless effrontery, blamed the nation for the German defeat," Niekisch says. The army accepted Hitler as a *Bildungsoffizier*. "The Reichswehr was lucky, for it was in the army that Hitler detected his gift for becoming a tribune and leader of masses." Papen's *coup d'etat* of July 1932 "brought the power of the state into the hands of the bourgeois, the Junkers and the army. . . . The road was free for Hitler."[118]

In the same year that Niekisch's pamphlet was published, a Prussian nobleman, Ewald von Kleist, published a pamphlet, *National Socialism, a Danger,* in which he said that the result of a National Socialist government could be "nothing but chaos."[119] He warned Hindenburg, whom he knew, against Hitler, and Hindenburg agreed with him. But not much later

Hindenburg sent for Hitler and offered him the chancellorship. Jochen Klepper entered in his diary: "Hitler is Reich Chancellor. Again that fateful alliance which Gustav Freytag called the greatest German danger has become a fact: the alliance between aristocrat and mob."[120] Papen, however, representative of a degenerated aristocracy, on November 2, 1933 boasted that he had been chosen by fate to transfer the power to Hitler on January 30, 1933: "God has blessed Germany by sending her such a leader in the days of her greatest distress."[121] Ludendorff, by now an adversary of Hitler, was of an entirely different opinion when he wrote to Hindenburg: "By nominating Hitler Reichs-Chancellor you have surrendered our holy German fatherland to the greatest demagogue of all times. I solemnly prophesy that this miserable man will bring our country to ruin and our nation into inconceivable misery, and that future generations will curse you in your grave for what you have done."[122] He was both right and wrong. Germany was ruined by Hitler but the Germans of today are still worshipping Hindenburg, "the Wooden Titan," as Mr. Wheeler-Bennett called him.

After the war Papen wrote a book full of lies in which he represents himself as an innocent lamb. When the East Germans made their abortive uprising against the Russians on June 17, 1953, he wrote: "Peasants and burghers revolted, ran with naked fists against panzers and machine guns, tore the pictures of the slave drivers from the walls and the red flags from the masts, thus proving that one can die for freedom even under a totalitarian regime."[123] If he and his like had done that in the last days of the German democratic republic or in the first days of Hitler's totalitarian regime, Germany would have been spared the twelve years of the Third Reich with all their catastrophic consequences. All the surviving "heroes" of those critical days are spreading yet another legend by asserting that in the last years before Hitler's advent Germany had only the choice between Communism and National Socialism. This is a brazen lie. The German Communists had not much influence in those days and were never a real danger to the republic. The real danger was the adherents of Hitler, coming from the right wing parties, the remnants of the Pan-Germans, the Soldiers' Leagues and the "unpolitical" Germans who had never bothered about politics and were the first to fall victim to the Pied Piper. "All Germans," Hermann Hesse said, "almost unanimously sabotaged the Republic and have never learned anything whatsoever."[124]

Most responsible of all were the German generals who alone had the power to stop that madman who ran amok among the Germans. Seeckt, a reactionary monarchist, called parliamentarism the cancer of the modern age, and all the generals of the decisive years between 1928 and 1933 were of the same opinion. They did nothing when the SA terrorized the country, and they did nothing when Hitler, contrary to the existing constitution, made himself president after the death of Hindenburg. On December 17, 1932, a law had been passed by a two-third majority providing that in the event of Hindenburg's death the president of the Reichs-Court should take up his office. On March 24, 1933, all parties, except the Socialists, voted to give Hitler the wide powers he had asked for. The Communists had already been arrested and taken to concentration camps—"to educate them," as Minister Frick had said on March 14, "to do fruitful work. They will have an opportunity to do this in the concentration camps."[125] Only because the Communist members of the Reichstag had been arrested could Hitler get a majority of votes for his program. The vote was thus invalid, unconstitutional. The parties who voted for this monstrous law have to share before history their responsibility for all that followed. But they expressly exempted the office of President from the law to which they had given their assent.

The army made no move when the Hitler gangs murdered

Generals Schleicher and Bredow nor when they murdered more than a hundred of their own men on June 30, 1934. General Fritsch did nothing to inform Hindenburg of the murder of the two Generals; he only said; "This man is German's fate, and fate must take its course to the end."[126]

General Blomberg said in 1937: "Born out of the National Socialist spirit, the *Reichswehr* is the champion of the National Socialist *Weltanschauung* and way of life."[127] On July 1, he thanked Hitler in the name of the government for the murders perpetrated on June 30. In 1935, Major Foertsch wrote that the army had "the same aims as the National Socialist Party." In 1936, Lieutenant-Colonel Foertsch wrote: "Adolf Hitler is our Führer. He who is faithful to him lives for Germany. . . . Hitler saw what the old army was lacking. He created a new German army. He had realized with great satisfaction that the Reichswehr had remained in good form in spite of the pacifism and defeatism, the treachery and demoralisation of the November republic, and very early he got in touch with the Reichswehr. The younger officers soon saw that here was a man who was able to restore the German army. The soldiers, too, knew this. No wonder that the army was full of enthusiasm when President Hindenburg made Hitler Chancellor. Any officer who does not approve of National Socialism from the depth of his heart, should quit the army."[128] He followed his Führer to Russia, was awarded a high order, and became a general. After the war he was accepted into the new army, and he wrote *Principiis obsta* in which he tried to evade his and his countrymen's responsibility by asking: "What is guilt? What is fate?"[129] And so they all speak and write today. Colonel-General Guderian, who had accepted a large sum of money from Hitler, for which he had tried to buy an estate in 1944, who had refused to participate in the plot against Hitler, and who, after the abortive plot, had become Supreme Army Commander and had compelled all officers to swear a new oath to the Führer and his ideas, said in 1950: "Both the West European and the American ideal is the freedom of man. The counterpoise against the Bolshevic tyranny lies in the free development of the personality, in the free spiritual, economic and industrial development, and in free scientific endeavours."[130] Only in 1950 did he discover this truth, a little late indeed.

Leo Lania said on February 25, 1933, "Germany marches with gigantic speed into a cultural prison,"[131] and fled into exile. Theodor Heuss, however, said a week earlier, on February 18, 1933: "Our nation will not endure for very long all this meanness." Professor H. J. Schoeps retorted after the war which he had spent in exile: "It endured it for twelve years."[132] Oskar Simmel S. J. reminds us of what Hitler said on February 28, 1926: "We must rid ourselves of the opinion that the masses can be satisfied by intellectual things. Knowledge is but a shaking platform. What is stable, that is hatred. The masses are feminine, and ask for a man in cuirassier boots who says: 'This is the right way.' What the masses must feel is the triumph of their own power, the contempt of the enemy." Simmel, who calls Hitler "a *Führer* into chaos," says: "Such ideas would not have impressed a more healthy nation than the Germans of the 1920's." Large parts of the educated populace had already been poisoned "by the racial and nationalistic gospels of Lagarde, Langbehn, Chamberlain, and others."[133]

In 1957, a retired general who had served Hitler as well as he could, Waldemar Erfurth, undertook the task to refute, in a lengthy book, the bad opinion the world has of the German generals. He thunders, of course, against the "shame" of Versailles, the "lie" of the German war guilt, the demilitarization of Germany in 1918. He calls Ludendorff "a powerful personality" and revives the stab-in-the-back legend. He wants us to believe that nothing could be done to prevent Hitler's rise to power, he belittles the famous Hossbach Protocol about Hitler's war aims, blames Great Britain for the guarantee she gave to

Poland, and asserts, quoting Professor Ritter, that the German General Staff "had certainly nothing to do with the militarism of the Third Reich." He also quotes Field-Marshal Montgomery as saying that "the essence of democracy is freedom, that of the army is discipline." It is apparently still all the same to him whether you serve a democracy or Hitler. Blomberg, according to him. will "remain a riddle for ever." Keitel was "a man of the highest sense of duty." Warlimont, another war criminal, was "an eminently intelligent and far-seeing member of the General Staff." In short: "It remains the glory of the German General Staff that they preserved, and, in time, developed, the secret of victory inherited from great predecessors." 1918? 1945? This unteachable man goes even further in applying to the German General Staff the famous words of Pericles: "We are rather the model for the others than their imitators. We shall be admired in the present and in the future."[134] The Prussian nobleman, von Kleist-Schmenzin, however, who was hanged in 1944, said several years before his death: "People will say in future: spineless like a German civil servant, godless like a Lutheran pastor, dishonourable like a Prussian officer."[135] And the poet Erich Kästner, who never served Hitler, who was not allowed to publish anything in the Third Reich, and who was twice arrested by its thugs, in 1933 wrote a poem in which German militarism and all the generals appear in a wholly different light. In a satirical variation of Goethe's poem "Know'st thou the land where the fair citrons blow?" he asked:

Know'st thou the land where cannons blow?

and gave a grim answer: It is the land where the babies are born with little spurs, where you are not born as a civilian, where you are promoted if you keep your tongue. "Know'st thou the land?" You can find there goodness and even true heroism now and then, "but not with many." Every other man there is infantile. Freedom does not ripen there, it remains always green.

"Whatever you may build it always turns out to be barracks. Know'st thou the land where cannons blow? You don't know it yet? You will know it."[136]

It is a pretty safe guess that more Germans agree with ex-General Erfurth than with Kästner.

Notes

1. *Briefe*, pp. 91, 95.
2. *Der deutsche Soldatenkalender*. Muenchen, 1954, p. 23.
3. *Preussische Jahrbuecher*, Berlin, July, 1919; Kruck, *op. cit.*, pp. 121, 126, 127, 149.
4. Kurt Pritzkoleit. *Das Kommandierte Wunder*. Muenchen, 1959, p. 710.
5. Erich von Ludendorff. *Der totale Krieg*. Muenchen, 1935, p. 13.
6. Margarete Ludendorff. *Als ich Ludendorffs Frau war*. Muenchen, 1929, p. 209.
7. *Deutsche Rundschau*. November, 1961.
8. H. Rothfels. *Zeitgeschichtliche Betrachtungen*. Goettingen, 1959, p. 74.
9. L. von Rudolph. *Die Luege, die nicht stirbt*. Nuernberg, 1959, p. 35.
10. *Die Fackel*, November, 1921.
11. *Die Luege, die nicht stirbt*, pp. 124, 135.
12. *Der totale Kreig*, pp. 5, 6, 9, 14, 17, 20, 21, 24, 83, 84.
13. *Der Quell* (a periodical), Paehl bei Weilheim, June 23, 1953.
14. *Nuernberger Nachrichten*, January 23, 1954.
15. *Von 1914-1939*. Leipzig, 1939, p. 27.
16. Pross. *Die Zerstoerung der deutschen Politik*, pp. 321-322.
17. *Sueddeutsche Zeitung*. Muenchen, October 13, 1956.
18. Kruck, *op. cit.*, 132.
19. Karl von Helfferich. *Reichstagsreden 1922-1924*. With an introduction by Count Westarp. Berlin, 1925, p. 17.
20. Kruck, *op. cit.*, p. 192.
21. *Deutsche Geschichte*. Leipzig, 1919, p. 9, 12, 49, 176, 298.
22. *Deutschlands Erneuerung* (a periodical), 1921, No. 6. Quoted in: Ritter. *Europa und die deutsche Frage*, pp. 183-184.
23. *Mein Damaskus*, pp. 55, 56, 68, 74, 121, 129, 140, 192, 194, 199, 205, 215, 240; *Zehn Jahre Kampf fuer Frieden*. Hamburg, 1929. Entries: April 17, 1921, January 15, 1922, June 2, 1922, December 17, 1922, February 24, 1923, August 4, 1923, September 7, 1925, June 10, 1928.
24. *Der Generalfeldmarschall und ihr Generalgeldmarschall*. Verlag fuer Gewerkschaftspolitik und Sozialwissenschaft, Berlin, 1953, pp. 12, 15-16.
25. *Weltpolitik*, pp. 26, 53, 54, 62-64, 126; *Mein Kampf gegen das militaristische und nationalistische Deutschland*, pp. 113, 124, 168.
26. *Vom Krieg der Zukunft*. Berlin, 1920, pp. 150, 237.
27. H. J. Schoeps. *Das war Preussen*. Honnef, 1955, pp. 13-17.
28. Curt Martens. *Verschwoerer und Fehmemoerder*. Berlin, 1926, p. 7.

29. *Das verlorene Afrika.* Berlin, 1919, pp. 6, 7, 9, 17.
30. *Die Kultur,* Muenchen, July 1, 1957.
31. E. von Salomon. *Die Geaechteten.* Berlin, 1935, p. 297.
32. G. W. F. Hallgarten. *Hilter, Reichswehr und Industrie.* Frankfurt, 1955, p. 13.
33. K. Pritzkoleit. *Wem gehoert Deutschland?* Muenchen, 1957, pp. 429-430.
34. P. Wiegler. *Literaturgeschichte.* Berlin, 1930, Vol. II, p. 463.
35. *Die Kultur,* Muenchen, August, 1961.
36. *Nuernberger Nachrichten,* March 15, 1962.
37. *Professor Bernhardi.* Berlin, 1912, pp. 50, 64, 123, 133, 148, 178.
38. Wilfried Daim. *Der Mann, der Hitler die Ideen gab.* Muenchen, 1958.
39. *Die Fackel,* October, 1913.
40. Martin Freud. *Glory Reflected.* London, 1957, p. 109.
41. *Die Fackel,* 1925.
42. Sigmund Freud. *Letters.* London, 1961, pp. 346, 413, 415, 443.
43. *Land im Strom der Zeit.* Wien, 1958, p. 12.
44. Lion Feuchtwanger. *Erfolg.* Berlin, 1930, p. 789.
45. *Briefe,* p. 246.
46. *Mein Kampf.* Muenchen, 9th edition, 1930, p. 252.
47. *Ibid.,* p. 272.
48. *Ibid.,* p. 145.
49. *Ibid.,* p. 253.
50. *Ibid.,* p. 702.
51. *New Statesman,* London, October 6, 1956.
52. Max Domarus. *Hitler: Reden und Proklamationen 1932-1945.* Neustadt, 1962, Vol. I, pp. 25-26.
53. *Mein Kampf,* pp. 99-100.
54. *Ibid.,* p. 438.
55. *Ibid.,* pp. 736-738, 740.
56. *Ibid.,* p. 154.
57. *Ibid.,* pp. 731-732.
58. *Ibid.,* p. 742.
59. *Ibid.,* p. 743.
60. *Das Reich der niederen Daemonen,* p. 45.
61. *Die Kultur,* Muenchen, August, November, 1960.
62. *Christ und Welt* (a periodical), Stuttgart, November 17, 1960.
63. *Deutsche Rundschau,* September, 1960.
64. *Kleine politische Schriften.* Vol. I, p. 208.
65. *Deutsche Schriften.* Goettingen, 1886, re-issued Muenchen, 1940, pp. 130, 132, 144-147, 500-501.
66. Kruck, *op. cit.,* p. 44.
67. *Ibid.,* p. 33.
68. Foerster. *Erlebte Weltgeschichte,* p. 314.
69. *Politische Anthropologie.* Leipzig, 1903, p. 298.
70. *Deutsche Politik,* 1905, Vol. I, pp. 53-54.
71. *Reines Deutschtum.* 1904, p. 210. Quoted by Ch. Andler. *Die all-deutsche Dewegung.* Lausanne, 1915, p. 24.

72. *Die neue Rundschau.* Berlin, 1907, pp. 753-754.
73. *Deutschland und der naechste Krieg,* pp. 79, 86.
74. *The Tablet,* London, March 31, 1962.
75. Ritter. *Europa und die deutsche Frage,* pp. 142, 147.
76. *Mein Kampf,* p. 742.
77. Thomas Mann. *Altes und Neues,* pp. 403ff.
78. Czeslaw Milosz. *Verfuehrtes Denken. Koeln,* 1953, p. 133.
79. W. Hegemann. *Fridericus oder das Koenigsopfer.* Berlin, 1926, motto.
80. *Deutsche Rundschau,* January, 1956.
81. *Neue Zuercher Zeitung,* mid-August, 1954.
82. K. Hierl. *Ausgewachlte Schriften und Reden.* Muenchen, 1941, p. 243.
83. *Ibid.,* Vol. I, pp, 224, 228, 248; Vol. II, p. 322.
84. *Im Dienst fuer Deutschland 1918-1945.* Heidelberg, 1954, p. 45.
85. *Die Kultur,* Muenchen, May 1, 1958.
86. *Altes und Neues.* Frankfurt, 1953, p. 365.
87. *Politische Novelle.* Berlin, 1928, pp. 34-36.
88. Leber, *op. cit.,* p. 100.
89. *Gegen die Brandung.* Zuerich, 1959, pp. 85-86.
90. *Gespraeche mit Hitler,* p. 237.
91. *Der Spiegel,* Hamburg, July 29, 1959.
92. F. Rasche. *Unruh. Hannover,* 1960, p. 222.
93. *Deutsche Rundschau,* July, 1947.
94. Domarus, *op. cit.,* pp. 68-90.
95. Walter Hofer. *Der Nationalsozialismus: Dokumente 1933-1945.* Frankfurt, 1957, p. 24.
96. *Die deutsche Katastrophe,* p. 105.
97. *Wider den Strom.* Leipzig, 1932, Introduction.
98. *Alldeutscher Verband—Wehrverbaende. Von einem deutschen Hochschullehrer.* Berlin, 1932, pp. 3, 10, 16, 23, 39, 40, 42-43, 48, 65, 91, 160.
99. Kruck, *op. cit.,* p. 177.
100. *Unter dem Schatten deiner Fluegel,* p, 18.
101. *Der Spiegel,* October, 1957.
102. *Deutsche Rundschau,* September, 1954.
103. P. A. Steiniger. *Der Nuernberger Prozess.* Berlin, 1958, p. 32.
104. L. Poliakov and J. Wulf. *Das Dritte Reich und die Juden.* Berlin, 1955, p. 36.
105. Steiniger, *op. cit.,* pp. 48-50.
106. *Gewagtes Leben,* p. 266.
107. *Die Welt,* Hamburg, June 11, 1957.
108. Domarus, *op. cit.,* p. 130.
109. *Ibid.,* p. 132.
110. G. Radbruch. *Rechtsphilosophie.* 4th edition, 1950, p. 354.
111. E. Otwald. *Deutschland erwache.* Wien-Leipzig, 1932, p. 353.
112. *Hitler—ein deutsches Verhaengnis.* Berlin, 1932, pp. 7-8, 12, 32, 35.
113. *Gewagtes Leben,* p. 382.
114. *Widerstand* (a periodical), Berlin, January, 1933.
115. *Gewagtes Leben,* pp. 27, 29, 30, 32, 160, 174, 277-278.

116. *Ibid.,* p. 331.
117. *Ibid.,* pp. 381, 383.
118. *Das Reich der niederen Daemonen.* Hamburg, 1953, pp. 11, 14, 16, 19, 20-21, 39, 74.
119. *Du hast uns heimgesucht bei Nacht.* Muenchen, 1954, p. 41.
120. *Unter dem Schatten deiner Fluegel,* p. 36.
121. Eduard Hemmerle. *Der Weg in die Katastrophe.* Muenchen, 1948, p. 270.
122. W. Breucker. *Die Tragik Ludendorffs.* Stollheim, 1953, p. 136.
123. *Europa, was nun?* Goettingen, 1954, p. 24.
124. *Briefe,* p. 238.
125. Domarus, *op. cit.,* p. 218.
126. *Daily Telegraph,* London, November 7, 1960.
127. Hemmerle, *op. cit.,* p. 362.
128. Foertsch, pp. 19, 21, 23, 35-36, 41; Foertsch. *Der Offizier der neuen Wehrmacht.* Berlin, 1936, pp. 13-14.
129. Foertsch. *Schuld und Verhaengnis.* Stuttgart, 1951, pp. 10, 18, 25, 215.
130. *Kam Westeuropa verteidigt werden?* Goettingen, 1950, p. 67.
131. H. J. Schoeps. *Konservative Erneuerung.* Stuttgart, 1958, pp. 16-17.
132. *Ibid.*
133. *Stimmen der Zeit* (a periodical), Muenchen, May, 1960.
134. W. Erfurth. *Die Geschichte des deutschen Generalstabs, 1918-1945.* Goettingen, 1957, pp. 65, 85, 148, 149, 182, 202, 209, 310, 311, 312, 313.
135. Ernst Niekisch. *Das Reich der niederen Daemonen,* p. 248.
136. *Die Kultur,* Muenchen, November 1, 1957.

13
Literary Seducers
and Warners (1916–1933)

THE INTELLECTUALS, TOO, THE WRITERS OF THE PERIOD FROM
1918 to 1933, formed two opposite camps. Oswald Spengler, in
Decline of the West, prophesied the coming of formless powers
without tradition, a new Caesarism, with democracy turning
into dictatorship and poetry and literature being replaced by
technology. Great individuals, he "scientifically" foretold, would
reign over "enervated fellahin, treating them like cattle for
slaughter."[1] We must either will the inevitable or nothing at all,
he said. Thomas Mann indicated his pessimism, fatalism, and
nihilism in sharp words, calling him a snob, "a mere defeatist
of humanity" who posed as a prophet and hurled a "malicious
dogmatism and hatred of the future" against mankind.[2] This
was by no means too strong an indictment because this
"prophet" not only foretold the inevitable downfall of European
culture but also the rise of Russia. Ours, he said with strange

satisfaction, will be the fate of ancient Rome which was "barbarian, disciplined, practical, Protestant, Prussian. . . . Those who do not realise that nothing can be done against this fate, that we must love it or else dispair of future and life; those who still cherish provincial idealism and the style of past ages; should give up all hope to understand history, to create history. . . . If, under the impression of my book, people of the new generation turn to technology rather than to music, to naval affairs rather than to painting, to politics rather than to epistemology, they will do what I wish they did and one can wish for no better thing."[3]

In *Prussianism and Socialism*, which Spengler later proudly called the origin of the "national movement," he called the revolution of 1918 "the most senseless act" of Germany history. Like Sombart during the war, he glorified Germany and spoke contemptuously of Great Britain. While the Britons had "no state" because a "liberal" state was no state at all, Prussian Germany was entirely different. "Power belongs to the whole which is sovereign. A few dictate and the rest obey. To serve—this is old Prussian style. No I but only We. The individual does not count, it is being sacrificed to the whole." Republicanism, parliamentarism, democracy were "empty phrases," according to him.[4] In 1924 he enlightened the national youth about its political duties. "The devotion to a Führer," he told them, would be "decisive" in the armies of the future. "The best Germans, and not only they, are waiting for a man into whose hands they can put the fate of our country." Hitler was then already making much noise. Spengler stated with satisfaction that the Germans had at last "learned to hate. He who does not hate is no man, and history is made by men. That the German can at last hate, is one of the few results of our time which guarantee us a future." What a prophet! He admonished the young "to educate themselves as material for great leaders and be ready for impersonal sacrifice. This, too, is a German virtue."[5]

Then came novelists who glorified the war and others who showed the horrors of war. Ludwig Renn, descendant of an ancient noble family, in *War,* and Erich Maria Remarque in *All Quiet on the Western Front* told, in the words of the latter, of "a generation which was destroyed by the war even if it had evaded the grenades."[6] Both had to flee into exile in 1933. Fritz von Unruh, another descendant of a noble family, came back shattered and utterly disillusioned from the Kaiser's war. During that war he wrote *The Way of Sacrifice* which could be published only after Germany's defeat in 1918. He described the horrors of war in telling words and asked: "To what purpose? For Verdun?" The result of all that false glory was "a bony picture."[7] In 1915 he wrote a drama in verse, *Before the Decision,* in which he again condemned the madness of war and said: "It seems to me to be impossible for a nation to win its finest cup by blood and weapons." He cursed all Prussian kings from Frederick William I to the romantic kings of the 19th and 20th centuries. The last words of this verse play are: "All false gods crumble down, and the sun shines again."[8] In a third book, in verse again, *A Lost Generation,* a mother cries because she must bear children to be killed in war. A war-mad Wilhelmian officer says to her: "It is my duty to kill you before you damage the mighty structure of the state."[9] Von Unruh, too, had to flee into exile in 1933.

Foremost among the writers who glorified the spirit of the war was Ernst Jünger, who had won the *Pour le mérite.* His *In Storms of Steel* ran into several editions. In the preface to the fifth edition Jünger said that Germany needed "a hard and inconsiderate generation in the years to come. We shall have to replace the pen by the sword, ink by blood, words by deeds." A brutal age was nearing. "Peace does not belong to cowards but to the sword."[10] In *War as an Inner Experience* Jünger assured the defeated Germans that war was "the most tremendous meeting of nations, a law of nature." And he waxed enthusiastic about "the thirst for blood when the flashing clouds of destruction hover above the fields of anger . . . the voluptiousness of blood hanging above the war like a red storm-sail above a black galley."[11] In *Forest 125* Jünger called war "the focus of life," and, looking into the future, he said: "The real core of our nation will, even if we should be defeated in war, never give up the opinion that the world cannot be all right if we are not the first. Our hour will come." What a prophet! In view of what the Germans did, when their hour came in 1933, what are we to think of these words of Jünger's: "We have regrettably less barbaric substratum than the world seems to think we have"?[12] In 1932, when millions hailed Hitler, he published *The Worker* in which he said that nations voluntarily impose on themselves dictatorships "in order that the necessary can be commanded." What was this necessary? "The assertion and the triumph, the preparedness, if necessary, for resolute destruction amidst a world threatened everywhere."[13] In 1934, when the Führer was already installed and preparing the Germans for their resolute destruction, Jünger published his *Total Mobilisation* in which he said that the 1914-18 war had been "the barrier which separates us from Europe," that in 1918 "something alien has got the upper hand" in Germany, that the idea of individualism had "always been questionable," and that the Germans must be proud of being regarded by the democratic West "as one of its greatest dangers."[14] Thus spoke Jünger in the years of Hitler's ascendancy. After Hitler's eclipse he tried to evade his responsibility by saying that he had only been a "seismograph," and that only primitives made the barometer responsible for the typhoon.[15]

Another of the war enthusiasts (we cannot mention them all) was Werner Beumelburg who in *Group Bosemüller, Douaumont,* and *Flanders* described the first German war as if it had been one single heroic event. In 1934 he published *The Iron Law* in which the German republic was called "a pigsty":

" 'You were in the war. But this must stop at last.'

'It will never stop, not as far as we are concerned. We can

only prepare it. The others will act, those who come after us.' "[16]

They came. Then Beumelburg said, alluding to Remarque, that there had "once" been a time when people said that the war had destroyed a whole generation, and that "that opinion had spread like an epidemic." The epidemic was, in reality, books like those by Jünger, Beumelburg, and others, who had helped to prepare Germany for Hitler and war. Beumelburg said so himself in his book *From 1914 to 1939:* "Those who have saved Germany and made her great again trace our age back with pride to the battlefields of the world war. Hitler has said so himself in his book when, filled with that soldierly spirit, he decided to become a politician. . . . Our generation has experienced the greatest grace of God. For the man who has regenerated and formed the Reich is flesh of their flesh, blood of their blood, spirit of their spirit, a soldier in thinking and acting."[17] *Die Kultur,* Munich, published this in March, 1956: "The road to our Inferno started with Wildenbruch and Dahn and continued with Beumelburg, Flex and Hans Grimm. This sort of literature found its way into the schools in 1933. Nobody need be surprised that the youth of those decades fell victim to the heroic myths of the Kaiser and Adolf Hitler. We are punishing the criminals of the concentration camps but we forget to weed out the intellectual weed which is responsible for the sadists."

Thomas Mann had foreseen all this in 1926: "You believe in the coming of war if you do not condemn it sufficiently."[18] And that exceptional general, Count von Schönaich, had said after the first war: "They do not allow the nation to know the true face of war. They prefer self-deception and hurrahs to the abhorrence of atrocities which could create peace. They think war is a sort of steel bath. But that famous steel bath has now become a quagmire in which the nations are threatened with suffocation."[19] Stefan George had said the same thing in 1917 when he said that he who has seen the golems of modern war crush his comrades to pulp and fragments "laughs grimly when false phrases of old time heroism are sounded. The ancient god of battle is no more."[20]

Then there were the novelists who searched the whole history of the world for Führers, to mirror in them the man whom millions were already acclaiming with their "Heil Hitler!" H. F. Blunck thus told the story of a certain Hein Hoyer, a north-German condottiere of the 15th century, showing how the revolutionary soldier becomes a statesman who builds a new community. Under Hitler, Blunck wrote *King Geiserich,* the story of the Germanic Führer of the Vandals and his march from the Elbe to Carthage. Will Vesper discovered an Icelandic Führer and glorified him. The Austrian Mirko Jelusich depicted Führers in *Caesar* and *Cromwell.* In 1940 he told his readers that Hitler had saved him from despair and that he had worked illegally for him under Dollfuss.

The writer Wilhelm Stapel in 1928 published a book, *The Fictitiousness of the Weimar Constitution,* expressly in order to undermine the democratic republic, and to clamor "with a good conscience" for "a Führer."[21] When Germany had found this Führer, he formulated his program in these words: "One nation must excel the others, one nation must lay down an imperial law and a European order. Only the German nation can be the embodiment of the new imperialsim. If only two Germans were to live in Poland, they would be more important than the millions of Poles. Only a Europe led by Germans can become a peaceful Europe."[22]

Yet another pace-maker for Hitler was the writer Edgar J. Jung who said in his book, *The Reign of the Inferiors,* that the democratic West knew no nations, but only "masses" for they had no idea of the formative power of "soil, blood and fate." Democracy was already condemned to death by history. Germany was the heart of Europe—"hence our duty and right to lead Europe to a new European order."[23]

Other pacemakers for Hitler were a number of literati around the *Tat* Circle who preached a radicalism compared with which Bolshevism and Italian Fascism appeared to be too liberal, and a wild nationalism and economic self-sufficiency. One of them, Hans Zehrer, editor of the periodical, *Die Tat,* said in 1932 that the parties no longer represented the new reality, parliamentarism was done for and so was liberalism. After Hitler had become master of Germany, Zehrer was pleased with the success of the young generation, and promised the assistance of his periodical. "Liberalism, parliamentarism and capitalism must be liquidated. We are striving for great unity of nationalism and socialism."[24] His friend Ferdinand Fried in 1931 preferred an alliance with the East to one with the West.[25] In 1932 he advocated the abolishment of liberalism, parliamentarism, democracy, internationalism, and capitalism. Consequently, he too was pleased with Hitler, and said about those Germans who had fled into exile: "All these birds have flown to Vienna, Prague or Paris but some are still here waiting anxiously for blows. National Socialism cannot be preached by these who persecuted it a year ago. In some periodicals Arnold Schönberg is still celebrated as a genius. It is still possible to see a Bergner film and publish books à la Remarque." He criticized those who opposed Adolf Hitler and was pleased that National Socialism had replaced a regime which had denied "all racial values." How was it still possible "to debase the honest endeavours of the National Socialist leaders"?[26] A third member of the radical *Tat* Circle was Giselher Wirsing who spoke in 1942 of Roosevelt's "fight for leadership in the world" and of "the new European unity" created by Hitler, whom he called "a powerful personality"; in 1944 he published an article about "the Jewish Problem in the Middle East" in Rosenberg's anti-Semitic periodical *Weltkampf.*[27] Zehrer, Fried and Wirsing are back again in West German journalism.

The poet Stefan George has been regarded as a forerunner of National Socialism. This is a complete misunderstanding. Very early in his career he said that the Germans should turn not to the Nordic spirit but to the South for "clarity, width and sunlight." Prussia he called "a powerful system but hostile to all culture and art." He always regarded the Kaiser's Empire, with its "megalomania" and the "empty arrogance" of Wilhelm and the governing classes, as a caricature of a "genuine state," and its downfall in 1918 as a "well deserved punishment." The leaders of the new republic were esteemed by him because they were "simple and unostentatious" and had courageously taken over "when everything was tottering and the chains of Prussian slavery had fallen to the ground." While millions of Germans were hailing their Führer, he said to his friends: "I cannot even hint at what I see coming. But you will all experience it and pay for it."[28] Göbbels offered him the membership of the Nazified Academy of Literature; he refused and left Germany. He died in Switzerland and his friends returned the flowers which the Nazi Ambassador in Berne had sent in the name of his government. But Professor Ernst Bertram, one of his circle and once also a good friend of Thomas Mann, praised him in Nazi Germany as the man who had "called for the gigantic realities of today and tomorrow," and waxed enthusiastic about the "Germanic ideal of government and service, leadership and followership," about the new youth which was out "to preserve the deeply endangered Nordic blood, the ancient Aryan blood-inheritance." A false humanism, he said, had "no feeling for the lofty mission" of National Socialism "to impose on the ageing world of Europe at the last possible moment the saving regeneration."[29] He also said this: "Once again we have witnessed what the 'omnipotence of undivided enthusiasm' of which Hölderlin once spoke can do—against all doubts of the clever and all derision of the cunning. We saw"—he quoted George—"that blessed dreams, deeds and sufferings gave birth to the one man who can help . . . under the restored flag of Bismarck's *Reich* and the ancient mythical swastika of the rejuvenation of the light. It was a second Tannenberg victory against Asia. If we should fail in our fight symbolised by the Tannenbergs of 1914 and 1933, the end of the white race would come."[30] Today the Germans are told that Bertram had been "wronged and dishonoured" in 1945, "thanks to the fanatical ignorance of a single officer of the army of occupation."[31]

George foresaw the possibility of such a betrayal of his Goethean humanism when, in a short poem, he answered the question: "He who circled in your orbit, Can he bear to break away?" with the words: "Some have drunk the wine of living, Others eaten of their death."[32]

In George's inner circle there were two kinds of followers, some more humanistic, others more nationalistic. He opposed Friedrich Wolters' essays "On Sacrificial Death for the Fatherland" and "Goethe as an Educator to Patriotic Thinking" because they came much too near the nationalism of the 1920's. Kurt Hildebrandt, too, moved far away from George's humanism in his books *State and Race* and *Norm, Degeneration, Decay* which were duly praised in the Third Reich as being "exemplary" and coming from "a wise teacher."[33] Rightly so, for Hildebrandt spoke of "the Nordic German race as the leading one," while the other nations were like "a rotten tree."[34] In 1933 this traitor drew a parallel between the Third Reich and Plato's ideal state. Then as now the political situation was ripe for "the savior of the nation. . . . In times of an undisciplined mixture of races it was necessary to draw attention to the conditions of human breeding." So Plato subjected it to a holy law because selection was "more important than mercy." Degenerates were allowed to mix with degenerates "but their children were killed. A heroic solution."[35]

Another strange man was Berthold Vallentin. He was of Jewish origin, and as such he is an example of how even Jews, though only two or three, succumbed to the hero-worship so characteristic of the Germans. In the years of an already rapidly growing National Socialism he said of Napoleon: "He violated nothing, he found nothing to violate. He saw no order which to attack would have been violence and invasion. He only saw material which he formed and welded together, just as any material longs to be shaped by the creative and universal genius. Only he himself is the judge of what is violation and what not. For since when do we measure the master and his deeds with a view to 'the inalienable rights' of the material? Since when is the stone permitted to cry when hit by the chisel? If it groans is it not hit all the harder? True, we have learned that human life, even the most wretched human life, has greater value than all the material and even the work of the world. But this is the teaching of dissolution, of real death. Fortunately, every hero feels an inborn urge towards form and work, while remaining utterly unconcerned with the arrogance of the sterile 'humane.' "[36] One can find the same ideas in *Mein Kampf* in less high-flown language. Vallentin spoke as if Hitler were not threatening Germany because, as Thomas Mann said, German intellectuals are never concerned with the possible consequences of their ideas in the field of practical politics.

The misunderstanding about George arose from his poem "The Poet in Times of Confusion," in which he spoke of a young generation which would again measure men and things by the genuine measures, and of a savior who would found "the new kingdom." This was the dream of a great poet who hoped for the renewal of a truly spiritual world. Nobody in his senses could ever have regarded Hitler as the man whose coming George had prophesied. One of George's true disciples, von Stauffenberg, who paid with his life for his attempt to kill Hitler, used to quote lines from George's poem *The Anti-Christ,* which he applied to Hitler. In this poem the Devil says:

> The sky has no marvels I cannot confer
> A hairbreadth amiss, but you do not concern
> The hoax, for your senses are blunted.

So were the senses of half a nation which hailed Hitler. They were, as the poem goes on, "charmed by demoniac ruse," and would in the end be "like cows when the barn is afire—and grimly the trumpet is sounded!"[37] Another true disciple, the poet Robert Böhringer, spoke of the cursed year when George left Germany and Hitler, who was to ruin Europe, became its master. The young generation of which George had spoken was "expelled, tortured and murdered. How many were left of the secret circle? As many as there had been just men in Sodom."[38]

On the extreme fringe of the George circle stood Ludwig Klages, who, in his pernicious book *The Intellect as Enemy of the Soul,* defamed all reason and intellectualism in an obscure language. He was also a fanatical anti-Semite and said of George: "What he has achieved in the field of literature he achieved with the help of Jewry. Jewish professors were his pace-makers and followers, and when he came to town, he lived in the houses of Jews or half-Jews."[39] Paul Ludwig Landsberg, who died in a concentration camp, attacked Klages's "paganism" in an article in 1923.[40] Thomas Mann spoke in 1929 of those who "deify the irrational out of spite and defame the spirit as henchmen of life," and inaugurate "Astarte feasts of dynamic romanticism."[41] A few years later he denounced those who extolled "as solely creative the powers of the unconscious, dynamic, chthonic" and "cursed reason as the murderer of life . . . Ten thousand lecturers of the irrational did not care a damn whether they seduced the nation to moral sans-culottism. . . . The masses heard that reason had been dethroned, and invented the term *Intellektbestie* . . . The result will be war, a general catastrophe, the end of civilisation."[42]

While so many irresponsible and contemptible "writers," in common with many unteachable politicians, were undermining the unstable young German democracy and preparing the way for Hitler, there was a small minority of honest German writers who in vain warned against the National Socialist danger that was hanging over Germany. Hermann Hesse grimly spoke of the Germans who had made of Goethe a beautifully stylized old master and national hero, and who read newspapers of "the party of militarists and war-mongers"[43] and allowed themselves to be incited and corrupted by the generals, industrialists, and politicians who were very satisfied with themselves and had no sense of responsibility whatsoever. They did not listen to him, they called him a chap without a fatherland who had ridiculed the Kaiser. "Mothers of heroes" wrote him nasty letters and spoke to him enthusiastically of the Führer. When he saw that the Germans "unanimously sabotaged their republic and had learned nothing," he returned his German citizenship and became a Swiss.[44]

Most outspoken of the German bishops who condemned National Socialism and its un-Christian racialism was Cardinal Adolf Bertram of Breslau, who spoke of the "seducers" who had "taken possession of the soul of the nation" and of the "black fogs" which were hovering over Germany. He condemned "the glorification of race," "the self-deification," "the fanatical nationalism," and exclaimed: "Beware of false prophets whose main weapons are inciting slogans! Stand together like a strong wall in defence of our most holy inheritance!"[45] If the Germans had listened to him, Breslau and Silesia would still be theirs.

The writer Lion Feuchtwanger depicted the scene in Germany, more especially in Bavaria, in his novel *Success*. We make the acquaintance of the nationalistic organizations which murder decent democrats ("Traitors have to be handed over to the Vehme"). One of them, who later becomes a gauleiter, derides his victim in these words: "He speaks of justice, humanity, civilisation, pacifism, but when he starts screaming, he gets intolerable"—and murders him. We hear of the slogans "master race" and "Nordic idea." A Bavarian minister says that Kant's idea of absolute ethics and justice was false. "Justice and soil, justice and climate—they are one and indivisible." The National Socialists are thundering against "the Jewish government of Berlin" and industrialists give Hitler money in exchange for a promise to keep down the trade unions. The industrialists get richer and richer by the inflation, while the ordinary people get daily poorer. We witness the Führer's abortive revolt. He is imprisoned by the wild agitation against "Rome and the Jews" continues. One of the National Socialist heroes of the day says: "Just as bacilli destroy the lungs, so international Jewry is destroying the German nation."[46] If Feuchtwanger had not escaped in time in 1933 he would have been tortured and murdered by the Nazis.

Professor E. R. Curtius in 1932 published a book, *German Spirit Endangered,* in which he warned against "the doctrinaire forms of nationalism" and against the Germans "appealing to irrationalism" which was "a dangerously two-edged weapon." That appeal, he warned, "does not pave the way to mystical vision but to psychological barbarism. All those who today form a front against the spirit do not promote the interests of the nation but the destruction of the German spirit by revolutionary chaos." As an example he quoted a sentence from a nationalistic novel: "The intellect is a danger to the character."[47] Another professor, H. A. Korff, praised Lessing's *Nathan* because it preached "tolerance against people of other creeds and different opinions. Thus we learn to judge everybody on his human qualities." *Nathan* proved "the independence of ethics from a particular denomination, a particular nation."[48]

The satirist Kurt Tucholsky, who fought Germany's false ways all his life, left his fatherland in the 1920's and settled in France. Later he emigrated to Sweden where he committed suicide in 1935. As early as 1907 he told the Germans the "Fairy Tale" of the Kaiser's epoch: "Once upon a time there was an emperor who reigned over a mighty, rich and beautiful country. And what did the emperor do with his country? He did not care a pin for it." Tucholsky reminded his fellow countrymen many times in the years both before the First World War and between the wars that the evil did not start with Wilhelm II. "The Crown glistened and the burghers cringed" since 1870. The Western World became "democratic, but Old-Prussia remained unchanged." General Moltke said: "We keep the army to clear the streets in case people should come too near to the Castle." Soldiers were treated "as only Germans allow themselves to be treated" because the Germans are "a nation of slaves."

They sang enthusiastically: "I am a Prussian and want to be a Prussian." In 1913 when nobody knew anything of Adolf Hitler tramping the streets of Vienna, Tucholsky wrote: "In every town some Napoleon brushes his black lock from his forehead." When the war of 1914 came, the Germans believed the lie "that Germany had been attacked." They spoke of "perfidious Albion" whose "sordid minds have no inkling of the depth of the German soul," and sang "We shall victoriously march into France," calling the French "decadent and lazy to the bones." H. S. Chamberlain wrote: "This is a war between barbarism and civilisation. It is the old war between day and night, between Ormuzd and Ahriman." And the slogan became popular again:

> *Denn es muss am deutschen Wesen*
> *Einmal noch die Welt genesen,*

while every tram conductor, every little doorkeeper was a "Ludendorff, Comander-in-Chief, Emperor and sergeant-major rolled into one."

After Germany's downfall in 1918 Tucholsky refused to say: "*De mortuis nil misi bene,*" but said instead: "First we must curse the old regime. Oh nation, discourage your caste arrogance, and trust those chaps never, never again!" But very soon he realized: "The revolution of November 9 was no revolution at all. Nobody settled accounts with the abuses of absolutism." The remnants of the imperial army, especially the officers, made much noise in order "to prevent the spread of the truth about

their war activities." Tucholsky also accused the Social Democrats, whose leader Scheidemann had greeted the German army
returning from the battlefield as "undefeated" soldiers. Nobody
liked to remember "that eighty million had marched as slaves of
the sword" all over Europe. *"Deutschland, Deutschland über
alles*—Europe, humanity, Christianity died under the boistering
chords of that song." Historians began to falsify German history
again. Great Britain was accused of having started the war "in
order to break the power of the only competitor," and Paris was
called "the centre of moral decay." General Seeckt said that it
was the aim of the new army "to keep alive the spirit which has
once led us to Sedan and over the battlefields in East and
West." The Social Democrats, who had formed a new government, misunderstood the intentions of the people—who were by
no means Bolshevistic and only aimed at liberal social reforms
—and left the old feudal classes untouched. One foul murder
followed the other. Karl Liebknecht, Rosa Luxemburg, Erzberger, and Rathenau were bestially murdered—but people said:
"Not the murderer, the murdered is guilty." Nearly all newspapers were in Pan-German hands, and by 1920 anti-Jewish
slogans were repeated: "Only the Jewish race is reigning us."
"Citizens, the lion is abroad! Who is guilty? The Jews." "All
woods are Jewish, Jesus Christ is Jewish. Germany must be
freed from the Jews." Tucholsky retorted: "A mixed race like
the Germans, descending in its Eastern parts from Wends,
Kashubs and Poles, has no reason to resent the mixing of races.
The anti-Jewish slogans only divert the attention of a severely
duped nation from its real criminals." In vain he reminded them
of the lines of the poet Georg Herwegh, who had to flee Germany in 1848:

> *Die Wacht am Rhein wird nicht genügen,*
> *Der schlimmste Feind steht an der Spree.*[49]

He asked his intoxicated countrymen: "Do you not see that the
Nazis condemn you to death. Germany is asleep, but we are

awake!" But again: "We do not care a damn for peace. We want war without which we are nothing on this earth."

Karl Kraus said in 1933: "Language can only stammeringly repeat what is happening."[50] And he quoted some of the things the Germans were saying in that year: "Adolf Hitler's mission is God-like," "We have learned to renounce all intellectualism not only in order to serve such a *Führer* but to love him," "That alien race which is *artfremd* to the blood of the Germans, those leeches who suck dry our unhappy nation—away with the Jews! The Jews have declared war on us, a nation of 65 millions. We want to be—away with the Jews!" But Kraus also quoted the words of the noble German poet, August Platen:

> *Aber einst aus unsern Knochen*
> *Wird ein Rächer auferstehn!*[51]

The two most outspoken warners against the threatening barbarism were Heinrich and Thomas Mann.

In 1919 Heinrich Mann published a lengthy essay, "Monarchy and Republic," in which he showed again how wrong German policy and the German way of thinking had been during the previous decades. The longing for unity had been taken up by "men of violence," the foundation of the Reich in 1871 was not at all a masterwork but rather "an ephemeral *coup de main*," and from then onward the motto had been "Might before Right" and *"Oderint dum metuant."* The ideology of the Reich was "an ideology of evil," realism to them was the cynical opinion that only evil was realistic. The Reich between 1871 and 1914 was characterized by arrogance, the madness of its rulers, the stupidity of servile subjects, hatred of men, commercial avarice, and shameless anti-spirituality. The new Reich had nothing in it which promised any future. It was even more vulgar than the France of Louis Philippe, and had the glittering façade of the empire of Napoleon III with its theatricality, prestige politics, and military absolutism disguised as constitutionalism. The Kaiser, a jack-of-all-trades with an eagle helmet and seventy uniforms, continuously incited the nation to get to the top and twice refused an alliance with Great Britain, because, true to Bismarck's principles, "he always wanted to be the senior partner of an alliance."

The soul of the age, Mann continued, was the Pan-Germans with their senseless and irresponsible demonstrations of power, the degenerated professors, generals, and industrialists who tried to absorb Europe "peacefully" in a manner that spelled war long before 1914. They spoke perpetually of their "dashing swords," of "the German army," of "German science," of "German music". It was their philosophical pride to have "overcome" morality by politics. Their slavery they called "liberty"; democracy was "a sign of decay," eternal peace but a dream—and not a beautiful one at that—human progress a lie.

Thus they roused nationalism and called themselves "an everlasting master race." The noise they made in 1913, when celebrating the centenary of Leipsic, implied "In the end it is we who are the victors." When war came they spoke of the nobility of their nation and of their infinitely higher mission. "That Reich had in it the seeds of defeat ever since," said Heinrich Mann. The curse of the victory of 1870 had brought them to 1914 and 1918 and to the downfall of "the arrogant adventurers." When the Germans clamored about the injustices of the Treaty of Versailles, he reminded them that they had shown by their Treaty of Brest-Litovsk that they would have behaved "much more intransigently" if they had won the war. As the word "revolution" was roared down in the Reichstag by monarchists, he added that that revolution had come about with little enthusiasm and had not brought about a genuine change of mind. "The lies of the monarchy have been taken over complete with its staff"; the worst warmongers felt the least responsibility. "But a nation must first realise its full responsibility before it can clamour for justice."[52]

Not many read this appeal with contrition. Nor did they listen to what Heinrich Mann told them in the following years, down to 1933. Your fathers, he reminded them, have, in the words of the Kaiser, led you toward "glorious days," they fed you "with hatred" both before and during the war. Never has the word "nation" been identical with "internal freedom." Personal responsibility has always been, and still is, unknown with us. "Democracy means the responsibility of everybody for everybody." But you follow "the knights of the past," nationalists like Ludendorff whose activities make the world around us doubt whether Germany's democracy is the real thing. These nationalists hated the French until "the incident of the victory" in 1870 eased their hearts. Then they began to hate Great Britain; the war of 1914 gave them an opportunity "to degrade all Europe." But for their anti-Semitism they have not yet found an outlet. "The anti-Semites cannot forget the time of their national disaster. Hence the super-emphasis on their national superiority." In reality they suffer from an "inferiority complex."[53] He foretold the nationalists and racialists: "Every dictator ends at some Waterloo."[54]

They refused to listen to him and called him one of the worst destroyers of the German spirit. In 1933 he had to flee into exile; he never returned to Germany. In 1946 he reminded his compatriots that they had never bothered about politics since the time of the romantics, who had turned to history instead. They developed the fatal fanaticism of *"Gott strafe England"* and the slogans "master race, living space, geopolitics," and racial madness. "A nation representing a mixture of old-German, Slav, Celto-Roman and Jewish races, with a sprinkle of Nordics, pretends not only to be a race but to be a master race, *the* master race."[55]

Thomas Mann began his fight against the German mentality of the post-war period in 1922. His political development was both so characteristic and so uncharacteristic of the development of German intellectuals as to warrant a closer description. Up to 1914 he was, or thought he was, an unpolitical, a sinfully individualistic writer, always concerned with the problems of his own spiritual existence, that is, decadence, pessimism, the questionability of writing, the relation of spirit and life, nihilism and the possibility of its conquest ("moral resoluteness beyond the depths of knowledge").[56] This individualistic attitude, he knew, was a Goethean heritage, as expressed in the words of Wilhelm Meister: "To form myself just as I am, was darkly, from my youth up, my purpose and my desire."[57] We find the same attitude in Stifter's *Indian Summer,* in Keller's *Green Henry,* Hesse's *Narciss and Goldmund,* and Thomas Mann's *The Magic Mountain,* all of them *Erziehungsromane,* not novels of social manners. But *The Magic Mountain* marks a turning point in Mann's spiritual life. He alluded to this fact when he said in 1923, before finishing the book, that he had "remained too long in the magic mountain of romantic aestheticism."[58] He was not understood, and Germany has now to bear the consequences. Aestheticism and barbarism, Thomas Mann said after the war, are twin brothers. And remembering his brother Heinrich's brave attitude during the first German war he paid apologetic homage to him on several occasions.

Before his change of mind, he had, as a disciple of Goethe and Schopenhauer, been an unpolitical man, and when, during the First World War, the problem of politics was forced on his mind, he looked around and found that "German education fundamentally lacks the political element."[59] As a pessimistic onlooker he saw that politics only made men doctrinaire, one-sided, narrow-minded, intolerant, self-righteous, fanatical, and, most of all, it requested them to believe in a man's good nature and progress. Schopenhauer had called all this "nefarious optimism." As an artist with his "inborn sense for mastership and aversion against bungling," he disliked everybody's talking of, and interfering with, everything.[60] It was this mental attitude, not a particular enthusiasm for the Kaiser, that forced him to decide for Germany in the First World War. He in time changed his romantic attitude, having realized, as he said much later, that politics was never something by itself, that it was something "bound up with the ethical, the aesthetic, with things seemingly intellectual and philosophic."[61]

When still defending his unpolitical pessimism, he stressed: "I do not belong to any party, I do not fight democracy."[62] It was the example of Kant which helped him to overcome his romantic passion, while still consciously confessing it. Kant's two main works, *Critique of Pure Reason* and *Critique of Practical Reason,* offered themselves as a symbol to him. In the first, Kant had radically demolished all metaphysics, but in the second he realized that no absolute morality was possible without metaphysics and he reintroduced belief in God into his argument. He restricted radicalism to the theoretical sphere, behaving toward life in a practical, ethical, anti-radical way. In the same manner Thomas Mann restricted his radical pessimism to the theoretical sphere—and began to advocate politics and democracy, because Germany's state of mind became very alarming and disturbing, so much so that he felt, like his brother, more at home on the other side of the Rhine than in authoritarian Germany.

All the reactionaries, who had up to then admired him because of his "unpolitical" ideas, immediately began to call him a traitor. They had not read his confessions closely enough; had they done so, they would have stumbled over this: "Conservative? I am not conservative, of course. In cases like mine destructive and conservative tendencies mix." He spoke of his "free, knowing, tender, spiritual, ironical conservatism."[63] They did not listen, they shouted "Traitor, deserter!" This was the rule in Germany; they never listened to the warnings of the few judicious men in their midst but defamed them and drove them into exile.

The murder of Rathenau in 1922 was the beginning. It was, as Mann then publicly called it, the mad misdeed of "uncouth racial"[64] vandalism, and a little later he spoke of a new "racial religion with antipathy not only against international Judaism but also, quite expressly, against Christianity," a "pagan folk-religion, Wotan cult, romantic barbarism."[65] Turning to the monarchistic reactionaries, he said that the new republic could be "something more German" than the glittering, saber-rattling monarchy which had been but an "imperial gala opera." He warned them not to misuse the present unavoidable misery for glorification of the discarded monarchy. He quoted Walt Whitman:

> For you these from me, O Democracy, to serve you, *ma femme,*
> For you, for you I am trilling these songs.[66]

Immediately, vicious attacks began to pour down on him, for, as he said years later, they "unanimously" called the democratic republic "a bad joke, and shrugged their shoulders."[67]

Even the composer Hans Pfitzner for whose fame Mann, in his extraordinary analysis of *Palestrina,* had done more than anybody else, turned against him. He wrote to Mann that he had to sever their friendship because of Mann's "approval of the Marxist November Republic."[68] The German republic had never been Marxist. The Social Democrats behaved very sensibly and patriotically and tried to remedy the mess into which the Kaiser and the reactionaries had brought Germany. Pfitzner —Thomas Mann did not know this at the time—had already been visited twice by Hitler, with whom he had discussed the war, its consequences, and anti-Semitism.[69] In 1933 Pfitzner organized a campaign against Mann and protested publicly, in common with Richard Strauss, Clemens von Frankenstein, Hans Knappertsbusch, and many other celebrities, against Mann's Wagner lecture, which he had given in Amsterdam. In their protest, published in various newspapers, they praised "the national rebirth of Germany" and said that Thomas Mann had "suffered the misfortune to lose his national persuasion when the republic was founded, exchanging it for a cosmopolitan and democratic one." They felt compelled, they said, to defend Richard Wagner against "defamation." Thomas Mann had not defamed Wagner by any means. He had only shown that Wagner and his music, a complex of mythology, psychology, and psychoanalytical insight (mother fixation, sexual desire, and fear), belonged to the romantic period of French and German music. What infuriated those protestants most was, as they put it, that he "presented himself abroad as a representative of the German spirit."[70] After Germany's downfall Pfitzner, "obstinately German and bitterly angry," as Mann called him, called Mann and Hermann Hesse "wretches" because they "did not believe that we Germans are the highest and noblest of peoples." Pfitzner still believed it and said the German nation was "a canary among a flock of sparrows," to which Mann retorted: "I was of course only a grey rationalistic sparrow among so many sentimental canaries from the Hartz mountains."[71] To Hesse he wrote that the Germans had been glad to get rid of him in 1933, and the consequence was "the inevitable ruin of unhappy Germany, which both of us foresaw."[72]

Thomas Mann was not deterred by Pfitzner and the other unteachable writers and politicians and went on warning the Germans against the new nationalism which was soon to become National Socialism. In the preface to *The Magic Mountain* he said that with the war so much had begun "which has scarcely yet ceased to begin."[73] He pictured an ideal of a civilized and enlightened humanity and depicted his hero's enthusiasm for "the friendliness, the mutual courteous regard these children of the sun showed to each other, a calm, reciprocal reverence wreathed in smiles."[74] He warned against growing anti-Semitism as represented by a certain Wiedemann. "The preaching of this negative gospel was the pride and content of his life."[75]

Thomas Mann said in 1953: "Very early I saw the terrible dangers looming over Germany, Europe and the world, at a time when the mischief could still have easily been stamped out. . . . It showed itself as a beautiful cult of the depths, conservative revolution and intellectual obscurantism, and prepared the road to disaster."[76]

When Mann was invited in 1926 to Paris to lecture there, he visited the Russian refugee writers Leo Schestow, Iwan Bunin, and Dmitry Mereshkovsky. "I felt sympathy, solidarity, a sort of possible comradeship. I do not doubt that circumstances may arise under which their fate might prove to be mine."[77] He was right. But he went on with his warnings. The National Socialists, he said, have adopted the idea of revolution while successfully masquerading "the most dead-and-buried ideas as the greatest novelty"; their hatred and barbarism, he said, would lead to war.[78]

The catastrophic result of the election of September 14, 1930 was hailed by millions, among them Professor Otto Koellreutter, who said: "It was a rebellion of the younger generation, representing the future of the German state, against a system which had no idea whatsoever of the state."[79] That election caused Thomas Mann to go to Berlin and deliver his *Appeal to Reason,* his strongest warning against the "orgiastic, nature-deifying, radically anti-humanitarian, intoxicated, dynamic, absolutely unbribled" National Socialists. He accused the many professors who, with their "Germanistic romanticism and Nordic creed," expressed "in an idiom of mystical probity and high-flown wishy-washy," had given the National Socialists an ideological superstructure and had poisoned the souls and stupified the brains of millions, much more than "the political romanticism that had led them into the war" of 1914. "It this German?" he asked. The Germans had a long emotional and intellectual history behind them—and now they were offered "a primitive, pure-blooded, blue-eyed simplicity that smiles and submits and claps its heels together." He differentiated between the Roman Catholic part of the population which had "remained safe in the bosom of the Church with her universal and super-national heritage, strongly rejecting all ethnic paganism,"[80] and the part that shouted "Heil Hitler!" These yelled and rioted during Thomas Mann's whole lecture, and he had to leave through a back door. A friend of the Enlightenment, he said in later years, regards the conception of "the folk" (in the racial sense of the word) as alarmingly anachronistic because it usually stirs up "all sorts of reactionary evils."[81]

In 1933, he left his barbarized country, with the words of his favorite poet, August von Platen, in his mind, that it is much better for a man who hates barbarism to leave his fatherland when slaves hail evil, then "to bear the yoke of the blind hatred of the mob."[82] While millions were hailing their Pied Piper from Braunau, and shouting "Germany, awake!" he entered in his diary: "Never has anything like this happened in the human sphere. What will become of the over-joyous, intoxicated and seemingly happy German nation? How many disappointments will it have to swallow? What physical and psychological catastrophes are in store for it? Their awakening will be ten times more terrible than in 1918."[83] In 1938 he wrote: "A nation which is taught 'to release the safety-catch of its revolvers,' if somebody speaks of culture, surely, that nation will be wrecked and perish."[84]

His letters of the years between the two German wars are full of the same warnings, condemnations, and forebodings. The Latin blood in his veins, "was reason enough for our literary Teutons to hate me"; the "Germanic and racialist world is always only separated from barbarism by three steps." Hindenburg's presidency was mere romanticism. How could the Germans be so instinctless as to choose a warrior of ancient times as head of their country? The nationalists were out for a war of revenge. Count Coudenhove-Kalergi, who "propagates the necessary with the clearest passion," only met "with the resistance and hatred of those who tried with godless faithfulness to live in the past." When Thomas Mann began to write his *Joseph* novels, his heart filled with joy about Jacob's blessing for his favorite son: "The Almighty who shall bless thee with blessings of heaven above, blessings of the deep that lieth under. . . ." In 1927, he wrote: "It is terrible to see how they hate in Germany today." The country was full of Fascists calling themselves revolutionaries. "What has this nationalism to do with fatherland? It is but a dynamic romanticism, the glorification of the catastrophe for catastrophe's sake." Some professors of Munich university had already said when Rathenau was murdered: "Bravo, one less!" In 1932 Mann wrote: "One shudders to think what defeats are in store for us, what desperate self-lacerations! We shall see what they will make of Germany." When, in 1933, Einstein applauded his courageous stand against the Nazis, he answered: "This is the most honorable thing that I have ever experienced in my life." That so-called revolution was no revolution at all. "It lacks all the characteristics of genuine revolutions which, however bloody they may have been, have won the sympathy of the world. To have warned against this moral and spiritual misfortune will once be our honourary title." In 1934 he wrote to Professor Ernst Bertram, who had betrayed him: "I want to be buried in Switzerland, as Stefan George had wanted it." When he saw Frenchmen of a little town in France celebrate the day of the Bastille, he asked himself "whether the Germans will once dance a whole day remembering the burning of the *Reichstag.*" In 1934 he wrote: "Miserable, miserable nation! I have long been praying that they should be scattered all over the world, as the Jews have been scattered with whom they are connected by many tragedies." When, in 1935, he was awarded an honorary degree by Harvard University, some five or six thousand people acclaimed the act. When a Swiss critic wrote in 1936 that only Jewish writers had left Germany he retorted:

"My brother Heinrich and I are no Jews. Nor are Leonhard Frank, René Schickele, Fritz von Unruh, Oskar Maria Graf, Annette Kolb, A. M. Frey, Gustav Regler, Bernhard Brentano and Ernst Glaeser. . . . One is not German if one is a racialist. Their hatred of Jews is not directed against the Jews alone. It is directed against Europe, against all better Germans, against the Christian and Greek fundaments of the Western civilisation." Remembering his *Joseph* novels, he felt deep sorrow "that the most characteristic and incommensurably German book had to be written in exile. . . . I hate those murderers of humanity and blood-thirsty fools from the bottom of my heart and wish them with all my soul the terrible end they deserve."[85]

These are the facts. But the Germans of today want us to believe that the Treaty of Versailles caused the rise of Hitlerism. In reality, as we read in *Through the Looking Glass:*

> I told them once, I told them twice:
> They would not listen to advice.

They have never given a thought to the old democratic wisdom that the price of freedom is eternal vigilance. Theodor Haecker entered in his diary of 1940: "This terrible man who ran amok could easily have been removed in the beginning."[86] He had already written in 1931: "Ever since the German Doctor Faust, by a grotesque rape of language, theological and philosophical language, translated the words 'In the beginning was the Word' (of God) by 'In the beginning was the Deed,' German genius fell into delirium without ending. The effect of this spiritual misdeed makes the effect of the whole Nietzsche a mere trifle, a mere consequence of that deed, of that misdeed by which generations were educated in a childish pride." The Germans "renewed the Promethean and Titanic by the Faustian, of which the old Goethe was shuddering a little in the end. The so-called Faustian man is a man hypertrophic in his instincts and atrophic in his intellect."[87] To judicious Germans (a tiny minority, as usual) it is clear beyond any doubt that National

Socialism was not a consequence of the Treaty of Versailles. Thomas Mann said in 1938: "The bottomless resentment, the deeply festering thirst for revenge of an unfit, impossible, ten times stranded and utterly frustrated man met with the (much less warranted) inferiority complex of a defeated nation which did not know how to make something sensible of its defeat."[88] In 1943 he said that National Socialism bore its mark from the very beginning and could never have had any other result. "This is Germany's great guilt, that she did not see it when there was still time to see it."[89] He reminded them again and again of his warnings and told them that their mad leaders would never lead them to victory. "If you are defeated, all spirits of revenge will fall on your heads for what you have done to the other nations."[90] And again: "You know the unspeakable crimes against Russians, Poles and Jews"; and he spoke of "the gigantic hatred which will fall on your heads one day. Hell came over you when these leaders came over you."[91] Professor Wilhelm Roepke, after the war, agreed with this: "All this could clearly have been foreseen long before National Socialism began to reveal its true nature to the world, if one had cared to look at the deeds and words of the National Socialists, at their faces, into their books." He refutes another lie, widely believed in postwar Germany, by saying that the great unemployment of 1929-1933 had nothing to do with the growth of National Socialism. "Decisive was their intellectual and moral constitution. They were very easily moulded and in political questions lacked all discernment."[92] When one of the German counsels in Nuremberg asserted that the German nation had been tyrannized by Hitler and had been his first victim, the judges referred him to *Mein Kampf*.

Professor F. W. Foerster, who had fought German militarism and anti-Semitism all his life and had spent both wars in exile, said that the Germans were again trying to mystify the world by their Versailles legend. "Hitler only popularised what had grown up in Germany for a hundred years, Prussian militarism and Pan-Germanism are two gigantic trees, the roots of which reach deep down into German history, and which become one in National Socialism. . . . The Germans have politically stopped at the age of puberty."[93] Professor Othmar Anderle is of the same opinion: "It is no mere chance, that Germany is the land of 'eternal boys.' Everything German is self-contradictory, unbalanced, *outré,* as is characteristic of all puberty." He sees a direct line going from the literary movement of the *Sturm and Drang* of the 18th century across the movement of the Wartburg students of 1817 and its renewal in the age of the Kaiser down to National Socialism.[94]

In 1956 German sixth form students were invited to listen to one of Hitler's raving speeches reproduced from a British record which had been lent to the school for that occasion. When asked for their opinion on what they had just heard the hesitated and stuttered that they could not possibly criticize the behavior of the Germans before the war. "We should have to say," one said, "that our parents were stupid." "You may safely say so, my boy," the teacher answered. "We have been stupid, and this is the least that can be said."[95]

To return to Thomas Mann, in 1936 he was deprived of the honorary degree which Bonn University had awarded him in 1919. The man who signed the letter of cancellation Professor K. J. Obenauer who in a book contrasted the literature of the pre-Hitler period with that of the Third Reich. The latter, he said, was racial and "Nordic-Germanic, the former rootless, unfamiliar with the problem of blood."[96] Thomas Mann answered in a lengthy letter which was smuggled into Germany and passed from hand to hand by Roman Catholic priests. In it he spoke of the barbarities daily committed in Nazi Germany and made this prophecy which nine years later was fulfilled to the letter: "Woe to the nation which, seeing no other way out, would in the end really plunge the world into a war equally hateful to God and men! This nation would be lost! It will be defeated so as never to rise again."[97] In his novel, *Lotte in Weimar,* he compared the Germany of Goethe with that of Hitler, Göbbels, Himmler, and Streicher, and cursed the Germans for having hailed a "fanatic scoundrel who appeals to their baser qualities, confirms them in their vices, teaches them that nationality means barbarism." Germans, Goethe says, must be open-minded mediators, but Hitler's Germans show a "pig-headed craving to be a unique nation." They glorify themselves and want to rule the world by stupidity. "Wretched nation, they will meet with a bad end because they do not want to understand themselves. But if you misunderstand yourselves this not only arouses laughter, but brings you into the greatest possible danger. I am sure they will be defeated because they betrayed themselves and did not want to be like the others."[98]

His warnings were ignored by the Germans but, most unfortunately, they were also ignored by the Western countries, France and Great Britain, as much ignored and resented as the warnings of Sir (then Mr.) Winston Churchill. In 1933 the latter drew attention to the barbarism prevailing in Germany, and in the same way Thomas Mann tried to arouse Great Britain's conscience against the persecution of Jews and Christians by the Nazis. He said in 1938 exactly what Mr. Churchill said after the Munich pact, namely that "peace can never be saved by treachery, by abandoning all honour. . . . When we warned against what threatened the world we were called warmongers."[99] But in justice to Great Britain, we must add today that it was France which violated her pact with Czechoslovakia. Great Britain had never concluded such a pact but might have come to the help of Czechoslovakia if France had been willing to fulfill her treaty obligations. Neville Chamberlain had disliked Germany throughout his life. "On the whole," he said in 1930, "I loathe the Germans." He saw very early that Hitler symbolized an aggressive Germany which encouraged "bloodshed and assassination for her own selfish aggrandisement and pride." He called Hitler "a lunatic," Goebbels "a vulgar common little mind," and Ribbentrop "so stupid, so shallow, so self-centred and self-satisfied, so totally devoid of intellectual capacity that he never seems to take in what is said to him." Chamberlain was also "horrified by the German behavior to the Jews." His policy of appeasement sprang from his love of peace and his belief that Hitler was in a stronger position than Great Britain. He erred in that, but it was not an ignoble belief.[100]

To state Great Britain's and France's responsibility, as Churchill and Thomas Mann have done, is one thing. But it is an entirely different thing to allow the Germans to shift their responsibility for Hitler onto Great Britain or to speak of Chamberlain's stab-in-the-back at precisely that moment when some German generals were about to arrest Hitler. If they thought that Hitler was a maniac out to destroy Europe, it was their duty to remove Hitler from the political scene. Or was it Great Britain's duty to act as governess to Germany and keep her on the path of virtue? It is intolerable to read what a certain Dr. Richard Thilenius (and many other unteachable Germans) have said: "It is indeed hard to understand why the foreign powers during the first six years of Nazism paid so little attention to the political programme published by Hitler only a few years earlier."[101] Why did the Germans not pay any attention to it and why did they shout "Heil Hitler!" in spite of the many warnings of their best compatriots?

In 1945, after Germany's ruin, Thomas Mann said: "To live there again—utterly impossible."[102] When the German novelist Walter von Molo, a writer of unimportant novels about the Hohenzollerns, Luther, and Schiller, invited him to return to Germany, he answered in an open letter on September 28, 1945, a letter which caused much uproar in his ex-fatherland. "Can these twelve years and their results," he asked, "simply be wiped off the black-board? Can one behave as if nothing had happened?" He reminded Molo of his years of wandering from one country to another, and of the oath of allegiance which so many writers had sworn to the Führer. Why did not all writers, composers, artists, teachers, and doctors do what he had done? "Why did they not rebel as one man against the barbarism?" He reminded Molo of the words of Hermann Hesse, who said that the Germans are "impossible as a political nation," and added that he, too, would have nothing to do with them, that he had already publicly declared long before Germany's downfall that he did not intend "ever to leave the United States." What happened in Germany was the result of the German character; therefore one must put up with the consequences and not simply say: "Please, come back, everything is forgiven!" He frankly declared: "An understanding between someone, who has witnessed the witches' sabbath from abroad, and you, who have shared in the dance and waited on the Devil, would be rather difficult." He suggested that the books which had been written in Germany between 1933 and 1945 should be destroyed—"a smell of blood and shame clings to them." But he also said: "I shall never cease to regard myself as a German writer." He mentioned the book he was just writing, a book about Germany, and added: "The pact with the Devil is a deep German temptation, and a German novel which deals with the sufferings of the last years, sufferings caused by Germany, must have that terrible pact as its topic."[103]

He strictly adhered to his resolution not to return to Germany, which had become utterly alien to him. In 1934 he had written to a man who had once been his friend and god-father to his youngest child but had betrayed him: "Unhappy, unhappy nation! I have been thinking long ago that the world-spirit may free them from politics, dissolve the nation and disperse them in a new world like the Jews."[104] When he left the United States he went to Switzerland, where he lies buried. Only twice did he visit Germany, for short periods, to lecture on

Goethe and Schiller, whose great humanistic heritage the Germans had shamefully betrayed. About his first visit in 1949 he wrote to a friend: "It was very likely at the last moment possible that I went to Germany—once and never again. Already this time a large number of detectives seemed to be appropriate."[105] Three years later he said: "The fatherland over there is highly uncanny, a dangerous land which terrifies me."[106] He settled down for good in Switzerland, where he had first found refuge in 1933, because Switzerland, as he said in 1945, was "far more European than the political colossus to the North" where the word "international" has long since been considered an insult and where arrogant provincialism had "tainted the atmosphere and made it stagnant."[107] He died in Switzerland in 1956 and lies buried in a village cemetery high above the lake of Zurich, near the Swiss poet and writer to whom he had felt akin, C. F. Meyer. Meyer, in his novel *The Temptation of Pescara,* makes the victor of Pavia in 1525 say about defeated Italy: "Twice she had seen liberty. . . . Now she stands on the threshold of slavery, because she has lost all honour and virtue. Nobody can help her, neither man nor God. How can lost freedom be won again? By a thrust and storm of the moral powers coming up from the depths of the nation."[108] Thomas Mann said much the same thing about his defeated nation.

Hitler thundered against Bolshevism, which he called Jewish, and imagined himself saving Germany and Europe from Communism, which was then threatening neither Germany nor Europe; he said in *Mein Kampf:* "Russian Bolshevism is to be regarded as the 20th century Jewish attempt to become master of the world."[109] Meanwhile in 1933 and 1939, Thomas Mann said that National Socialism was "a philistine Bolshevism in the midst of Europe, a morally inferior form of Bolshevism, an anarchic revolution threatening the fundaments and pillars of all Western morality and civilisation, a revolution of mere violence, of spiritual nihilism—the worst kind of Bolshevism, different from the Russian by a complete lack of ideas."[110] While Hitler pretended he was saving European culture, Thomas Mann called him "a henchman of culture, a ravisher of culture."[111] While Colonel-General Guderian, who served Hitler to the last, is of the opinion that Hitler's dictatorship was only "a feeble copy of that of Stalin,"[112] Professor Roepke, who refused to swear an oath of allegiance to Hitler, who left Germany in 1933, and who is still teaching at Geneva, calls National Socialism "the most repulsive tyranny of all times. No totalitarian regime has more devilishly corrupted men than National Socialism. It has ruined and degraded Germany and dragged her into the mire, and brought our whole western culture to a point from where it cannot be said yet whether it will recover again."[113] Thomas Mann spoke in 1940 of "the most infamous tyranny that has ever threatened the world" and said that Hitler had come "to replace the teaching of the brotherhood of all men under God by a creed murderous for bodies and souls." In 1941 he said that National Socialism "had deep roots in German history, it was the virulent degeneration of ideas which had in them the seed of murderous corruption." In 1942 he spoke of "the revolutionary philosophy of bestialism" which was committing crimes "so shamefully, so hopelessly, so unforgetably that one could not see how the Germans could live in future among the other nations as one of them."[114] After the war, Thomas Mann thanked his good genius for having left a nation "which all its spirituality and all its music could not prevent from hailing the basest barbarity and threatening the foundations of European civilisation."[115]

When General Sir Brian Horrocks uncovered one of those "horror" camps south of Bremen in the spring of 1945 he was "physically sick within five minutes, and the sight of those human skeletons in those awful striped pyjamas will remain with me to the end of my days. . . . My whole attitude towards

Germans has changed." He said to the German general who surrendered to him: "The world will never forgive Germany for these camps."[116] On April 12, 1945, the American General George rang General Omar Bradley to come and see "how bastardly these Krauts can be." So Generals Bradley, Eisenhower, and Patton went to the "pesthole" of Ohrdruf. They saw 3,200 naked, emaciated corpses with lice crawling over their skin; starving soldiers had torn out the entrails of the dead for food. Eisenhower's face became white, Patton was sick in a corner. "Here death had been so fouled by degradation that it both stunned and numbed us."[117]

National Socialism, says Thomas Mann, was the political fulfilment of ideas which had haunted the German nation for at least 150 years. "A patriotism which asserted that a blood state like that was so foreign to our national character that it could not take root among us: such a patriotism would seem to me more high-minded than realistic."[118]

Many a decent German fully agrees with him. Professor Ewald Wasmuth, a Roman Catholic philosopher, says that he and his Christian friends saw during the years "when the dark birds of disaster darkened Germany and the Germans greeted the unholy as their salvation," the explanation for this is in a hymn of Hölderlin's:

> *Wer hub es an? Wer brachte den Fluch? Von heut*
> *Ist's nicht und nicht von gestern, und die zuerst*
> *Das Mass verloren, unsre Vaeter,*
> *Wussten es nicht und es trieb der Geist sie.*[119]

(Who started it? Who brought the curse? It is not of today nor of yesterday. Those who had first lost the measure, our forefathers, did not know it when the spirit drove them on.)

Max Pribilla, another Roman Catholic writer, speaks of "the political immaturity of the Germans. A nation which is so clumsy as to arouse the enmity of the whole world twice in one generation can of course not claim to be politically gifted. The

Third Reich was the best proof of its political absurdity and brought about the most terrible catastrophe in German history." He quotes what *Das Schwarze Korps* wrote on February 8, 1940: "If we consider the political events of the last few years, as the *Führer* has been explaining them again and again both persuasively and simply, we can only be astonished at how little important the role of reason is in the evaluation of those events." Pribilla compares this with what Sir Winston Churchill said in the House of Commons on November 11, 1947, namely that the British, in their long history, have learned more than any other nation that they must control their politicians.[120]

Reinhold Schneider, a Roman Catholic poet, novelist, and essayist, says that the government of the Third Reich did not come about "by chance" but had been "potentially inherent in German history. How else could it have met with such undeniable approval?" Just as *Don Quixote* was a critique of the Spanish nation, so Goethe's *Faust* was a critique of the Germans. Faust was "the great hero of the downfall which we are experiencing now." Did Goethe in his wisdom not warn the Germans by his poem? But the Germans did not heed the warning. They called themselves "Faustian," spoke of Faustian culture, Faustian ages. This Faustianism means "the guilty flight of the foundering, insatiable spirit through all the space of the universe, the abyss, and history."[121]

Professor Eduard Hemmerle, yet another Roman Catholic, says Hitler would never have succeeded in Germany "if he had not found the soil prepared for his grains of seed. It had been prepared by philosophers and politicians who had idolized the state and prevented the Germans from maturing towards independent thinking and acting."[122] Professor Karl Heim, a Lutheran theologian, said after Germany's downfall that only the Germans, with their professors, judges, and generals, who "have but a minimum of political insight," were capable of surrendering themselves and their fate "unconditionally" to the

"*Führer,* that corporal," and allowing themselves to be brought to complete ruin.[123]

Professor Wilhelm Roepke says that "romantic mysticism in all its forms has been at the bottom of the German spirit through centuries, so much so that the German could be called the eternal romantic. There lurks in German romanticism a want of moderation, unruliness and savageness which broke through five times in the last two centuries: in the storm and stress of the 18th century, in the romantic movement, in the young Germany movement, in the movement of the youth and, in the extreme, in National Socialism." The latter is "not only Prussianism but also the extreme degeneration of the mystical romanticism of the Germans." It was, therefore, that he said to them: "Do not think it is enough to call the National Socialists criminals with whom you have nothing to do! There is no doubt whatever that National Socialism was the outcome of conditions peculiar to Germany alone. . . . In order to germinate, the seed of Hitlerism had to find favourable soil. We must stress the fact with the utmost vigour that the Third Reich has deep roots in German history, and is the catastrophic end of the fatal development which began with the brutal unification of Germany by Bismarck." Professor Roepke therefore speaks of a "collective guilt of which only a minority of the nation can regard itself free with a good conscience, a guilt of the most hideous and bestial cruelties which men can invent and commit, a guilt of the painful death of millions."[124] Comparing the Germans with the British, Professor Roepke says: "The German inclination to self-pity is connected with their great touchiness as individuals and as members of their nation. They are very little gifted with the precious gift of self-irony and self-criticism, and, consequently, they are lacking the fine art of laughing at themselves. A burlesque description of their own history, such as the English love, has, up to now, been impossible in Germany."[125] The Bishop of Osnabrueck said to General Sedgwick in 1945: "You Englishmen can do what we never have learnt to do, laugh at yourselves."[126] Another German who visited Great Britain after the war wrote in a German newspaper "that the English dislike all boasting and showing off, preferring to appear ten degrees too small to appearing one degree too big."[127] A German woman who visited Great Britain after the war said to the BBC correspondent in Bonn after her return to Germany: "You British are twenty seconds in the minute slower than the Germans, but you are two hundred years ahead in your attitude to life."[128] Hugo Preuss, who in 1918 drew up the Constitution of the German Republic, called the Germans "the most excitable nation in the world. They are not accustomed nor willing to act against the will of authority."[129] Professor Michael Freund said after the last war: "Latitudinarianism took the least roots in Great Britain, Scandinavia and the Netherlands. In Great Britain the former leader of the Labour Party, Earl Attlee, could pride himself on the Bible being the programme of his party. In Great Britain no 'Christian' parties arose because it would make no sense, where everybody is Christian, to call a particular party Christian. In Great Britain Communism is almost non-existent, and so is radicalism. The conservative parties there need not fear that socialism might topple over to the left, nor need the leftist parties fear that conservatism might topple over to the right."[130] Professor Hans-Oskar Wilde wrote a book of 600 pages in praise of Great Britain's "middle way" through the last three centuries. He quotes Dean Inge who once said: "The Englishman, like a sailor on shore, preserves his equilibrium by rolling heavily from side to side, still keeping somewhere near the middle of the road." Even English socialism, says Professor Wilde, "is different from both German and French socialism" because it always betrays "strong tendencies of liberalism and monconformism." Thus Great Britain succeeded in the middle of our century in peacefully bringing about "one of the greatest social revolutions which in its depth, efficiency and character can only be compared with the glorious English revolution of 1688." Why? "The English idea of liberty always remained concrete and embedded in English life and tradition." The English, he says, "can laugh at themselves and at their history," theirs is "a patience of listening and waiting, goodness, humaneness, modesty."[131]

Now let us listen to three Austrians. Professor Alois Melichar who, as an anti-Nazi, was deprived of his position as conductor of the Berlin Philharmonic orchestra, speaks of "the well-known habit of the Germans uncritically to accept every ideology from Frederick II to Adolf I."[132] Professor Stefan Blaskowitz says that the deeper German guilt lies in a constantly frustrated revolution. Luther's reformation was a frustrated social revolution. The German princes misused the revolutionary powers for their own interests, and very soon the "strong hand" of Prussia began to work. The Prussian Elector soon became a Prussian King who expelled the Roman Emperor, representative of a unified Europe, and became Emperor himself. The idea of a universal Christian Reich was replaced by a nationalistic state, the fulfilment of which was National Socialism. Hitler's advent was neither the result of Germany's first defeat nor of the Treaty of Versailles. He was the result of a long development: Prussia above the other princes, Prussia above the universal monarchy, Prussia above Europe, Prussia above all the world. Hitler, obsessed with the idea of a great Reich, was the fulfilment of those mad ideas and thought himself chosen to unite all power and all the world; he regarded himself as the embodiment of Germany, Europe, the world—he had come to replace God. German *hubris* was directed politically against Europe, ideologically against Western ideas, Judaism and Christianity, and nationally against nations and races. This ended in Germany's destruction.[133]

Friedrich Heer, an Austrian historian, finds the vestiges of Erasmus everywhere in Great Britain, "from the 16th century to this very day, in all things where a certain understatement, intelligent and circumspect modesty, quiet culture of spirit and heart, and common sense reign." He speaks of "the free English climate which preserved the Erasmian tradition from the days of Thomas More to the many non-conformist movements.[134] Wilhelm Herzog, a Jewish writer of German origin, says of Erasmus: "What would have become of him in Germany? He would have been imprisoned in a concentration camp to atone for his pacifism, treacherous internationalism, love of tolerance and humanism, his free European outlook. Did this anti-patriot not pronounce: the whole world is my fatherland?"[135]

Lord Herbert Samuel, who blames Germany for two world wars, says of the Germans that they did not follow the humanism of Goethe but the barbaric philosophies of Hegel, Fichte, Treitschke, Spengler, and their successors.[136] Dr. G. P. Gooch, the historian, said in 1945 that the central paradox of German history is "the co-existence through the centuries of a community almost slavishly docile to constituted authority and of a rich, critical, creative cultural life." Comparing Great Britain with Germany he said that "modern Germany has thought primarily in terms of the might and majesty of the state, modern England primarily in terms of the rights and liberties of the citizen."[137] Did not, asks Dr. Gooch in his autobiography, Hegel and Treitschke deify the Prussian state? Austen Chamberlain, he reminds us, once said that Treitschke had revealed to him the narrow-minded, proud and intolerant chauvinism of Prussia. Bismark's triumphs, continues Dr. Gooch, killed German liberalism. The German danger began to reveal itself in 1908, and when British statesmen tried to come to an agreement with Germany on naval rearmament, the Kaiser declined because he was as proud of his navy as a child of his new toy. When Hitler became Chancellor, Dr. Gooch thought of Spengler's prophecy that Germany would never produce another

Goethe but a new Caesar. That now Caesar brought untold misery upon the world and devastation and defeat upon Germany.[138]

Notes

1. Thomas Mann. *Bemuehungen,* p. 242.
2. *Ibid.,* p. 243-248.
3. *Der Untergang des Abendlandes.* Muenchen, 1919, 15th edition, 1920, Vol. I, pp. 36-37, 53-54, 57.
4. *Politische Schriften.* Muenchen, 1933, pp. ix, 9, 11, 15, 32-33, 35, 55-57, 70-71.
5. *Ibid.,* pp. 133, 145, 147, 155.
6. *Im Westen nichts Neues.* Berlin, 1919, 326th edition, 1929, p. 5.
7. *The Way of Sacrifice.* New York, 1928, p. 144.
8. *Vor der Entscheidung.* Berlin, 1919, pp. 26, 140.
9. *Ein Geschlecht.* Muenchen, 1922, p. 66.
10. *In Stahlgewittern.* Berlin, 1929, 10th edition, p. xiv.
11. *Der Kampf als inneres Erlebnis.* Berlin, 1922, pp. 9, 36.
12. *Das Waeldchen 125.* Berlin, 1925, pp. ix-x, 18-19, 50-51, 176, 178-179, 184-185.
13. *Der Arbeiter.* Hamburg, 1932, pp. 11, 13, 20, 121, 253, 256.
14. *Die totale Mobilmachung.* Berlin, 1934, pp. 5-7, 12, 19, 20, 21-23, 28-29, 34-35.
15. *Deutsche Kommentare* (a periodical), Berlin, April 2, 1955.
16. *Das eherne Gesetz.* Berlin, 1934, 30th edition, 1941, pp. 37, 73.
17. *Von 1914-1939,* pp. 3, 28, 36-37, 42.
18. *Der Zauberberg,* Vol. II, p. 69.
19. *Zehn Jahre Kampf fuer Frieden,* August 1, 1922.
20. *Das Neue Reich,* p. 30.
21. *Die Fiktionen der Weimarer Verfassung.* Hamburg, 1928, pp. 49-51, 102, 112.
22. *Der christliche Staatsmann.* Hamburg, 1932, pp. 25-30, 252-254.
23. *Die Herrschaft der Minderwertigen.* Berlin, 1930, pp. 114, 118, 209, 273, 277, 647, 682.
24. *Die Tat* (a periodical), March, 1932, March, April, 1933.
25. *Ibid.,* July, 1931.
26. *Ibid.,* April, 1934.
27. *Der masslose Kontinent: Roosevelts Kampf um die Weltherrschaft.* Jena, 1942, pp. 24, 449-450.
28. R. Boehringer. *Mein Bild von Stefan George,* pp. 43, 150-151; Edgar Salin. *Um Stefan George.* Muenchen, 1954, pp. 184, 225, 255, 264, 274, 312-314.
29. *Deutsche Gestalten.* Leipzig, 1934, pp. 246, 264, 271, 279.
30. Schonauer, *op. cit.,* p. 55.
31. *Die Welt,* Hamburg, May 8, 1957.
32. *Das neue Reich,* p. 112.

33. *Vom Schicksal des deutschen Geistes.* Berlin, 1934, an advertisement at the end of the book.

34. *Staat und Rasse.* Breslau, 1928, pp. 7, 8, 11, 51.

35. *Platon.* Berlin, 1923, pp. 135, 244-246.

36. *Napoleon und die Deutschen.* Berlin, 1926, pp. 38-39.

37. *Der siebente Ring,* pp. 56-57.

38. Salin, *op. cit.,* p. 327.

39. Franz Schonauer. *Stefan George.* Hamburg, 1960, p. 88.

40. *Hochland* (a periodical), October, 1923.

41. *Altes und Neues,* p. 160.

42. *Achtung, Europa!,* pp. 84-92.

43. *Der Steppenwolf. Gesammelte Schriften,* Vol. IV, pp. 266-267.

44. *Briefe,* p. 238.

45. "Ein offenes Wort in ernster Stunde." *Germania,* December 31, 1930.

46. *Erfolg,* pp. 565, 583, 587, 599, 646, 649, 661. And similar ideas on many other pages.

47. *Deutscher Geist in Gefahr,* pp. 19, 20, 24, 84.

48. *Geist der Goethezeit.* Leipiz, 1930, Vol. II, pp. 156-158.

49. "To watch the Rhine will not be enough; the enemy stands at the Spree." *Gesammelte Werke.* Hamburg, 1960, 3 vols., on many pages.

50. *Deutsche Rundschau,* January, 1958.

51. "But a revenger will one day rise from our bones." *Die dritte Walpurgisnacht,* pp. 15, 46, 127, 254.

52. *Macht und Mensch,* pp. 205-207, 210-211, 216-219, 221-222, 229-230, 234-235, 239, 242, 259, 261, 268.

53. *Sieben Jahre.* Wien, 1929, pp. 58, 142, 144, 152, 225, 367, 368, 370, 553 ff.

54. *Ibid.,* p. 229.

55. *Ein Zeitalter wird besichtigt.* Stockholm, 1946, pp. 29, 35-36, 58.

56. *Novellen.* Berlin, 1922, Vol. II, p. 536.

57. Thomas Mann. *Bemuehungen,* 1925, p. 20.

58. *Neue Freie Presse,* Wien, December 30, 1923.

59. *Betrachtungen eines Unpolitischen,* p. 79.

60. *Ibid.,* p. 223.

61. *Lotte in Weimar.* Stockholm, 1939, p. 270.

62. *Betrachtungen eines Unpolitischen,* p. 321.

63. *Ibid.,* p. 606.

64. *Bemuehungen,* pp. 146, 151.

65. *Ibid.,* p. 136.

66. *Ibid.,* pp. 158, 166.

67. *Doktor Faustus,* p. 558.

68. W. Abendroth. *Hans Pfitzner.* Muenchen, 1935, p. 261.

69. *Ibid.,* p. 252.

70. *Muenchner Post,* February 11, 1933; *Fraenkischer Kurier,* April 17, April 19, 1933; *Frankfurter Zeitung,* June 2, 1933.

71. *Altes und Neues,* p. 226.

72. *Ibid.,* pp. 225-226.

73. *Der Zauberberg,* Vol. I, p. 10.

74. *Ibid.*, Vol. II, p. 253.

75. *Ibid.*, Vol. II, p. 576.

76. *Altes und Neues*, p. 13.

77. *Pariser Rechenschaft.* Berlin, 1926, p. 75.

78. *Die Forderung des Tages*, pp. 212 ff.

79. *Der Sinn der Reichstagswahl vom 14. September 1930.* Tuebingen, 1930, p. 5.

80. *Achtung, Europa!*, pp. 50-53, 55, 57-58.

81. *Doktor Faustus*, p. 59.

82. *Briefe 1889-1936.* Frankfurt, 1961, Vol. I. p. 413.

83. *Leiden um Deutschland.* A private printing, pp. 4, 6.

84. *Mass und Wert* (a periodical, edited by Thomas Mann), Zuerich, II/1.

85. Thomas Mann. *Briefe*, pp. 207, 228, 239, 249, 257, 263, 267, 278-281, 319-320, 331-332, 346-349, 367, 395, 409-413, 427, 431.

86. *Tag-und Nachtbuecher*, p. 167.

87. *Vergil.* Leipzig, 1931, pp. 83-84, 105-106.

88. *Altes und Neues*, p. 623.

89. *Deutsche Hoerer!*, p. 100.

90. *Ibid.*, p. 25.

91. *Ibid.*, p. 44.

92. *Die deutsche Frage*, pp. 18, 53, 216.

93. *Neue Zuercher Zeitung.* Quoted in: *Die deutsche Frage, von draussen und drinnen gesechen.* Hannover, 1947, pp. 6, 8-9.

94. *Das universalhistorische System Arnold Toynbees.* Frankfurt and Wien, 1955, pp. 11-12.

95. *Die Zeit*, Hamburg, March 8, 1956.

96. *Volkhafte und politische Dichtung.* Leipzig, 1936, p. 8.

97. *Achtung, Europa!*, p. 106.

98. *Lotte in Weimar*, pp. 328-330, 337.

99. *Altes und Neues*, p. 403.

100. *Sunday Times*, London, October 22, 1961.

101. R Thilenius. *Die Teilung Deutschlands.* Hamburg, 1957, p. 11.

102. In a letter to a life-long friend now living in London.

103. *Aufbau* (a periodical), New York, September 28, 1945.

104. *Briefe an Ernst Bertram.* Pfullingen, 1960, p. 185.

105. In a letter to the author of this book.

106. In another letter to the author of this book.

107. "Deutschland und die Deutschen."

108. *Die Versuchung des Pescara.* Re-issued, together with *Der Heilige*, by Knaur, Berlin, p. 259.

109. *Mein Kampf*, p. 751.

110. *Deutsche Rundschau*, January, 1958; *Altes und Neues*, pp. 634, 653-654; *Das Problem der Freiheit.* Stockholm, 1939, pp. 30-31.

111. *Deutsche Hoerer!*, p. 90-92.

112. *Kann Westeuropa verteidigt werden?*, p. 28.

113. *Die deutsche Frage*, p. 17.

114. *Deutsche Hoerer!*, p. 15-17, 20, 36, 49.

115. *Altes und Neues*, p. 648.

116. *A Full Life*. London, paperback edition, 1962, p. 239.
117. Omar N. Bradley. *A Soldier's Story*. London, 1951, pp. 539-540; George S. Patton. *War as I Know It*. London, 1948, pp. 292, 300.
118. *Doktor Faustus*, p. 731.
119. *Zeit und Stunde*. Salzburg, 1955, p. 8.
120. Max Pribilla. *Deutsche Schicksalsfragen*. Frankfurt, 1950, pp. 92, 102-103, 314.
121. *Verhuellter Tag*. Koeln, 1955, p. 207; *Daemonie und Verklaerung*. Vaduz, 1947, pp. 15-43.
122. Hemmerle, *op. cit.*, p. 8.
123. *Ich gedenke der vorigen Zeiten*. Hamburg, 1956, pp. 263, 274.
124. *Die deutsche Frage*, pp. 68, 108-109, 155-159.
125. *Ibid.*, p. 132.
126. H. Portmann. *Cardinal von Galen*. London, 1957, p. 21.
127. *Die Welt*, Hamburg, May 24, 1957.
128. *The Listener*, London, June 7, 1956.
129. Georg Lukacs. *Die Zerstoerung der Vernunft*, p. 49.
130. *Die Zeit*, Hamburg, February 9, 1956.
131. Hans-Oskar Wilde. *England—Weg der Mitte*. Stuttgart, 1959, p. 349.
132. *Schoenberg*. Wien, 1960, p. 194.
133. In a letter to the author of this book.
134. F. Heer. *Die dritte Kraft*, pp. 133, 620.
135. *Grosse Gestalten der Geschichte*. Bern, 1950, Vol. I, p. 180.
136. *The Listener*, London, December 18, 1958.
137. G. P. Gooch. *The German Mind and Outlook*. London, 1945, p. viii.
138. *Under Six Reigns*. London, 1958, pp. 5, 36-37, 140, 142, 279, 283, 297, 310.

14
The Third Reich

1. Hitler's Generals, Writers, and Professors.

This half-crazy barbarian was hailed by seventeen million voters at a time when they could still have listened to the warnings of the best Germans and voted differently without any danger to their personal security; as the years went by more and more millions hailed him as long as he seemed to win. Today they have forgotten it all. A little too much fuss is made about the German resistance. A few hundred or thousand men and women behaved very honestly and bravely, revolting against Hitler and facing his criminal judges. They have saved the honor of their country and deserve to be praised, even if their political programs for the future of a liberated Germany were rather naïve and nationalistic. While paying tribute to their memory we must not forget that they were only a very tiny minority among many millions shouting "Heil Hitler."

Hitler was acclaimed by almost all the generals and they all spoke his barbaric language. General-Admiral Raeder spoke of the enthusiasm of the German nation for National Socialism born out of the spirit of the German soldiers of the Kaiser's war. "We follow the symbols of rejuvenation with deep love and fanatical passion. Therefore we fight relentlessly against Bolshevism and international Jewry whose nation-destroying activities in our national body we have sufficiently experienced."[1] General-Admiral Dönitz asked what would have become of Germany without Hitler; she would have been "permeated with the disintegrating poison of the Jews."[2] Field-Marshal Reichenau told his soldiers that in a war against Russia, they were "bearers of an inexorable racial idea and avengers of all crimes committed against Germans and *artverwandte* nations. Therefore the soldiers must have full understanding for the necessity of a hard but just retribution meted out to the subhuman Jews."[3] Field-Marshal Manstein said the same in an order of November 20, 1941: the Jews were the go-betweens between the enemies behind the German front and the Russians who were still fighting. They held key points in commerce and the crafts and were the center of all possible disorders and revolts. They should never again be allowed to interfere in Europe. The German soldier was the representative of a racial idea and had to revenge all crimes perpetrated against the Germans. It was also necessary to use the food of Russia for the German army and export the rest (as much as possible) to Germany. The Russians will have to go hungry; it would be an unnecessary humanity to give it to the Russians or the Russian prisoners of war. "The Jewish-Bolshevist system must be exterminated. The soldier must have understanding for the necessity of a hard retribution against the Jews."[4] When he was brought before the judges of Nuremberg and shown this order, he said that he had forgotten all about it. He was prematurely released from prison. When a German colonel saw how Jews were dragged to their death in the Ukraine, some women being shot on the way, he shrugged his shoulders and said: "This is perhaps hard but the Jewish problem cannot be solved in any other way."[5] A decent German said after the war that the German army looked at these barbarities "with a fatalism which did no credit to the officers in whose vocabulary the clean shield of honour played too prominent a part. Their careers depended on the benevolent passivity with which they buried their heads in the sand. Those who keep their tongues in view of certain things are guilty, too."[6] A decent Austrian officer, Hanns H. Pilz, a pupil of Professor F. W. Foerster, who witnessed one of these massacres, wrote after the war: "Having no doubt in our minds that what we had seen was the most horrible thing in all our lives, we burnt that night almost all the books we had brought with us, including the works of Goethe, as all the prattle about *Kultur* seemed to us a downright shameful lie."[7] A German Jewess who had escaped abroad in time speaks of the last visit she paid to two friends living in a home for elderly Jewish people at Berlin: "They were sitting in the sun in the courtyard and reading Goethe. Goethe's countrymen fetched the two women to their death the next day."[8] About those Jews who had escaped in time Professor Alfred Marchionini said: "It was not words from Lessing's *Nathan* or lines from Goethe's *Iphigenie* which the German Jews took with them as the last memory of the old fatherland, but the shouts, orders and curses of inhuman SS men."[9] The greatest Jewish philosopher of German origin, Hermann Cohen, said during the First World War: "The German spirit is the spirit of classical humanism and of true world citizenship. Which nation possesses the spiritual unity of such heroic poets as Lessing, Herder, Schiller, and Goethe, who make our spiritual history a living reality! Which nation possesses that unity of classical literature and philosophy!"[10] He died soon after the first war. Had he lived to see 1933, he would have realized that the great German writers had never succeeded in really civilizing their nation.

Many German generals gave terrible orders which brought them into prison and to the gallows. One of them, General Reinecke, said that all nations had combined against "the racial idea of National Socialism. Our enemies fight us with an infernal hatred, heated by Jewish inventions and the Bolshevist instinct of destruction."[11] Even as late as October, 1944, all General-Field-Marshals in an order proclaimed it as their duty "to bind the army to Hitler's high ideals so that every soldier becomes an even more fanatical fighter for the National Socialist future of our country."[12]

Many of the surviving generals have written books in order to show that they were innocent lambs and to blame their Führer for everything that has happened to Germany. However, Dr. Joseph Scholmer, whom the Russians abducted in 1945 and brought to Workuta, far away in Northern Russia, found there thirty captured German generals whose behavior in captivity gave him the answer to the question: "How could the army tolerate a hysterical neuropath as their supreme commander? Hitler's war was the best chance of their lives. Without them he could never have played the game of his military madness. Even now, five years after the most complete disaster which has ever befallen an army, the moral of the downfall was completely lost on them. They have learned nothing and never will."[13] Field-Marshal Rundstedt was captured by the British army. When in captivity he was asked by General Sir Brian Horrocks whether he had any complaints; he answered that some of the German generals in his prisoner-of-war camp were "not the sort of people" with whom he was used to mix, and that he would be "grateful" if they could be removed to another camp. Who were these undesirable generals? "General Doctors and General Engineers. It is most unpleasant for us real Generals to be forced to live with people like that."[14]

Turning to the Nazi writers, we can fully realize what Karl von Tschuppik meant when he said that a nation of 65 millions can never be barbarized against its will. Eighty-eight writers swore an oath of allegiance to Hitler and declared: "Our deep conviction of our duty to resurrect the Reich, and our resolution to do nothing that is not in accord with our and the fatherland's honour cause us, Herr Reichskanzler, to vow the most faithful obedience to you in this serious hour."[15] A number of important but racially or politically undesirable writers were excluded from Göbbels' newly consititued Chamber of Writers: Alfred Döblin, Bruno Frank, Leonhard Frank, Ludwig Fulda, Georg Kaiser, Bernhard Kellermann, Jakob Wassermann, Alfred Mombert, Alfons Paquet, Rudolf Pannwitz, René Schickele, Fritz von Unruh, Thomas Mann, Heinrich Mann, Franz Werfel. The leading woman writer, Ricarda Huch, left the Nazified Chamber and wrote on April 3, 1933: "What the present government prescribes as national opinion is not my sort of Germanness. Compulsion, brutal methods, defamation of different opinions, boastful self-praise, I do not consider to be German, but fatal. . . . I herewith withdraw my membership of the Academy."[16] Karl Kraus, in Austria, declared in a moving little poem: "The world died when that world awakened."[17] In prose he said that "the obscene misuse of our language has led to the horrors of blood."[18] The Swiss professor Walter Muschg says of Karl Kraus today: "You can recognize the genuine prophets when their vision of the future comes true." He was a representative of "the classical tradition of the Jews." When he was still fighting, his many enemies called him "mad" and spoke of his "megalomania" and, as he was a Jew, they spoke of his "nihilism." His *The Last Days of Mankind,* published after the First World War, was "not only the greatest poem against the war, but also a religious *theatrum mundi* . . . an accusation of an age which had destroyed all human values. . . . The still more terrible catastrophes of the Second World War which he did not live to witness and the consequences of which nobody can foresee, were the retribution which Kraus prophesied."[19]

One of the writers who remained in Nazi Germany and served Hitler as best as he could, Hans Johst, became President of the Nazified Chamber of Writers. In 1928 he published *I Believe*, an enthusiastic declaration in favor of National Socialism. In *The Voice of the Reich* (1942), describing a journey to occupied Poland in the company of Himmler, he said: "The Führer needs soldiers and workers for his victory. Our hearts and bones are at your service, my fatherland. . . . At lunch I sat between Minister Frank, Governor General of Poland, and the District Chief of Lublin in whose region the German Jews will be crowded together." The Poles he called "a nation which thought it could tyrannize Germans with impunity."[20] In 1957 he published a book, *Blessed Transitoriness,* in which he said: "I do not know whether the war has robbed us of much, but I know for certain that it has given us much."[21]

The second president of the Chamber of Writers was H. F. Blunck. In 1921 he prophesied that one day Germany would awake and the other nations would "tremble before your mere name."[22] After that prophecy had come true he prayed to God to bless the Führer so that he might "raise the Reich from the dust."[23] He was full of joy that "the Germanic blood in us had become alive again. We Germans show the world a new way of life and a new creed."[24] He looked back in anger at the decay of the liberal age with its asocial idea of freedom. "We live now amidst a miracle, a good miracle. Let Great Britian and France defend a decaying world—we begin anew."[25] After his world had fallen to pieces he had the effrontery to call Heinrich Mann "a grave-digger of the German Republic."[26]

Guido Kolbenheyer addressed a poem to the Führer in which he described him as a man who "in the fateful storm of the nations had opened for his nation a road towards the light. He knows that, high above all intrigues, his nation would prove a master race. His will is purposeful, hard and pure like crystal."[27] In lectures, Kolbenheyer spoke about what the war of liberation, the awakening of the German spirit, meant to German literature. The liberty of art is only guaranteed, he said, "when the high and purifying biological function of art regulates the life of the nation."[28] Germans and Italians, he asserted, the one under Hitler, the other under Mussolini, had reached "the highest cultural maturity and at the same time possessed the most vigorous inner life." They have found "the racial concentration for a new communal life" and thus have overtaken the other nations.[29] Kolbenheyer was awarded the Cultural Prize of the Sudenten Germans in 1958.

Ina Seidel wrote in 1942 for the Führer's birthday: "Where we now stand as Germans, as fathers and mothers of the future of the Reich, we gratefully and humbly feel that in our efforts and our activities we are integrated into the work of the one chosen man of the generation—Adolf Hitler."[30] Today a dozen schools are called after her and she was awarded a price of DM 10,000 by the state of North-Rhine-Estphalia. R. G. Binding, who was awarded the Goethe Prize of 1932, said in 1933 in an answer to protests of Romain Rolland: "Do you want to tell Adolf Hitler and the whole nation what is really German? Goethe is as damned German as is Goering or Goebbels or SA-man Müller or I myself." In a poem, he imagined Goethe applauding him for "not having heinously said *adieu* to the fatherland, not having escaped like a coward in Germany's greatest distress."[31]

Many "poets" deified the Führer and his Reich in blasphemous poems. The poet Gerhard Schumann, who had become a high SA officer, extolled Hitler and prayed to God "to make our souls hard and powerful, to watch over the Führer and our country."[32] Josef Weinheber, master of the great forms of poetry, odes and hymns, addressed a paean in immaculate lines to Hitler.[33] In 1938, at a meeting of Nazi poets in Weimar he said: "We are the mouthpiece of our nation but the Gods speak through our mouths. Today we know again what we are here for. I do not believe that there is a nation in the wide world today which honors, appraises and loves its poets as much as the German nation."[34] The greatest poets and writers had fled into exile, the few genuine poets and writers who had not left in time and cursed the Third Reich lived in the shadow of its gallows. Alfred Mombert was in a concentration camp. The poet and sculptor Ernst Barlach was living as an outlaw in his Mecklenburg home; Nazis wrote threatening letters to him and smashed his windows. When Jochen Klepper, another of the outlawed writers, saw Barlach's portrait by König he saw in it "all the paralysed horror of the old and spiritual in view of the outbreak of such a new time."[35] Barlach died lonely in October, 1938. In one of his last poems he speaks of "the murderers who are roaming through the streets and throw fire. . . . An angel takes me by the hand . . . he will nurture me with songs."[36] After Barlach's death Klepper entered in his diary: "Over his last years, too, was written an *In tormentis*. What has the Third Reich done to him who had once been awarded the *Pour le mérite!*"[37]

Gottfried Benn, who had never uttered a word against the approaching National Socialist danger—on the contrary, he had indirectly encouraged it by his penchant for the archaic and apocalyptic—described the Third Reich as "perhaps the last great conception of the white race, very likely one of the greatest realisations of the world spirit. . . . Even if the apocalypse came to break the seals of this German man, the possession of the new vision of humanity would remain."[38] He wrote this to Klaus Mann, who had warned him: "First one hails irrationalism, afterwards barbarism—and you are already with Adolf Hitler." But Benn was of another opinion: "I think you would understand the events in Germany far better if you did not regard history as a balance sheet which your bourgeoise nineteenth century brain presents to Creation. You amateur of civilisation and troubadour of Western progress!"[39] He said on the radio on April 24, 1933: "We accept the fact of a perfectly logical victory of the national idea nourished by genuine human values. History does not act in a democratic but in an elementary manner. She presents a new biological type to act and suffer, and to create the idea of his generation. He acts, this new biological type, and certain sociological conditions change, of course, certain stalls are swept clean. . . . Freedom of thought? Young people have enough of it. It means freedom for decomposition, and anti-heroic ideology."[40] He also said that the National Socialist spirit was alive "as one and the same command in the poems of George and in the march rhythms of the brown battalions." After the apocalyptic end of the Third Reich he became fashionable again in Germany, inaugurated a new fashion of highly intellectual poetry, was fully rehabilitated and received honors and prizes. He shook off all responsibility with cynical sayings like these: "If somebody speaks of your aestheticism and formalism, study him with interest: he is the caveman and his words show the beauty-appreciation of his club and apron."[41] Thomas Mann, however, said that aestheticism and barbarism are twin brothers. The Swiss professor, Walter Muschg, was disgusted that Benn "succeeded in getting rehabilitated."[42]

The writer Bruno Brehm praised Hitler in these words: "When princes and masters, scholars and priests see no way out, a simple man, called by nobody and longed for by everbody, steps forward from the despairing multitudes and saves them all. The nation looks at that man and knows that he has come at the very last moment, it recognises itself in him and all at once knows what it wants. It sees in the deeds of this man, as in a mirror, how great, how just, and how beautiful it is, it respects itself and also compels the other nations to respect it."[43] In 1941 he said in Weimar: "Do we not now understand why we had to remove from our midst those carriers of infection, the Jews? Do we not now understand why we shall never again tolerate these people in Europe?"[44] After the war he shook off all responsibility with these words: "Only the bad recognise the bad immediately. The good are blind."[45]

The writer August Winnig published in 1937 his *A German's Thoughts About Europe,* in which he offered the Germans a mixture of Chamberlain's *Foundations of the Nineteenth Century* and Hitler's *Mein Kampf.* He had enthusiastic words about "the heroic mind" and "warlike spirit" of the Germans, and said about the Jews: "What does Europe know of the Jews? Only the Germans and the Russians know them. Nobody has experienced them as we have, as the destroyers of nationhood. Who would give aliens the right to misuse the order of the house where they are only tolerated guests?" Like Hitler he said: "The idea of Bolshevism is of Jewish origin," and saw only one alternative: "Either culture-destroying Bolshevism or culture-saving authoritarian government! Bourgeois freedom cannot be saved, it is perishing with the age of which it is part." He spoke of Bolshevism without realizing that he spoke of National Socialism: "Man has become a vessel of eternal fear, he has become a liar, a hypocrite, a traitor under this pressure. At last you only see a gang of guilty criminals and a docile mass held together by fear."[46] After the downfall of Germany he posed as a man of the resistance who had always seen through Hitler and his regime. He published a second edition of his book on Europe and said in the introduction: "I have only deleted a few sentences in which I spoke of the role of the Jews. They are as true today as they were then. But out of reverence for the fate of the Jews I have deleted that paragraph."[47] The University of Göttingen in 1953 awarded him the honorary degree of a Doctor of Theology.

Only a few examples can be given on these pages of what many professors said in praise of the Third Reich. In a manifesto they wrote in 1933 they said: "The *Führer* has called us to vote for him. He asks nothing of the nation, he rather leaves to them the most free decision about whether they want to exist or not. The nation will tomorrow vote for nothing less than its future. Is this a relapse into barbarism? Certainly not! It is the clear avowal of untouchable independence. It is the rejuvenation of a refined youth. The nation wins back the truth of its being. We have renounced the idolization of a thinking not based on soil and power. We see the end of all that philosophy. National Socialism does not replace one party by another, but our revolution means a complete change of our German existence."[48]

One of the most notorious literary "critics" in pre-Hitler days was Adolf Bartels who was, accordingly, visited by Hitler when the party meeting of 1926 was held in Weimar, where the aged Bartels lived. In 1909 he had called Thomas and Heinrich Mann Jews and, when forced to admit his error, had said that they had "creole blood" in their veins and that what they wrote was "essentially Jewish" anyway.[49] In 1920 he published his essays on *Race and Nationhood* with chapter headings like: Racial Pride; Racial Discipline; State, Nation and Race; Germanic Christianity. In a sonnet (for he was also a poet) he said: "Nationhood and race—no, this is no false pride! One blood, one spirit must permeate the whole nation."[50] In 1921 he said that "narrow-minded people like we German racialists are" know for certain "that no Jew can ever become a German writer and that Germans who mixed socially with Jews lost their best qualities." He denounced Hofmannsthal, Wassermann, Thomas Mann—whom he called "an enemy of Germany" —Gerhart Hauptmann, Richard Dehmel. "Do we still have any German spiritual life at all?" he exclaimed and sought consolation with "the two anti-Semites Adolf Stöcker and Theodor Fritsch" and the racialists H. S. Chamberlain and Ludwig Woltmann.[51] When he published his *Jewish Origin and Literary Science* in 1925 a decent German suggested that a monument be erected to Bartels with the inscription *Destructor et Compromitator Patriae*. This man foresaw the year 1945 in 1925.[52]

Albert Soergel in 1919 praised Thomas and Heinrich Mann as the two most "important novelists of today" and said of Alfred Mombert, a mystic poet of Jewish origin, that his poetry had made "the ears of many people more sensitive."[53] In 1934, however, he excused himself for having neglected "the writers of Aryan persuasion." He dated the new edition of his work from "the second week in November 1933 when our Führer had admonished all Germans to concentrate," and spoke now only of those writers who were "prophets and shapers of a German community, selfless moulders of a new German face," not pan-Europeans and utopians but "makers of a new German nation, a new Reich." He spoke only of those who "had the same blood in their veins and were Nordic men," and, consequently, conjure up the hero whom "the recent past had murdered. The German heroic man has been reborn." He praised his predecessor Adolf Bartels, the stubborn fighter "for a German literature as an expression of the racially pure, racially conscious Germans."[54]

Professor Julius Petersen rejoiced over the appearance of "the prophesied and longed-for Führer. "We can now envisage our last aim. The new Reich has been established." He agreed with Chamberlain and Rosenberg that "Nordic traits were visible in the teachings of Christ," and ranked Goethe's autobiography, *Poetry and Truth,* with Hitler's *Mein Kampf.*[55]

Professor Herbert Cysarz asserted with satisfaction that all values had been revalued by National Socialism. "Creative man had revolted against the man of commerce, the uprooted knowers of everything had been replaced by national men, individualism by the dictatorship of the community, the personality in the style of Goethe or Humboldt by leadership." In a book dedicated by many other contributors to the Führer on his 50th

birthday, he said that "our eyes have been widened and sharp-
ened for the rebirth of our German origins in the age of Luther,
in the age of Herder." Jews were "eliminated" because they had
darkened true Germanness. Everybody was now concerned with
the racial past and was looking "for a racial state-will, for the
political roots of mythical prophecy."[56] In 1950, forgetful of
his racist past, he began to speak of "the sin of totalitarianism,"
and was concerned about the disappearance of "the age of the
comparatively sovereign individual." He is a very interesting
example of the split mind so characteristic of many Germans.
Now Cysarz is speaking contemptuously of "the millenarian cult
of Führer and heroism," of "anarchic supermen" and of
"amorphous masses" clamoring for "idols of their own making," and of the many who had been "persecuted, imprisoned,
ostracised because of their creed." Now he tells us that National
Socialism was "the enemy of all the world" because it "persecuted with fire and sword humanism, internationalism, pacifism" and "destroyed, for the first time in Central Europe, the
dignity and grandeur, the modern face of man." The height of
cynicism is reached when he says: "He who today says the
opposite of what he said yesterday should either not have been
taken seriously yesterday or should not be taken seriously
today."[57]

One of the most contemptible "historians" of literature was
Professor Josef Nadler; he re-wrote his *History of German Lit-
erature* three times between 1924 and 1950. Most interesting is
the fourth volume of the Nazi version of his *Reich* (*1914-1940*)
with chapter headings like "The Missed World" and "The
Unborn Reich," meaning that in the pre-Hitler days the Swiss
Germans, the Austrian Germans, the Sudeten Germans and the
Carpathian Germans formed no part of Germany. But thanks to
Hitler, he could add two more chapters with the headings
"From State to Reich" and "From Reich to World Reich." He
summed up the development under Hitler in these words: "The
German revival had, of course, effects on all Germanic coun-

tries. One age has died away and another begins. The ascent of the world state is guaranteed by the New Reich." Of the leader of that Reich he said that he "would lead to peace and bring freedom. His acts have encouraged literature and given her new topics. The Reich itself is like a poem, visible and audible in the community of nations." Hitler's *Mein Kampf* is "the design of a new age"; it has "no predecessor nor example in German literature." The National Socialist movement, "a spiritual movement," was accompanied by the songs of its poets, by Dietrich Eckart's "Germany, awake," Horst Wessel's "Song of the Flag," and the poems of Baldur von Schirach. Nadler also spoke enthusiastically of the war books of Jünger and others who had shown "the heroism," "the metaphysics" of war. "War is the meaning of a manly life, war is the order of a new world. . . . It is the Nordic race which is operating in this soldierly life-philosophy of the Lower Saxon tribe."[58] (Jünger, Dwinger, and Salomon came from Lower Saxony.)

Of the Jews he said that the German nation "could only recover by a hard will to inevitable measures, by a resolution to the most extreme consequences." He was contemptuous of "the three Jews, Bergson, Freud, and Husserl." Rathenau he called "a Jewish tempter of the most dangerous kind" who wanted to bind the Germans to "nothing but the spirit" because he was "antipathetic to blood and soil. How did the German youth answer this attempt? Rathenau was shot by young hands. The shots hit the man who had given the Germans poison which looked like medicine." (One of those young men was the Lower Saxon Salomon, now a very rich writer living in Western Germany.)

Adolf Bartels, however, received high praise from Nadler because he had "by his racial vigour" opposed "international rationalistic eduation and Jewry as the carrier of un-racial spirit," and because he believed "in the Aryan ancestry of Christ, Germanic peasants, and a German saviour."[59]

He, too, is a very instructive example of German schizophrenia. After his master's downfall he said of literary criticism: "It does not deduce the notion 'literature' from the reality 'nation' but deduces the notion 'nation' from the reality 'literature.'" And he asserted that his Nazistic history of literature had "nothing at all to do with racial psychology" but aimed only "at objectivity." In 1950, he deleted all Nazi obscenities from his book, saying with utter cynicism: "Shortening is an art, too. A good many writers, representatives of the then official creed, had to be taken out. They fell with the mantle of the Duke." (Duke=Duce=Führer). "The finder of a truth is not responsible. He cannot be made responsible for the fact that two times two adds up to four."[60]

Professor Heinz Kindermann, who was allowed to return to Vienna University in 1955, spoke of the occupation of Austria as "a homecoming" and called the occupation of Czechoslovakia "a wonderful act of our Führer's," leading to a "renewal of the old and eternal glory of the Reich." He edited an anthology of National Socialist "poets" of Austria and the Sudetenland, full of rubbish in praise of Hitler.[61]

Now for the professors and lecturers of other disciplines who represent a still lower form of German degradation and barbarism in the Third Reich. Only a few examples from more than a thousand can be indicated in this book. The books written by all Hitler scientists, historians, and jurists might fill a library.

Christian Lichtenberg, a professor at Göttingen University, said in the 18th century that there are two kinds of prostitutes, the girls of easy virtue and the German professors. On August 3, 1870, Professor Emil du Bois-Raymond, while calling the French "an immoral peace-murdering nation," proudly pronounced: "Berlin University, situated opposite the Royal Palace, is the intellectual bulwark of the Hohenzollerns."[62] There have been exceptions, of course. In 1837 seven professors at Göttingen University protested against the Duke of Cumberland, who had made himself king of an independent Hanover and abolished the liberal constitution, replacing it with the reactionary one of 1819. The names of those professors became famous in Germany: Albrecht, Dahlmann, Ewald, Gervinus, Weber, and Jacob and Wilhelm Grimm. All were ordered to leave the new kingdom within three days. When several hundred students greeted their professors enthusiastically, they received their answer: "True we seven sacrificed much in the eyes of the world. But we did it with joyous courage." The police arrested 50 students. Friedrich Wilhelm III said: "Actors, whores, and professors can be got everywhere for money." Jacob Grimm answered publicly: "This independence has strengthened my soul. It resists dishonorable demands which want to injure my clean conscience." He was very sorry for the other professors at Göttingen University who behaved like cowards. "I should have expected that at least the theologians among them should have emptied the chalices of their rage and freed themselves from all trinity of doubt."[63]

What happened in 1837 was repeated in Germany in 1933 when twelve Jewish Nobel Prize winners and many Jewish professors were forced to leave Nazi Germany, never to return. The famous Professor Max Planck said to the Führer in 1933 that it would amount to "self-mutilation" if he forced Jews of importance to emigrate because "we badly want their scientific knowledge, and now the foreign countries will benefit from them." Hitler did not listen to him, and Planck called Hitler's reaction his "worst high treason."[64] Planck's son Erwin was hanged because he had taken part in the abortive revolt against Hitler. Professor J. Bronowski said of Max Planck: "He had taught the world a new physics; but two wars and the Nazi terror had shown how little a great patriot could teach Germany."[65] Professor Norman Bentwich writes: "From 1933, the lights of the humanities and science were going out in one country after the other of Central Europe. But they were rekindled in the countries of the rest of the world." He quotes what Sir Winston Churchill said in 1940: "Since the Germans drove the Jews out of Germany and lowered their technical standards, our science is definitely ahead of theirs."[66]

More than 1,200 scientists left Germany in 1933. One of the very few decent German newspapers of today, the editor of which spent six years in Hitler's prisons, wrote in 1954: "None of the German Nobel Prize winners who were forced to immigrate from the Third Reich has returned to us after the war. They represent a loss for German science. This is one of the worst consequences of the Hitler regime."[67]

Not all Jewish professors left in time. Professor Max Fleischmann committed suicide in 1943, when in danger of being transported to Auschwitz. Professor Victor Klemperer, a cousin of the famous conductor, survived the Third Reich by a miracle and told of his experiences between 1933 and 1945 in his book, *Lingua Tertii Imperii*. He was robbed of all his books and forced to leave his house. When a Dresden Gestapo man found in his house Rosenberg's *Mythus*, which his "Aryan" wife had borrowed from a public library, he battered his head with it for several minutes. After September 19, 1941, Professor Klemperer, like all other Jews, was forced to wear a yellow Jewish star visible on his clothes, and a German who saw him crossing a street one day said to his son: "Look at him, Horst, he is responsible for everything!" In 1943 Klemperer was forced to work as a factory hand in Dresden. One day he was picked up in the street and brought to the headquarters of the Gestapo to be searched for "fleas." He had to wait for fifteen minutes, his face turned towards the wall, before he was told to go upstairs and report: "Here is the Jew Paul Israel Filthybeast." The man upstairs said to him: "Oh, you are a professor? You want to teach the like of us? For this insolence alone you deserve to go to Theresienstadt." They found nothing in his clothes, neither rations nor cigarettes, and released him with these words: "Off with you! Now you will probably pray at home for a Jewish victory, won't you? Isn't this your war?" On February 13, 1945, Klemperer, like some other Dresden Jews with "Aryan" wives, received an order to report next morning at Gestapo headquarters. He immediately knew what this meant: deportation to Auschwitz, or being murdered somewhere, since Auschwitz was already in Russian hands. "On the evening of February 13 Dresden was hit by a catastrophe: bombs came down from heaven, burning beams fell on Aryan and non-Aryan heads, and the same stream of fire killed Jews and Christians. For those of the 70 star-bearers who survived, however, the bombing spelt salvation."[68]

Professor Wilhelm Roepke, one of the very few "Aryan" professors who declined to serve Hitler and fled abroad, says that the German universities of the 1920's were full of "brutal" nationalism, "silly" national pride, "idiotic" hatred of the victors of 1918 against whom "a passionate war of revenge" was preached, an "inhuman" contempt of international law, anti-Semitism, anti-democratism, anti-liberalism.[69] In 1939 Professor Walther Schultze praised "that small group of men of learning" who, in the unhealthy days of the democratic republic, "had early found their way to Adolf Hitler and had helped the ideas of the Führer to a full victory in the realm of science" in spite of being hated and derided by their enemies. Their behavior, he said, had been justified by events, and now scientists worked "shoulder to shoulder with all the other soldiers of the Führer's at the new German idea of culture." Liberalism was done for, the facts of race were at variance with the so-called liberty of the individual and the idea "that all men are alike. Germany opposes today the democratic and Marxistic madness of Jewish falsehood."[70] In Austria, Professor Othmar Spann prepared the way to totalitarian thinking in a similar manner. He preached a sort of state mysticism, a state of the élite in which parliamentarism could have no place. A Führer and his paladins would take over. In 1933 he praised Mussolini's Fascist order. But as early as 1921 he had said that "the true statesman is a soldier and an official at the same time, more of a soldier than of an official." In 1933 he said that "the realistic spirit of Fascism and organic National Socialism gives to the idea of the state a new meaning which also applies to international law."[71] Spann was predestined to play a rôle in the Third Reich but Rosenberg saw a competitor in him and had him arrested after the occupation of Austria.

Another Austrian pacemaker of Hitler's was Professor Hans Eibl who considered himself a Roman Catholic. In 1928 he said to the French professor Count Robert d'Harcourt, a genuine Catholic, that Germany was representative of the moral forces of the universe and solely graced by God while the rest of Europe was in a state of mortal sin. D'Harcourt thought this preposterous and called Eibl even then "a visionary, a poet of pan-Germanism." In 1932 Eibl said that National Socialism was aiming at "a racial ennoblement of German man. By extolling the Germanic man as the ideal of a disciplined man the National Socialists are closing a gap in the order of values."[72]

Professor Joseph Lortz deserves to head the shameful list of German professors because he is the only Roman Catholic professor who tried, as early as 1933, to combine Roman Catholicism and National Socialism. He blamed Roman Catholic politicians, among whom the most famous in the last years of the democratic German republic was Dr. Brüning, because of their "really tragic ignorance of the supreme positive ideas and aims of National Socialism as they had been authentically outlined in *Mein Kampf* in 1925." He spoke of "a fundamental kinship between National Socialism and Catholicism. It is a shame to have been shortsighted enough not to see it earlier. There can be no doubt that National Socialism has already transformed life in Germany to a large extent. We can be sure that it will accomplish its task and create a new type of man. National Socialism is not only the rightful power in Germany but it represents the large majority of Germans—a double duty of our conscience to say an unqualified Yes to it."[73] This strange man was allowed to return to his post after the war.

Professor Ernst Krieck, whose name Thomas Mann once said reminded him of *Krieg* (war), was of the opinion that "science does not produce knowledge which is valid everywhere and at all times. Science is racially determined. There is no such a thing as pure reason, absolute science. We have a science and truth which is valid for our race, our nation and our historical position and task." Hitler's Minister of Science, Rust, said that "the new Germany did homage to the spirit of true science"; he denied that "we were intolerant against the free spirit of science, that National Socialism made science the servant of political power, but the new Germany had to be intolerant against the former ideology of unconditioned science being misused for un-German plans. For this reason "all those had to be eliminated who are not our blood and essence."[74]

Professor Philipp Lenard of Heidelberg University was an adherent of Hitler in 1924. He said in the opening words of his *German Physics* (1936): "German physics? one might ask. I could also have spoken of Aryan physics or the physics of Nordic man. 'But is not science international?' This is a mistake. In reality, science, like everything else, is racially conditioned. Nations of other races have a different way of scientific endeavour." International physics was Jewish physics, its main representative being "the pure-blooded Jew Albert Einstein. The Jew strikingly lacks all understanding for truth."[75] Professors Johann Stark and Wilhelm Müller agreed fully with him in their book, *Jewish and German Physics*. They called Einstein's theory of relativity "a great Jewish world bluff presented as a redeeming formula to the German nation in the days of their greatest shame." They accused Planck of having "supported Einstein for many years" and attacked Professor Heisenberg for having said even in 1936 that "the theory of relativity is, of course, the fundament of all scientific research." They differentiated between "Jewish dogmatism" and "German pragmatism" based on "the great and clear ideas of the Führer."[76]

Dr. Theodor Vahlen, in *German Mathematics,* called the idea of "pure and international mathematics without any presuppositions a terribly dangerous one. Our fanatical belief in National Socialism proves to us the absolute falsehood of those inherited liberal opinions."[77]

Professor Martin Staemmler formulated the main principles of racial culture in these sentences: "Liberation of the racially conscious nation from inferior people who are only an impediment for the whole nation. Keeping the race unpolluted. Elimination of alien races who have had an unwholesome influence on the psychological structure of our nation. These demands are hard in many respects but we must never forget that the existence of our nation is at stake and that every suitable means to save it is allowed."[78] Professor W. Gross wrote books about *Racial Education, The German Idea of Race and the World, Racial Theories in Modern History*. Professor Dr. Hirsch said that all pressure from without would only have the effect that "those few who still keep aside flock into the camp of Adolf Hitler. Try it and you will only unite Germany and National Socialism all the more."[79]

Professor Max Wundt wrote a *Textbook of Racial Thinking,* Professor Adolf Köhler wrote *Ethics as Logic: A Fundamental Problem of National Socialist Philosophy,* Professor H. A. Grunsky wrote on *Intrusion of the Jews into Philosophy*. Professor Alfred Klemmt, in *Science and Philosophy in the Third Reich,* said that "there existed no such thing as a general science of mankind or a general human culture because all true culture is racially conditioned," and that National Socialism had taken up "the fight for the salvation of European culture and civilisation." Logic, allegedly unchangeable for ever, will be replaced by a German logic which "does justice to reality." As to ontology, it was only a libelous assertion of refugees of alien race that National Socialism had "replaced spirit by race." The National Socialists had only replaced "the bloodless, abstract, rootless spirit of mankind" by "a racially conditioned, organically rooted spirit." As to ethics, he asserted that National Socialism did not deny any of the values of "European culture."[80] Professor Paul Heyse made of Kant a National Socialist who had "renewed Germanic life."[81] Professor Kurt Huber however, who had revolted against Hitler, said to his criminal judges who sentenced him to death, that he had revolted with a view to Kant's categorical imperative. "No judgment more terrible about a community is imaginable than the confession which we must all make that nobody is secure from his neighbour, no father from his sons."[82] Professor Ferdinand Weinhandl thought differently when he expressed his agreement with "the saying of the Führer that to be German means to be clear," as our science is "clear and simple, plain and profound."[83]

One of the most contemptible professors of philosophy was Alfred Baeumler, with whom Thomas Mann had already quarrelled in 1926.[84] On May 10, 1933, he said from his chair in Berlin University: "Hitler is not less than the idea [of Plato], he is more than the idea because he is real . . . We have no Pope today but we have a Führer."[85] We have left behind us "the age of individualism and free conscience." A year later he called "the discovery of race the Copernican deed of modern time."[86] In 1935 he derided humanism (the first, the second, and the third) which had been replaced by "National Socialism, the only spiritual power in Germany."[87] In 1943 he published *The New Order in Europe as a Problem of the Philosophy of History*. Only the idea of race, he asserted, can really make us understand world history. Democratic states were no states at all, their slogans were contemptible, and the Germans fought a war "so that the decrepit sham order can be replaced by a truer order. A millennium has come to an end; in the dawn of the rising day there emerges Europe."[88] In 1944, Baeumler spoke about the Führer idea in history. He called Homer's word that "one should be ruler" "the formula of Indo-Germanic leadership." In 1918 the German army had returned "undefeated" and was forced "to give up the fight." Chaos reigned but "a simple soldier of the great war" decided to become a politician. "The decision of the Führer was the origin of the Reich. He goes down in history, along with Theoderic and Charlemagne, as the founder of Greater Germany."[89]

More than a hundred professors submitted to Hitler a book on the occasion of his 50th birthday. They called it *Festival Gift of German Science* and "accounted" in it for what they were doing in honor of *Führer* and *Reich*. Count Schwerin (of Munich University) outlined how "National Socialist Jurisprudence has been rejuvenated by becoming conscious of its Germanic way." Professor Tackenberg (Bonn University) called "the founding of chairs for the study of German prehistoric times in ten universities a cultural deed of National Socialism." Professor Eugen Fischer (Berlin University) gave the Führer the testimonial that he had saved "the German soul" at the very last moment by the insight "that race and heritage are the most important, the only valuable things in the life of nations." Professor Walter Franck (Berlin University) called historiography "a political science" and defined its present aim as teaching how "to look at national and world history from the viewpoint of the revolutionary experience of National Socialism." Professor Spindler (Munich University) praised National Socialism for having "recognised the indestructible tie of blood between the German and English nations as the two leading Germanic peoples on earth." Professor Blume (Kiel University) dealt with "Music Research and Race," which should aim at "laying the foundations" on which a "theory of racial music research could be built." Professor Pinder (Berlin University) asserted that in the days before Hitler there was only a "sham science"

which regarded "the world of art forms as something independent," while "the history of art is the history of the particularly
characteristic expressions of our race."[90]

In February, 1941, Hitler's historians met at Nuremberg.
Professors W. Platzhoff and Th. Mayer there proclaimed that
"the German historians are conscious of their duty to deliver
the historical weapons for the main problem of the present war
and the imminent new order of Europe."[91] Professor K. A. von
Müller delivered these weapons in the once famous and now
Nazified *Historische Zeitschrift*. "Our German nation," he said,
"has been called up and rejuvenated by a great creative Führer.
. . . It is the duty of today's science to carry forward the new
spirit which has come to life in our nation, into the battlefield of
science." He wrote an introduction to *Anti-Semitism in the Late
Middle Ages* by Dr. Wilhelm Grau, a falsification of history of
the most obscene sort, in which Grau spoke of "the final solution
of the Jewish problem." When Grau became Director of the
Munich Institute for Jewish Research Professor Müller celebrated him by an oration.[92] English history, he said, was full of
"mercilessness and blood-stained cruelty up to the latest centuries—how much more powerful was the achievement of the
Germans in the same time!" England hated the Germany of
Bismarck. Germany lost the war of 1914-1918 because the
Kaiser's policy lacked visionary aims, but even in the seeming
hopelessness "what a power of rejuvenation!" Parliamentarian
democracy was done for. "An age of socialism and new authoritarianism has begun, and we are its foremost representatives."
Hitler, "the *Führer* of our nation, has a new, visionary aim."
Austria and the Sudeten region are part of Germany and form
"the nucleus of a new and greater Germany." Hitler's Germany
and Mussolini's Italy are "the young nations" who will create
"a new order. . . . Our racial power is stronger and younger
than that of Great Britain."[93] When Müller was seventy-five in
1957, he was called "one of our best countrymen."[94]

Another historian, Professor Fritz Hartung, praised the

authoritarian German state as something specifically German and opposed to Western parliamentarism. He praised Hitler for having "enhanced the old-Prussian tradition of a powerful state by creating a totalitarian state. After the glorious beginning of the war of 1939-40, the German nation can look into the future with quiet poise."[95] What a prophet! He has forgotten everything he said then, and now condemns National Socialism as "the inexorable enemy of all human rights" which, with its theory of the inequality of men and races, "has brought misery onto the whole world." Now he says that there is "a grain of truth" in the belief of foreigners that "the submissiveness of the German nation to Hitler was the expression of a weakness characteristic of the whole of German history. It is characteristic of our constitutional history that the civilian element has played a much smaller part in it than in Western Europe or in the United States."[96]

Professor Johannes Haller, whom we met in the First World War among the Kaiser's adulators, lived long enough to see Hitler's advent and downfall. In 1922 he published his very Prussian *Epochs of German History,* by which he hoped "to strengthen the belief and the will of our nation to a better future so that a new generation can again give some meaning to German history." When, ten years later, his book appeared in a new edition he expressed the hope that he would be able to say at the end of a third edition "that the day which we have been longing for has come." In the third edition (1939) he stated: "Sooner than could have been expected by the boldest this wish has come true. What had once been belief and hope has beome reality. The day has come. The night in which we lived has been followed by a new dawn."

Forgetting that he had once accused Great Britain as an aggressor he now said that Bismarck's followers had "affronted Russia and driven her into the arms of France." Instead of seeking an alliance with Great Britain the German politicians pursued "a policy of pin-pricks, challenging Great Britain by a naval policy which was bound to frighten her and make any agreement impossible." It was, he said, the German politicians themselves who "wove the net of encirclement with their own hands." Bulow was "a statesman without ideas, false and untrue to the core, without any responsibility and conscience, a criminal." But, he added, one cannot blame him alone, the whole nation was responsible because it never tried to remedy things. "Germany must blame herself for her fate and not try to shift the responsibility to a single individual."

All this sounds sensible enough, but why did he hail Hitler's advent? Why did he, who had once advocated a *Pax Germanica,* complain of the Treaty of Versailles and the allegedly high reparations, just as Hitler had done? Hitler, he said, "is the symbol of our nation and our unity. His ascendancy is the victory of the national idea." He praised him for the rearmament of the German nation and for bringing Austria "home, thus healing the wound which Bismarck had once been forced to inflict on German hearts." Czechoslovakia, he said, had "voluntarily put itself under German protection in order to become part of the German Reich."[97]

Another of these Hitler professors was Paul Schultze-Naumburg. In a book which he dedicated to "his friend," the infamous racialist F. K. Günther, he complained about "the catastrophic de-nordification" of the Germans and their "obnoxious intermarriages with alien, especially Jewish, blood." He also blamed Christianity which, "by teaching the equality of all men had destroyed the moral principles of Germandom. No wonder that it destroyed the Nordic ideal of beauty, too. . . . There is only one way to restore that beauty. The *Führer* has shown it." In an article in 1944 he said that Greece went down because "the principle of leadership died by the poison of democracy." Rome suffered in the same way and for the same reason. "Nobody did more to realize this historic truth than our Führer. He foresaw prophetically the necessities of a future crisis in *Mein Kampf.* As long as the German nation follows his

teaching, it will remain invincible and its life will last eternally."
Fredelind Wagner says of him: "He specialized in extolling the
Nordic race. Indeed he liked the type so well that he married
four blond Nordic women in fairly quick succession. . . . His
photographs of the Aryan and non-Aryan breasts were very
popular."[98]

Now for Hitler's jurists. Again a few examples must suffice.
Professor Georg Eisser said: "The epoch-making racial theory
of law leads us back to the law of our forefathers which we have
learnt to recognise and admire, and to new, never before
trodden paths.[99]

Professor E. R. Huber praised Hitler for having abolished
such old-fashioned 19th century ideas as "constitution, *contrat
social,* constitutional law. The Führer creates out of the natural
unity of the nation the conscious and politically active nation
and the racial state. From this fact he derives his totalitarian
power." Characteristic of such a state, he said with satisfaction,
was "the non-existant neutrality of any sphere of life." Democratic elections were nonsense, because "the will of the nation
can be purely and unadulteratedly expressed only by the Führer." The "independence" of judges was an absurd liberal invention, jurisdiction must closely be related "to the racial and political whole." The judge must be subordinated to "the will of the
Führer who is the expression of the highest law." The idea of
mulla poena sine lege had been abolished. Freedom of science
and art were obsolete ideas, too. "The universities have been put
under stern political leadership in order to free them from old
traditions and prepare them for their new tasks." As to foreign
policy, National Socialist Germany was waging war in order "to
lay the foundations of a new Europe which will secure lasting
peace and uninterrupted security for all nations."[100] Today he
is again professor of social sciences at the University of
Wilhelmshaven.

Professor G. A. Walz equally condemned Marxism and liberalism because of their "abstract logistic dialectics" with the help of which one could prove anything needed "for the last political struggle." National Socialism had done away with all those "fatal illusions." No "sphere of state life is now free as in the liberal state." Only "a new Germanic order" can overcome the European chaos. The "dogma" of an executive independent of the legislature and administration was replaced by "a new vision of law which will become the standard of all National Socialist science of law."[101] Professor Karl Larenz said that for centuries Western philosophy had been "the great tempter" of the German way of thinking but Germany was now about to create "a new, a specifically German idea of law."[102]

Professor Friedrich Grimm rejoiced when Hitler overran Austria and spoke of "Hitler's German Mission." He cried out: "One nation, one Reich, one Führer! The dream of all Germans come true!" He rejected as horror propaganda the assertion of foreigners that the Third Reich was "no state of justice, no state of culture." In the same year (1938) he dedicated a book to the memory of the hanged murderers of the Austrian Chancellor Dollfuss, in which he said: "Why do we honour Planetta and Holzweber? Because of their sacrifice. They died for an idea, for Germany and the Führer. They died as heroes. How great are these things, and how mean is the propaganda which attacks National Socialism because we pay homage to Planetta and Holzweber." When, two years earlier, he defended the *gauleiter* Wilhelm Gustloff, who had been murdered by David Frankfurter in Switzerland for what was being done to the Jews in Germany, he said that Frankfurter must not be acclaimed "as a new David who had killed the giant Goliath." Forgetting what was going on in his beloved Führer's Germany, he asked the Swiss judges: "Are people in a constitutional state permitted to give full vent to their hatred?"[103]

Professor Otto Koellreutter celebrated "the racial order of life" as "the fundament of any political and cultural achievement." He said that in a Führer state there existed no unrelated justice. The elimination of the Jews, for instance, "is unjust according to liberal and democratic ideas" but it is right according to "the claims of a racial justice for which the preservation of the race must be the supreme law." Jurisprudence, he went on, "must go back to the racial ideas of right." Did not Roland Freisler—the chief prosecutor of the Supreme Court, who was killed by an American bomb—say: "It is not the judge's concern to create justice. He must draw it from the fountain of norms set by the Führer in the name of the nation"? Koellreutter celebrated the "National Socialist state of justice" in several books. In the age of individualism, he argued, the feeling of what constitutes a "genuine state of justice" had got lost but Hitler had "destroyed the form of the sterile liberal state of justice" and "rejuvenated the experience of national unity in the Germans. The National Socialist state of justice is the highest form and fulfilment of our revolution." According to Germanic thinking "leadership had always been racially conditioned. . . . The German racially-conscious judge must be grateful to the National Socialist movement for having created a racial German justice the norms of which he has to apply." Of one of the most famous experts of international law, "the Jew Hans Kelsen," he said that he adhered to liberal and democratic ideas which were alien to a genuine conception of the state.[104] Kelsen was also attacked by Professor E. Tatarin-Tarnheyden because he was "corrupting German youth by his identification of democracy and a people's state." Tatarin quoted as his own witnesses Hegel, Lagarde, Gobineau, Wagner, and Chamberlain.[105]

Professor Friedrich Berger wrote several books in praise of the Third Reich, was an intimate friend of Ribbentrop's, and ambassador extraordinary. In 1940 he wrote: "France reaped what she sowed," and derided the defeated country because it was "incapable to understand the great world-historic events in Germany." After the war he got a chair of international law at

Munich University. An honest German protested that chaps who were responsible for the Nazi horrors, "who, as publicists, artists, scientists, and pedagogues, had paved the way for, and justified, war and mass murder, have become outwardly democrats and have been accepted again as civil servants. The new state is in need of experts, and the academic youth needs —models."[106]

Now we come to the man whom the Nuremberg judges called the main protagonist of the Nazi jurists, Professor Carl Schmitt. On August 25, 1933 the very decent Professor Vossler wrote to Benedetto Croce: "Heidegger and Schmitt reveal themselves as the two spiritual catastrophes of the new German state."[107] Heidegger said in his high-flown existentialist language that "the beginning had passed over our heads as the greatest event. The beginning has fallen into our future and it will be our duty to catch up with its greatness. . . . The march of our nation into its future. We will this ourselves. For the young and youngest power of the nation has already decided upon it."[108] Professor Heidegger is today again acclaimed in Germany as one of the leaders of existential philosophy.

Schmitt, after the ghastly events of June 30, 1934 published a justification of those murders under the title "The Führer Defends Justice."[109] General Beck, who later became a martyr of the Third Reich, was "horrified" by those events and said that a Führer who committed such beastly crimes was "capable of anything in the field of foreign politics."[110] Schmitt derided the liberal separation of legislature, executive, and judiciary and said that Hitler had "proved himself as the highest Führer and judge" on that day. "He is his own master." When people abroad thought his behavior monstrous he retorted that their clamoring was only proof that Hitler had found "the right word" at the right moment.[111]

In 1934 Schmitt called "state, movement, and nation" a "triad." He condemned the liberal state in which many spheres of life were free from state interference, and said that a certain German law theory had undermined the leadership principle of the Prussian state in which the soldiers "swore an oath of allegiance to the monarch, not to the constitution." Hitler, however, had made true the words "All power derives from the nation," which had only been a false slogan of the liberal state. Now "Führer and followers are of the same kind, and this prevents the power of the Führer from becoming an arbitrary tyranny." How true! He went further and said that "a Führer state built by German soldiers could never compromise with a constitutional state controlled by its citizens."[112]

In 1935 he said that it was "self-understood that justice also reigned in the National Socialist state, even more so than in a constitutional state with its many norms." Men like Ministers Frick and Frank—both hanged at Nuremberg—had proved this. (He said this in a *National Socialist Handbook of Law and Legislature,* edited by Frank, to which many other law experts also contributed.)[113]

In 1941 Schmitt wrote *International Law and the Order of Large Spaces,* that is Hitler's Europe. Other norms, he said, were needed than those which were valid between different states which were democratic and had no notion of race. The National Socialist starting point was "the concept of the Reich founded on a certain *Weltanschauung* and excluding the interference of other powers which do not belong to Europe. The deeds of the Führer gave reality, historical truth and a great future to the idea of our Reich."[114]

Schmitt presided over a meeting of National Socialist professors of law in October 1936 in which the "pernicious" influence of Jewish jurists in Germany was discussed. Streicher sent a congratulatory telegram and Frank said to the assembled professors that the state expected them "to become genuine fighters for the awakened racial spirit in their scientific research" and to develop "a science which serves the nation as it comes from the nation. You have the great luck to be active as jurists in the most creative age of Germanism, in the time of Adolf Hitler."

How did they respond to this challenge? Professor Schmitt gave them three mottoes, one from *Mein Kampf:* "By fighting the Jews I do the work of God"; second, Frank's words: "Remain alert to the Jewish danger"; third, a saying of one of those who fell in Hitler's abortive revolt of November 9, 1923. Schmitt added a contemptuous word about those "Jewish emigrants" who had "called the wonderful fight of *gauleiter* Streicher something 'unspiritual.'" The papers the professors read had titles like "Jews and Economics," "The Criminality of the Jews," "The Influence of the Jews on State Theories," "The Influence of Jews on German International Law," etc. Professor K. Klee said that Jewish jurists had had "a fatal influence on the theory and practice of the Penal Code," and "tried to undermine the authority of the punishing state" by recommending "a humanitarian application of punishment," that is prisons should be "institutes of re-education instead of penitentiaries"; fortunately that "excessive humanitarianism was abolished by National Socialism." Professor Karl Siegert complained that Germany was still lacking "an all-round picture of the fatal influence of the Jews." He did his best to correct things by saying that "an abyss" existed "between German and Jewish jurisprudence," and that "the gross Jewish individualism is racially conditioned," that Jewish spirituality aimed at becoming "pure spirit." They had stressed "the idea of humanism" in order "to get the upper hand in national cultures which are alien to them." But now "we have eliminated the Jews from theoretical and practical jurisprudence and broken the Jewish supremacy. It is, however, our larger aim to destroy all Jewish power by exterminating all Jewish spirit in our jurisprudence."[115] Schmitt told the assembled Nazi jurists always to remember "every word which Adolf Hitler had said about the Jews in

Mein Kampf" because he had "revolutionised our knowledge while earlier times had been dazzled and been without any idea" of the Jews. It remains a riddle why Schmitt was not accused as a war criminal and imprisoned. After the war he called himself "a Christian Epimetheus," and when reminded of his criminal behavior he characteristically retorted: "My scientific endeavours have nothing to fear from a spiritual forum, nothing to hide, nothing to regret. The road of the spirit can lead to errors but spirit remains spirit even when it errs."[116]

The writer Theodor Plievier depicted in *Berlin,* in the third volume of his trilogy of Germany's defeat in the East, a Hitler professor whom he calls Hasse, perhaps remembering the Pan-German leader of the same name. While Berlin is burning the Hitler professor complains only of defeatism and corruption, is angry with his "stupid Ukrainian domestic," and calls not Hitler but Churchill "a Devil in the shape of a man."[117]

Some professors behaved even worse. Franz Six, a philosopher, said in April, 1944 that the physical extermination of the East European Jew would deprive the Jews of their biological reserves. Himmler made him an *SS-Obergruppenführer* for his extraordinary services. When brought to trial he said that the killing of Jews was no disgrace because it had been done on the order of the Führer. He was given a long sentence but was released far too soon for the cynical reason of expediency. Professor Spanner invented a method for making soap from the fat of human corpses. Professor Hirt asked for a hundred Jewish skeletons to complete his collection, giving detailed suggestions of how to sever the heads from the bodies; 115 Jews were murdered in the concentration camp of Struthof.[118]

Professor Walter Schreiber told the Nuremberg judges of a secret meeting of the German High Command in July, 1943 at which various professors were present. The new military situation after the defeat at Stalingrad, they argued, made new things necessary and new "weapons" should be put into practice, that is to say, bacteriological warfare. A committee was founded and the professors Schuhmann, Richter, Kleive, and others undertook to prepare this new kind of warfare. Professor Blome was the president of the committee. But they did not get very far with their preparations; Professor Blome came along one day and reported that the Russians were nearing Posen. The professors were forced to flee and had not even time to have their institute demolished. But other professors had time to do other things. Professor Karl Gebhardt performed operations on the skulls of living Russian prisoners of war and had them killed in stages in order to study the changes in the bones of the skulls. Professor Holzlöhner and Dr. Kramer reported in the autumn of 1943 of experiments on inmates of the concentration camp of Dachau. All sorts of experiments (high altitude, freezing, malaria, mustard gas, sulfanilanicide, bone and muscle regeneration, sea water, sterilization, spot-fever, gas oedema, etc.) were performed on helpless Jews, Poles, and Russians. The "Nordic" heroes were, as far as is known, the Professors Gebhardt, Schilling, Mrugowsky, Schroeder, Rose, Eppinger. They were given long years of imprisonment after the war. Professors Brickenbach and Haagen were each sentenced to twenty years by a French court for their experiments on inmates of the concentration camp Struthof. Professor Alexander Mitscherlich said after the war that 350 professors and doctors had taken part in these crimes.[119] Professor Georg Hohmann wrote: "Those experiments had nothing to do with science. Even in the Third Reich laws against the torture of animals existed. But it was not animals against which these people sinned, but only human beings. If the Baal priests in ancient times, in their fanaticism, sacrificed innumerable men to their god Dagon, this had been a barbaric and primitive cult."[120]

Thomas Mann in March 1933 spoke of the unforgettable cowardice of the German universities, deadly to the honor of the German spirit."[121] In 1937 he wrote: "The German universities share a heavy responsibility for all present distresses. . . . They allowed their soil to nourish the ruthless forces which have devastated Germany morally, politically, and economically."[122]

The reader is now asked to compare the shameful and criminal behavior of more than a thousand professors and university lecturers with the brave behavior of some students, Hans and Inge Scholl, Christoph Probst, and Alexander Schmorell, who opposed Hitler by distributing leaflets in Munich University against "this state with its terrible madness of extermination" and who lost their young lives under the executioner's axe. "The German name," they wrote, "will remain disgraced for ever if German youth does not revolt at last, revenging and atoning, smashing their torturers and finding a new spiritual Europe."[122] They died "with joyful acceptance." With them died their friend, Professor Kurt Huber, who said to his judges that if everybody did what he had done, "order, security, confidence would return to our state. Every morally responsible man would raise his voice with ours against the reign of mere power against justice, mere arbitrariness against the morally good. My intentions and my deeds will be justified by the inexorable march of history."[123] They were.

2. Paganism

"On January 30, 1933 we declared our apostasy from God as a nation."[124] These words are to be found in the secret diary of the writer Theodor Haecker.

Pope Pius XI said in his encyclical, *Mit brennender Sorge* (1937), who deified race or state or the ruler of a state and makes them the highest norm, perverts the order of things created by God. He condemned it as heresy to speak of "a national God, a national religion," and called it madness "to imprison God, the creator of the universe, with the frontiers of a single nation, the blood-conditioned narrowness of a single race."[125] But millions of Germans kept on shouting "Heil Hitler!" "Thanks to our Führer." In September, 1938 he received in audience pilgrims from Belgium, and spoke to them of German anti-Semitism. He read to them some chapters from the Bible and said to them with tears in his eyes: "There can be nothing better in the world than these words. How can a Christian be an anti-Semite? No Christian can have anything in common with anti-Semites, for we are all Semites in spiritual matters."[126]

Roman Catholics from Europe who had found refuge in the United States said in 1943 that the deification of race and blood amounted to a new paganism which necessarily resulted in "a denial of Christ and the God of Jewish-Christian tradition."[127] The most fanatical of all German post-war fanatics, Hans Grimm, applied to Hitler and his role in the Germany of 1933 to 1945 these words of Luther: "I cannot resist, I must take care of poor, miserable, forsaken, despised, betrayed and sold-out Germany."[128]

In 1933 Cardinal Faulhaber said: "The German nation will either be Christian or it will not be. The apostasy from Christianity is the beginning of the end of the German nation. Our Fatherland is better served by devout disciples of the gospel than by warlike old Germans." One of the most sinister National Socialists, Professor Johannes von Leers, who after the war fled to Egypt and there organized Nasser's war propaganda against Israel, answered the Cardinal with these words: "Many things in Christianity are so repulsive and intolerable to Nordic Germans that they are entitled to reject them in their own and their children's name."[129] Professor Eugen Rosenstock, now living in the United States, remembers that Pastor Schirmacher, aide-de-camp to Hitler's Bishop Müller, said to him in 1933, "Hitler is Christ," and says: "What Hitler did in Germany that people adored him like the beast from the abyss, this means that we should not talk of God's things for a while after they have so been misused."[130] Professor Karl Thieme, a leading German Roman Catholic, reminded the Germans that "dozens of small Jewish school children" were marked down for suicide "from 1934 onwards" because they "could no longer stand the tortures inflicted on them by their schoolmates."[131] He explains German anti-Semitism by reminding us that "dull masses of Nordic nations" had been baptised "more or less forcefully without really understanding their new faith."[132]

But not even the Roman Catholic Church spoke with one voice in Nazi Germany. The censor of the diocese of Münster gave his *Nihil obstat* to the shameful little book by the Catholic Professor Joseph Lortz, mentioned on an earlier page. On July 20, 1933, the Holy See concluded a concordat with Nazi Germany in order to pin Hitler down to a minimum of Christian honesty and force him to respect the Catholic Church and its activities. But, unfortunately, Secretary of State Cardinal Pacelli (later Pope Pius XII) saw fit to declare: "If totalitarianism is understood in such a manner that all citizens without exception should be subject to the state and its lawful government in everything which belongs to the state because it is an essential part of the state, there is no doubt that we must say yes to this."[133] This was said of a state and government which had extirpated democracy, crushed the trade unions, imprisoned many German opponents of Hitlerism, and preached hatred of the Jews. No wonder then that the Catholic bishops officially declared in 1935 that Hitler's order to the civil servants to swear an oath of allegiance to the National Socialist state "without any reservations and qualifications,"[134] corresponded with the teaching of the Church about the oath. No wonder, either, that Cardinal Faulhaber, forgetting all he had said in 1933, said in a sermon in 1936: "Pope Pius XI was the best, in the beginning even the only, friend of the new Reich. Millions of foreigners who mistrusted it at first began to trust the new German government after the concordat had been concluded."[135] In

1936, the German bishops declared: "The second weapon of the Church is the word, the word that does not just criticise, lament and notice only the bad things, but unifies all the divergent powers to a communion of the Church and strengthens the trust in the Führer. Your bishops want to work with the state in peace and with confidence and also recognise what is good and great in the work of the Führer."[136] Compare with this what the Jewish village priest Matthatias the Maccabee said to the emissary of King Antiochus in the market-place of Modin eighteen centuries ago: "Though all the nations that are under the King's dominion obey him and fall away everyone from the religion of their fathers and give consent to his commandments, yet will I and my sons and their brethren walk in the covenant of our fathers."[137]

In 1935 Archbishop Gröber of Freiburg said this: "You have no right at all to ask whether a war is waged for the sake of right or crime. Catholic theologians have never allowed the individual with his shortsightedness and his emotions, when a war breaks out, to argue about its rights and wrongs, but left it to authorities to decide."[138] In a *Vademecum* for Roman Catholic soldiers, approved by the authorities of Münster on November 8, 1938, one could read this: "The *Führer* embodies the unity of nation and Reich. It is the duty of a Christian to obey him. His faith tells him to recognise in the personality of the ruler the glory and honour bestowed on him by God." In an approved book of prayers and songs for Roman Catholic soldiers published in 1940 one could read: "Soldiers made Germany great. Military service is a school of fortitude, the cradle of great soldiers. Remember the word: with God for our *Führer,* nation and fatherland!"[139] The Roman Catholic Bishop Franziskus Justus said this to the soldiers on July 29, 1941: "Comrades! Who can doubt that we Germans have now become the main nation of Europe? As so often, Germany has become the saviour of Europe. This war in the East will prove to you that it is an unspeakable luck to be a German."[140] On December 10, 1941, the German bishops said this: "We follow our soldiers with our prayers." When Hitler marched into Austria and the Jews were trembling with fear (a good many committed suicide), Cardinal Innitzer and all the Austrian bishops declared "from the depths of our hearts and on the occasion of these historic events that National Socialism had done, and is still doing, great things for the national, social and economic reconstruction of the German Reich and nation. . . . It goes without saying that it will be the national duty of all bishops on election day to vote for the German Reich, because we are Germans."[141] The representatives of the Lutheran Church of Austria followed suit: "We say an unconditional Yes to the work of the Fuehrer and thank God that he saved the German nation in its most difficult hour!"[142] Even after the Nuremberg racial laws had been promulgated on November 8, 1938, the day when a few hours later hundreds of synagogues burned all over Germany, the censor of the diocese Münster gave his *Nihil obstat* to a book about the oath, in which Roman Catholic soldiers were told things like these: "What we understand by the word *Reich* is an orderly government in which the will of the Führer not only embodies the actual power but also the will of the nation in the noble form of obedience and followership. The Führer represents the unity of nation and *Reich,* he is the highest authority of the state. A Christian German is compelled to obey him by his conscience, even without an oath. 'Let every soul be subject unto the higher powers. For there is no power but of God: the powers that be ordained are ordained by God. Whosoever, therefore, resisteth the power resisteth the ordinance of God.' Paul said this in his Epistle to the Romans, chapter 13. This unqualified affirmation of the power of the state was addressed to Christians who were inclined to see in their state the expression of a power inimical to their faith. The apostle denied in these words the individual Christian the right to tie up his obedience to the state with arbitrary qualifications. If the German soldier finds it easy to swear an oath of allegiance to the Führer and Commander-in-Chief because the Führer regards it as the task of his life to add to the greatness and honour of his nation, the Christian soldier will swear his oath in all seriousness and with a gay heart because his faith tells him to recognise in the person of the ruler, beyond his human faculties and achievements, the power and the glory which God has given him."[143]

Even in 1942, a Roman Catholic Archbishop, in a Christmas message to "the worthy army chaplains and all German soldiers of the Roman Catholic faith," said this: "The efforts which are crowned by victory will ask for much strength and devotion. Our Führer and Commander-in-Chief is our glorious example. We shall achieve the aim for which we are fighting if we have unshakable confidence in him. The aim is the highest and noblest possible: home, freedom, fatherland, and living space for our nation."[144]

It was therefore that Dr. Schweitzer said: "During the great build-up of anti-Semitism by the Hitlerites the churches did nothing. Their silence was mortifying. For the doctrine of the Church Fathers that God wanted to punish the Jews for the crucifixion of Jesus had already become the accepted doctrine."[145] Dean H. Gruber said that most Germans had seen or known how the Jews had been persecuted and tortured during the Nazi regime, but, like the Christian churches, most Germans had remained silent, and "thus become accomplices in the Nazi crimes."[146]

The National Socialists called Adolf Hitler "charismatic" and even their "savior." *Mein Kampf* was called "the holy book of National Socialism and the New Germans."[147] Or they spoke of "a holy flame grown out of an ancient historic mission, realised by a God-sent Führer in a moment when 'the time was fulfilled.'"[148] They even said this: "Just as Jesus freed man

from sin and hell, so Adolf Hitler saved the German nation
from ruin. Jesus and Hitler were persecuted but while Jesus was
crucified Hitler was made Chancellor of the Reich."[149] The
new savior from Braunau called the men who were killed during
his abortive revolt in 1923 "my apostles."[150] Göring said of
him: "We all, from a simple SA man up to the Prime Minister,
stem from Adolf Hitler and exist through Adolf Hitler."[151]
Jodl said that Christianity and Bolshevism were "identical."[152]
The poetess Gertrud von le Fort, however, considering the
crimes perpetrated by Hitler and his adherents, put these words,
while the Third Reich was still in being, into the mouth of
Jesus:

> It was I who was choked in the poisonous chambers of crime.
> I was tortured and cried but no heart broke.[153]

They violated all the Ten Commandments given on Sinai, as
Count von Galen, Bishop of Münster, told them from the pulpit.
In 1944 a book was published in the United States under the
title *The Ten Commandments. Then Short Novels of Hitler's
War Against the Moral Code.* The authors were Thomas Mann,
Rebecca West, Franz Werfel, Jules Romains, André Maurois,
Sigrid Undset, H. Willem van Loon, and Louis Bromfield.
Thomas Mann's contribution, *The Tables of the Law,* contains
these words about Hitler: "Blood shall flow in torrents because
of his black stupidity, so much blood that the redness shall
vanish from the cheeks of mankind."[154] He said that Hitler
had come "to put himself in the place of Jesus and to replace
his teaching of the brotherhood of all men under God by a creed
of body and soul-murdering violence."[155] As early as 1922 he
had uttered his disgust with the "pagan folk-religion, Wotan
cult . . . [and] romantic barbarism" in which many Germans
were indulging.[156] Ten or twelve years later, Hitler said: "We
shall replace the dogma of the suffering and death of a godly
redeemer by the life and deeds of a new law-giving Führer who
frees his adherers from the burden of free decisions."[157] Poets

adhering to his creed said: "There are many who have never seen you but they know that you are their savior."[158] Many periodicals cropped up in the Third Reich opposing the cross of Christ with the crooked cross of Hitler and speaking of German piety. What was meant by this can be seen from these words: "The Church of the Germans wants to combine the racial renaissance of the nation with the eternal values of the gospel but it rejects a Jewish and alien Christianity." Or from these: "We aim at an evangelical church of the German nation. We want to strengthen the Führer idea." Or from these: "The national Christian movement of the 'German Christians' is following Führer and Reich absolutely. It adheres unreservedly to the National Socialist *Weltanschauung*. Service to the nation is service to God!"[159] They baptized the children in the name of the nation.

The prelude to Kolbenheyer's novel *Paracelsus* was highly praised by Hitler's high priest, Alfred Rosenberg, because Wotan and Christ are shown in it as "One-Eyed and Beggar." Wotan says to Christ: "There is no nation like this which has no gods and is eternally longing to see the god." Then, in the words of Rosenberg, Wotan lifts "the tired Christ, who lies begging in the road, with his strong arms and carries him through the German lands. And the miserable and tortured Christ inhales the strong breath of this German genius and becomes stronger and healthier." The one-eyed Wotan says of the Germans: "They no longer worship me, for they have voices only for their eternal gods who bear the seal of death, but they live me. How many ancient rivers are still flowing in the blood of this nation! They are bound to be the longing ones among the nations." Rosenberg's comment on that prelude was that it had not been written as a piece of mere art; he who would think it was would only prove that he knew nothing of "German art."[160] National Socialist critics like Nadler and Fechter repeated these blasphemies.

Professor Hermann Gebhardt said that Hitler in 1933 had laid the foundation stone to a racial German religion. The Third Reich was different from "the Kingdom of God which Jesus had once brought" and which was "international." It was a Lutheran theologian who spoke like this, and it is what Hans Grimm meant by saying after the war that Hitler perfected what Luther had begun. That Lutheran theologian changed the meaning of the Lord's Prayer to read like this: "The German Christian swears to be a citizen of the Kingdom of God, he swears particularly to visualise the invisible Kingdom of God in the visible Third Reich. . . . The daily bread must grow on German soil. And this soil must yield to the Germans as much as to the English, the French and the Dutch. . . ." The seventh prayer he disliked because it was "unheroic." The German Christian must know "that his nation is immortal and that the world will be saved by Germanness." The first commandment must read: "Hallowed be thy race." Nobody, he said, could prove that Jesus was "a full-blooded Jew. . . . That must not be so. Jesus cannot have been a Jew."[161] When National Socialist poets prayed for their Führer in their poems, whom did they pray to? Albert Soergel gave this answer: "These poets are pious. But theirs is a Nordic and Germanic piety. They search for the German god and one of them has made this equation: God is identical with the German nation."[162]

Professor J. W. Hauer saw in the Third Reich the last stage of the old fight between Semitism and Indo-Germanism. Goliath, he said, had been one of those "Indo-Germanic heroes slain perfidiously by the Semitic David." The Nordic German does not want to have anything to do with the Christian idea of sin. This was an "alien" idea, and an alien religion is "disastrous for a nation," causing "confusion and spiritual derangement. . . . Semitic alienisation" has been "the ruin of our nation."[163]

Professor Hermann Schwarz, in the Third Reich called "the philosopher of the German rejuvenation," spoke of "the miracle of National Socialism" and praised Hitler for having taught the Germans "the nobility of the Nordic race," so that we are his and he ours, "no longer under the sign of Jahve or the martyr-cross but under the sun-wheel." The Germans, he said, had three times been alienated from their own being, at about 700 A.D. by Christianity, which robbed them of "their inner light," after the Thirty Years' War by the French and English philosophers, and in the 19th century by an un-German natural science. All this was the original sin of the German spirit. Now National Socialism had begun a process of purification so that "a racial German philosophy could awake and start its bold flight." As precursors of this he named all sorts of German philosophers, including Hegel who had said that "when a state is threatened by annihilation only a great leader can save it. These are the seeds of German spirit which have blossomed out in our time." He baptized the blossoms "heroic faith in blood and soil" and "unswerving fidelity to the Führer."[164]

The university lecturer Herbert Grabert spoke about "the incompatibility of Germandom and Christianity." Nordic Germans had never loved Christianity but "the road to freedom has been long and arduous." As liberators he praised Alfred Rosenberg, who had shown the way to "a new, Germanic attitude and faith," and Professor J. W. Hauer, who had fought "against Christianity and the Church" because he knew that the Germans were "not Christians." What Luther had done was only half a deed. "Where he did not succeed we shall succeed, freeing ourselves from an alien creed for a German creed." Christianity had been "the handicap of the Germans." What could Nordic men do with a supernatural God "who has torn up the abyss of sin between himself and the world and 'forgives' out of pure grace and pity"?[165]

The blasphemies outlined on the foregoing pages did not start with Hitler; they, too, have deep roots in a certain German mentality. In the 1890's the racialist periodical *Heimdall* suggested the erection of "a temple of German cult." In "the holy of holies" the gods of the Germans, Wotan and the others, should sit "on a throne", and during the service "Wagnerian music" should be softly played.[166] Jesus, these forerunners of Nazism said, did not want "his gospel to be preached to all nations because he knew only too well that only Aryans, only Germans could be genuine Christians."[167] A few years later H. S. Chamberlain complained: "Olympus and Valhalla became empty, and Jahve became the God of the Indo-Europeans."[168] In 1931 Professor Bergmann exclaimed: "How great and powerful would Germany be if she had never known the religion of the fall of man." If Widukind, Duke of the pagan Saxons, had defeated Charlemagne, instead of the other way around, and if Boniface had not felled the holy oak but the holy oak killed Boniface, "our present frontiers would lie in Siberia."[169] Hitler's renewed march of the medieval German knights comes immediately to mind.

These things must be recalled, at least in brief, if we really want to understand what genuine German Christians, notably Roman Catholics, said in the Third Reich and after Germany's collapse.

Count von Galen, Bishop of Münster, said in his pastoral letter of March 19, 1935: "What a noise the pagans make! There are pagans again in Germany, German compatriots who call themselves pagans, even worse, who are proud of being pagans."[170] Count Galen's sermons were resented as "an attack upon state and party,"[171] because "National Socialist and Christian ideas are incompatible. Our National Socialist ideas of the universe are much higher than those of Christianity, the main tenets of which have been inherited from Judaism."[172] But Count Galen, in his Easter message of 1934, said that the German pagans aimed at a national religion which was not based on revelation "but on ideas of blood and race. Be prepared against the inducements of the enemies from the beginning." And: "If the reign of the Queen of Justice should not be restored, our German nation and our fatherland will perish of inner rottenness in spite of the heroism of our soldiers and all the boastful victories."[173] Devout Roman Catholics distributed "chain letters" in which they said to each other: "The Hour draws near when you will be needed. Be fully prepared to be thrown into the fire as the last log."[174] God was despised and rejected by millions of Germans who encouraged their children to shout behind the backs of chaplains "We do not care for the catechism any longer,"[175] and who wrote: "We shall have no peace before the last Jew hangs on the gut of the last priest."[176] Devout Catholics and Protestants, however, called the Third Reich "the gigantic work of the Devil," "the product of Satan."[177] The Roman Catholic priest Paul Schneider, to mention but one of the many priests murdered in concentration camps, was terribly beaten up in Buchenwald because he failed to salute the Nazi flag. When, on another occasion, he shouted out of the window of his prison cell: "People are being murdered and raped here. Brothers, pray for me!"[178] an SS doctor killed him with a poisonous injection. The worst criminals in those camps were the SS doctors, a number of whom are practicing again in West Germany.

Many churches and monasteries were shut down and confiscated. Count von Galen on July 13, 1941 protested against the "fight against monasteries" in Austria, Southern Germany, Westphalia, Luxembourg, Lorraine, and the East, and prophesied "that Germany will perish because of such injustice."[179] Girls of the *Bund deutscher Mädchen,* when giving birth to illegitimate children, would write home: "Do not beat me when I come back with a child or else I shall denounce you to the party." The leader of a labor camp was happy to be able to tell the parents of a girl that she and five other girls would "present the Führer with a child.[180] Devout Christian women, on the other hand, were often brought to concentration camps and went through all the horrors, "bearing witness," as one said, "to the Kingdom of Jesus." They asked themselves "whether Dante had been to a concentration camp before describing the Inferno."[181] Many priests, Lutheran clergymen, and sectarians, who would not join Hitler's army, died in those camps.

On July 13, 1941, after the Allies bombed Münster, Count von Galen preached on "the meaning of God's visitation" and warned the Germans "not to proceed on a way which would call forth divine judgment and lead to the ruin of our nation."[182] As they did not listen to him, he blamed them on August 3, 1941 for the violation of all the Ten Commandments given by God on Sinai and said, quoting the Gospel: "The days shall come upon thee when thine enemies shall lay thee even with the ground, and thy children with thee, and they shall not leave in thee one stone upon another because thou knewest not the time of the visitation."[183] It took barely four years before this came true. The Nazis did not dare to imprison the courageous Bishop, but when three young chaplains distributed his sermons among civilians and soldiers they were caught and executed.

At about the same time Theodor Haecker, that staunch Roman Catholic writer, entered in his diary: "Does anybody doubt that all this will end in blood and dirt? Else there is no God and the non-existence of God is proved. . . . The religion of the German *Herrgott* is the religion of a stony heart. They will be crushed, they will be pulverised to dust, and then they will want a heart of flesh again."[184]

All the time they kept on saying that the feeling of sin was "unworthy" of a Nordic man, that their morality was free from "oriental self-denial and longing for redemption,"[185] and they murdered some twelve million innocent men, women, and children.

What happens to a nation which denies God was described, with a view to what was going on in Nazi Germany, by the poet and novelist Franz Werfel in 1937 in *Jeremias*. "No man," we read there, "can undo what God has created." The prophet, seeing the sinfulness of his people, knows (like Count von Galen) "that perhaps only one moment is available to stay the punishing hand of God." And exactly like the brave Bishop of Münster he says in the name of God: "My people has forsaken me. It turned away from the well of quick water and drinks from pools, puddles and burst graves." False prophets, like those of Hitler, shout *"Heil! Heil!"* and sing "the delusive song which blinds, deafens and intoxicates every nation and brings it to ruin." One of the true prophets, Urijah, is murdered by King Jojakim, and when Jeremiah sees this he picks up a big earthenware pot and throws it down again so that it falls to pieces, and exclaims: "I shall crush this nation and this city like this earthen pot which nobody can make whole again." When Nebuchadnezzar approaches Jerusalem Jeremiah says, as did Count von Galen: "You ask why God has brought all this upon us. The Lord answers: Because your fathers have forsaken me and have followed only the pride of their hearts, and did not listen." Nebuchadnezzar destroys Jerusalem and abducts the population to Babylon. Jeremiah says: "What He has built through many generations He crushes now. Verily, into a stinking pool He has thrown the daughter in her purple clothes and jewelry and presumption."[186] Franz Werfel said exactly the same of Germany in 1945. Thomas Mann, to whose warnings against Hitler the Germans had refused to listen, said, in the words of Jeremiah: "We have transgressed and have rebelled: Thou hast not pardoned. Thou hast covered with anger and persecuted us: Thou hast made us as the offscouring and refuse in the midst of the people."[187]

Professor Ewald Wasmuth, too, speaks of the German fate in 1945 in terms of the Bible. He and his friends, he confesses, learned in the bleak years of the Third Reich better to understand the teachings of the prophets Isaiah and Jeremiah, and applied their words to Hitler's Reich. It makes no difference, he argues, whether you fight a war with horses and vehicles or with tanks. "The same sun of punishment shines over all ages of disaster." Man has the freedom to change his ways so that God may permit him to stay in his home, as Jeremiah said, as the prophets and Jesus taught. "If, however, we do not change our ways," we remain "under the laws of God, the Father, which have not been abolished by Jesus." He continues that the Greeks meant the same by the word *nemesis*. "All men believe that guilt, a fault in man's relation to God, calls for disaster, and that that disaster comes upon the heads of guilty and innocent alike."[188] When King Maximilian of Bavaria asked Ranke about *nemesis* in history "when not only the government but the whole nation has committed a crime that has injustice as its basis," the historian answered: "The whole nation will have to suffer for it."[189]

3. Writers in Exile and Writers of the Inner Resistance

On May 10, 1933, the books of "un-German" writers were publicly burned by the students of all German universities.

German students had already burned books in 1817 when they celebrated the fourth centenary of Luther's rebellion, which had led to the Thirty Years' War. "Judgment has come," one student said then, "for bad books which dishonour our fatherland and ruin our spirit." The title of each book was called out—and the students shouted: "Into the fire! Into the fire! To the devil with it!" In 1819, in a proclamation to the German nation, this was said: "Brothers in Christ! Arm yourselves with courage and vigour against the enemies of our faith! The time has come to suppress the evil murderers of Christ who deride our creed. We are still powerful enough—so let us pass judgment upon them as it is written: His blood upon us and our children! Do not hesitate. . . . These Jews are like all-devouring locusts, and they threaten to destroy all our Prussian Christianity; they are the descendants of those who once shouted: Crucify! Crucify! Our shout must be! Hepp! Hepp! Hepp!! Death to all Jews! Fly or die!" In about 1820 Professor Fries told the students to renounce the humanitarian ideals of the enlightenment and expel the Jewish students as "enemies of our nation."[190] This remained the normal thing among German students in the 19th and 20th centuries—most students were feudal adherents of the Kaiser and became the admirers of Hitler's burning "un-German" books.

The Bavarian writer Oskar Maria Graf was considered "German" enough and his books were not burnt. So he addressed an open letter to the barbarians, "Burn Me Too," in which he said sarcastically: "They call me a representative of the New German spirit. By what did I earn this insult? Almost all great writers have been exiled, and the Third Reich has dissociated itself from the true German literature. They dare to claim me for their 'spirit.' I did not deserve this shame! I have a right to ask that my books should be delivered to the pure flames of the stake. Burn the works of the German spirit which will live for ever as your ignominy will be remembered forever!"[191]

He left Germany and fled to the United States. In 1944, in a lecture to American professors of German which he gave at Princeton University, he called the German language his *"unverlierbare Heimat"* and remembered the writer Detlev von Liliencron who, although a Prussian Junker, had left Germany after 1870 and spent five years in the United States as a shoeblack, piano teacher, painter, and stable-boy, and had written to a friend: "I find the disgust with so many lies and submissiveness of our pompous and rich bourgeois intolerable."[192] After Germany's downfall in 1945, Graf asked: "Where have we got to with all our honour of a civilised nation, with our spirit, with our great artists and writers? Every intellectual saw that beastly Hitler barbarism long before it established itself." But many of them have to shoulder their guilt because they remained "unpolitical and let things develop, without resisting them. They pretended to be unworldly only to submit to the dictatorship of irresponsible chaps." He remembered "the insolent and challenging *Deutschland, Deutschland über alles*" the result of which "blind hubris was the devastation of our inner world which we witnessed terrified in the Hitler years." Presidents Wilson and F. D. Roosevelt. however, "conceived and realised the idea of the United Nations."[193] So O. M. Graf has remained in New York up to this day. In 1960 he said: "I should regard it as a shameless betrayal ever to forget all this!"[194]

Professor Krieck, rector of Frankfurt University, published this in the early days of May 1933: "The Free Corps of the students invite all professors to the burning of Marxist and corrupt books which will take place on May 10. The students would very much like to see all professors there in view of the great symbolic importance of this ceremony."[195] The students came along. A chorus of students. The first said: "I throw into the flames the books of Marx and Kautsky." The second: "I throw into the flames the books of Heinrich Mann, Ernst Glaeser and Erich Kaestner." The third: "I throw into the flames the books of Friedrich Wilhelm Foerster." The fourth: "I throw into the flames the books of Sigmund Freud." The fifth: "I throw into the flames the books of Emil Ludwig and Werner Hegemann." The sixth: "I throw into the flames the books of Theodor Wolff and Georg Bernhard." The seventh: "I throw into the flames the books of E. M. Remarque." The eighth: "I throw into the flames the books of Alfred Kerr." The ninth: "I throw into the flames the books of Tucholsky and Ossietzky."[196] In Berlin, Professor Baeumler led the university students to the *auto-da-fé* and said to them: "You are marching out now to burn the books in which a spirit alien to us has misused the German word in order to combat it. . . . We do not burn men."[197] Heinrich Heine, however, knew from his history books: "Where you burn books, you will soon also burn men."[198] When Erich Kästner in 1957 received the Georg Büchner Prize he spoke of the many German writers whose prizes had been "persecution and prohibition" (he had been one of them), whose diplomas had been "cancellation of citizenship" and whose academies had been "prison and concentration camp. And even higher honours, the last honours, were not held back."[199] On May 10, 1958, he said in Hamburg: "A Doctor of Philosophy, a pupil of Gundolf, told the German university students to burn the German spirit. It was murder and suicide in one. Intellectual Germany committed suicide." Kästner reminded his audience of what Professor Martin Heidegger, "the greatest philosopher of our century," had told the students of Freiburg University on that day: "Not propositions and ideas should guide your lives. The Führer himself and alone represents the reality of today and tomorrow and its law."[200] Not long after Germany's downfall, he had written: "Of all the books that ought to be written about the Third Reich, the most fascinating and the most tragic will have to deal with the degeneration of the German character."[201] "Madness is reigning now, barbarism governs men," said Ernst Toller. Klaus Mann wrote: "Masses of writers have left Germany. Never in history has a nation lost so many of its literary representatives within a few months."[202] Seven writers committed suicide in exile: Walter Benjamin, Walter Hasenclever, Ernst Toller, Kurt Tucholsky, Ernst Weiss, Alfred Wolfenstein, and Stefan Zweig. More than 20 writers were murdered in Nazi-occupied Europe. One of them was Jizchak Katzenelson from Warsaw, who was murdered at Auschwitz. In his *Song of the Last Jew,* written in Yiddish, we read: "Not one was saved. Was this just, ye heavens? If just, tell me for whom? for whom? for us? What for? We are ashamed of you and of the guilt of the world. . . . Ye heavens, do you still remember Moses? Do you remember Joshua? Do you know us any longer? Have we changed? Or have you yourselves changed? We are the nation which has propagated the word of God, a nation which is God's witness, and our fathers were saints. My holy nation hangs on the cross and atones for the guilt of the earth. Ye heavens, do you see how the murderers of my nation lead children to their death? Millions of children who in fear lift their hands to you. But you are neither moved by the groans of fathers or the weeping of mothers. Enjoy yourselves, ye heavens, with the Germans! And the Germans, may they enjoy themselves with you!"[203]

More than two thousand poets, too, some of "Aryan" and some of Jewish origin, left their barbarized fatherland. Berthold Viertel, in a moving poem, described his experience in questions and answers: "What did you do when you were still living?"— "Oh, I wrote." —"What for?" —"I wanted to keep the wound open." —"The wound?" —"Yes, that it should not close."[204] One of the most amiable exiled poets was Max Hermann-Neisse, a descendant of Silesian peasants, who died in London. His poems are full of the agony of an exile, but he never regretted having fled from his barbarized fatherland, because, to save his conscience, he had left behind "a fatherland which was turned into a hell. . . . I was once a German poet, now my life is as ghostly as my poems. . . . When misery and shame become too heavy to bear there remains only despair and the Last Judgment."[205] Max Barth spoke of "the bitter bread of exile" and the beggar-like, isolated life of the exiled poets, who roamed aimlessly through the streets of South American towns and had the feeling that people were trying to avoid them, saying inwardly: "Leper, Leper!" So they had to bear "your shame, oh Germany!" in isolation. When one or the other of the strange people inquired: "Where, among millions, are your three just men?" they could only feel "hatred and contempt" for the German name and knew that they would never again call "brothers those who have raped our mother."[206] Paul Zech, descendant of Westphalian peasants, a noble poet who fought Hitler from the very beginning, in 1933 was forced to hide and to flee. His books were burned, his wife and daughter committed suicide in Germany. In South America, where he had fled, he had to earn a frugal living by playing the piano in an obscure harbor bar. In his *Argentine Sonnets* he settled his account with barbarized Germany. His poems are full of the anguish and despair of an exile and often he was forced "to eat the bread offered by kind hands." When life became unendurable he remembered that its "emptiness" had to be endured "for the sake of those murdered" by the Nazis, and thinking of the fate of Sodom he said: "I believe in the three just men."[207]

Gustav Regler, another "Aryan" writer who had fled to the United States, wrote to his son in Germany in a seemingly critical manner, as he was sure the German censor would read his letter: "A strange country. They are so obsessed with their private life that they cannot understand that you are fond of being soldiers. They do not believe that you have cleaned your libraries of corrupting literature and burned the books of Heine, Marx and other Jews. They say auto-da-fés are part of the Middle Ages. If they speak of Germany, they are silly enough to refer rather to the emigrants than to the *Führer* who made Germany great."[208]

Arnold Hahn, who died in Great Britain, wrote *The People Messiah,* seven times seven sonnets in praise of the Jews, describing what the Jews have done for mankind from the days of Moses and Jesus to Albert Einstein, and what they had to suffer through the centuries and were still suffering in barbarized Germany and Europe. "A curse on those who hunt down the Jews so that their own nation may be 'awakened.'"[209] Karl Wolfskehl, whose forefathers had lived in Western Germany for more than a thousand years, wrote in the years of his exile many poems, most notable among them his song cycles *Mare Nostrum, Song from Exile,* and *Hiob.* The whole Jewish race had become Hiob under the hands of the Ger-

man barbarians: "Love is poison! He who is a man hates!"[210]
Wolfskehl also depicted the future fate of Germany in what
blinded Hiob Simson does at Gaza to the overlords of the Philis-
tines, who have brought him out from prison "in order to drink
his sufferings like a delicious intoxication."[211] Simson pulls down
the pillars of the palace of his enemies, and "one death" buries
him and them. Wolfskehl also also addressed a lengthy poem
"To the Germans" in which he told them that his forefathers
had come to Germany at the time of Charlemagne but "your
ways are no longer mine," you have betrayed "your great
heritage. The German spirit is where I am."[212] He also said to
them: "If you knew what I know, cold sweat would run down
your foreheads and eyelids, and your limbs would shake as if
lashed with rods."[213] He condemned their lie about a Nordic
race which denied Jesus, and added: "Although you utter a
thousand words, the Word, the Word is dead."[214] In his letters
we read: "Full of ice-cold disgust and hot anger I have decided
to go as far away as this small planet allows me to do. An
expelled poet does not creep back."[215] He lies buried in Auck-
land, New Zealand. On his tombstone are the words *"Exul
poeta."* None of the expelled writers returned to Germany. The
painter Fred Uhlman, said: "I cut myself off completely from
Germany."[216] In his book *The Making of an Englishman,* he
says that it had been the tragedy of the German Jews that they
wanted first to be Germans and only afterwards Jews. To give
but one example of this tragedy, we deal a little with Rudolf
Borchardt, a German poet and essayist of Jewish origin to
whom Benjamin Disraeli was a mere "Oriental." He had been
brought up "in faithfulness to the King" of Prussia and volun-
teered for the Kaiser's war in 1914. During the war he wrote
that Wilhelm II represented "the type of a young king" and
"satisfied our longing for a symbolic and typical personality." He
compared the creation of the Kaiser's fleet with the creation of
the Prussian army by Friedrich Wilhelm I, but Germans like

Philip Scheidemann, Fritz von Unruh and Professor F. W. Foerster were not to his liking. Even as late as 1927 he praised those German Jews who had embraced Christianity in order "to disappear" among the rest of the German nation, "to hope their hopes, to believe in their beliefs, to love their loves . . . and to die for their state."[217] He nearly died at the hands of the Nazis.

The Swiss professor Walter Muschg after the war wrote a book which he entitled *The Ruin of German Literature*. "The German literature," he said in the preface, "has been so utterly ruined that they are unable to recognise its ruin."[218] No writer of any standing has appeared in the post-war generation of German writers, none who can in the least be compared with the writers of the pre-Hitler days. The couplet in Wagner's *Mastersingers,*

> Through Holy Roman Empire sink to dust
> There still survives our sacred German art

can only be applied to the great literary past of Germany, not to the present day. It is highly characteristic that sensitive German youth regard Paul Celan, a Rumanian Jew, as the most gifted post-war German poet. But he prefers to live in Paris because his parents died in one of the German concentration camps. In a terrible poem, "Death Fugue," he describes what the Hitlerites did in those camps.[219] In another poem he says: "My blonde mother did not return home. My quiet mother cries for all."[220]

While the barbarized Hitler writers and professors were defaming the German name, a number of honest and brave men, though only a tiny number, proved by their behavior that it was also possible to remain an honest writer in the face of the most hideous tyranny. They chose the same method as Heinrich Mann during the Kaiser's war, the method of indirect and hidden criticism.

The poet and translator R. A. Schröder lectured in 1935 on

Horace as a political poet and illustrated his opinions by care-fully chosen quotations, the real meaning of which was grasped by intelligent listeners and readers; for instance the following lines: "Woe, woe! We rue the wounds, we rue the blood and our brothers! Woe, thou hard generation, what has remained un-touched by thine impudent hands! What has remained holy, whom does youth still revere? Which altar has remained pure of our crimes?" He even added courageously: "These words sound like an exhortation to our days. For while history never repeats itself, the fundamental laws of life are few, the fundamental notions of the human heart remain the same throughout the ages." In another context he said that "all unworthy things last a short while, but what is destined to survive the changes of the centuries must be made of another stuff." He looked into the future of Nazi Germany and quoted: *"Quidquid delirant reges plectuntur Achivi"* and even translated the words: "What the madness of kings perpetrates, their peoples bear the conse-quences."[221] He let one of his own poems secretly pass from hand to hand and even read it to audiences in Leipsic, Göt-tingen, Tübingen, and Erlangen. It runs: "Look down on your sad ones, O Lord! Have mercy on your sad ones, O Lord! They are burdened and beaten down, their burden becomes heavier every day. Thine adversary moves through our land, no longer at night, nay, in broad daylight. He wears as crowns all the plagues which Thou hast banned to hell."[222]

Ernst Wiechert said in 1936 in a lecture to students of Munich University: "It is certainly possible for a nation to cease differentating between right and wrong. But such a nation stands on a precipitously inclined plane and the law of its down-fall has already been passed. On each wall the hand will appear, writing letters of fire."[223] For this speech he was sent to Dachau. In 1937 he published a short story, *The White Buffalo,* which he also read before audiences. His hero, Vasudeva, an "Aryan" Indian of an entirely different kind from the Nordic

"Aryans" of the Third Reich, even as a youth raises "his arrow against injustice," and later dies as a martyr because he had said to the autocratic ruler of his country: "Power does not satisfy. Everybody worships you but I do not worship you, so you know how powerless you are. You cannot compel me, you can only kill me.... That man who killed my buffalo was worth less than the murdered animal. He murdered the gods by murdering it.... The powerful is responsible for each single tear which is shed in his country."[224]

Theodor Haecker, a devout Roman Catholic, kept a diary in which he entered all his forebodings and prophecies. Here are just a few of these entries:

The Germans adhere to the words of their dear Martin Luther: *Peccare fortiter—mentiri fortiter.*

Since the Prussians established their hegemony which reaches its climax today, the Germans have been conditioned by the slogan: *Oderint dum metuant.*

The Germans will not be defeated by the power of men. They are the strongest and most terrible nation on earth. God himself will defeat them.

They wage this war as slaves of an apostate government powerful by the passions of despair. *Ruimus in servitutem.*

It is a war against Western religion.

The French Revolution spoke of freedom, equality, brotherhood. What are the ideas of National Socialism? Exactly the opposite, no doubt. There is only *one* race which is superior to all others. There are nations like Jews and Poles which are *Untermenschen.*

Salus ex Germanis, not *salus ex Judaeis.*

The German *Herrgott* announces that right is what serves the German nation.

Prussian idealism robbed the Germans of their human hearts and gave them an iron heart. The communion of duty with empty phrases meant the dehumanisation of man. Already Frederick II's word of the first servant of the state was an empty phrase. He spoke more truly when he confessed that he had attacked [Austrian] Silesia out of vanity and greediness of glory.

I have no doubt that the religion of the most primitive nations is infinitely more deep than the religion of the German *Herrgott,* the shallowness and brutality of which has no equal.

National Socialism succeeded overnight in subjugating the Norwegians who have been free men for a thousand years.

General Field-Marshal Brauchitsch said God has blessed us and God will not forsake us in future as long as we do not forsake ourselves.

The Russian soil drinks blood since June 22.

They tell us today that every Jew will have to bear a yellow star, the Star of David, from September 19. The day may come when the Germans will have to bear a swastika which is the sign of Antichrist.

One can already clearly hear the howling and wailing of the demons. If we do not win the war the Party will be lost—*ergo* we shall win it. God gave us victory during three years; it would not make sense not to help us any longer—*ergo* we shall be victorious. Or more simply: we must win the war, *ergo* we shall win it. And still more simply: we have already won the war long ago, but the enemy has not realised it yet.[225]

Dr. Rudolf Pechel, editor of the *Deutsche Rundschau,* for nine years waged a clandestine war against Hitler. He invented various methods of indirect criticism and condemnation. In April, 1933 he said, with reference to a famous word of Bismarck's: "The lack of civil courage is indeed one of the national German vices. Therefore it is necessary to say to the German bourgeois loudly and honestly: Gentlemen, more civil courage!" Pechel wrote, for instance, about Tsarist Russia, but his readers understood whom he meant: "If everybody is suspect, a very elaborate system of spying is the inevitable consequence of such a state of affairs, and it leads to a demoralisation of the whole nation. It makes no difference whether the 'suspect' fellow-citizens are already in concentration camps or still at 'liberty.'" On another occasion he said about Robespierre, meaning Hitler: "In the opinion of the French if he was not regarded as a madman thursting for blood, a maniacal tyrant, he could only be a priest gone astray who was experimenting with some pseudo-religion, Rousseau being his prophet, and cutting off the heads of everybody who opposed his religion. Robespierre was, no doubt, a democrat, as the term was understood then, but he was not a liberal and did not care for the French ideal of humanity. . . . He made the revolution the terror of Europe and all mankind. His paradise was a prison without light. . . . The moral disintegration of the nation progressed rapidly. The moral decay of the nation became an abyss."

Or Pechel would deal with Napoleon, meaning Hitler, by contrasting what the hero-worshipper Nietzsche had said about him with what the humane and skeptical Swiss historian Burckhardt had said. Nietzsche, Pechel said, praised Napoleon "as an ingenious man of power, a *Herrenmensch* full of contempt for all Christian virtues. Napoleon's indifference as regards human sacrifices was, in Nietzsche's opinion, further proof of his 'nobility.' The great goal at which, according to him, Napoleon was aiming was a united Europe." This was written in 1941. Burckhardt, however, continued Pechel, was a conservative historian and regarded "an individual who stepped forward with immoderate claims and reckless inconsiderateness, as did Napoleon, as something 'unnatural in the highest degree.' Under his regime everybody was barbarised." The following is very apt: "He was particularly sensitive to critisism in the foreign Press, which the English bore in mind, provoking him again and again, so that he got white-hot in the face." Burckhardt, Pechel continued, regarded Napoleon as "an enemy of Europe," because that conservative historian cherished "freedom, moderation, and humaneness." He also quoted Coulaincourt's words about Napoleon: "If there is a God in heaven, that man will not end on the throne." In 1939 Pechel prophetically foretold what Hitler was to say in 1945, remarking that Napoleon "said with regard to his inevitable downfall by way of excuse that he had been too great for the French."

When depicting Nietzsche as an inspirer of Nazism, Pechel

reminded his readers that there had also been another Nietzsche who said things like these: "When I try to imagine a man who goes against all my instincts it is always a German." And: "In all my deepest instincts I am averse to everything German." And: "It was always a sign of the best of our nation to turn towards the un-German." And: "Not to associate with anybody who has a share in the race swindle."

He wrote an article about "Demonism of Power" and used as a motto these lines from *Troilus and Cressida:*

> Then everything includes itself in power,
> Power into will, will into appetite;
> And appetite, an universal wolf,
> So doubly seconded with will and power,
> Must make perforce an universal prey,
> And last eat up himself.

In another article he said: "Megalomania is one of the most dangerous illnesses of the mind." And added: "The most illustrious Germans have again and again, and with pitiless pungency, drawn the attention to these dangers. They could never penetrate the pleasing legend. Never was the cleavage between the conscientious critics and the majority of the nation bigger than in the last years before the [1914-18] war when the legend about the Kaiser and the glorious and invincible German nation was celebrated with flags, fanfares and drums. Every German has the livery of a lackey in his knapsack."

Pechel also published quotations from Manzoni, Gracian, Boëtius in order to criticize the Third Reich, this one, for instance, from Boëtius: "I can see the whole ignominy with my eyes: the witches' kitchens of the criminals full of joy and jubilation, the most depraved chaps threatening us with new and despicable denunciations." He also quoted Madame de Remusat's words: "The army has become the accomplice of tyranny."

Pechel found brave collaborators who published other indirect denunciations of the Hitler regime in his periodical. Ernst

Samhaber, for instance, unearthed a South American dictator, Francisco Lopez, and pictured the Führer in that madman. This courageous German wrote in the days of Stalingrad: "With blind confidence in the power of his weapons Lopez entered into a political course which was to find a tragic end and bring about a terrible collapse of his nation. He was fond of being regarded by his entourage as a demi-god. Inclined towards conceit by nature, the flatterings and incense of continuous admiration intoxicated him and he ceased to see the reality as it was. In 1865 the catastrophe came. His plans were bound to miscarry: Lopez' dream came to an end, his army was smashed to pieces, his power ceased. His ambition, his madness had ruined state and nation. The Paraguayans had to experience the bitter end."[226]

In April, 1942, Pechel was arrested and taken to the concentration camp of Sachsenhausen. On his record card were written the words: "Must not leave the camp alive." His son, who served as an officer in the German army, tried several times to get his father released—in vain. In the spring of 1945 he succeeded, by a pretense, in forcing his way into the presence of the almighty and very much dreaded *SS-Obergruppenführer* Müller who decided life and death for the inmates of the concentration camps of the region. When he asked him to release Dr. Pechel, the Nazi boss told him angrily that this prisoner had never repented and had remained an enemy of the Third Reich; he would therefore never be released. Young Pechel, resolved to shoot himself on the spot if Müller should ring for his aide to have him arrested, said in a stern voice: "Let us be frank, Müller. The Third Reich is doomed. In three weeks the Russians will be in Berlin. Would you not like on that day to have a couple of good marks?" Müller did not ring for anybody but said he would consider the case. Next morning Rudolf Pechel was set free. Müller was probably killed by Russian shells when trying to flee from Berlin.

Jochen Klepper, banned from public literary life and forbidden to publish anything because he declined to separate from his Jewish-born wife, wrote a novel on Friedrich Wilhelm I, *Der Vater,* and succeeded in getting permission to publish it; the Nazi bosses did not grasp its real meaning. True, he idealized that Prussian king, depicting him as a God-fearing man; but his many readers understood immediately (and wrote to him about it) that he contrasted a truly Christian king with the pagan rulers of the Third Reich. He interspersed his narrative with many quotations from the Bible to the effect that God hated injustice and that governments could be consolidated only by justice. The novel was a great success, but a Nazi critic called it an effrontery that a man who "had married a Jewess with two Jewish daughters shortly before 1933" should dare to write about "the father of Frederick the Great."[227] Klepper looked with despair at what was going on his barbarized country. He was the son of a pastor and filled his diary with quotations from the Old and New Testaments, and he was sure that Hitler's Reich would end in disaster. Here are but a few of the many thousands of entries in his diary, which was published after the war.

June 10, 1933: I am completely living in exile now.

August 21, 1933: It is very difficult to have to hate one's own nation which one has naturally loved before.

February 26, 1935 (from a statement of the leader of the German Youth): If the new generation will have passed through the Hitler Youth for ten years, it will hardly know anything of Jesus.

November 26, 1937: They pride themselves on having excluded 30,000 Jews from the cultural life in Germany, and they tell us how happy the German writers are today.

February 12, 1938: One shudders at the sight of the hubris of this poor nation.

March 14, 1938: It is a Reich of the highest activity, but of extreme hubris.

March 16, 1938 [after the seizure of Austria]: 70 million Germans have now finally conquered 950,000 Jews.

August 17, 1938: The Tower of Babel and the elimination of the Jews: one is terrified to death.

November 23, 1938: The SS, 'the Order of National Socialism,' hate the Jews to a degree that they ask for ghettos, the Yellow Star, and even extermination of criminal Jewry by fire and sword.

March 20, 1939 [after the seizure of Prague]: Hatred against Germany is unimaginable.

September 2, 1940: Another division of the minds: some are delighted that Germany will be provided for by what comes from the occupied countries, others fear for the future of these nations.

December 20, 1941: We hear of the mass murder of Jews in the East.

August 18, 1942: More and more deportations. Families are being separated.

Of anti-Hitler writers, he often met Reinhold Schneider who said to him, "We have no fatherland any longer,"[228] and that "not to be spoken of is the best thing that can happen to people like us."[229] Klepper excerpted these words from Schneider's book on Portugal: "It is the tragedy of prophets and their countries that those who love most see the downfall the surest—that deepest devotion feels the gliding down, while the rioters on the surface think they are ascending."[230]

He knew that the deported Jews were murdered in the East, so before his wife and his younger stepdaughter (the older was already in Great Britain) could also be deported, they decided to die together. His friend, Reinhold Schneider, says: "When there was no longer any justice or protection he took his wife and daughter by their hands and hurried before the Judge, the terrible Father, knowing himself guilty and sure of infinite grace."[232] The last entry in his diary reads: "December 10, 1942. We shall die together tonight. Above us in our last hours is the picture of the Blessing Christ who fights for us."

Schneider, a devout Roman Catholic, published a novel, *Las Casas Before Charles V*, in which he condemned the barbarities committed by Cortez and his men against the defenseless Indians, alluding, of course, to the Nazi's behavior against the Jews, Poles, Czechs, and Russians. The Spanish *gauleiters* say that they "are of a higher and more civilised race." In this book we are made to look into the eyes of tortured Indians "which seemed to shine with abysmal floods of tears." We read of "slave hunters" and are reminded of Sauckel, Rosenberg, and Speer. One of these heroes says: "We did not care whether we separated parents from children, husbands from wives. Everybody wanted strong workers." Unfortunate slave workers did what the slave workers of Krupp, I. G. Farben, etc., did, they "fled in spite of the heavy penalties which awaited them when recaptured." We are reminded of the fate of the Jews in the Third Reich when we hear Las Casas, a Catholic priest, say: "Our nation has sinned against the commandment to love our neighbour against no one more severely than against these unfortunate creatures. . . . I felt day and night the unspeakable despair of exterminated nations and saw with my mind's eye the picture of our Lord derided on all roads. . . . I also saw much, much worse things which no human brain can think of, no lip can tell." This priest, this writer, the conscience of barbarized Germany, calls "aggressive wars illegal, tyrannous and hell-like." He asks himself anxiously how the perpetrators of all these crimes will defend themselves "before our Judge some day in the future," and is sure "that God's judgment will come over this country. Unspeakable crimes will be punished in an unspeakable manner."[232]

Schneider also wrote many poems, mostly sonnets, during those years and had them secretly passed from hand to hand. In them he spoke of "my enslaved nation" and "voices of prophets burning with heresies." Madness constructed "clay palaces," and celebrated "noisy feasts," but "this mad *Reich* will fall to pieces overnight, and we shall hear the terrible question of our Judge whether we have ever entered His *Reich*." While the others rejoice over the glory, he said in another sonnet, I see only "night, evil, and death, and how downfall is looming in victories, and how the corrupters clothe themselves in false glory. O my people, how will the eternal judge weight our deeds

in accordance with eternal justice if he does not consider what
we have silently suffered." He represented Hitler as Satan in one
of his most powerful sonnets. "He clothes himself in the shape
of God and speaks His holy language and dares to assume His
rôle as a judge—and nobody sees that it is Satan who speaks.
But when he tries to ascend towards the light he will be struck
by lightning from the highest circle throwing him into the darkness from which he came." One can imagine with what satisfaction decent Germans read these words. To his people he said in
1943: "Change your hearts before God's lightning answers your
deeds!" And: "A curse on us who are destroying ourselves."[233]
In 1940 he published an essay on *"Franz Grillparzer's
Epilogue on History,"* conjuring up the Führer in some lines
from one of Grillparzer's dramas. The Emperor Rudolf II
speaks of "a monster" which has come up from the deepest
depths "hankering after everything and not satisfied with anything." No Scyths nor Chazars, says the Emperor, are threatening us, no other nations; "the barbarian has come from our own
loins," undermining everything great: art, science, state, the
Church. . . ."[234]

For this courageous and uncompromising behavior Schneider
was later made a Honorary Doctor of Münster University.

The poet and novelist Werner Bergengruen, who had been
excluded from the Chamber of Writers, in his novel *The Grand
Tyrant and the Judgment* put these words into the tyrant's
mouth: "Would you not permit me to handle justice in such a
way that it serves the continuation of our powerful and pros-
perous community as its highest aim, even though the small
claim on justice of a huckstress may suffer?" The answer given
is: "I have learnt and believe that that régime remains most
secure under which not one huckstress is denied her right."
These words, too, were clearly understood as an allusion to the
terrible reality of the Third Reich: "He who tries to imitate
Christ must be prepared not only to follow in His steps but also

do the deed with which He concluded His earthly life, that is to offer himself voluntarily as an atoning sacrifice for many."[235] Bergengruen had several of his poems secretly passed from hand to hand. In one of them, which was found on some German prisoners of war who were brought to Great Britain, he says: "Who will distinguish the pure from the guilty? Who of the pure has not soiled himself? The sickle will cut both wheat and weed when the verdict of the harvesting day is pronounced."[236]

Prelate Romano Guardini spoke in the second edition of *Religious Characters in Dostoevsky's Work* of "deified nature," of "the hubris of the superman," of "idolized nationhood."[237] Father Alfred Delp, executed after the plot against Hitler, said in 1943 in *Man and History:* "The picture of history is more darkened by injustice, perjury, and violence than by misfortune. Ships with black sails, ships of pirates; freebooters of life sail on the waters of history, and their sails are bellied out by favourable winds and their storerooms are full—and quietly and securely they sail from crime to crime."[238] For a time. While that time lasted the poet Rudolf Hagelstange spoke of the Nazi "drunkards" who did not even so much as look up when, in the middle of their feast, a hand appeared "writing the *menetekel* on your wall."[239]

Hermann Hart, a fanatical enemy of Hitler, collected, from the very first day of the Third Reich, press cuttings about the Devil's regime in Germany and had them secretly printed. He called them "a collection of pictures of the millennium," and we can now read what he collected from 1931 to 1943. A picture published by the Berlin newspaper, *Vorwärts,* on November 27, 1931 shows prophetically what was to come: the barbarians of the SA and SS plunder and murder; slave workers, connected by chains around their necks, are being driven to work by an SS man who carries a whip in his right hand and a gun in his left. Göring said on March 10, 1933: "I thank God that I do not know what objectivity is." Minister Frick said in 1935: "As far as we National Socialists are concerned, everything is good that serves the Germans, and everything is bad that harms them." Hitler said of Churchill and Roosevelt on January 30, 1942: "Churchill, that chatterbox and drunkard, that liar and sluggard, is one of the most wretched Herostratusos of world history. Of his accomplice in the White House I better say nothing for he is only a pitiful madman." On February 12, 1936, Hitler said, "Not even one murdered adversary lies on the path of our movement. From the first day we declined to fight with such weapons." Dr. Hart retorted: "Except in Potempa, except in the concentration camps, except in the case of Dollfuss, except the innumerable judicial murders, except the murder of hostages in the occupied countries, except the mass extermination of Jews in Germany and the occupied countries." With relish Dr. Hart quoted Hitler's address to the Germans on January 30, 1943, ten years after his accession to power: "New life will blossom from the ruins of our cities and villages, for we fight for a Teutonic State of the German nation, the eternal National Socialist Greater Germany." Pope Pius XII, however, said on September 1, 1943: "Woe to those who build their might on injustice! Woe to those who suppress the powerless and innocent! God's anger will fall on their heads without pity."

Dr. Hart mentions a book, *Genghis Khan* by M. Prawdin, which was published in Germany in 1934, and quotes from it passages which he applied to Hitler's Reich: "The soldiers were jubilant when they heard that their victorious Kha-Khan would lead them into a rich country where they would find more booty than they had ever seen. Genghis Khan alone had an inkling of the magnitude of this adventure."[240]

A number of German professors deserve very much to be praised. Professor Dietrich von Hillebrand left Germany and went to Vienna where he said in a Catholic periodical that it was impossible to hope that National Socialism could ever free itself from its depravity. "Its ideology has from the very beginning been a product of mean and dangerous instincts, intellectual stupidity and half-education. It is, foremost, a terrible heresy, utterly anti-Christian, anti-religious, and blasphemous. Only one word is suitable for it: *Ceterum censeo Carthaginem esse delendam.*"[241] Another Catholic professor, Johannes Maria Verweyen, said in Dresden in 1935: "All blue eyes and blonde hair are no substitute for culture." After his lecture the editor of the periodical, *The Jew-Expert,* addressed him in these words: "Citizen Verweyen! You have been very clear, and we have understood!" The sentence of his lecture: "It is only a matter of time when the avenging demons will arrive," was answered with: "We have always thought that Professor Verweyen entertained good relations with certain demons."[242] He was brought to Belsen where he died a few days before the Allied armies reached that institution of German culture.

We cannot agree with Professor Ritter on anything he said after the war but we must pay homage to him for his behavior in the Third Reich. In his book, *Power State and Utopia,* he seemed, on the surface, to condemn Macchiavelli's theories, but in reality he was out to condemn the theories and practices of Hitlerism. We have always known, he said, of terrorism, cruelty, malice in history—"What is new is the experience that all this is inseparable from the nature of a political fight for power." He spoke of "notorious methods of purposeful hypocrisy, cruel hardness under the mask of condescension, love of peace, and love of man, of cunning, underhand tricks, fraud and treason of all sorts." Speaking of Napoleon, but meaning Hitler, Ritter said: "The misuse of the ideals of national freedom and greatness as a smoke screen put over the bare, egoistic lust for power aroused, in the end, secret opposition within his own nation and, above all, the rebellion of the suppressed nations."[243] Professor Ritter received many letters from understanding readers approving of his "unmasking of political demonism."[244] After July 20, 1944, he was sent to a concentration camp.

A number of other decent professors criticized the Hitler régime in veiled or open words in their lectures, others did so at least in private conversations, like Professor Wilhelm Schüssler, who said that Grillparzer's word, "From humanism through nationalism to bestialism," had come true in the Third Reich, adding: "Idealism ended in the paroxysm of Hegel, nationalism in the paroxysm of Hitler."[245] Professor Paul Kahle, world famous as an authority on the history of the text of the Bible, helped Jewish colleagues as much as he could, was threatened by the Nazis, and fled to Great Britain, where he spent the whole war.

Notes

1. *Deutscher Bundestag, 140th Sitzung,* April 18, 1956.
2. International Military Tribunal (IMT), Nuremberg, May 10, 1946.
3. IMT, January 7, 1946.
4. IMT, August 10, 1946.
5. H. Gollwitzer. *Und Führe uns, wohin wir nicht wollen.* Muenchen, 1952, p. 159.
6. *Nuernberger Nachrichten,* November 5, 1955.
7. Foerster. *Die juedische Frage,* p. 113.
8. *Bulletin des Leo Baeck Instituts.* Tel Aviv, No. 2-3, p. 106.
9. *Muenchner Nenesle Nachrichten,* May 9, 1958.
10. *Bulletin des Leo Baeck Instituts,* No. 7, p. 13.
11. *Offiziere des Fuehrers* (a periodical), 1944, 1st issue.
12. Max Pribilla. *Deutsche Schicksalsfragen,* p. 132.
13. J. Scholmer. *Die Toten kehren zurueck.* Koeln, 1954, pp. 72-73.
14. *A Full Life,* p. 165.
15. *Frankfurter Zeitung,* October 26, 1933.
16. *Neue Presse am Sonntag,* October 9, 1955.
17. *Die Fackel,* July, 1934.
18. W. Kraft. *Karl Kraus.* Salzburg, 1956, p. 189.
19. *Von Trakl zu Brecht.* Muenchen, 1961, pp. 176, 177, 178, 185, 194, 196.
20. *Die Kultur,* August 1, 1957.
21. *Ibid.*
22. *Die Zeit,* Hamburg, May 30, 1957.
23. *Ibid.*
24. Will Vesper. *Deutsche Jugend.* Berlin, 1934, p. 1.

25. *Deutsche Kulturpolitik.* Muenchen, 1934, pp. 20, 21, 29-30.

26. *Die Zeit,* Hamburg, May 16, 1957.

27. H. Kindermann. *Heimkehr ins Reich.* Leipzig, 1939, p. 402.

28. *Lebenswert und Lebenswirkung der Dichtkunst in einem Volke.* Muenchen, 1935, p. 21.

29. *Der einzelne und die Gemeinschaft.* Muenchen, 1939, pp. 11-12.

30. *Bulletin of the Association of Jewish Refugees,* London, February, 1959.

31. Kraus. *Die dritte Walpurgisnacht* p. 149; *Deutsche Blaetter,* Santiago de Chile, March, 1945.

32. W. Vesper. *Die Ernte der Gegenwart.* Muenchen, 1941, p. 384.

33. *Das innere Reich* (a periodical), 1939-1940, Issue I.

34. Walter Muschg. *Die Zerstoerung der deutschen Literatur.* Bern, 1956, p. 88.

35. Klepper. *Unter dem Schatten deiner Fluegel,* p. 501.

36. Friedmann. *Deutsche Literatur im 20. Jahrhundert.* Heidelberg, 1954, p. 145.

37. Klepper, *op. cit.,* p. 669.

38. Kraus. *Die dritte Walpurgisnacht,* pp. 67-77.

39. Schonauer, *op. cit.,* pp. 47-48.

40. *Kunst und Macht.* Stuttgart, 1934, p. 98.

41. Muschg, *op. cit.,* pp. 55, 62.

42. *Ibid.*

43. Kindermann. *Heimkehr ins Reich,* p. 263.

44. *Das innere Reich,* 1941, p. 406.

45. *Am Rande des Abgrunds.* Graz, 1950, p. 215.

46. *Europa.* Berlin, 1937, pp. 5, 7, 11, 17, 48, 49, 73, 74, 80-82.

47. *Die Welt der Arbeit* (a periodical), Koeln, November 21, 1955.

48. Pross. *Die Zerstoerung,* pp. 98-100.

49. *Geschichte der deutschen Literatur.* Leipzig, 1909. Vol. II, p. 542; *Deutsches Schrifttum.* Weimar, 1910, p. 94; *Die deutsche Dichtung der Gegenwart.* Leipzig, 1910, pp. 307-308.

50. *Rasse und Volkstum.* Weimar, 1920, p. 320.

51. *Die deutsche Dichtung der Gegenwart: Die Juengsten.* Leipzig, 1921, pp. 37-38, 76-77, 89, 93, 102, 129.

52. *Juedische Herkunft und Literaturwissenschaft.* Leipzig, 1925, pp. 208-209.

53. *Dichtung und Dichter der Zeit.* Leipzig, 9th edition, 1919, pp. 483, 579, 797, 808.

54. *Dichter aus deutschem Volkstum.* Leipzig, 1934, pp. 7, 11, 12, 16, 18-19, 75.

55. *Dichtung und Volkstum* (a periodical), 1934; *Die Wissenschaft von der Dichtung.* Berlin, 1939, p. 374; Jonas Fraenkel. *Dichtung und Wissenschaft.* Heidelberg, 1954, pp. 262-263.

56. *Dichtung im Daseinskampf.* Karlsbad, 1935, pp. 31, 33, 43-44, 48, 36-38.

57. *Neumond des Geistes.* Wien, 1950, pp. 14, 15, 57, 70, 123, 164.

58. *Berliner Romantik.* Berlin, 1920, pp. 5, 44; *Literaturgeschichte des*

deutschen Volkes. Berlin, 1941, Vol. IV, pp. 212-213, 240, 259-261, 381-382, 436-438.

59. *Ibid.,* pp. 5, 221, 225.

60. *Kleines Nachspiel.* Wien, 1954, pp. 88-90, 91, 93, 174.

61. *Heimkehr ins Reich,* p. vii.

62. *Reden.* Leipzig, 1886, Vol. I, p. 418.

63. W. Schoof. *Jacob Grimm.* Bonn, 1961, pp. 249, 287-288, 300, 303-305.

64. H. Hartmann. *Max Planck,* pp. 68-70.

65. *Observer,* London, April 27, 1958.

66. *The Rescue and Achievement of Refugee Scholars.* The Hague, 1953, pp. 8, 73.

67. *Nuernberger Nachrichten,* December 10, 1954.

68. *Lingua Tertii Imperii.* Berlin, 1949, pp. 15, 17, 18, 86, 92, 152, 177, 183-184.

69. *Die deutsche Frage,* pp. 77, 82.

70. *Erste Reichstagung der Wissenschaftlichen Akademiker des NSD-Dozentenbundes.* Muenchen, 1939, p. 14.

71. W. Ferber. *Geist und Politik in Oesterreich.* Konstanz, 1955, pp. 12-18.

72. *Ibid.,* pp. 5-12.

73. *Katholischer Zugang zum Nationalsozialismus.* Muenster, 1933, pp. 5-7, 9, 16, 26.

74. Minister Rust and Professor Ernst Krieck. *Das nationalsozialistische Deutschland und die Wissenschaft.* Hamburg, 1936, pp. 13, 14, 18, 20, 24, 27.

75. *Deutsche Physik.* Muenchen, 1936. Foreword, pp. IX-X.

76. *Juedische und deutsche Physik.* Leipzig, 1941, pp. 6, 11-12, 14, 16, 21-24, 55.

77. *Deutsche Mathmatik.* Leipzig, January, 1936, p. 5.

78. L. Poliakov and J. Wulf. *Das Dritte Reich und seine Diener.* Berlin, 1956, p. 19.

79. L. Poliakov and J. Wulf. *Das Dritte Reich und seine Denker.* Berlin, 1959, p. 106.

80. *Wissenschaft und Philosophie im Dritten Reich.* Berlin, 1938, pp. 6-7, 9-14, 16-19, 22-24, 26-29.

81. *Erste Reichstagung der Wissenschaftlichen Akademiker des NSD-Dozentenbundes.* Muenchen, 1940, pp. 23-32.

82. W. Hofer. *Der Nationalsozialismus,* pp. 327-932.

83. *Erste Reichstagung,* etc., p. 42.

84. *Pariser Rechenschaft,* pp. 58 ff.

85. *Maennerbund und Wissenschaft.* Berlin, 1943, pp. 126-127, 137.

86. *Politik und Erziehung.* Berlin, 1937, p. 41.

87. *Ibid.,* p. 57.

88. *Die neue Ordnung Europas.* Berlin, 1943, pp. 22, 23, 28.

89. *Offiziere des Fuehrers* (a periodical), 1944, Issue I.

90. *Deutsche Wissenschaft. Dem Fuehrer Ueberreicht als Festgabe der deutschen Wissenschaft zu seinem 50. Geburtstag.* Leipzig, 1939.

91. F. Hartung. *Das Reich und Europa.* Leipzig, 1941, Preface.

92. *Der Aufbau,* New York, February 7, 1958.

93. *Deutschland und England.* Berlin, 1939, pp. 16-17, 38, 41, 42-44, 46.

94. *Das Tegernseetal* (a periodical), Muenchen, winter, 1957.

95. *Volk und Staat in der Geschichte.* Leipzig, 1940, pp. 26 ff.

96. *Die Entwicklung der Menschen-und Buergerrechte von 1776-1946.* Berlin, 1948, p. 19; *Deutsche Verfassungsgeschichte.* Stuttgart, 1950, pp. 352-353.

97. *Die Epochen der Weltgeschichte.* Stuttgart, 1940, Preface and pp. 6, 382-387, 390, 403.

98. *Nordische Schoenheit.* Muenchen, 1937, pp. 9, 11, 202; *Offiziere des Fuehrers,* 1944, Issue I; Friedelind Wagner. *The Royal Family of Wagner,* p. 142.

99. L. Poliakov and J. Wulf. *Das Dritte Reich und seine Diener,* p. 290.

100. *Wesen und Inhalt der politischen Verfassung.* Hamburg, 1935, pp. 15, 82-83; *Verfassungsrecht des grossdeutschen Reiches.* Hamburg, 1937, pp. 151, 153, 159, 194, 197, 210, 237, 240, 276-277, 279-280, 481-483; *Bau und Gefuege des Reichs.* Hamburg, 1941, p. 14.

101. *Volkstum, Recht und Staat.* Breslau, 1937, pp. 6, 13-16, 28-29.

102. *Deutsche Rechtserneuerung und Rechtsphilosophie.* Tuebingen, 1934, pp. 4-5, 16, 20, 26, 34, 38.

103. *Hitlers deutsche Sendung.* Berlin, 1938, pp. 62; *Politischer Mord und Heldenverehrung: Vortrag,* August 27, 1938, pp. 3-4, 6, 44, 46, 48; *Politische Justiz, die Krankheit unserer Zeit.* Bonn, 1953, pp. 49, 107.

104. *Grundriss der allgemeinen Staatslehre.* Tuebingen, 1933, pp. v, 39, 50-51, 85, 163-164; *Der deutsche Fuehrerstaat.* Tuebingen, 1934, pp. 7, 17, 19-20, 29; *Der Nationalsozialistische Rechtsstaat,* Vol. I, 16, pp. 3, 35, 11, 12; *Volk und Staat in der Weltanschauung des Nationalsozialismus.* Berlin, 1935, pp. 16, 20, 22-23.

105. *Das Judentum in der Rechtswissenschaft. Tagung der Reichsgruppe Hochschullehrer des NSRB.* Berlin, 1936, in 9 vols., Vol. V, pp. 25-30.

106. *Deutsche Rundschau,* October, 1955.

107. B. Croce und C. Vossler. *Briefwechsel.* Frankfurt, 1955, p. 343, letter of August 25, 1933.

108. Muschg. *Die Zerstoerung der deutschen Literatur,* p. 98.

109. *Deutsche Juristenzeitung,* August 1, 1934.

110. W. Foerster. *Ein General Kaempft gegen den Krieg,* p. 26.

111. *Deutsche Juristenzeitung,* August 1, 1934.

112. *Staatsgefuege und Zusammenbruch des zweiten Reiches.* Hamburg, 1934, pp. 13-14, 49.

113. Hans Frank. *Nationalsozialistisches Handbuch fuer Recht und Gesetzgebung.* Muenchen, 1935, p. 32.

114. *Voelkerrechtliche Grossraumordnung.* Berlin, 1941, pp. 47-48.

115. *Das Judentum in der Rechtswissenschaft. Reichsgruppe Hochschullehrer des NSRB.* Vol. I, pp. 10, 13-16, 33; Vol. IV, pp. 5-18, 19-38.

116. *Ex Captivitate Salus.* Koeln, 1947, pp. 12, 22.

117. *Berlin.* Muenchen, p. 212.

118. *Achtung, Europa!,* p. 99.

119. *Wissenschaft ohne Menschlichkeit.* Heidelberg, 1949, p. v.

120. *Ein Arzt erlebt seine Zeit.* Muenchen, 1954, pp. 171-172.

121. *Altes und Neues,* p. 603.

122. *Suedwestdeutscher Rundfunk,* June 8, 1951; Inge Scholl. *Die weisse Rose.* Frankfurt, 1952, p. 44; *Vierteljahrschefte fuer Zeitgeschichte.* Muenchen, October 1954, p. 331.

123. *Du hast uns heimgesucht bei Nacht.* Muenchen, 1954, pp. 254-255.

124. *Tag-und Nachtbuecher,* p. 202.

125. *Aeta Apostolica Sedis.* Rome, 1937, and Muenster, 1946. Also: *Reichspost,* Wien, March 25, 1937.

126. Foerster. *Die juedische Frage,* p. 77.

127. *Deutsche Blaetter.* Santiago de Chile, January, 1943.

128. *Warum, Woher—aber wohin?,* p. 133.

129. Johannes von Leers. *Der Kardinal und die Germanen.* Hamburg, 1934, pp. 6, 18, 56-57.

130. *Juden, Christen, Deutsche,* pp. 199-200.

131. *Ibid.,* p. 314.

132. *Ibid.,* p. 313.

133. *Das Andere Deutschland,* Hamburg, September 18, 1959.

134. *Blaetter fuer deutsche und internationale Politik,* Koeln, September, 1959.

135. *Das Andere Deutschland,* September 18, 1959.

136. *Blaetter,* Koeln, September, 1959.

137. Rabbi Dr. S. Rappaport. *Jewish Horizons,* pp. 3-6.

138. *Blaetter,* Koeln, September, 1959.

139. *Ibid.,* May, 1958.

140. *Ibid.,* May, 1958.

141. Kurt Pritzkoleit. *Das Kommandierte Wunder.* Muenchen, 1959, p. 695.

142. *Ibid.*

143. *Blaetter,* Koeln, September, 1959.

144. *Ibid.*

145. *Observer,* London, December 31, 1961.

146. *Jewish Chronicle,* London, March 23, 1962.

147. Victor Klemperer. *Lingua Tertii Imperii,* p. 123.

148. Vesper. *Deutsche Jugend.* Berlin, 1934, p. ix.

149. W. Hofer. *Der Nationalsozialismus.* Frankfurt, 1957, p. 128.

150. V. Klemperer, *op. cit.,* p. 120.

151. *Ibid.,* p. 122.

152. H. Gollwitzer. *Und fuehre, wohin du nicht willst.* Muenchen, 1952, p. 128.

153. *De Profundis.* Muenchen, 1946, p. 108.

154. Thomas Mann. "Das Gesetz." *Erzählungen.* Frankfurt, 1958, p. 875.

155. *Deutsche Hoerer!,* p. 20.

156. "Goethe und Tolstoi." *Bemuehungen,* p. 136.

157. Müller-Claudius. *Deutsche und Juedische Tragik,* p. 172.

158. Klemperer, *op. cit.,* p. 122.

159. Wilhelm Niemoeller. *Die Protestantische Kirche im Dritten Reich.* Bielefeld, 1956, pp. 93, 187-188.

160. *Der Mythos des 20. Jahrhunderts.* Edition 1943, pp. 439-441.

161. *Das Buch von der deutsch-voelkisch-christlichen Religion.* Breslau, 1934, pp. 7-9, 52, 56-60, 62, 87-88, 146, 173.

162. *Dichter aus deutschem Volkstum.* Leipzig, 1934, pp. 19-20.

163. *Deutsche Gottschau.* Stuttgart, 1934, pp. 2, 4, 12-13, 22-24, 45, 47, 52, 110, 133.

164. *Grundzuege einer Geschichte der artdeutschen Philosophie.* Berlin, 1937, pp. 7-9, 12, 37-38, 78; *Christentum, Nationalsozialismus und deutsche Glaubensbewegung.* Berlin, 1938, pp. 18-19.

165. *Der protestantische Auftrag des deutschen Volkes.* Stuttgart, 1936, pp. 19, 37, 41, 67, 237, 247, 253; *Krise und Aufgabe des Voelkischen Glaubens.* Berlin, 1937, pp. 5-10, 15, 17, 21, 26-28, 30; *Die Voelkische Aufgabe der Religionswissenschaft.* Stuttgart, 1938, pp. 7, 9, 14, 18, 20, 23-27, 31, 45-50.

166. Otto Baumgarten. *Das Echo der Alldeutschen Bewegung in Amerika.* Jena, 1917, pp. 23-24.

167. *Heimdall* (a periodical), 1899, p. 130.

168. *Die Grundlagen des 19. Jahrhunderts.* Muenchen, 6th edition 1906, p. 404.

169. Foerster. *Erlebte Weltgeschichte,* p. 275.

170. Max Bierbaum. *Das Leben des Kardinals von Galen.* Muenster, 1955, pp. 161-162.

171. Heinrich Portmann. *Dokumente um den Bischof von Muenster.* Muenster, 1948, p. 100.

172. *Ibid.,* p. 293.

173. Heinrich Portmann. *Bischof Graf von Galen Spricht!* Freiburg, 1946, pp. 23, 52.

174. Portmann. *Dokumente,* p. 99.

175. Portmann. *Kardinal von Galen.* Muenster, 1948, p. 162.

176. Kurt von Schuschnigg. *Ein Requiem in Rot-Weiss-Rot.* Zuerich, 1946, p. 146.

177. Portmann. *Kardinal von Galen,* p. 99.

178. *Nuernberger Nachrichten,* June 19, 1958.

179. Portmann. *Dokumente,* p. 87.

180. Ulrich von Hassell. *Vom Anderen Deutschland.* Zuerich, 1946, p. 62.

181. Gertrud Ehrle. *Licht ueber dem Abgrund.* Freiburg, 1951, pp. 110-111.

182. Portmann. *Bischof Graf von Galen spricht!* p. 48.

183. *Ibid.,* pp. 75-76.

184. *Tag-und Nachtbuecher,* pp. 55, 220-221.

185. Portmann. *Bischof Graf von Galen spricht!,* pp. 35, 37, 40.

186. *Jeremias.* Re-issued Frankfurt, 1956, pp. 37, 74, 92, 270, 339, 346, 427, 453, 479, 529, 543, 546.

187. *Doktor Faustus,* p. 551.

188. *Zeit und Stunde.* Salzburg, 1955, pp. 8-9, 19-20.

189. *Deutsche Blaetter,* Santiago, January, 1943.

190. H. Pross. *Vor und nach Hitler.* Freiburg, 1962, pp. 49, 53, 253-254.

191. *An Manchen Tagen.* Frankfurt, 1961, pp. 14-15.

192. *Ibid.,* p. 48.

193. *Ibid.*, pp. 20, 26, 28.
194. *Ibid.*, p. 17.
195. *Die Kultur,* Muenchen, May 1, 1957.
196. Kraus. *Die dritte Walpurgisnacht,* p. 132.
197. Pross. *Die Zerstoerung,* pp. 101-102.
198. *Maennerbund und Wissenschaft.* Berlin, 1943, p. 137.
199. *Rede Zur Verleihung des Georg Buechner-Preises 1957.* Koeln, 1958.
200. *Ueber das Verbrennen von Buechern.* Koeln, 1959.
201. *Times Literary Supplement,* London, June 19, 1959.
202. *Autobiographien und Bibliographien, P.E.N. Zentrum Deutschsprachiger Autoren im Ausland. Sitz London,* pp. 1, 3.
203. M. Schloesser. *An den Wind Geschrieben.* Koeln, 1960, pp. 158-161.
204. *Dichtungen und Dokumente.* Muenchen, 1956, p. 57.
205. *Um uns die Fremde.* Foreword by Thomas Mann. Zuerich, 1936, pp. 56, 77, 84.
206. *Deutsche Blaetter,* Santiago, 1943, Issue 2.
207. *Neue Welt.* Buenos Aires, 1939, pp. 25, 32, 42.
208. *Deutsche Blaetter,* Santiago, July, 1945.
209. *Das Volk Messiah.* London, 1943, Sonnet XLVI.
210. *Sang aus dem Exil.* Heidelberg, 1953, p. 13.
211. *Hiob.* Hamburg, 1950, p. 12.
212. *An die Deutschen.* Zuerich, no year of publication given.
213. Gert H. Theunissen. *Zwischen Golgatha und Auschwitz,* p. 23.
214. *Sang aus dem Exil,* p. 16.
215. *Buecher-Kommentare,* Berlin, 1961, Issue I.
216. B.B.C., London, October 8, 1960.
217. Werner Kraft. *Rudolf Borchardt.* Hamburg, 1961, pp. 37, 408, 412.
218. *Die Kultur,* Muenchen, May 15, 1959.
219. K. Fassmann. *Gedichte Gegen den Krieg.* Muenchen, 1961, pp. 204-205.
220. M. Schloesser. *An den Wind geschrieben.* Darmstadt, 1960, p. 194.
221. *Reden und Aufsaetze.* Berlin, 1939, Vol. I, pp. 90-91, 95, 103.
222. *De Profundis,* p. 373.
223. *An die deutsche Jugend.* Muenchen, 1951, pp. 83-84.
224. *Der Weisse Bueffel.* Muenchen, 1949, pp. 73, 77-78, 82.
225. *Tag-und Nachtbuecher,* pp. 59, 68-69, 73, 83-84, 86, 90, 105, 108, 111, 119, 131, 193.
226. *Zwischen den Zeilen.* Wiesentheid, 1948, pp. 29, 94-98, 147-150, 225, 238-240, 247-255, 256-267, 303.
227. *Unter dem Schatten deiner Fluegel,* p. 460.
228. *Ibid.,* February 21, 1938.
229. *Ibid.,* April 28, 1935.
230. *Ibid.,* April 30, 1935.
231. *Ibid.,* p. 7.
232. *Las Casas vor Karl V.* Leipzig, 1938, pp. 10, 18, 31, 70, 71, 87, 88, 99, 114, 125, 139, 148, 157, 172-173.
233. *Die Sonette von Leben und Zeit, im Glauben und der Geschichte.* Koeln, 1954.

234. *Doemonie und Verklaerung.* Vaduz, 1940, p. 353.

235. *Der Grosstyrann und das Gericht.* Re-issued Muenchen, 1947, pp. 115, 170.

236. *De Profundis,* p. 42.

237. *Religioese Gestalten in Dostojewskis Werk.* Muenchen, 1939, pp. 31-32, 105.

238. A. Delp. *Kaempfer, Beter, Zeuge.* Berlin, 1955, p. 13.

239. *Venezianisches Credo.* Wiesbaden. *Inselbuecherei* No. 609, p. 19.

240. *Attila der Letzte.* Volkbach bei Wuerzburg, many pages, especially pp. 66, 94, 142, 209, 219-221.

241. *Der Christliche Staendestaat,* Wien, April 3 and July 8, 1934.

242. Karl Kamps. *Johannes Maria Verweyen.* Wiesbaden, 1955, p. 29.

243. *Machtstaat und Utopie.* Muenchen, 1941, 2nd edition, pp. 24-25, 30, 33, 45, 123.

244. *Die Gegenwart* (a periodical), Muenchen, December 24, 1945.

245. August Winnig. *Aus Zwanzig Jahren.* Hamburg, 1948, p. 66.

15
The Atrocities
Against the Slav Nations

HITLER HAD HARDLY SETTLED DOWN IN THE REICHS-CHANCELLERY when he began to put his program, as outlined in *Mein Kampf,* into practice. He had already said in 1932 to Dr. Rauschning that "we must regain the good conscience to be cruel and compel the Germans to greatness" if they are to realize their historic mission. "I know that I must be a hard educator."[1] War was life and the origin of all things. He did not care a bit for international law and agreements. The Germans were a chosen people which, unless it had had power over Europe, would perish. In 1933 Hitler said to Dr. Rauschning: "Yes, we are barbarians! It is an honourable title. It is we who will rejuvenate the world."[2] He revealed his policy in detail to Rauschning because he thought he could trust him. He would, he said, proceed step by step and wait with iron determination for the correct moment to strike. He would not miss it, he would use all his energy to bring it about.[3] He would do away with Jewish Christianity with its effeminate morality of pity and replace it by a belief in a God who lived in the blood and destiny of the Germans. National Socialism would even liberate the Americans from their ruling class. Rauschning fled in terror and never returned to Germany; he is still living in the United States.

National Socialists, in the meantime, thanked God, who had "sent them a saviour in their deepest affliction," the most wonderful personality of all times. It was clearly the will of God that "the whole world should be freed from those parasites who, for more than two thousand years, had been the cause of almost all pains and catastrophes which divided and enslaved the nations"—the Jews.[4] Hitler himself said on March 29, 1933: "The Jews must know that a Jewish war against Germany will fall back on the German Jews with full severity."[5] The *Völkischer Beobachter* wrote on May 2, 1933: "Those who saw the jubilation and the ecstasy of our redemption, who witnessed the march of millions, saw the flags shine and heard the songs roar, do not worry about the future of Germany!"[6]

As early as 1932 a certain Ewald Banse published a book, very soon translated into English, entitled *Germany, Prepare for War*. The future, said Banse, would stand in the sign of the Third Reich, the most creative nation of the world, the Germans would become masters of the world. Nordic Germans did not wage war in order to live but lived to wage war. The British, however, had no understanding for the glory of war. He outlined a detailed plan of how Great Britain would be invaded by the Germans, for the first time since 1066. After a victory in the West the Germans would turn to the East. The Nazis disowned Banse as an irresponsible dreamer but Hitler made him a "Defense" professor at Braunschweig.[7]

On February 3, 1933, Hitler outlined his program to the commanders of the army and navy at the house of General von

Hammerstein-Equord. He proposed first to rebuild the German army. To what purpose? Germany's living space was too small. He spoke of the "conquest of new living space in the East, and the ruthless Germanisation of it." The youth and the whole nation must be orientated towards war, because only war could rescue the German nation from the abyss; a strictly authoritarian rule was necessary, the cancer of democracy must be eliminated.[8] The generals and Admiral Raeder listened and did nothing against it.

During the first Party Reunion after Hitler's coming into power, held in Nuremberg in the summer of 1934, the Führer went about with a blood-stained flag in his hand—allegedly the flag carried by one of his "apostles" who fell in the abortive revolt of 1923—and blessed all the other flags by touching them with the holy relic. Hess said to him afterwards: "My Führer, when all the flags and standards which you see here today have rotted away then only will all the Germans realise what you have meant for Germany." Indeed. The Führer said: "We are happy to know that the future is ours. We want one day to see *one* Reich." Streicher said: "A nation which does not keep its race pure will perish."[9]

On August 2, 1934, Hindenburg died, leaving a testament which disappeared mysteriously. Hitler, leaving the grave, reminded the Field-Marshal of the battle at Tannenberg. "This was a victory unequalled by any other victory in world history. Dead general, enter now Valhalla!"[10] On August 27, 1933, he visited the Tannenberg memorial in East Prussia and said there: "Nineteen years have elapsed since those glorious days when the German nation, after centuries, heard again of Tannenberg, a name covered with shining glory. This was our salvation. Germany was saved. Fate allowed me at the time to fight as a simple musketeer among my brothers and comrades for the liberty of our nation. I feel today it is gracious Providence which gives me an opportunity to express to you, *Herr General-*

feldmarshall, my most humble thanks in the name of a unified nation on the most glorious battlefield of the Great War."[11]

A devout Roman Catholic, Karl Otmar, Baron of Aretin, describes, in what he calls "a study in the moral decay of the officers of the Reichswehr," how General Blomberg and Colonel Reichenau used the political confusion to enforce a new-fangled oath, not to the state but to Hitler personally, which was without any legal basis. The Reichswehr had been sworn in not to the President but to the Constitution.[12]

Many Germans continue up to this day to spread the legend that Hitler wanted friendship with Great Britain; they do not care to read what Austen Chamberlain said on July 5, 1933: "Can we be really friendly with a nation which proscribes, on racial grounds, a race within its borders, and refuses to treat its own citizens as equals and fellows? The spirit shown within Germany to Germans is a menace to every nation beyond her borders, and to any other race over which she might ever succeed in establishing her domination."[13] Professor Julian Huxley called the idea of an Aryan race a crazy and dangerous myth. General Blomberg said on June 29, 1934: "The Wehrmacht, which proudly carries the signs of the German renaissance on their steel helmets and uniforms, stand together with the whole nation, in discipline and faithfulness behind the leader of the state, Adolf Hitler."[14]

This madman and his fellow madmen, forgetting *Mein Kampf,* tried to lull their neighbours into the same forgetfulness. Hess said in 1933: "The leaders of the state want to let the world know that no serious man in Germany entertains the idea to violate the independence of another state."[15] Hitler said on May 27, 1933, that "National Socialism rejects the idea of germanizing other nations. We reject the policy of changing our frontiers at the cost of other nations. We shall never try to subjugate any other nation."[16] On October 15, 1933, he repeated that his only aim was "to work peacefully for the recovery of an unhappy world, but the world has been persecuting us for months with a flood of lies and calumnies. The men who govern Germany today have nothing in common with the paid traitors of November 1918."[17] On May 21, 1935, he assured the world: "National Socialist Germany wants peace from the innermost convictions."[18] In *Mein Kampf*, however, he had said: "With Great Britain alone covering the back a new German march could begin"[19] towards Russia. He even told Ribbentrop in 1937 to approach Churchill and submit this idea to him. Ribbentrop asked Great Britain for a free hand in Eastern Europe because White Russia and the Ukraine were indispensable to the future of Germany. Churchill's answer was that Great Britain would never give Germany a free hand in the East. Ribbentrop then said bluntly that Germany would wage a war to achieve her aims, and that nobody would be able to stop her. Hitler told Göring, Neurath, Generals Blomberg and Fritsch, and Admiral Raeder on November 5, 1937 that after four and a half years of deliberation he had reached the conclusion that Germany must conquer more living space for her growing population. This would involve risks; the attacker always met with resistance by the attacked.[20] On November 23, 1937, in a secret meeting at the *Ordensburg Sonthofen,* he told the political leaders of his party that, as compared with the British Empire and Russia, Germany was in a desperate situation, the result of many centuries. Germany had once been the dominant race and power, and it was her mission to become such a power again. Might was right. Who cared whether the other nations loved Germany? Enough if they respect us. Who cared whether they hated us? Enough if they fear us.[21] Ludendorff, however, said in the same year, shortly before his death: "When Hitler directs everything himself, woe to Germany! There will be war and that war will end with our enemies shaking hands in the middle of a devastated Germany."[22]

Hitler constantly spoke of his will to peace but broke the

Locarno Pact which he had recognized in 1935 and marched into the demilitarized Rhineland. He said he would never attack Austria or Czechoslovakia while secretly developing his plans of attack. He invaded Austria in 1938 where, it is true, he was greeted so enthusiastically by so many Austrians that the *Neue Basler Zeitung* wrote: "The scenes of jubilation which could be seen when Hitler came defy all description." Even Cardinal Innitzer visited Hitler to express "his pleasure at the reunification of Austria with the Reich," and promised "the serious collaboration of the Austrian Catholics."[23] When the Western Powers acquiesced, Hitler began to clamor for the Sudeten Germans, meaning the Skoda Works. When he got them at the shameful conference of Munich, he said publicly that he wanted no Czechs, but secretly to his friends that he had never meant to stick to the Munich Treaty. He directed his stooge Konrad Henlein to provoke disturbances which would give him an excuse to intervene. On November 5, 1937 he told Henlein: "In order to improve our military situation we must, in case of war, aim at the destruction of Czechoslovakia and Austria at the same time. It must be done in a lightning manner."[24] He hoped to win there food for five to six million Germans, especially if two million Czechs and one million Austrians were expelled.

He marched into Prague and soon afterwards he started troubling Poland. In 1934 he had said to Dr. Rauschning that he did not want a settlement with Poland. He spoke to his generals several times about his plans to conquer the East. He stated them openly on August 11, 1939 to the High Commissioner of Danzig, Carl J. Burckhardt.[25] But in German books Great Britain is blamed for giving a guarantee to Poland, thereby making a (never intended) peaceful arrangement with Poland impossible. It is always the others who are responsible, never the Germans. Göring said in December, 1939: "Great Britain wanted this war."[26] But Count von Galen, the famous Bishop of Münster, said on the day of the outbreak of the war: "*Finis Germaniae*—the end of Germany."[27] When the Führer was opposed by General Beck in the late summer of 1938, Hitler said: "The Wehrmacht is an instrument of our policy. I shall give the army my order at the right moment. The army must obey, not argue whether the orders are right or wrong." General Beck answered: "This point of view is unacceptable to me as Chief of the General Staff. I cannot accept the responsibility for orders of which I cannot approve."[28] He was the only general to oppose Hitler and had to shoot himself in 1944.

On May 23, 1939 Hitler told Göring, Raeder, Halder, Brauchitsch, Keitel, Warlimont, Milch, Bodenschatz, Jeschonnek of his plans to attack Poland. Right or wrong, it was a question of life and death for 80 million Germans. He said: "I shall give a propagandistic reason for the outbreak of war, whether plausible or not. Right does not matter in war—only victory."[29] On August 22, 1939, he told his generals: "I have issued the order to shoot anyone who utters even one word criticising the principle . . . the physical extermination of the enemy." He had ordered his *Totenkopf* divisions "to kill without mercy or pity any man, woman or child of Polish descent speaking the Polish language. Poland shall be depopulated, and be settled by Germans."[30] Seven years later, the judges at Nuremberg said of the accused generals: "They have been responsible in large measure for the miseries and suffering that have fallen upon millions of men, women and children. They have been a disgrace to the honorable profession of arms. Without their military guidance the aggressive ambitions of Hitler and his fellow Nazis would have been academic and sterile."[31] General Beck had already said on July 16, 1938: "History will make the highest officers of the Wehrmacht responsible for this bloody guilt, if they do not act in accordance with their expert and political knowledge and conscience. Their duty to obey ends when their knowledge, conscience and responsibility forbids them to obey an order."[32]

From his first appearance on the political scene Hitler had

raved against "Jewish Bolshevism," but on March 23, 1933 he suddenly changed his tune and said that he intended to entertain friendly relations with Soviet Russia which would be fruitful to both countries. In 1936 he changed his tune again and said of Germany and Russia: "They are two different worlds which can only move away from each other but can never meet."[33] On January 30, 1937, he said: "Bolshevism is a pestilence to us."[34] On September 13, 1937, he spoke again of "Jewish Bolshevism" and called it "a general attack against the social order of today. The Jews carry the torch of Bolshevik revolution into the democratic world. Their final aim is the Bolshevik revolution" in order to "exterminate the *arteigenen* nations. What will remain as the last representative of a miserable intellectual knowledge is the Jew."[35] Secretly, however, he felt more akin to totalitarian Stalinism than to the democratic West. In 1934 he had said to Dr. Rauschning: "I am not only the conqueror but also the fulfiller of Marxism if you divest it from its Jewish-Talmudistic dogmatism. I have learnt a lot from Marxism. I confess it without hesitation. The whole National Socialism is in it."[36] In 1943 he said to General Jodl: "Roosevelt and Churchill—what manner of men are they! The first is a cripple, and the other smokes and drinks himself to death. But Stalin? You know, I still esteem him. He realised his programme consistently and without restraint. I should have learnt more from his recklessness."[37]

The Russians never forgot what he had said in *Mein Kampf*. Nor had they forgotten it when they accepted the pact which Hitler offered them in 1939 to bluff the West. Hitler apparently did not remember what he had said thirteen years before: "You do not conclude a pact with a partner whose only interest it is to annihilate the other."[38] Such a pact would mean the end of Germany. It did indeed. The Russians sang a couplet about that pact:

Spassibo Jasche Ribbentropu,
Schto on otkryl akro w Ewropu.[39]

They thanked Joachim Ribbentrop "for opening for them a window to Europe." Ribbentrop, however, said at Koenigsberg, now Kaliningrad: "We National Socialists know all: What our Führer does is right. This was also proved this time."[40] Jochen Klepper, that devout Christian writer, entered in his diary on August 26, 1939: "What a torment to see in the newspapers the laughing pictures of Ribbentrop and Stalin, who was only yesterday called an 'Asiatic criminal' and 'the enemy of the world!' "[41] But in some German books one can find the legend that Hitler had been forced to wage a preventive war against Russia. They avoid rereading Göbbels' speeches after the attack against Russia, in one of which he triumphantly announced that the German soldiers had conquered the most important granary in the East. "While we were a nation without living space before, this is no longer the case."[42] And Hitler said on April 20, 1941, outlining to Rosenberg his plan of attacking Russia: "When the Soviet Union has broken down, within a few months, under the mighty onslaughts of our armies, the immense economic resources of the East will be ours. This will enable us to compel Great Britain to make peace and build up a German Empire."[43] A decent German said in 1955: "When Hitler spoke of Bolshevism, he meant the corn of the Ukraine. It was Hitler who, by his wanton attack on Russia, brought Communism to Central Europe."[44]

In innumerable German books and articles one can still find the legend that National Socialism wanted to put up a dam against the Russian danger. But did not Thomas Mann say in 1933 that National Socialism was an inferior brand of Bolshevism? Hitler's last Chief of Staff, Colonel General Guderian, after the war spread the lie: "Our soldiers fought and fell for Europe."[45] Thomas Mann, however, said during the war: "Freedom is the light and soul of Europe. Love and the praise of history will belong to those who fell for it, not to those who killed it with their tanks."[46] And to his barbarized countrymen he said: "As slaves of Hitler's miserable fanaticism you continue to fight like Berserks for his horrible New Order in Europe."[47] Many Germans still regard the Waffen SS as the first European army, a precursor, as it were, of the NATO army. It consisted of National Socialists and of those Norwegian, Danish, Dutch, Belgian, French, and Swiss traitors who betrayed their fatherlands and joined the Führer, such as the Blue Division which Spain had sent to Germany. In the meantime Hitler's henchmen murdered many of their compatriots who worked in the European resistance. Their last letters have been collected and edited in a book, *And the Flame Shall Not Consume You,* which was published in Switzerland and prefaced by Thomas Mann. These victims of German barbarism, he says, were "the true European youth, internationally unanimous in their resistance against the German degradation of their fatherlands, against the ignominy of a Hitlerite Europe, the horror of a Hitlerite world." One of those brave young men, hardly nineteen, wrote home shortly before his execution: "I could have saved my life but I preferred to do or say nothing which would have been a betrayal of my fatherland."[48] A Greek student wrote on June 5, 1942: "We shall be executed today. We are worthy of our forefathers and of Greece."[49] A Norwegian wrote before his execution: "I bear something in my heart which is greater than Hitler's Grossraum." A Rumanian: "Only a small consolation remains. To add your grave to the graves of the forefathers. Knowing that the cathedrals of Chartres or Reims will live by your death." A Serb to his still unborn child: "Keep in your heart the hunger after knowledge, keep the hatred of all lies and evils. I know I must die. I am ashamed of leaving you in an awkward world. Good night, my child, good morning and a bright awakening."[50]

German Christians who were forced to fight for Hitler often said: "What sense does our war make? We are fighting against Bolshevism abroad but for Bolshevism in our country."[51] E. M. Remarque pities the honest German soldiers who became "food for guns and manure for Hitler's millennium," and makes one of these soldiers say to a Jew who flees from one hiding place to another that he is compelled to go on fighting "so that the criminals who are hunting you can retain their power a little longer." The SS, he says, burned everything on their retreat from Russia and shot everybody they met on the way, behaving "like Attila and Gengis Khan."[52] The novelist H. H. Kirst makes an honest colonel say that God would have "nothing to do with this Germany, those criminals by instinct and murderers with a *Weltanschauung*. Soldiers fight—but do they murder Jews? Do they plunder whole districts, do they execute hostages by the dozen?"[53] A precursor of Hitler, Field-Marshal Count von Haeseler, said, long before Hitler: "It is necessary for our civilisation to erect its temple on mountains of corpses, on oceans of tears and to the death rattle of innumerable dying people."[54]

The Czechs had hated the Austrians and the Germans since, at the beginning of the Thirty Years' War, a combined army of Austrians and Bavarians under General Tilly had crushed a Czech army in the battle of the Weisser Berg in 1620 and slaughtered the Czech nobility. Nations have long memories. When the Czechs aimed at national independence under the Habsburgs about 1848 they were suppressed by Metternich. A Czech writer, Carel Havliček, criticized the suppression of his nation in a camouflaged way by writing about the suppression of the Irish nation. At the beginning of the First World War the Austrian authorities imprisoned many Czech leaders; Masaryk and Beneš managed to escape. Various Czech regiments deserted to the Russians on the Eastern front. The Good Soldier Schweik, who the Czech writer Jaroslav Hašek invented, was no invention at all; he is the symbol of the Czech attitude to the war of the Habsburgs. After the war President Masaryk spoke of the 60,000 Czechs, Serbs, Rumanians, and Italians who had been executed by the Austrian authorities. He reminded the

Germans that not Kant, Herder, and Schiller, but Hegel, Hartmann, and Nietzsche had become the leaders of the Prussian-
ized Germans, one of whom, Werner Sombart, defined Prussian
militarism as "Faust, Zarathustra and Beethoven in the
trenches." The pan-Germans threatened to exterminate or Germanize Czechs and Poles, and proclaimed: "The Germans,
thanks to their culture, have the right and even the duty to
subjugate the world, they are a master race, the only and absolute master race. Germany will become the redeemer of Europe
and all humanity."[55]

Hitler told Dr. Rauschning in 1932 that he would remove the
Czechs from Europe to Siberia or to the Volhynian swamps.
The famous Czech writer Karel Čapek, however, called Hitler's
Germany "the greatest cultural debacle of history: a whole nation, an entire *Reich* professes the belief of animals, an entire
nation, including professors, pastors, writers, doctors and
jurists, believes in race and other nonsense."[56] In 1936, Professor K. Bittner of the German University of Prague reminded
the Czechs that in the Middle Ages they had represented the
lower strata of society and that the presence of Germans in
Bohemia was only part of the German drive towards the East.
Sudeten Germans started the whole Munich troubles with their
clamor, and their leader, Konrad Henlein, announced over the
German radio that he would "bring the Sudeten Germans home
into the Reich." In a conversation with the German Lieutenant-
Colonel Köchling he defined the aim of the German Free Corps
in Czechoslovakia as "the maintenance of disorders and the
precipitation of clashes."[57]

When the Germans moved into the Sudetenland they began
almost immediately to plunder the Czech libraries and to con-
fiscate all industrial concerns belonging to Czechs and Jews.
They removed to Germany raw materials, food, railroad cars,
locomotives, and even rails; also paintings and sculptures.
When, breaking the agreement of Munich, they moved into the

Czech regions and into Prague, they were received with joy by most Germans but with tears and clenched fists by the Czechs. The population lining the streets of the capital suddenly surged forward, bringing the first German tank to an abrupt standstill, and sang the age-old hymn of Slav defiance, "Thunder and hell, your rage is in vain." The Germans plundered the Czech National Museum and the Gallery of Modern Art and carried away all the foreign currency and all the gold (23,000 kilograms) of the National Bank. Not a penny was returned to the Czechs after the war. The Czech peasants were driven away from their soil and German settlers moved in. Innumerable Czechs were arrested, tortured, and killed. Many professors and teachers were brought to German concentration camps where most of them died in terrible circumstances. The university and many high schools were closed, the laboratories plundered. No pupil ever received a lesson about Czech history but had to listen to Nazi ideology for sixteen hours a week. K. H. Frank, a Sudeten German schoolmaster, was lord over the life and death of everybody. He developed a plan partly to drive out the Czechs and partly to make them serfs to the German *Herrenrasse*. The *Völkischer Beobachter* wrote that there were too many educated Czechs; so the Nazis in Prague began to destroy all the cultural life of the subjected nation. On November 17, 1939 many Czech students were murdered. While they were tortured and put into ice-cold water they were forced to shout: "We thank you." Then they were tied to stakes and shot. Many girl students were raped; Nazi barbarians burnt their breasts with the tips of cigarettes, compelled them to drink urine, and then shot them.[58] When the Czechs asked their enemies to reopen Prague University they received this answer from K. H. Frank: "If Great Britain wins the war, you will reopen your university yourselves. If we win, a primary school will be good enough for you."[59] Thomas Mann spoke during the war of Himmler's plans to exterminate all Czechs if they should rebel against the

Herrenrasse, and called the Czech Protectorate as hellish as the Polish General Government. The Nazis, he said, know very well that universities are breeding places of human pride and liberty.[60] The first Lord Protector who came to occupied Prague was the diplomat Neurath. In August, 1940 he sent his and Karl Hermann Frank's plans for the subjected Czechs to Hitler. Neurath wanted to Germanize some of the Czechs and expel the rest while Frank, a Sudeten German, wanted to exterminate all of them. SS *Obergrupponführer* Reinhard Heydrich, a typical result, as his English Biographer, Charles Wighton, shows, of the *Befehl ist Befehl* mentality prevailing in Germany since the days of Frederick II, was "the most demoniac of all" Nazis. He foresaw the day when Adolf Hitler "will occupy the same position in Germany that Jesus Christ has now," he arranged the burning down of all synagogues in Germany on November 9, 1938, and was the chief executive of the annihilation of the Jews. When he came to Prague he immediately began to terrorize the Czechs, whom he regarded as *Untermenschen* like the Poles and the Russians. Two Czechs murdered him one day. Hitler rushed to Prague and praised him as one of the best champions of Greater Germany, and an orchestra played the Funeral March from Wagner's *Goetterdaemmerung*—another Siegfried stabbed in the back by a dark enemy. In reprisal, 100,000 Czechs were arrested, 100 intellectuals shot, and the 173 males of the completely innocent village of Lidice murdered and the women were brought to concentration camps where most of them perished. The children disappeared completely; some of them reappeared at Nuremberg to testify against the murderers.[61]

Ulrich von Hassell, who was later hanged by Hitler's henchmen, speaks in his diary of 1939 of "the criminal adventurers who lead us, and of the shame they bring on the German name by their war in Poland, the brutal activities of the air force, the horrid bestialities of the SS, especially against the Jews." On

March 16, 1941, he entered in his diary: "Nasty things reported from Poland, Norway and Holland. They arouse indescribable hatred." And on August 1, 1942: "Terrible terror by Heydrich. Two places exterminated. All men were shot, women deported, and children abducted to compulsory education. Terrible things are going on in Poland causing me nightmares and reddening my face with shame."[62]

Now for the Poles. The Austrian historian Friedrich Heer says that "the original sin of German history" began with the German King Conrad II concluding a pact with Jaroslaw of Russia to attack Poland, "that bulwark against Russia, Byzantium and the Turks."[63] In the 18th century Poland was divided up three times. Professor Foerster says: "Russia, without the collaboration of Prussia and Austria, would never have dared to dismember Poland." That upright German nobleman, Count vom Stein, called the destruction of Poland a crime.[64] Frederick II of Prussia expropriated from the Poles many of the newly acquired provinces and settled Germans there. He compelled the Poles to become Germans by decreeing that only German-speaking servants could be employed. In the 19th century Constantin Frantz, Bismarck's great antagonist, called the divisions of Poland "a crime against international law." He accused the Prussian Government of having broken the solemn promises given when acquiring parts of Poland and having turned them "into Prussian provinces without much ado and germanised them by violent means."[65] He prophesied that they would lose these provinces again one day. Yet the violent Germanization of the Poles was continuing all the time. In the Frankfurt Parliament of 1848 the liberal Robert Blum said that the Germans who despised the Poles and spoke of their "vices" should remember that the Germans themselves were responsible for them. "If, after eighty years, those whom we have trodden into the dirt with our feet appear dirty, we should not lay the blame at their door."[66] In the 19th century many Polish priests were arrested because they resisted the order that all priests must learn German. Bismarck, as the friend of Tsarist Russia, was inimical to the Polish uprising of 1863. In later years he forbade the teaching of the Polish language to Polish children. In 1885 he expelled 30,000 Poles who had for generations resided in Prussia: they were expelled "with brutal inconsiderateness," as von Holstein said.[67] Poles, like Catholics, Social Democrats, and Guelphs, were, in the eyes of Bismarck, "enemies of the Reich." More and more Germans were settled in the Polish provinces of Prussia. In 1906 some 10,000 Polish children went on strike because they wanted religious instruction in their own mother tongue. Even Stresemann hated the Poles at the beginning of his career. General Seeckt said in a memorandum addressed to the German government on September 11, 1922: "The existence of Poland is unbearable and contradictory to the vital interests of Germany. It must, and it will, disappear. . . . To achieve this must always be the main aim of German politics. It can be achieved—achieved, of course, only through Russia and with her help."[68]

Then came Hitler, who told Frank, even before the attack on Poland, that as Governor Frank would be given a "devilish" task. After the defeat of the Poles General Hammerstein said "that Himmler's hordes were hurled at the Poles and worked havoc among them. They execute the intelligentsia and decimate the population. Whole villages have been exterminated."[69] General Ulex wrote on February 2, 1940: "The evacuation of the population causes an ever growing alarm in the whole country. It is clear that the starving population, threatened in its very existence, must look with the greatest anxiety at those newcomers who have been evicted from their homes in the dead of the night and arrive hungry and almost naked and without any means. It is only too clear that their feelings grow to immeasurable hatred when they see the many dead children, who have died during the journey and the trains full of frozen corpses." The decent German who quoted these things complained: "Hardly a German history book gives a correct description of the expulsion of the Poles from the German-occupied provinces while describing at full length the expulsion of the Germans from the provinces behind the Oder-Neisse line. Was the expulsion of the Poles less criminal? Why do those books not mention that Hitler was the first to invent a gigantic expulsion machinery? The Poles were expelled in the most cruel manner."[70]

Major Johann-Adolf, Count of Kielmannsegg, boasted that he had sat on the seat of the head of a state which "we have not only defeated militarily but wiped out from history . . . a state which has been condemned by history already one hundred and fifty years ago. 'World-history is world-judgment': this profound word of Schiller has once again come true."[71] General von Küchler, later sentenced as a war criminal, said, in an order dated July 22, 1940, that soldiers and especially officers must refrain from any criticism of measures taken against Poles and Jews. "The racial final solution of our national war asks for particularly stern measures."[72] Ulrich von Hassell entered in his diary on October 8, 1940: "Every Pole must bear the letter P on his clothes, and to defend this procedure they say that there is an honest Pole as seldom as there is an honest Jew. Hungry workers are getting weaker and weaker, Jews are systematically exterminated, and a devilish war is waged against the Polish intelligentsia with a declared purpose to annihilate it. There is no doubt possible that, if this system should be victorious, a terrible time is waiting for Germany and Europe."[73] And Theodor Haecker entered in his diary at about the same time that, according to Hitler, there were three sorts of men in existence: supermen, men, and *Untermenschen*. "The Führer of the Germans is always the Führer of the supermen; the Jews are *Untermenschen*. The Poles come nearest to them and then, perhaps, the negroes."[74]

The Poles were humiliated in the most barbarous manner and

deprived of all human rights. The civil population was deliberately murdered during and after the military operations, unspeakable tortures were inflicted upon innumerable prisoners,
rapes were organized, the Polish peasants were expelled from
their soil and deported as slave laborers to Germany. "Not even
a centimeter of the land which we have conquered," *Gauleiter*
Greiser boasted in a poster, "will ever belong to a Pole again.
Poles can work for us, but not as rulers, only as serfs!"[75] Many
university professors, teachers, priests, judges, lawyers, and
doctors were taken to concentration camps where most of them
died of hunger or tortures. Cardinal Hlond told Pope Pius XII:
"The monasteries have been methodically suppressed. The cathedrals, palaces of bishops, seminaries, the houses of the clergy
and the money of the seminaries have been stolen by the
intruders."[76] The Polish culture was systematically destroyed.
The Germans asserted that they were a *"Herrenvolk"* and the
Poles contemptible. "No German," they said, "may say that he
knows a decent Pole. There are no decent Poles, just as there
are no decent Jews."[77] These quotations have partly been
taken from a book published by the exiled Polish Government.
It is illustrated by many terrible pictures: Poles being shot and
hanged, blindfolded Poles being led to death, others being led to
concentration camps, Poles being forced to dig graves for murdered Poles. Jews being forcibly shaved by grinning German
soldiers, Jews wearing the yellow armlet with the Star of David,
old Jews being forced to dig earth under supervision of German
soldiers, the wall of the Warsaw Ghetto being built, Polish children rendered homeless and hungry under the German rule,
the monument of the great Polish poet, Adam Mickiewicz,
being pulled down, a poster showing the ruined Polish capital—
the caption: 'England, thy work'—a crowd of Poles rounded up
by Germans for slave labor in Germany. Thomas Mann in 1941
spoke over the British radio of "the unspeakable things done to
Poles and Jews" and of "the gigantically growing hatred which
will one day fall upon your heads."[78]

How Governor General Frank went about his devilish task can be read in the many volumes of his diary now kept in the Warsaw Museum of German Atrocities. Here are a few specimens:

If one considers that 540 million zloty banknotes of the Polish Bank have been taken over by the Governor General without any return service of the Reich, this is a tribute of half a milliard which the Governor General has given to the Reich. [The Poles never received a penny back after the war.]

If I ordered that one should hang up posters for every seven Poles shot, there would not be enough forests in Poland out of which to make the paper for these posters.

Before the German nation is allowed to suffer hunger the occupied territories and their inhabitants must suffer hunger. The consequences must be drawn with icy coldness and without pity.

When we have won the war then mincemeat can be made of Poles, Ukrainians, and everybody who runs about here.[79]

Professor Kurt Boeme advocated "special treatment" for 35,000 tubercular Poles, and practices again today at Dortmund. An SS man lectured at a conference of military medicine in 1943 on gas-gangrened wounds which he had inflicted on Polish women prisoners, and his lecture was attended by important members of the German medical service.[80]

The Polish writer Czeslaw Milosz says that the Germans regarded the defeated Poles as an inferior race which had to be exterminated, and adds that what he witnessed in Poland transcended the boldest and most cruel fantasy. "Germany threatened the Poles by war and contempt."[81] A German nobleman, Bodo Freiherr von Maydell, ashamed of what Germans did, said that he would never forget the sight of Auschwitz, of those almost naked women, their hair shorn and their bodies wrapped in rags, coming from, and going to, their work. "On a Saturday I saw an endless procession of hopeless people over a wide plain entering through a gate from which there was no return, and I saw from midday till evening the thick cloud of 'the Jewish fire' above the forest."[82]

He was under the impression that only Jews were murdered at Auschwitz; he could not know that quite as many or even more Poles lost their lives there. The Polish Prime Minister, Josef Cyrankiewicz, spent years in Auschwitz and was saved only by a miracle. Captain H. J. Delargy, M.P., said: "Auschwitz was the nadir of all human wickedness. Thousands of Germans were directly and personally guilty of it: the engineers who built the railroads; the scientists who devised the gas-chambers and incinerators; the doctors who made their grisly experiments; the dentists who extracted the gold fillings; all the foul administrators and guards and torturers—they were all personally responsible. And most of them exulted in it. There are thumbscrews on show in Auschwitz which proudly bear the name of the manufacturers."[83] Many of those Anschwitz criminals were captured and sentenced to death. Among the accused was an SS doctor, Moench; when he was brought before the judges, the former Polish inmates of Auschwitz who were in the audience attested gratefully that he had been the only German who had behaved decently toward them and had saved many from certain death. As a matter of fact, Dr. Moench had a Jewish wife and only joined the SS to hide this. One of the German professors, Johannes Kremer, Doctor of Medicine and Philosophy, who had used Poles as guinea pigs for worthless experiments, was sentenced to death by a Warsaw Court but his sentence was commuted to imprisonment for life. In 1958, after twelve years, he was released. When he returned to Münster, his birth place, the Rector of the University of Munster, Professor Wilhelm Klemm, and Professor Count Fuerstenberg visited him to bring him the official greetings of the University.

The Poles keep Auschwitz in the same state as it was found by the Russians in 1945. Up to the spring of 1957 more than two million visitors saw the mountain of human bones, the pile of cut hair of women, and innumerable ghastly photographs taken by the Germans themselves. In 1957 former inmates of Auschwitz from about twenty nations met there at the most somber reunion of all history, and in due course a memorial will be erected there to the Polish and other victims of German barbarism. A special museum in Warsaw contains a substantial collection of original German documents with complete files of *Gauleiters* Forster and Greiser, and many other war criminals, and the forty volumes of Governor Frank's diaries; also many books telling what innumerable Germans have done to innumerable Poles.

In 1950 Minister Strauss said: "We are not prepared to defend with our blood the frontier which was created by the stupidity of others."[84] It is always the others who are to be blamed for the German fate. Professor Carlo Schmidt, of the Social Democratic party, said in 1957 that the Germans must learn again to regard the Poles as a great European nation—but is it not a little late to say so? Will fine words bring to life again those hundreds of thousands of Poles murdered by the Germans? A Polish Roman Catholic from Warsaw, Anna Niklewicz, said: "Poland had to reckon with the German problem for a thousand years. Ever since the creation of our state we have been threatened by the *Drang nach Osten* of a bigger nation—a nation with some virtues, no doubt, but these virtues have been misused by many of its leaders for bad and criminal purposes. Hitler's policy resulted in the division of Germany. The reader of what I say may be interested to know that I wrote this from the point of view of a Roman Catholic."[85]

Now for the Russians. We heard at Nuremberg of Count Schulenburg's warnings that Russia did everything to avoid a conflict with Germany and adhered loyally to the conditions of the economic pact which she had concluded with Germany.[86] August Winnig tells us in his autobiography that Stalin gave this message for Hitler to a German merchant who visited Russia:

"Tell him that I advise him not to make a mistake. I possess fifteen million soldiers who are well equipped. And I have so many panzers and aeroplanes that he will experience a surprise if he should attack me."[87] Hitler, however ordered his generals on December 18, 1940 "to crush Soviet Russia in a quick campaign. . . . The ultimate objective is to establish a defence line against Asiatic Russia from a line running approximately from the Volga River to Archangel."[88] Colonel General Halder reported on June 22, 1941: "Tactical surprise of the enemy has apparently been achieved along the entire line."[89] Hitler said that he would stress again, as he had done in the case of Norway, Denmark, Holland, and Belgium, that he had been forced to go to war. He would not show his hand, but the "final solution," all the shooting and expelling, would of course follow later on.[90] Before attacking the Russians, Hitler told his generals that the war between Germany and Russia was "a racial war," and since the Russians were not members of the Hague Convention, Russian prisoners of war and political commissars would not have to be treated in accordance with that convention.[91]

When his armies invaded Russia on June 21, 1941, the SS, those fighters for European culture, wrote, taking up Hitler's slogans of *Mein Kampf:* "The new march of the Germans, this is the work of our Führer, the Führer of all Germans. Now the Eastern frontier of Europe is safe forever. The history of three thousand years finds its glorious full stop. The Goths ride again, every one of us a German fighter!"[92] The Russians are alleged to have given this answer in 1945: "The regions have been won back for the Slavs who have been robbed of them by the German knights in the 13th century."[93] In 1942 Hitler said: "Our aim was to rob the enemy of his great areas of wheat and coal and to come near to his oil. Now we want to conquer Stalingrad. And you can rest assured that nobody will be able to dislodge us from there."[94]

His audience at the Sport Palace in Berlin applauded enthusiastically. Although Guderian complained in 1945 that a thousand years of German colonization had been wiped out, the democratic General von Schoenaich, a pupil of Professor F. W. Foerster, had in 1926 reminded Count Freytag-Loringhoven, one of the nationalist grave-diggers of the Weimar Republic, that the "vast estates" belonging to him and his fellow Junkers had only come into their possession because their forefathers had "intruded into the land of the Latvians and robbed them of their soil."[95]

Two months before Hitler's attack on Russia, Rosenberg called Russia "not a subject of European policy," but a mere "object of German world policy." In his and many other Germans' eyes Hitler's attack was a revision of the invasion of the Huns in A.D. 375. Professor Dr. Konrad Meyer of Berlin University said at the opening of the exhibition, "Planning and Reconstruction of the East" in Poznan on October 23, 1941: "Everybody who has been called upon to work at the New Order in the East must have faith, fantasy and courage." At a meeting of February 12, 1942, attended by Professors Gerhard von Mende, B. K. Schultz, Eugen Fischer, a discussion took place on what to do with the subjugated nations. More detailed plans we know from a document of some thirty pages, dated April 27, 1942. The Baltic states, Poland, and large parts of adjoining Russia up to a line stretching from Lake Ladoga to the Valdai Hills and further south through Bryansk to the Black Sea would be colonized by millions of Germans. As to the "alien races" of the East, the greater part, 30 to 50 million people, would be evacuated to Siberia, a minority of racially "desirable" Poles and Czechs would be "Germanized," the Jews would be exterminated. It was necessary to Germanize the "Nordic" types because of "the loss of the best German blood on the battlefields," and because so much undesirable blood had found its way into the German nation by the slave workers.

"The German woman plays not a very honorable role at all in that matter. . . . The most fatal danger which could ever threaten the German nation would be a victory of the pan-European idea, the consequence of which could only be a great European racial morass."

Professor Wolfgang Abel of Berlin University warned the Nazi bosses especially against the Russian danger. The Russians, he said, had much 'Nordic' blood in them and were biologically stronger than the Germans. If Germany were oblivious of these facts, it might have to fight another war against the Russians in 25 or 30 years. The best thing, the Nazi bosses thought, would be to lower the Russian birth rate by gigantic propaganda, by lectures, pamphlets, by press, cinema and radio. Contraceptives should be praised, artificial abortion should be allowed and midwives trained to do the job. The mortality of infants should not be combatted, voluntary sterilization should be supported.[96]

Hitler said in November, 1941 that he would populate the Russian *Raum* with Germans. In 1942 he said that it would not be opportune to teach Russians, Ukrainians and the other nations of the East to read and write, because the more intelligent among them would acquire historical knowledge and become enemies of the Germans. In May, 1942 he said: "If we want to get the oil of the Caucasus we must subject it to the strictest discipline." The Crimea would have to be remodelled in a way "that even the Germans of later generations could not be caused by anything to give up that piece of German endeavour." On April 12, 1942 he said: "If we win the war, the milliards we spent of the *Wehrmacht* do not matter in the least. They would be outweighed by the ore alone which has fallen into our hands in the last year in the Russian *Raum.*"[97]

In January, 1941, Himmler told a gathering of SS officials at Weselburg that the destruction of thirty million Slavs was a prerequisite for German planning in the East.[98] On October 4,

1943, he said to a number of SS leaders at Poznan: "It does not matter to me in the least how the Russians or the Czechs are getting on. Whether the other nations are living in prosperity or perish by hunger is only of interest to me insofar as we need them as slaves for our *Kultur*. Whether 10,000 Russian women fall down exhausted or not when digging a panzer ditch is only of interest to me insofar as that ditch must be dug in time. . . . It is a crime against our own blood to worry about them and to bring to them ideals which will cause our sons and grandsons to have even more difficulties with them."[99]

Hitler said a nation which knew its mission had a right to conquer and colonize the East. The Russians, he said, were *Untermenschen* and he treated them as such. The Lutheran theologian Professor Helmut Gollwitzer said after the war: "It was one of the greatest crimes to call the Russians *Untermenschen*. They are not only 'men like ourselves,' they are peasants with natural feelings, strong passions, alert intellect and very often admirably fine tact."[100] One of the German counsels at Nuremberg, who had been in Russia as a soldier, tells of how much he was moved by the friendliness of the Russians and the virtue of the Russian women. When German soldiers had reached a Russian village after a long march, the peasant women brought them milk and helped the suffering out of instinct because they themselves had suffered all their lives.

Even before crossing the Russian frontier Keitel and Jodl drew up an order to murder all Russian commissars who fell into German hands, and hundreds of those commissars in Russian uniform lost their lives. "It is impossible," says the Earl of Birkenhead, "not to compare Napoleon's onslaught on Russia with that of Hitler. Both aggressions were the brain children of men consumed by monstrous egotism. . . . The similarities between Napoleon's attack on Russia and Hitler's were that both were treacherous, both clandestine, and both inspired by a false strategy which took too little account of space and climate. The

difference between them surely resides in the fact that Napoleon
was not a monster like Hitler. He was free from that repulsive
hatred and contempt of the Slavs which led Hitler into sending
his *Einsatzgruppen* in the wake of his armies to carry out
wholesale massacres."[101]

Himmler said that it was not their task to Germanize the
East, as it had once been done; only really German Germans
with German blood should populate it. The end of the war
would open a free road to the East and see the creation of a
Germanic *Reich* of 120 million Germans who would be the only
mighty power in Europe.[102] Field-Marshal Reichenau said that
it would be superfluous friendliness to feed the civilian population and prisoners of war. Field-Marshal Manstein said the
same. Ribbentrop said that humanitarian sentimentality toward
the Russians would lead the Germans nowhere. Göring wrote to
Ciano in 1943: "In the camps for Russian prisoners they have
begun to eat each other. This year alone between twenty and
thirty million people will die of starvation. Perhaps this is as
well, for certain nations must be decimated."[103] Göring's so-
called "Green Folder" contained Hitler's order to strip Russia
of everything that might be useful for the German war machine.[104] Göring's Economic Staff plundered all of occupied
Russia although they knew that millions of Russians would
starve to death.[105] Göring told them on October 5, 1942 not to
forget that they had robbed the Russians of their most fertile
provinces: they would find there eggs, butter, flour in unimaginable quantities.[106] General von Graevenitz ordered that Russian prisoners of war who could not work should be shot. Generals Warlimont and Jodl ordered that political commissars
should be shot. Innumerable Russian prisoners were left in open
fields without food and medical treatment. Many died of epidemics; starving soldiers ate the flesh of their dead comrades.
Paul Waldman, an SS man, told the Nuremberg Court that at
one time 840,000 Russian prisoners of war were murdered and

burned at the concentration camp Sachsenhausen.[107] Reichs Commissar Erich Koch, said: "We are a master race. I have not come here to give my blessing. The simplest German worker is a thousand times more valuable racially and biologically than a Russian."[108] SS-Obergruppenführer Hofman, chief of the Office of Racial Colonisation, wrote in 1942: "There is enough soil available for everyone willing to colonise. Even the children of our soldiers and their children will find enough soil in the years to come. Nobody need to be afraid of coming too late."[109] They destroyed 1,700 towns, 70,000 villages, 1,700 churches, 530 synagogues, a number of the most famous medieval monasteries. They plundered all museums and libraries and stole very precious Persian, Abyssinian, and Chinese manuscripts.

Gauleiter Sauckel got the task of bringing slave workers to Germany. If they do not come voluntarily, he said on April 20, 1942, they must be forced to come to the Reich. Male and female German agents hunted the Russians down and packed them into unheated trains without any sanitation; people who died on these journeys and children who were born in the trains were thrown out of the windows.[110] In order to make life easier for German mothers with many children 400,00 to 500,-000 especially strong Russian girls were forcibly brought to Germany.[111] On April 14, 1943, Sauckel reported to Hitler ("My Führer!") that after one year of hunting 3,500,000 Russians worked for the German war machine and so did 1,500,000 Russian prisoners of war.[112] On another occasion Sauckel reported that—from November, 1941 to January, 1942—500,000 Russians had died.[113]

Gauleiter Alfred Rosenberg, whose 39 volumes listing his plundering of art treasures in France were captured after the war, said in 1941 that the war could only be won if the whole German Army lived on what food they found in Russia; if millions of Russians died, this would have to be accepted without undue feelings. The Hague Convention was no longer valid as the USSR had to be regarded as dissolved. The fate of Russian prisoners of war in Germany was a great tragedy; many died, others too weak to march on were shot before the eyes of the population.[114] As to the Jews, Rosenberg wrote: "The Jewish problem which has not been solved by the nations of Europe during 2,000 years would be solved by the National Socialist revolution."[115]

Field-Marshal Milch found it very amusing that Russians had to serve German cannons.[116] General Keitel promulgated an order to shoot 50 to 100 Russians for one German soldier killed,[117] and ordered the soldiers to use every possible terror, even against women and children.[118] Before the concentration camp of Dachau was reached by the American armies all inmates who had been brought there in accordance with Keitel's Night and Fog Order were murdered; people too ill to walk were carried on stretchers to the crematorium.[119] Professor Gebhardt murdered Russian prisoners of war by opening the skulls to watch the pathological changes in the bones of the victims.[120]

Dr. Eugen Kogon says: "The German generals in France and in the East, while behaving like madmen thought their behavior was *Realpolitik*. In reality, by strangling the laws of humanity, they strangled the interests of the Germans: *Ex ossibus ultor—* from the corpses of the hostages thousands of avengers arose."[121] A speaker on the Bavarian radio on February 7, 1956 said that high German officers took part in the deportations, liquidations, and murders punishable even by the Nazi laws. General Geyr von Schweppenburg said: "National Socialism ruined the German *Wehrmacht*. Those crimes ruined also the military value of the German army and hastened the downfall of the Third Reich."[122]

In March, 1945, 208 Russian slave workers (among them 77 women and two children) were brutally murdered by the SS.

The main culprit, SS General Kammler, committed suicide in 1945. When the other SS criminals early in 1958 were brought before German judges, one of their lawyers called Kammler a great and strong personality who would go down in the history of the Second World War. In defense of the other accused men he used the same arguments which had been used at Nuremberg, namely that the Hague Convention had become outmoded by total war and that the accused had to obey the orders of their superiors. SS-Obersturmführer Wetzling received only a sentence of five years' imprisonment. A decent member of the German Parliament called this sentence "a criminal miscarriage of justice dishonoring Germany," and a German newspaper wrote: "Twelve days for each murder. Wetzling acted out of lust for murder purely and simply, out of the convictions of a Nordic SS superman. It makes you cry with disgust."[123] At about the same time a railway employee was sentenced to four years of hard labor because he had stolen 18 marks. When, at another trial, one of the murderers was asked whether he had cross-examined the murdered to find out whether they were guilty or not he answered: "I did not think it opportune to hear each of those miserable creatures."[124] The Catholic periodical, *Wort und Wahrheit,* complained: "The change in the German juridical practice is a scandal without parallel. If we allow, tolerantly and with the help of our judges, the dyke to be breached at one point only, there will one day be successors to Hitler."[125] Dr. Hans-Bodo Gorgasz was released from prison after a few years. In 1947 he had been sentenced to death because he had helped to poison some 10,000 inmates of concentration camps, children of mixed marriages, and incurables. The sentence was commuted to imprisonment for life. When he was released after ten years decent Germans cried out and reminded the public that this man used to look impassively through a window at the painful dying of his victims. The minister responsible for his early release defended his action by saying that many doctors had been released earlier "who have perhaps done worse things and are following their professions unchallenged."[126] More than 300 concentration camp doctors are practicing again in Germany.

Many Russian (and Polish) prisoners of war were used as guinea pigs in concentration camps, maimed for life, or murdered right away. In Russia, children of six or eight years of age died because they had been robbed of their blood. Field-Marshal Küchler had 230 incurable Russian invalids murdered at Christmas, 1941. Field-Marshal von Rundstedt ordered that Russian prisoners of war should be made to clean up mines "to save German blood."[127] Dr. Wilhelm Jaeger told the Nuremberg judges of how the slave workers were treated in the Krupp factories. They had to live in overcrowded huts and only received 1,000 calories of food daily, much less than the German workers; one of the two daily meals consisted only of a watery soup. Many slave workers fell ill, most of them suffered from skin diseases, many from starvation, oedema, and nephritis.[128] On February 19, 1946, the judges were shown photographs from Auschwitz, including a photograph of seven tons of hair removed from dead women to be used for industrial purposes. A firm called Strem received human bones to be used for making superphosphates. Bills addressed to that firm spoke of tons of flour made of human bones. Professor Spanner made soap out of human fat and collected human skins for some purpose. But a German, Karl Epting, said in a book after the war that "no other nation has done so much for other nations and helped them in spite of their own sufferings" as the Germans, "by the work for prisoners of war and foreign workers. The German nation proved in the last war that it could be a genuine mediator."[129]

There were decent Germans who tried to warn against the consequences of this barbarous behavior in Russia, for instance Count von Schulenburg, General Henning von Tresckow and

General Helmut Stieff. All three later became martyrs of the Third Reich. Today the Germans, who once hailed Hitler by the millions, are constantly complaining about what Czechs, Poles, and Russians did to them in 1945. Hans Grimm sold 300,000 copies of his books by saying: "The German nation has done absolutely nothing to the world."[130] Guderian, Hitler's last Chief of Staff, in March, 1945 convened German and other journalists, protested against "the Russian violence," and appealed to "the chivalry of our enemies."[131] When, however, Admiral Canaris protested to General Keitel on September 15, 1941 because of the German barbarities against Russian prisoners of war and stressed the fact that, although Russia was not a member of the Geneva convention, "the principle of international law with regard to the treatment of prisoners of war" must still be adhered to, Keitel brushed this warning aside, saying haughtily: "These scruples are in accordance with the ideas of a chivalrous war. But we are concerned with the extermination of a *Weltanschauung*. Therefore I approve of these measures and accept responsibility for them."[132] General Guderian complained even after the war that the Western Powers had weakened German resistance against the East by "concluding a pact with Russia." He never stopped to remember that Hitler had forced the West to conclude that alliance with Russia in order to fight Hitler and all he stood for. He only complains that a "thousand years of German history, German colonisation, German culture and civilisation has been wiped out in Central Europe."[133] He apparently does not know what General Eisenhower said in 1945: "To no one man do the United Nations owe a greater debt than to Marshal Zhukov."[134]

The Germans have published many books and articles about what was done to them in 1945 by the humiliated and decimated Eastern nations, saying that not only all German politicians should read them but also the politicians of the West. But they have not published, translated even one of the many English, Polish, Czech, and Russian books in which the unspeakable crimes perpetrated by innumerable Germans against the nations of Eastern Europe are described. When an International Congress of Scholars in 1955 debated "Europe: Its Heritage and Task" at Mainz, Professor Max Beloff (Oxford) remarked that much had been said about the horrors of Bolshevism but that the crimes of the Nazis and, throughout history, of the Catholics were rapidly glossed over although the massacres of ten to twelve millions of innocent civilians were much more horrible.

Did they expect the Poles, Czechs, and Russians simply to say "Thank you, German master race"? Human nature being what it is, terrible revenge was inevitable and was foreseen long before by men like Sir Winston Churchill and Thomas Mann. One of the greatest German writers, Friedrich Schiller, says: "This is the curse of every evil deed that, propagating still, it brings forth evil."[135] Who of us can be really sure that he would not have behaved like the Eastern nations if the Germans had committed these terrible crimes against his family, his nation, his country? If the Germans cared to remember their own proverbs—such as: As you prepare your bed, so you will lie; The soup which you have prepared you must eat; Do not unto others what you would not like to be done by; He who soweth wind will reap the whirlwind; What you shout into the wood is shouted back to you—they would understand what happened to them in 1945. But the Germans do not care to remember anything. In the words of Mr. Brian Connell in his *Watcher on the Rhine:* "It is almost as if the Germans have no mind. And if they have, then it is a schizophrenic mind."[136]

The German bishops never protested as a body against the persecution of the Jews between 1933 and 1945; since when they asked after the war was it permitted to take revenge on innocent people? And a group of Americans said that "something has been happening in Europe which is new in the annals of recorded history."[137] Although it is said in the Bible that to take such revenge is not permitted, that was done in Europe to Czechs, Poles, Russians, and Jews was also something without precedent in recorded history. Harrison P. Salisbury, author of *Stalin's Russia and After,* says: "The wonder is not that the Germans met defeat in Russia, the wonder is that any of them survived or were permitted to survive."[138]

We must here remind the reader of the many war speeches of Sir (then Mr.) Winston Churchill from 1941 to 1945, in which he said that many proud and once happy nations kept down by the brutal force of the Prussians learn to hate the name of National Socialism more than anything else; that firing parties were executing Dutchmen, Norwegians, Frenchmen, Belgians, Czechs, Serbs, Greeks every week; that the crimes committed against the Poles, the destruction of their houses, the affronts against their religion, surpassed everything done in other subjugated countries; that a deep hatred against the German name had been aroused by Hitler's armies and Gestapo which would remain in the memory of mankind for centuries; that the German General Staff should have been exterminated after the First World War; that, when the signal is given, the revenging nations would hurl themselves against their enemy and murder the most cruel tyranny which has ever stood in the way of human progress; that it was the heroic Russian armies which tore the guts out of the German military machine; that the Jews had suffered indescribable tortures at the hands of the Nazis; that Germany must realize that she hopes in vain to divide the Allies.

After the war Brian Connell wrote: "Vengeful Slavs visited centuries of reckoning on the modern Germans who had murdered millions of Poles and Jews in the death factories of Mauthausen and Auschwitz. Some ten million Germans reaped the whirlwind Hitler had sown."[139] The Bonn correspondent of the London *Times* wrote, on January 6, 1959, that "nowhere is

there a word about the unfortunate millions who were driven
from their homes, and to their mass graves, by Germans. Oblivious of the victims of Hitler, they are stridently articulate
about their own sufferings. Polish and Czech revenge after the
war was often terrible, but cause and effect are ignored. In a
country with probably the largest Church membership in Europe retribution is apparently unknown."[140] Unknown even
though one of the few decent German professors who had remained in Hitler's Germany, Karl Reinhardt, had told them in
1955: "What we did to others was done to us."[141] The
Deutsche Blätter, a South American periodical edited by German refugees, had said in 1944: "Now the people of Russia,
huge armies, are invading the Nazi stronghold bringing with
them revenge and terrible retribution! These armies have covered thousands of kilometers and everywhere seen nothing but
extermination, devastation, and human cruelty. They knew
what the war of extermination means which the Nazis have
brought to perfection.[142] A Russian woman who, because of
some "deviation," had been deported to Workuta, said there to
a German woman deported by the Russians in 1945: "The
Germans regarded us as beasts, not as human beings. The
humiliations which we had to endure were too terrible for not
awakening in all of us, even in the most bitter enemies of the
government, a desire for revenge."[143] Such, unfortunately, is
human nature. Here are two examples which help to illuminate
this point. In a small town on the river Bug the Germans played
a film, *Germany Conquers,* and requisitioned the last two musicians who had remained there, a Jew, Mendel Harb, former first
violinist of the defunct orchestra of the town, and his accompa-
nist, Sokolko. After the film the German officers danced and the
two musicians had to play for them. Mendel Harb somehow
managed to smuggle some dynamite into the hall and hid it
under the piano. At a prearranged signal Sokolko jumped out of
the window. Harb lit the dynamite with his cigarette, killing

himself and all the German officers in the hall.[144] Rabbi Dr. Leo Baeck, however, whom the Germans had deported to Theresienstadt and who had been of great religious help to the Jews in that concentration camp, persuaded his camp-mates not to revenge themselves on the captured German guards when the Russians, who had occupied the camp, permitted and even invited them to do so.

The Russians did not revenge themselves in all cases. Mrs. Lali Horstmann, whose husband was abducted and probably murdered by the Russians, saw from the window of her country house east of Berlin how a Russian soldier dismounted from his bicycle, offered it to a wretched German prisoner of war who could hardly move, and helped him mount it, as Frau Horstmann says, out of brotherly compassion.[145] Nobody has ever reported a German soldier doing the same for a Russian prisoner of war. The theologian Gollwitzer says that the system of "complete unlawfulness and humiliation of man which made hells of German concentration camps was unknown in Russian prisoner of war camps."[146] He must know, for he spent several years in those camps. Of the 95,000 prisoners the Russians took in Stalingrad only 6,000 survived. They were full of praise for Russian doctors and nurses, some of them Jewish, sacrificing their lives in selfless care for the German prisoners, some even catching typhoid fever and dying themselves. The German actor Heinrich George had been deported by the Russians; seriously ill in a Russian camp, he was haunted by terrible nightmares of a mass grave into which his corpse might be thrown. A Russian orderly, a Jew and a theater enthusiast who knew who George was, succeeded in persuading the camp commandant to let the German actor have a coffin and a separate grave.

When the German prisoners of war, diplomats, and civilians (men, women, and children abducted by the Russians) returned in 1955 to Germany and were interned in a prepared camp at Friedland, the reporter of a leading Hamburg newspaper wrote that the earth of Friedland camp "could tell the most terrible story of modern times."[147] What happened in German concentration camps did not seem to him worth remembering. All who had returned were received with the same enthusiasm—so that a decent newspaper complained that it made no difference to the Germans whether an innocent child or men "who had constructed the gas chambers of Auschwitz had come back. In none of the speeches by which they were greeted was the name of Hitler mentioned."[148] Another decent newspaper wrote that ministers greeted "men of the SS responsible for unimaginable crimes and Hitler diplomats who had helped him to subjugate Europe."[149] About the returned Hitler generals a German mother had this to say: "They are the same men who committed crimes against humanity and ruined our country. I only heard again the old phrases of heroism and soldierly obedience, and none of them said: 'I am sorry.' They have not changed a bit."[150] A Jew complained that the former commandant of Warsaw, "in whose area 250,000 Jews were murdered," had appeared on television.[151]

After the First World War German history for most Germans began with the Treaty of Versailles; for most Germans of today German history begins in 1945. They have completely forgotten that millions, in spite of the warnings of the best Germans, once shouted "Heil Hitler!," "All Power to the Führer!," "We shall march on till everything goes to pieces. Today Germany is ours, tomorrow the whole world."

They are criticizing the unconditional surrender policy of the Allies, completely forgetting that in 1918 they boasted that their armies had returned "unbeaten in the field." Remarque tried in vain to remind them that they had called traitors those decent but stupid Germans who had come forward in 1918 to sign the armistice while the Kaiser's responsible generals kept in the background. "No such thing can happen today. Totalitarian government—total defeat."[152] Field-Marshal Montgomery told

Admiral Friedeburg in May, 1945 that he could accept the unconditional surrender only of the German armies in the West, the Eastern armies must surrender to the Russians. When Friedeburg expressed fear that the Russians might murder all Germans, Montgomery retorted that they should have thought of this before attacking the Russians.[153] Schiller, the greatest German dramatist, makes Werner Stauffacher, as representative of the oppressed Swiss, say this:

> Yes! there's a limit to the despot's power!
> When the oppress'd for justice looks in vain,
> When his sore burden may no more be borne,
> With fearless heart he makes appeal to Heaven,
> And thence brings down his everlasting rights,
> Which there abide, inalienably his,
> And indestructible as are the stars.[154]

About the refugees from Nazi oppression who found asylum in Great Britain, Schiller makes his Marquis de Posa say to totalitarian Philip II:

> Already thousands have your kingdom fled,
> In joyful poverty. . . .
> See, with a mother's arms, Elizabeth
> Welcomes the fugitives, and Britain blooms
> In rich luxuriance from our country's arts.[155]

Of Germany in 1945, the Marquis, "a citizen of ages yet to come," says:

> All Europe,
> Exulting, sees its foe oppress'd with wounds,
> By its own hands inflicted![156]

Warped as their minds were by the Führer who broke every pact except the one with the Devil, the Germans expected in all seriousness in 1945 that the Allies would betray their Russian ally and allow Germany to fight the Russians. Hitler was the first to say, when everything seemed lost, that he would conclude a separate pact with whoever reached him first, the Russians or the Western powers, in order to fight the other. Papen, one of the main culprits, tried his luck with Roosevelt with a similar project. Colonel-General Rendulič, one of the most fanatical Austrian National Socialists, who had already been punished for his National Socialist sympathies by the Dollfuss Government, offered his services against the Russians to the American general who took him prisoner. The Hitler writer Bruno Brehm, who had said in 1941, "We had to fight the Russians and know we shall defeat them," wrote after the war: "All men of honour [!] in Germany had hoped to the last that they would be allowed to defend themselves against the East."[157] Guderian said after the war that he had hoped the West would grant Germany an armistice by which they could "defend themselves against the East with the rest of their armies."[158] The writer E. E. Dwinger, who had once hoped to enter Petrograd or Moscow with the German army, makes the Russian general Vlassow say in a novel of his that nobody had a right to strengthen Stalin so that he could crush Hitler. Why not? Because what the West had to expect after Hitler's victory might have been bad but what it had to expect after Stalin's victory was "nothing but horror."[159] German logic! In reality Vlassow had once said to the Germans that the Russians would never allow themselves to be reduced by the Nazis to the status of a colonial people. Ulrich von Hassell, who was hanged in 1944, entered in his diary on October 8, 1940: "If this system should be victorious, Germany and Europe have to expect terrible times."[160] Professor W. Steller, however, said that "the Americans and other European nations who had allied themselves with the Soviets in a 'crusade against Germany' had opened Europe to Bolshevism by breaking the back of the European nation in the middle of its fight against Bolshevism."[161] Guderian even asserted in May, 1945, without troubling to find out the true military position, that "the Western Allies had it in their power to hold back the Russian steam-roller."[162] The Germans prefer listening to these and other paladins of Hitler to reading what G. R. Kennan said about this matter, even though his words have been translated into German. He said that the Americans would not have been able to prevent the Russians from overrunning the whole East in the years 1944 and 1945 because they had not sufficient military strength to do so. The German theologian Helmut Gollwitzer, who saw the Russian army in Bohemia in 1945, was so impressed by it that he wrote: "So these were Stalin's 'last reserves,' children and old men, as German propaganda would have us believe during the last two years when we kept on retreating."[163] M. W. Gauss, a by no means unbiased German historian of the Yalta Conference, is forced to admit: "The Red Army was at that time victoriously progressing on a wide front towards Central Europe. This put Stalin into a position to dictate his own terms. . . . The appearance of the Red Army at the door of Berlin was the dominant fact at the conference."[164] Thomas Mann said on January 14, 1945 that the Germans had not only murdered and burned millions, they "ground and pulverised their bones and used them for fertilising the German soil—the holy German soil which German armies still thought they must defend, they were allowed to defend against violation by the enemy,"[165] and that "Germany, the Reich, everything German has become intolerable to the world."[166] Hermann Hesse told the Germans after the war: "You have lost your mad and satanic attack against your neighbors because German lust for conquest and murder has once again become intolerable to the whole world."[167]

But the Germans do not listen to such words of their best men; they write books about the "crimes" of Teheran, Yalta, Potsdam. These "crimes" include the expulsion of the Sudeten Germans, who, in protest, have used envelopes on the back of which is shown a divided Germany. The caption reads: "Roosevelt, Churchill, and Stalin signed at Yalta and Potsdam an 'agreement' under which 17 million Germans were, under terrible cruelties, expelled from their homes where they had been living for seven centuries. We claim our homes!" They do not read what Thomas Mann had to say about Roosevelt: "I have always admired Roosevelt as the born and conscious antagonist of the unredeemingly wicked diabolism to which Germany has given herself and by which she has become so dangerous to the world. The world which has produced this politician of the good, was saved by him, and so was man and liberty."[168] In his *Joseph* novels he paid homage to Roosevelt's New Deal. And Heinrich Mann called Roosevelt the most inspired president the United States has ever had.

No German is willing to listen to what a sensible and God-fearing minority of Germans tries to convey to him. The young German writer Kirst said in Oslo: "Our curse is our readiness to believe, even if it is in a Kaiser, a Chancellor or a Hitler. This belief has led us into the First World War, and into the abyss of the Second."[169] E. M. Remarque says: "We are a master race! And even in our dreams we obey all orders."[170] Dr. Pechel, who spent three years in a concentration camp, says that "the frantic joy of a great part of the German nation" ended "in complete ruin which cost the lives of millions, threatened the nation's very existence and loaded it with well-earned hatred by the whole world."[171] The poet Hans Carossa says: "Without Hitler's policy the Russians would not be in Berlin today."[172] The Austrian Chancellor Kurt von Schuschnigg, whom Hitler dragged from one concentration camp to another, says: "Without Hitler's war there would have been no world alliance against Germany, and without Hitler's war against Russia the Russians would not have become the masters of Europe."[173] The poet Hans Brandenburg calls Hitler "the grave-digger and disgracer of Germany."[174]

Professor Hermann Heimpel says that Germany was united in 1938 but that this unity was "gambled away in 1939. It was we ourselves who divided Germany." Since Germany's one-sided and excessive nationalism had degenerated into an imperialism which trampled down the rights of other nations, "all patriotic slogans stick in our throat." He says that Germany was out of touch with the ideas of the 19th century and was united by Prussian and authoritarian monarchists in contrast to the ideas of 1789 and without the German revolutionaries of 1848.[175] Professor Walter Hofer says: "The Third Reich did not last a thousand years. But its twelve years sufficed to undo the history of a thousand years."[176]

As the Germans coined the slogan, "Right to a Homeland," and repeated it more and more passionately, Professor Ludwig Dehio retorted: "What about the very same right of other nations in Europe before 1945?"[177] That is to say that a nation which had degenerated from Goethe and Schiller to Hitler and Himmler, from Bach and Beethoven to the "Horst Wessel song" —a nation which, in spite of the warnings of the best Germans, had hailed a barbarian who hated Jews, Christians, liberals, and social democrats, who promised to renew the march of the medieval German knights to the East, and whose Nordic heroes had murdered twelve million innocent men, women, and children—cannot possibly claim any rights in connection with the outcome of the last war. "Germany," Professor Dehio continues, "was truly the midwife of Bolshevism during the First World War, before she became its pacemaker in the Second." He reminded his compatriots of the words of the Prussian historian Otto Hintze before 1914 that the Germans would, if worse came to worse, let themselves "be buried under the ruins of European civilisation." Words like these, says Dehio, "cast their shadow into the future."[178] Professor Karl Jaspers reminded the Germans that German unification was enforced "by violence" in 1871 and greeted enthusiastically even by many liberals, although no political freedom was achieved at the time. "Consideration tells us to accept the consequences of a war for which are responsible. . . . A reunited Germany is unacceptable for both Russia and Poland." One cannot base any rights on something which no longer exists. "The state of Bismarck is irrevocably a thing of the past."[179]

That Hitler could undertake his aggressive war and destroy both Germany and Europe is the responsibility mainly of the German generals. A judicious minority of Germans stresses this fact. Infuriated by the flood of memoirs written by generals who try to shift the sole blame to Hitler, one German wrote: "The German nation owes it to its generals that Hitler could remain at the helm to the bitter end. They already knew after Stalingrad in January, 1943 that the war was lost. They alone had enough military power and the possibility to unite and end the Nazi ré-gime, without risking more than the soldiers at the front. Their wrong notions of honour and duty and their lack of political insight and resolution resulted in the one revolution by a few out of their own ranks being crushed and the war going on in blind obedience to a madman up to the unconditional surrender. The Russians would certainly not sit in the very heart of Ger-many today, and we who have been driven out from our East-ern soil would have remained in our homes if the German gen-erals had soon after Stalingrad or in July, 1944 taken the same step that Hindenburg took when the First World War was lost in 1918. But these generals get big pensions, write memoirs and want us to believe that they have no responsibility for the ter-rible end of the war."[180]

We need only read the books of Colonel-General Guderian or Field-Marshal Manstein to realize how right this German victim of their criminal folly is. The latter ascribes the *Lost Victories* to Hitler's interference and tells us that the German soldiers fought with a heroism unparalleled in history. He compares their fight with the stand of the ancient Greeks against the Persians. In his eyes Hitler's war apparently was a war to save European civilization. Kunrat von Hammerstein, a decent Ger-man officer, sums up his indictment of Manstein (and the other German generals now posing as innocent lambs) in these warning words: "The stab-in-the-back legend after the first war has its equivalent now in a Field-Marshal myth which is being used in order to throw a veil over the true causes of our defeat."[181] Neither the Hitler generals nor the German people like to be reminded of the warnings of General Beck on July 16, 1938 to General Brauchitsch that history would make the highest officers of the German army responsible because their obedience as soldiers must have a limit where their knowledge, conscience, and honor should forbid them to execute mad orders.

Another sensible German, Helmut Lindemann, says: "All of us are guilty who were grown-ups in 1933 and remained more or less passive, looking more or less disgustedly at the course of events without resolutely resisting it. . . . Now people seem to think they can wipe out from their memory the ignominious chapter of the German history which began in 1933 and ended in 1945, simply by ignoring it. Even during the Second World War by far the greater part of our nation approved of Hitler's policy." Whole German provinces had been burnt and devastated "as Hitler had devastated whole Russian provinces. Millions had been driven out from their soil and their homes, as Hitler had started uprooting and expulsion in 1940. Never in modern history has any saying come true in such a terrible manner as the one: Do not do unto others what you would not like to be done by."[182]

Yet another judicious German, Professor Eppo Steinacker, reminds us of the many German compounds with *deutsch*, from *altdeutsch* to *alldeutsch* and *volksdeutsch*, which Hitler coined. "This last and shrill chord brings before our inner eye cemeteries, mass graves, concentration camps, millions of uprooted lives. . . . Did not the Second and even more so the Third Reich for ever discredit any Reich mysticism, any Reich theology? It certainly did."[183]

Yet another God-fearing German, Jürgen Thorwald, after describing on many terrible pages the inferno through which the

Germans in the East had gone in 1945, sums up in these words: "History will say that what was done to us is no worse than the expulsion and extermination of the Jews by the Germans but a just answer to the crimes which were committed first."[184] The chief of the Pan-German movement, Heinrich Class, said in 1911, forgetting everything he had preached up to that moment, that a rapacious aggression did not correspond with his ideas, and that "punishment for a reckless attack seems to me justified even if it should be made in the harshest form [evacuation]."[185]

Theodor Haecker, in 1941, when Hitler was the master of an enslaved Europe, entered in his diary with the unfailing certainty of a devout Christian: "The Germans are digging graves for many a nation but they will fall into all of them themselves. They are shoveling a grave for Greater Germany."[186] After the war Professor F. W. Foerster, who for five decades had fought German militarism, chauvinism, and anti-Semitism and therefore had to spend both German wars in exile, said this: "All Germany resounded of furious lamentations about the sufferings of the refugees from the East which certainly deserved our greatest sympathy. But where is the pious memory of five years of pitiless plundering and torturing of the nations which, after many terrible years, are ridding themselves forever of the Germans who had heartily collaborated with the intruders? What about your own guilty shudders?"[187] He accused his countrymen of reserving their horror and moral indignation for what had been done to them by their victims. When he visited Germany for a short time (he is living now in Switzerland), he got in touch with the German expellees, and when he asked a young student whether he hated the nations who had expelled him and the others, he received the answer: "Not at all. We know only too well that we have to thank Hitler for all this."[188] Professor Foerster accuses the Germans of having "betrayed all great German traditions" and fallen "victim to the fatal error that they could become the masters of the world if they could only by such madness betray all their great spiritual heritage."[189] He, like Professor Dehio, says that the Germans cannot treat the problem of their return to the lost provinces as "a question of right because they would risk being answered: What right have you to rights? How can you claim any rights after for decades having derided the idea of justice and replaced it by the madness of power?"[190]

Heinrich Mann, whose warnings against Hitler the Germans ignored and whose books they burned in 1933, said in 1946 that the Germans had abducted millions "into misery for the greatness of the master race." In 1945 they hoped to evade "the revenge of the tortured nations. . . . Their last rapacious war cost the Germans their country."[191]

These are German voices crying in the wilderness of German forgetfulness. They are listened to as little today as were the warners against Hitler in the years before 1933.

Now we must hear what non-Germans have to say on the matter of the expulsion of the Germans.

Anthony Rhodes, a *Daily Telegraph* correspondent who visited Czechoslovakia in 1958, found anti-German feeling there even among violent anti-Communists. They dislike the Russians but point out that the Russians have never gassed Czechs nor behaved like Heydrich, Henlein, and their like. All Czechs are convinced that the Germans cannot be trusted. Having lived under all sorts of Teutonism for a thousand years and through the experience of Lidice in more recent times, they refuse to differentiate between good and bad Germans.

J. B. Hutak, a Czech refugee living in Great Britain, said in 1957 in his book *With Blood and With Iron:* "All those mothers and fathers, brothers and sisters, winding their way from Auschwitz to Mauthausen, from Theresienstadt to Ravensbruck left one obligation, one testament, one command behind them: Never forget." He attacked the meetings of the Sudeten Germans who are clamoring for return and their speakers, Lodgman von Auen, a nationalist who, after the rape of Austria, called Hitler "a unifier of all Germans," and Dr. Hans Seebohm, member of the German liberal party and minister in the German government, who said: "The reality of this unity down the centuries means that the lands of the Czech crown, Bohemia, Moravia and Silesia, should for ever remain united to the Reich." What infuriates Mr. Hutak most is that the Germans constantly talk of what they had to suffer in 1945 and forget the far worse brutalities the Czechs had to suffer at the hands of the Germans from 1939 to 1945. He is sure that a hundred Lidices would not teach the Germans anything and speaks of the intellectual illness from which the Germans are suffering, a sort of schizophrenia, which enables them to produce men like Goethe, Kant, Beethoven, and Thomas Mann, and, on the other hand, men like Heydrich and Frank, Hitler and Himmler, and the thousands of SS men who tortured innumerable human beings "daily for many years in Belsen, Auschwitz, Mauthausen, and Ravensbrück."[192] The Czechs, whether Communist or anti-Communist, are not prepared to forget the past and to look only to the future. They have not forgotten that the West betrayed their country in 1938 and sacrificed it to Hitler, nor are they willing to forgive the crimes the Hitlerites have committed against them. "The Czechs," says Charles Wighton, "see in Bonn high officials and generals of Hitler's Third Reich holding key appointments and offices. . . . They read with genuine horror of statements of the German aim to liberate the satellites."[193]

As to Poland, we must remember that it was carved up again by Ribbentrop and Stalin in 1939 after it had been carved up three times in the 18th century by Tsarist Russia, Prussia, and Austria. When Great Britain negotiated with Stalin in 1939 she was not prepared to pay the price he asked for. But Hitler paid the price asked by Stalin for a pact with Germany, offering him the Eastern part of Poland. The Poles recovered the Russian and Austrian parts of their former territory in 1918, the Prussian part in 1945. Silesia, which in former centuries had also belonged to Poland, later came under the rule of the Habsburgs. Frederick II, in the Hitlerian manner, robbed Austria of Silesia, although his father had warned him in his testament "not, for heaven's sake, to start an unjust war and become an aggressor. Read history and you will see that unjust wars do not end well. You are a great man on earth but you will be held responsible by God for an unjust war and the blood which you have shed."[194] Maria Theresa said about Frederick's Prussia that "this terrible system will conquer us all, one after the other, if we do not resist it with firmness." Professor Foerster, who quoted these words after the last war, added that nobody resisted and one after the other was conquered; "and the story is perhaps not finished for a long time yet."[195]

The Poles have published a book, *We Remember* which is full of ghastly photographs. Its jacket shows a reproduction of a Nazi order informing the unhappy Poles how many of their fellow citizens had been executed on a certain day in a certain district "because of crimes committed against the reconstruction of the General Government,"[196] as they called subjugated Poland. The Poles, who are mourning for more than five million countrymen murdered by the Germans and have to provide for five million orphans, say that the deepest German dream seemed to come true during the war: the conquest of Europe from the Atlantic to the Volga and the Caucasus. It is their deepest disappointment now that they have not only lost the territories subjugated during the war, but also the provinces they had conquered since the 12th century. Now they say: "The German territorial status in 1945—incontestable from the point of view of international law—must be the initial point of any negotiations concerning the German frontier."[197] The Poles note with concern and contempt the existence of many German institutes editing a flood of revisionist pamphlets and books and cherishing wild dreams never refuted by the German Government.

At another occasion Gomulka said: "The Germans have lost the right to decide their frontiers themselves. That right was buried by the Hitlerites under the ashes of the crematoriums."[198]

It is not only Polish Communists who say so; Polish Catholics agree. Stanislaw Stomma, leader of the Catholic party in the Polish parliament, spoke in March, 1958 of the nationalist German youth of the 1880's who "idolised" Bismarck after his victories over Austria and France and sang: *"Graudeamus igitur animo ex toto/ Nam in Germanorum gente/ Celebratur grata mente/ Cancellarius Otto."* The same youth "followed Hitler enthusiastically" fifty years later. "The vicinity of so dynamic and great a nation as the Germans, with all their traditions," he continued, "must inevitably remain a threat to us." His consolation is that things are no longer what they used to be in the times of Bismarck or Hitler. "We are now more powerful than the Germans, than we had been during the last three centuries," when the Poles again and again were the object of aggression. German imperialism has broken down within the time of one generation; Prussia disappeared after Germany's second defeat; Poland is a member of an alliance "which makes any further German aggression impossible." Furthermore, "two German states were established *de facto*." The Poles would not forget the injustices they had suffered in the past, and if the Germans wanted a friendly coexistence with Poland, they must "turn away from the traditional Prussian policy. The question of the Oder-Neisse frontier has been settled once for all." Certain German circles were still full of "hatred against Poland" and advocated "a continuation of the policy of the *Drang nach Osten*," and even leading politicians of West Germany agreed with this in their official utterances. Only a complete change of mind on the side of those Germans can pave the way to laying "the dreadful ghosts of the last war."[199] Cardinal Wyszynski, in a sermon in the George chapel in Marienburg, said on August 18, 1960: "You have heard the echo of the threats uttered in haughty West Germany by an enemy against the land of our forefathers and our liberty, and fear of the future may have crept into some hearts. But look at these powerful castles once inhabited by such haughty people relying on iron and steel. Where are they now who once ruled over us with power and hatred from these castles? God has led the Christian Poles back into the country which once belonged to them."[200] On the occasion of the 25th anniversary of Hitler's accession to power judicious men said things like this: "On January 30, 1933, the march into our ruin started. Adolf Hitler ruined the *Reich,* and Europe lost its old hegemony for ever." The result of the Nazi era? Instead of a "Greater Germany a Germany divided into three parts." "We shall march on until everything falls to pieces. . . ."

Sensible Germans agree with what the Poles say. Dr. Rauschning says: "Whatever we Germans may say about the cruel expulsion and that crimes cannot be remedied by new crimes—all this is of no avail. Germany is responsible for the disaster of the Second World War. The loss of a large part of our territory is justified as retribution and atonement."[201] Paul Wilhelm Wenger, a Roman Catholic columnist, reminds the Germans of the criminal German history since the days of Bismarck; Donoso Cortes, Spanish ambassador to the King of Prussia, said in 1853: "I love neither Prussia nor her policy nor her aggrandizement, not even her existence. Since the first day of her existence I see in Prussia a satanic power, and when considering the peculiar and puzzling development of this state I am convinced that this will remain so in future." Crown Prince Frederick wrote on December 31, 1870 that the world regarded the Germans, once a nation of thinkers, poets, artists, and idealists, as a nation of conquerors and destroyers. He blamed Bismarck for his "policy of blood and iron" and added: "What is the use of all power, all martial glory and splendour, if we meet hatred and mistrust everywhere. Bismarck made us great and powerful, robbed us of our friends, of the sympathy of the world, robbed us of our conscience." German megalomania, continues Wenger, returned in the words of Professor Werner Sombart during the First World War: "Just as the German bird, the eagle, soars high above all other birds, so the Germans should regard themselves above all other nations which surround them, and which they see below them in a bottomless depth. . . . It is the loftiest characteristic of our German way of thinking that we realise unity with God already down here on earth." Paul de Lagarde said much earlier: "The nations in the vast empire [of the Habsburgs] are, with the exception of the Germans and the Slavs of the South, all politically without any value, only material for Germanic colonisation." After the well-deserved catastrophe of 1918, Hindenburg said "that the weakened German front was stabbed in the back by the home front, as Siegfried had been stabbed by the cunning spear of dark Hagen." In spite of this, the retired General was chosen President, who, a few years later, "in the *Garnisonskirche* at Potsdam, invested the proletarian from the banks of the Danube with the Prussian tradition and legitimized him to call Frederick II and Bismarck the godfathers of his policy." The "German spring" of March 21, 1933 was followed by "the macabre weeks of July 1945 at Potsdam." Wenger quotes Talleyrand's words: "German unity—this is their slogan, their doctrine, their religion, and they confess it with true enthusiasm. Who can surmise the consequences, when the united German masses will become aggressive? Who can say when such a movement is going to stop?" Wenger adds: "Hitler gave the answer at Tobruk, Narvik, in the Caucasus, in Vienna, Prague, Athens, Paris, Belgrade, Rome, and Bucharest, and, above all, in Auschwitz and Theresienstadt."

Hitler's Eastern colonial policy brought "the Russian frontier from Brest Litovsk close to Fulda. . . . The frontiers of Bismarck's Reich were gambled away in 1917 when Germany refused the mediation of Pope Benedict XV for a peace without annexations. The frontiers of 1919 were gambled away when the bankrupts of the First World War called for Hitler to revise them, and when he marched into Vienna, Prague, and Warsaw. In 1939, Poland was carved up again. After the war against Poland was finished Hitler said: 'The result was the annihilation of all Polish armies and the dissolution of the Polish state.' Can we really claim a total indemnification in the name of international law, wl.ich we have brutally trodden under our feet, without heaping red-hot coals upon our own heads?"[202]

The *Westfälische Rundschau* stated in May, 1959 that the Germans tried "to belittle the crimes of the Third Reich. No book informs us of the measures taken to exterminate the Polish intelligentsia during the last war."[203] Paul Schallück, in his novel, *The Forgotten Guilt,* tries to remind the Germans of their behavior since 1918, when they said that the Imperial army had not "really" been beaten on the front but "cowardly stabbed in the back by the nation at home." They destroyed the democratic republic and hailed Hitler, marching "into a future of a thousand years" and saying, "Praised be what makes us hard," and addressing their Führer in poems like this: "We know your work will succeed because God has enlightened your heart." In 1940 they defeated the decadent nation in the West and rode "against the East to put up an insurmountable barrier against the hordes of Slavs" who surmounted it all the same in 1945. Between 1941 and 1945 they exterminated millions, and all that remained of the victims was a 30-foot-high hill of the hair of "Jewish women"—"hideous crimes, gassing and burning, deeds for which the language has no words "those in use being useless." Germans who resisted the Hitler regime were tortured to death in concentration camps. One of those of whom Schallück speaks in greater detail said: "One just man could have saved Sodom, if found there. I do not consider myself to be that just man, and I cannot save Germany." He also says, quoting the Gospels: "The day will come when your enemies will come upon you and turn everything upside down because you did not recognise the time when you were visited."[204]

Golo Mann, Thomas Mann's gifted son, who still remembers that "the great majority of Germans" disliked the republic of 1918, that General Seeckt favored a German-Russian alliance, and that Hitler's policy had been "anti-Russian from beginning to end," says: "The Russians have experienced from 1941 to 1944 what German political and military independence can do to the Russian nations. No unbiased man can take it amiss if the Russian statesmen are out to prevent the reappearance of such an independance at all costs." Looking to the West he says: "The victors of 1945 have little interest, and little possibility, to undo the consequences of the [German] defeat of 1945."[205]

Englishmen who have not forgotten the German past, agree both with the Poles and the sensible Germans. Lord St. Oswald said on January 1, 1959 that we compensated the Poles at the expense of Germany in 1945. "It certainly did not seem an unwarranted sanction against Germany, who had started the war by attacking Poland, and whose savage conduct of that war was vivid in everyone's mind. . . . To weep for the Germans as the only or even the principal sufferers from this exchange is to mock history. It is mistaken to think that the Polish occupation and the German evacuation of this zone conflicted with Article II of the Atlantic Charter. Mr. Winston Churchill, in a speech in the House of Commons in February, 1944, said: 'There will be no question of the Atlantic Charter applying to Germany as a matter of right and barring territorial transferences or adjustments in enemy countries.' Those transferences took place" and "are now a European fact."[206] Dr. D. W. Crowley, in *The Background to Foreign Affairs,* says: "The German minorities still kept up something of the air of being the bearers of Teutonic civilisation to the backward Slavs. In fact there have been echoes of this posture in the slogans of the refugee organisations; and this is not a healthy attitude. The German minorities have always been a source of trouble in Eastern Europe; Russia has on the whole done Europe a good turn in expelling them. The dreams of the refugees have been an alarming and dangerously unrealistic element in the post-war European situation."[207] Peter Kirk, M.P., said in a German weekly that "the overwhelming majority" in Great Britain regards the Oder-Neisse frontier as permanent and would not lift a finger to change it. The frontier must be regarded as a *fait accompli*.[208]

By attacking and devastating Russia, Hitler brought Communism to what is called the East Zone in Germany today. When a high official of the Hitler Youth, whom the Russians had brought to Workuta in 1945, was worried about his children in the East Zone, another German prisoner of war, apparently no Hitler enthusiast, said to him: "They have long since become Communist pioneers. When you return after a couple of years they will be experts in political economics. They will ask you: 'Papa, do you know the law of surplus value?' and be disappointed should you be unable to answer this question." Whereupon the National Socialist: "If I knew that for certain, I should be sorry for not having smashed their heads against a wall in 1945." The other: "It would have been better if you had done that to Hitler in good time."[209] But the Germans as a whole are apparently unwilling to learn from their past. Dr. von Brentano, Foreign Secretary when the millenary celebrations of the battle of the Lechfeld were held at Augsburg on June 10, 1955, said this: "The problems of one thousand years ago are clearly identical with the problems which face us again today. In those days nomadic heathen hordes of the East stood at the gates of Europe threatening ruin and disaster. Today once again the masses from the East stand not very far from this city and once again we are facing the danger that the West will be overrun and fall into their hand."[210] A member of the German Reichstag, Herr Jaeger, said that the Russian system "is essentially as demonic and diabolical as it was in its first hour. We think that the power of evil in world history has never shown itself so drastically as in the forty-three years of Soviet policy."[211] When Minister Ehrhard said that "the imperialism of totalitarian Communism was worse than colonialism," the Russian ambassador in West Germany retorted: "The German murdered 20 million Russians,"[212] and a decent German, Conrad Ahlers, wrote: "The Russians are apparently unwilling to leave such reproaches unanswered any longer. We have no right whatever to play the role of public prosecutors. For it is we ourselves who sit in the dock of world history."[213]

Professor Franz Paul Schneider wrote in 1959: "The best Germans, after the unconditional surrender in 1945, hoped for a thorough conversion, change and spiritual revival, but the high hopes of 'the other Germany' have not come true. . . . The German gods retreated to Valhalla. But the political and social powers which coined the ideas and ideals and aims of the Kaiser's era, which systematically destroyed the Weimar republic and lifted the Austrian comedian into the saddle, have reoccupied their positions long ago. The guilty men have not been punished. You find them in the administration, the judiciary, the keypoints of our ecomomy, the academies and universities. Communism is again the deadly enemy No. 1. The continuity of Hitler's foreign policy has been fully restored. . . . Many of the best were murdered in concentration camps. Those who emigrated did not prove willing to return."[214] Helmut Lindemann said: "The past lives on in the present, in our anti-Bolshevism. The innocence with which many Germans indulge in a doctrinaire anti-Communism can only be explained by our forgetting our recent past. . . . We Germans attacked Russia in 1941 and tortured and devastated her—and we did so under the flag of anti-Bolshevism. We should remember that that anti-Bolshevism was a smoke-screen behind which Hitler tried to realise his excessive dreams of a Greater Germany extending to the Ural."[215] Giselher Wirsing, who once praised Hitler and denounced Roosevelt as a world conqueror, has since very much changed his mind and says: "The German soldiers who found newly erected schools even in the farthest corners of the Caucasus were forced to admit that the Russian nation had been raised to a new level by a gigantic effort."[216] Thomas Mann, who had no need to unlearn anything, says to-day what he had already known in 1933, that Hitlerism was "a stupid imitation of Communism, a sham revolution without any relation to the idea of humanity and its future. Nobody can deny such a relation to the great Russian revolution." Bourgeois democracy was unknown in Russia, which has always been despotic. But the revolution of 1917 "put an end to impossible anachronistic conditions. It raised a nation of analphabets intellectually and socially. That revolution was the great social revolution after the political revolution of 1789, and, like this one, it will leave its marks on all human affairs." He tries to remind the West "that, to save their lives, they stood together with Russian Communism in the war against the Nazis. Today, however, people think it necessary to stamp out the last memory of yesterday as high treason."[217]

Mann said in 1943 that Germany will "never become a decent liberal and democratic republic," and knew in 1944 that "victory will be lost this time to an even larger measure than last time." From 1947 on he saw with deep misgivings the growing "friendliness towards Germany" and "the remorse for having defeated Germany with the help of Russia and not rather Russia with the help of Germany." He remembered that Ernst Wiechert had spoken of "that hopeless nation," 60 or 80 per cent of which would accept Hitler, if he came back, with "open arms."[218] And he said in 1947: "Is the sense of guilt quite morbid which makes one ask oneself the question how Germany, whatever her future manifestations, can ever presume to open her mouth in human affairs again?"[219]

Professor Alexander Mitscherlich, who has published a book about the crimes committed by German professors and doctors against helpless inmates of concentration camps, speaks of the "unadulterated madness" of the Germans of the Third Reich and of "a nation-wide toleration" of that madness. When Germans protested against the murder of their relatives, inmates of psychiatric hospitals, this was stopped by the authorities. But "no one in Germany stood up in a similar manner for the Jews. Much of the previous anti-Semitism has been transmuted in the current German anti-Communism."[220] Professor Hans Rheinfelder says: "We have learnt nothing, absolutely nothing, from our guiltful defeat. We think it right that German soldiers attacked and devastated Russia twice, feel no remorse about the crimes of Hitler's wars and are rather inclined to praise, and give honours to, Hitler's henchmen."[221]

Dr. Adenauer, after his audience with the Pope in 1960, said: "We are the last bastion of Western civilisation against the barbarism of the East. Our German soldiers are the soldiers of God. We have a mission in the world." But Dr. Hermann Rauschning, author of *Hitler Speaks* and *The Revolution of Nihilism,* retorted: "This missionary role which the Chancellor claims for West Germany against Communism, not only reminds us of the old proud word that the world will once be saved by Germandom, but also of Hitler who bellowed into Schuschnigg's ear that Germany had a historic mission."[222] And a Roman Catholic member of the Polish parliament, State Councillor Zawiejski, retorted: "We hear that God has given a special mission to the German nation in the battle between East and West. This is first a misuse of the name of God and secondly it is a false arrogance in the name of a nation."[223] Dr. Rauschning says that a new wind "blows coldly and soberingly into our faces." The German future starts with the knowledge "that there will be two German states, not one. One is tempted to quote the words: *'Tu l'as voulu, George Dandin'* to the German 'economic miracle' citizens who follow the dreamers of Bonn with the same uncritical and unteachable feudal faith as they followed quite recently the Shaman drummer from Braunau." The policy of "roll-back" and of the liberation of the "captive nations" has become meaningless, but the Germans run the risk of becoming the mischief-makers in Europe while the United States and Russia try to come to an agreement. West Germany refused to listen to reason when, a few years ago, neutralism could have solved the German problem. "The time has been missed when the Germans could have offered something towards releasing the tension. Today their hands are empty." If they want reunification, "the only possible solution is a confederation of the two German states whose existence as equal partners is unshakable. Even if that 'unity' should be a very questionable thing for the time being, it should not be pooh-poohed as a possible beginning of a closer unity and cooperation."[224]

Dr. Rauschning also said that Germany only succeeded in somewhat reducing the mistrust of the West by arousing the mistrust of the East. "It sided with the West although the unprovoked attack on Russia weighed infinitely more than the war against the West." And it did this with the same hatred of Russia which was so characteristic of Hitler, of Alfred Rosenberg and his *gauleiters* for the East.[225] It will be helpful to remind the reader of what Dr. Rauschning told the world of Hitler's ideas as far back as 1940. Because he thought he could trust him, Hitler said to him before the war: "A nation of eighty or a hundred million Germans! It will be my first task to accomplish this. And this will not only make us invincible but secure us the decisive superiority for all future. For this we need Austria, Bohemia, Moravia, Western Poland, the Baltic States. All these regions are mostly inhabitated by alien tribes and it will be our duty to eliminate them. It is the secret of our success to have made the law of genuine *Herrentum* the center of our political fight. The German nation has the mission to give to the world this new *Herrentum*."[226]

It is therefore that Dr. Rauschning said in the summer of 1962: "It is not good enough to have led the German nation out of the depth of the Hitlerian catastrophe to richness and self-indulgence but to leave it spiritually amidst the ruins of the values which Hitler has destroyed." A policy, "approved by a Hitlerian majority of the nation must lead to a new catastrophe which will not be smaller but worse than that of Hitlerism." The policy of the Kaiser and of Hitler has returned today as "the policy of strength." People still dream of the liquidation of Russia as a world power and of "erecting Germany's hegemony" again. "I wish," Dr. Rauschning says, "a man of the stature of Emile Zola stood up and hurled his new *J'accuse* against the mystification and corruption of the Germans."[227]

Professor Hagemann is perfectly sure that the Western Allies will not start a war for Germany to regain the lost provinces beyond the Oder and Neisse, but the leaders of the German expellees go on repeating the slogan of "an unalienable right to a fatherland" after Hitler denied that right to millions of *"Untermenschen,"* and behave "as if no Third Reich had ever existed." He fears that that sort of behavior might lead to another "nationalistic explosion." Russia, he says, "will never accept a strong Germany directed against her, in the midst of Europe, after it had been brought to the brink of destruction twice in one generation" by the Germans. She was willing to accept a reunified Germany in 1952 at the price of Germany being "neutralized." Germans had "little gift for democracy. Again and again hopeful attempts at political self-determination have come to nothing," in 1815, in 1848, under the Kaiser, and in the Weimar Republic. Now West Germany's politicians indulge again in Hitler's anti-Bolshevism, "which, being still alive in many German hearts, has become virulent again in an un-paralleled resurrection." Both German anti-Communism and German anti-Semitism "come from the same root of hatred and self-righteousness, they were indivisible in the Third Reich." But all this, argues Professor Hagemann, is doomed to failure because Russia is a world power today. "We cannot undo what we have done." Germany must pay "an adequate price for the gigantic guilt which Hitler's barbaric regime has brought on Germany's head." In other words, it must give up the illusion that there exists no other German state, and try to come to an agreement with it on the basis of "a confederation of the two states and so overcome the disastrous national division."[228]

Professor Ludwig Dehio asked: "Would it not be like believing in miracles if we thought we could by mere diplomatic skill throw off our shoulders the consequences of the most terrible war—*our* war, which destroyed the lives of 50 million people and the liberty of many more millions and changed the whole globe?"[229]

Professor Albrecht von Rantzau, by no means a Communist, quoted the following words by Goethe before assessing the German problem of today: "The heart of the nation has been trodden into the mire and is no longer capable of any noble feeling." Who, he asks, can guarantee to the Russians, who are very suspicious of the Germans, that a unified Germany within the framework of NATO would not "one day renew Hitler's *Drang nach Osten* or become the platform for an American 'crusade for the liberation of the Eastern nations'?" The Russians, he says, know that a reunited Germany would opt for the West and this option would mean "unconditional surrender" for them. But such unconditional surrender of the Russians is very unlikely. Rantzau therefore advocates negotiations of Western Germany with the masters of the Eastern zone to find out what sort of unification of the two zones might be possible. As the Germans of the West keep on saying that they cannot negotiate with dictators, Rantzau reminded them that they are enter-taining diplomatic relations with Franco and Salazar.[230]

Dr. A. Niehans writes: "The Russians will never be willing to free the Eastern zone of Germany by negotiations. As we can-not use force without ruining Europe still further, we must ac-cept the consequences and resign. What the Russians have brought into their sphere of influence they will keep, and they have the power to do so. At the most they will agree to a confederation of two states with equal rights and different social orders. It is utopian to think that the Western powers will work out something for us or if necessary, use force. They have no real interest in a change of the *status quo*. They still feel Hitler too much in their bones."[231]

The pacifist Otto Lehmann-Russbüldt, who spent Hitler's millenium in Great Britain, says: "The gigantic waves of the Third Reich and the Second World War rolled crushingly over the nations of Europe."[232] Professor Helmut Gollwitzer says "that our depotism was the most bestial of all in modern times, and it was approved of by large parts of our nation."[233] Pro-fessor Karl Jaspers says: "National Socialism meant the most radical destruction of communion between man and man. It exterminated everything that was true and good in the German nation. . . . All Germans, with very, very few exceptions, wanted a German victory."[234]

Professor Hans Joachim Iwand, a Protestant theologian, says: "I knew in 1933, and said so, that our policy would lose us the German East. Today I experience the same. If we go on behaving as we do, this means our end. We do not fight against Communism, this is only a smoke screen. We fight against the mighty hand of God before which we refuse to bow in spite of two defeats. This hand will smash us completely. And no voice is raised to pull us back."[235]

Pastor Herbert Mochalski says: "A direct road leads from the assassination of Rathenau to Stalingrad and Auschwitz.

After the First World War, Theodor Plievier wrote *The Kaiser Went, His Generals Remained*. Today we say: Hitler is dead, but those who served him are in high positions again. Hitler's generals who worked out his aggressive wars, are generals of the Bundeswehr. General Heusinger told us: 'Attack, wherever we get a chance: the West should oppose the East by this method of warfare.' "[236]

Notes

1. H. Rauschning. *Gespraeche mit Hitler*. New York, 1940, p. 22.
2. *Ibid.*, p. 78.
3. *Ibid.*, pp. 16, 33, 113, 118.
4. *Die dritte Walpurgisnacht*, pp. 12-13.
5. Domarus, *op. cit.*, p. 28.
6. Hart. *Attila der Letzte*, p. 148.
7. *Raum und Volk im Weltkriege*. Oldenburg, 1932.
8. *Vierteljahrshefte fuer Zeitgeschichte*, Muenchen, October, 1954, pp. 434ff.
9. *Triumph des Willens*. An original German film of 1933, shown in London after the war.
10. Domarus, *op. cit.*, pp. 437-438.
11. *Ibid.*, pp. 293-294.
12. *Der Eid Auf Hitler. Politische Studien*. Muenchen, November, 1956. The words quoted from the subtitle of the book.
13. *Friends of Europe Publications*. London, No. 7, p. 5.
14. H. Foertsch. *Die Wehrmacht im nationalsozialistischen Staat*. Hamburg, 1935, p. 25.
15. Kraus. *Die dritte Walpurgisnacht*, p. 147.
16. Domarus, *op. cit.*, p. 279.
17. *Ibid.*, p. 310.
18. *Ibid.*, p. 506.
19. *Mein Kampf*, p. 154.
20. F. Hossbach. *Zwischen Wehrmacht und Hitler*. Wolfenbuettel, 1949.
21. H. Picker. *Hitlers Tischgespraeche im Hauptquartier, 1941-1942*, pp. 443-444.
22. Breucker. *Die Tragik Ludendorffs*, p. 149.
23. Domarus, *op. cit.*, pp. 822, 825.
24. *Deutsche Rundschau*, December, 1960.
25. *Die Zeit*, Hamburg, August 30, 1956.
26. *Der Voelkische Beobachter*, December 31, 1939.
27. Portmann. *Kardinal von Galen*, p. 230.
28. F. von Schlabrendorff. *Offiziere Gegen Hitler*. Zuerich, 1946, p. 26.
29. IMT, July 26, 1946.
30. *Zachodnia Agencja Prasowa*, Warszawa, June, 1958.

31. IMT, January 1, 1946; IMT Document PS 795.
32. Goerlitz. *Der deutsche Generalstab*. Frankfurt, 1950, p. 469.
33. Hart. *Attila der Letzte*, p. 188.
34. *Ibid.*, p. 188.
35. Domarus, *op. cit.*, pp. 727-728.
36. *Gespraeche mit Hitler*, p. 174.
37. Adolf Heusinger. *Befehl im Widerstreit*. Tuebingen, 1950, p. 252.
38. *Mein Kampf*, p. 750.
39. Erich Kordt. *Nicht Aus den Akten*. Stuttgart, 1950, p. 409.
40. Hart. *Attila*, p. 154.
41. *Unter dem Schatten deiner Fluegel*, p. 792.
42. *Der Voelkische Beobachter*, October 19, 1942.
43. J. Thorwald. *Wen sie verderben wollen*. Stuttgart, 1952, p. 15.
44. *Frankfurter Allgemeine Zeitung*, October 31, 1955.
45. *Kann Westeuropa verteidigt Werden?*, p. 30.
46. *Deutsche Hoerer!*, p. 29.
47. *Ibid.*, p. 21.
48. *Und die Flamme soll euch nicht versengen*. Zuerich, 1955, pp. ix, xii.
49. *Nuernberger Nachrichten*, April 6, 1962.
50. *Blaetter*, Koeln, April, 1962.
51. *Du hast mich heimgesucht bei Nacht*, p. 64.
52. E. M. Remarque. *Zeit su leben und Zeit zu sterben*. Koeln, 1954, pp. 24, 42, 318.
53. *0815*. Muenchen, 1954, Vol. II, pp. 327, 412.
54. Foerster. *Erlebete Weltgeschichte*, p. 349.
55. T. G. Masaryk. *Das Neue Europa*. Berlin, 1922, pp. 13, 74.
56. Schonauer, *op. cit.*, p. 49.
57. Steiniger. *Der Nuernberger Prozess*, Vol. II, p. 126.
58. *German Cultural Oppression in Czechoslovakia*. Edited by the Czechoslovak National Committee. London, 1940 (a pamphlet).
59. Steiniger. *Der Nuernberger Prozess*, Vol. II, p. 424.
60. *Deutsche Hoerer!*, p. 39.
61. *Heydrich: Hitler's Most Evil Henchman*. London, 1962, pp. 27, 66, 82, 90, 162-163, 225, 245-246, 278.
62. *Vom anderen Deutschland*, pp. 187, 272-273.
63. *Europaeische Geistesgeschichte*. Stuttgart, 1953, p. 80.
64. *Erlebte Weltgeschichte*, p. 179.
65. *Deutschland und der Foederalismus*. Re-issued 1921, Stuttgart, p. 114.
66. Robert Blum. *Ausgewaehlte Reden und Schriften. Heft 5. Blum und die polnische Frage*. Leipzig, 1879.
67. *Times Literary Supplement*, London, July 5, 1957.
68. Pross. *Die Zerstoerung*, p. 298.
69. Winnig. *Aus zwanzig Jahren*, p. 115.
70. *Welt der Arbeit*, Koeln, February 19, 1960.
71. *Panzer Zwischen Warschau und dem Atlantik*. Berlin, 1941, p. 81.
72. *Vierteljahrshefte fuer Zeitgeschichte*, Muenchen, October, 1953.
73. *Vom anderen Deutschland*, p. 166.
74. *Tag-und Nachtbuecher*, p. 151.

75. *The German New Order in Poland.* Published for the Polish Ministry for Information. London, 1942, p. 407.
76. Steiniger. *Der Nuernberger Prozess,* Vol. II, p. 428.
77. *The German New Order in Poland,* p. 415.
78. *Deutsche Hoerer!,* p. 44.
79. Steiniger. *Der Nuernberger Prozess,* Vol. II, pp. 405ff; IMT, January 10, February 15, 1946.
80. *Daily Telegraph,* London, April 13, 1962.
81. Czeslaw Milosz. *Verfuehrtes Denken.* Koeln, 1953, p. 146.
82. *Die Stieglitz aus Arolson.* Neustadt an der Aisch, 1956, p. 91. Van Maydell is a descendant of Jews who had adopted Christianity in the 18th century. He knew nothing of it until he was told the truth by his parents during Hitler's reign.
83. *Observer,* London, May 11, 1958.
84. *Die Kultur,* May 1, 1958.
85. *Blaetter,* Koeln, April, 1960.
86. IMT, December 10, 1945.
87. *Aus zwanzig Jahren,* p. 142.
88. John Erickson. *The Soviet High Command.* London, 1962, p. 561.
89. *Ibid.,* p. 563.
90. IMT, December 17, 1945, February 8, 1946.
91. IMT, February 13, 1946.
92. Hofer. *Der Nationalsozialismus,* p. 250.
93. Bruno Brehm. *Am Rande des Abgrunds,* p. 447.
94. *Deutsche Woche,* Muenchen, January 1962.
95. *Zehn Jahre Kampf fuer Frieden,* May 27, 1926.
96. *Vierteljahrshefte,* July, 1958.
97. Picker. *Hitlers Tischgespraeche,* pp. 45, 72-73, 82, 91, 102, 116, 141-142.
98. *Bulletin of the Wiener Library,* London, Nos. 3, 4.
99. IMT, December 11, 1945.
100. Gollwitzer. *Und Fuehren, Wohin du nicht willst.* Muenchen, 1952, p. 280.
101. *Daily Telegraph,* London, April 3, 1959.
102. IMT, December 14, 1945.
103. Terence Prittie. *Germany Divided.* London, 1961, p. 49.
104. IMT, February 8, 1946.
105. IMT, December 17, 1945.
106. IMT, February 8, 1946.
107. IMT, November 30, 1945, February 13, February 19, 1946.
108. IMT, December 11, 1945.
109. *Vierteljahrshefte,* July, 1958.
110. IMT, July 6, 1946.
111. IMT, December 12, 1945, February 8, 1946.
112. IMT, December 13, 1945.
113. IMT, April 10, 1946.
114. IMT, December 18, 1945, April 17, June 7, 1946.
115. *Weltkampf* (a periodical), April-September, 1941.
116. IMT, July 26, 1946.

117. IMT, April 6, 1946.
118. IMT, July 26, 1946.
119. IMT, January 11, 1946.
120. IMT, August 26, 1946.
121. *Der SS-Staat.* Stockholm, 1947, p. 406.
122. *Erinnerungen eines Militaerattachés,* p. 63.
123. *Sueddeutsche Zeitung,* Muenchen, February 8, 1958.
124. *Nuernberger Nachrichten,* May 15, 1958.
125. *Ibid.*
126. *Sueddeutsche Zeitung,* February 8, 1958.
127. Steiniger. *Der Nuernberger Prozess,* Vol. II, p. 365.
128. IMT, December 12, 1945.
129. *Generation der Mitte.* Bonn, 1953, pp. 216-217.
130. H. Grimm. *Warum,* p. 199.
131. *Erinnerungen eines Soldaten.* Heidelberg, 1951, p. 380.
132. IMT, April 6, 1946.
133. *Kann Westeuropa verteidigt Werden?,* pp. 23, 29.
134. J. Gunther. *Inside Russia Today.* London, 1958, p. 146.
135. *Wallenstein,* Part II.
136. Brian Connell. *Watcher on the Rhine,* p. 21.
137. *The Land of the Dead.* Committee Against Mass Expulsion, New York.
138. In a letter to his publisher in London about *German Rule in Russia* by A. Dallin.
139. Connell, *op. cit.,* p. 18.
140. *Times,* London, January 6, 1959.
141. *Die Neue Rundschau* (a periodical), Frankfurt, 1955, Issue I.
142. *Deutsche Blaetter,* Santiago, 1944, Issue VII.
143. Brigitte Gerland. *Die Hoelle ist ganz anders.* Stuttgart, 1954, p. 33.
144. *Deutsche Blaetter,* February, 1942.
145. Lali Horstmann. *Unendlich viel ist uns geblieben.*
146. Gollwitzer, *op. cit.,* p. 112.
147. *Die Welt,* Hamburg, October 8, 1955.
148. *Sueddeutsche Zeitung,* October 29, 1955.
149. *Allgemeine Wochenzeitung der Juden,* Duesseldorf, October 28, 1955.
150. *Sueddeutsche Zeitung,* December 17, 1955.
151. *Allgemeine Wochenzeitung der Juden,* Duesseldorf, October 28, 1955.
152. *Zeit zu leben und Zeit zu sterben,* p. 391.
153. *The Listener,* London, June 10, 1954.
154. Schiller. *Wilhelm Tell,* Act II, Scene 2.
155. Schiller. *Don Carlos,* Act III, Scene 10.
156. *Ibid.*
157. Brehm. *Unser Kampf im Osten. Sinn und Sondung.* Weimar, 1941, p. 40; *Am Rande des Abgrunds,* p. 492.
158. *Erinnerungen eines Soldaten,* p. 364.
159. *General Wlassow.* Frankfurt, 1951, p. 160.
160. *Vom Anderen Deutschland,* pp. 166, 186-187.

161. W. Steller. *Wiedervereinigung, der erste Schritt zur Heimat.* 1957, p. 2.

162. *Kann Westeuropa verteidigt werden?*, p. 27.

163. *Und Fuehren, Wohin du nicht willst*, p. 21.

164. *Der Weg nach Jalta.* Heidelberg, 1952, pp. 115, 247.

165. *Deutsche Hoerer!*, p. 118.

166. *Doktor Faustus*, pp. 517-518.

167. *Briefe*, p. 249.

168. *Altes und Neues*, p. 657.

169. *Die Kultur*, March 8, 1958.

170. *Zeit zu leben und Zeit zu sterben*, p. 335.

171. *Deutsche Rundschau*, January, 1958.

172. *Ungleiche Welten*, p. 30.

173. *Requiem in Rot-Weiss-Rot*, p. 458.

174. *Trost in Traenen.* Muenchen, 1955, p. 6.

175. *Frankfurter Allgemeine Zeitung*, May 25, 1955.

176. W. Hofer. *Der Nationalsozialismus*, p. 367.

177. *Deutschland und die Weltpolitik*, p. 145.

178. *Ibid.*, pp. 19, 145, 152.

179. *Die Zeit*, Hamburg, August-September, 1960; *Deutsche Woche*, August 24, 1960.

180. *Sueddeutsche Zeitung*, July 21, 1956.

181. *Frankfurter Hefte*, May, 1956.

182. *Stuttgarter Zeitung*, January 26, 1954.

183. *Zeit und Stunde*, pp. 197-198.

184. J. Thorwald. *Das Ende an der Elbe.* Stuttgart, 1950, p. 384.

185. *Wenn ich der Kaiser wär*, p. 141.

186. *Tag-und Nachtbuecher*, pp. 134-135.

187. *Erlebte Weltgeschichte*, p. 307.

188. *Ibid.*, p. 177.

189. *Die juedische Frage*, p. 52.

190. *Groesse und Gefahr des Westoestlichen Gegensatzes.* Quoted in *Der Schlesier*, Whitsun, 1956.

191. *Ein Zeitalter wird besichtigt*, pp. 28-29, 103-104, 109.

192. *With Blood and Iron.* London, 1957, pp. 9, 155-156; E. Wiskemann. *Germany's Eastern Neighbours.* London, p. 203.

193. *Heydrich*, p. 244.

194. G. Ritter. *Staatskunst und Kriegshandwerk.* Muenchen, 1954, Vol. I, pp. 28-29.

195. *Erlebte Weltgeschichte*, p. 363.

196. *Pamiętamy.* Warszawa, 1958.

197. *Zachodnia Agencja Prasowa.* Warszawa, June, 1958.

198. *Blaetter*, Koeln, September 25, 1960.

199. *Dokumente.* Koeln, June, 1958.

200. *Nuernberger Nachrichten*, October 8, 1960.

201. *Blaetter*, Koeln, February, 1959.

202. *Wer Gewinnt Deutschland?* Stuttgart, 1959, pp. 61, 70-72, 137-138, 148, 184, 193-194, 273-274; *Die Kultur*, June 1, 1959.

203. *Westfälische Rundschau*, Dortmund, May 7, 1959.

204. *Engelbert Reinecke. Die Vergessene Schuld.* Frankfurt, 1959, pp. 19, 26, 37, 42, 47, 50, 55, 64, 102, 108, 127, 131, 132, 164, 174.

205. *Geschichte und Geschichten,* pp. 16, 227-229, 237, 240, 250, 337.

206. *Daily Telegraph,* London, January 26, 1959.

207. Desmond Crowley. *The Background to Current Affairs.* London, 1961, p. 196.

208. *Deutsche Woche,* August 10, 1960.

209. J. Scholmer. *Die Toten Kehren zurueck.* Koeln, 1954, p. 97.

210. *Bulletin des Presse-und Informationsdienstes der Bundesregierung.* Bonn, July 14, 1957.

211. *Blaetter,* Koeln, July 25, 1960.

212. *Nuernberger Nachrichten,* October 22, 1960.

213. *Blaetter,* Koeln, October 25, 1960.

214. *Geist und Zeit,* Darmstadt, 1959, Issue III.

215. *Deutsche Rundschau,* August, 1959.

216. *Schritt aus dem Nichts.* Frankfurt, 1951, p. 152.

217. *Meine Zeit.* Frankfurt, 1950, pp. 29-30.

218. *Die Entstehung des Doktor Faustus.* Amsterdam, 1949, pp. 62, 72, 101, 187.

219. *Doktor Faustus,* p. 730.

220. *The Listener,* London, March 10, 1960.

221. *Blaetter,* Koeln, September, 1959.

222. *Ibid.,* March, 1960.

223. *Ibid.,* March, 1960.

224. *Ibid.,* October, 1959.

225. *Ibid.,* August, 1962.

226. *Ibid.,* August, 1962 (quoted from *Gespraeche mit Hitler*).

227. *Ibid.,* August, 1962.

228. *Das Wagnis des Friedens.* Koeln, no year of publication given.

229. *Deutschland und die Weltpolitik,* p. 155.

230. *Deutsche Rundschau,* January, 1958.

231. *Ibid.,* August, 1958.

232. *Deutsche General-Felmarschaelle und ihr General-Geldmarschall.* 1953, p. 9.

233. *Mannheimer Hefte,* 1955, Issue III.

234. *Philosophie und Welt,* pp. 355, 384.

235. *Blaetter,* July, 1960.

236. *Geist und Zeit,* Stuttgart, 1959, Issue IV.

16
The Atrocities
Against the Jews

THE GERMANS HAVE NOT ONLY FORGOTTEN WHAT THEY DID TO POLES,
Czechs, and Russians; most of them have also forgotten, and
do not want to be reminded of, what they have done to the
Jews. They use, as Dr. Reitlinger has intimated by the title of
his second book, *The SS as Their "Alibi."*

As a matter of fact, it was not only the SS who committed
those crimes. Many high officials, state secretaries and under-
secretaries of state of the various ministries, and many professors prepared the atmosphere, many generals approved of the
murders and many professors and doctors took active part in
them. On earlier pages we have quoted what the Hitler professors and Hitler generals, such as Reichenau and Manstein, and
the Grand Admirals Raeder and Doenitz said against the Jews.
Here are a few more of such utterances. State Secretary Weizsaecker sent this telegram to Hitler's ambassador, Ludin, at

Pressburg on July 29, 1942: "It would surprise in Germany if the evacuation of the Jews would be stopped, the more so as the collaboration of the Slovaks in the Jewish problem has been very much appreciated here."[1] Councillor Dr. C. Zeitschel said: "The Jews can be transported to the East even during the war. We shall have no difficulties after the war as all the Jews in the [Polish] General Government could be transported in vehicles on the roads."[2] Councillor Rademacher, another "Aryan" hero, wrote about the result of his journey to Belgrade: "All male Jews will be shot by the end of this week. The rest (women and children) and 1,500 gypsies, the males of whom will also be shot, should be kept in the gypsy quarters."[3] Rademacher was reinstalled in the German Foreign Office after the war but honest people found him out and he was tried in 1952, the Foreign Office advising the judges to treat his case with discretion. He was sentenced—and disappeared with the help of Nazi friends. General Jodl sent the following telegram to the Foreign Office in 1943: "The deportation of the Jews will be executed by Himmler."[4] Colonel-General Salmuth called for Ohlendorf's SS to massacre Jews at Kodyma and sent 300 of his own soldiers to help them. Ambassador Benzler (Belgrade) said in a telegram to Ribbentrop on September 28, 1941: "The solution of the Jewish problem is at present the most important task. . . . General Boehme has asked me again and pressingly to deport the Jews as quickly as possible from this country."[5] The Polish-Jewish Professor Graubard, now living in West Germany, said in 1959: "I saw how the German Wehrmacht marched into Poland and what it did there. I saw how they entered the houses and threw the people out of their rooms. It cannot be said that such things would have been possible anywhere else. The German nation had lacked the courage since 1933 to say that their regime was criminal. We Jews had the courage to say there is something higher, there is a law that is more important than the will to survive. Without this law, life is not worth living. The Germans did not show that courage, probably because they did not feel bound by God's laws."[6] Many officers of the German army went to look at the execution of Jews as if it were a spectacle. General Helmut Stieff was the only laudable exception. He could not do anything against the barbarities of his fellow generals and fellow countrymen, but he said in one of his letters describing the crimes against the Jews: "This must, I am sure, be revenged on us, and rightly so."[7]

Prelate Hermann Maas, who visited Israel several times after the war, was deeply moved by "Rachel's weeping for the millions of her children slain by the heavy fist of hateful persecutors; she would not be comforted." In the face of almost every Jew he found "a hidden secret connected with the terrible fate of the Jews."[8] He looked into those faces and said to himself: "All these people are survivors who have escaped! All these should have been dead by now in accordance with the will of our leaders whom our nation has applauded enthusiastically for years. It is not our merit that these people are still alive. With the exception of a few, we have all collaborated, not resisted those terrible murders. Many of us were quite willing to throw millions of Jews into the hands of Adolf Hitler to satisfy his pleasure."[9]

And the Germans? There follows what decent Germans had to say about their countrymen after the war. Hermann Hesse: "What the Germans did to the Jews has no parallel in the modern history of any other nation in the world."[10] Prelate Romano Guardini: "How monstrous the events have been can be seen from the attitude of the Germans after the war. It is a matter of great alarm how little our people thinks about what has happened. How can they go on living as if all this had not happened?"[11] Stefan Andres, a Catholic writer: "The number of those who see in the devilish attempt to exterminate a whole nation not an evil deed but the act of a politicial genius is great and steadily growing."[12] Professor Michael Freund: "The reaction of the Germans towards the atrocities of the Third Reich is not at all neurotic. It is awfully 'healthy,' and the good conscience of Germany is at times uncanny."[13] About those of their compatriots who returned from Russia in 1956, however, the Germans say: "Those who have escaped from that hell will not forget the horrors till the end of their days."[14]

They are so occupied with what was done to them that they have no time to spare for a thought for their victims. Some 40,000 Nazi torturers and murderers are still at large in Germany, living under assumed names, but no serious attempt has ever been made to find them out and bring them before judges. Nor have any of the thousands of engineers who built the railroads in Auschwitz or the scientists who devised the gas chambers and incinerators been brought before a court. "The murderers are among us," wrote the *Deutsche Rundschau,* "executioners and criminals have exchanged their brown and black uniforms for the distinguished civilian clothes of honourable men who deserve a pension."[15]

The Germans simply refuse to be bothered. When a decent German showed the *Night and Fog* film on German television, he received many letters of protest like this: "Are the Jews innocent of the things that happened? What about the crimes the Jews have committed during the last two thousand years?" And: "We who have a good conscience want to be left alone." One German wrote that he agreed with the showing of the film on television and said so publicly, but was "afraid of being lynched."[16] When Dr. Rudolf Pechel dealt with the reappearance of National Socialism and anti-Semitism in Germany he received letters like this: "Herr Pechel! Cursed hireling of the Jews! Old snout, get out. Our patience is exhausted." And: "We shall settle our account with you in due course." And: "What you are doing is well-poisoning." And: "Are you perhaps a Jew? Then everything is understandable." And: "I am for historical justice and just therefore I cannot pity the Jews."[17] Official sources—the *Bundesamt für Verfassungsschutz*—registered 389 anti-Semitic and National Socialist outrages in 1961 alone.[18]

The Catholic writer, Michael Müller-Claudius, after the war

told the story of how the burghers of Regensburg in days gone by rescued the Jews from the persecution by the anti-Semitic nobleman Rindfleisch and his imitation SS and passed this resolution: "The inhabitants of Regensburg who want to save the honour of their town herewith forbid to persecute or kill Jews without a judgment of the Court."[19] Nothing of this sort happened in any German town during the Third Reich. But in Holland and Denmark many Jews were rescued by their Christian friends, who gave them shelter and food while Hitler's Danish Lord-Lieutenant, Dr. Best, told the SS that Germany was eliminating the Jews and abolishing the wrong ideas of democracy and liberalism at the same time (he, too, is a free man in post-war Germany). A group of Danes, after the Nazis had murdered a number of Jews on the Jewish New Year, organized the rescue of the Danish Jews and secretly transported them to Sweden. The head of this organization says that he and his friends did it in the sense of these two lines by Schiller:

And deep be the stake, as the prize is high—
Who life would win, he must dare to die![20]

Dr. Ernst Mayer, Professor Jaspers's brother-in-law, lived with his family for three years, "cared for by the humanity and sacrificial courage of a Dutch lady, Maria van Boven and a group of Dutch resistance fighters." In that house he wrote *Dialectics of Non-Knowledge*.[21] A courageous Dutch woman, Mrs. Wijsmuller, saved thousands of Jewish children from Nazi persecution; she also helped Jews to escape to Spain.[22] Patriarch Kiril, the head of the Orthodox Church in Bulgaria, saved hundreds of Jews during the Nazi era. When he visited Israel in 1962 he was greeted by many Jews and by Rabbi Kahane, Director-General of the Ministry of Religious Affairs. He visited Yad Vashem and lit a memorial light at the shrine in memory of the six million dead.[23] The French Abbé Fournier risked his life in helping Jews and Frenchmen to escape to Switzerland from occupied France.[24]

A few Germans in Germany and the occupied countries acted like those heroes, for instance the Catholic Oskar Schindler in Moravia, who rescued more than 1,100 Jews and sacrificed for their sustenance 95 per cent of his wealth. Provost Bernard Lichtenberg said to his Berlin community: "Do not be misled by un-Christian feelings but act in accordance with the strict commandment of Christ: Love thy neighbour as thyself."[25] He died in Dachau. But, as a whole, neither Roman Catholic nor Lutheran Church ever protested against the persecution of the Jews by the Nazis. So devout a writer as Reinhold Schneider said after the war: "On the day when the synagogues were burnt the Church should have sisterly stood by the Synagogue. It is of decisive importance that it failed to do so."[26]

The Austrian writer Franz Theodor Csokor, who, although an "Aryan," left Austria when Hitler entered, after many adventures got to Yugoslavia. There he heard the story of a Jewish hawker who had, shortly before Hitler's attack, been murdered by the son of the mayor of Borodin. The inhabitants of that village decided therefore to fast (in the Greek Orthodox manner) for two months. After that all the councillors of the village went to confession and communion, and collected a sum to be distributed among the poor of the district. "Where," asks Csokor, "is that place where the life of a Jewish hawker is still valued so highly? That place where it was still felt that guilt is as common as life and death?"[27] The writer Friedrich Sieburg wrote in the spring of 1959: "The knowledge of history is rapidly declining in Western Germany." The Jews realized "that our memory is getting worse and the story of their recent sufferings begins to lose the sharp outlines which ought to be preserved, if only for the sake of the moral order of things. . . . The Germans have decided to have no past."[28] Yet another German, Paul Schallueck, a writer of the young generation, quoted the words of a French professor, who explained that in the phrase *"la tuechtigkeit allemande"* the German word *tuechtig-*

keit was untranslatable, that it meant an efficiency lacking in all grace, all moderation, all joy of life, allowing of no amiability, of no time to think of the past. "A large majority of the nation—with the conscious or unconscious help of politicians, teachers and clergymen—has forgotten everything that happened between 1933 and 1945." Signs of shame and remorse have been replaced by indolence of heart, self-conceited thoughtlessness, thoughts of success and comfort. People who have somehow managed to escape the hangman are cold-shouldered again, anti-Semitism becomes more and more insolent, while the churches, universities, and schools are not doing nearly enough against it. The provincial press, read by the majority of the nation, avoids mentioning the past; the same is the case with the illustrated periodicals. A good many nationalistic and neo-National Socialist newspapers and periodicals are full of anti-Semitic statements, and their editors are "still riding against the East." Most films present heroes who are fatalistic, evade personal responsibility, and resign before the authorities of state and family. "Anonymous powers are responsible for everything." These films suggest to the public that the solution of political problems is something beyond their control. They never deal with the National Socialist past, with German anti-Semitism, with the concentration camps. "The murderers are amongst us," said Schallueck. "I do not feel at all happy in our West German present."[29]

In a novel, Schallueck makes a former Nazi say to the son of a murdered decent German that nobody cared any longer about any German's past "now that so many Nazis are back in ministries and offices." That former Nazi had once called the murdered German "a sinister democrat" and "a cultural Bolshevist," and had spoken enthusiastically of a Europe "pacified under German hegemony." Today he speaks of "a Western community" and is proud of the German "economic miracle which nobody can imitate." Schallueck also portrays some of the reinstated Nazi teachers who once made their pupils translate *Mein Kampf* into Caesar's clean Latin and spoke contemptuously of "the Ostic-Baltic races of Russia." Today they say that "the old stories" of the Third Reich must not be mentioned again. When an honest teacher, son of a murdered decent German, tries to tell his pupils "the old stories," the headmaster rebukes him:

"If I think it right not to give any exact figures, only to speak of some hundreds of thousands, I find it very annoying that you insist on six millions."

"But, Sir, it was six millions, six million Jews alone, not to mention the others."

"Dear colleague, why do you make your position in our school still more difficult with such trifles?"[30]

In the spring of 1956 a German visited the Belsen memorial in the company of two German boys, war orphans, one fifteen, the other thirteen. He did not tell them anything and let them find out the truth for themselves. They began to read the inscription, and suddenly the older boy turned around terrified and said:

"Thirty thousand dead! All murdered! And all this was done by the Russians? When did it happen?"

"What makes you think of the Russians? How did this occur to you?"

"Well, all these evil and cruel things are done by the Russians. Are they not?"

Then the old German told them who had done these things. The boys were shattered: "Germans like you, like our father? Is this possible?"

They were advised: "Remember this and tell it to your school colleagues. Ask your teachers to tell you more about it!"[31]

When the German professor Rudolf R. Degwitz, who had been abroad for some time, returned to Germany, he was forced to admit that "the majority of school children know nothing of the extermination of the Jews, the concentration camps, the Gestapo, and the world war started by Hitler in a criminal manner." The parents complained when some teachers tried to tell their pupils the truth. They again think, says Professor Degwitz, that it is their "national duty" never to admit what the nation has done, just as they have persuaded themselves after the first war that "we have not been beaten in the field" and that "traitors have stabbed the victorious army in the back."[32]

In a much used German textbook of history "the old stories" were treated as follows. In the edition of 1949, 41 pages were devoted to the history of the Third Reich—two and a half to the burning of the Reichstag, three to the persecution of the Jews, five to concentration camps, two to the persecution of religion. In the edition of 1958 only 13 pages were devoted to the Third Reich, only 14 lines to the persecution of the Jews, only four and a half lines to the persecution of religion; the burning of the Reichstag and the concentration camps were not mentioned at all.

The trade unions complain that most textbooks "promote nationalism. The same facts which in the case of foreign countries are exposed as imperialism and injustice are, in the case of Germany, represented as self-evident action to safeguard legitimate interests." They also complain of the lack of any correct account of the way the Poles were treated by Nazi Germany; Poles are never stated to have been expelled but "evacuated" or "re-settled. . . . How is the young German to know what's what if he is not told about the cause of Germany's present condition?" The presentation of the extermination of the Jews is "truly humiliating." The line generally taken by so-called historians, namely that "only few Germans knew of those atrocities," is refuted as a "barefaced lie." Did not the Nuremberg Laws, the 1938 pogrom, the Yellow Badge make "perfectly obvious to all Germans that the Jews were treated like outcasts. . . . As long as we call Hitlerism a result of Versailles we deceive the young generation and distort the causes of two German catastrophes. Something is foul in our state and in our nation. This must be said so that the youth may not repeat the old errors. This is the main duty of our new history books. But most of them fail in this respect. It is an established fact that the authoritarian state lasted longer in Germany than in any other Western state." The chance which 1848 gave the Germans was missed. A large part of the political intelligentsia emigrated in 1849, as they did in 1933. But the textbooks tell the youth nothing of all this. Nor do they tell anything of the policy of the generals and the extravagant Pan-German war aims, of the terrible peace treaty of Brest, of the nationalism after 1918, or of Hindenburg, who congratulated Hitler after the massacre of June 30, 1933. The textbooks also fail to mention that there was an economic crisis in the late 1920's in Great Britain, France, and the United States, too, but that only Germany produced a Hitler whom Hugenberg and other nationalists helped into the saddle.[33]

Professor Albert Jan Rasker, who teaches Christian ethics at Leiden University, wrote in 1962: "Germany could already in 1918 and, more especially, after 1945 have grasped her chance to become a region of coexistence and mutual understanding between East and West. But she failed to realise this mission. German unity lasted a hundred years, but the unity of the German power state was a German dream and a European nightmare. Again the world sees a Germany which clamours for the unity of such power. What is most depressing is that the Germans make the others, always the others, responsible for the division of Germany. Nobody says with candour: We ourselves have caused all this by our self-chosen and—thank heaven—lost war. Who knows, who wants to know, that they have despised the freedom, the human existence of the nations of the East and tried to exterminate them? Why do they say on all good and bad occasions that only a few Germans took part in the crimes of Hitler? The other nations ask with astonishment how such a great and such a gifted nation could have been seduced by a few criminals. Would it not be better and more honest as well as more reassuring if they confessed: Not only Hitler and his paladines, but my nation, we all have done all this? They talk again of German honour, German power, German self-assertion. As long as German unity lasted it was a German dream and a European nightmare."[34]

When President Luebke said to the young generation that Germany must show the world "that we shall never put up with the dismemberment of our country," he received this answer from a sensible young German: "We are sorry that the President did not tell the youth how and why this 'dismemberment' came about. We are sorry that the youth is told nothing of the Weimar republic and Hitler's millennium."[35] Schoolboys give such answers today: "Hitler promised the unemployed work, so most of them followed him." "Hitler ordered *Autobahnen* to be built which was a good thing." "Hitler was afraid that the Jews might become too powerful. They also had most of the money."[36] One student, visiting Belsen, said: "My father was a Nazi, and when I asked whether he knew of the mass murder of the Jews, he said: No. But can I believe him?" Another student said: "Our parents and teachers evade the issue when we ask them whether they knew anything and why they did nothing against it."[37] Other students said: "Eleven years after Germany's defeat, seventeen years after September 1, 1939, twenty-three years after January 30, 1933, German boys and girls know hardly anything of these dates. Most grown-ups refuse to hear anything about these dates. The conscience of the German people does not keep pace with the new big buildings and the frigidaires, with television and football world championships. Nor did it keep pace with the story of 1933-1945, the twelve blackest years in German history, worse than the Thirty Years' War, worse than the years of plague and famine."[38]

A speaker on the Bavarian radio complained in 1955: "Just as the German Blitz victories filled the world once with astonishment, the German economic mirade is today admired everywhere."[39] A few months later he said: "One should watch what our teachers tell their pupils about the German past and present, what the newspapers and the radio tell us—and what they do not tell us."[40] It is, therefore, not surprising that pupils say things like these: "It is not true that five million Jews were burnt. It was only a few hundred thousands. The Jews behaved in such a way that they have only themselves to blame for their fate."[41] "My history teacher told us that Hitler was a genuine leader, and my math teacher told me that Hitler would have lead us to greatness but for such traitors as the Scholls. My father also said that the Jews governed Germany before 1933. Whom can I believe?"[42]

A decent German wrote in 1958: "People do not go to lectures about National Socialism, books dealing with it remain unread."[43] Dr. Rudolf Pechel wrote in 1959: "If you make inquiries you learn again and again that pupils both of grammar and high schools know almost nothing of the past."[44] Professor Franz Boehm complained: "We professors heard from students that they never succeeded in finding out in schools or in their parents' houses what happened in the Third Reich. 'We have' they said, 'the impression that the entire older generation consists of cowards.' Of course, many of the teachers belong to the class of cowards."[45] Young Israelis who visited West Germany left disappointed because the Jewish question occupied only the minds of a small group of active Germans, while the rest had "suppressed" the past and the fate of the European Jews."[46]

A German Jew who returned to Germany for a short while wrote in a German newspaper: "It is remarkable how little the young generation knows of the relation of the past to the problems of the present. . . . I missed any real discussion among the young generation." How different, he says, are American students, "who sit around the lecturer and torment him with their questions." A young politician told him: "The powers of reaction are about to occupy the hills, while we are standing in the valley."[47] A German student at Munich University wrote in a letter addressed to the older generation on May 20, 1960: "You have systematically stultified the youth by the mirage of the economic miracle. We ask ourselves who had helped Hitler into the saddle, if you have all been against him from the very beginning."[48] Roman Catholic Bishop Walter Kampe gave the answer: "There are many hot irons which nobody dares to touch. The main difficulty of our resistance against the Nazi influence lies in the fact that our nation has not conquered National Socialism spiritually. Our nation did not reject Hitlerism because it recognised its moral baseness, but only because of the catastrophic consequences it brought with it."[49]

After having preached the collective guilt of the Jews for more than a hundred years, after having hailed Hitler, who preached the collective guilt of the Jews in *Mein Kampf,* and after having shouted "Germany awake—perish Judah" and "Tremble, ye nation of Mazzoth devourers, the night of the long knives draweth near" for fifteen years before and after Hitler's accession to power, the Germans repeat more and more frequently: "We knew nothing." This has been refuted by the judges who tried the criminal German jurists. They drew attention to the fact that a large part of German Jewry was transported to the East, that millions disappeared from Germany and the occupied countries without leaving any trace behind them, that the thousands of German soldiers and Gestapo and SS men who took part in those deportations returned home from time to time. Was it possible that none of them ever whispered a thing into the ears of the Germans? Did not Hitler say in the Reichstag in 1938 that he would exterminate European Jewry? The Germans do not even listen to Michael Müller-Claudius, who reminded them that Hitler had said "Conscience is a Jewish invention," and had preached "the deliverance from the Jews" and would, without his anti-Semitism, "never have got his seventeen million votes in 1933." He asks himself why racial anti-Semitism "could have become so uniquely powerful in our country" and gives this answer: "Unlike the Western democracies, the Germans have never severed their ties with the idea of an autocratic state," they got stuck "in autocratic and militaristic feelings," the inherited idea of their state was regarded by them as "an unchangeable racial substance." So when a democratic state was established in 1918 it seemed to most Germans a betrayal by "seducers of an alien race." Hitler saw in democracy and parliamentarism an instrument of that race which, because of its secret aims, had to fear the sun. Only the Jews, he said, can praise an institution which is as dirty and deceitful as they are themselves."[50] Müller-Claudius tells the Germans that they were killed and driven out from the East in 1945 "only because they were Germans," as the Jews had been driven out and murdered by their compatriots "only because they were Jews."[51]

They knew nothing? Here are a number of unmistakable utterances of their leaders between 1929 and 1943 proving that of all their lies this is the greatest.

Streicher in 1925: "Make a start today so that we can exterminate the Jews."

Streicher in 1934: "For fourteen years we have been shouting into the German lands: German people, recognise your true enemy! It fell to our movement to unmask the Jews as mass murderers. The Jews are carriers of illnesses who, in the interest of mankind, must be destroyed." After fifty years the graves of the Jews would "show that this nation of murderers and criminals has at last met its well-deserved fate."[53]

Göring in 1938: "If the Reich should be involved in a conflict with foreign nations in the near future, then it is self-understood that we shall first settle our account with the Jews in Germany."[54]

Hitler in the Reichstag on January 30, 1939: "If international financial World-Jewry within the borders of Europe or outside should succeed in plunging the nation into another world war, the result will not be the Bolshevisation of the earth and the victory of the Jews but the extermination of the Jewish race in Europe."[55]

In 1942 Hitler reminded the Germans of his speech of January 30, 1939, and added: "The hour will come when the most evil enemy of the world will play his last card for a thousand years at last."[56]

Streicher in 1943: "Now, in the fourth year of this war, World Jewry begins to realise that the fate of the Jews is being solved by German National Socialism."[57]

In a pamphlet circulated in 1944 we read: "The Jews destroy every national order of life. Jewry aims at world domination. The Jews contaminate the life of the nations among which they live. The Jew destroys the national [völkische] order of all communities with the help of freemasonry, revolutions, democracy and parliamentarism. The Jew poisons all national culture, he undermines morality. The criminal nature of the Jew destroys justice and law. The Jew is the originator of the present war."[58]

The judges at Nuremberg said about Hitler's threats against the Jews that they were no empty words, and that nobody who knew Hitler's speeches and remembered the violent methods he adopted against real or imaginary adversaries had reason to think that they were mere rhetoric. SS-General Erich von dem Bach-Zelewski said at Nuremberg that an explosion of this kind was bound to come "if one has preached for years, for decades that the Slavs are an inferior race and that the Jews are no human beings at all."[59] Hitler had already read in H. S. Chamberlain's, his teacher's, *Foundations of the Nineteenth Century* that the Jews had been the greatest misfortune of world history, while the Germans were its greatest blessing. Full of enthusiasm, Chamberlain saw in his fantasy those Germanic "barbarians who were most happy when going stark naked into battle," those "savages" who were the legitimate heirs of antiquity. "I was high time that the saviour appeared. We can only regret today that the German has not more thoroughly exterminated wherever his victorious arm reached."[60] Hitler acted in accordance with the advice of his teacher not only against Jews but also against Czechs, Poles, Russians. When Eichmann boasted to his colleague, SS-Hauptsturmbannführer Dieter Wisliceny, that he would laughingly jump into his grave, because he was exceedingly satisfied to have five million men on his conscience, Wisliceny answered: "May God give our enemies no opportunity to do the same to the German nation."[61] The world knows what happened in 1945.

"Why did we not know anything?" Professor Helmut Gollwitzer asked his countrymen. "Were we not able or not willing to know?"[62] He added that they had done nothing against it while it happened. "Even the little that everyone knew should have sufficed to arouse such a wave of revolt in the whole nation that the régime would have been forced to change or disappear. Fifteen centuries of Christian preaching did not result in a protective wall being built around the persecuted Jews by devout Christians." Far from it; this régime, "the most bestial of modern times," was hailed by a vast majority of Germans seduced by "the phrase of the *Herrenvolk*" who were "not loath to build the happiness of our nation on the tears of even one Jewish child." Therefore Professor Gollwitzer told them what they do not want to hear: that they must remember 1933 whenever they think of the events of 1945.[63] Professor Jaspers told them: "It is our guilt that we are alive. We are responsible before history for the misdeeds of the régime which we allowed to get to the top."[64] He also said: "All those who once criticised the Jews and did not speak of them with the deep respect which they deserve because of their historical greatness, their tragedy and the great number of noble Jews—are guilty today."[65] Pastor Niemoeller told them: "The excuse 'I did not know' is untrue with any grown-up person."[66] He blamed the Church for the six million murdered Jews because it did not unmistakably protest against the anti-Semitism of the Hitler régime. Ex-pastor Albert Goes makes a German say in a moving short story set in the time of Hitler: "One must not know everything,"—whereupon his wife runs out and into the church of St. Peter's which still stood. "I remained at the entrance for a moment and listened to the singing, and knew already what would come, and it really came six years later."[67] Professor Theodor Litt wrote: "The Germans could have foreseen the terrible crescendo of the devilish crimes against the Jews if they had only wanted to see it. But far too many did not want to see it. In everything Hitler said and wrote glowed a hatred of Jews which was never satisfied by its furious invectives."[68]

But it is all in vain. Everything said by decent, God-fearing men falls flat. The writer Friedrich von Reck-Malleczewen, who was murdered by the Nazis, foresaw this in 1944 when he exclaimed: "You miserable German nation, you are about to deny the hour of self-communion, and to forget that only self-communion gives you the ultimate key to your future."[69] In 1942 he entered in his secret diary: "Oh shame, oh life without honour, oh thin crust which divides us from the inner kernel of the earth where the dark fires of Satan burn! Satan has got loose and the Lord has given him much power!" In 1944: "I never saw Germany so degenerated. Even the Communist rule in Munich [in 1919] was exemplary if compared with what Herr Hitler will behind him."[70]

Anti-Semitism is not dead in Germany; it smoulders everywhere beneath the surface. Again and again, more than a hundred times since 1945, Jewish cemeteries have been desecrated, again and again Germans assert that the Jews and other victims of the Third Reich have grown fat in the concentration camps and that not enough Jews have been gassed. Peter Stonier, who worked for eight months in one of Germany's biggest steel plants, tells this story. Two hundred and fifty tons of steel were slowly cooking at a temperature of around 3,000° F. When the command was given, "*Achtung!* Furnace No. 5 will be tapped in four minutes' time," a 55-year-old refugee from East Germany shouted to him: "If I had my way, furnace No. 5 would be full of bloody Jews and not with H.S.B. steel just about now." The others laughed their appreciation. "To me the lingering, smouldering hate for the Jews that is still in Germany is not an object of fun." Another day, when travelling by car from Hanover to the Ruhr, Stonier heard these words from his driver, an engineer: "So the Jews are pulling out for good. The rats are leaving the sinking ship. Now, perhaps, we shall be able to see who has been gnawing the holes in the hull."[71] And so it will no doubt go on.

The representatives of the German Jews declared early in 1959: "The Board of Jews in Germany observes with growing concern the development of German affairs expressing itself in anti-Semitism. The return of former National Socialists to key positions in the Government has, no doubt, contributed to it. It is a tragedy that we are forced to utter serious warnings fourteen years after the collapse of a totalitarian régime which has brought Germany and Europe to the brink of destruction."[72] J. J. Baschinski, a Jew living in Germany, wrote in the spring of 1959: "The so-called collective shame has only remained an empty phrase. Popular rather is the sentence: 'Not enough Jews have been gassed.' Some say: 'Never again'; but the older generation remembers a similar 'Never again' after the First World War. It had no effect and did not prevent the Second World War. The warners were sent to concentration camps and were bestially murdered or ended their lives in gas chambers."[73] How right he was! From 1954 to 1959 many Jewish churchyards and synagogues were desecrated and many Nazis were punished for anti-Semitic utterances. When Jewish cemeteries were desecrated in 1957, a German wrote: "There is either an ineradicable criminal inclination in the German nation, unknown among other nations, or our police have been infiltrated by former Nazis who lack the energy to prevent and combat these crimes."[74] How right Baschinski was was proved on Christmas Eve, 1959, when the walls of Cologne Synagogue were smeared in red and black paint with the words "Germans, we demand—Jews get out." Within a few days of this shameful crime, similar incidents occurred in some fifty other places of West Germany; swastikas were painted on park benches, fences, trees, lampposts and barn doors. Some Jews received letters that they would be liquidated. When the German authorities pretended to be surprised by these happenings, Rudolf Pechel, editor of the *Deutsche Rundschau,* took them to task and reminded them of the warnings by the Bavarian radio about the "Renazification of the Federal Republic," the warnings of the monthly publications *Enemies of Democracy,* the warnings in *La Voix de la Resistance* (Paris), *La Voix Internationale de la Resistance* (Brussels), *Bulletin of the Wiener Library,* and *Bulletin on German Questions* (London). Pechel also reminded them of his own warnings since 1953, when he had said: "You have underrated the Nazis before they came. You must on no account underrate them now. They are everywhere, in Government and municipal offices, in the political parties, in the press, in publishing houses."[75] The Roman Catholic writer Stefan Andres wrote: "The Churches have never declared heretical racial hatred which was directed against the First Commandment. After our collapse, the Churches opened their gates widely for those who have hailed the Howling Monkey without ever asking for something like penance and an adequate period of probation. The map of the German soul is a *terra incognita* and therefore it has a good conscience. Now that the vermins come out of their hiding places, you cry: Communism. Many prominent fighters, collaborators and fellow travellers of the blessed Fuehrer are back again in the highest places."[76]

What things are really like in post-war Germany can best be judged after a closer look at how Nazi victims have been compensated. One of the very few decent German newspapers published an article, "If Anne Frank Were Still Alive Today," describing how many forms she would have to fill out and how many oaths she would have to swear before she could submit her case to the restitution authorities. "How good," she says, "that I died in Bergen-Belsen. So at least my diary remains. The story of dead Anne Frank is believed even without an oath."[77]

One day in 1958, Herr Fritz Schaeffer, then German Minister of Finance, announced that the compensation of the Jews was endangering the value of the German mark, and found immediate support from unteachable Germans. Even a German pastor said: "Once the Jews had fewer rights than the Aryans. Today an unfortunate indemnification has turned right into its opposite."[78] The facts are these: in 1958 Jews got 945,000,000 marks, German war victims 3,945,000,000,000 marks, and pensioned-off Nazis 1,371,000,000,000 marks. Among the latter were 15 former State Secretaries, 7 presidents of Hitler's highest courts, 67 ambassadors and high-ranking ministry officials, 245 ministers resident, 777 high-ranking ministry officials, 1,551 Hitler generals. Dr. Nehemiah Robinson wrote: "West German restitution to Jewish victims of Nazism is a small fraction of the actual loss suffered by European Jews in property, assets, and income. The total loss is placed at $27,000 million at values applicable during the time of despoilation, but worth, at today's levels, between $40,000 million and $50,000 million. The value of restituted property and payments in reparations, restitution and compensation, principally by West Germany, is about $6,000 million."[79] Paul Schallueck, that very decent post-war German writer said: "The muddled anti-Semitic brains regard the sums of restitution to the Jews in Germany, Israel and other countries as immeasurable, as unjust, as blood-sucking."[80] The German-Jewish writer Hermann Kesten wrote: "The Germans are still hating the Jews more than the Nazis. A great part of the population prefers to pay a rent to an SS general than to a Jew or a concentration camp victim. The Nazi murderers, as far they were not hanged by the allies, they give a hundred times more. Almost the whole population listens humbly to a general, a minister, an industrialist rather than to a writer, a professor, a moralist."[81]

Here are a few examples. Field-Marshal Manstein, sentenced as a war criminal (in an order he had spoken of the just retribution meted out to the Jews), receives a monthly pension of 1,281 marks. Manstein, however, refused to take part in the plot against Hitler, and in 1944 looked, like Guderian, for an estate in Silesia or Pomerania, which he intended to buy with the money with which Hitler had presented him. Today he is praised as "one of the best brains of the former German General Staff";[82] and when the post-war Germany army was reorganized, it was no other than Manstein who was asked for his expert advice. A room in the new defense ministry was put at his disposal and an active major acted as his aide-de-camp. When honest Germans protested, the very characteristic answer given by the ministry officials was that, according to an old Prussian tradition, a Field-Marshal always remained a Field-Marshal—even if convicted for war crimes.

General Admiral Raeder, on release from prison, got 7,000 marks as "indemnification for late homecomers," and now receives a monthly pension of 1,600 marks. In his unrepenting autobiography he calls Hindenburg "one of the greatest men of our age" and asserts that Hitler wanted peace with Great Britain. He regarded him as "an extraordinary man, capable of leading a nation."[83] He now asserts that he had always been "only a soldier," and compares himself to Admiral Lord Cunningham: "He fought for his country, I for mine."[84]

General-Admiral Doenitz, too, after his release got 7,500 marks as "indemnification for late homecomers" and receives a monthly pension of 1,300 marks. A decent German protested against this shameful act in these words: "What will be more remunerative after the next war—to be a victim of fascism or a victim of anti-fascism? What pension does a man get who has lost his eyesight in the service of the Führer? What did a school-teacher, a country doctor, an artist, a scientist earn in Doenitz's glorious days, and what pension may they get today?"[85] In his glorious days Doenitz spoke of Jewish poison and was furious about "the criminal plot against our beloved Führer who was rescued by divine providence."[86] Shortly before July 20, 1944, Doenitz had pronounced: "Within a year at the latest, perhaps even this year, Europe will recognise that Adolf Hitler is the only European statesman with a great personality."[87] On May 1, 1945, he addressed the Germans with these words: "German men and women! Soldiers of the German Wehrmacht! Our Führer Adolf Hitler is dead. The German nation bowes its heads in deep distress and awe. Hitler's heroic death in the capital of the German Reich ends a life of fight and an unerringly just road."[88]

Field-Marshal Erhard Milch, Göring's deputy, who took an active part in forced labor, receives a monthly pension of 1,300 marks. The widows of Roland Freisler, President of the People's Court, and butcher Heydrich each receive 1,000 marks monthly. "Heydrich," the judge said, "was killed on active service."[89] When Minister Oberlaender was forced to resign at last, he was awarded a monthly pension of 3,000 marks. "Once again," a decent German commented, "the German politicians have proved that they have no feeling for moral values in political life."[90] State Secretary Professor Franz Schlegelberger, author of a Nazi law for the treatment of Poles and Jews and of the Night-and-Fog Order, sentenced to imprisonment for life for his war crimes and prematurely released after five years, was awarded a monthly pension 2,849 marks only eight weeks after his release. After eight years the courageous Minister of Finance of Schleswig-Holstein stopped Schlegelberger's pension. But this Nazi appealed to the law courts, and he found a judge who said that Schlegelberger did not know that he was doing anything wrong when he delivered a 74-year-old Jew to the Gestapo for execution, and gave him back his full pension. "Justice in Schleswig-Holstein,"[91] a decent German Catholic wrote, and another decent German ironically reminded his readers of what the Prime Minister of Schleswig-Holstein, Kai-Uwe von Hassel, had said on December 14, 1959: "We have endeavored to win friends abroad, as we are the most hated nation in the world. If we look at our Schleswig-Holstein, we must say that we have regained our political stability, our political peace."[92]

Dr. Kurt Matthaei, chief of the National Socialist police in Schaumburg-Lippe, receives a monthly pension of 795 marks, Erich Stolleis, Lord Mayor of Ludwigshafen, 900 marks, Dr. Hans Wildgassen, Lord Mayor of Osnabruck, 950 marks. Under the heading of "compensation," these heroes of the Third Reich received high sums: Anton, Police Counsellor of Lubeck, 14,100 marks; Budde, Mayor of Bielefeld, 21,000 marks; Otto Hellmuth, *gauleiter* of Lower Franconia, 5,600 marks; Rudolf Jordan, *gauleiter* of Saxony-Anhalt, 6,000 marks; Anto Kaessler, SS Colonel and commandant of the concentration camp Sachsenhausen, 6,000 marks; Dr. Pagenkopf, Lord Mayor of Dortmund, 42,000 marks; Dr. Plaza, SS doctor in Buchenwald, accused of mass murder by Professor Kogon, an inmate of the camps, 4,000 marks; Eggert Reeder, SS group leader, responsible for deportations in Belgium, 26,000 marks; Walter Schroeder, president of the police in Lubeck, 65,000 marks. Dr. Ernst Lautz, former Public Prosecutor at the People's Court and responsible for the death of Goerdeler, Field-Marshal Erich von Witzleben, and many other decent Germans, received until recently a monthly pension of 1,692 marks. Many protests were raised against this shameful state of affairs and in the end his pension was reduced by half. Devout Germans pointed out that he still receives more than the victims of the Hitler régime. The highest pension for such a victim is 600 marks a month. Dr. Erich Gritzbach, SS Oberführer and author of a book on Göring, receives a monthly pension of 1,293 marks. Professor Dr. E. Meier said long ago, with a view to these scandals: "National Socialism has lost the war but it is just about to win the peace."[93] Many widows and sons of executed resistance fighters get monthly pensions of only 250 marks.

None of the survivors of Jewish victims of the Nazis gets an indemnification nearly as high as the pensions of the heroes of the Hitler régime. A German Jew who survived Hitler complained that he was too young, only fifty, to reckon on a speedy settlement of his indemnification case, while Dr. Marin Hellinger, sentenced as a war criminal by a British Court in 1947, received 10,000 marks "indemnification for his imprisonment" only three months after his premature release.[94] SS officer Hans Eisele, a doctor in Buchenwald, was sentenced to death by an American court after the war and released after seven years. He received 4,000 marks "indemnification" from the German authorities and a loan of 25,000 marks free of interest. A speaker on the Bavarian radio said long ago: "The persecutors have been provided for sooner than the persecuted, the executioners sooner than the survivors of the hanged."[95] These words were used as a caption to two pictures showing the shooting site at Auschwitz and a mass grave of naked corpses. Austria, mistakenly declared by the Allies the first victim of Nazi aggression in spite of the fact that about half of its population had clamored for Hitler and hailed him when he overran their country, refuses to pay any compensation to Jewish victims. She has only set aside a comparatively small sum from which elderly people in bad health are to benefit. When the Austrian Foreign Secretary,

Bruno Kreisky, defended the rights of the Austrian minority in South Tyrol, Dr. F. L. Brassloff, an ex-Austrian refugee living in Great Britain, retorted: "One wonders whether Austria has the moral right to pose as a defender of human rights and dignity as long as she fails to honour her obligation to recompense the surviving victims of Nazi persecution in and from Austria for their suffering and losses."[96]

Dr. C. I. Kapralik, a former Austrian, complained about the legal Western fiction that Austria had not been a willing tool of Hitlerism but a victim of its aggression. "Our greatest difficulty has been that neither the Germans nor the Austrians will accept responsibility for what had been done to the Jews in Austria."[97]

The Germans, who, during six terrible years, looted and starved the whole of Europe, have been clamoring for a long time for the return of their confiscated assets in the United States, and, as usual, the loudest voices are those of Germans who once praised Hitler. The United States has already taken steps to comply with the German wishes, although the Germans still refuse to compensate non-German victims of the Nazis, those hundreds of thousands of Danes, Norwegians, Dutchmen, etc., whose lives were broken in concentration camps. Great Britain and France, in common with nine other nations, have repeatedly urged the German government to compensate all victims, Jewish or not, but nothing has happened so far. France claims compensation for 180,000 Frenchmen deported to concentration camps. Representatives of the British Jews have urged the German government many times to compensate the Jews who had been forced to flee Austria when Hitler invaded that country, but in vain. However, when Professor Heuss went to Great Britain in 1958 he boasted that Germany did all she could to compensate all victims. On February 10, 1960, Mr. B. Janner, M.P., reminded the Secretary of State for Foreign Affairs of the eleven-Power démarche and asked him to tell the

West German Government "that all persons who are British subjects at present and who have been persecuted and have suffered in consequence of Nazi victimisation at any time and in any place should be included within an agreement as to provide for compensation if they are not receiving compensation under the German compensation law."[98] Nothing has been heard of it since. In September, 1961, Anselm Reiss, President of the World Federation of Polish Jews, said at a meeting of the Association of Jews of Polish Origin in Great Britain: "We do not envy those Jews who have benefited from German restitution and compensation. But we regard it as our obligation to raise our voice in protest against the unparalleled inequity committed against the Jews in Eastern Europe, who were deprived of the right of compensation."[99]

Most unfortunately, the West, too, seems to have forgotten everything. The American professor, Herbert Muller, said that "German historians are fond of talking of the lusty original genius of the Teutonic peoples and their potentially splendid culture." Germany "has failed catastrophically in two attempts to dominate the continent. . . . American leaders seem to have forgotten the millions slaughtered by Germany in the last war."[100] Philip Toynbee complained at the end of 1957: "Hardly anybody nowadays seems to talk anymore about the extermination of the European Jews, except perhaps in Israel."[101] And Storm Jameson, the novelist, said in 1960: "The memory of the concentration camps and the gas ovens is fading. Unconsciously or consciously, we are beginning to think of these things as an aberration. . . . They were no accident, no passing aberration, but the wilful act of men who knew what they were doing."[102] Mr. John Alldridge protested against this forgetfulness by reminding us of Hitler's words: "A stronger race will drive out the weaker ones, for the vital urge in its ultimate form will break down the absurd barriers of the so-called humanity of individuals to make way for the humanity of

Nature, which destroys the weak to give their place to the strong." He also reminded us of the oath of the Nazis: "I pledge eternal allegiance to Adolf Hitler. I pledge unconditional obedience to him and to those appointed by him." The result? "In this way Hitler was able to gain control of Germany. In this way they gained the experience and training that later made them the scourge of occupied Europe. The enslavement of millions, the murder and ill-treatment of prisoners of war, the mass executions of civilians . . . it all began with the oath of eternal allegiance to Adolf Hitler." Mr. Alldridge also reminds us of what Himmler said: "We shall take care that never again in Germany will the Jewish-Bolshevistic revolution of sub-humans be kindled from the interior or through emissaries from outside."[103] Professor Gerhard Gollwitzer adds: "Far too many Germans, especially educated Germans, have become guilty by their slogan: Führer, give your orders and we shall obey."[104] The Germans have been using the word *Wiedergutmachung* when speaking of the financial reparations to German (not Austrian or Polish) Jews; an Israeli writer protested against this in a Hebrew novel based on his own experience in Auschwitz. Yechiel De-Nur, in *The Clock Overhead,* makes his K-Z prisoner No. 135633 say: "Before my sister was burned in the crematorium of Auschwitz, they shaved off her hair. In a shipment of hair, in sacks or in rectangular bales, tight-pressed like cotton from rich plantations, my sister's hair was sent to Germany. It was unloaded at a factory to make blankets, soft club chairs, upholstery. Somewhere in Germany, a young *Fräulein* now covers herself with a blanket. A single hair of gold, unprocessed, thrusts out of the blanket's weave. The *Fräulein* stretches out a bare arm, pulls, pulls—*Fräulein!* Give me back that hair! It's out of my sister's golden locks. . . . My sister, now they want to give money for you. How can I take money for my sister, the 'Field Whore,' from you—and not be a pimp?"[105] Prelate Hermann Maas says: "No human *Wiedergutmachung* is

possible of the terrible crimes done to Israel by National-Socialist Germany, the murder of six million people. . . . Only God's
judgment and God's grace can here make good."[106]

The famous German poet Hans Carossa after the war appealed to the Jews to recognize "the deeper meaning of the hour
and refrain from revenge."[107] Nobody knows whether the
Jews, if they had had a chance, would have revenged themselves
in the same way as the Czechs, Poles, and Russians. But in the
course of my studies I came across various utterances by Jews
which must be recorded here for the sake of historical truth.
Anne Frank entered in her diary: "What a nation, these Germans! The British radio speaks of gas chambers, but this is
perhaps the quickest extermination method. . . . Nobody is
excepted, old people, babies, pregnant women, ill people . . . all,
all must join this death dance!" About the fate of the Dutch
Anne Frank notes, on January 13, 1943: "Many children run
about in thin blouses, with bare feet, without overcoats, caps or
gloves. They have nothing in their stomachs and chew a car-
rot. Things have gone so far in Holland that children beg for a
piece of bread in the streets. The Jews are waiting, the Christians, the nations and the whole world is waiting . . . many are
waiting for death."[108] Martin Buber, when awarded a prize by
German book-sellers after the war, said: "Who am I to be as
bold as to 'Forgive'!"[109] Professor Joachim Schoeps, who had
left Germany in time, said that his father, a high-ranking army
doctor, had refused to leave Germany because he could not
believe that the authorities would harm a man who had faithfully served his nation throughout many years. He was taken to
Theresienstadt where he died. "He has paid for this error with
his life, Prussia however with her existence."[110] The writer
Kate Werner said: "Germans always talk in superlatives; they
are the best artisans, the most industrious workers, the most
intelligent scientists. . . . Nobody wants this. It would be much
nicer if they showed a little humanity."[111] Jewish refugees

from Nazi oppression say almost unanimously that Germany has never reached the cultural level of the West, and are more or less indifferent to the fate of Germany. Wilhelm Raabe, of whom we spoke on earlier pages, in a short story about the terrible consequences of the Thirty Years' War, makes an old Jewess who is beaten to death by an enraged mob say this to her frightened grandchild: "Our Kings were shepherds but their flocks grazed under palm trees. The sun of the Lord shone upon us, and the land of our forefathers smelled of myrrh and incense. What can the people rob us of as nothing is left to us but our misery?" And to a Roman Catholic monk old Leah says: "Our forefathers have never known peace since the days of the Emperor Titus. What do I care for what you have made of your country?"[112] She expresses the approximate feelings of the Jews of today. Some Jews even say that but for the grace of God Germany would have suffered the fate of Sodom. Very few of them (only elderly people) have returned to the country of their origin. Michael F. Michaels wrote to the London *Daily Telegraph* on August 18, 1958: "On August 18 it will be exactly 25 years since I came to this country as a refugee from Nazi oppression. . . . This country has given me tenfold what Hitler tried to take away from me—a home, happiness and self-respect."[113] He expressed the feelings of thousands of German and Austrian refugees.

Wilhelm Unger, a Jewish refugee who in 1957 returned to Germany after 20 years, said in 1960: "I had thought during the last three years that the Germans have changed. But the recent events have caused me to think that my hope was an illusion. Even two million British fascists—I can say this after a twenty years' stay in Great Britian—could never infect the whole nation. In Germany, however, 50,000 or even less fascists could again bring chaos to Germany. Great Britain is a solid democracy after all."[114] Heinrich Böll, a Roman Catholic German writer of the post-war generation, said in 1960: "If I were a descendant of a Jewish family, and my parents, my brothers and sisters had been murdered by the Nazis, I think I could not return to Cologne. My feelings, my memories would prevent me from returning to Germany."[115] Another Jew who returned to Germany for a short time said: "It was no 'home-coming,' comparable with what a prisoner of war may feel on returning home. The language which the people speak is no longer our language. Almost everyone of them prefers to talk of his experiences in the war and post-war years when he was hungry, without realising that people like me cannot regard their suffering as indelible as the injustice done to us, as the extermination of a by no means worthless minority, while almost all Germans looked on, passively at best, who now regard the events from 1933 to 1945 as a regrettable trifle."[116] Jews refuse to return to Germany because, like A. J. F. Taylor, they are afraid that people they meet in the streets of German towns may have taken part in crimes. "If you go to Germany for a holiday and fall ill," Mr. Taylor said, "you may be treated by a doctor who not long ago was rubbing glass into the wound of a child—a wound he had himself caused."[117] Jews of the DP camps in Germany had exactly the same feelings when they said in the final issue of their mimeographed camp newspaper: "We have given the world the will and testament of those who perished: 'Do not put your faith into European civilisation. In the Stygian chambers of inhuman persecution we signed the divorce. We are handing the divorce papers over to you. Return to the sources of Jewish morality!'"[118] Rabbi Zvi Asaria, a survivor of a concentration camp, was Chief Rabbi of Cologne for some time, received many threatening letters during the Eichmann trial, and left Germany in 1961 to settle in Israel. He said: "I strongly doubt whether there will be a Jewish community in Germany in twenty years."[119]

British Jews, mostly descendants of Polish-Russian Jews, have said that they would always remember what had been done to their race in Europe, and that the vast majority of Germans supported Hitler. Forgive? This can only mean to refrain "from exacting vengeance," but no more. If the word should be taken to mean "that we without qualification regard the Germans now as our brethren in the great human family, then we must, with regret but without hesitation, refuse."[120] One of them, Reuben Ainsztein, said: "Germany was the chief source of anti-Semitism in the Middle Ages, the exporters of Jew-hatred to Eastern Europe, and the creator of the modern forms of anti-Semitism in the 19th and 20th centuries. Hitler's anti-Semitism was not an accident, but the culmination of the work of permanent evil forces in German history."[121] When Frankie Vaughan, a Jewish artist, stated on television that it was time for the Germans to be forgiven for their crimes against the Jews, Marcus Shloimovitz gave this answer: "In a Dachau concentration camp the following is written on a wall: 'Forgive them not, for they knew what they did.' Two thirds of the Jews of Europe have been exterminated. Men, women and children were pushed into the gas ovens. Remember that, Mr. Vaughan."[122] Another British Jew, M. Esther: "It is only decent human nature that should prevent Mr. Vaughan and other so-called Jewish entertainers from bringing laughter into the hearts of those who have brought tears into ours. . . . I do agree that we must learn to forgive, as stated in the Torah, but at the moment I think we are justified in still preserving our hatred of the nation which killed six million of our brothers and sisters, especially when one knows that many of these German criminals are still ailve today."[123] Rabbi Immanuel Jakobovits, former Chief Rabbi of Ireland, said in the United States that the Jewish "centre of gravity" has moved from Eastern Europe and Germany to England in recent years.[124]

Sir Lewis Namier, remembering his descent from the famous Gaon of Vilna, when asked whether he had visited Germany after the war, answered that he had millions of reasons not to go there. Thirty years ago he had already called the Germans "a nation, hardworking and intelligent, even though uncouth and, in a deeper sense, not altogether civilised." In 1941 he called them "the only European nation which glories in the barbaric period of its history." The British, freedom loving and democratic as they have been for generations, feel "respect for the individual, for human rights. . . . This is the basis of English Monarchy, of English Conservatism and English progress." The pattern forms of the British are "Parliament and the team, of Germany the State and the army, or perhaps rather the army and the State." Characteristic of Germany is "the utter conscious subordination of the individual, their iron discipline which they inforce . . . and their resultant inhumanity." Frederick William I started it all and Frederick II became "the idol of generations of Prussians, indeed of the entire German nation." In the Prussian state everyone was "both slave and master; the less personal life and freedom the German enjoys, the more important it is for him to feel as a member of a master nation, of a *Herrenvolk*." Hitler was the result of this development. The Germans, "temperamentally unfit for revolution," have, from Hegel and Fichte down to Treitschke, "defied State and nation" and spoken of *deutsche Treue, deutsche Wissenschaft, deutsche Arbeit, deutsche Waelder, deutsche Eichen*. The ultimate expression of all this was "Hitler's maxim that whatever benefits the German nation is morally good and just." Hitler "understood the German people which has found its full self-expression under his leadership." His rise to power was "due to the fact that he has given expression to some of the deepest instincts of the Germans." His *Lebensraum* theory, outlined in *Mein Kampf*, was begun by the medieval Teutonic Knights and preached by many Germans before him, especially the Pan-Germans who claimed to be a *"Herrenvolk"* with a mission as *"Kulturträger."* "They talked '*Urgeschichte*,' Nordic trash, and Nietzschean amorality." Hitler, in his turn, "became the leader and pacemaker of the anti-Semites through East-Central and South-Eastern Europe." The atrocities have been "systematically planned and organised from above ... hundreds of thousands of men have participated in them, and tens of millions have watched them with approval, or at least with connivance."[125]

Paul Johnson wrote: "In Central Europe, the irreplaceable Jewish leaven, which played a vital historic role in the crystallisation of the continental culture, has virtually disappeared, leaving unimaginable dullness behind."[126] No wonder that the British Jews read with great satisfaction what Pope John XXIII said to the British Prime Minister in an audience in 1960: "We salute in your person the noble British people, who are dear to our heart for their high moral qualities."[127] Could the same be said of the Germans?

When the question arose in Israel of German tourists being allowed to come there, many Jews let it be known: "The mere thought that our streets would be swarming with Germans whose fathers have burnt six millions of our nation after bestially murdering them is repulsive."[128] When the international PEN Congress was held at Frankfurt in 1959, Jewish writers from Israel declined to attend. Rabbi Mordechai Nurok protested against the import of German books and films into Israel and called all advances to Germany "a moral shame for the Jewish nation."[129] Israeli resistance fighters even declined to meet German resistance fighters at an international gathering. When the Mayor of Berlin, Willy Brandt, a welcome visitor because he spent the twelve years of Hitlerism in exile, came to Tel Aviv to attend a Congress of the International Union of Local Authorities, the German flag was not raised outside the Congress building, the Habimah Theater, because of fear of demonstrations. The town council of Jerusalem unanimously declined to entertain "cultural relations" with Munich. "Certainly not with Munich," they said, "the cradle of Nazism." The

Mayor, Ish-Shalom said: "We cannot forget that a third of our nation has been murdered."[130] The music of Richard Wagner, one of the main teachers of Hitler, cannot be played in Israel to this day. "In the career of Hitler's favourite composer," Colin Welch wrote, "the bold immodesty of the romantic artist reaches heights not surpassed till Hitler himself did so."[131] The poet Werner Kraft, who emigrated from Germany to Israel, says: "Only he is a genuine poet who knows that Goethe's poem to the moon contains a condemnation of Hitler, and also knows that a poem to the moon, written today, must speak of the millions of murdered Jews and Christians, even it does not mention them."[132] Dr. Arieh Kubory, Chairman of Yad Vashem, at a meeting of the Council in Jerusalem, condemned Israeli's apparent eagerness to show friendliness to German visitors, and his views were endorsed by the majority of those present. He went on to say that there was evidence that even the most enlightened German liberals have not yet come round to facing the necessity of teaching their youth the harsh and bitter truth that their holocaust was unparalled in history.[133] Dr. Heinz Flügel, a leading German Lutheran who saw in a museum in Israel soiled scrolls of the Bible, handbags and waistcoats made of holy scrolls, was so moved that he said to a Jew: "Jesus is crucified again and again by all nations, by all men. He was tortured and crucified in the most terrible manner in Belsen and Maidanek." To his compatriots he said: "It has surprised me again and again that many a Christian who tries to explain away the collective guilt of the Third Reich, can still as ever burden the Jews with the unforgivable guilt for the crucifixion of Jesus two thousand years ago."[134] A young German, Hans Jürgen Schultz, says: "The common history of Jews, Christians and Germans has been destroyed by unparalleled crimes."[135] Professor Carlo Schmid, remembering the nationalism of the German romantics and the German racialists with their "blood mysticism," says that the curse of the terrible crimes of the nation was bound to fall on guilty and innocent alike. . . . "Those murdered in the gas chambers cannot be revived again, and the expelled will not return. Who can blame them? We are all guilty."[136]

The Jews in Israel remember Hannah Szenes, a 23-year-old Hungarian-Jewish girl, who, when the British army in Palestine had agreed to send small groups of Jewish volunteers to occupied Europe to contact Jewish underground fighters, pleaded to go to rescue her mother in Hungary. She jumped into northern Yugoslavia by parachute and crossed the frontier secretly into Hungary. She was arrested shortly afterwards, tried and found guilty by a German military court. She refused to plead for mercy; she declared in open court that she would not ask for mercy from "murderers who were prepared to destroy their own country by acting as tools of the Nazis." When the firing squad levelled their guns, Hannah began to sing the Jewish hymn, the "*Hatikvah*." After her death, Hebrew poems and essays were found among her belongings. One poem reads:

> Blessed is the match that is consumed
> in kindling flame,
> Blessed is the flame that burns in
> the secret fastness of the heart.
> Blessed is the heart with strength to
> stop its beating for honour's sake.
> Blessed is the match that is consumed
> in kindling flame.[137]

Young Israelis who visited West Germany in the autumn of 1960, left it disappointed. The Jewish problem, they said, occupied only a small number of active Germans, most Germans having forgotten the past and "suppressed" the fate of the European Jews. When some Germans got a cheap sentimental feeling out of performances of the falsified story of Anne Frank, a Jewess from Israel protested: "Stop these performances, for they tell only half the truth. This is syrup." She gave the true facts: The daughter of a Jew who had died in a concentration camp saw Anne Frank in October, 1944 in Belsen, in the dark of the night; otherwise the SS guards would have shot them. Anne, in prisoner's clothes, and with a bald head, was hungry and freezing, and whispered that she did not want to live any longer, as her parents were dead and her sister lay dying from typhoid fever.[138]

But this is not the end of the story. Jews have something more to say. They see these things before their inner eye:

One day we received the message that the SS had murdered seven thousand Jews at Borissow. One group of Jews were forced to dig a big grave. After this was done, the same group had to put off all their clothes, age or sex being disregarded. The Jews were told to lie down in that grave whereupon the SS shot them dead with their machine guns. Immediately after the next group had to enter the grave. In that manner they all lay one upon another—seven thousand poor, tortured people.[139]

This trench [at Kerch], one kilometer in length, four meters wide, and two meters deep, was filled to overflowing with bodies of women, children, old men, and boys and girls in their teens. Near the trench were frozen pools of blood. Children's caps, toys, ribbons, torn off buttons, gloves, milk bottles and rubber comforters, small shoes, galoshes, together with torn off hands and feet, and other parts of human bodies, were lying nearby. Everything was spattered with blood and brains.[140]

At that time, when the greatest numbers of Jews were exterminated in the gas chambers, an order was issued that the children were to be thrown into the crematory ovens, or into the crematory ditches, without previous asphyxiation with gas. . . . The children were thrown in alive. Their cries could be heard all over the camp.[141]

They killed them with their parents, in groups, and alone. They killed them in children's homes and hospitals, burying them alive in graves, throwing them into flames, stabbing them with bayonets, poisoning them, conducting experiments upon them, extracting their blood for the use of the German army, throwing them into prison and Gestapo torture chambers; the children died from hunger, torture, and epidemic diseases."[142]

Not even the most fanatical enemy of Communism has ever reported such things of the Russians. Of the 15,000 children who passed through Theresienstadt, only one hundred were rescued alive. One of the murdered children wrote: "We got used to being smacked without any reason, we got used to tortures and executions, to seeing people dying in their own excrements, to seeing coffins full of corpses."[143] Mr. Sydney Silverman, M.P., described in Parliament on February 10, 1960, what he had seen at Auschwitz: "I saw the huts, the incinerators, the crematoria, the death wall, the museum, the piles of shoes, the glass case, from floor to ceiling filled with human hair, the collection of eyeglasses, the battered old suitcases and handbags with the names and initials of the victims. There were four million people deliberately put to death in that camp; three million of them were Jews, but we claim no monopoly in persecution or martyrdom. There were plenty of others."[144] The others were gypsies, Czechs, Poles, Russians. Twelve million innocent men, women, and children were murdered by the Germans, as was stated at Nuremberg.

Can anyone expect the Jews to forget and forgive this? Captain Malcolm Hay, a Scottish Roman Catholic, says: "The German crime of genocide has its logical roots in the medieval theory that the Jews were outcasts, condemned by God to a life of perpetual servitude."[145] He also says that the sermons of St. John Chrysostom could have been preached beside the mass graves in Eastern Europe. For this saint, called golden-mouthed said things like this: "See how Judaea is deserted, and how all is desolation and ruin in that nation! Your situation, O Jewish people, becomes more and more disastrous, and one cannot see showing on your foreheads the slightest ray of hope." And: "But it was men, says the Jew, who brought these misfortunes upon us, not God. On the contrary it was in fact God who brought them about. If you attribute them to men, reflect again that, even supposing men had dared, they would not have had the power to accomplish them, unless it had been God's will."[146]

As it was Jews who have been murdered by the Hitlerian Nordic heroes, six million Jews—the greatest crime in all history—we must listen to what their representatives have to say about it. The Jews read in their Bible, which is also the Bible of the Christians: "For this commandment which I command thee, this day, it is not hidden from you, neither is it far off. . . . See, I have set before thee this day life and good, and death and evil. . . . But if thine heart turn away, so that thou wilt not hear . . . I denounce unto you this day, that ye shall surely perish. I call heaven and earth to record this day against you, that I have set before you life and death, blessing and cursing: therefore choose life, that both thou and thy seed may live."[147] God told the Jews: "Love the stranger, for ye were strangers in the land of Egypt. God loveth the stranger." In the Psalms we read: "Precious in the sight of the Lord is the death of his saints."[148] The prophet Amos makes God say to the Jews: "You only have I known of all families of the earth; therefore I will punish you for all your iniquities."[149] The Prophet Micah says the same in different words.[150] The prophet Jeremiah says: "Our fathers sinned and are not, and we bear their iniquities."[151] An early rabbi said: "With what measure ye mete, it shall be measured to you again."[152] Jesus said the same. It is therefore that a London rabbi, whose entire family had been murdered, said when Eichmann was captured: "There is no punishment fit for Eichmann and the German people."[153] Rabbi Isidore Epstein says: "The world still recalls today with horror the cruelties and beastliness perpetrated by the Germans in the concentration camps. These deeds were not committed by primitive barbarians and savages, but by civilized and educated men and women. But these civilised men and women had a false philosophy of life, a philosophy founded on the doctrine of blood, race and soil, and that brought their conduct to a depth of degradation such as humanity had never witnessed before. He reminds us that the "sin of pride as the cause of all catastrophes in history is the recurring theme of the Bible," and says of Germany: "The collapse of Germany is but the result of the disregard of the claims of morality in international relations which has characterised German politics for almost a century. For a time it paid and brought in rich dividends, making Prussia the nucleus of a united German nation and the leading military power of the old world. But a limit was ultimately set by the judgment of history to German injustice and aggressiveness, leading to the Nemesis that has overtaken the Hitler Reich in our days." Rabbi Epstein quotes what Professor John Macmurray said: "Jewish reflection thinks history as the act of God." He quotes the Rev. Reinhold Niebuhr: "Judgment in history falls heaviest on those who come to think themselves gods." He also quotes the historian Froude: "Justice and truth alone endure and live. Injustice and falsehood may be long-lived, but doomsday comes at last to them, in French revolutions and other terrible ways." He lastly quotes Dean Inge, who wrote in 1940: "The Jews have stood by the graves of all their oppressors in turn. They may yet say to their latest persecutors: 'The feet of them that buried Assyrians, Babylonians, Greeks, Romans and Spanish Inquisitors are at the door and shall carry thee out." As for Israel, however, Rabbi Epstein quotes Sir Winston Churchill, who said in 1949: "The coming into being of a Jewish State in Palestine is an event in world history, to be viewed in the perspective, not of a generation or a century, but in the perspective of one thousand, two thousand, or even three thousand years."

In liberated Auschwitz, a photograph of fifteen rabbis was found. Some of these rabbis were murdered in Auschwitz and other camps. Others were murdered in Warsaw, together its half a million Jews. Many of these Jews died slowly of hunger.[155] A film of the scene was made by the Nazis themselves showing scantily clothed Jews, so emaciated that they are indistinguishable from skeletons, lying in the streets waiting to die, their skin covered with sores and boils, their hair filled with lice. Naked bodies were wheeled away and tipped into a pit as if garbage, the individual corpses being indistinguishable, the limbs hideously intertwined. "I want to share the fate of my brethern," one rabbi said. "I enjoin you not to despair on the way to death. Do not refrain from singing the melody: 'I believe with a perfect faith in the coming of the Messiah,' and like Rabbi Akiba die with the words 'the Lord is One!' "[156]

The revolt of the Warsaw Ghetto began on April 19, 1943. The last words of the Jewish fighters from burning Warsaw were: "The Germans blast the blocks of houses in which Jews are resisting. The Ghetto burns. Clouds darken the whole town. Men, women and children who are not burned alive, are being slaughtered in masses."[157] The German heroes of these crimes, as far as is known, were the SS generals Juergen Stroop and Heinz Reinefarth. Stroop, who proudly told the Führer "The Jewish quarter of Warsaw has ceased to exist,"[158] was hanged by the Poles. Reinefarth escaped punishment and, only a few years later, became Mayor of Westerland, on the Isle of Sylt. The German government refused to look into his past at first, but when under pressure by public opinion Reinefarth was brought before some judges, they set him free again. The leading Jewish newspaper in Germany had this to say: "It is necessary to fill books with judicial scandals by now. One of the most terrible examples of miscarriage of justice is the case of SS Obergruppenführer Reinefarth whose crimes are among the worst ever committed. He was set free although a member of the Polish resistance had declared that every ruin of Warsaw is proof of his crimes. A high official of the Ministry of Justice of

Sleswig-Holstein, Rhode, spoke in favour of Reinefarth, but he himself is responsible for criminal judgments as Nazi judge at Prague. Instead of punishing these judges they were reinstated. In the Weimar Republic such judges helped fascism into the saddle."[159]

The American-Jewish writer Zvi Kolitz, in a Job-like monologue of a Jew in burning Warsaw, makes him say to God: "I am happy to belong to the most unhappy nation in the world. You say we have sinned, of course, we have sinned. But I want you to tell me whether there is a sin in the world which would warrant such punishment. You say you will repay our enemies. I am sure you will repay them without pity. I do not doubt this. But I want you to tell me whether there is a punishment in the world which could atone for the crime committed against us." This unhappy Jew, Jossel Rackower, also says: "I feel and know now that my heart is jubilant at the thought that our God has been a God of revenge for thousands of years."[160] With these last words he refers to Psalm 94: "O Lord God, to whom vengeance belongeth; O God, to whom vengeance belongeth, show thyself. Lift up thyself, thou Judge of the earth: render a reward to the proud. Lord, how long shall, how long shall the wicked triumph?" After all, the Psalmist was a Jew, not a Christian. A number of God-fearing Germans agree with what the Jews said. Pastor Dietrich Bonhoeffer, murdered by the Nazis in 1945, said in 1941: "I pray for the defeat of my fatherland because only by this defeat can we atone for the terrible crimes which we committed against Europe and the world. Christians do not wish to escape punishment or chaos, if it is God's will to bring them about. As Christians we must accept God's judgment."[161] The Lutheran theologian, Professor Hans Joachim Iwand, said: "We Germans carry the mark of Cain on our foreheads. Who will take this guilt from us one day and from our forefathers with whom it all began? In this question we find the reason why so many of us flee into amusements, money-making, achievements, into all things which make us forget. How can a nation become innocent again which revolted against Israel and God?"[162] A German lady, Marie Sturm, a Roman Catholic, said after the war: "You can hear again and again: 'Well, the German rulers committed grave crimes, but the German nation is not responsible for them.' Of course it is. They used the most general franchise to vote for a dictator who preached hatred of the Jews from the beginning. Now we find many who feel no guilt because they did not commit murder themselves. But they hated together with the others and are guilty of the crimes which the others committed."[163] Professor Foerster cried out of the depths of his heart: "Who can take the memory of this gigantic guilt from my soul and my conscience? Nobody can. But what is much worse is the fact that this gigantic guilt has fallen into oblivion. The sulphurous fumes of these crimes went up much higher to high heaven than the explosion of a H-Bomb."[164] Professor H. R. Trevor-Roper (Oxford) says: "This unique, purposeless, but systematic crime was not the work of a party. It was a national act. Disguise it as they may, the Germans were involved in it as a nation. The German bureaucracy, German business, the German army and German society itself played their silent but positive part and made the tragedy possible. . . . And when the machinery began to run out of Jewish fuel, other human beings—gypsies, Poles, 'a-socials' —were stuffed in to feed it. For the Germans there were no *crise de conscience:* on the contrary, the murder satisfied the German conscience. . . . Can it be that some peoples have a 'national' love of destruction? German history offers plenty of evidence for such a view." Professor Trevor-Roper finds the same hatred of life in the Spanish Inquisition, the expulsion of the Moors and Jews, and the terrible slaughter in the more recent Spanish Civil War.[165]

Surely, it is not good enough to say, as some Germans do: "Words cannot describe the macabre Inferno of the Third

Reich."[166] Such utterances seem hopelessly inadequate in view of what really decent and devoutly Christian Germans have to say and what the German masses refuse to listen to.

Professor Gollwitzer told them this: "We Germans have, in our words and deeds against Jews and Poles, heartily accepted the inhuman term of collective guilt before we became the object of this term." He added: "Now *the* Germans have been measured with the same measure with which they measured *the* Jews. Will they realise the connection?"[167] Toward the end of the war, when some German soldiers spoke to Gollwitzer of the extermination of the Jews, of which they knew, and said to him, "If there is a God, this will be punished," Gollwitzer answered: "There is a God, and it has been punished."[168]

Sister Teresa Benedicta a Cruce, author of two books, posthumously published, *Science of the Cross* and *Finite and Eternal Being,* was born a Jew. When she took the veil a few years after embracing the Roman Catholic creed, many famous German Catholics witnessed the ceremony with deep emotion. Dr. A. Donder, the Provost of Münster Catheral, called her "a blessed soul, quiet like a beam of God," and others said of her that she was shining like a star "at a time which loved darkness more than light." In 1933, when she was still living in the Carmelite nunnery in Cologne and heard of the plight of the Jews, she said: "All this will be revenged one day." And, on a later occasion: "Woe when God's punishment for what is done to the Jews overcomes this town and this country." When her stay in Cologne seemed too dangerous her superiors removed her to a Carmelite nunnery in Holland. But the Nazi thugs found her out there, tore her and her sister from the nunnery, removed them to the East, and murdered them there. The German professor, Martin Grabmann, wrote that Catholics hoped that she will be declared a saint one day, "to shine as a model of the knowledge and love of God and be called upon for intercession."[169]

The Lutheran writer Jochen Klepper, who regarded himself as living "entirely as an exile" within Nazi Germany and knew from the beginning that "the daring adventure to which this miserable nation has encouraged mad visionaries" would end in disaster, entered in his diary on August 21, 1938 a verse from an old German church hymn which asserts that God is warning us, day in, day out, by signs. "His punishment is already at our doorstep. Germany, listen to this, repent in time while God is still willing to show you grace."[170]

The Catholic writer Theodor Haecker, entered in his diary in 1944: "A German saviour wants to replace Christ. . . . By their persecution of the Jews the Germans are coming nearer and nearer to the Jews and their fate. They crucify Christ today for a second time, as a nation."[171]

The Catholic poet Werner Bergengruen in 1944 wrote his poem, "The Last Epiphany," which he secretly distributed and which was found on some German prisoners of war who reached Great Britain. The poet makes Christ say in this poem:

> Ich klopfte bei Nacht, ein bleicher Hebräer,
> Ein Flüchtling, gejagt, mit zerrissenen Schuhn,
> Ihr riefet dem Schergen, ihr winktet dem Späher
> Und meintet noch Gott einen Dienst zu tun.
>
> Verwaister Knabe auf östlichen Flächen,
> Ich fiel euch zu Füssen und flehte um Brot.
> Ihr aber scheutet ein künftiges Rächen,
> Ihr zucktet die Achseln und gabt mir den Tod.
>
> Ich kam als Gefangner, als Tagelöhner,
> Verschleppt und verkauft, von der Peitsche zerfetzt.
> Ihr wandtet den Blick von dem struppigen Fröner.
> Nun komm ich als Richter. Erkennt ihr mich jetzt?[172]

Perlate Hermann Maas who visited the Holy Land after the war—invited there because he had brought himself into danger by saving Jews from the Nazis—saw there "parts of the European synagogues which had been burnt and destroyed, scrolls of

Holy Scripture half-burnt, blood-stained, desecrated, torn to pieces, witnesses of the sport the Nazis had made of them; they had stuck together a fancy-dress from pieces of scrolls. As a matter of fact, there were inscribed on those pieces God's curses for those who mock him." Prelate Maas does not mention the soap made of the fat of murdered Jews, some of which is still kept in an Israeli museum. But he tells us that the Arabs of an ancient place in Palestine had protected the ancient synagogue during the Israeli-Arab war of 1948 and had not allowed it to be destroyed. They hid the two scrolls of the law in a cave and returned them to the Jews after the war. Prelate Maas also visited the Dead Sea, the site of Sodom, "a city visited by God's punishment," and when some Jews asked him how the Germans could have succumbed to such devilry he was so moved that he could not answer. No "cheap answer," he thought, was permissible at such a moment, "especially after one has seen one of the most horrible places of God's punishment. It is the Bible which gives the last answer."[173] Our thoughts go back to the last letter of General Henning von Tresckow, written before he shot himself in order not to fall alive into the hands of the SS and be tortured by them for his part in the plot against Hitler. "As God once promised Abraham," he wrote to his wife, "not to destroy Sodom in case he should find ten just men in it, it is my hope that God will not destroy Germany either for the sake of us."[174]

The Catholic poet and novelist Maria Mathi in 1941 wrote a poem about the Jews of Hadamar which could, of course, not be published in Nazi Germany; it remains unpublished to this very day. It is a dialogue between a Jewish child and mother. The child asks where Poland is and receives the answer: "Where our forefathers are—in eternity." Does one carry there the grapes on the shoulders and on yokes? "The harvest in Poland, my son, is heavier still." Do we cross there the Red Sea which Jehovah divides for us? "The wave of blood is towering high as heaven." And when I grow up and return here? "No-body will know you and you will know nobody." But it will not take so long till I am grown up. "The stars will move differently then. Listen, the bell of Hadamar tolls for our de-parture."[175] After the war, Maria Mathi wrote the story of the Jews of Hadamar, which, characteristically enough, she had to submit to some fifty German publishers before one dared to publish it because she tells the story of the burning of the Jews of that town. One of the last Jews of Hadamar, on his way to the burning oven, says to a German woman he meets: "What is done to us can be done to all of you. But what will be done to you can no longer be done to us. He who weeps last weeps most bitterly."[176]

The Catholic poet Hans Carossa said after the war that there is no European nation which has not been labelled by the Germans with some negative word. The French were degenerated and an arch-enemy, the Italians were malicious, the English shopkeepers or cranky globe-trotters, all Slav nations inferior, the Russians candle eaters, the Americans soulless, the Jews "hateful as such." The "powerful" Germans believed in the value of one race and the unworthiness of others and thought that they had more right to live than other nations. They hailed a Führer "who arrogated to himself the right to decide which race should be allowed to live. A few years pass by, and mil-lions of innocent men, women and children are caught together, poisoned in gas chambers and killed by machine guns and flame-throwers. One day, however, a terrible retribution falls upon that proud and mighty nation."[177] In a poem he said: "On everything lies the shadow of an unatonable guilt."[178]

Kurt Ihlenfeld, a devout Lutheran poet and novelist, one of the few friends of Jochen Klepper who dared to follow his coffin, in *Thunderstorm in Winter* makes a devout Lutheran lieutenant compare the fate of the Germans with that of the ancient Jews. "People asked then," he says, "why all this has happened, and we do the same today. The answer was given by the prophets. No pleasing answer, no flattery, no prospect of glory and a glorious millenium." They had told the Jews in unmistakable words what would come, namely that the enemy would take and destroy Jerusalem and abduct the inhabitants of the holy city and the other cities and villages into captivity. "This was truly done," the lieutenant says, "the prophets did not exaggerate. Just as your neighbours, friends and relatives have set out on their wandering this morning, in the same manner the Israelites had to wander into an alien land. Tomorrow or the day after tomorrow the enemy will have crossed the Oder and then he will move very rapidly. And it will be like a river bursting over its banks and destroying all dykes."[179]

The poet Hans Brandenburg speaks of Germany's punishment in terms of the Nibelungs: "That ancient story—did it come true again? The ancient story of the *Götterdämmerung*— did it turn into *Menschendämmerung?*"[180] This reminds us of what Hitler, speaking of Germany's possible downfall, said— that he would take the world with him to hell. He called this by the ancient German word *Muspili,* the burning of the world, and hummed a tune from his favorite composer's *Götterdämmerung.*

Notes

1. Poliakov and Wulf. *Das Dritte Reich und seine Diener,* p. 71.
2. *Ibid.,* p. 119.
3. *Ibid.,* pp. 32-33.
4. *Ibid.,* p. 388.
5. *Ibid.,* pp. 28-29.
6. *Was bedeutet Aufarbeitung der Vergangenheit. Bericht ueber die Erzieherkonferenz am 6. und 7. November 1959 in Wiesbaden.* Edited by the Board of the Societies for Christian-Jewish Collaboration, Frankfurt.
7. Poliakov und Wulf. *Das Dritte Reich und seine Diener,* p. 530.
8. Hermann Maas. *Und will Rachels Kinder Wieder bringen in das Land.* Heilbronn, 1955, pp. 7, 37.
9. H. Gollwitzer. *Israel und wir.* Berlin, 1958, p. 15.
10. *Briefe,* p. 382.

11. *Die Verantwortung.* Muenchen, 1952, p. 30.
12. *Ansprache im Titaniapalast,* Berlin, February 17, 1952.
13. *Der Monat,* Berlin, February, 1954.
14. *Nuernberger Nachrichten,* January 15, 1955.
15. *Deutsche Rundschau,* October, 1955.
16. *Die Zeit,* Hamburg, March 7, 1957.
17. *Deutsche Rundschau,* July, 1957.
18. *CrP. Informationsdienst,* Koeln, April, 1962.
19. Müller-Claudius. *Deutsche und juedische Tragik,* p. 73.
20. Aage Bertelsen. *October 43.* London, 1955, pp. 110, 159.
21. Jaspers. *Philosophie und Welt,* p. 328.
22. *The Jewish Chronicle,* London, March 16, 1962.
23. *Ibid.,* April 13, 1962.
24. *Deutsche Rundschau,* April, 1959.
25. *Du hast uns heimgesucht bei Nacht,* p. 36.
26. *Mannheimer Hefte,* 1955, Issue III.
27. *Auf fremden Strassen.* Muenchen, 1955, p. 7.
28. *Frankfurter Allgemeine Zeitung,* Frankfurt, May 11, 1959.
29. *Zwanzig Jahre: 9. November 1938.* Koeln, January, 1959; *Zum Beispiel.* Frankfurt, 1962, pp. 7-8, 10-14, 17, 20-22.
30. *Engelbert Reinecke,* p. 27, 123, 174.
31. *Deutsche Rundschau,* March, 1956.
32. *Sueddeutsche Zeitung,* February 4, 1956.
33. *Welt der Arbeit,* Koeln, February 19, 1960.
34. *Blaetter,* Koeln, May, 1962.
35. *Die Liga,* Wuppertal-Vohwinkel, July, 1960.
36. *Sueddeutsche Zeitung,* Muenchen, July 26-27, 1958.
37. *Die Zeit,* Hamburg, March 21, 1957.
38. *Blaetter des Bielefelder Jugend-Kulturringes,* Bielefeld, September, 1956.
39. *Bavarian Radio,* June 7, 1955.
40. *Ibid.,* April 10, 1956.
41. *Die Kultur,* April, 1956.
42. *Ibid.,* September 1, 1956.
43. *Nuernberger Nachrichten,* April 7, 1958.
44. *Deutsche Rundschau,* April, 1959.
45. *Der Monat,* Berlin, June, 1959.
46. *Nuernberger Nachrichten,* September 27, 1960.
47. Kurt R. Grossmann, *Rheinischer Merkur,* September 18, 1959.
48. *Die Zeit,* Hamburg, May 20, 1960.
49. H. Jaeger. *The Reappearance of the Swastika.* London, 1960, p. 43.
50. *Deutsche und juedische Tragik,* pp. 96, 98-108, 125-126, 131.
51. *Ibid.,* pp. 55-56.
52. IMT, July 26, 1946.
53. IMT, April 29, 1946.
54. *Deutsche Rundschau,* April, 1954.
55. R. M. W. Kempner and Karl Haensel. *Das Urteil im Wilhelmstrassen-Prozess.* Schwaebisch-Gmuend, 1950, p. 90.
56. *Ibid.,* p. 90.

57. IMT, April 29, 1946.
58. Hofer. *Der Nationalsozialismus*, p. 34.
59. Poliakov and Wulf. *Das Dritte Reich und seine Diener*, p. 512.
60. *Die Grundlagen des 19. Jahrhunderts*. Muenchen, 6th edition 1906, p. 500.
61. *Daily Mail*, London, May 25, 1960; IMT, January 3, 1946.
62. Gollwitzer. *Und Fuehren, Wohin du nicht willst*, pp. 159-160.
63. "Stunde der Besinnung." *Mannheimer Hefte*, 1955, Issue III.
64. *Rechenschaft und Ausblick*. Muenchen, 1951, p. 138.
65. *Ibid.*, p. 190.
66. *Die Zeit*, Hamburg, October 11, 1956.
67. *Das Brandopfer*. Frankfurt, 1954, pp. 8, 10.
68. *Der Monat*, Berlin, Issue 165.
69. *Du hast uns heimgesucht bei Nacht*, p. 252.
70. *Tagebuch eines Verzweifelten*, Stuttgart, 1947, pp. 162, 194.
71. *The Jewish Chronicle*, London, November 18, 1960.
72. *Blaetter*, Koeln, July, 1959.
73. *Aufbau*, New York, May 29, 1959.
74. *Nuernberger Nachrichten*, April 25, 1957.
75. *Deutsche Rundschau*, March, 1960.
76. *Die Kultur*, February, 1960.
77. *Nuernberger Nachrichten*, March 19, 1957.
78. *Der Spiegel*, Hamburg, January 29, 1958.
79. *The Jewish Chronicle*, London, April 6, 1962.
80. *Geduldet oder Gleichberechtigt*. Koeln, 1960, p. 27.
81. *Die Kultur*, August, 1960.
82. *Frankfurter Allgemeine Zeitung*, December 10, 1955.
83. *Mein Leben*. Tuebingen, 1957, p. 110.
84. *Ibid.*, pp. 318-319, 322.
85. *Die Kultur*, November 1, 1956.
86. *German Bundestag*. Session of April 18, 1956.
87. *Ibid.*
88. *Ibid.*
89. *Blaetter*, Koeln, April, 1960.
90. *Deutsche Rundschau*, May, 1960.
91. *Rheinischer Merkur*, November 25, 1960.
92. *CrP. Informationsdienst*, Koeln, December, 1960.
93. *Nuernberger Nachrichten*, March 1, 1956.
94. *Allgemeine Wochenzeitung der Juden*, Duesseldorf, October 28, 1955.
95. *Bavarian Radio*, Muenchen, November 9, 1954.
96. *Spectator*, London, December 12, 1961.
97. *The Jewish Chronicle*, London, April 20, 1962.
98. *Parliamentary Debates*. London (Hansard), February 10, 1960.
99. *The Jewish Chronicle*, London, September 15, 1961.
100. Muller. *The Uses of the Past*, pp. 95, 135, 202.
101. *Observer*, London, October 27, 1957.
102. *The Jewish Chronicle*, London, October 28, 1960.
103. *The Jewish Gazette*, London, July 29, 1960.
104. *Blaetter*, Koeln, June, 1959.

105. *The Jewish Quarterly*, London, autumn, 1961.

106. *Und will Rachels Kinder wieder bringen in das Land*. Heilbronn, 1955, p. 203.

107. Hans Carossa. *Ungleiche Welten*. Wiesbaden, 1956, p. 31.

108. Anne Frank. *Diary of a Young Girl*. Entries for October 9, 1942, November 19, 1942, January 13, 1943.

109. *Das echte Gespraech und die Moeglichkeiten des Friedens*. Heidelberg, 1953, p. 5.

110. *Die Ehre Preussens*. Stuttgart, 1951, p. 7.

111. *Die Zeit*, Hamburg, September 23, 1954.

112. *Hoexter und Corvey. Saemtliche Werke, Zweite Serie*. Vol. IV, 1915, pp. 173, 196.

113. *Daily Telegraph*, London, August 16, 1958.

114. *Geduldet oder Gleichberechtigt*, p. 39.

115. *Ibid.*, p. 19.

116. *Deutsche Rundschau*, April 1959.

117. *Sunday Express*, London, October 19, 1958.

118. *Guardian*, London, December 9, 1960.

119. *The Jewish Chronicle*, London, October 20, 1961.

120. *Ibid.*, September 16, 1955.

121. *Jewish Observer*, London, January 15, 1960.

122. *Jewish Gazette*, London, July 29, 1960.

123. *Ibid.*

124. *Observer*, London, November 13, 1960.

125. *In the Margin of History*. London, 1939, p. 62; *Conflicts*. London, 1942, pp. 3, 6, 34-38, 79-82, 85, 88, 90, 145, 163, 188 ff; *Diplomatic Prelude*. London, 1948, pp. 8, 9, 21, 24.

126. *New Statesman*, London, September 10, 1960.

127. *Daily Mirror*, London, November 24, 1960.

128. *Die Welt*, Hamburg, May 22, 1957.

129. *Rhein und Neckarzeitung*, Heidelberg, March 15, 1959.

130. *Nuernberger Nachrichten*, September 27, 1960.

131. *Daily Telegraph*, London, November 7, 1960.

132. Werner Kraft in *Almanach des Fischer Verlags*. Frankfurt, 74th year.

133. *Bulletin of the Association of German Jews in Great Britain*, London, January, 1961.

134. *Juden, Christen, Deutsche*, p. 102.

135. *Ibid.*, p. 6.

136. *Ibid.*, pp. 27-28.

137. *The Jewish Chronicle*, London, November 11, 1960.

138. *Der Monat*, Berlin, August, 1957.

139. F. von Schlabrendorff. *Offiziere Gegen Hitler*, p. 50.

140-42. M. Hay. *The Foot of Pride*, pp. 8, 314, 315.

143. *Kinderzeichnungen und Gedichte aus Theresienstadt*. Statni Zidovsk Museum, Prague, 1959.

144. *Parliamentary Debates*. London (Hansard), February 10, 1960.

145-46. Hay, *op. cit.*, pp. 4, 30.

147. Deuteronomy 30:15, 19.

148. Psalm 116, verse 15.
149. Amos 3:2.
150. Micah 6:8, 13.
151. Lamentations 5:7.
152. Herford. *Pharisaism*, p. 117.
153. *Evening Standard*, London, May 27, 1960.
154. *The Faith of Judaism*. London, 1954, pp. 24, 75, 260-265, 275-276, 305.
155. *The Jewish Chronicle*, London, August 5, 1960.
156. *Daily Telegraph*. London (no date traced); and *The Jewish Chronicle*, London, August 5, 1960.
157. H. J. Schoeps. *Juedische Geisteswelt*. Koeln, 1960, p. 314.
158. *Die Zeit*, Hamburg, October 11, 1956.
159. *Blaetter*. Koeln, September, 1962.
160. *Neue deutsche Hefte*, Berlin, January, 1956, pp. 757-764.
161. H. Rothfels. *Die deutsche Opposition gegen Hitler*. Krefeld, 1949, p. 169.
162. *Blaetter*, Koeln, May 25, 1960.
163. *Rundbrief*, Freiburg, August, 1950.
164. *Ibid.*, September, 1959.
165. *New Statesman*, London, March 2, 1962.
166. *Die Zeit*, Hamburg, October 11, 1956.
167. *Stunde der Besinnung*. Mannheimer Hefte, 1955, Issue III; *Und fuehren, wohin du nicht willst*, p. 18.
168. *Und fuehren, wohin du nicht willst*, p. 160.
169. Teresia Renata de Spiritu Sancto. *Edith Stein*. Nuernberg, 1952, pp. 7, 8, 108, 194, 195; Hilda Graef. *Leben unter dem Kreuz*. Frankfurt, 1954, p. 137.
170. *Unter dem Schatten deiner Fluegel*, p. 630.
171. *Tag-und Nachtbuecher*, pp. 119, 244.
172. ("I, a pale Hebrew, knocked at a door at night, a fugitive, persecuted, with torn shoes. You called a henchman, you winked a spy, and thought you were serving God.
"An orphaned boy somewhere on the Eastern steppes, I fell at your feet and begged for bread. You shied away from a future revenge, you shrugged your shoulders and murdered me.
"I came as a prisoner, a day-laborer, abducted and sold, hacked to pieces by a whip. You turned away from the dirty slave. Now I come as a judge. Do you recognize me now?") *De Profundis*, p. 39.
173. *Und will Rachels Kinder wieder bringen in das Land*, pp. 71, 28, 157-158.
174. Schlabrendorff. *Offiziere gegen Hitler*, p. 153.
175. Presented to the writer of this book.
176. Maria Mathi. *Wenn nur der Sperber nicht kommt*. Gueterslok, 1955, p. 301.
177. Hans Carossa. *Ungleiche Welten*. Wiesbaden, 1951, p. 235.
178. *Ibid.*, p. 220.
179. *Wintergewitter*. Witten, 1952, p. 748.
180. *Trost in Traenen*, p. 12.

17
The Two
Post-War Mentalities

IN 1922 THE POET RILKE TOLD THE GERMANS: "GERMANY COULD, in the moment of her breakdown, have shamed and moved the world by an act of repentance and deep truth. . . . She has not rejuvenated from the very bottom, she has not realised that dignity which has its roots in a deep humility."[1] Professor Wilhelm Roepke, who went into exile in 1933, told the Germans in 1945 that they had committed "physical, political and moral suicide," and admonished them to recognize the "immense guilt they had incurred and the bitter necessity to do penance. . . . The only hope lies in the recognition of your guilt."[2] The leaders of the Lutheran Church published this on October 18, 1945: "We know we are not only in a great national community of suffering but also in a solidarity of guilt. We confess in deep distress that we brought infinite sufferings on many nations and countries. We fought for many years, in the name of Jesus, against the spirit which found its terrible expression in the National Socialist terror. But we must accuse ourselves for not having spoken more courageously, prayed more faithfully and loved more burningly."[3] Sir David Maxwell Fyfe, the British Prosecutor at Nuremberg, said on August 29, 1946 that the only hope for Germany and the world lay in the acknowledgement by the Germans of their responsibility for what had been done in their name, and in their atonement. The German poet and novelist Reinhold Schneider, a courageous resistance fighter, said in 1944 in one of his sonnets, which were secretly passed from hand to hand or orally: "Do penance, pray and keep silent. . . . Your guilt crouches in every corner."[4] Fritz von Unruh, returning from his exile, said in 1946: "The only right the Germans have today is the right to contrition."[5] The young poet Heinz-Winfried Sabais said: "We go the hard road without lament and atone silently for our guilt and shame."[6] The poet Bernt von Heiseler reminded his nation in a dirge, "In Memoriam Patriae," that they had once hailed Hitler, and said: "How deeply are we guilty? You too and I too. Only if we confess our guilt and shoulder it, our right is shining in God's light, a community of all Germans. Confess and do penance!"[7]

Did the Germans listen to these exhortations? It is best to hear the answers given by the decent German minority. Dr. Eugen Kogon, who spent seven years in Hitler's concentration camps, said that the Germans regard it as indecent to be told that their past should have a bearing on their present, they prefer to indulge in anti-Communism rather than in self-examination. Miracles of economic resurrection do not make up for moral disaster. When German newspapers in 1956 made a great fuss about the centenary of Heine's death, one of their few decent writers said that the revolutionary poet would no doubt be a *persona non grata* in post-war Germany because he would not remain silent and would become obnoxious by every word of criticism he uttered. "How could a reactionary Germany dare to call Heine one of their precursors, her prophets?"[8] Professor Joachim Schoeps, one of the very few Jewish exiles who returned to Germany after the war, had to state that the economic miracle had made the Germans forget their guilt, and added with bitter sarcasm: "We are, of course, towering high above 'the Bolsheviks.' All this is nauseating. . . ."[9]

When Thomas Mann in 1949 visited Germany to give a lecture on Goethe, he could not fail to see that the Germans had thought it necessary to guard him with many policemen and detectives. He wrote: "I have been there probably at the last possible moment. The country is rapidly moving backwards (direction 1930), and their moral attitude is disgusting."[10] When a critic of his *Doctor Faustus,* completely misjudging its moral and religious meaning, complained that he could find in it no help for a moral regeneration, Mann retorted: "Is he the last one not to notice that the Germans do not want to regenerate themselves at all?"[11]

When the poet Walter Bauer saw how many Nazi writers and journalists had returned into public life and realized that "the dawn we had hoped for had not come but restoration by reactionnaries," he felt that the sight of a majority of unteachable Germans was like "shackles around my hands"[12] and he emigrated to Canada, preferring to be a dishwasher there than a poet in an unregenerated Germany. In one of the poems he wrote in Canada he says that he is cleaning glasses, silver plates, knives, and forks from 7 P.M. to 4 A.M. for $28 and a free evening meal a week. In another poem he says that he left the fatherland "loaded with the memory of too much death, poisoned with guilt for which I am—though more and more hesitatingly—searching for a judge who has failed us." He remembers the millions murdered at "Auschwitz, Theresienstadt, Belsen, Buchenwald," and whenever he thinks of these places, "the beloved language of my fatherland tastes of ashes."[13]

A German of Jewish origin who had left Germany and gone

to Australia, returned to Germany in 1957 to see whether he could live there again. After a few months he wrote to a friend in London: "The longer I live here the more I am longing to live again among English-speaking people."[14] What got on his nerves most was that the Germans did not see any of the things he saw, and that their moral condition was utterly disgusting. He left Germany again. The American writer Norbert Muehlen who visited Germany a few years ago said in a book that the Germans are trying to forget or whitewash their past and are feeling as little responsible for the Nazi period as for any other period of their history. They identify Hitler's anti-Communism with the anti-Communism of the West. The American ex-diplomat Charles Thayer says in *The Unquiet Germans* that they only remember their sufferings during the first post-war years and blame the Western Allies for them, not the Nazi regime, which was responsible for infinitely more suffering. This forgetfulness and the new German assertiveness frightened Mr. Thayer.

Those Englishmen and Americans who visited Germany for a short period and wrote books or articles about how fine a democracy West Germany is, give a very untrue picture of Germany, for the sloth of German hearts is crying to heaven. The poet Hans Brandenburg knows his people better. In a very impressive poem he says: "The masses shouted and were jubilant finding the mass-idol in you. And those who did not belong to the masses and are awake today behave like those who do not remember what they did in their intoxication. They rub their eyes and say: It was not me."[15]

This sort of sloth started in May, 1945. The Allied armies entering Germany uncovered many concentration camps full of unspeakable horrors. One need only read what the Generals Eisenhower, Bradley, and Patton found in Ohrdruff and how they reacted then, only twenty years ago. When the Mayor of Ohrdruff and his wife were shown the horrors of that camp, they went home and cut their wrists; life seemed to them intolerable after they had seen what innumerable of their countrymen had done. The Allied armies also found some 500 slave labor camps in Germany with 14 million half-starved slave workers from more than twenty nations. The Germans, however, as Professor M. J. Proudfoot, who worked several years with UNRRA, said, "in a very little while succumbed to an overwhelming surge of self-pity over their own post-war inconveniences, and the agonies of their former captives were conveniently forgotten."[16] The composer Hans Pfitzner, for instance, who had once quarrelled with Thomas Mann because Mann had spoken in favor of "the Marxist republic," as Pfitzner put it, complained in 1945: "We live miserably in a small room and must be glad to have found refuge in a hospital." In 1946 he wrote: "Now in the evening of my life, I sit unhonoured, forbidden, undesirable, suppressed in an old people's home."[17] And he complained about "what Herr Thomas Mann deemed right to say about Germany to the world."[18] Others complained that "the whole of Germany had become one gigantic concentration camp" because the Allies had interned every German suspected of crimes against humanity. "One must, however," the Germans added, "not call it a concentration camp."[19] They complained that life in the internment camps was "as narrow as a coffin."[20] The louder a German had once hailed Hitler, the louder was his lament in 1945. In many books they pitied themselves in heartbreaking words, all these Hitler writers and Hitler generals of whom we spoke on earlier pages. Some even wrote that the inmates of the concentration camps "got 1,675 calories daily even in the worst times."[21] Ernst von Salomon found many readers for his cynical book, *The Questionnaire,* in which he described the SA leader Ludin, who was executed as a war criminal by the Czechs, as a noble idealist. When the courageous Bishop of Münster, Count von Galen, complained to the British authorities about some murders committed by released slave workers against Germans, the commanding British general answered politely that he would look into the matter; but he asked the bishop to consider that these foreign workers had for several years experienced that might went before right and were hating the Germans now—he could not possibly keep these foreign workers behind barbed wire any longer. The poet Hans Carossa thanked the Allied armies for their discipline, which alone saved the German nation from the revenge of those slave workers who "had been treated very harshly and starved terribly."[22] No one of those who complained so bitterly, he added, had asked himself "what Hitler, Himmler, Heydrich and Kaltenbrunner would have done to a defeated Great Britain, a defeated Russia and a defeated America." Professor Johannes Klein said that if a nation, after losing a war, suffers hunger because of the hardness of the victors, "everyone shoulders the 'collective guilt.' He suffers for those who have committed crimes, he suffers for the reputation of his nation."[23] A Christian humanist wrote that the Second World War had been unlike any other war; it was "a punitive expedition of world-wide scope undertaken by the civilised world to punish an unspeakable gang of criminals who had seduced a whole nation to committing the most hideous crimes."[24]

Professor F. W. Foerster, seeing that the post-war Germans did not want to be reminded of "disagreeable facts" and that many former Nazis have returned to "influential posts," takes great pains to remind them of all sorts of things. He calls himself "political doctor and psychiatrist who, after an experience of decades, has come to the conclusion that the German war illness cannot be compared with anything in the world." The Germans betrayed their European heritage when Bismarck came along with his principle of blood and iron, when even the small minority of German liberals were perfectly willing to sell their freedom "to a state which had sold justice to power."

Constantin Frantz, Bismarck's enemy, wrote at the time: "The maxim of *oderint dum metuant* may one day bring into being a great coalition against the new *Reich*." Treitschke, however, said in 1870 that Germany should show no "forbearance and magnanimity towards a defeated France. A miraculous grace hands us down a wreath which we should seize with courageous hands." When Nicholas II of Russia suggested to the Kaiser complete disarmament, the latter retorted: "If he says this to me personally I shall smack his face." And Professor Wilhelm Kahl wrote: "The ancient Germans would turn in their graves at the idea of complete disarmament." More and more German industrialists, politicians, and generals clamored louder and louder for "a European extension of the German *Reich*." General Bernhardi wrote: "We should not be blinded by English approaches. Let us use them to win time for the necessary and inevitable war until we can wage it with reasonable hope of victory." Professor Foerster remarks: "The mad belief in the invincibility of the Prussian military system was shared by only too many in the highest quarters."

But, after the defeat in 1918, the Germans clamored passionately against "the lie of our war guilt," and murdered Commander Hans Paasche, who had written: "Very few Germans know the gulf which separates them from the rest of the world. The 'German idea' is dead." The conservative historian Hans Delrueck wrote in 1926: "Responsible for our downfall is this and this alone: militaristic and nationalist hubris which, in foreign affairs, prevented the policy of a negotiated peace, and internally, a compromise long overdue." But to this very day, Professor Foerster remarks, "millions of Germans cling to the mad idea of a perfidious Albion which started a war against Germany out of financial envy." The Treaty of Versailles "gave Germany a providential opportunity to rid herself of her mad militarism," but the Germans very soon rearmed secretly and their generals collaborated with the Red Army. Colonel Hierl wrote in 1929: "There is a certain pacifism which is a political weapon and serves for preparing war. You lull the enemy into security by peaceful phrases, he neglects his armament, and you put a smoke screen around your own armament. Pacts to outlaw war must be looked at from this angle."

Professor Foerster says, therefore: "The German inclination towards exaggeration, their want of moderation, their extremism, culminated in the cult of the total state and total war." Thomas Mann said of the Third Reich: "This is no state and no social order, it is the wickedness of hell. War against it is a holy war of humanity against the Devil himself." Professor Foerster: "The murder of ten to twelve million innocent people burdens the German name forever. No hellish fantasy can describe what happened in the burning of the Warsaw Ghetto when Germans shot dead women and children who had fled to the roofs of the burning houses." The German nation "does not realise its betrayal of all moral principles from 1933 to 1945, a betrayal which can only be called satanic." They excuse themselves by saying: "It was only Hitler—and a few others." Professor Foerster asks: "Why did the Germans vote for Hitler's party from 1930 onwards and went on voting for it until it reached 44 per cent? . . . All mass expulsions and murders of the Second World War had been recommended decades earlier by the Pan-Germans." Even worse: "What was destroyed of the German cultural heritage between 1933 and 1945 is the result of the Prussian confusion since Frederick II. . . . Hitler was only one of innumerable Germans full of confused Prussian and Pan-German ideas. He sealed the destruction of the German idea which has been reigning for a thousand years." Professor Foerster quotes Professor Hans Rothfels: Hitler "was no isolated phenomenon of German history but the catastrophic product of the German inclination to deification of the state and convenient submission to state authority." The Germans did not succeed in "conquering the mistrust against their war of conquest against Russia. . . . We must understand that the memory of the victims is better than that of the forgetful West."[25]

Ernst Glaeser, whose books were burned in 1933, speaks today of German schizophrenia. In the German soul "good and bad have perennially been fighting each other. I often think the Germans were always searching for paradise, and when they do not find it, they are so enraged with themselves that they take refuge with the Devil." Another decent German says the Germans can "suddenly become enraged against everything, now under the Prussian, now under the brown jackboot. What a divided nation, a conglomeration of many nations! They spoke so much about race because they have none."

We read in his novel of the German peculiarity of rapidly forgetting unpleasant things. In professorial circles "they hardly touch the years of the Third Reich. The students, with few exceptions, know nothing about them and are not eager to know anything." One German of the older generation is against bringing up the past. "After all, we have indemnified the Jews, and the Russians have pilfered enough." But Ernst Glaeser reminds them of everything they have done: the extermination of the Jews, the Russian slave-workers, the plundering of Russia and so on. He also sees how all the industrialists, scientists, and politicians bury themselves in work. "After the intoxication of the war, the Germans have flung themselves into the intoxication of the peace. What has been suppressed by a cunning military state which, in the end, sold itself to political cannibalism explodes now into an unchecked individualism valuing nothing except rattling money. It was a flight from the hollow spaces of false ideals into berserk work." We make the acquaintance of various specimens of the Hitler era. High school teacher Joblanski, who once lectured in the Skoda works of occupied Czechoslovakia, is now "a realistic politician" and says: "Our great duty lies, as ever, in the East which was once civilised by our medieval kings and the German Knights." Hugo Pflantler, who once took snapshots of the Jewish ghettoes and published them in the *Völkischer Beobachter*, has become a millionaire by publishing stories of "the heroic deeds of the *Luftwaffe*, the desert war, the Siberian prisoner of war camps." Of course, "all officers and soldiers are fine chaps, courageous men who only did their duty." An industrialist says: "They destroyed our factories but we built new ones and beat them on the markets by our superiority." But he also says this: "Our nation has always been divided. It consists of hexerogeneous tribes who never were one. Unification was forced on us by blood and iron."[26]

Gudrun Tempel, a young German of the post-war generation, has this to say: "If we look back at the last thirty years, we see a large herd of ostriches: Ourselves. We evade the truth. Of all nations I know, the Germans evade the truth more than all the others. If you ask me for one word which characterises the German, I should call him the eternal Evader. What he evades more than anything else, is responsibility. This explains Hitler's great success. Does the German care for anything at all? With his whole personality? Yes, for one thing, efficiency and obedience. Take away his efficiency, what remains of him?"[27] He only cares for hard work, not for his past. He still wants "to be told what to do." A cry from her heart: "My generation of Germans has such bitter feelings about the generation before ours because they refused to take on responsibility exceeding the limits of their own four walls. They were not really interested in resistance, they were concerned with the largest slice of the cake. The majority of Germans are still utterly devoid of the capability of political reasoning. They worship the god of efficiency above all other gods."[28]

The most outspoken critic of Germany's post-war behavior was Hermann Hesse. When, during the war, some German soldiers from the Russian front—which the poet called "a rapacious march through half of Russia"—wrote to him that they stood in the Caucasus to defend those highest values of the

German spirit as part of which they regarded his work, he pushed the letter aside as "immature nonsense," because these poor heroes "helped some beasts to ruin everything genuinely German." When others wrote him after the war about what they had to suffer, he asked them why they made no mention of what "they had for years done as German soldiers to the world," and why they "felt no guilt." When somebody asked him what they could have done against Hitler, he retorted: "Why did you find out Hitler only after 1933? Could you not have found him out after his Munich revolt at the latest? Why did you almost unanimously sabotage the German republic, the only gratifying fruit of the First World War? Why did you unanimously vote first for Hindenburg and later for Hitler?" Germany's misery, he told those unteachable Germans, did not start with Hitler, it started in the summer of 1914 when "the drunken joy of the German nation about Austria's mean ultimatum to Serbia could have awakened you." When others told him that they had had one foot in a concentration camp, he answered that he "could only take seriously those enemies of Hitler who had been in concentration camps with both feet, not with one foot there and with the other foot in the party." When they complained of the bombing of Germany and indicated how valuable they themselves were and how worthless the enemies of Germany, he retorted: "The German nation feels no responsibility for what it did to the nations of the world." They should stop praising the German soldiers. He had for years "prayed for the defeat of the glorious soldiers." When they showed concern for the public morals of the Norwegians who had condemned Knut Hamsum, he told them not to moralize for other nations. In France, Hamsum would have been one of the first to be shot for collaboration; he was not only a friend of the Nazis, but most of his books reveal him as a bitter enemy of the spirit. Hesse spoke angrily about the nationalism of those for whom the word "German" had still a sentimental and "holy" ring. Has dignity, he asked, or courageousness more value when it bears the label "German"? Do we not find the same dignity, courageousness, perseverance, chivalry in good Japanese, Chinese, Mohammedans? "As soon as Germany sees some possibility of getting powerful again you will be tempted by those who speak of holy Germany, her holy distress, her holy suffering and her eternal manliness, and very soon the soldiers will be there again and Germany's claim to power, to an empire and to being the chosen vessel." He condemned German forgetfulness in angry words, saying: "It is a German vice to speak so loudly of the rope in the house of the hanged. No one has learnt anything, everybody expects pity, help, understanding, but nobody indicates that he feels guilty for anything, not only for Hitler but for many things as well." To another German he wrote that he could not agree with the German opinion that "nations are not responsible for what they do." They could have found out Hitler in 1923 but they preferred to sabotage the republic. "You must accept the consequences for having attacked the world like robbers and turned it into a hell by your satanic methods."[29]

Hesse repeated these accusations in an Open Letter addressed to all Germans, with the result that he was told that he had no right to criticize the Germans because he had lived quietly in Switzerland all the time, having given up his German citizenship when the Germans refused to listen to his warnings in the years before Hitler. He retorted: "Many a thing is today as it was once at the end of the First World War. Just as all my German friends are today unanimous in the condemnation of Hitler, so they were unanimous in the condemnation of militarism, war and violence when the German republic was founded. But a few years later Hitler could already attempt his Munich revolt. Therefore I do not take seriously today's unanimity in condemning Hitler nor do I see in it the slightest guarantee of a political change of heart or even political understanding."[30]

The Germans had hardly recovered from their defeat when

they began, more and more loudly, to criticize the behavior of the Allies before and during the war and to make them responsible for Germany's fate. Highly remarkable in this respect is the popularity among post-war Germans of Captain Russell Grenfell's odd book, *Unconditional Hatred*. They were very pleased to read, in a German translation, that Austria is not to be blamed for the outbreak of the First World War because Serbia's answer to the Austrian ultimatum had by no means been as conciliatory as the British want us to believe. As for Germany, it was in reality Sir Edward Grey who is the culprit, because he had authorized secret military conversations with France in 1906. The allegation that Germany had started the war of 1914, is "but a myth." Hitler, in his turn, had always been very anxious to come to an understanding with Britain, and up to the British declaration of war he had done her no harm. Britain was very imprudent, first to allow herself "to become involved in the German dispute with Czechoslovakia," and then to commit the blunder of letting herself be "pushed by interested clamour into making a gesture to stop Hitler by guarantee to Poland against Germany." This, according to him, was the "true" origin of the Second World War. Britain's vital interest had neither been consulted in 1914 nor in 1939, or else we should have had no wars at all. But propaganda by Sir Winston Churchill and other British politicians, editors of newspapers, and bishops had made us believe "that Germany started the last two wars." As to the conducting of the Second World War, he blames Great Britain for the bombing of German towns, glosses over the German crimes against all European nations (if the Germans were monsters—"but who is not?"), blames Sir Winston for giving, at Yalta, German territory to the Poles, and for the division of Germany.[31]

Naturally the Germans fell for such nonsense; many unteachable German writers are telling their countrymen the same things. They listen with satisfaction to Grenfell, but refuse to listen to the few judicious German historians who tried to convey to them the stark truth about Germany. The publisher of the German translation of the late Captain Grenfell's book announced proudly that 22,000 copies of it had been sold in the first seven months.

Hitler's deputy press chief Helmut Sündermann, too, praises Sir Oswald Mosley. In 1941 Sündermann wrote that Hitler's victory "would mean the end of all Jewish dreams of world hegemony." In 1940 he wrote about "the end of the Jews in Europe" and said: "The last bastion of international Jewry still stands. But this last tower of refuge is tottering under the annihilating blows of the German army. The time is nearing when the fateful invasion of the Jewish bastards into Europe, which has lasted for two thousand years, will be part of the bad past."[32]

This criminal was not imprisoned by the Germans after the war but was allowed, under the pretense of democratic freedom, to found a publishing firm. He used this freedom to publish a number of Nazi books, Ribbentrop's memoirs, Hess's letters to his wife, a book by the former Nazi Lord Mayor of Berlin, Lippert, who had been imprisoned by the Belgians for eight years because of his war crimes, and who had said in 1933: "The Jew is not a human being. But which animal could I offend by comparing it with a Jew?" Of Albert Einstein Lippert said in 1941: "He looked like a Galician carpet dealer who had not washed for a year."[33] In 1955 Sündermann published his own book, *Old Enemy—What Now?* The question is addressed to Great Britain, which he blames for both world wars. The Jews, he says, were deported because they had committed "acts of sabotage."[34] When some courageous journalists found a German judge who confiscated these books, Suendermann appealed against the sentence and found another judge who said that the books were all right and released them.

Many generals who helped Hitler to destroy the whole of

Europe have published war memoirs in which they figure as innocent lambs. Colonel-General Hausser of the *Waffen-SS* sang the praise of these soldiers in a book, *Waffen-SS in Fight,* and E. G. Kraetschmer wrote a book about *The Bearers of the Knights' Cross of the Waffen-SS.* The war criminal Kurt Meyer of the Waffen-SS wrote a book, *Grenadiers,* and yet another book showed the *Waffen-SS in Pictures.* Many other books glorify the German campaigns in Russia, Greece, Norway, and the successes of Hitler's air force and navy.

Apart from the publishing firm of Druffel, the general manager of which is Helmut Sündermann, the Goettinger Verlagsanstalt, Plesse Verlag, Vowinckel Verlag and Stocker Verlag also specialise in publishing neo-Nazi books which find many readers in Germany. One of the worst Nazi publishing firms, J. F. Lehmann, began to publish books again in 1950. The books published by this firm between 1890 and 1930 helped to bring about both world wars. Between the two wars he published books by the Pan-Germans Heinrich Class and Count Reventlow, and books with titles such as *Unconquered at the Front* and *The Responsibility of the Jews for Germany's Ruin.* Under Hitler, J. F. Lehmann published the books of the racialist H. F. K. Guenther, *The German Race, The Jewish Race* which, the publisher said, "contains the clue to the Jewish problem."

Many illustrated papers are specializing in white-washing the German past; the same is the purpose of the periodical *Nation Europa,* the editor of which, Arthur Erhardt, was a high officer of the SA after 1933 and later Sturmbannführer of the SS.

Many neo-Nazi organizations have openly or secretly established themselves in Germany and are glorifying the past in periodicals, calendars for soldiers, and leaflets. Many heroes of the Third Reich are contributors to these publications. Some of these periodicals are published abroad—many Nazis escaped in 1945 to Spain, Argentina, South Africa, Egypt, and the Middle

East—and are smuggled into Germany. One can read in these periodicals that the true Germans are against the criminal state which was established with the help of victors who have imported an alien culture into Germany. Yesterday, they assert again and again, Greater Germany had been a gigantic reality, and tomorrow it will become a new reality. Because the name National Socialism is discredited all over the world, they prefer to call themselves "Europeans" and are in touch with similar "Europeans," a lunatic fringe in many countries. On West German soil many Hungarian, Rumanian, Croatian organizations have established themselves, remnants of the admirers Hitler once found in those countries. The writer Stefan Andres complained a few years ago: "Our National Socialist heroes who were hibernating have awakened again, they travel abroad and come back, hold meetings, defame the resistance and tell their astonished but soon enthusiastic audiences—for everything is possible again now—that they have remained faithful to the Führer and his ideals and that it was high time that Germany awake again."[35] The set German answer to such warnings is the same as in the early 1920's: it is only a tiny minority. It took only a few years for the minority of the 1920's to become a majority; if Germany's economy should one day suffer a setback or if Germany at last realizes that the lost Eastern provinces are lost forever, nationalism will rapidly grow again and become hysterical. There is no possible doubt about this.

Most of Hitler's professors and novelists wrote books after the war and found publishers for them. But the books of such an eminent pre-war writer as Jacob Wassermann have not been reprinted in West Germany.

The Germans have written a number of books, and innumerable articles, about the bombing of Germany, but not even one book about the bombing of Warsaw, Rotterdam, London, Coventry, Plymouth, Belgrade by the German air force. They have always asserted that it was Great Britain which started the bombing of open towns. They forget that Admiral Canaris had warned Keitel against the bombing of Warsaw because it might invite retaliation from the Western Powers; Keitel had answered that the order had been given by Hitler personally.[36] The Polish writer Czeslaw Milosz said that Warsaw had been turned into "a heap of rubble and ashes, a city of the dead" by the German bombing,[37] and Ulrich von Hassel, who died the death of a martyr in 1944, entered in his diary in October, 1939 that Hitler's war against Poland had brought shame upon the German name, partly by the brutality of the German air force and partly by the ghastly bestialities of the SS, especially against the Jews. "Those who saw Warsaw with its devastated districts and the many thousands of corpses in the streets were terribly impressed by it."[38] F. T. Csokor witnessed in Poland "that new way of waging war when the hinterland becomes the front."[39] He had to flee from Poland and in the end got to Yugoslavia where he witnessed, and survived, the bombing of Belgrade, where, he says, there were "28,000 people in deep sleep not knowing yet that they will have to die this very night."[40] Theodor Haecker entered in his diary on April 6, 1941: "Occupation of Yugoslavia. The Yugoslavs declare Belgrade an open city, we called it Fortress Belgrade and bombarded it three times 'with great success.' The German heart is jubilant."[41] General Jodl entered in his diary on March 27, 1941: "It is politically very desirable to attack Yugoslavia with inexorable severity. It will be the main task of our *Luftwaffe,* starting as early as possible, to destroy their grounded air force and exterminate Belgrade by continuing attacks."[42] On June 30, 1940, Jodl signed an order in which he said: "Coupled with propaganda, terror attacks against England—to be declared as retaliation—to weaken and destroy the resistance of the population and compel the government to capitulate."[43] Fritzsche, Hitler's war commentator, announced over the radio: "When fire once rained on Sodom and Gomorrah only seventy-seven just men remained alive. It is very questionable whether seventy-seven just men are alive in London." But Theodor Haecker entered in his diary: "I already know many reasons why Germany will not win this war. One of them is this word by Fritzsche."[44] Fritzsche remained unpunished.

When Goebbels announced that "300,000 Kilograms of bombs crashed down on Birmingham tonight," Haecker wrote: "The depravity and curse of a nation are revealed more loudly and unmistakeably by these words than by its deeds."[45] When Luebeck was bombed in the spring of 1942, the Lutheran pastor Karl Friedrich Stellbrink told his community in his Sunday sermon "to listen to the voice of God and follow Him." He was arrested and executed. When Münster was bombed in October, 1943, Monsignore Heinrich Portmann, Count von Galen's secretary, was reminded of the prophecy of the godly Anna Katharina Emmerick that a rain of fire would set the roof of Munster Cathedral on fire in 1940. He thought also of Hitler's words: "I shall erase their cities," and asked: "Can one reap love if one sows hatred?" He reports Count von Galen as saying, when Hitler declared war against Great Britain and France: *"Finis Germaniae*—the end of Germany."[46] Thomas Mann said in 1943 in one of his radio speeches addressed to his barbarized nation: "Who would not think of Warsaw, Rotterdam, London and Coventry, and the triumphant descriptions full of cruel satisfaction which the Germans newspapers published of these bombings?"[47]

When Munich was bombed, the writer Friedrich Reck-Malleczewen said: "Under the burning heaven we see a gigantic shadow, the question of our guilt."[48] Victor Mann, Thomas and Heinrich Mann's brother, whose situation in Nazi Germany was more than awkward because of his brothers' uncompromising fight against the Third Reich, said: "Stronger than my sorrow when I saw dear old Munich burning and crumbling was my knowledge of a superhuman power. *Gladius Dei super terram cito et velocitor*."[49] These Latin words are from one of Thomas Mann's early short stories.) When Annette Kolb, the famous novelist who had left Germany in 1933, returned to Munich after the war and saw how it had been devastated by bombs, she simply said: "They should have listened to me."[50] The poet Hans Carossa said: "It was ourselves who have asked for the grey swarms of demons which are galloping through our night-skies and spreading horror."[51] Whenever he passed a certain rubbish heap in Munich after the war he remembered the pretty building which had once stood there and the fine chemist's shop which, being a doctor, he had often visited. He remembered especially the morning of March 5, 1933, when the young chemist's assistant told him with hectic passion of the destruction of the Social Democratic newspaper building, *Muenchner Post*, in the night before the election; it had been, he said, "the happiest night of his life." "Does that young man perhaps today know the connection between that gay night of destruction and the later nights of horror when beautiful Munich was laid in ruins?" asked Carossa.[52]

Theodor Plievier, who had to flee from Germany in 1933, says about the bombing of Dresden, which the Germans have resented most: "Oradour-sur-Glane, Lidice, Treblinka, Auschwitz, the Gas Zyclon B, the Night-and-Fog Order, Mountains of human skeletons from the fire-ovens and the gas chambers and hundreds of thousands marked down for annihilation, genocide as a principle of the state—it ill behooves us to speak of terror."[53] Victor Count von der Lippe, one of the Nuremberg Counsels, says that the bombing of Dresden should make the Germans ask themselves "whether the suffering of so many innocent Germans has not a moral side, whether it cannot be regarded as a sort of retribution for the suffering caused by the Germans."[54]

Professor Gollwitzer summed up the bombing of Germany in these terrible sentences: "Children jumping into the Elbe and the Wupper as blazing torches of phosphorus, children frozen to death in a ditch, skeletons of children running towards their liberators in Belsen and Auschwitz, naked children of gypsies and Jews, crowded together and dying heart-renderingly in flowing gas, Jewish schoolchildren in 1933, standing anxiously and without understanding in a corner of the school yard, evaded and insulted by the other children who had played with them only yesterday. With the year 1933 we stand at the beginning and this is the year of which we must think when we say 1945. It is our duty to remember, even if, and just because, it pains us."[55] The Lutheran theologian Karl Barth, who refused to swear an oath of allegiance to Hitler and left Germany to return to his native Switzerland, says: "A National Socialist victory would have been our worst imaginable defeat. Better a devastated Germany."[56]

One of the saddest chapters of the post-war history of Germany is her attitude regarding the Nuremberg trials. Pater Max Pribilla, S.J., as early as April, 1933 quoted publicly the words of St. Augustine, *"Remota iustitia quid regna nisi magna latrocinia,"*[57] and Cardinal Count von Galen, quoted those words again in a sermon on September 6, 1936. The Germans never listened to these men while Hitler's millennium lasted, nor have they taken the trouble to read the many volumes of the Nuremberg Proceedings or, at least, the utterances of a few of their own experts.

They prefer to listen to what unteachable politicians and journalists had to say about Nuremberg from 1945 to 1957. Göring, who had said on March 4, 1933, "My job is not justice, but to exterminate and annihilate,"[58] said afterwards: "We have lost the war. This is our war crime."[59] General Guderian said that "the defenders of Europe" had been tried in Nuremberg. "One may say about Hitler's deeds what one likes. If we look back, he fought for Europe."[60] General Rendulić, another fervent Hitler general said: "All orders which were declared illegal by the courts of our former enemies, were orders of

Hitler, that is to say not orders simply, but laws of the state."
He therefore speaks of "the so-called war criminals."[61] Walter
Goerlitz, historian of the Second World War, also speaks of "so-
called war-criminals" and of "biased judges."[62] In a textbook
for high schools one can read: "the German nation looks criti-
cally at these trials because many of the sentences were unjust."[63] The Germans have always complained that no German
judges were allowed to take part in the court proceedings. But
what German judges would have done at Nuremberg we can see
by what they did when a war criminal was caught later and
brought before a German Court. August Heinrich Kolb, commandant of the concentration camp Sachsenhausen, was sentenced to only four years and three months. Emanuel Schaefer,
an SS officer, who reported to Hitler that "Serbia is free from
Jews" and was responsible for the death of five or six thousand
Jewish women and children, received only a sentence of six and
a half years. The German judge said that he had been too weak
to resist evil. Councillor Rademacher, responsible for the shooting of 1,300 Jews in Yugoslavia, received a sentence of only
three years and five months. At the same time, Germans who
maltreated their fellow prisoners in prisoner of war camps received much heavier sentences, very often ten, twelve, fifteen
years or life sentences.

Let us now look back into the German past and remember
what some Germans said long ago. Professor Adolf Lasson
wrote in 1871: "The dream of a law between and above the
states is a confused and nonsensical dream born out of cowardice and false sentimentality." Professor Gerhard Ritter, who
quoted this sentence after the last war, added: "Such teachings
were much appreciated especially in military circles. The historian Heinrich von Treitschke told them in the 1880's to his
students who spoke of the 'godly majesty' of war."[64] One of
Hitler's innumerable scribes wrote in 1934 that similar ideas of
right only stemmed from "similar racial *Artung*," and that "no

parallel was possible between national and international law." All right was conditioned by race, and as the races were very different "no body of law was possible which would be appreciated by everybody."[65] Another Hitler scribe, Dr. Hans-Helmut Dietze, said in 1936 that "not the dreams of people without race could be the foundation of a realistic international law, but only the racial order of mankind. . . . It is a sign of courage to break with outmoded international ideas. National Socialism applies it to all questions of our life."[66]

Judicious Germans held, of course, very different ideas. J. K. Bluntschli, a very famous jurist, wrote in 1878: "Other states have a right to interfere in the name of international law when 'human rights' are violated to the detriment of a race."[67]

Let us now go back to the Nuremberg trials themselves, of which Dr. Eugen Kogon, who spent seven years in Hitler's concentration camps, said after the war: "The German nation should read, with that objectivity which had once been its pride, what truth is to be discovered in those proceedings, and ask itself: Where have we got to? How was this possible? What can we do?"[68]

The Nuremberg judges quoted on various occasions the Hague and Geneva Conventions, in which the rules of warfare are clearly defined. They tell all politicians and generals what they are, and what they are not, allowed to do during a war. In case of doubt which might arise in the future, this was laid down: "Until a more complete code of laws of war has been issued, the high contracting parties deem it expedient to declare that, in cases not included in the regulations adopted on them, the inhabitants and the belligerants remain under the protection and the rule of the principles of the law of nations, as they result from the usages established among civilised peoples, from the laws of humanity, and the dictates of the public conscience."[69] The judges also drew attention to Paragraph 234 of the German penal law, published in 1942, which provided that "whoever seizes another by ruse, threats of force in order to expose him in a state of helplessness, or to deliver him into slavery, bondage, or a foreign military or naval service shall be punishment for kidnapping by confinement in a penitentiary."[70] Further, the judges drew attention to the Kellogg-Briand pact of August 27, 1928, signed by Germany, by which war, as Secretary of State Stimson outlined in 1932, had been declared illegal.

Nobody in Germany bothered to explain these things to a wider public. Only the hairsplitting paradoxes of the German counsel for the defense seem to have got stuck in the minds of the Germans. Professor Jahrreiss, who conveniently forgot that millions of Germans, in spite of many warnings, had shouted "All power to the *Führer*," told the judges that all power lay in the hands of Hitler and that his orders had to be obeyed by the hierarchy of the German state. It did not matter whether this or that order of Hitler was against international law—Professor Jahrreiss was sorry, but this was the state of affairs. Dr. Servatius was of the opinion, shared by Dr. Thoma and Dr. Stahner, that Germany was fighting a war of life and death, a war in which all values have been revalued—we remember Nietzsche!—and could therefore not adhere to international law. Dr. Laternser, who defended the accused generals, repeated Dr. Jahrreiss' "arguments."

A few decent German experts have published their opinions about the justification of the Nuremberg trials but they failed to arouse the interest of the general public. Professor Dr. Herbert Kraus said that no moral man will doubt that the terrible crimes which had been revealed at Nuremberg "cried out for punishment before God and men." The crimes of which the war criminals were accused "constitute without exception acts which are regarded as crimes by the laws of all civilised states."[71] Professor Dr. Wilhelm Grewe, too, said that the Nuremberg Court dealt with "acts which are not only morally wicked but also criminal and punishable according to the clear wording of the law."[72] The former Bavarian Prime Minister, Dr. Hans Ehard, said: "These crimes would have met with deserved punishment in accordance with the laws of most states, including Germany. What a shame to see unrefutable proof of how cowardly, dog-like obedience of followers of Hitler and mad frenzy have trodden all honour and humanity under their feet and squandered the German prestige."[73] Dr. August von Knieriem, who was himself accused in connection with the proceedings against the I. G. Farben but was acquitted, reminded the Germans (in vain, of course) that, according to Livy, the Romans had punished their general Quintus Pleminius because of his war crimes against the Locri during the Second Punic war. Livy (XXIX, 16) quotes what the Locri said: they called Pleminius "a pestilential monster" who had turned all his captains and soldiers into Pleminii. "They rob, plunder, wound and murder. They rape women, girls and children whom they tear from the embrace of their parents." The Locri say that there are gods who will punish the criminals. Again, in 1474, the judges at Breisach needed no codified international law when they sentenced Peter Von Hagenbach to death, who, as Lord-lieutenant of Charles the Bold, "had trodden all God's and human laws under his feet"; it was of no avail to him that he said that he had to obey the orders of his king.[74]

Dr. Otto Nelte, contradicting Professor Jahrreiss, said that if what the latter had asserted was right, one would come to the conclusion "that a Caesarian maniac could in his frenzy decide what is right and what wrong. The principles of humanity need not be codified, they are absolutely valid.[75] Professor Gustav Radbruch, one of the most famous German jurists (he was duly dismissed from his post in 1933), quoted the words of St. Augustine and said: "Where justice is not even aimed at, where the equality of all men, which is the core of all justice, is consciously denied, the promulgated laws are not just 'incorrect laws' but they lack all qualities of laws. The most outstanding quality of Hitler was his lack of a sense of truth and justice. In the beginning of his career there was his telegram of sympathy to the murderers of Potempa, at the end the horrible degradation of the martyrs of July 20, 1944."[76] A high German judge, Dr. Erdsiek-Celle, when reviewing Professor Radbruch's book, *The Spirit of English Law,* sums up its deductions by saying that the continental positivism with regard to law cannot be applied to English law because in England people think of the substance of justice, not of the letter of the law. The Germans, however, uncritical as to the meaning of the law, regard as right what is expressed in the law, even if it is only the authoritarian order of a state disregarding every right."[77]

Dr. Knieriem reminded the Germans of the provision of the Hague Convention of October 18, 1907 that the governments who have signed the convention should promulgate laws which regulate warfare in accordance with that Convention. The idea that war crimes should be punished is expressed in the American *Instructions for the Government of Armies of the United States in the Field* (1863) and in the regulations of the German General Staff of 1871, in which is said: "Those who act against certain rules of warfare will, if captured, be punished." Knieriem says: "What use is the positive law if a state possesses a law which forbids murder, and compels its citizens to commit murder?" He quotes Professor Radbruch, who asks: "If the law compels the courageous and the coward to lay down his life rather than to desert, can it not expect everybody to sacrifice his life rather than become a slave to the most cruel barbarism and the most terrible in humanity?"[78]

Professor Kraus says: "There are things which cannot be ordered and done by any sovereign law."[79] The accused German generals, however, repeated again and again that they had to obey orders, and their Defense Counsel, Dr. Laternser, quoted English and American military laws as saying that a soldier must obey orders. He often quoted the famous British expert on international law, Oppenheimer, as saying the same, and "the Jew" Oppenheimer all of a sudden became "one of the most famous jurists" of Europe.[80] But this famous jurist had already strongly disapproved of the behavior of Germans during the First World War and had hoped for their defeat. Can anybody in his senses think that Professor Oppenheimer intended to concede to the German generals of the Second World War the right to commit hideous war crimes when he said that a soldier must obey orders? Dr. Laternser asserted: "We realise now the sins of the past when people omitted to promulgate clear and exhaustive rules of the rights of an occupying power in war time. For this sin of omission both the Hague Convention and the League of Nations are responsible."[81]

When the accused generals asserted that a refusal to obey military orders was a thing unknown in the Prussian tradition, they simply and cowardly lied. When Frederick William I inspected a regiment and, for some small slip, beat a major with his crutch-stick, the major drew his pistol, fired it into the sand, and said: "This shot was meant for Your Majesty."[82] Then he shot himself. Colonel Ludwig von der Marwitz had, in the Seven Years' War, disobeyed an order of Frederick II to plunder the castle of the Saxon Minister Bruehl. Marwitz refused to do something which he regarded as unworthy of himself. On his gravestone in the village churchyard of Friedersdorf (Brandenburg) are engraved, visible to all, these words: "Saw Frederick's heroic age and fought in all his wars, but chose disgrace when obedience meant dishonour."[83] General von Seydlitz refused to obey Frederick II when the king gave him a senseless order in the campaign of Zorndorf, and when the King threatened to have him shot, he answered: "My head is at Your Majesty's disposal after the campaign."[84] When Frederick II ordered his Minister of Justice, Baron von Muenchhausen, to annul a lawful verdict of the courts, the decent Prussian nobleman answered: "My head is at Your Majesty's disposal but not my conscience."[85] Count von Galen quoted this example in his sermon on July 20, 1941, and added: "Are noblemen like him extinct? Obedience to God and our conscience may cost us life, liberty and home but let us rather die than commit sin."[86] General York von Wartenburg disobeyed Frederick William III, concluded his famous convention of Tauroggen with the Russians on December 30, 1812, and wrote to the king: "I lay my head willingly at Your Majesty's feet, if I have done wrong." He became famous in Germany for his "World-historically important deed" which was the beginning of the end of Napoleon.[87] (Many descendants of these famous noblemen took part in the revolt against Hitler on July 20, 1944.) General von Lossow (in the autumn of 1923) disobeyed an order by the democratic War Minister Gessler to suppress the *Voelkischer Beobachter* in Bavaria.

Lieutenant-General Helmut Friebe reminded the Germans of the question of a soldier in the Kaiser's army: "What have I to do if His Majesty should give me an order to shoot every tenth prisoner of war?" His colonel told him that his question was irrelevant because such an order could never be given to a German soldier.[88] The young novelist Kirst makes one of his characters ask: "Why do we obey when this Fuehrer gives an order?" and another answer: "A national character trait—orders are sacrosanct with us. All orders, whether given by honourable men, idiots or criminals."[89] Remarque makes one of his characters say: "We are a master race! And obey every order even in our dreams!"[90] The poet Werner Bergengruen praised Dr. Rudolf Pechel for his fight against the Third Reich "in which no marshal titles, no marshal cheque books and no marshal notations nor 'oak leaves and swords' could be won, but only a rope and the axe."[91]

As some high British personalities have expressed doubts about whether it was right to hang German generals, it will be good to recall what a younger counsel at Nuremberg, Carl Haensel, said: "A soldier who receives an order from an officer to kill a man, must not obey. Every soldier knows this. This is no new principle of law but an ancient rule."[92] As hardly any ordinary German has ever taken the trouble to read the many volumes of the Nuremberg proceedings, nobody in Germany seems to know that the judges drew attention to Paragraph 47 of the German Military Law of 1926 which expressly said that both the commanding officer and the obeying subordinate are to be held responsible for the execution of a military order which is contrary to the law. Colonel-General von Mackensen, when asked at Nuremberg whether he, as a high officer, recognized a higher law than obedience to the oath sworn to Hitler, answered: "Yes, there is a higher order, namely: Thou shalt obey God more then men."[93] Count von Galen said from the pulpit in 1934: "Human authorities can only give us orders when acting as servants of God in accordance with and subject to the will of God."[94] In 1936 he said that obedience which enslaved the soul and was contrary to conscience, the holy of holies of human freedom, was "rudest slavery." He reminded the congregation of the early Christian martyrs who had disobeyed a Roman emperor who gave them blasphemous orders, and "willingly accepted death because they knew that one must obey God more than men."[95] He himself was quite prepared to become a martyr, if God willed it so. *Gauleiter* Alfred Meyer of Westphalia would have liked to martyr him and Bormann would have liked that too, but they were afraid of a revolt of the Catholics of Westphalia. So they decided to hang him after the war. On August 3, 1941, Count Galen said again from the pulpit: "Woe to men, woe to our German nation, if we break the holy commandment: 'Thou shalt not kill; which God gave us on Mount Sinai under thunder and lightning."[96] On more than one occasion he foretold the Germans their fate.

A glimpse of the "other" Germany will show that devout

Christians acted in accordance with Count Galen's sermons. The priest Franz Reinisch, when called up refused to swear the oath of allegiance to Hitler with these words: "The present Government is not willed by God, it is a nihilistic Government which has come into power by violence, lies and fraud."[97] He was executed on July 7, 1942. Hans Berndt von Häften said to Freisler at the People's Court: "I see in Hitler the representative of evil in history."[98] He was executed. Many members of a Christian sect roughly the equivalent of Jehovah's Witnesses were terribly maltreated and murdered in concentration camps because they refused to join Hitler's army. Father Alfred Delp, imprisoned after July 20, 1944, and tortured by the SS in prison, wrote with his shackled hands: "Bread is important, freedom is more important. But the most important thing is the never-broken faithfulness and the unbetrayed reverence."[99] He was executed.

The young chaplains Johannes Prassek, Hermann Lange, and Eduard Mueller died on November 10, 1943 "for the truth of Christ," as Bishop Wilhelm Berning said, for trying to demoralize the army, as the Nazis said; they had distributed the sermons of Count von Galen both among civilians and soldiers. When the Bishop visited them in their cells after they had been sentenced to death, he noticed "a holy peace in their eyes." They told him that they were "happy beyond words to be allowed to sacrifice their lives for Christ, our King." Chaplain Prassek entered in his Bible after returning to his cell: "Praise be to God! I have been sentenced to death today." Chaplain Lange wrote to his parents a few hours before his execution: "Oh, look wherever you like, always we meet with the joy at the grace of being God's child. Today is the day of the great return into the house of my Father. How could I be otherwise than joyful and full of expectation?" Chaplain Mueller wrote to his sister: "My last word: Christ, our King, eternal faithfulness!" When Prelate Bohnen three years later held a memorial service for these three martyrs he said: "I have suddenly a vision. I see the men in the dock at Nuremberg."[100]

The mass of the Germans are unconcerned with these things; they continue to speak of the injustice of Nuremberg to this very day. A few years ago they stopped speaking of "war criminals" and now only speak of "the war condemned." For years they have been clamoring for the release of the war criminals, and the Western Powers have complied with their wishes for reasons of cynical expediency, thus encouraging the Germans in their belief that these criminals were wrongly condemned. Hitler generals like Kesselring and Manstein and the Waffen-SS General Hausser wrote to the President of Italy to release the war criminal Walter Reder, sentenced for the murder of 3,000 Italian civilians. He had to obey orders, they said. When many war criminals in 1956 returned from Russia to Vienna and the Minister of Justice ordered their arrest, the Austrians cried out: "They were obeying orders!" So a general amnesty was declared in Austria. Sir Hartley Shawcross, British Prosecutor at Nuremberg, said in 1955 that it was wrong to release war criminals prematurely because their crimes had been of a nature that asked for a full atonement.[101]

Professor Wilhelm Roepke said in 1945: "All those who after this event"—Hitler's telegram of sympathy to the SA murderers of Potempa in 1932—"still adhered to the party of such a man have condemned themselves. At least, none of them should in future have a place in the public life of their nation."[102] Did the Germans perhaps listen to this warning? In 1948 one could read in a German newspaper: "The author of the prayer for children: 'God help our Führer!,' the author of the first National Socialist novel, the spiritual fathers of the racial laws, the notorious representatives of the SS biology—they have all long since returned and enjoy the best publicity. . . ."[103]

A great many National Socialists who served in Ribbentrop's

Foreign Office, and others as well, have returned to the Foreign Office of West Gemany.

Dr. Gerhard Schroeder, First Minister of the Interior, now Foreign Secretary, once wrote: "Our fight for the rejuvenation of science aims at eliminating the so-called objective uninhibited sciences and to replace them by disciplines which, like all other things of our life, are grounded in the politics of race and get their value and standard from the values of National Socialism. If we ask for a *Weltanschauung* in our historical judgment, we mean a German *Weltanschauung,* born of soil and blood, fight and suffering, work and fate of our nation."[104]

Under-State Secretary Dr. Wilhelm Grewe, for a time ambassador in Washington, wrote in 1940: "In the reconstruction of the *Generalgouvernment* [i.e., occupied Poland] just as in the entirely different *Protektorat* [i.e., occupied Czechoslovakia] we can see that, within the might realm of Greater Germany, a new political order is becoming reality."[105] In 1941 Grewe spoke of Hitler's "great world-historic mission" and his "big super-national task," seeing only in Russia, not in Nazi Germany, a state which is fundamentally different from all other states "in its political, social, spiritual and cultural substance."[106]

In 1942 he said about Hitler's war against Russia: "A mighty exertion of all our strength will be necessary to conquer this *Raum*. Once conquered, the world-political struggle against the Anglo-Saxons will be decided in our favor."[107] The diplomat Bargen, now ambassador in Iran, said under oath before a German court that Ribbentrop's Foreign Office had had nothing whatever to do with the deportation and murder of Jews, whereupon the judges showed him the draft of a deportation order which he had signed. Almost all State Secretaries, Under-State Secretaries, and heads of departments of the Nazi Foreign Office from Weizsaecker down had seen and signed the infamous order against the Jews. Dr. Otto Braeutigam wrote on November 11, 1942, from somewhere in the East: "On the order of the Military Commander 15,000 men, women and children have been deported. As many Jews, alarmed by rumours of the slaughtering of Jews, did not obey the order to come forward to work for us they were captured in raids and single actions."[109] When this became known in 1955, the Foreign Office, under pressure from decent Germans, was forced to retire him. Long before he had to leave, he had tried to bring into the Foreign Office his former boss in Rosenberg's East Ministry, Dr. Georg Leibbrandt, who took part in the discussions about the "Final Solution" on January 20, 1942. Dr. Braeutigam was interrogated by a commission of the Bundestag and, naturally, was exculpated. He is now in the Foreign Office again. Dr. Eberhard Taubert returned to the Foreign Office, East Department, although he had worked in the same capacity in Göbbel's Ministry of Propaganda and, as judge in the People's Court, had sentenced the resistance fighter George Walter to ten years' imprisonment. Dr. Herbert Dittmann, who in 1952 was declared by a commission of the Bundestag "not fit for a leading position in the Foreign Office"[109] because of his past, was recalled from his post as Counsul General in Hong Kong in 1957 and promoted to Under-State Secretary and head of four departments (Europe, West, East, Commerce). Dr. Braeutigam went to Hong Kong in his place. Chief of Protocol Dr. Guenther Mohr, who joined the Nazi Party since 1935, was sent as ambassador to Berne in spite of the campaign of several Swiss newspapers against him. Werner von Grundherr is now German ambassador in Athens although "he approved of the terror regime of SS *Obergruppenführer* Dr. Best in Denmark. When Best informed him of the plan to sweep down on 6,000 Jews and deport them, he only asked: "How many SS men do you need for the job?"[110]

About 85 per cent of the higher staff of the present German Foreign Office are former Nazis. Many of them had to do with the deportation and extermination of the Jews, in which also Ribbentrop's Foreign Office was involved.[111]

A member of the opposition party, Fritz Erler, therefore said a few years ago: "Restorative tendencies are certainly to be found everywhere but during the three years of my political life in this Parliament I have never seen a Ministry which regards itself with so much justification as a direct descendant of the Berlin Foreign Office, as the present Foreign Office."[112]

Dr. Fritz Schaeffer became Minister of Finance although he had been prepared to enter Hitler's Cabinet in 1933 and had said in May, 1933: "The task which Adolf Hitler has been called upon as rejuvenator of the *Reich* is so immense that it will be necessary to concentrate all our strength that the Chancellor succeeds in this gigantic task for the sake of Germany. Nothing could be more mad than to speculate on this failure."[113] Joachim von Meerkatz has become a minister although he once said this: "The liberal, democratic and parliamentarian state is decaying while a new political unity has come into being by the revolution of a responsible and vigorous government. The political expression of this cultural development is the *Führerstaat*."[114] Professor Theodor Oberlaender became Minister for Refugee Problems. A member of the Nazi party in 1933, he rose to the rank of *Hauptsturmführer* in the office of *Gauleiter* Erich Koch in the Ukraine. At times he was director of the Nazi Institute for East European Economy in Koenigsberg, and, in 1936, as director of the organization "German East," praised National Socialism as defender of Europe. Oberlaender said in 1954: "The expulsion of the Germans from the East annuls all German war crimes. We are morally absolutely quits."[115] When he criticized Professor Schmidt's journey to Poland, calling his and his friends' policy toward Poland a crime against Germany and Europe, he was reminded that he "had himself collaborated with the truly criminal Eastern policy of the National Socialists."[116] A decent German, Helmut

Hammerschmidt, said over the Bavarian Radio that Ober-laender had "gathered around him in his Ministry a phalanx of former high SA and Hitler Youth leaders. The bankrupts of yesterday have been recalled to their desks."[117] He added, thinking of all the other post-war ministries: Who pretends that it was impossible to find a few thousand intelligent, characterful, politically clean men and women for our higher posts? A few thousand in a nation of fifty millions?"[118]

Under-Secretary of State in Dr. Adenauer's Reich Chancellory was Dr. Hans Globke. When Cardinal Count Preysing called him "a devoted Roman Catholic whose life and deeds were ruled by the principles of the Roman Catholic faith,"[119] did he know all the facts? In 1932, as an official in the Ministry of Interior, Globke was instrumental in working out an order to prevent Jews from changing their names in order to hide their "non-Aryan" origin. Count Bismarck, dissatisfied with the fact that Jews of East European origin had "adopted very noble German names," suggested that Globke study the matter more closely. Globke agreed and sketched an order by which Jews were deprived of "protected" German names like Siegfried and Thusnelda; the document shows the names of Himmler and Globke near each other. On August 30, 1935, State Secretary Dr. Wilhelm Stuckart, with whom Globke remained in close contact till the end of the Third Reich, suggested to the higher authorities that Globke should be made a *Ministerialrat* because of his clear judgment, quick decisions, and perfect reliability. On September 9, 1935, the "Law for the Protection of German Blood and Honour" was promulgated, and in March, 1936 Stuckart's and Globkes's authoritative *Commentary* to this law was published. It was based on Hitler's words in *Mein Kampf*: "The fundament of the German State is the Nordic race." The racial laws, Stuckart said in the introduction, were based "on natural laws willed and given by God. The leadership of the National Socialist State is deeply convinced to act in accordance with the almighty creator of the world when it tries to express the eternal and iron laws of life and nature in the order of the Third Reich. . . . National Socialism sets against the belief in the equality of all men and the fundamental, unrestricted freedom of the individual the hard but necessary knowledge of the natural inequality of men." Jews, by their blood and innermost character, are "alien to Germandom [*dem Deutschtum artfremd*]."

Globke explained in his *Commentary:* "Of *artfremd* blood in Europe are only Jews and gypsies as a rule. Every nation endangers its life by receiving *artfremd* blood." On August, 1938, all German Jews were forced to add the name Israel and Sarah to their names; it was Globke who sketched that particular order which forced on newborn Jewish children names like Abieser, Ahasver, Asahel, Assur, Esau, Herodes, Hiob, Itzig, Jethro, Kaiphas, Korah, Laban, Moab, Sabbatas, Uria, Uriel, Chinke, Dewaara, Driesel, Fradel, Gole, Jezabel, Machle, Pesse, Rause, Reitzge, Scharne, Schlämche, Tetze, Zerel, Zirel, Zorthel. Jochen Klepper entered in his diary on August 23, 1938: "The list of names for newborn Jewish children is a sadistic derision."[120] But Globke was in the same year of shame awarded the Cross of Honour, "for faithful services." Stuckart, too, was awarded this Cross. Globke also worked out the racial laws to be applied in Poland. There exists a photograph showing Minister Frick (later hanged at Nuremberg), State Secretary Stuckart, and Globke, all three in National Socialist uniforms, being greeted in occupied Pressburg by little girls who present flowers to them. Another photograph shows these heroes and some other dignitaries raising their right arms before some National Socialist monuments. Globke's monthly salary in 1942 amounted to 1,199 marks. In the same year he was awarded another order of merit "as a sign of acknowledgement for services in the war which had been enforced on us." In 1942, Globke and Stuckart were awarded the "Star of Rumania."

Globke knew of the extermination of the Jews, just as did State Secretary von Weizsaecker, who posed as an innocent lamb before his judges in Nuremberg. A more decent German quarrelled with Stuckart and left the service. He was duly arrested. Globke, however, survived the war in freedom in a Bavarian Villa. The opposition party protested against Globke's comeback; Willie Mellies quoted a sentence from Stuckart-Globke's commentary and called it "a serious heresy."[121] Rightly so, for the sentence reads: "According to the National Socialist creed, not single individuals but races and nations form the order of this world as God has willed it." A few years later, seeing Globke still in office and even promoted, Dr. Arndt said in a parliamentary debate that the racial laws of Nuremberg meant "murder" and reminded the House that wherever Stukkart and Globke went in the occupied countries to discuss the deportation of the Jews, "a track of blood of the tortured and murdered Jews went, as all the world knows, from these discussions to the death-camps of Auschwitz and Maidanek." Outside Parliament he said that it was as impossible "to write a juridical commentary about the Nuremberg Laws as about the status of a criminal gang or the regulations of a brothel."[122] Adenauer completely ignored this criticism, and Globke remained in office until he was 65. He was even sent to Rome to congratulate Pope Pius XII on his 80th birthday. Professor Eduard Wagner protested against this scandal in these words: "What has Herr Globke to do in Rome? Should some tender coyness not better have kept him, with such a past as his, in the background? But tender coyness—and our worthies of yesterday who have risen so high again!! Tender coyness? Not at all. It was not a Canossa pilgrimage for him in sack and ashes to do penance."[123] But when it became known that Globke was to go to the United States, American Jews threatened that they would make demonstrations, and this time Globke stayed home. When Adenauer, however, invited the protesting professors of Goettingen in order to discuss with them the political aspects of German

H-bombs, Globke and General Speidel were present as "experts." When some Germans tried to whitewash Globke, Peter Miska, a simple but decent German, wrote about his commentary to the racial laws: "It is not disagreeable to read it—it is disgusting. Now we know you, Herr Globke. It does not happen everyday that a jurist lends his hand to comment on laws which are obviously criminal, as you did."[124] Another German wrote: "The author of this pornography did not die of delirium tremens; he was not hanged; nor did he commit suicide, but he is the almighty state secretary in the office of the Chancellor."[125] It was of no avail. Dr. Globke remained Dr. Adenauer's right hand. Other officials of the Third Reich also wrote commentaries to these laws, and they, too, are back again in post-war Germany: Dr. Knost is president of the district of Braunschweig. Dr. Massfeller, who represented the Ministry of Justice at the conference dealing with the "Final Solution" on April 6, 1942, is today in the Ministry of Justice at Bonn.

In all political parties we meet with former Nazis and anti-Semites, and as one party cannot blame the other for these scandals without blaming itself at the same time, all parties have a gentleman's agreement to be silent. Take, for instance, Dr. Heinrich Schneider, now a leading politician in the Saar. On February 18, 1934, he was photographed in his Nazi uniform swearing his oath of allegiance to Hitler with raised hand, standing near Vice-Chancellor Papen.

Many Nazi judges responsible for the death of many Poles, Czechs, Belgians, have become judges again in post-war Germany; Pastor Herbert Mochalski complained in 1959: "Our courts are full of judges and public prosecutors who as special judges of Hitler supported his criminal terror. And if they have not become judges again, they get high pensions."[126] On March 15, 1958, Gert Ledig, author of a novel with the telling title *Retribution,* published an open letter, "In the Name of the Gassed Children," in which he accused the present High Judge

THE TWO POST-WAR MENTALITIES 549

Muhs at Hamm (Westphalia) of being an accomplice to the murder of two Poles and three children. Muhs, he revealed, on June 25, 1943, at Radom, sentenced the Pole Bazyl Antoniak to death because this honest man had hidden two children, who should have been gassed in the Ghetto of Glinice. He also sentenced to death, on April 4, 1944, the Pole Wladyslaw Tyczinski for hiding a child which also was to have been gassed. "I call for justice for those three children. I accuse Muhs who now wears the robe of a judge in our republic. Muhs pronounces judgment today again in the name of the German nation. Law and justice are humiliated and defiled."[127] Danish resistance fighters protested in October, 1958 against the return in Germany as a high judge of Dr. Ernst Kanter, who had been the highest judge of the German court-martials in occupied Denmark. "It is incompatible with a democratic development," they wrote to the German authorities, "to allow men like Kanter to become judges again."[128] When a German denounced two Hitler judges, Dr. Lau and Dr. Cramer, who had become high judges again, a German lady, Ruth Andreas, asked: "But how many Wohrmanns are still in office?"[129] Two others who were reinstated after 1945 were Herman Markl and Max Rothang. In 1942, attorney Markl called 69-year-old Leo Katzenberger, one of the most esteemed Jews of Nuremberg, a dangerous enemy of the Germans. "The Jews are our misfortune. . . . the Jews are responsible for the war." Dr. Max Rothang condemned Katzenberger to death because he had acted against Hitler's racial laws. "The only possible answer," he declared, "to the frivolous attack of the accused against the German blood, the German honour and the body of a German woman is the death sentence."[130]

In the summer of 1962, Dr. Wolfgang Immerwahr Fraenkel was made Attorney General of West Germany, and some newspapers praised him as a strong enemy of every form of dictatorship. Who is this man? He had joined the Nazi Party in 1933 and became one of Hitler's judges in 1936. As such, he was not satisfied with the judgments of other judges who condemned Jews or Slavs to several years of imprisonment for imaginary crimes; he had them condemned more severely, in one or two cases to death. When decent Germans protested against the reinstatement of Dr. Fraenkel and asked how a man of his past could have been reinstated at all, the official explanation was: We asked him whether he had been a Nazi and he said no. He had to be retried and was given a good pension. A number of other Hitler judges were retried in 1962; all received good pensions but none was punished. Professor Franz Boehm said at the exhibition, "Unpunished Nazi-judges," in 1962: "These were no single crimes, they were a never-ending chain of misdeeds during the whole regime of Hitler. The reinstatement of so many guilty men in a civilised and free society is a political problem."[131]

General Speidel is back again after making the Free World believe that it is only Communists who are trying to defame him today. The truth is, as existing German documents prove beyond doubt, that, when Chief of Staff to General von Stuelpnagel, the German Commander in France, he had full knowledge of the murder of many Frenchmen and Jews who were shot in a barbaric system of reprisals and hostages. He reported all this in a matter-of-fact tone to his superior. People demonstrated against him in Paris, Copenhagen, and Oslo, but not in London. The appointment of this man as Commander of the NATO land forces in central Europe is inexcusable and a sad sign of the willingness of Western politicians to forget everything.

Also back in high positions are many industrialists who served Hitler with enthusiasm. Huge industrial concerns, disbanded after Germany's defeat because they helped Hitler to exploit and enslave all Europe, are slowly combining again in contradiction to the existing laws about the deconcentration of

German heavy industry. It is Dr. Adenauer himself who tries to get the permission of the Western Allies to annul the Paris agreement of 1954 about deconcentration. The Krupp and Thyssen concerns have become very powerful again; the latter is today the biggest German producer of steel. Also many Nazi directors of industrial concerns have again managed to secure high posts for themselves. Dr. Otto Ambros of I. G. Farben at Ludwigshafen, for instance. On April 12, 1941 he wrote about the plunderings in the East: "Dr. Eckell has very well stood the test, our new friendship with the SS proves to be a blessing. During the dinner which the leader of the concentration camps gave us, we have settled all the questions regarding the affiliation of the really magnificent works of the concentration camp with the Buna works."[132] Today Dr. Ambros is a director of three industrial companies. His friend, Walter Duerfeld, once director of the works of Auschwitz-Monowitz, is today director of a chemical factory.

Charles Wighton, who made a special study of Heydrich's and Neurath's behavior in occupied Czechoslavakia, says that "hundreds of the accomplices of Heydrich are still at liberty in Germany—unpunished." A high official of the North-Rhine Westphalia government asked him: "What about the *Bundes-Kriminalamt* and the *Sicherheitsgruppe* in Bonn where there are former top members of the SS who were involved in shooting and other crimes?" Charles Wighton adds that many Ruhr industrialists and bankers who once "swarmed into the protectorate to exploit the Czech colony" are today holding dominant positions in West German commercial life.[133]

Back already in 1947 were a number of despicable Hitler professors, whom Ursula Maria Martius, a devout Catholic German, denounced in the *Deutsche Rundschau*. "Hardly three years have passed since I stood before a barbed wire of the concentration camp where my father was kept imprisoned," when she found at the annual meeting of the Physical Society at

Goettingen "men who are still haunting me in my nightmares." They sat in the first row in civilian clothes, not in Nazi uniforms with the *Hakenkreuz*: Professor Stuart, who once came to his university lectures in SA uniform, today is in Hanover; Professor Schumann, once addressed as "Herr General," Professor Schober, who once prided himself on having been in the Aryanization Commission of the University of Vienna and who is now back in Hamburg.[134] Professor Pascual Jordan, whom that German lady was deeply disturbed to find again in Goettingen, wrote in 1941 that Hitler had not only united Nationalism and Socialism but also done away with all the things which disunited Germany. Hitler's war, he said, had brought about one definitive decision: "Parliamentarian and democratic thought is dead. Authoritarian and dictatorial governemnts are the mark of our age, expressing the insight that the unheard-of achievements of a technocratic mankind can only then be kept in order if the will of a Führer of extreme severity and hardness disciplines all the scattered forces. Only one thing matters: Not every nation has been presented with the vigour of a volcano." Therefore, he added, "we are not willed to see a misuse in the connection of science with military power because our military power has proved its constructive vigour by creating a new Europe."[135] In 1957 he had the insolence to attack the famous non-Nazi atomic scientists, Otto Hahn, Max Born (a Jew who unfortunately returned to Germany), and Werner Heisenberg, who had given warning of Germany's intention to start making atomic bombs. The grateful Christian-Democratic party put Professor Jordan up as a candidate for Parliament and he is now a member of the Bundestag. So it was perfectly in vain that Miss Martius said in 1947, of him and the other Hitler professors: "They have no right whatever to be educators today. There are enough others."[136]

Back also is Professor Erich Rothacker, who wrote in 1934 that it was important "to meditate about the gigantic event which we have witnessed. We were allowed to see how chaos gave birth to a new star." He praised "the victory of the national revolution" while deriding "liberal easy going." Hitler, "with the instinct of a great statesman," has in *Mein Kampf* made "the idea of a unified nation the highest value." Professor Rothacker despised all those "who had tried to veil the obvious physiognomic difference of the Jews."[137] Alfred Riewald, a high official in a ministry of Lower Saxony, was made Professor at Goettingen although, under Hitler, he had praised the idea of "blood" and despised liberalism, which protected "the individual too much." National Socialism allows no secrets in any sphere of life. "The Jews are no Germans."[138] Professor Wilhelm Helmich is back at Kiel University even though he wrote in 1939: "Children can see National Socialism embodied in the Führer. Their belief and their love are not satisfied by a mere ideal, they want a hero of flesh and blood. Our literature must bring the picture of the Führer before the eyes of the reader; it must stress the unity of blood between the Führer and the nation for the sake of racial education."[139]

Professor Hans Sedlmayr is back again, even though he said under Hitler: "We are united under the symbol of the *Haken-kreuz*. The future teachers of the German youth shall be taught faith in the banners of the Führer. We have gathered under these banners, and under these banners we march on. This is the total mobilisation of bodies, hearts and spirits for the fight for Führer and Reich."[140] Professor Theodor Maunz is a minister in the Bavarian government. He had praised Hitler's state in these words: "With its coming to power National Socialism has inaugurated a gigantic movement. Its aim is to rejuvenate German jurisprudence which has been falsified by alien ideas, and German juridical science which has been paralyzed by an alien idealism." In 1936 he lectured about "The Jews in Juridical Science."[141] Professor Peter Heinz Seraphim, who lectures today about East European economy, was in the days of Hitler a member of the Institute of German Eastern Activities and a member of the Institute for the Elucidation of the Jewish Question. Arthur Eisenbach, the historian of the Jewish Historical Institute at Warsaw, says about Professor Seraphim "that he wrote many papers about the Jews of Eastern Europe and played a criminal part in the preparation of the material used for the extermination of the Jews."[142]

Professor Karl Jaspers wrote in 1951: "The crime against the spirit of science was committed when professors falsified truth and served the interests of the Party. Truth and National Socialism are incompatible. Science was ruined by professors. It is the disgrace of our universities that this could have happened."[143] Rudolf Pechel wrote in 1956: "We stand on the threshold of an uncertain future, before the doors of new barracks and the menacing thunderstorms of a new concentration of racialists. Our public life is being renazified silently and without opposition. Power is no longer seized, it is obtained by underhand influence. The prominent intellectual forerunners of Fascism return more or less secretly."[144]

Back and in the new German army are many men of the SS and Waffen-SS, members of organizations, which was declared criminal by the judges of the International Court in Nuremberg—those men whom Dr. Werner Best, later Hitler's Lord-Lieutenant in Denmark, said in 1940 were subordinated to Himmler "for special duties in peace and war."[145] The world knows now what special duties were alloted to them. During the last German election almost all parties spoke of the need for a rehabilitation of all former Nazis and for "an honourable reconciliation."[146]

Completely forgotten is the Allied law of 1945: "All members of the Nazi party who have been more than nominal participants in its activities . . . shall be removed from public and semi-public office."[147] Thirteen years later Dr. Rudolf Pechel said: "The poison has penetrated too deeply into the national body and into our thoughts to be regarded as definitely conquered. Allegedly converted, half-converted or unconverted National Socialists are everywhere to be found in Bonn, in the *Laender,* in the town councils, in the parties, in economic life, at the universities. . . . Court proceedings of the last few months have proved beyond doubt that no genuine change of mind has occurred in many quarters."[148] A German who hides behind the initials P.R. agreed with this when he said in a south German newspaper in May, 1958: "We evade all serious discussion about National Socialism even today, which is perhaps due to the fact that many former Nazis are back again in leading positions."[149] Robert Neumann, a German refugee writer living in Switzerland, said in an interview with a decent German journalist: "It is Germany's tragedy that after the downfall of the Nazis there has been no revolution but a restoration which has led to the conservation of the ruins of the regime."[150] Listening for only a quarter of an hour to the debate in the German parliament about Germany's rearmament with nuclear weapons, he heard more than once the voice of Hitler—for he is, as he explained, "as sensitive to the cadences of voices as a Geiger counter is to radioactivity."[151]

Thomas Mann, the most famous of all German refugees, said in Wagnerian terms—Hitler loved Wagner's ideas and music and regarded himself as a new Siegfried stabbed in the back by world-Jewry—in 1947: "Our love belongs to fate—to any fate, if it only be one, even if it be the end of the world which kindles heaven with the redness of the twilight of the gods."[152] The poet Hans Brandenburg agrees, saying: "The ancient myth—does it once again, mysteriously whispering, explain the more ancient myth turning the twilight of the gods into the twilight of men?"[153] One of the German counsels at Nuremberg said it had been the deep tragedy of the German nation that it did not sublimate its belief of having come too late for the division of the worldly possessions, into securing and bettering its honorable place in the world of the spirit and the applied sciences. A Viennese professor sums up Germany's fate by saying that her deeper guilt lies in the fact that a real revolution has never been allowed to take place on her soil. Luther's reformation was a social revolution which was sabotaged by the German princes, who misused the revolutionary energies for their own interests. Very soon "the strong arm" of Prussia appeared on the scene. The Elector of Brandenburg became King of Prussia and, in due course, supplanted the Emperor—representing the unifying idea of Europe—and was created Emperor of a unified Germany.

Hitler's accession was neither the consequence of the Treaty of Versailles nor of the circumstances prevailing in Germany after the First World War. He is a product of a long development: Prussia above all the other Princes, Prussia above the German Reich, Prussia above Europe, Prussia above the whole world! Hitler, obsessed by the idea of a great Reich, represents, with his idea of having the mission to embody in himself all power, all justice, all authority, the culmination of an old megalomania. He regarded himself as the embodiment of Germany, Europe, the world, and—ultimately—the man who could replace God. He was the personification of Germany's idea of power. Germany's presumption turned against everybody and everything—politically, against Europe; ideologically, against Judaism and Christianity; nationally, against nations and races. This is the reason for Germany's downfall.[154]

Because Thomas Mann was the most famous German adversary of Hitler and because the Germans refused to listen to his warnings against National Socialism, his must be the honor of summing up the German problem. He reminded the Germans, who prefer to blame the Treaty of Versailles for the growth of Hitlerism, that they never took seriously the German democratic republic of 1918 but dismissed it as a bad joke, hating it as the result of their well-earned defeat. He reminded

them of the great responsibility of the majority of their intellectuals. Instead of fostering the idea of liberty they offered the
nation an old-new teaching "in which the values bound up with
the idea of the individual—truth, freedom, law, reason—were
entirely rejected . . . or else had taken on a meaning quite
different from that given them for centuries."[155] They ridiculed
the belief in free scientific research without any preconceived
assumptions; freedom was only given "to thought that might
justify force."[156] These professors did not believe in free institutions since, so they thought, the concept of freedom was "self-
contradictory"; they approved of "despotic tyranny over the
masses" which would be "provided with mythical fictions . . .
insane visions, chimaeras which needed to have nothing to do
with truth or reason or science in order to be creative, to deter-
mine the course of life and history."[157]

Thomas Mann was terrified watching this fateful development and warned against it with all the vigor of his word. He
knew that such an ideology would initiate a period of wars
"which would probably take us back far behind the Christian
civilisation of the Middle Ages" into the barbaric age of priest-
medicine men and priest-wizards. As a symbol for this state of
affairs he uses the musical term of the glissando, "a barbaric
rudiment from pre-musical days. . . . I have always been inclined to sense in it an anti-cultural, anti-human appeal."[158]

German youth was fond of totalitarian ideas long before Hitler. We can see this from their conversations in the novel *Doctor Faustus,* which takes place in the early years of the 20th
century. The language they use is a typical German jargon of
Hegelian vintage, which Goethe ridiculed in his time and which
is full of insurmountable obstacles for the English translator.
The English translations of such words as *sakraler Raum,
Strukturprinzip, Wesensfrage, ontische Naturhaftigkeit* lack the
original ironical effect which Thomas Mann wishes to convey.
These hopeful young men are convinced that liberalism is out-

moded, that nobody is any longer beguiled by the idea of freedom; they can only find "two possibilities of religious [!] reali-
sation: the social and the national."[159] A decade or two later,
these possibilities established, accompanied by the jubilation of
millions of young and not-so-young men and women, the "religion" of National Socialism. One of the young men in *Doctor
Faustus* utters a warning that it is not enough to call oneself
National and German because it all depends on how many
"Germanies" one embodies "in a personal—that is, in a qualita-
tive sense."[160] In a Goethean sense, one may add.

Thomas Mann's Faust is a composer; it is Mann's opinion
that the old Faustus legend and Goethe's tragedy are not really
representative of the German character insofar as they lack the
musical element. "Music is the domain of demonism,"[161] as
Kierkegaard knew perfectly well. (One of Kierkegaard's most
interesting essays, on Mozart's *Don Juan*, plays an important
part in the scene where Adrian is visited by the Devil.) Music,
romantic music especially, had a devastating effect on the German mind. Mann quotes Balzac as saying in 1839: *"Les Al-
lemands, s'ils ne savent pas jouer des grands instruments de la
liberté, savent jouer naturellement de tout les instruments de
musique."*[162] ("If the Germans do not know how to play the
great instruments of liberty, they know naturally how to play all
the instruments of music.") The musician Adrian says of his
new method of composing music that it is "bound by a self-
imposed compulsion to order, hence free." Zeitblom, ironically:
"Well, the dialectics of freedom is unfathomable."[163]

The Catholic Zeitblom, in all political respects the mouthpiece of Thomas Mann and, like him, an uncompromising
enemy of the Third Reich, says that the Germans plunged the
world into war and that the Hitler regime had made Germany
intolerable to the rest of the world by turning a European-
minded Germany into the mad dream of "a German Europe."[164] They spoke of Germany, says Zeitblom, as of a Eu-

ropean fortress while, in reality, it was as a madhouse, a prison "suffocatingly full of foul air."[165] A German defeat, he argues, will be terrible, but still more terrible would be a German victory.

The main motive of *Dr. Faustus* is the pact with the Devil. On one of the first pages we read of the "terrible bargain";[166] and everything preceding the scene in which Adrian argues with the Devil as well as everything following that scene is related to the main motive. Like Goethe's Faust and, even more, like Marlowe's Faustus, Germany was out to conquer the world by virtue of a pact with the Devil, and, like Faust, she was carried off by the Devil.

The Devil's main characteristic is his pride—*"Non serviam"*. The Germans, too, were driven by pride and arrogance.

Thomas Mann castigated this pride in his *Joseph*. The Germans are, he said in 1936, "so absurdly vain because they were born in the land of 'men,' the only true birthplace of the gods," that they "would have laughed to scorn the slightest doubt passed upon the superiority of their civilisation over that of any of the surrounding countries."[167] A few years later, in one of his radio messages to Germany—to which a good many Germans secretly listened at the risk of their lives—Mann spoke of Germany's "megalomania," and in *Doctor Faustus* we read of God's enemy, the Devil, "His foe . . . fallen through pride."[168] Adrian is full of "arrogance," and the Devil says to him: "Your vain glory aspired to the elemental . . . we are in league and business."[169] Adrian's fellow students once spoke of the plunge into the elemental. One of them, characteristically bearing the name of Deutschlin, says: "The Russian have profundity but no form. And in the West they have form but no profundity. Only we Germans have both."[170]

The Devil allows Adrian, allows the Germans "good time, devilishly German time, great time, mad time, quite bedevilled time in which the fun waxes fast and furious."[171] The Third

Reich is the Devil's domain, which no words can adequately describe; "that is the secret delight and security of hell that it is protected from speech."[172]

Many millions rejoiced in 1933, intoxicated by a false religion which betrayed itself to any intelligent person as a regime of crudity, vulgarity, gangsterism, sadism, filthiness. They committed unspeakable crimes against the nations of Europe, degraded man in a manner which the history of civilization has never known before, and made an abomination before God and the world. What use was their Goethean humanism if Hitler could trample Europe under his feet while calling himself the savior of Europe! A thousand years of German history are refuted by their collapse. "Everything German, even the German mind and spirit, German thought, the German word stands forth as an abomination and an example of evil." German history has ended "in a plunge into hell lighted by a dance of roaring flames."[173]

Doctor Faustus shows the Germans what they have to do. True contrition, we read, is not just feeling sorrow and shame, as some Germans say they do. Genuine contrition is a complete disbelief in the possibility of mercy, "the conviction of the sinner that he has acted too grossly for even the Everlasting Goodness to be able to forgive his sin."[174] We have seen how remote most (nearly all) Germans are from such feelings, although only a contrition of this kind can pave the way to salvation. The hero of *Doctor Faustus,* the representative of Germany's pride, confesses in the end: "Guilt like mine is too great to find forgiveness."[175] These are the words of Cain, the first murderer, and they were quoted by Count von Galen on August 3, 1941, from the pulpit. Cain, he said, plagued by his conscience, confessed his unpardonable guilt.

Only after Adrian has confessed to the guilt of Cain, Mann, in the last sentence of *Doctor Faustus,* says: "God be merciful to thy poor soul, my friend, my Fatherland."[176]

Thomas Mann's great novel made no impact whatever on the Germans of today. Some Germans heaped honors on Thomas Mann when he gave his lecture on Schiller in Stuttgart in 1955. The German Ministers of Culture presented him on his 80th birthday with a large sum which he was at liberty to give to needy German writers, victims of the Nazis, and when, shortly after his 80th birthday, he fell ill, they conferred on him the order *Pour le mérite*. This cost them nothing. The nation as a whole, forgetting everything and unrepentant behind the thin façade of democracy, refuses to listen to anything he said in *Doctor Faustus* or in his post-war essays. What Theodor Haecker entered in his diary as early as 1939 has literally come true: "One can expect that the Germans will do everything to forget all that they are saying, writing and doing today, as quickly as possible." He added: "But God will have to say something about it."[177]

Notes

1. O. M. Graf. *An manchen Tagen,* p. 194.
2. *Die deutsche Frage,* pp. 9, 60, 67.
3. In a letter from H. E. Holthusen to the author of this book, February 23, 1962.
4. *Die Sonette von Leben und Zeit, dem Glauben und der Geschichte.* Koeln, 1954, p. 141.
5. *Neue Zeitung,* May 18, 1948.
6. *De Profundis,* p. 313.
7. A. Closs. *The Harrap Anthology of German Poetry.* London, 1957, p. 541.
8. *Rhein-und Neckarzeitung,* Heidelberg, February 18, 1955.
9. H. J. Schoeps. *Die letzten dreissig Jahre.* Stuttgart, 1956, p. 163.
10. In a letter from Thomas Mann to the author of this book, September 15, 1949.
11. In another letter, October 15, 1951.
12. *Deutsche Rundschau,* 1955.
13. *Die Kultur,* September 15, 1957; *Nachtwachen des Tellerwäschers.* Muenchen, 1957, pp. 13, 38.
14. In a letter, December 5, 1956.
15. *Trost in Traenen,* pp. 6, 7.
16. Malcolm J. Proudfoot. *European Refugees 1939-1952.* London, 1957, pp. 316-317.

17. *Reden, Schriften, Briefe.* Berlin and Neuwied, 1955, letter of November 2, 1945 to Walther Abendroth, and letter of October 5, 1946 to Bruno Walter.

18. *Ibid.*, letter to Walther Abendroth, November 23, 1945.

19. Peter Kleist. *Auch du warst dabei*, p. 396.

20. Richard Euringer. *Die Sargbreite Leben.* Hamm, 1952.

21. Kleist, *op. cit.*, p. 396.

22. *Ungleiche Welten*, pp. 234, 240.

23. *Geschichte der deutschen Novelle.* Wiesbaden, 1954, p. 352.

24. *Die Besinnung,* Nuernberg, April-May, 1954.

25. *Deutsche Geschichte und politische Ethik.* Nuernberg, 1961, pp. 7, 19, 21, 49, 61-62, 69, 85, 109, 113, 124, 131, 150, 154, 169, 182, 192-194, 197-198, 205, 209, 223, 226, 234.

26. *Glanz und Elend der Deutschen.* Muenchen, 1960, pp. 72, 77, 90-91, 134, 212-213, 344, 345, 367, 386.

27. *Die Kultur,* February, 1962.

28. *Sunday Times,* London, November 19, 1961, November 26, 1961.

29. *Briefe,* pp. 244-247, 266-267, 286, 301; *Gesammelte Schriften,* Vol. VII, pp. 447-448.

30. *Gesammelte Schriften,* Vol. VII, p. 451.

31. *Unconditional Hatred.* New York, 1954, pp. 35, 65, 75, 93, 114, 184, 187, 243, 246.

32. *Cottbuser Anzeiger,* November 8, 1940.

33. *Die Kulter,* July 1, 1956.

34. *Alter Feind, was nun?* Muenchen, 1955.

35. "Es gibt Untaten, ueber welche kein Gras waechst." A speech given in Berlin, February 17, 1952.

36. IMT, November 30, 1945.

37. Milosz. *Verfuehrtes Denken,* p. 208.

38. Ulrich von Hassell. *Vom anderen Deutschland.* Zurich, 1946, p. 92.

39. F. T. Csokor. *Auf fremden Strassen,* pp. 38, 73.

40. *Ibid.*, p. 117.

41. T. Haecker. *Tag-und Nachtbuecher,* pp. 227-228.

42. IMT, June 6, 1946.

43. *Ibid.*

44. Tag-und Nachtbuecher, p. 242.

45. *Ibid.*, p. 169.

46. Portmann. *Kardinal von Galen,* pp. 209, 230.

47. *Deutsche Hoerer!,* p. 99.

48. *Du hast uns heimgesucht bei Nacht,* p. 252.

49. *Wir waren fuenf.* Konstanz, 1949, p. 545.

50. *Die Zeit,* Hamburg, September 1, 1955.

51. *Ungleiche Welten,* p. 45.

52. *Ibid.*, p. 25.

53. Theodor Plievier. *Berlin.* Muenchen, 1954, p. 13.

54. Viktor Freiherr von der Lippe. *Nuernberger Tagebuchnotizen.* Frankfurt, 1951, p. 168.

55. *Mannheimer Hefte,* 1955, Issue III.

56. Grimm. *Warum,* p. 417.

57. ("If justice has been removed what are governments but great robbers?") Pribilla. *Deutsche Schicksalsfragen*, p. 25.

58. Eugen Kogon. *Der SS-Staat*. Stockholm, 1947, p. 24.

59. H. Springer. *Das Schwert auf der Wage: Hans Fritzsche ueber Nuernberg*. Heidelberg, 1953, p. 28.

60. *Kann Westeuropa verteidigt werden?* Goettingen, 1951, p. 30.

61. *Glasenbach, Nuernberg, Landsberg*. Graz, 1953, pp. 13, 38.

62. *Der Zweite Weltkrieg 1939-1945*. Stuttgart, 1951, p. 16.

63. F. Simonson. *Lebendige Vergangenheit*. Stuttgart, 1953, p. 144.

64. *Europa und die deutsche Frage*, p. 104.

65. G. Kraaz. *Nationalsozialistisches Voelkerrechtdenken. Reichs und preussisches Verwaltungsblatt*. Vol. 55, 1934, pp. 9-11.

66. *Europa als Einheit. Zeitschrift fuer Voelkerrecht*, 1936, pp. 294, 300.

67. *Das Moderne Voelkerrecht der civilisierten Staaten*, 1878, 3rd edition, p. 220.

68. *Der SS-Staat*, p. 405.

69. *Das Juristenurteil*. Hamburg, 1948, p. 133.

70. *Trial of War Criminals Before the Nuernberg Military Tribunal Under Control Council Law No. 10*. Vol. II, p. 371.

71. *Gerichtstag in Nuernberg*. Hamburg, 1947. pp. 8, 19.

72. W. Grewe and O. Kuester. *Nuernberg als Rechtsfrage*, pp. 30-31.

73. *Sueddeutsche Juristenzeitung*, July, 1948, columns 355, 358, 364.

74. Carl Haensel. *Das Gericht vertagt sich*. Hamburg, 1950, pp. xi-xii.

75. *Die Generale, das Nuernberger Urteil und die Schuld der Generale*. Hannover, 1947, p. 6.

76. *Rechtsphilosophie*. Stuttgart, 1950, pp. 347-357.

77. Radbruch. *Der Geist des englischen Rechts*. Heidelberg, 1947, pp. 9-10, 15, 17, 65-66.

78. *Nuernberg*. Stuttgart, 1953, pp. 68, 92, 93, 284, 366.

79. *Kontrollgesetz No. 10*. Hamburg, 1948, p. 121.

80. *Bilanz des zweiten Weltkrieges*, p. 409.

81. *Verteidigung deutscher Soldaten*. Bonn, 1950, p. 237.

82. *Merkur*, Stuttgart, July, 1954.

83. *Sueddeutsche Zeitung*, July 20, 1954.

84. Leo Freiherr Geyr von Schweppenburg. *Gebrochenes Schwert*. Berlin, 1952, p. 16.

85. *Bischof Graf von Galen Spricht!*, p. 32.

86. *Ibid.*, p. 60.

87. J. G. Droysen. *Das Leben des Feldmarshalls Grafen York von Wartenburg*. Leipzig, 1913, p. 367; W. V. Voss. *Yorck*. 1906, p. 89.

88. Herbert Kraus. *Die im Braunschweiger Remer-Prozen erstatteten Gutachten*. Hamburg, 1953, p. 53.

89. *0815*. Vol. II, p. 313.

90. *Ibid.*, p. 138.

91. Rudolf Pechel. *Zwischen den Zeilen*. Wiesentheid, 1948, p. 6.

92. Haensel. *Das Gericht vertagt sich*, p. 73.

93. Hans Laternser. *Verteidigung Deutscher Soldaten*. p. 66.

94. *Bischof Graf von Galen Spricht!*, p. 29.

95. *Ibid.*, p. 31.

96. *Ibid.*, p. 72.
97. *Du hast uns heimgesucht bei Nacht*, p. 62.
98. *Ibid.*, p. 241.
99. *Alfred Delp: Kaempfer, Beter, Zeuge.* Berlin, 1954, p. 11.
100. Josef Schaefer. *Wo Seine Zeugen Sterben, ist Sein Reich.* Hamburg, 1946, pp. 7-8.
101. *Der Spiegel*, Hamburg, May 4, 1955.
102. *Die deutsche Frage*, p. 18.
103. *Die Zeit, Hamburg,* October 18, 1948.
104. *Blaetter*, Koeln, May, 1959.
105. "Harzburger Front." *Blaetter*, March, 1960.
106. *Monatshefte fuer auswaertige Politik*, 1941, pp. 748-749.
107. *Harzburger Front.*
108. H. Hammerschmidt and M. Mansfeld. *Der Kurs ist falsch.* Muenchen, 1956, pp. 39-40.
109. *Nuernberger Nachrichten*, February 2, 1958.
110. Hammerschmidt, *op. cit.*, pp. 38-39.
111. *Ibid.*, pp. 24 ff.
112. *Die Kultur*, March, 1956.
113. "Harzburger Front."
114. Hammerschmidt, *op. cit.*, p. 61.
115. *Koelnische Rundschau*, November 26, 1954.
116. *Nuernberger Nachrichten*, March 19, 1958.
117. *Bavarian Radio.* Munich, February 7, 1956.
118. Hammerschmidt, *op. cit.*, p. 70.
119. *Dr. Hans Globke: Aktenauszuege.* Edited by R. M. Strecker, Hamburg, 1961, pp. 1, 28, 34, 44, 52, 64, 65, 68, 94, 126, 127, 130-131, 153, 181, 186, 213, 221, 229, 231.
120. *Unter dem Schatten deiner Fluegel*, p. 631.
121. *Die Kultur*, March, 1956.
122. Bundestag, Session of March 12, 1956; and *Nuernberger Nachrichten*, March 5, 1956.
123. *Sueddeutsche Zeitung*, March 24, 1956.
124. *Suedwest-Rundschau*, Freiburg, March 15, 1956.
125. *Die Freiheit*, Mainz, March 19, 1956.
126. *Geist und Zeit*, Darmstadt, 1959, Issue IV.
127. *Die Kultur*, March 15, 1958.
128. *Nuernberger Nachrichten*, October 22, 1958.
129. *Der Spiegel*, Hamburg, July 29, 1959.
130. *Blaetter*, Koeln, September, 1962.
131. *Ibid.*
132. Poliakov and Wulf. *Das Dritte Reich und die Juden*, p. 67.
133. *Heydrich*, pp. 258, 279.
134. *Deutsche Rundschau*, November, 1947.
135. *Deutsche Rundschau*, November, 1947. Reprinted November, 1957.
136. *Ibid.*, November, 1947.
137. *Geschichtsphilosophie*, pp. 3, 57, 145-146.
138. *Blaetter*, Koeln, October, 1958.
139. *Cr. P. Informationsdienst*, Koeln, August, 1960.

140. *Blaetter,* Koeln, October, 1958.
141. *Ibid.*
142. *Ibid.*
143. *Rechenschaft und Ausblick.* Muenchen, 1951, p. 186.
144. *Deutsche Rundschau,* January, 1956.
145. *Die Deutsche Polizei.* Berlin, 1940.
146. *Deutsche Rundschau,* May, 1955.
147. *Gesetz zur Befreiung vom Nationalsozialismus und Militarismus.* Muenchen, 1946.
148. *Deutsche Rundschau,* January, 1958.
149. *Nuernberger Nachrichten,* May 3, 1958.
150. *Die Kultur,* May, 1958.
151. *Ibid.*
152. *Doktor Faustus,* p. 269.
153. Hans Brandenburg. *Trost in Traenen.* Muenchen, 1955, p. 17.
154. In a letter to the author of this book.
155. *Doktor Faustus,* p. 563.
156. *Ibid.,* p. 563.
157. *Ibid.,* p. 560.
158. *Ibid.,* pp. 566-571.
159. *Ibid.,* p. 191.
160. *Ibid.,* p. 190.
161. "Deutschland und die Deutschen."
162. *Ibid.*
163. *Doktor Faustus,* p. 300.
164. *Ibid.,* p. 266.
165. *Ibid.,* pp. 49, 390.
166. *Ibid.,* p. 11.
167. *Joseph und Seine Brueder.* Vol. III, p. 217.
168. *Doktor Faustus,* p. 134.
169. *Ibid.,* pp. 383-384.
170. *Ibid.,* p. 139.
171. *Ibid.,* p. 356.
172. *Ibid.,* pp. 378-379.
173. *Ibid.,* pp. 270, 462, 687, 730; *Deutsche Hoerer!,* p. 121.
174. *Doktor Faustus,* p. 382.
175. *Ibid.,* p. 761.
176. *Ibid.,* p. 772.
177. *Tag-Und Nachtbuecher,* p. 24.

Bibliography

W. Abendroth. *Hans Pfitzner*. München, 1935.

S. Adler-Rudel. *Ostjuden in Deutschland*. Tübingen, 1959.

Alldeutsche Verbände-Wehrverbände. Berlin, 1932.

Anderes Deutschland. Hamburg, September 18, 1959.

O. Anderle. *Das universalhistorische System Arnold Toynbees.* Frankfurt, 1955.

T. Adorno. *Versuch ueber Wagner*. Frankfurt, 1952.

———. *Prismen*. Frankfurt, 1955.

Allgemeine Wochenzeitung der Juden, Duesseldorf, October 28, 1955.

C. Andler. *Die alldeutsche Bewegung*. Lausanne, 1915.

S. Andres. *Aussprache im Titaniapalast*. Berlin, February 17, 1952.

K. O. Aretin. *Der Eid auf Hitler*. Politische Studien, Muenchen, 1956.

E. Arndt. *Germanien und Europa*. Altona, 1813.

K. Assmann. *Deutsche Schicksalsjahre*. Wiesbaden, 1950.

B. Auerbach. *Briefe an Jakob Auerbach*. Frankfurt, 1884.

Aufbau, New York. September 28, 1945; February 7, 1958; May 29, 1959.

Aussenpolitik, Stuttgart. Dec., 1954.

Autobiographien und Bibliographien, P.E.N. Zentrum deutsch-sprachiger Autoren im Ausland. London. No year of publication given.

A. Baeumler. *Nietzsche, der Philosoph und Politiker.* Leipzig, 1931.

———. *Politik und Erziehung.* Berlin, 1937.

———. *Maennerbund und Wissenschaft.* Berlin, 1943.

———. *Die Neue Ordnung Europas.* Berlin, 1943.

H. Bahr. *Selbstbildnis.* Berlin, 1923.

E. Banse. *Volk und Raum im zweiten Weltkriege.* Oldenburg, 1932.

A. Bartels. *Geschichte der deutschen Literatur.* Leipzig, 1909.

———. *Deutsches Schrifttum.* Weimar, 1910.

———. *Die deutsche Dichtung der Gegenwart.* Leipzig, 1910.

———. *Rasse und Volkstum.* Weimar, 1920.

———. *Die deutsche Dichtung der Gegenwart: Die Jüngsten.* Leipzig, 1921.

———. *Jüdische Herkunft und Literaturwissenschaft.* Leipzig, 1925.

W. Bauer. *Nachtwachen des Tellerwaschers.* Muenchen, 1957.

O. Baumgarten. *Das Echo der alldeutschen Bewegung in Amerika.* Jena, 1917.

G. Barraclough. *The Listener,* London. May 27, 1954.

Bavarian Radio, Munich. Nov. 9, 1954; June 7, 1955; Feb. 7, 1956; Apr. 10, 1956.

R. Beer-Hofmann. *Der Graf von Charolais.* Berlin, 1905.

———. *Jaakobs Traum.* Berlin, 1918.

G. Benn. *Kunst und Macht.* Stuttgart, 1934.

N. Bentwich. *The Rescue and Achievement of Refugee Scholars.* The Hague, 1953.

F. Bernhardi. *Deutschland und der nächste Krieg.* Stuttgart, 1912.

A. Bertelsen. *October 43.* London, 1955.

A. Bertram. *Ein offenes Wort in ernster Stunde*. Germania, Dec. 31, 1930.

E. Bertram. *Deutsche Gestalten*. Leipzig, 1934.

W. Bergengruen. *Der Grosstyrann und das Gericht*. Re-issued, Munich, 1947.

Besinnung, Nurenburg, April-May, 1954.

W. Beumelburg. *Das eherne Gesetz*. Berlin, 1934.

W. Beumelburg. *Von 1914-1939*. Leipzig, 1939.

M. Bierbaum. *Das Leben des Kardinals von Galen*. Muenster, 1956.

L. Bittner, et al. *Oesterreich-Ungarns Aussenpolitik von der Bosnischen Krise 1908 bis zum Ausbruch des Krieges 1914*. Wien, 1930.

Blätter des Bielefelder Jugend-Kulturringes, Bielefeld, Sept., 1956.

Blaetter fuer deutsche und europaeische Kultur, Koeln, 1958-64. All post-war issues.

S. H. Blanck. *Prophetic Faith in Isaiah*. Cincinnati, 1958.

F. H. Blunck. *Deutsche Kulturpolitik*. Munich, 1934.

H. Bluntschli. *Das moderne Voelkerrecht der civilisierten Staaten*. 1878.

R. Boehringer. *Mein Bild von Stefan George*. Munich, 1951.

F. Boettger. *Theodor Storm in seiner Zeit*. Berlin, 1959.

O. N. Bradley. *A Soldier's Story*. London, 1951.

E. Brandenburg. *Von Bismarck zum Weltkrieg*. Leipzig, 1933 and 1939.

H. Brandenburg. *Trost in Troenen*. Munich, 1955.

J. Braunthal. *Geschichte der Internationale*. Hannover, 1961.

B. Brecht. *Fluechtlingsgeschichte*. Frankfurt, 1961.

B. Brehm. *Unser Kampf im Osten. Sinn und Sendung*. Weimar, 1941.

———. *Am Rande des Abgrunds*. Graz, 1950.

W. Breucker. *Die Tragik Ludendorffs*. Stollheim, 1953.

B.B.C., London, Oct. 8, 1960.

C. Brinitzer. *Lichtenberg*. Tuebingen, 1956.

C. Brunner. *Der Judenhass und die Juden*. Berlin, 1905.

———. *Deutschenhass, Judenhass und der Judenhass der Deutschen*. Berlin, 1919.

———. *Unser Christus*. Koeln, 1958.

H. Brunner. *Die Wirtschaftsphilosophie Fichtes*. Nurenberg, 1935.

M. Buber. *Das echte Gespraech und die Moeglichkeiten des Friedens*. Heidelberg, 1953.

Buecher-Kommentare. Berlin, 1961.

Bulletin of the Association of Jewish Refugees. London, Feb., 1959; Jan., 1961.

Bulletin of the Leo Baeck Institute. Tel-Aviv, 1958.

Bulletin des Presse-und Informationsdienstes der Bundesregierung. Bonn, July 14, 1957.

Bulletin of the Wiener Library. London. All issues.

Karl Buchheim. *Leidensgeschichte des zivilen Geistes*. Munich, 1951.

Bundestag, Bonn. Sessions of March 12, 1956, and April 18, 1956.

W. Bussmann. *Treitschke*. Goettingen, 1952.

H. Carossa. *Ungleiche Welten*. Wiesbaden, 1951.

P. Cassel. *Wider Heinrich von Treitschke*. Berlin, 1880.

———. *Der Juden Gott und Richard Wagner*. Berlin, 1881.

———. *Die Antisemiten und die evangelische Kirche*. Berlin, 1881.

———. *Ahasverus: Die Sage vom ewigne Juden*. Berlin, 1885.

H. S. Chamberlain. *Die Grundlagen des 19. Jahrhunderts*. Munich, 1899. 6th edition 1906.

———. *Idol und Macht*. Munich, 1916.

———. *Demokratie und Freiheit*. Munich, 1917.

———. *Lebenswege Meines Denkens*. Munich, 1919.

———. *Rasse und Persönlichkeit*. Munich, 1925.

———. Englische Politik. Essen, 1938.

Christlicher Staendestaat, Wien, Apr. 3 and July 8, 1934.

Christ und Welt, Hamburg. Nov. 11, 1960.

H. Class. *Grosse Gegenwart—groessere Zukunft.* 1913.

———. *Deutsche Geschichte.* Leipzig, 1919.

———. *Wider den Storm.* Leipzig, 1932.

A. Closs. *The Harrap Anthology of German Poetry.* London, 1957.

Club republikanischer Journalisten (CrP.), Koeln. June, 1957; August, 1960; Dec., 1960; Apr., 1962.

B. Connell. *Watcher on the Rhine.* London, 1957.

Contemporary Review, London. Dec., 1950.

Cottbuser Anzeiger. Nov. 8, 1940.

H. Coudenhove-Calergi. *Das Wesen des Antisemitismus.* Berlin, 1901.

B. Croce unc C. Vossler. *Briefwechsel.* Frankfurt, 1955.

D. Crowley. *The Background to Current Affairs.* London, 1961.

F. T. Csokor. *Auf fremden Strassen.* Munich, 1955.

O. Culmann. *The Christology of the New Testament.* London, 1959.

E. R. Curtius. *Deutscher Geist in Gefahr.* Stuttgart, 1932.

H. Cysarz. *Dichtung im Daseinskampf.* Karlsbad, 1935.

———. *Neumond des Geistes.* Wien, 1950.

Daily Mail, London. May 25, 1960.

Daily Mirror, London. Nov. 24, 1960.

Daily Telegraph, London. July 16, 1955; Aug. 16, 1958; Jan. 26, 1959; Apr. 3, 1959; Sept. 11, 1959; Dec. 12, 1961; Nov. 7, 1960; Sept. 2, 1961; March 15, 1962, Apr. 13, 1962; June 1, 1962.

W. Daim. *Der Mann, der Hitler die Ideen gab.* Munich, 1958.

L. Dehio. *Deutschland und die Weltpolitik.* Munich, 1955.

R. Dehmel. *Saemtliche Werke.* Berlin, 1913.

A. Delp. *Kaempfer, Beter, Zeuge.* Berlin, 1954.

Deutsche Blaetter, Santiago de Chile. Feb., 1942; 1944, second issue.

Denk ich an Deutschland. Munich, 1956.

De Profundis. Munich, 1946.

Deutscher Horizont (a periodical of the early 19th century).

Deutsche Juristenzeitung. Aug. 1, 1934.

Deutsche Kommentare, Berlin. Apr. 2, 1955.

Deutsche Polizei. Berlin, 1940.

Deutsche Rundschau, Stuttgart. All post-war issues.

Deutscher Soldatenkalender. Munich, 1954.

Deutsche Wissenschaft. Dem Führer Ueberreicht als Festgabe der deutschen Wissenschaft zu seinem 50. Geburtstag. Leipzig, 1939.

Deutsche Woche, Munich. All post-war issues.

Deutschlands Kriegsziele. Leipzig, 1917.

H. H. Dietze. *Europa als Einheit. Zeitschrift fuer Voelkerrecht,* 1936.

Demokratie, Koeln. June, 1958; Feb., 1959.

M. Domarus. *Hitler: Reden und Proklamationen 1932-1945,* Wuerzburg, Vol. I, 1962; Vol. II., 1963.

F. Dostoevsky. *The Brothers Karamazov.* London, 1912.

A. Drews. *Das Markusevangelium als Zeugnis gegen die Geschidatlichkeit Jesu.* Jena, 1921.

——. *Der Ideengehalt von Richard Wagners dramatischen Dichtungen.* Leipzig, 1931.

——. *Deutsche Religion.* Munich, 1935.

A. Droste. *Die Judenbuche.* Works re-issued, Munich, 1952.

J. G. Droysen. *Das Leben des Feldmarschalls Grafen York von Wartenburg.* Leipzig, 1913.

E. Duehring. *Die Ueberschaetzung Goethes.* Karlsruhe, 1881.

Du hast uns heimgesucht bei Nacht. Munich, 1954.

Durch Kampf zum Frieden. Tuebingen, 1914.

E. E. Dwinger. *General Wlassow.* Frankfurt, 1951.

J. P. Eckermann. *Gespräeche mit Goethe.* Leipzig, 1837.

G. Ehrle. *Licht ueber dem Abgrund.* Freiburg, 1951.

J. Eichendorff. *Collected Works.* Re-issued Stuttgart, 1961.

I. Epstein. *The Faith of Judaism.* London, 1954.

W. Erfurth. *Die Geschichte des deutschen Generalstabs 1918-1955.* Goettingen, 1957.

J. Ericksen. *The Soviet High Command.* London, 1962.

Richard Euringer. *Die Sargbreite Leben.* Hamm, 1952.

Erste Reichstagung der wissenschaftlichen Akademiker des NSD-Dozentenbundes. Munich, 1939.

E. Eyck. *Geschichte der Weimarer Republik.* Zurich, 1954.

Fackel, Vienna. Oct., 1913; Jan., 1919; Nov., 1921; 1925; July, 1934.

K. Fassmann. *Gedichte gegen den Krieg.* Munich, 1961.

W. Ferber. *Geist und Politik in Oesterreich.* Konstanz, 1955.

L. Feuchtwanger. *Erfolg.* Berlin, 1930.

G. Fichte. *Reden an die deutsche Nation.* 1845-1846.

F. W. Foerster. *Politische Ethik und politische Paedagogik.* Munich, 1918.

————. *Weltpolitik und Weltgewissen.* Munich, 1919.

————. *Mein Kampf gegen das militaristische und national-sozialistische Deutschland.* Stuttgart, 1920.

————. *Die deutsche Frage, von draussen und drinnen gesehen.* Hannover, 1947.

————. *Erlebte Weltgeschichte.* Zurich, 1953.

————. *Die juedische Frage.* Freiburg, 1959.

————. *The Jews.* London, 1961.

————. *Deutsche Geschichte und politische Ethik.* Nuernberg, 1961.

————. *Ein General kämpft gegen den Krieg.* Munich, 1949.

H. Foertsch. *Die Wehrmacht im nationalsozialistischen Staat.* Hamburg, 1935.

————. *Der Offizier der neuen Wehrmacht.* Berlin, 1936.

————. *Schuld und Verhängnis.* Stuttgart, 1951.

T. Fontane. *Briefe an Friedlaender.* Heidelberg, 1954.

J. Fraenkel. *Dichtung und Wissenschaft.* Heidelberg, 1954.

A. Frank. *Diary.* Oct. 9, 1942; Nov. 19, 1942; Jan. 13, 1943.

H. Frank. *Nationalsozialistisches Handbuch fuer Recht und Gesetzgebung.* Munich, 1935.

Frankfurter Allgemeine Zeitung. Oct. 31, 1955; May 25, 1955; Dec. 10, 1955; May 11, 1959.

Frankfurter Hefte. May, 1956.

Frankfurter Zeitung. June 2, 1933; Oct. 26, 1933.

Frankfurter Kurier. April 17 and 19, 1933.

C. Frantz. *Deutschland und der Foederalismus.* Helleran, 1917. Re-issued 1921.

Freiheit, Mainz. March 19, 1956.

M. Freud. *Glory Reflected.* London, 1957.

S. Freud. *Letters.* London, 1961.

G. Freytag. *Soll und Haben.* Leipzig, 1886.

H. Friedmann. *Deutsche Literatur im 20. Jahrhundert.* Heidelberg, 1954.

D. Fryman. *Wenn ich der Kaiser waer.* Leipzig, 1913.

R. Furneaux. *The Other Side of the Story.* London, 1953.

M. W. Gauss. *Der Weg nach Jalta.* Heidelberg, 1962.

H. Gebhardt. *Das Buch von der deutsch-voelkisch-christlichen Religion.* Breslau, 1934.

Gegenwart, Munich. Dec. 24, 1945.

Geist und Zeit, Darmstadt. 1959, issue III; 1959, issue IV; Aug. 1960; 1961, issue III.

B. Gerland. *Die Hoelle ist ganz anders.* Stuttgart, 1954.

German Cultural Oppression in Czechoslovakia. London, 1940.

German New Order in Poland. London, 1942.

S. George. *Der Siebente Ring.* Berlin, 1926.

———. *Das Neue Reich.* Berlin, no year of publication given.

Gesetz zur Befreiung vom Nationalsozialismus und Militarismus. Munich, 1946.

L. Geyr v. Schweppenburg. *Erinnerungen eines Militaerattachés.* Stuttgart, 1949.

———. *Gebrochenes Schwert.* Berlin, 1952.

E. Glaeser. *Glanz und Elend der Deutschen.* Munich, 1960.

J. Glueck. *Ein Wort an Heinrich von Treitschke.* Berlin, 1880.

J. A. Gobineau. *Der arische Mensch.* Kampen, 1940.

H. Gollwitzer. *Und führen, wohin wir nicht wollen.* Munich, 1952.

———. *Israel und wir.* Berlin, 1958.

W. Goerlitz. *Der deutsche Generalstab.* Frankfurt, 1950.

——. *Der zweite Weltkrieg 1939-45.* Stuttgart, 1951.

J. W. Goethe. *Grosse Weimarer oder Sophienausgabe seiner saemtlichen Werke.*

——. *Gespräche ohne die Gespraeche mit Eckermann.* Leipzig, no year of publication given.

G. P. Gooch. *The German Mind and Outlook.* London, 1945.

——. *Under Six Reigns.* London, 1958.

——. *French Profiles.* London, 1961.

H. Grabert. *Der protestantische Auftrag des deutschen Volkes.* Stuttgart, 1936.

——. *Krise und Aufgabe des voelkischen Glaubens.* Berlin, 1937.

——. *Die voelkische Aufgabe der Religionswissenschaft.* Stuttgart, 1938.

H. Graef. *Leben unter dem Kreuz.* Frankfurt, 1955.

O. M. Graf. *An manchen Tagen.* Frankfurt, 1961.

F. C. Grant. *Ancient Judaism and the New Testament.* Edinburgh, 1960.

R. Grenfell. *Unconditional Hatred.* New York, 1954.

W. Grewe and O. Kuester. *Nuernberg als Rechtsfrage.* Stuttgart, 1947.

F. Griese. *Nietzsche, die Erfuellung.* Tuebingen, 1934.

F. Grimm. *Hitlers deutsche Sendung.* Berlin, 1938.

——. *Politischer Mord und Heldenverehrung.* 1938.

——. *Politische Justiz, die Krankheit unserer Zeit.* Bonn, 1953.

H. Grimm. *Warum, woher—aber wohin?* Lippoldsberg, 1954.

Grosse Politik der europäischen Kabinette 1871-1914. Berlin, 1927.

K. R. Grossmann. In *Rheinischer Merkur.* Sept. 18, 1959.

Guardian, London. Dec. 9, 1960.

R. Guardini. *Religioese Gestalten in Dostojewskis Werk.* Munich, 1939.

——. *Die Verantwortung,* Munich, 1952.

H. Guderian. *Kann Westeuropa verteidigt werden?* Gottingen, 1950.

——. *Erinnerungen eines Soldaten.* Heidelberg, 1951.

F. Gundolf. *Dichter und Helden.* Heidelberg, 1921.

——. *Caesar im 19. Jahrhundert.* Berlin, 1929.

J. Gunther. *Inside Russia Today.* London, 1958.

T. Haecker. *Vergil.* Leipzig, 1931.

——. *Tag- und Nachtbuecher.* Munich, 1947.

C. Haensel. *Das Gericht vertagt sich.* Hamburg, 1950.

R. Hagelstange. *Venezianisches credo.* Wiesbaden. No year of publication given.

W. Hagemann. *Das Wagnis des Friedens.* Koeln, no year of publication given.

K. Hahn. *Das Volk Messiah.* London, 1943.

J. Haller. *Die Epochen der Weltgeschichte.* Stuttgart, 1940.

G. W. F. Hallgarten. *Hitler, Reichswehr und Industrie.* Frankfurt, 1955.

W. Hammerschmidt. *Der Kurs ist falsch.* Munich, 1956.

H. Hart. *Attila der Letzte.* Volkbach bei Wuerzburg, 1944.

H. Hartmann. *Max Planck.* Basel, 1953.

T. Hartmann. *Grundsaetze des orthodoxen Judentums.* Rostock, 1935.

F. Hartung. *Volk und Staat in der Geschichte.* Leipzig, 1940.

——. *Das Reich und Europa.* Leipzig, 1941.

——. *Die Entwicklung der Menschen- und Buergerrechte von 1776-1946.* Berlin, 1948.

——. *Deutsche Verfassungsgeschichte.* Stuttgart, 1950.

U. Hassel. *Vom anderen Deutschland.* Zurich, 1946.

J. W. Hauer. *Deutsche Gottesschau.* Stuttgart, 1940.

G. Hauptmann. *Till Eulenspiegel.* Berlin, 1918.

M. Hay. *The Foot of Pride.* Boston, 1950.

F. Hebbel. *Collected Works.* First Series: Plays. Vol. I. Re-issued Berlin, 1911.

F. Heer. *Europaeische Geistesgeschichte.* Stuttgart, 1953.

————. *Land im Strom der Zeit.* Wien, 1958.

————. *Die dritte Kraft.* Frankfurt, 1959.

G. Hegel. *Volk, Staat, Geschichte.* Re-issued Stuttgart, 1942.

W. Hegemann. *Fridericus.* Berlin, 1926.

————. *Entlarvte Geschichte.* Leipzig, 1933.

K. Heim. *Ich gedenke der vergangenen Zeiten.* Hamburg, 1956.

Heimdall, 1899.

H. Heine. *Collected Works.* Leipzig, no year of publication given.

K. Helfferich. *Reichstagsreden 1922-1924.* Berlin, 1925.

E. Hemmerle. *Der Weg in die Katastrophe.* Munich, 1948.

R. T. Herford. *Pharisaism.* London, 1912.

————. *The Pharisees.* London, 1924.

M. Hermann-Neisse. *Um uns die Fremde.* Zurich, 1936.

H. Hertz. *The Pentateuch and Haphtoras.* London, 1937.

W. Herzog. *Grosse Gestalten der Geschichte.* Bern, 1950.

H. Hesse. *Briefe.* Frankfurt, 1954.

————. *Collected Works.* Frankfurt, 1957.

A. Heusinger. *Befehl im Widerstreit.* Tuebingen, 1950.

E. Heyck. *Luther.* Bielefeld, 1933.

K. Hierl. *Ausgewählte Schriften und Reden.* Munich, 1941.

————. *Im Dienste für Deutschland 1918-1945.* Heidelberg, 1954.

K. Hildebrandt. *Platon.* Berlin, 1923.

————. *Staat und Rasse.* Breslau, 1928.

Hilfe. 1917.

G. Hilger and A. G. Meyer. *The Incompatible Allies.* New York, 1953.

Historische Zeitschrift, Munich. Issues of 1950, 1951, and 1955.

A. Hitler. *Mein Kampf.* Munich. 9th edition, 1930.

Hochland, Munich. Oct. 1923.

W. Hofer. *Der Nationalsozialismus.* Frankfurt, 1957.

H. Hoffmann. *Hitler—wie ihn keiner kennt.* Berlin, 1940.

H. v. Hofmannsthal. *Collected Prose Works.* Frankfurt, 1955.

G. Hohmann. *Ein Arzt erlebt seine Zeit.* Munich, 1952.

E. Hoppe. *Ricarda Huch*. Stuttgart, 1951.

B. Horrocks. *A Full Life*. London, 1962.

L. Horstmann. *Unendlich viel ist uns verblieben*. Munich, 1954.

F. Hossbach. *Zwischen Wehrmacht und Hitler*. Wolfenbuettel, 1949.

E. R. Huber. *Wesen und Inhalt der politischen Verfassung*. Hamburg, 1935.

———. *Verfassungsrecht des grossdeutschen Reichs*. Hamburg, 1937.

———. *Bau und Gefüge des Reichs*. Hamburg, 1941.

R. Huch. *Das Zeitalter der Glaubensspaltung*. Zurich, 1937.

A. Huebscher. *Von Hegel zu Heidegger*. Stuttgart, 1961.

A. Hutak. *With Blood and with Iron*. London, 1957.

K. Ihlenfeld. *Wintergewitter*. Witten, 1952.

Inneres Reich. Issues 1939, 1940, 1941.

International Military Tribunal, Nuernberg, 1945-1946. German and English Editions. Nov. 30, 1945; Dec. 10, 11, 12, 13, 14, 17, 18, 1945; Jan. 1, 3, 7, 11, 1946; Feb. 8, 13, 1946; Apr. 6, 10, 17, 29, 1946; July 10, 16, 17, 26, 1946; Aug. 10, 26, 1946; Dec. 13, 19, 1946.

H. Jaeger. *The Reappearance of the Swastika*. London, 1960.

K. Jaspers. *Rechenschaft und Ausblick*. Munich, 1951.

Jewish Chronicle, London. Aug. 5, Oct. 21, Oct. 28, 1960; Nov. 11, 18, 1960; Jan. 13, Febr. 17, Sept. 15, Oct. 20, 1961; March 16, 23, Apr. 6, 20, 1962.

Jewish Gazette, London. July 29, 1960.

Jewish Observer, London. Jan. 15, 1960.

Jewish Quarterly, London. Summer and Autumn, 1961.

Juden und Christen. Unterwegs, Berlin, 1960.

Judentum in der Rechtswissenschaft. Berlin, 1936.

E. Juenger. *Der Kampf als inneres Erlebnis*. Berlin, 1922.

———. *Das Waeldchen 125*. Berlin, 1925.

———. *In Stahlgewittern*. Berlin, 1929.

———. *Der Arbeiter*. Hamburg, 1932.

————. *Die totale Mobilmachung*. Berlin, 1934.

E. Jung. *Die Herrschaft der Minderwertigen*. Berlin, 1930.

E. Kaestner. *Rede zur Verleihung des Georg Buechner-Preises 1957*. Koeln, 1958.

————. *Ueber das Verbrennen von Buechern*. Koeln, 1959.

E. Kohler. *Die Verantwortung des Geistes*. Frankfurt, 1952.

K. Kamps. *J. M. Verweyen*. Wiesbaden, 1955.

A. Kantorowicz. *Thomas und Heinrich Mann*. Berlin, 1956.

R. M. Kempner and Karl Haensel. *Das Urteil im Wilhelm-strassen-Prozess*. Schwaebisch-Gmuend, 1956.

G. Kennan. *Das amerikanisch-russische Verhaeltnis*. Stuttgart, 1954.

O. Kernholt. *Vom Ghetto zur Macht*. Leipzig, 1921.

J. A. v. Kielmannsegg. *Panzer zwischen Warschau und dem Atlantik*. Berlin, 1941.

H. Kindermann. *Heimkehr ins Reich*. Leipzig, 1939.

Kinderzeichnungen und Gedichte aus Theresienstadt. Prag, 1959.

H. H. Kirst. *0815*. Munich, 1954.

J. Klein. *Die Geschichte der deutschen Novelle*. Wiesbaden, 1954.

A. Klemmt. *Wissenschaft und Philosophie im Deitten Reich*. Berlin, 1930.

V. Klemperer. *Lingua Tertii Imperii*. Berlin, 1949.

J. Klepper. *Unter dem Schatten deiner Fluegel*. Stuttgart, 1956.

A. Knieriem. *Nuernberg*. Stuttgart, 1953.

O. Koellreutter. *Der Sinn der Reichstagswahl vom 14. September 1930*. Tuebingen, 1930.

————. *Grundriss der allgemeinen Staatslehre*. Tuebingen, 1933.

————. *Der deutsche Fuehrerstaat*. Tuebingen, 1934.

————. *Der nationalsozialistische Rechtsstaat*. Berlin, 1938.

————. *Volkund Staat in der Weltanschauung des Nationalsozialismus*. Berlin, 1935.

Koelnische Rundschau, Nov. 26, 1954.

F. Koenig. *Christus und die Religionen der Erde*. Freiburg, 1956.

W. Kohlschmidt. *Form und Innerlichkeit*. Munich, 1955.

H. Kohn. *German History. Some New German Views*. London, 1954.

G. Kolbenheyer. *Lebenswert und Lebenswirkung der Dichtkunst in einem Volke*. Munich, 1935.

———. *Der einzelne und die Gemeinschaft*. Munich, 1939.

E. Kordt. *Nicht aus den Akten*. Stuttgart, 1950.

E. Kogon. *Der SS-Staat*. Stockholm, 1947.

G. Kraaz. *Nationalsozialistisches Voelkerrechtsdenken. Reichs- und preussisches Verwaltungsblatt*. Vol. 55, 1934.

W. Kraft. *Karl Kraus*. Salzburg, 1956.

———. *Rudolf Borchardt*. Hamburg, 1961.

———. *Almanach des Fischer-Verlags*. Frankfurt, 74th year.

H. Kraus. *Gerichtstag in Nuernberg*. Hamburg, 1947.

———. *Kontrollgesetz No. 10*. Hamburg, 1948.

———. *Die im Braunschweiger Remerprozess erstatteten Gutachten*. Hamburg, 1953.

H. J. Kraus. *Philosophie und Welt*. Munich, 1958.

K. Kraus. *Weltgericht*. Leipzig, 1919.

———. *Die letzten Tage der Menschheit*. Wien, 1922.

———. *Die dritte Walpurigsnacht*. 1933. Re-issued Munich, 1952.

———. *Untergang der Welt durch schwarze Magie*. Re-issued Munich, 1960.

———. *Worte in Versen*. Re-issued Munich, 1959.

———. *Unsterblicher Witz*. Munich, 1961.

Kriegsschriften des Kaiser Wilhelm-Dank. Berlin, 1914.

A. Kruck. *Geschichte des alldeutschen Verbandes*. Wiesbaden, 1954.

Krupp und die Hohenzollern. Berlin, 1956.

R. Kuehlmann. *Erinnerungen*. Heidelberg, 1945.

Kultur, Munich. All post-war issues.

P. Lagarde. *Deutsche Schriften*. Goettingen, 1886. Re-issued Munich, 1940.

K. Larenz. *Deutsche Rechtserneuerung und Rechtsphilosophie*. Tuebingen, 1934.

H. Laternser. *Verteidigung deutscher Soldaten.* Bonn, 1950.

A. Leber. *Das Gewissen steht auf.* Berlin, 1954.

J. Leers. *Der Kardinal und die Germanen.* Hamburg, 1934.

O. Lehmann-Russbueldt. *Die Generalfeldmarschaelle und ihr Generalgeldmarschall.* Berlin, 1953.

E. Lepprand. *Heinrich von Treitschke im deutschen Geistesleben. des 19. Jahrhunders.* Stuttgart, 1935.

P. Lenard. *Deutsche Physik.* Munich, 1936.

W. Leppmann. *The German Image of Goethe.* Oxford, 1961.

G. E. Lessing. *Dramatic Works.* London, 1878.

———. *Works.* Ed. by F. Bornmueller, Leipzig, no year of publication given.

———. *Nathan der Weise.* 1962.

K. N. Lichnowski. *Meine Londoner Mission.* Berlin, 1919.

C. Lichtenberg. *Reden.* Leipzig, 1886.

H. Lietzmann. *Der Prozess Jesu.* Berlin, 1931.

Liga. *Wuppertal-Vohwinkel,* July, 1960.

G. Linden. *Der Sieg des Judentums ueber das Germanentum. Eine Wiederlegung.* Leipzig, 1879.

V. Lippe. *Nuernberger Tagebuchnotizen.* Frankfurt, 1951.

Listener, London. Oct. 9, 1952; June 10, 1954; June 17, 1954; March 10, 1955; June 7, 1956; Dec. 18, 1958; March 10, 1960; Sept. 10, 1960; Nov. 10, 1960; Nov. 2, 1961.

H. Maas. *Und will Rachels Kinder wieder bringen in das Land.* Heilbronn, 1955.

G. Mann. *Geschichte und Geschichten.* Frankfurt, 1960.

H. Mann. *Der Untertan.* Leipzig, 1918.

———. *Macht und Mensch.* Munich, 1919. Re-issued Wien, 1929.

———. *Sieben Jahre.* Wien, 1929.

———. *Ein Zeitalter wird besichtigt.* Berlin, 1946.

T. Mann. *Buddenbrooks.* Berlin, 1900. Re-issued 1920.

———. *Betrachtungen eines Unpolitischen.* Berlin, 1922.

———. *Rede und Antwort.* Berlin, 1922.

———. *Der Zauberberg.* Berlin, 1924.

———. *Bemuehungen.* Berlin, 1925.

————. *Pariser Rechenschaft.* Berlin, 1926.

————. *Die Forderung des Tages.* Berlin, 1930.

————. *Joseph und seine Brueder.* Vols. 1 and 2 Berlin, 1933 and 1934. Vol. 3, Wien, 1936.

————. *Leiden um Deutschland.* A private print, 1933.

————. *Achtung, Europa.* Stockholm, 1938.

————. *Lotte in Weimar.* Stockholm, 1939.

————. *Das Problem der Freiheit.* Stockholm, 1939.

————. *Deutschland und die Deutschen.* Stockholm, 1945.

————. *Adel des Geistes.* Stockholm, 1945.

————. *Doktor Faustus.* Stockholm, 1947.

————. *Neue Studien.* Stockholm, 1948.

————. *Die Entstehung des Doktor Faustus.* Amsterdam, 1949.

————. *Goethe, das deutsche Wunder.* Berlin, 1949.

————. *Meine Zeit.* Frankfurt, 1950.

————. *Luther.* Wiesbaden, 1951.

————. *Altes und Neues.* Frankfurt, 1953.

————. *Nachlese.* Frankfurt, 1956.

————. *Briefe an Ernst Bertram.* Pfullingen, 1960.

————. *Briefe 1889-1936.* Frankfurt, 1961.

V. Mann. *Wir waren Fünf.* Konstanz, 1949.

Mannheimer Hefte. 1955, issue III.

H. Marr. *Der Sieg des Judentums ueber das Germanentum.* Bern, 1879.

C. Martens. *Verschwoerer und Fehmemoerder.* Berlin, 1926.

W. Martini. *Das Ende aller Sicherheit.* Stuttgart, 1954.

T. G. Masaryk. *Das neue Europa.* Berlin, 1922.

Mass und Wert. A periodical issued by Thomas Mann in Zurich. All issues.

M. Mathi. *Wenn nur der Sperber nicht kommt.* Guetersloh, 1955.

B. v. Maydell. *Die Stieglitz von Arolsen.* Neustadt an der Aisch, 1956.

H. Mayer. *Von Lessing bis Thomas Mann.* Pfullingen, 1959.

F. Meinecke. *Kuehlmann und die poepstliche Friedensaktion von 1917.*

———. *Die deutsche Katastrophe.* Wiesbaden, 1947.

W. Meister. *Judas Schuldbuch.* Munich, 1919.

A. Melichar. *Schoenberg.* Wien, 1960.

C. F. Meyer. *Die Versuchung des Pescara.* Re-issued Berlin, no year of publication given.

S. Meyer. *Ein Wort and Herrn von Treitschke.* Berlin, 1880.

Merkur, Stuttgart. May, July, and Aug., 1954.

C. Milosz. *Verfuehrtes Denken.* Koeln, 1953.

J. Milton. *The Poetical Works.* London, 1961.

A. Mitscherlich. *Wissenschaft ohne Menschlichkeit.* Heidelberg, 1949.

Monat, Berlin. Aug. 1949; Febr. 1954; Aug. 1957; June, 1959; and Issue 165.

Monatshefte fuer auswaertige Politik, 1941.

J. Mueller. *Die Entwicklung des Rassenantisemitismus in den letzten Jahrzehnten des 19. Jahrhunderts.* Berlin, 1940.

M. Montgelas und W. Schuecking. *Deutsche Dokumente zum Kriegsausbruch.* Berlin, 1919.

G. A. Mueller. *Regierte der Kaiser?* Goettingen, 1959.

H. J. Mueller. *The Uses of the Past.* London, 1957.

K. A. Mueller. *Deutschland und England.* Berlin, 1959.

M. Mueller-Claudius. *Deutsche und juedische Tragik.* Frankfurt, 1955.

Muenchener Neueste Nachrichten. May 9, 1958.

Muenchener Post. Feb. 11, 1933.

W. Muschg. *Tragische Literaturgeschichte.* Bern, 1948.

———. *Die Zerstoerung der deutschen Literatur.* Bern, 1956.

———. *Von Trakl zu Brecht.* Munich, 1961.

J. Nadler. *Berliner Romantik.* Berlin, 1920.

———. *Literaturgeschichte des deutschen Volkes.* Berlin, 1941.

———. *Kleines Nachspiel.* Wien, 1954.

L. Namier. *In the Margin of History.* London, 1939.

——. *Conflicts.* London, 1942.

——. *Diplomatic Prelude.* London, 1945.

——. *In the Nazi Era.* London, 1952.

National and English Review, London. Jan., 1957.

O. Nelte. *Das Nuernberger Urteil und die Schuld der Generale.* Hannover, 1947.

A. Neubauer and S. R. Driver. *The Fifty-Third Chapter of Isaiah.* Oxford, 1877.

Neue deutsche Hefte, Berlin. Jan., 1956.

Neue Freie Presse, Wien. Dec. 23, 1923.

Neue Rundschau, Berlin. 1907; Oct. 1945; 1st issue 1955.

Neue Welt, Buenos Aires. 1939.

Neue Zuercher Zeitung, Aug. 18, 1954.

New Statesman, London. Oct. 6, 1956; March 7, 1959; Sept. 10, 1960; March 2, 1962.

H. Nicolson. *The Age of Reason.* London, 1960.

E. Niekisch. *Hitler—ein deutsches Verhaengnis.* Berlin, 1932.

——. *Das Reich der niederen Daemonen.* Hamburg, 1953.

——. *Gewagtes Leben.* Koeln, 1958.

J. M. Nielen. *Christlicher Antisemitismus.* Koeln, 1962.

M. Niemoeller. *Die protestantische Kirche im Dritten Reich.* Bielefeld, 1956.

F. Nietzsche. *Jenseits von Gut und Boese.* Leipzig. Re-issued 1924.

——. *Zur Genealogie der Moral.* Re-issued 1924.

——. *Menschliches-Allzumenschliches.* Re-issued 1925.

——. *Der Wille zur Macht.* Re-issued 1928.

C. R. North. *The Suffering Servant.* London, 1956.

Nordic Twilight. London, 1940.

Nuernberger Nachrichten. All post-war issues.

K. J. Obenauer. *Volkhafte politische Dichtung.* Leipzig, 1936.

Observer, London. Oct. 23, 1957; March 23, 1958; Apr. 27, 1958; May 11, 1958; Nov. 22, 1959; Sept. 18, 1960; Nov. 13, 1960; Dec. 31, 1961; April 22, 1962.

Oesterreichische Nation, Wien, Apr. 1956.

Offiziere des Fuehrers. Berlin, 1944 (the only issue).

J. Orabuena. *Gross ist deine Treue.* Paderborn, 1959.

E. Ostwald. *Deutschland erwache.* Wien, 1932.

H. Paasche. *Das verlorene Afrika.* Berlin, 1919.

Pamietami, Warszawa. June, 1958.

F. Papen. *Europa—was nun?* Goettingen, 1954.

J. Parkes. *The Foundations of Judaism and Christianity.* London, 1960.

Parliamentary Debates. London (Hansard), Feb. 10, 1960; Nov. 1, 1960.

B. Pascal. *Pensées.* Everyman's Library, London, 1960.

L. Pastor. *Geschichte der Paepste.* Freiburg, 1913.

G. S. Patton. *War as I Knew it.* London, 1948.

R. Pechel. *Zwischen den Zeilen.* Wiesentheid, 1948.

———. *Deutsche Gegenwart.* Darmstadt, 1953.

G. H. Pertz. *Das Leben des Freiherrn vom Stein.* Berlin, 1849.

J. Petersen. *Die Wissenschaft von der Dichtung.* Berlin, 1939.

H. Pfitzner. *Reden, Schriften, Briefe.* Berlin, 1955.

W. Picht and K. v. Tippelskirch. *Bilanz des zweiten Weltkriegs.* Oldenburg, 1953.

H. Picker. *Hitlers Tischgespraeche im Hauptquartier 1941-1942.* Bonn, 1951.

Pius XI. *Mit brennender Sorge.* Rome, 1937.

A. Platen. *Collected Works.* Re-issued Leipzig, 1910.

T. Plievier. *Berlin.* Munich, 1954.

L. Poliakov and J. Wulf. *Das Dritte Reich und die Juden.* Berlin, 1955.

———. *Das Dritte Reich und seine Diener.* Berlin, 1956.

———. *Das Dritte Reich und seine Denker.* Berlin, 1959.

H. Portmann. *Bischof Graf von Galen spricht!* Freiburg, 1946.

———. *Dokumente um den Bischof von Muenster.* Muenster, 1948.

———. *Cardinal von Galen.* London, 1957.

Preussische Jahrbuecher, Berlin. July, 1919.

M. Pribilla. *Deutsche Schicksalsfragen.* Frankfurt, 1950.

T. Prittie. *Divided Germany.* London, 1961.

K. Pritzkoleit. *Die neuen Herren.* Munich, 1955.

———. *Wem gehoert Deutschland?* Munich, 1957.

———. *Das kommandierte Wunder.* Munich, 1959.

Propylaeen-Weltgeschichte. Berlin, 1960.

H. Pross. *Die Zerstoerung der deutschen Politik.* Frankfurt, 1959.

———. *Vor und nach Hitler.* Freiburg, 1962.

M. J. Proudfoot. *European Refugees 1939-1952.* London, 1957.

Quell. June 23, 1953.

W. Raabe. *Der Hungerpastor.* Re-issued, Berlin. No year given.

———. *Der heilige Born. Complete Works.* Series I, vol. 3. Berlin, 1913.

———. *Hoexter und Corvey. Complete Works,* 1915. Series II., vol. 4.

G. Radbruch. *Der Geist des englischen Rechts.* Heidelberg, 1947.

———. *Rechtsphilosophie.* Stuttgart, 1950.

A. Raeder. *Mein Leben.* Tuebingen, 1957.

L. Ragaz. *Juden und Christentum.* A Pamphlet. 1922.

S. Rappaport. *Jewish Horizons.* Johannesburg, 1959.

F. Rasche. *Unruh.* Hannover, 1960.

H. Rauschning. *Gespraeche mit Hitler.* New York, 1940.

F. Reck-Malleczewen. *Tagebuch eines Verzweifelten.* Stuttgart, 1947.

Rhein- und Neckarzeitung, Heidelberg. Febr. 18, 1955 and March 15, 1959.

Rheinischer Merkur, Koeln. Nov. 25, 1960.

E. M. Remarque. *Im Westen nichts Neues.* Berlin, 1919.

———. *Zeit zu leben und Zeit zu sterben.* Koeln, 1954.

L. Rendulič. *Glasenbach, Nuernberg, Landsberg.* Graz, 1953.

G. Ritter. *Machtstaat und Utopie.* Munich, 1941.

———. *Europa und die deutsche Frage.* Munich, 1948.

———. *Luther.* Munich, 1950.

——. *Staatskunst und Kriegshandwerk*. Munich, 1954.

R. Rochefort. *Kafka*. Wien, 1955.

W. Roepke. *Die deutsche Frage*. Zurich, 1945.

——. *Gegen die Brandung*. Zurich, 1959.

A. Rosenberg. *Der Mythos des 20. Jahrhunderts*. Edition 1943, Munich.

J. Roth. *Juden auf Wanderschaft*. Berlin, 1927.

H. Rothfels. *Die deutsche Opposition gegen Hitler*. Krefeld, 1949.

——. *Zeitgeschichtliche Betrachtungen*. Goettingen, 1959.

L. Rudolph. *Die Luege, die nicht stirbt*. Nuernberg, 1959.

F. Ruehs. *Ueber die Ansprueche der Juden an das deutsche Buergerrecht*. Berlin, 1816.

Rundbrief, Freiburg. All post-war issues.

B. Russell. *Wisdom of the West*. London, 1959.

B. Rust and E. Krieck. *Das nationalsozialistische Deutschland und die Wissenschaft*. Hamburg, 1936.

E. v. Salomon. *Die Geaechteten*. Berlin, 1935.

——. *Der Fragebogen*. Hamburg, 1951.

G. Salzberger. *Christlicher Antisemitismus*. Koeln, 1962.

Sammlung, Goettingen. May, 1957.

J. Schaefer. *Wo Seine Zeugen starben, ist Sein Reich*. Hamburg, 1946.

P. Schallueck. *Engelbert Reinecke*. Frankfurt, 1959.

——. *Zwanzig Jahre: 9. Nov., 1938*. Koeln, 1959.

——. *Geduldet oder gleichberechtigt*. Koeln, 1960.

——. *Zum Beispiel*. Frankfurt, 1962.

P. Scheidemann. *Memoiren eines Sozialdemokraten*. Dresden, 1930.

L. Schemann. *Die Rassenfragen im Schrifttum der Neuzeit*. Munich, 1931.

F. Schiller. *Complete Works*. Berlin, no year of publication given.

F. Schlabrendorff. *Offiziere gegen Hitler*. Zurich, 1946.

M. Schloesser. *An den Wind geschrieben*. Koeln, 1960.

W. Schmid. *Hegel und die Idee der Volksordnung.* Leipzig, 1944.

C. Schmitt. *Staatsgefuege und Zusammenbruch des zweiten Reiches.* Hamburg, 1934.

————. *Voelkerrechtliche Grossraumordnung.* Berlin, 1941.

————. *Ex Captivitate Salus.* Koeln, 1947.

O. A. H. Schmitz. *Das Land ohne Musik.* Munich, 1914.

R. Schneider. *Las Casas vor Karl V.* Leipzig, 1938.

————. *Daemonie und Verklaerung.* Vaduz, 1947.

————. *Die Sonette von Leben und Zeit, im Glauben und der Geschichte.* Koeln, 1954.

————. *Verhuellter Tag.* Koeln, 1955.

L. v. Schoenaich. *Mein Damaskus.* Berlin, 1926.

————. *Zehn Jahre Kampf fuer Frieden.* Hamburg, 1929.

H. J. Schoeps. Juedisch-christliche Gespraeche. Berlin, 1937.

————. *Das andere Preussen.* Stuttgart, 1952.

————. *Das war Preussen.* Honnef, 1955.

————. *Die letzten dreissig Jahre.* Stuttgart, 1956.

————. *Juedisch-christliche Glaubensgespraeche.* Berlin, 1957.

————. *Konservative Erneuerung.* Stuttgart, 1958.

————. *Juedische Geisteswelt.* Koeln, 1960.

I. Scholl. *Die weisse Rose.* Frankfurt, 1952.

J. Scholmer. *Die Toten kehren zurueck.* Koeln, 1954.

W. Schoof. *Jacob Grimm.* Bonn, 1961.

F. Schonauer. *Stefan George.* Hamburg, 1960.

————. *Deutsche Literatur im Dritten Reich.* Olten, 1961.

L. Schroeder. *Die Vollendung des arischen Mysteriums in Bayreuth.* Munich, 1911.

R. A. Schroeder. *Reden und Aufsaetze.* Berlin, 1939.

H. J. Schultz. *Deutsche, Juden, Christen,* Stuttgart, 1961.

P. Schultze-Naumburg. *Nordische Schoenheit.* Munich, 1937.

K. Schuschnigg. *Ein Requiem in Rot-Weiss-Rot.* Zurich, 1946.

H. Schwarz. *Grundzuege einer Geschichte der artdeutschen Philosophie.* Berlin, 1937.

———. *Nationalsozialismus und deutsche Glaubensbewegung.* Berlin, 1938.

G. B. Shaw. *The Perfect Wagnerite.* London, 1898.

F. Sieburg. *Die Lust am Untergang.* Hamburg, 1955.

F. Simonson. *Lebendige Vergangenheit.* Stuttgart, 1953.

A. Soergel. *Dichtung und Dichter der Zeit.* Leipzig, 1919.

———. *Dichter aus deutschen Volkstum.* Leipzig, 1934.

W. Sombart. *Die Juden und das Wirtschaftsleben.* Leipzig, 1911.

———. *Haendler und Helden.* Leipzig, 1915.

Sonntag, Berlin. Aug. 7, 1949.

Spectator, London. Dec. 12, 1961.

Spiegel, Hamburg. May 7, 1955; Oct. 1957; Jan. 29, 1958; July 29, 1959.

Spectrum Austriae. Wien, 1937.

O. Spengler. *Der Untergang des Abendlandes.* Munich, 1919.

———. *Politische Schriften.* Munich, 1933.

T. R. de Spiritu Sanctu. *Edith Stein.* Nuernberg, 1962.

H. Springer. *Das Schwert auf der Wage.* Heidelberg, 1953.

H. Srbk. *Geist und Geschichte des deutschen Humanismus bis zur Gegenwart.* Munich, 1951.

W. Stapel. *Die Fiktionen der Weimarer Verfassung.* Hamburg, 1928.

———. *Der christliche Staatsmann.* Hamburg, 1932.

J. Stark und W. Mueller. *Juedische und deutsche Physik.* Leipzig, 1941.

P. A. Steiniger. *Der Nuernberger Prozess.* Berlin, 1958.

W. Steller. *Wiedervereinigung, der erste Schritt zur Heimat.* 1957.

W. Stigand. *Life of Heine.* London, 1875.

Stimmen der Zeit, Munich. May, 1960.

A. Stoecker. *Das moderne Judentum in Deutschland.* Berlin, 1880.

R. M. Strecker. *Hans Globke.* Hamburg, 1961.

Stuttgarter Zeitung. Jan. 26, 1954.

Sueddeutsche Juristenzeitung, July, 1948.

Sueddeutsche Monatschefte, Munich, Dec. 1921.

Sueddeutsche Zeitung, Munich, Aug. 2, 1958, and many other post-war issues.

Sueddeutscher Rundfunk, Stuttgart, June 8, 1951.

Suedwestdeutsche Rundscheu, Freiburg, March 15, 1956.

H. Suendermann. *Alter Feind, was nun?* Munich, 1955.

Sunday Express, London. Oct. 19, 1958; Nov. 19, 1961.

Sunday Times, London. March 30, 1958; July 12, 1959; Nov. 6, and March 13, 1960; July 16, 13, Oct. 22, Nov. 19 and 26, 1961.

Tablet, London. March 31, 1962.

Tat, Hamburg. March 1932; March and April, 1933.

Tegernseetal, Munich, Winter, 1957.

Telegraf, Berlin. Feb. 18, 1956.

G. Tergit. *Effingers*. Hamburg, 1951.

G. Theunissen. *Zwischen Golgatha und Auschwitz*. Koeln, 1959.

R. Thilenius. *Die Teilung Deutschlands*. Hamburg, 1957.

J. Thorwald. *Das Ende an der Elbe*. Stuttgart, 1950.

———. *Wen sie verderben wollen*. Stuttgart, 1952.

Times, London. Jan. 6, 1959.

Times Literary Supplement, London. July 5, 1957; June 19, 1959.

A. Toynbee. *A Study of History*. London, 1955-1961.

H. Treitschke. *Deutsche Geschichte im 19. Jahrhundert*. Leipzig, 1874-1894.

———. *Politik*. Leipzig, 1897.

H. R. Trevor-Roper in *Foreign Affairs*. New York, Jan. 1953.

Trial of War Criminals Before the Nurenberg Military Tribunal under Control Council Law No. 10. Washington, 1950.

E. Troeltsch. *Deutscher Geist und Westeuropa*. Tuebingen, 1925.

Und die Flammen sollen euch nicht verzehren. Zurich, 1955.

F. Unruh. *Vor der Entscheidung*. Berlin, 1919.

———. *Ein Geschlecht*. Munich, 1922.

———. *The Way of Sacrifice*. New York, 1928.

T. Vahlen. *Deutsche Mathematik*. Leipzig, 1936.

V. Valentin. *1848*. London, 1940.

B. Vallentin. *Napoleon und die Deutschen*. Berlin, 1926.

W. Vesper. *Deutsche Jugend*. Berlin, 1934.

———. *Die Ernte der Gegenwart*. Munich, 1941.

B. Viertel. *Dichtungen und Dokumente*. Munich, 1956.

Vierteljahrshefte zur Zeitgeschichte, Munich. All issues.

Voelkischer Beobachter, Munich. Dec. 31, 1939; Oct. 19, 1942.

F. Wagner. *The Royal House of Wagner*. London, 1948.

T. Walker. *Jewish Views of Jesus*. London, 1931.

G. A. Walz. *Volkstum, Reich und Staat*. Breslau, 1937.

Was bedeutet Aufarbeitung der Vergangenheit. Bericht ueber die Erzieher-Konferenzen am 6. und 7. Nov. 1959 in Wiesbaden.

Jakob Wassermann. *Das Gaensemaennchen*. Berlin, 1915.

———. *Lebensdienst*. Leipzig, 1928.

M. Weber. *Gesammelte politische Schriften*. Munich, 1921.

F. Wedekind. *Chansons*. Re-issued after the war, Munich, no year of publication given.

Welt, Hamburg. Oct. 8, 1955; Oct. 6, 1956; May 8, 1957; May 22, 1957; May 24, 1957; June 11, 1957.

Welt der Arbeit, Koeln. Nov. 21, 1955 and Feb. 19, 1960.

Weltkampf. Apr.-Sept., 1941; Jan-March, 1942.

P. W. Wenger. *Wer gewinnt Deutschland?* Stuttgart, 1959.

F. Werfel. *Jeremias*. Re-issued Frankfurt, 1956.

Westfaelische Rundschau. Dortmund. May, 7, 1959.

J. S. Whale. *The Protestant Tradition*. Cambridge, 1955.

Widerstand, Berlin. Jan. 1933.

P. Wiegler, *Literaturgeschichte*. Berlin, 1930.

E. Wiechert. *An die deutsche Jugend*. Munich, 1951.

———. *Der weisse Bueffel*. Munich, 1949.

C. Wighton. *Heydrich*. London, 1962.

H. O. Wilde. *England—Weg der Mitte*. Stuttgart, 1959.

A. Winnig. *Europa*. Berlin, 1937.

———. *Aus zwanzig Jahren*. Hamburg, 1948.

P. Winter. *On the Trial of Jesus.* Berlin, 1961.

G. Wirsing. *Der masslose Kontinent: Roosevelts Kampf um die Weltherrschaft.* Jena, 1942.

——. *Schritt aus dem Nichts.* Frankfurt, 1951.

J. Wolf and G. Salomon. *Der Charakter des Judentums.* Leipzig, 1817.

K. Wolfskehl. *An die Deutschen.* Zurich, no year of publication given.

——. *Hiob.* Hamburg, 1950.

——. *Sang aus dem Exil.* Heidelberg, 1953.

L. Woltmann. *Politische Anthropologie.* Leipzig, 1963.

World Jewry, London. Nov. 1960.

Zachodnia Agenzja Prasowa, Warszawa. June, 1958.

R. Zedlitz-Truetzschler. *Zwoelf Jahre am deutschen Kaiserhof.* Stuttgart, 1924.

Zeit, Hamburg. All post-war issues.

Zeit und Stunde. Edited by J. Zangerle. Salzburg, 1955.

L. Ziegler. *Das heilige Reich der Deutschen.* Darmstadt, 1925.

Index

How is it that the nation of Goethe and Beethoven was also the nation of Hitler and Goebbels, that the Germany Of Himmler was also the Germany of Thomas Mann? How could this highly civilized nation have plunged into the nightmare of barbarism that was the Third Reich? Historian and layman alike have been asking these questions since the beginning of World War II and its attendant horrors. If these questions are put to Germans themselves today, many prefer to talk of "the unsolved riddle of the Third Reich," or of "blind fate" which brought about National Socialism. Utterances like these have been published in innumerable variations in post-war Germany. But everything on earth has its roots and causes; could Hitler and Nazism have sprung from nothing?

In this book Jonas Lesser attempts to explain the German present (the Third Reich and the post-war period) by the German past, and to put things into their proper perspective. "Very few people," says Mr. Lesser, "seem to know anything of the German past of the last ten or fifteen decades, not only the political but also and more so the intellectual history, and hardly anyone knows what a decent German minority has always said about and against German developments since the days of Goethe or even Luther. Nobody seems to know anything of what the decent German minority of today has to say about consequences of Hitlerism and the German post-war behavior. Their voices are constantly drowned in the noise which German politicans and newspapers make day in and day out